FC95 .F79 2003
013410574
Frye, North
 1912-1991.
Northrop Fr

  c2003.

Collected Works of Northrop Frye

VOLUME 12

Northrop Frye on Canada

The Collected Edition of the Works of Northrop Frye has been planned and is being directed by an editorial committee under the aegis of Victoria University, through its Northrop Frye Centre. The purpose of the edition is to make available authoritative texts of both published and unpublished works, based on an analysis and comparison of all available materials, and supported by scholarly apparatus, including annotation and introductions. The Northrop Frye Centre gratefully acknowledges financial support, through McMaster University, from the Michael G. DeGroote family.

Editorial Committee

General Editor
Alvin A. Lee

Associate Editor
Jean O'Grady

Editors
Joseph Adamson
Robert D. Denham
Michael Dolzani
A.C. Hamilton
David Staines

Advisers
Robert Brandeis
Eva Kushner
Jane Millgate
Paul Gooch
Ron Schoeffel
Clara Thomas
Jane Widdicombe

Northrop Frye on Canada

VOLUME 12

Edited by Jean O'Grady
and David Staines

UNIVERSITY OF TORONTO PRESS
Toronto Buffalo London

© Victoria University, University of Toronto 2003
Toronto Buffalo London

ISBN 0-8020-3710-0

∞

Printed on acid-free paper

National Library of Canada Cataloguing in Publication

Frye, Northrop, 1912–1991
Northrop Frye on Canada / edited by Jean O'Grady and
David Staines.

(Collected works of Northrop Frye ; v. 12).
ISBN 0-8020-3710-0

1. Canada – Intellectual life.   I. O'Grady, Jean, 1943–
II. Staines, David, 1946–   III. Title.   IV. Series.
FC95.F79 2003   971.06   C2002-904212-7
F1021.F79 2003

This volume has been published with the assistance of a grant from
the Gelber Foundation.

University of Toronto Press acknowledges the financial assistance to
its publishing program of the Canada Council and the
Ontario Arts Council.

University of Toronto Press acknowledges the financial support for
its publishing activities of the Government of Canada through the
Book Publishing Industry Development Program (BPIDP).

Contents

Preface
xiii

Credits
xvii

Abbreviations
xix

Introduction
xxi

1 Lord Dufferin
3

2 *Characters in Cadence*
5

3 Canadian Art in London
7

4 Canadian Water-Colours
10

5 Gordon Webber and Canadian Abstract Art
12

6 Canadian and Colonial Painting
14

7 *Contemporary Verse*
17

8 Canadian Chapbooks
19

9 Canadian Writing: *First Statement*
21

10 Canadian Poets: Earle Birney
23

11 Canada and Its Poetry
26

12 *A Little Anthology*
39

13 *Direction*
40

14 Water-Colour Annual
41

15 *Unit of Five*
44

16 Undemocratic Censorship
47

17 Canadian Authors Meet
49

18 *Green World*
51

19 Promising Novelist
53

20 The Narrative Tradition in English Canadian Poetry
55

21 Canadian Poet
64

22 *Canadian Accent*
66

23 *The Flowing Summer*
67

Contents　　　　　　　　　　　　　　　　　　　　　　　　vii

24 *Other Canadians*
68

25 Duncan Campbell Scott
69

26 David Milne: An Appreciation
71

27 Canadian Dreiser
75

28 Editorial Statement
77

29 Dean of Critics
79

30 *The Book of Canadian Poetry*, Second Edition
81

31 *The Varsity Story*
83

32 The Pursuit of Form
85

33 Culture and the Cabinet
88

34 Letters in Canada: Poetry
91

35 Pelham Edgar
230

36 New Liberties for Old
235

37 John D. Robins
236

38 Turning New Leaves: *Folk Songs of Canada*
238

39 English Canadian Literature, 1929–1954
243

40 Introduction to *I Brought the Ages Home*
251

41 Preface to an Uncollected Anthology
255

42 Culture and the National Will
272

43 Poetry
280

44 Preface and Introduction to Pratt's Poetry
293

45 Introduction to *The Stepsure Letters*
306

46 John George Diefenbaker
313

47 Haliburton: Mask and Ego
316

48 Governor-General's Awards (I)
321

49 Governor-General's Awards (II)
324

50 Ned Pratt: The Personal Legend
327

51 Silence upon the Earth
331

52 Opening Ceremonies of the E.J. Pratt Memorial Room
334

53 Conclusion to the First Edition of *Literary History of Canada*
339

54 Foreword to *The Prospect of Change*
373

55 A Poet and a Legend
377

56 Edwin John Pratt
380

57 Silence in the Sea
383

58 Lawren Harris
398

59 America: True or False?
403

60 Dialogue on Translation
406

61 Rear-View Crystal Ball
408

62 Preface to *The Bush Garden*
412

63 Canadian Scene: Explorers and Observers
421

64 Lester Bowles Pearson, 1897–1972
426

65 *Cold Green Element*
429

66 Douglas Duncan
433

67 Canada: New World without Revolution
435

68 Conclusion to the Second Edition of *Literary History of Canada*
448

69 View of Canada
466

70 Haunted by Lack of Ghosts
472

71 National Consciousness in Canadian Culture
493

72 Canadian Culture Today
508

73 Culture as Interpenetration
521

74 A Summary of the "Options" Conference
531

75 Introduction to *Arthur Lismer*
541

76 Roy Daniells
544

77 Across the River and out of the Trees
547

78 Beginnings
564

79 Criticism and Environment
567

80 Introduction to *A History of Communications*
582

81 The Chancellor's Message
596

82 E.J. Pratt
598

83 Margaret Eleanor Atwood
611

84 Culture and Society in Ontario, 1784–1984
614

85 Tribute to Robert Zend
629

86 Opening of Lawren Harris and Arthur Lismer Exhibitions
632

87 Barker Fairley
634

88 Don Harron
637

89 Speech at the New Canadian Embassy, Washington
639

90 Afterword to *Hetty Dorval*
655

91 Foreword to Viola Whitney Pratt Papers
658

92 Italy in Canada
659

93 Tribute to Don and Pauline McGibbon
661

94 The Cultural Development of Canada
665

Appendix: Canadian Criticism
673

Notes
675

Emendations
703

Index
705

Preface

This volume contains almost all of Frye's published articles on Canadian culture, along with a number of hitherto unpublished speeches, such as those on E.J. Pratt (nos. 52 and 82) and on the Governor-General's awards (nos. 48 and 49), and two unpublished introductions (nos. 75 and 80). The chief omission is an article in Spanish, "La poesia anglo-canadiense" (no. D81 in Robert D. Denham's *Northrop Frye: An Annotated Bibliography*), which appeared in *SUR* in 1956. This article recapitulates ideas expressed more fully elsewhere; Frye's English original could not be found. Several works that bear particularly on Canada are to be published elsewhere in the Collected Works. Frye's review of *Voices: A Critical Quarterly*, Canadian issue, ed. Ralph Gustafson, is part of a longer review in the *Canadian Forum* (1943) and will appear in the volume on twentieth-century literature. His student review of Pelham Edgar's *The Art of the Novel* for *Acta Victoriana* (1933) deals with novel theory in general and is to form part of the first volume of works on critical theory. *The Modern Century* (1967), which was given on the occasion of Canada's centenary and reflects on Canadian culture, appears in the volume on modern culture, as do a number of articles on Canadian foreign relations, particularly in the 1940s. Reports Frye made in connection with his work on the then Canadian Radio-Television Commission can be found in volume 10 of the Collected Works, *Northrop Frye on Literature and Society, 1936–1989*. Frye also makes many references to Canada, its culture, and its role in his own life in the interviews that will make up a later volume of the Collected Works. The items in the present volume are arranged chronologically according to the date of first publication; when articles were originally given as speeches, however, the date is that of delivery of the speech, though the text may be taken from the printed version.

Headnotes to the individual items specify the copy-text, list all known reprintings in English or French of the item, and also note the existence of typescripts and where they can be found in the Northrop Frye Fonds in the E.J. Pratt Library of Victoria University. The copy-text chosen is generally the first edition, which was often the only one carefully revised and proofread by Frye himself. In some cases he did reread essays for inclusion in his own collections, such as *The Bush Garden* or *Divisions on a Ground*, and such revised versions have some claim to becoming the authoritative text. Most of the revisions to the articles on Canada, however, consist of omissions; the surveys of Canadian poetry in the *University of Toronto Quarterly*, in particular, were drastically cut down for inclusion in *The Bush Garden*. We have therefore chosen the fuller, original version as copy-text in most instances. All substantive changes to this version are noted in the list of emendations. All authoritative versions have been collated.

Inevitably, repetition in this volume is increased by the reinsertion of omitted passages. Such repetition is endemic to a collected works organized by theme. As Frye himself said to the Association for Canadian Studies in the United States at Washington, D.C., he was often asked to speak about Canadian culture. "The subject itself no doubt is inexhaustible, but my comprehension of it is not; and I find that each time I speak many of the same points insist on being repeated" (508). Nevertheless, those points enter into new contexts or are re-envisioned in each autonomous speech or essay. And, as Frye assured his Washington audience, "whatever I repeat I believe to be substantially true."

In preparing the text, we have followed the general practice of the Collected Works in handling published material from a variety of sources. Since the conventions of spelling, typography, and to some extent punctuation derive from the different publishers' house styles rather than from Frye, we have regularized them silently throughout the volume. For instance, Canadian spellings ending in -our have been substituted for American -or ones, commas have been added before the "and" in sequences of three, and titles of poems have been italicized.

Notes identify the source of all quotations we have been able to track down, except for certain references within references, especially when Frye is quoting other critics in the *Literary History of Canada*. In the case of short Classical identifications, the section number, from the Loeb edition, has been placed in square brackets in the text. Notes provided by Frye himself are identified by [NF] following the note. Authors and titles

Preface   xv

mentioned in passing are not annotated, but life dates, when they can be ascertained, and date of first publication of books are provided in the index.

The introduction is in two parts. The first, by David Staines, describes the changing focus and intellectual context of Frye's Canadian writings, while the second, by Jean O'Grady, surveys the critical reaction to them.

Acknowledgments

A number of people have helped us in the preparation of this volume. The articles were originally expertly typed or scanned by Carrie O'Grady and Kelly Quinn, and checked over by Margaret Burgess, our editorial assistant, with her accustomed eagle eye. Monika Lee transcribed material from tape. We thank them and also Judith Williams, the copy-editor for the Press. Marc Plamondon, our graduate assistant, has done wonders with looking up notes and chasing down the dates of obscure Canadian poets; his help with this volume has been invaluable. Michael Happy, Nicholas Halmi, Jan Gorak, Christopher Jennings, Jay Macpherson, Elisabeth Oliver, Ian Parker, Ian Singer, and Helen Smith have also been helpful. We owe special thanks to Alvin Lee, the general editor of the Collected Works, for his support and patience, and to Walter O'Grady for his helpful reading of the introduction.

Credits

We wish to acknowledge the following sources for permission to reprint works previously published by them. We have not been able to determine the copyright status of all the works included in this volume, and welcome notice from any copyright holders who have been inadvertently omitted from these acknowledgments.

Association for Canadian Studies in the United States, for "Canadian Culture Today," from *Voices of Canada/Voix du Canada*, © 1977, The Association for Canadian Studies in the United States.

Arizona State University and Professors John Evans and Peter Horwath for "Criticism and Environment," from *Adjoining Cultures As Reflected in Literature and Language*, ed. John X. Evans and Peter Horwath (1983).

Canadian Broadcasting Corporation for "Opening Ceremonies of the E.J. Pratt Memorial Room" (1964); and for the lecture "E.J. Pratt" (1982).

Canadian Poetry Magazine for "Silence upon the Earth" (1964).

Elvehjem Art Center, Madison, for "Canadian Scene: Explorers and Observers," from *Canadian Landscape Painting, 1670–1930* (1973).

English Studies in Canada for "Roy Daniells" (1979). Reprinted with kind permission of *English Studies in Canada*.

Italian Institute of Culture (Dr. Francesca Valente, Director) for "Preface," from *Italy in Canada* (1990).

Lugus Productions for "Foreword," from *Viola Whitney Pratt: A Testament of Love*, and *Viola Whitney Pratt: Papers and Speeches*, both ed. Mildred Claire Pratt (1990).

The Dean of Arts and the Department of English Language and Literature, Memorial University of Newfoundland, for *Silence in the Sea* (1969).

Oberon Press for "America: True or False," from *Notes for a Native Land*, ed. Andy Wainwright (1969).

Dr. William Riggan, Editor, *World Literature Today*, for "English Canadian Literature, 1929–1954," from *Books Abroad* (1955).

Royal Society of Canada for "Preface to an Uncollected Anthology," from *Studia Varia: Royal Society of Canada, Literary and Scientific Papers*, ed. E.G.D. Murray (1957); for "Edwin John Pratt," from *Proceedings of the Royal Society of Canada* (1965); for "National Consciousness in Canadian Culture," from *Transactions of the Royal Society of Canada* (1976); and for "Canada: New World without Revolution," from *Preserving the Canadian Heritage/La préservation du patrimoine canadien*, ed. Keith J. Laidler (1975).

University of Toronto Press for "Letters in Canada: Poetry," from *University of Toronto Quarterly* (1951–60); for Frye's tribute to Douglas Duncan from *Douglas Duncan: A Memorial Protrait*, ed. Alan Jarvis (1974); and for the conclusions to *Literary History of Canada: Canadian Literature in English*, ed. Carl Klinck, 1st ed. (1965) and 2nd ed. (1976).

All other works are printed by courtesy of the Estate of Northrop Frye/ Victoria University.

Abbreviations

AC   Northrop Frye, *Anatomy of Criticism* (Princeton: Princeton University Press, 1957)
Acta   *Acta Victoriana*
BG   Northrop Frye, *The Bush Garden: Essays on the Canadian Imagination* (Toronto: Anansi, 1971)
D   *The Diaries of Northrop Frye, 1942–1955*, ed. R.D. Denham. CW, 8. Toronto: University of Toronto Press, 2001.
DG   Northrop Frye, *Divisions on a Ground: Essays on Canadian Culture*, ed. James Polk (Toronto: Anansi, 1982)
EAC   Northrop Frye, *The Eternal Act of Creation: Essays, 1979–1990*, ed. Robert D. Denham (Bloomington: Indiana University Press, 1993)
ECLI   *Mythologizing Canada: Essays on the Canadian Literary Imagination*, ed. Branko Gorjup (New York: Legas, 1997)
LS   *Northrop Frye on Literature and Society, 1936–1989: Unpublished Papers*, ed. R.D. Denham. CW, 10. Toronto: University of Toronto Press, 2002.
MC   Northrop Frye, *The Modern Century* (Toronto: Oxford University Press, 1967)
NF   Northrop Frye
NFC   *Northrop Frye in Conversation*, ed. David Cayley (Concord, Ont.: Anansi, 1992)
NFF   Northrop Frye Fonds, Victoria University Library
RCLI   *Reflections on the Canadian Literary Imagination* (Roma: Bulzoni Editore, 1991)
RW   Northrop Frye, *Reading the World: Selected Writings, 1935–1976*, ed. Robert D. Denham (New York: Peter Lang Publishing, 1990)

StS   Northrop Frye, *The Stubborn Structure: Essays on Criticism and Society* (Ithaca: Cornell University Press, 1970)
TSE   Northrop Frye, *T.S. Eliot* (Edinburgh: Oliver and Boyd, 1963)
WE   *Northrop Frye's Writings on Education*, ed. Jean O'Grady and Goldwin French (Toronto: University of Toronto Press, 2001).

Introduction

I

When the poet Dennis Lee, an editor at House of Anansi Press, invited Northrop Frye in 1970 to collect for publication a selection of his Canadian writings, Frye happily accepted the invitation. He gathered together most of his articles, then he and Lee together made the final selection. In his introduction to what became *The Bush Garden*, Frye observed that the collection consisted of "episodes in a writing career which has been mainly concerned with world literature . . . and yet has always been rooted in Canada and has drawn its essential characteristics from there" (412).

Born in Sherbrooke, Quebec, Frye received his primary and secondary schooling in Moncton, New Brunswick. He then moved to Toronto and to Victoria College, the United Church College in the University of Toronto. The journey from New Brunswick to Toronto took him through a world he later described.

> I would take the train to Montreal, sitting up overnight in the coach, and looking forward to the moment in the early morning when the train came into Lévis, on the south side of the St. Lawrence, and the great fortress of Quebec loomed out of the bleak dawn mists. . . . Here was one of the imaginative and emotional centres of my own country and my own people, yet a people with whom I found it difficult to identify, what was different being not so much language as cultural memory. But the effort of making the identification was crucial: it helped me to see that a sense of unity is the opposite of a sense of uniformity. . . . Real unity tolerates dissent and rejoices in variety of outlook and tradition, recognizes that it is man's

destiny to unite and not divide, and understands that creating proletariats and scapegoats and second-class citizens is a mean and contemptible activity. Unity, so understood, is the extra dimension that raises the sense of belonging into genuine human life. (416–17)

For Frye, this ideal of unity became the force to which he owed his loyalty, and "a distrust of such a loyalty is rooted in a distrust of life itself" (417).

Victoria University became Frye's home for the rest of his life. First as an undergraduate student at Victoria College (B.A. 1933), then as a theology student at Emmanuel College, the United Church's theology college on the western side of the Victoria campus (he was ordained in 1936), and lastly as a professor, he found his true roots. "I enrolled at Victoria College in Toronto with the ministry in mind. But as soon as I got to university I knew that was where I wanted to stay. I found myself in a community where I felt I had something to contribute. I plunged into everything: the dramatic society, the debating society. It was a sudden, extroverted reaction from my rather withdrawn adolescence" (566).

At Victoria College he met three teachers who would serve as role models and mentors. The first was John D. Robins (1884–1952), professor first of German and then of English at Victoria College, and an authority on German philology and the Teutonic languages. Robins authored two books, *The Incomplete Anglers* and *Cottage Cheese*, and edited two anthologies, *A Pocketful of Canada* and *A Book of Canadian Humour*. He was a powerful force in the cultural life of his country, seeing "perhaps more clearly than anyone else has seen, the shaping and growth of Canadian writing and painting out of the conditions of Canadian life" (237). An active contributor to the *Canadian Forum*, he introduced Frye to this important repository for reviews and articles. In 1939 he was responsible for bringing his student back from Oxford University to the faculty of Victoria College.

Pelham Edgar (1871–1948), professor first of French and then of English at Victoria College, taught Frye his second-year Shakespeare course. From that time on, he took a sincere interest in his young student's well-being. He showed the way of balancing one's academic interests (Edgar had written two full-length studies, *Henry James, Man and Author* and *The Art of the Novel*) with a passionate commitment to the contemporary: "His strong and constant interest in the contemporary was part of his feeling ... that literature helps to create the standards and values of life,

Introduction

xxiii

and that consequently the appearance of a new good poem or novel is a significant historical fact" (231). This is especially true in regard to the literature of Canada: "Dr. Edgar worked hard for Canadian literature without forgetting that good writing is no better for being Canadian; he studied the classics of two literatures, taught them, and maintained the standards implied by them, without losing touch with his own community" (234).

E.J. Pratt (1882–1964), the third mentor for the young Frye, became a lecturer in the Department of Psychology in the University of Toronto in 1913. Edgar appointed him to the Department of English at Victoria College in 1919, and he remained there until his retirement in 1952. As well as being a writer, he was a full-time teacher and scholar. As a prolific poet he captured the moods and tensions of his time, echoing in his works the Canada of the past as well as the Canada of the present. "He has never been afraid to be topical, is in fact rather impatient with poets of 'still life,' and he has accepted both the responsibilities and the risks that go with being a kind of unofficial laureate" (304). From Pratt, Frye found a mood that encapsulated the times and the values he would sustain throughout his life:

> To write and to teach in Ned's generation meant defending the values of the imagination through a depression and a war, and this took courage of a kind that he not only celebrated but, very unostentatiously, possessed. Some of us grew up in that generation and tried to hold on to the kind of liberal values that are not simply the values of the left as against the right, but are the values of human dignity as opposed to stupidity and hysteria. (330)

Robins, Edgar, and Pratt. These were the figures who guided the young Frye into the academic life: "no one who knew the teachers I had at Victoria: Pelham Edgar, Pratt himself, and J.D. Robins, would be in the least surprised at any student's wanting to pursue the careers they were so brilliant an advertisement for" (384). All three men

> had in common a sense of the contemporary which, I think, was extraordinary. All over Canada and the United States, students were being placidly informed in classrooms that many of the contemporary writers, such as D.H. Lawrence or James Joyce or T.S. Eliot, were either obscure or obscene, and that, in a properly regulated society, they would be either in jail or in a madhouse. But this imperturbable Methodist institution, in the persons of

Edgar and Pratt and Robins, informed their students that these people were serious writers who should be investigated. And they all had in common too an extraordinary sense of the vitality and promise of Canadian literature. (335–6)

All three had "a keen and generous (often very practically generous, as many could testify) interest in younger Canadian writers, and a desire to do what they could to foster the creative talent around them" (385). Under their tutelage and concern, Frye came into the academic life aware of the beauty and power of the word. He brought to his calling a keen interest in the contemporary and a strong passion for the creative talent in Canada. And he fostered among his students the same qualities he found in the three. When Frye returned from Oxford to Canada in 1939 to accept a full-time position among his colleagues and friends at Victoria College, he began a career that would last more than fifty years.

Frye began his critical work as a reviewer in the pages of *Acta Victoriana*, the Victoria College undergraduate literary magazine, and later in the pages of the *Canadian Forum*, the journal of left-wing opinion with which Robins was closely associated. As a reviewer, he saw himself "as a nurse, that is, as somebody bringing along a culture that was not yet wholly mature but showed so many signs of it."[1] The reviews in the *Canadian Forum* and his role from 1948 to 1950 as managing editor of the magazine form the first period of Frye's Canadian writings. At the beginning of this period Frye was working busily on his book on Blake, *Fearful Symmetry*, published in 1947. Ever since his third-year course on the Romantics with Edgar, he was increasingly concerned, indeed obsessed, with uncovering the many patterns that stand behind the work of the poet and graphic artist. While Blake consumed Frye's critical attention, the Canadian writings were forming a constant background.

In this group of thirty-three essays and reviews, Frye examines Canadian paintings, poetry, and some fiction to find the underlying themes and symbols that seem to characterize his own culture, moving quickly from the canvas or the text to generalized observations. In "Canadian Art in London," written when he was only twenty-six, he examines briefly the Group of Seven in language that will be repeated and developed in his later writings: "The Group was not badly represented, though I should have preferred bigger and better MacDonalds, and at least one Lawren Harris abstract picture, not only for its own merit but to show that the Group effected a revolution in rhythm and outline as well as in colour" (8).

Introduction

Two years later, a comparison of the paintings of Tom Thomson and Horatio Walker begins no longer with the paintings themselves but with the abstract concepts and even archetypal patterns suggested by them:

> The countries men live in feed their minds as much as their bodies: the bodily food they provide is absorbed in farms and cities: the mental, in religion and arts. In all communities this process of material and imaginative *digestion* goes on. Thus a large tract of vacant land may well affect the people living near it as too much cake does a small boy: an unknown but quite possibly horrible Something stares at them in the dark: hide under the bedclothes as long as they will, sooner or later they must stare back. Explorers, tormented by a sense of the unreality of the unseen, are first: pioneers and traders follow. But the land is still not imaginatively absorbed, and the incubus moves on to haunt the artists. It is a very real incubus. . . . I propose to compare Tom Thomson with Horatio Walker. (14)

In a later article, Frye turned to the world of Canadian poetry (no. 11):

> When I was still a junior instructor, the first edition of A.J.M. Smith's *Book of Canadian Poetry* appeared (1943), and my review of it in the *Canadian Forum* was perhaps my first critical article of any lasting importance. It is hard to overstate my debt to Mr. Smith's book, which brought my interest in Canadian poetry into focus and gave it direction. What it did for me it did for a great many others: the Canadian conception of Canadian poetry has been largely formed by Mr. Smith, and in fact it is hardly too much to say that he brought that conception into being. (417–18)

Frye's remarks about poetry recall his earlier remarks about Canadian painting:

> Canadian poetry is at its best a poetry of incubus and *cauchemar*, the source of which is the unusually exposed contact of the poet with nature which Canada provides. Nature is seen by the poet, first as unconsciousness, then as a kind of existence which is cruel and meaningless, then as the source of the cruelty and subconscious stampedings within the human mind. (36–7)

The complementary article, "The Narrative Tradition in English Canadian Poetry," owes its origins, too, to the Smith anthology.

These two review-articles mark the beginning of Frye's lifelong commitment to the study of Canadian poetry. In the first article he isolates the prevalent theme that appears to dominate much of Smith's anthology: "the fact that life struggles and suffers in a nature which is blankly indifferent to it. Human beings set a high value on their own lives which is obviously not accepted in the world beyond their palisades. They may become hurt and whimper that nature is cruel to them; but the honest poet does not see cruelty: he sees only a stolid unconsciousness" (34). And in the second, he pursues this theme by developing its roots in the earliest Canadian poet, Charles Heavysege, and following it through the poetry of Pratt. It is a bleak country, overcome by a "feeling of the melancholy of a thinly settled country under a bleak northern sky, of the terrible isolation of the creative mind in such a country, of resigning oneself to hardship and loneliness as the only means of attaining, if not serenity, at least a kind of rigid calm" (56). Frye recognized, too, the issue that would dominate much of his later writing on Canadian poetry: "the striking predilection of Canadian poets for narrative" (65), which becomes "a curious predilection of Canadian poets for narrative and descriptive verse which seems to be peculiar to Canada" (82).

In these articles Frye is already defining his sense of the distinctive Canadian literary voice:

> the anthology thus unconsciously proves the existence of a definable Canadian genius (I use this word in a general sense) which is neither British nor American but, for all its echoes and imitations and second-hand ideas, peculiarly our own. . . . no one who knows the country will deny that there is something, say an attitude of mind, distinctively Canadian, and while Canadian speech is American, there is a recognizable Canadian accent in the more highly organized speech of its poetry. (28)

The wisdom and sanity of Frye's voice were almost unique in a country whose creative output was moving, again to use Frye's distinction, from writing to literature. Poets in Canada—and the number was steadily increasing—became aware of an informed critical voice whose standards were Canadian yet also international, whose knowledge was encyclopedic, and whose natural understanding of Canada was sympathetic and resonant. "His mere presence among us," George Johnston recalls, "has lifted the intellectual level of the country and given Canadian poets something both Canadian and for all time to think about."[2]

After the publication of *Fearful Symmetry* (1947), Frye "thought at first

Introduction

of writing my second book on Spenser, but the pull of contemporary literature was too strong and the theory of literature too chaotic, and I was drawn to a more general and theoretical approach which ultimately became the *Anatomy of Criticism* (1957)" (418). During his sabbatical leave on a Guggenheim Fellowship in 1950, he was approached by J.R. MacGillivray, then editor of the *University of Toronto Quarterly*, to take over the annual survey of poetry in its "Letters in Canada" issue, an important and appropriate duty for someone who had written in his notebooks a few years earlier, "I have never been actively interested in fiction."[3] The second group of Frye's Canadian writings centres on the 1950s when he took over this responsibility from a dying E.K. Brown—and he did regard it as a responsibility. Brown, a scholar whom Frye regarded highly, had been the founding reviewer of poetry from 1935 until 1950. He died on 23 April 1951.

In his second review in this series, Frye pays tribute to Brown, "my predecessor in this survey, whose tact, skill, erudition, and comprehensiveness in making it I had long admired, and am now fully in a position to appreciate, if somewhat wryly" (101). He would later comment:

> E.K. Brown was the first critic to bring Canadian literature into its proper context. Before him, the main question asked was "Is there a Canadian literature?" After him, the question was rather "What is Canadian literature like?" He started out with an interest in contemporary literature which in his generation marked a quite unusual originality, and he worked at first mainly on American authors, including Edith Wharton and Willa Cather. Thus, when he came to Canadian literature, he was able to see it, not simply as a local product growing in the surrounding woods like a hepatica, but as a literary development within, first, its North American context, and, secondly, in its international context. He was aware of the British and colonial affinities of earlier Canadian literature, but did not exaggerate their importance as earlier critics had tended to do.[4]

The reviews for the *University of Toronto Quarterly* demanded a more constant and more detailed attention to Canadian poetry than did those reviews of the preceding decade. They also provided him with an opportunity to read closely the increasing body of poetry being produced in Canada. The ten reviews reveal Frye as a practical critic, sharing his insights while working out his larger theories.

Given the task of reading all the poetry published in Canada each year, Frye approached it as an occasion to work out his growing understanding of mythic patterns within the specific parameters of one art form in one country. These reviews were, as he later reflected, "an essential piece of 'field work' to be carried on while I was working out a comprehensive critical theory. I was fascinated to see how the echoes and ripples of the great mythopoeic age kept moving through Canada, and taking a form there that they could not have taken elsewhere" (418–19). Deliberately and, I suspect, happily, he "dealt with Canadian poetry for the reader of the *Quarterly* as though no other poetry were available to him."[5] As a reviewer, he remained the committed consistent writer, seeing his function as a constructive critic, as a "nurse" helping writers and, more importantly, readers:

> The reviewer knows that he will be read by the poets, but he is not addressing them, except indirectly.... The reviewer's audience is the community of actual and potential readers of poetry. His task is to show what is available in poetic experience, to suggest that reading current poetry is an essential cultural activity, at least as important as keeping up with current plays or concerts or fiction.... The reviewer must take poetry as he finds it, must constantly struggle for the standards of good and bad in all types of poetry, must always remember that a preference for any one kind of poetry over another kind is, for him, laziness and incompetence.... The reviewer is not concerned with the vague relativities of "greatness," but with the positive merits of what is before him. And every genuine poet is entitled to be read with the maximum sympathy and concentration. (227–8)

In this final review, Frye concluded: "The appearance of a fine new book of poems in Canada is a historical event, and its readers should be aware that they are participating in history. To develop such awareness it is an advantage to have a relatively limited cultural horizon. *Ubi bene, ibi patria*: the centre of reality is wherever one happens to be, and its circumference is whatever one's imagination can make sense of" (228).

For these reviews, which constitute "a record of poetic production in English Canada during one of its crucial periods" (418), Frye read the volumes of poetry published each year, took copious notes, then penned his long critical appreciation of the year's work. His commentaries reveal a thorough familiarity with all the books and a careful yet evaluative reflection of each. Now that these reviews are printed here in their entirety, it is possible to obtain a full appreciation of all Frye did.

P.K. Page's *The Metal and the Flower*, for example, "has a competent elegance about it that makes even the undistinguished poems still satisfying to look at, and the book as a whole is as consistently successful in reaching its objectives as any book I have read since I began this survey" (132). And Irving Layton's *A Red Carpet for the Sun* is "a volume of great importance. . . . [H]is refusal to be content with the merely poetic, to make aesthetic pearls out of his irritations, has not landed him outside poetry but into the realization that 'all poetry . . . is about poetry itself'" (216).

At the same time, there are negative statements about quite a few poets. Frye wrote in his diary:

> I got out some books of Canadian poetry and started looking at *that* job. What a job. Here's Philip Child gone and written a long poem that's complete bullshit from beginning to end, and who am I to say so?—a friend of Philip Child's. However, the growth of hypocrisy in public criticism doesn't alarm me as much as it did. What some people regard as a loss of honesty is often just an outgrowing of their own emotional attachment to symbols of their emancipation from mediocrity. Anyway, if I get through this job without outraging either the people who write Canadian poetry or the people who read it, if any, I'm going to apply for the honorary degree of D.C.L. (Doctor of Canadian Letters). (*D*, 482–3)

Reading the review of Child in the light of this statement illuminates Frye's remarks: "In the narrative itself one regrets a rather self-deprecatory melancholy, a gentleness that often seems merely tentative, and, more technically, a mannerism of quoting too many tags from Shakespeare" (96).

In a continuation of his earlier pattern, there is a strong interest in painting in the poetry criticism: "Poetry, like painting, has two poles: the pole of content or subject-matter, the thing represented, and the pole of form, the conventional structure of the art. Painting may be very formal, as in geometrical ornament or abstraction, or it may be very representational, as in illusion-painting or *trompe l'oeil*" (137). And in these reviews, too, Frye is theorizing in greater detail about Canada:

> a Canadian is an American who rejects the Revolution. Canada fought its civil war to establish its union first, and its wars of independence, which were fought against the United States and not Europe, came later. We

should expect in Canada, therefore, a strong suspicion, not of the United States itself, but of the mercantilist Whiggery which won the Revolution and proceeded to squander the resources of a continent, being now engaged in squandering ours. There is in Canada, too, a traditional opposition to the two defects to which a revolutionary tradition is liable, a contempt for history and an impatience with law. The Canadian point of view is at once more conservative and more radical than Whiggery, closer both to aristocracy and to democracy than to oligarchy. (106)

While studying Canadian poets in their own environmental context, Frye also placed them, slowly at first, but with increasing emphasis as the 1950s progressed, in an international or nonnational context, the context of all literature. His greatest achievement as a reviewer, for Malcolm Ross, was "to have given our writers some strong and honest assurance that they were at last out of the parish and standing with their peers on high, new ground."[6] And Margaret Atwood recalls:

> The only "influence" Frye had on those of us who wanted to be writers, and it was a considerable one, was to take us seriously.... In a society still largely provincial, where the practice of literature and the arts generally was regarded with a good deal of suspicion—immoral if not a frill—he made literature seem not only an honourable calling but a necessary one.... He always made it quite clear that it was the job of writers to write but it was certainly not the job of critics to tell them what to write.... He was not prescriptive.[7]

In his reviews, which reflect his genuine interest in his country's poets, Frye offered a firm example of the caring critic.

At the end of the decade, Frye announced his retirement from publicly observing Canadian poetry: "if I could go on doing such a job indefinitely it would not have been worth doing in the first place. At a certain point diminishing returns set in for both reviewer and reader" (229). He would later comment, "by a combination of good luck and instinctive cunning I retired just before it became humanly impossible to continue it, because of the phenomenal increase in quantity. During this period I acquired my own sense of the context, in time and space, that Canadian culture inhabits.... [T]he Canadian scene became a kind of cultural laboratory in which to study the relation of criticism to its environment" (567–8).

Introduction

During the 1950s Frye was reading Canadian poetry, teaching a pass course on Canadian literature,[8] and writing his *Anatomy of Criticism*; he had little time left for other duties. Nevertheless, in this period he also wrote a few important poetic studies that developed further his earlier two review-articles. In 1956 he published his answer to A.J.M. Smith's volume, "Preface to an Uncollected Anthology" (no. 41), which reiterates and broadens the many ideas of his earlier pieces. In his article on "Poetry" for *The Arts in Canada* (no. 43), he explores the Canadian scene from new perspectives he has only hinted at in the other three major essays, bringing his theories up to the present with many allusions to the volumes he has been reading in the 1950s.

For Frye, the reviews of the 1950s, like his earlier reviews, serve the same function in his Canadian writings as does his study of Blake in his non-Canadian writings. "I think it advisable for every critic proposing to devote his life to literary scholarship," Frye wrote, "to pick a major writer of literature as a kind of spiritual preceptor for himself, whatever the subject of his thesis. I am not speaking, of course, of any sort of moral model, but it seems to me that growing up inside a mind so large that one has no sense of claustrophobia within it is an irreplaceable experience in humane studies. Some kind of transmission by seed goes on here too."[9]

For Frye's non-Canadian studies, the major writer was, of course, Blake, and Frye worked his way through Blake's poems to become the creator of *Anatomy of Criticism*. The earlier account of the order and structure of Blake's symbology in *Fearful Symmetry* led directly to Frye's next book, for *Anatomy of Criticism* studies on a grand scale the archetypal or mythic patterns in literature through critical techniques already explored in *Fearful Symmetry*. But Frye, the reviewer of Canadian painting and literature, did not have "a major writer of literature as a kind of spiritual preceptor" in his own country. In lieu of the absent masterworker, he collectively made the paintings and books he reviewed his spiritual preceptor, and these works of art serve as his literary training, which in turn prepared for the third and final group of his Canadian writings, those later commentaries that embody a full vision of his country, its history, its culture, and its future. Through his essays, Frye became a cultural theorist who articulated the myths he saw shaping the paintings he examined and the books he read. This third group, which begins in the 1960s, includes no further reviews. Now Frye devotes himself to commentaries on the cultural life of Canada.

The year 1965 saw the appearance of the encyclopedic *Literary History of Canada*. Frye had been approached by Carl Klinck in the 1950s to join the editorial committee for a history of English Canadian literature, and his membership included the preparation of a thorough conclusion to this masterly work. "The conclusion which I wrote for this history repeats a good many conceptions worked out earlier during the poetry reviews, but it is closely related to the rest of the book in which it first appeared, and is heavily dependent on the other contributors for data, conceptions, and often phrasing," he wrote later (419). With the intention of showing "how the verbal imagination operates as a ferment in all cultural life," Frye realized that the literary history "tends to confirm me in most of my intuitions on the subject: the advantage for me is that this attempt at conclusion and summary can involve some self-plagiarism" (341, 340). The conclusion offers a fine occasion for Frye to bring together many of the themes that have characterized his understanding of the Canadian imagination.

"Canada has, for all practical purposes, no Atlantic seaboard. The traveller from Europe edges into it like a tiny Jonah entering an inconceivably large whale, slipping past the Straits of Belle Isle into the Gulf of St. Lawrence, where five Canadian provinces surround him, for the most part invisible," Frye begins. "Then he goes up the St. Lawrence and the inhabited country comes into view, mainly a French-speaking country, with its own cultural traditions. To enter the United States is a matter of crossing an ocean; to enter Canada is a matter of being silently swallowed by an alien continent." And once the settler has made his home in Canada, "he then becomes aware of the longitudinal dimension, the southward pull toward the richer and more glamorous American cities" (343–4).

Here are Frye's many and by now famous observations about the development of a Canadian literature. There is "a tone of deep terror in regard to nature . . . not a terror of the dangers or discomforts or even the mysteries of nature, but a terror of the soul at something that these things manifest. The human mind has nothing but human and moral values to cling to if it is to preserve its integrity or even its sanity, yet the vast unconsciousness of nature in front of it seems an unanswerable denial of those values" (350).

The garrison emerges as a central feature of Frye's portrait of the struggling literary voice. "Small and isolated communities surrounded with a physical or psychological 'frontier,' separated from one another and from their American and British cultural sources: communities that provide all that their members have in the way of distinctively human values, and that are compelled to feel a great respect for the law and order that holds them together, yet confronted with a huge, unthinking, menacing, and formidable physical setting—such communities are bound to develop what we may provisionally call a garrison mentality" (350–1). And this mentality changes as the centre of Canadian life moves to the metropolis, the garrison mentality beginning "as an expression of the moral values generally accepted in the group as a whole, and then, as society gets more complicated and more in control of its environment, it becomes more of a revolutionary garrison within a metropolitan society" (355).

It is in the conclusion to this compilation that Frye first observed that the Canadian sensibility is "less perplexed by the question, 'Who am I?' than by some such riddle as, 'Where is here?'" (346). But the *Literary History* closed its survey at the end of the 1950s, and the accuracy of Frye's observation on earlier literature should not blind historians to the fact that the 1950s were also the time when Canada's colonial literary mentality gave way to a postcolonial mentality no longer obsessed or even perplexed by the meaning of *here*.

For Frye, the conclusion meant a great deal more than his observations. Just as the writers featured in the compilation have identified the habits and attitudes of the country, just as they "have also left an imaginative legacy of dignity and of high courage" (372), so, too, the conclusion gave Frye the occasion to reiterate his themes in the context of a vision of Canada that arises from the pages of the texts themselves: "The reader of this book, even if he is not Canadian or much interested in Canadian literature as such, may still learn a good deal about the literary imagination as a force and function of life generally" (341). In adding his detailed conclusion, Frye presented a paradigm of the literary patterns that stand behind English Canadian literature.

With the publication of the *Literary History* Frye suspended his involvement with Canadian literature. The years of the *University of Toronto Quarterly* reviews had exhausted him, and his work with the *Literary History* committee had now ended. Between 1963 and 1971 he published twelve books; three of them were collections of previously published writings, the third one being *The Bush Garden: Essays on the Canadian Imagination* (1971). In this last he published many of his Canadian essays, and the core of the book is his magisterial conclusion to the *Literary*

History. Only one essay from his post-conclusion writings appeared in the book, his introduction to a study of Lawren Harris (no. 58).

When Frye did return to Canadian literature, he was not content to reiterate his previous statements. In the new conclusion to the second edition of the *Literary History* (1976), he focused on Canada within the North American continent. "It is difficult to know what to say, as a general conclusion, to this part of the *Literary History* that is not already said or implied in my previous conclusion," he began. Of course, so much had happened in the quantity of the literature: "nearly every contributor says or implies something about the colossal verbal explosion that has taken place in Canada since 1960," he notes (448–9). But then he turns for the better part of his new conclusion to Canada as part of North America. Not a continentalist himself, he argues that an "independent Canada would be much more useful to the United States itself than a dependent or annexed one would be, and it is of great importance to the United States to have a critical view of it centred in Canada, a view which is not hostile but is simply another view" (452).

Frye's perspective on the United States is seminal to an understanding of his view of Canada. In the second conclusion he developed at length the contrast he had established in the *University of Toronto Quarterly* reviews and the first conclusion between the Whiggish and a priori American revolutionary tradition and the more pragmatic, ad hoc, and conservative Canadian attitude. The United States "found its identity in the eighteenth century, the age of rationalism and enlightenment. It retains a strong intellectual fascination with the eighteenth century: its founding fathers are still its primary cultural heroes, and the bicentenary celebrations of 1976, from all accounts, will be mainly celebrations of the eighteenth century rather than of the present day" (453). Canada, on the other hand, "had no enlightenment, and very little eighteenth century. The British and French spent the eighteenth century in Canada battering down each other's forts, and Canada went directly from the Baroque expansion of the seventeenth century to the Romantic expansion of the nineteenth" (454). It now appeared to him that the two nations were beginning to exchange identities: after the traumas of the Vietnam War and Watergate, the United States was engaging in questioning and self-examination, whereas Canada was experiencing a period of cultural flowering and confidence. In the essays from the 1970s these essential distinctions between Canada and the United States persist.

In 1974, while Frye was Charles Eliot Norton Professor of Poetry at

Harvard University, I invited him to return the following year and present a paper for my new course on Canadian literature. He readily accepted, adding that the paper he would like to give would be a detailed study of Canadian painting; he wanted to explore a variety of artists and pursue his sense of the varied features that seem to represent the patterns of landscape painting. A year later, I asked him for the title, and he regretted that he did not have sufficient time to write his projected paper on landscape; instead, he offered "Haunted by Lack of Ghosts: Some Patterns in the Imagery of Canadian Poetry." But his obsessive interest in Canadian painting marks another distinctive feature of his later essays.

"Painting is by far the most interesting art in Canada up to almost 1960," Frye announced in 1977 (528), and in 1980 he reiterated, "painting was perhaps the liveliest of all Canadian arts up to about 1960 at least, and is still very much in a foreground position" (562). In the later essays he often returns to painting, the subject of many of his early essays, to solidify his theories in an inclusive way: "Once again it is painting that gives us the clearest sense of the contrast. If we turn from the Group of Seven to the Quebec landscape painters, to Maurice Cullen, Suzor-Côté, Clarence Gagnon, and the very little of Morrice that was done in Canada, we are in a world of softer and gentler outlines where the sense of being lived in shows through" (513). And in Lawren Harris, he may well be presenting the ideal he himself follows: "He is missionary as well as explorer: not a missionary who wants to destroy all faith that differs from his own, but a missionary who wants to make his own faith real to others. Just as a new country cannot become a civilization without explorers and pioneers going out into the loneliness of a deserted land, so no social imagination can develop except through those who have followed their own vision beyond its inevitable loneliness to its final resting place in the tradition of art" (402).

Many of the later essays are explorations of Canadian culture. All the time he was writing his books on the Bible, Frye was continually drawn back to his own country, now as the spokesperson for a vibrant Canadian culture, "the indestructible core of a human society, so far as it is a human society and not a mere aggregate of atoms in a human mass" (671). In these essays Frye is a careful critic of Canada, a land that has occupied his attention all his life. He could not write the definitive book on Canadian literature or culture because, as he notes in his conclusion to the second edition of the *Literary History*, "It would be an affectation for me to pretend not to notice that I am extensively featured in this book myself" (449).

Frye was the most respected critic of his country's literature; as he himself sensed, he was a vital participant in his country's cultural evolution.

David Staines

II

Frye's substantial contribution to the development of Canadian literature and its criticism is made abundantly clear by a consideration of the critical reaction to his Canadian writings. In what follows I have chosen a thematic organization and concentrated on those aspects that have appeared puzzling, problematic, or contradictory to his readers, not in a polemical spirit but as a way of exploring the arguments. Frye is a notoriously "poetic" thinker,[10] and his penchant for holding diametrically opposed ideas simultaneously is a challenge to more linear minds. The fact that his pronouncements have called forth a diversity of responses among Canadian critics emphasizes the degree to which he has dominated the Canadian cultural scene for many years.

A convenient starting-point is Frye's influential and widely quoted assertion that "nature is consistently sinister and menacing in Canadian poetry" (37) in his review of Smith's *Book of Canadian Poetry* in 1943. Frye developed this idea in the conclusion to *Literary History of Canada* (1965) and the preface to *The Bush Garden* (1971) when he described the "garrison mentality" of settlers barricading themselves inside their small centres of civilization against both nature and human attack. Opposition to these notions has been expressed by some of the poets supposedly characterized. In a symposium following Frye's delivery of "Canadian Culture Today" (no. 72) in Washington, for instance, both Ralph Gustafson and Douglas LePan repudiated the suggestion that they were "terrified" or "fixated on survival."[11] Some critics, too, have questioned the adequacy of this characterization of the dominant note in earlier Canadian literature. For these writers, Frye does less than justice to the literary responses to the startlingly beautiful aspects of nature, which they see as also quintessentially Canadian. Wayne Grady argues that, far from being terrified of an alien nature, some writers "walk[ed] boldly into it, compelled by its seeming limitless beauty to express our response in a literature that is filled with wonder and respect."[12] For Susan Glickman, what Frye characterizes as terror was a component of the response to the sublime, and could be a positive, life-enhancing encounter with otherness.[13] Sandra Djwa maintains that in early Canadian poetry, nature is as often beneficent as fearsome. She traces the note of terror Frye discerns to his propensity to read through the lens of E.J. Pratt's poetry, which inherited from such writers as Thomas Hardy a sense of the stark indifference of nature to human concerns.[14]

As if anticipating this charge of biased vision, in his review of Smith's anthology Frye dismisses the idea that the sombre "unity of tone" (28) he discerns may have been imposed by the anthologist's selective criteria. But his own selective criteria may well be at work, making him respond aesthetically to those poems that display the chosen attitude and to dismiss others as conventional expressions of the appreciation of nature. Thus, "Canadian poetry is at its best a poetry of incubus and *cauchemar*" (36); "the better the poem the more clearly it expresses it" (37). The chronological organization of the present volume makes it clear that, though Frye may have seen the theme in Canadian poetry on first looking into Smith's anthology, he was predisposed to find it there. As Staines points out, in his 1941 essay on "Canadian and Colonial Painting" he had already used the incubus figure for the inability to absorb the menacing vacant land imaginatively (14). It is worth noting, too, that this distrust of nature is very similar to that expressed in *Fearful Symmetry*, which he was writing at the time of the Smith review. In 1953 he first used the Jonah's-whale figure described by Staines for the way the traveller becomes swallowed by Canada (102). Since this Leviathan image is his Blake- and Bible-derived figure for "the monster of indefinite time and space" (485) from which humankind needs to be delivered, Canadian nature acquires even more negative, and typically Frygian, overtones.

As time passed, both Frye's perception of the artistic response to Canadian nature and his own views of nature evolved. He learned from scientific theorists such as David Bohm and from the environmental movement that man and nature form a continuum rather than being opposed entities.[15] In the 1960s his comments on Canadian artists take on a new tone. Even in the conclusion to the *Literary History of Canada* he recognized the presence of two attitudes to nature in Canadian poetry, one of terror and one which constructs a pastoral myth. The latter is no longer a mere reflection of social mythology, but has a "genuinely imaginative form" in which nature, "though still full of awfulness and mystery, is the visible representative of an order that man has violated, a spiritual unity that the intellect murders to dissect" (364, 367). In 1968, he praised Pratt's ability, as a Newfoundland poet, to see not just the ferocity and destructiveness of nature, but also "the unquenchable energy and the limitless endurance which unite the real man with real nature" (396). In 1969 he remarked in relation to Lawren Harris that the artist's mind seeks a responding spirit in nature, "the quality in nature which for the artist ... contains what can be identified with the searching intelligence" (401). In his later theorizing, as we shall see, he came to reinterpret the sense of terror before the vacant land, which he still maintained was predominant in earlier literature and painting, as part of the problem with the colonial mentality that needed to be overcome if a mature culture was to develop.

Critics nevertheless continue to identify Frye with his earlier and less nuanced formulation regarding the perceived threat of nature because of its power and memorability. It has become a cultural icon, a historical marker in the evolution of Canadian consciousness. As Desmond Pacey asserts, the Smith review "has become one of the classics of our criticism."[16] Staines refers to the first conclusion to the *Literary History* as "an immediate classic, the single most-quoted essay in Canadian literary criticism."[17] The conclusion had an unusual distinction: written for the first edition, it was hailed as a Canadian myth in the second (of which it still formed a part), when Malcolm Ross declared that "Frye, in attempting to specify a temper peculiarly Canadian, is at the same time making for us a myth."[18] Towards the end of his life Frye remarked that his phrase "garrison mentality" had been somewhat over-exposed, "its specific historical context being usually ignored" (647).

The fecundity of Frye's concept of the Canadian poet's response to nature can be seen in the studies of Canadian literature indebted to it. Such works include D.G. Jones's *Butterfly on Rock: A Study of Themes and Images in Canadian Literature* (1970), Marcia B. Kline's *Beyond the Land Itself: Views of Nature in Canada and the United States* (1970), Margaret Atwood's *Survival: A Thematic Guide to Canadian Literature* (1972), John Moss's *Patterns of Isolation in English-Canadian Fiction* (1974), Jay Macpherson's chapter "This Swan Neck of the Woods" in *The Spirit of Solitude: Conventions and Continuities in Late Romance* (1982), and perhaps even Dennis Lee's *Savage Fields: An Essay on Literature and Cosmology*

(1977). These works do not servilely echo Frye; for instance, a whiff of D.H. Lawrence blows through Jones's chapters, nature appearing often as a source of vital instinctual life repressed by the conventional civilization of the garrison. But in spite of their individual differences, these works are similar in that they all probe the characteristic attitudes associated with the imaginative presentation of the Canadian environment as Frye had done. Written coincidentally with the establishment of the academic study of Canadian literature, they were taken up immediately into university courses, along with the writings of Frye himself, and became part of the established contours of the subject.

Criticism of such studies began with Frank Davey's "Surviving the Paraphrase" (first given as a speech at the founding conference of the Association for Canadian and Quebec Literatures in 1974) with its complaint that in "thematic" criticism of this type, "the critic extracts for his deliberations the paraphrasable content and throws away the form."[19] In a further reaction against what was conceived of as the reigning orthodoxy in Canadian literary studies, Barry Cameron and Michael Dixon, in their introduction to the 1977 special issue of *Studies in Canadian Literature*, complained that thematic criticism, which reduced Canadian literature to a single theme, failed to do justice to the richness of the literature. Frye's thematic approach was relevant at the time he wrote his conclusion, they argued, but became a "dated letter" as that literature developed. Rather than being studied as specifically Canadian, our literature should be treated "as part of the autonomous world of literature."[20] The latter phrase has such a Frygian ring that it is evident the authors are using Frye's general critical theory to suggest limitations in his purely Canadian writings. Davey had done the same in pointing out the alternatives to thematic study, one of which was the archetypal criticism of Frye himself. Paul Stuewe's *Clearing the Ground* is a later, less temperate attack on the supposedly negative effect of Frye's thematics.[21] But as early as 1978, Russell Brown was arguing in his essay "Critic, Culture, Text: Beyond Thematics" that thematic considerations were still relevant as long as they were incorporated into a more comprehensive critical schema. Thus common themes might be seen as part of the grammar of the Canadian imagination, used as "a structural feature ... to give form to a work."[22] And Heather Murray argues that thematic criticism at its best was a "serious if over-extended and under-equipped attempt to form ... a criticism both literary/aesthetic and social/historical, a criticism attentive to both the text and its culture."[23]

"Attentive . . . to the culture": this phrase highlights another of the difficulties with Frye's "garrison" theme. By concentrating on the Canadianness of Canadian literature, Frye appeared to be practising a form of "environmental determinism,"[24] arguing (in contradiction to all his theoretical work) that literature was defined by its place of origin. Leon Surette has coined the term "topocentrism" for this belief.[25] Here I want to note one particular subset of this criticism, that which links Frye with a specifically North American determinism. In 1971, Eli Mandel viewed Frye's emphasis on the wilderness rather than on the institutions inherited from Britain and France as an extension of the "frontier theory" of Frederick Jackson Turner, in which the native North American environment is seen to exercise a decisive influence over American history.[26] In his 1976 essay "Northrop Frye and the Continentalist Tradition" David Jackel also linked Frye to this North American context, complaining that Frye thereby negated the Canadian particularity while claiming to define it; while Frye often recognized an east-west or "Laurentian" axis in Canada (414) and a series of north-south axes linking Canada to the United States, he underplayed the east-west axis.[27] The frequency of contrasts between the United States and Canada in Frye's later writings, however, disposes of this contention.

Whereas some critics complained that Frye paid too much attention to the environment out of which Canadian culture arose, others (or sometimes the same ones) introduced a diametrically opposed set of considerations when they discussed the relation between Frye's more general theory of literature and his remarks on Canadian poets: Frye was thought to be fostering a school of poets who used universal, transcultural myths and archetypes rather than reflecting the world around them. The least attractive form of this complaint posits a self-reflexive coterie or mythopoeic mafia. According to Jackel, Frye elaborated a particular, myth-centred theory which was reflected in the poetry of former students such as Margaret Atwood, Margaret Avison, Dennis Lee, Jay Macpherson, and James Reaney. Such poetry was then praised by Frye in his reviews for revealing the importance of myth. George Bowering castigated an unworldly set of "Northrop Frye poets" who huddled apart from the mainstream, to wit those who were more open to the currents emanating from the United States.[28] Obviously the topic of Frye's influence is an enormously complex one, but in practice it tends to centre on the more manageable question of the relation between his poetry reviews in the *University of Toronto Quarterly* (no. 34) and the

Introduction

ideas in *Anatomy of Criticism*, which he was then producing. One of Jackel's arguments was that Frye selected, for reprint in his influential *Bush Garden*, those portions of the *UTQ* reviews that bring out the mythological dimension of poetry.[29] The reader of the present volume, where sections omitted in *The Bush Garden* are in braces, will see a different principle of selection. The sections omitted are those concerning minor or amateur poets, some anthologies, and most chapbooks, even when the latter two involve well-known authors such as Dorothy Livesay, Louis Dudek, and Earle Birney, or mythopoeic poets such as Macpherson.

A reading of the uncut reviews will cast doubt on Mandel's notion that in them one "repeatedly" reads about "symbolism," "mythical and metaphorical," and even "apocalyptic," a complaint first aired by Louis Dudek.[30] In the *Anatomy* Frye remarked that popular literature "affords an unobstructed view of archetypes" (*AC*, 116), yet the word "archetype" is used only twice in the 139 pages of reviews, once in relation to another critic's method (159, 191). Far from trying to favour one particular school, Frye goes out of his way (in the inclusive spirit of *Anatomy*) to recognize the genre being attempted and to help poets to find their individual voices. In an analysis of the approach Frye takes in "Letters in Canada," Milton Wilson has shown that both the system-making impulse and the interest in archetypes so prominent in *Anatomy* are muted here. He argues that in the reviews Frye calls upon his deepest-rooted resource as a reader of poetry, his sense of verbal texture and rhythm. As "field work" for *Anatomy*, his studies of this poetry contribute most to Frye's understanding of rhetoric, or the *melos*, *lexis*, and *opsis* of the Fourth Essay.[31] Perhaps his most basic concern is for poetic sincerity. It may seem odd at first glance to find him speaking out for the heartfelt over the formulaic, for "fresh experience" (94) and lyrics in which the poet "speaks directly" (96). But "repeating ready-made formulas is one thing; working within a convention is quite another" (98): a conventional form may be the best means of releasing genuine emotion, as it is in Jay Macpherson's poetry (147). The distinction rests in the quality of the rhetoric, with much scope for Frye's favourite, question-begging word "genuine." Frye is delighted to recognize genuineness in any guise; as a sympathetic, helpful reviewer attentive to craft, he could not be faulted.

There remains the larger question of whether, through his new theoretical understanding, Frye did encourage a "mythopoeic" type of poetry. He vigorously denied that he did, pointing out that a critic cannot influence an artist directly in this way (450). He went too far, however, in polemically maintaining that there is no such thing as mythopoeic poetry, all poetry being equally so; here he is using the word "myth" with the special, restricted meaning of "the structural principle of a poem." At other times he uses the word in its more conventional sense and admits there can be more or less mythopoeia in poetry, speaking for instance of three great mythopoeic periods in English literature (418). In the edition of *Literary History* in which Frye thanks George Woodcock for putting paid to the notion of a "Frye school of mythopoeic poetry" (450), Woodcock points out that the idea of such a school is one of our potent myths. He also maintains, however, that the poet-critics associated with Frye were influential in spreading the theory of a new kind of allusive poetry.[32] In a previous article he had posited not so much a direct influence from Frye as a kind of synchronicity, with a general revival of interest in mythology in literature at this time.[33] One might cite in support of him James Reaney's editorial inaugurating the periodical *Alphabet* (1960), which hails the use and study of iconography as one of the most exciting developments of the century and a particularly noticeable phenomenon in Canada.[34] Though he is not mentioned by name, Frye's presence hovers over the discussion. Reaney does mention Macpherson and also Hope Lee, who later edited anthologies for schools based on Frye's principles.[35] In his theoretical work, which shared the poets' vision and shaped it in rational form, Woodcock argues, Frye "did stimulate a generation of poets by clarifying their poems for them and . . . liberating their imaginations for further efforts."[36]

The most immediately controversial feature of *Anatomy* was its assertion that the critic's function was not to judge the work in front of him. Several critics have pointed out that in his *UTQ* reviews Frye does act as a judge, though they have generally recognized that he made a distinction between the public critic, or reviewer, and the critic proper, or theorist.[37] In a late interview, Frye confessed that the necessity a reviewer is under to say, "This is a permanent thing, which you will want to go back to, and this is expendable," was "rather what got me down" about the job.[38] More impressive as an example of the application of his nonjudgmental stance is *Literary History of Canada*. Djwa has shown that Frye was no mere accessory, brought in at the last to read the manuscript and draw together a conclusion; rather, he was a collaborator of Klinck's from the inception of the project in 1956, involved in many practical decisions. In particular, Frye's "Preface to an Uncollected Anthology" (no. 41) gave Klinck the rationale for his nonevaluative approach to

Canadian literature, in which the critic is "somewhere between" the social scientist who merely describes and the critic who upholds ordinary literary values.[39]

No one would deny that *Literary History of Canada* heeds Frye's dictum even to excess, in that at times it reads like a mere catalogue of the good, the better, and the best forgotten. But Frye's conclusion is another matter. Murray points out through a careful analysis of Frye's ambiguous use of the term "literature" the contradictions inherent in his stance. Frye both denies evaluation, when he says that one's idea of literature needs to be widened when looking at the Canadian writing scene, and at the same time evaluates according to the traditional idea of literature, when he argues that it is easier to see what literature is trying to do in "a literature that has not quite done it" (341).[40] In that Frye's conclusion addresses the problems inherent in dealing with a minor literature, it thus provides a way into a last major topic, the question of colonialism.

Frye's reflections on the colonial "frostbite at the roots of the Canadian imagination" (30) were contested mainly because they sorted so oddly with his general theory. In *Anatomy*, Frye presents literature as an autonomous verbal universe organized by archetypes. Though he does not deny that individual works have a descriptive meaning which relates to the external world, he argues that the final direction of attention is inward to the patterns established by verbal relations within the work (*AC*, 74). In studying a poem, the natural progression is to move from the individual work, to other poems by the same author, and thence to the context of literature as a whole. The intermediate context is more likely to be all the literature written in the poet's language than all the literature of his nation. Poetry, Frye says, is written from other poetry: poets draw on the tradition of their craft for their shaping form, while their actual environment, if used at all, is mere content. What does it matter, then, where a poem was written? Why not be colonial—are not all poets, in this sense?—and what is the difference between being colonial and writing literature fully informed by the literary tradition of one's language?

Some critics have seen advantages in living at the periphery. A.J.M. Smith comments on the many models available to the Canadian poet because of "his position of separateness and semi-isolation."[41] Milton Wilson, in an article which Frye quotes (492), also muses that "I even wonder whether colonialism may not be, in theory at least, the most desirable poetic state. . . . The Canadian poet has all the models in the language (not to mention other languages) at his disposal, but lacks the deadening awareness that he is competing with them."[42] Mandel takes this remark to be "the result either of quiet desperation or of irony,"[43] but I think it is neither. Nevertheless, in spite of all this potential, there is a sense (much studied of late) in which a colonial literature does appear to be derivative, minor, or less than compelling to outsiders. Frye never denied that literary excellence has some relation to the social conditions under which it is produced; he simply denied that we know what that relation is (577). In his studies of particular authors he takes into account politics, history, and the climate of ideas, though it is true that geography does not feature prominently. His Canadian writings offered an opportunity for one knowing the conditions intimately—indeed living in and through them—to approach this question of the background of literature and to come up with some tentative suggestions, which is all he intends his remarks to be.

Surette discerns two contradictory theories among Frye and his followers regarding the problematical relation of the colonial poet to the literary tradition of his native language. On the one hand, the poet is seen as cut off, unable to enjoy the wealth of models because of geographic distance. In this vein Frye argues that the English poet is part of a tradition extending back to Homer and the Old Testament, whereas to the Canadian poet, "broken off from this linear sequence and having none of his own, the traditions of Europe appear as a kaleidoscopic whirl with no definite shape or meaning" (32). To this Surette remarks that "the resident of High Wycombe ignorant of Greek and Hebrew is much more cut off from the hypostatized 'linear sequence' than the resident of White Horse who is conversant in both languages,"[44] and wonders, like Smith and Wilson, why a colonial poet should be considered "cut off."

This is not an argument that Frye pursues far, though by stressing the need for urban centres (624) he implies that a writer may be cut off, not only by lack of texts, but also by lack of a literary community to discuss them with. But the second and opposite explanation of colonialism, which Surette sees in D.G. Jones but does not investigate in Frye, is more important to Frye. In this view, the poet is connected with his tradition, but situated in a new land to which that tradition is unsuited. Frye's doctrine is linked to his idea that the poet's quest is not to see, even imaginatively, but to give form to what he sees (268). Frye sometimes uses the word "form" in the sense of "imaginative shape," or the poet's pattern of images. In this sense he opposes poetry to the versified rhetoric which is likely to emerge from a garrison; this has the same audience-facing characteristics here as it does later in *Words with Power*, and is an apt characterization of much earlier Canadian verse. At other times "form" refers to the more traditional "verse forms." We are reminded that the theory of modes in the First Essay of *Anatomy* is "environmental," in that dominant modes, genres, and themes are appropriate to the prevailing social organization. A colony is out of step, in that a sophisticated social system and the most primitive wilderness coexist. Thus we have the odd phenomenon Frye likes to dwell on, that of an Anglo-Saxon imaginative sense trying to express itself in late Romantic forms (265–6). Pratt is so successful partly because he has some of the characteristics of the Anglo-Saxon oral poet (385). As Ross remarks, for Frye Canadian writers have failed first as readers, not having digested the literary tradition and seen the possibilities in earlier forms.[45]

These thoughts about the relation of the colonial writer to his tradition are characteristic of Frye's earlier period. He enlarged his views enormously in what Staines calls a third period of cultural criticism in which he began to probe history, particularly what Canada shared and did not share with the United States. By this time, Canadian literature had outgrown its colonial status and was admired worldwide, and Canada itself had become fully independent of Britain, so that he was studying a process of change and maturing. The most notable feature of his new awareness—and one that seems insufficiently studied by critics—is his emphasis on the Cartesian consciousness that, along with Baroque Christianity, dominated European settlement of the new world. This mindset, which Frye characterizes as rational and individualistic, proclaimed the supremacy of the human consciousness, looked on nature only as an external environment to be subdued and exploited, and thus helped to fuel the "garrison mentality." In October 1975, in a major address to the Royal Society's symposium on preserving the Canadian heritage (no. 67), he deplored the result of this inherited predatory and imperialistic attitude: "many of our major social problems are those of ecology, the extinction of animal species, the plundering of forests and mines, the pollution of water. . . . We are the grave robbers of our own resources, and posterity will not be grateful to us" (435–6). A few months later he wrote that "we are . . . Cartesian ghosts caught in the machine that we have assumed nature to be" (478). Of course the remedy for Frye is not exactly to accept nature as it is, though there is a strain of this idea in some of his later writings. Rather it is to humanize nature by entering into imaginative contact with it: in the final analysis, by making myths. When Frye in later years praises recent poetry for its "professionalism," what he has in mind are its mythopoeic qualities. And one feature he prizes particularly about this new poetry is its ability to draw from Canada's native traditions, the myths of those who have always belonged here: "We are no longer an army of occupation, and the natives are ourselves" (520). Once this sense of belonging is established, then the poet is able to absorb rather than simply to imitate his or her cultural tradition. The whole process is described in "Haunted by Lack of Ghosts" (no. 70), which ends by endorsing Wilson's notion of the simultaneous presence of all the elements of the tradition, but for the mature rather than the colonial poet.

An often noted feature of this criticism has been the shift in emphasis from nation to region, a shift with both political and cultural aspects.[46] Politically, Frye declared in 1977, Canada had gone "from a prenational to a postnational phase of existence without ever having been a nation" (532); its containing form was "coming apart at the seams" and its future arrangements were unclear. In cultural terms, he saw a more positive evolution from a colonial or provincial culture to a mature, regional one without an intervening national stage. A favourite image of his for the imagination had always been the vegetable, "something that needs roots and a limited environment" (576). In "Canada and Its Poetry" he had suggested that the nation is the right size of plot for this particular vegetable (28). In his 1966 essay "Design as a Creative Principle in the Arts," however, he argued that "whatever the merits of the art produced in our time, it will certainly be an international art, and decentralizing theories seem at present to be a hopeless anachronism. . . . [T]he extent to which Canadian culture can grow out of the Canadian soil I realize in advance to be an exceedingly limited one."[47] In *The Modern Century* (1967) he again repudiated "cultural nationalism," though confessing "that I held a version of it myself, or thought I did, when I was beginning to write in Canadian periodicals" (*MC*, 53). In his later pronouncements he combined the international perspective with a theory of regionalism: "A world like ours produces a single international style of which all existing literatures are regional developments. This international style is not a bag of rhetorical tricks, but a way of seeing and thinking in a world controlled by uniform patterns of technology, and the regional development is a way of escaping from that uniformity" (554). Thus Canada shows its maturity by the liveliness of its localized cultures. And there is a hint here of a reconciliation of his environmental with his theoretical criticism. Frye had always declared, though somewhat unconvincingly before, that the poet's environment provided "mere content." For mature writers, form is derived from literature as a whole, while what is shared with writers of the same region is extraliterary content; as expressed in "Culture as Interpenetration," the literature is provincial in "articulate content" rather than in "inarticulate form" (530).

Frye's regionalism has been contested by Ross, who argues for an overall sense of national identity characterized precisely by the tolerance of, as well as tensions between, these regions.[48] The difference is perhaps similar to that between those who see Canada as a "community of communities" and those who espouse a strong central government. In this volume the reader will find Frye taking a variety of attitudes to the political situation. To mention the extremes, in the "Options" conference on the future of Canadian Confederation in 1977 (no. 74), Frye appears to be a federalist, whereas in "Canadian Culture Today" in the same year he seems to look with equanimity on political, economic, and technological dependence on the United States (514). But one of his main tenets is that political and cultural situations need not be congruent: no matter what the fate of Canada's polity, its culture may retain its distinctiveness, and to him "the fight for cultural distinctiveness . . . is a fight for human dignity itself" (495). Ross had argued that if Canadian culture were purely regional it would be impossible to discuss "Canadian literature" at all. But at the opening of the Canadian Embassy in Washington in 1989 Frye made the point that "the *aggregate* of writers in Canada will produce a Canadian body of literature, which is felt by both Canadian and non-Canadian readers to be distinctive of the country" (645) though it may be impossible to characterize precisely. In his last statement on the theme, characteristically, he stressed the outstanding need for cultural Reconfederation along multicultural lines, with a hope that a renewed political Reconfederation will be its basis (667).

The sense of liberation from a white, European tradition into multiculturalism is one of the most prominent themes in Frye's last papers. Both for this reason and because of the contradictions and tensions in his Canadian writings, Frye may be read in a postcolonial context, as Murray and also Wang Ning have done.[49] These tensions are hailed by Linda Hutcheon as evidence of postmodern complexity and both/and thinking.[50] In this sense Frye's Canadian writings may prove to be more congenial than his "modernist" theoretical works to a world that he calls "post-American, post-British, post everything except the world itself" (371).

It is not necessary, however, to validate Frye by assimilating him to the predominant discourse. In some ways he is more fruitfully read as part of his time, part of the development of Canadian culture in its Ontario-centred phase, and himself a monument in it. This collection includes many of his classic statements, those which will always be read and which naturally attract most comment. But the virtue of an inclusive Canadian volume is that it also shows the myriad, noncanonical ways in which Frye contributed to Canadian culture: the introductions to others' works, the summaries, the reviews, the tributes, the endless reading for the Governor-General's Awards. This tireless work, as well as his more monumental pieces, aided the flowering of Canadian literature that he prized as one of the most significant developments of his lifetime.

As part of that "verbal explosion" (449), to what extent was Frye a product of his Canadian environment? Are *Anatomy* and *The Great Code*, for instance, typically Canadian products? Canadians are by reputation so apologetic and mild-mannered—what Frye calls "incoherent, inarticulate, proceeding by hunch and feeling" (459)—that one's first impulse would probably be to deny it. Nevertheless Eleanor Cook has argued that *Anatomy* is a typically Canadian hybrid form in its combination of magisterial anatomy and personal confession.[51] Margaret Atwood has located the Canadianness of *Anatomy* in its attempt to see the larger framework, an impulse she connects with the status of the smaller observer-nation.[52] In "Northrop Frye as a Canadian Critic," A.C. Hamilton has set out to show that every key aspect of Frye's criticism, including his stress of humanity's need to construct an imaginative world out of nature, his desire to "probe into the distance," his inductive method, and his inclusiveness, may be linked to aspects of the Canadian environment and history.[53] Certainly Frye never doubted that "scholarship ... grows out of a specific environment and is in part a response to it" (558), and that if he had left Canada, his own work "would have been quite different in tone and in context."[54] Many of the remarks he makes about Canadian artists illuminate his own genesis. Perhaps the most striking part of his Canadian heritage was his ability to live in a country based from the first on different languages and cultures, clashing regions, and ad hoc compromises, a country which he ventured to surmise might "serve as a pilot project for an emerging new mode of human life" (532).

Jean O'Grady

Northrop Frye on Canada

1

Lord Dufferin

April 1938

Review of Helen's Tower, *by Harold Nicolson (London: Macmillan [Constable], 1937). From* Canadian Forum, *18 (April 1938): 458.*

Mr. Nicolson is planning to write his autobiography as a series of biographies of the important people he has met. *Helen's Tower* is thus partly a biography of his uncle Lord Dufferin and partly a scattered series of recollections of his own childhood, with special reference to a governess named Miss Plimsoll. This idea, it may be said at once, has very little to recommend it. Almost any fair-to-middling novelist could give us a good sketch of childish experiences and impressions, possibly sparing us the patronizing sneers at the wretched little governess. Nor is this really necessary to the book: the author's infancy has essentially very little to do with his subject, and merely gets in the way of it.

That subject, Lord Dufferin, is an important man well worth writing about. He was the Governor-General of Canada in the difficult post-Confederation period, Viceroy of India when Russia was turned from collision with British to collision with Japanese interests and when Burma was conquered, key man in the negotiations with Turkey which led to the seizure of Egypt, ambassador to Russia, Turkey, Italy, and France at various critical times, and author, in his younger days, of a book in Everyman's Library, *Letters from High Latitudes*. He was a Liberal, in the sense in which Edmund Burke was a Whig, an aristocrat in a period of declining aristocracy convinced of the importance and responsibility of his class. Such an attitude in so oligarchic an age had something romantic about it, and Dufferin was strongly influenced in his youth by two very important phenomena of Romanticism, the novels of Scott and the

Anglo-Catholic movement headed by Pusey. His memorial tower to his mother, from which the book gets its name, decorated with the poems extracted from Tennyson and Browning about it,[1] the author takes as a symbol of this Romanticism. Dufferin's class prejudices were blinkers which helped him to do sincerely and competently the jobs given him by his government, while shutting out the disturbing impressions which might have interfered with that competence. In the history of the blind, half-unconscious seizure of world markets by English merchants he is a typical figure and by no means an unattractive one.

The author is perhaps too much in sympathy with his hero to look at him objectively—he tries to at first, but soon gets tired of it, and his interpretation of his material is generally about on a level with *Cavalcade*.[2] One will also have to get used to a humour which sees fit to employ such words as "agglutinative," "striated," and "amalgam" when the subject is hair-oil, and to a certain amount of this sort of thing:

> His own attitude was one of old-fashionable chivalry. He would rise when she entered a room and open the door for her when she left. He would pay her little compliments which brought the blush to her cheek. "Oh little Lal," he would say when he was over seventy, "how well that gown becomes you! How beautiful you look to-night!" [144]

These and other faults excepted, the book is a readable and entertaining account of a man all Canadians ought to know something about.

2

Characters in Cadence

April–May 1938

Review of Characters in Cadence *by Louise Morey Bowman (Toronto: Macmillan, 1938). From* Canadian Bookman, *20 (April–May 1938): 49.*

The author of this volume of poems is a Canadian representative of the Amy Lowell school of imagism. Her work reflects the rather precious style of interior decorating and the affinity with vegetable life characteristic of this type of poetry. She is at her best when writing of quiet forests and the more whimsical aspects of fantasy:

> There was overtone and undertone
> of the tide's low moan;
> there were birds that called
> in the wood at the end of the town;
> in the tops of the trees there was sound
> but none in the soft brown ground
> of the wood at the end of the town—
> but now they have cut the wood down. [*Fugue*, final stanza]

We recognize a tenuous but perceptible charm, sincere emotion, and a knack of getting a real aesthetic value out of the vague and undefined impression. She is at her worst, however, when sententious and discursive, her range of ideas being rather commonplace. Her anecdotes, character sketches, and aphorisms are not very successful, and even the more objective poems are injured by the obtrusion of vague abstract words and ideas.

The most serious fault is a lack of precision in imagery, phrase, or rhythm. There is scarcely a poem without a cliché or some ready-made poetic formula, and this laziness is the more irritating in that the poet seems capable of giving her work a much higher finish. With a more relentless conscience, she may contribute something distinctively romantic to Canadian poetry.

3

Canadian Art in London

January 1939

From Canadian Forum, *18 (January 1939): 304–5. The holograph article is in Helen Frye Fonds, 1991, box 2, file 4. Frye was reviewing the exhibition "A Century of Canadian Art," which ran at the Tate Gallery from 14 October 1938 to 2 January 1939.*

The Canadian Exhibition at the Tate Gallery was opened by a somewhat puzzled Duke of Kent, who said, according to the *Times*, that Canadian painting was very interesting, and that the really interesting thing about this exhibition was that it gave the English a chance to see this painting.[1] It consisted of five rooms of pictures, one a water-colour room, and a sculpture court. In the first there were British Columbia totems and a few French Canadian wood-carvings, good as far as they went but rather skimpy—the English can see better totems in the British Museum, and surely Jobin, one of the greatest artists Canada has ever produced, should have more prominence.[2] Then there was a lovely portrait of a negro slave by an eighteenth-century French Canadian called Beaucourt, some Paul Kane, who, though a fine artist to Canadians, is hardly an exportable one, and some nostalgic Old World painting, designed to make Canada look as much like Europe as possible. Krieghoff was of course the best of these: his adaptation of the Brueghel tradition to Canada is something that could be followed up. Then there was a room full of nineteenth-century painting and pictures by artists who constitute what is euphemistically known as the "conservative school." A brilliant Horatio Walker painting of turkeys and four Morrices stood out. The water-colour room had good things in it, but the sculpture was disappointing, Stephen Trenka's work being perhaps the most arresting.

The two other oil rooms held Thomson (notably *Jack Pine* and *Spring Ice*), the Group of Seven, and their successors. The Group was not badly represented, though I should have preferred bigger and better Mac-Donalds, and at least one Lawren Harris abstract picture, not only for its own merit but to show that the Group effected a revolution in rhythm and outline as well as in colour. And a good chance to make something of Varley, who seems to me subtler and more emotionally precise an artist than Morrice, was passed up. Of the rest, while there were a few bad pictures which parodied and spoiled the effect of the good ones, still most of the important people were at least nominally represented by something fairly typical. I can think of a dozen more to make room for whom I should gladly have cleared a space in the preceding room, but choosing such an exhibition for so hopelessly mixed a public can hardly be an easy job.

What the intelligent English public thinks of the exhibition I am not sure, but the printed criticism of it is inadequate and slovenly. There are good critics on English periodicals, and one wonders if this is merely a recurrence of the celebrated English Transatlantic Snuffle, aggravated by a country which is colonial as well as American. Most contemptuous of all, of course, was the *New Statesman*, in some ways the most dogmatically insular of all English magazines. The others were vague and patronizing, not much interested in any of the work which had got beyond the colonial into the independent stage, though the *Times* liked an Emily Carr and the *Observer* David Milne.[3] Of course there were difficulties in the critical path. So much Canadian painting is landscape, setting forth a country and an atmosphere very different from that of England (this, of course, was frequently noted, in a gently reproving sort of way). Very little good Canadian or American painting has been shown in England, much of it comparatively independent of European influence, and practically every younger Canadian was represented by only one or two pictures. Still, one feels that the right place to exhibit Canadian art is New York.

It is easy to say that Canadian art lacks subtlety. It would be equally easy to answer that what modern art needs is not subtlety so much as the rediscovery of the obvious. Nor does that altogether dodge the issue. The Group of Seven put on canvas the clear outlines of the Canadian landscape in the hard Canadian light, and provided a formula for a bright posterish painting, often with abstract tendencies. That much of this painting would be facile and insensitive is of course true; but there is a corresponding virtue, the virtue of good humour. There is a life and buoyancy in Canadian painting, of a kind not often found outside France, and fading there, a pleasure in bright colour and adventurous outline for its own sake, and I think that if that quality persists it is capable of absorbing what other qualities are necessary for mature craftsmanship. Whether art will survive in Europe or not depends on whether the cause which nearly every genuine artist there is supporting wins or not. If that cause is defeated, Canada will be one of the few pockets of creative activity left. I have seen only the illustrated catalogue of a recent showing of approved German art, but I am nevertheless ready to state on oath that however bad Naziism may be it cannot be so bad as it is painted. If Canadian artists can keep their chins up for the next decade or so, they will deserve a monument as well as the heroes of Vimy Ridge, and will perhaps be able to design a better.

4

Canadian Water-Colours

April 1940

From Canadian Forum, 20 (April 1940): 14. *Frye was reviewing an exhibition of water-colours in the Print Room of the Art Gallery of Toronto, which ran from January to April 1940.*

The excuse for writing about a show in the Toronto Art Gallery in a nation-wide magazine is that this particular collection of water-colours comes from all over the dominion. But a water-colour show is its own justification in Canada. The only thing like a tradition in Canadian painting is that which attempts to portray the primitive grandeur of the Canadian scene in solemn and stentorian oil. The room of Thomson, MacDonald, and Harris in the National Gallery gives the impression that all Canadian art has been inspired by *Finlandia*. Many of the Group of Seven and their contemporaries began as commercial artists, and their pictures were for the most part organized posters. (Need I say that this is nothing against them?) The normal development of Canadian painting from there would have been the absorption of, at any rate, some of it into industry and commerce: murals or panel paintings, like Comfort's Nipigon studies, resulting. The similar movement across the line fostered by the WPA is not a desperate unemployment measure but part of the organic evolution of American painting.[1] But the twentieth century is not an era of sound development but of frustrated and throttled creative effort all over the world, and the consequence in Canada has been an overproduction of tepidly interesting landscapes, certainly different but not organically or significantly different from those of Thomson and his associates.

Now oil painting tends to a convention and the importance of this show, apart from its novel catholicity, is not that it exhibits a genius or a masterpiece or a promise of either but that it brings out the fact that some Canadians are trying apologetically and in water-colour to find an outlet for some less conventional impulses to paint. There is humour in this show: humour in Fred Hagan's lively Susanna-and-the-Elders parody;[2] humour in Lismer's *Three Graces*, a little picture of African idols which proves that even a contemporary of Picasso does not have to make a fetish of a fetish: humour in Ada Killins's delicate *Aspiration*, a country church with an impossible pointed window, worthy of Grant Wood at least. And with humour goes a sense of the importance of the random impression: Milne's *Bread with Blue Wrapper* is only the best of several attempts to record a haphazard perception of interesting pattern and colour. There are a number of watchful and observant genre studies which may mean that Canadian eyes are slowly rising from the vegetable kingdom into human life.

5

Gordon Webber and Canadian Abstract Art

February 1941

From Acta Victoriana, *65 (February 1941): 39–42. The article was accompanied by four illustrations: Lawren Harris's* Country North of Lake Superior, *J.E.H. Macdonald's* Solemn Land, *Paul Nash's* Void, *and Vasily Kandinsky's* Gaiety.

At the Picture Loan Society there is a group of abstract paintings by Gordon Webber, a young Toronto artist who has fallen under the spell of Moholy-Nagy and the Chicago Bauhaus. They are stated to be the product of a railway journey and in some of them the derivation from the landscape is quite clear: others are arabesques on themes suggested by telegraph wires, signal posts, and gasometers. The artist is interested in the way the window keeps framing what one sees into orderly rectangles and in the possibility of bringing out something of the different emotional qualities behind vision, whether calm and speculative, or worried and inattentive.

Canadian landscape painting has to deal with a sharp hard light and solid blocks of clear colour: consequently a tendency to conventionalize outlines has been inherent in it from the first. Thomson, being interested in problems of linear distance and in the breaking up of light which they suggest, dodged this tendency, but it is strong in Jackson and Emily Carr, and of course far stronger in Lawren Harris, who saved himself from dropping into a facile formula (like Rockwell Kent) by turning to out-and-out abstract painting.

This last began (if we ignore a long tradition stretching back through the Mohammedans to the Scythians) with the so-called "cubist" geometrical analysis of form started by Picasso and Braque after the last war, as a kind of logical complement to Impressionism. It has since attracted an important and increasing body of artists. Its main point is that by being restricted wholly to formal relationships abstract painting attains the concentration and integrated detachment of music; and that the fortunate possessor of an abstract picture is not tied down to a single response, as cows in a field would tie him down. On the other hand it is hard not to feel that painting completely detached from any form of representation becomes merely a piece of interior decorating, and belongs with streamlined pipe-chairs, indirect lighting, and oppressively chaste and sterile colours, just as the cows in the field go with velvet curtains, cut glass, gloom, and mangled mahogany. If this is true, then abstract painting is rather a dead end, like the painter in Huxley who got so abstract he finally produced a bare canvas, and announced that the art of painting was finished.[1] It is at any rate an argument to cover an inner resentment at not knowing a good abstract from a bad one.

Perhaps some such feeling is behind what I think is perhaps the most important fact in modern painting: the merging of abstraction with surrealism, in the work say of Klee, Miró, Paul Nash, and Henry Moore. Here surrealism escapes the feeling of being simply disjointed narrative, like a *Derby Day* done with centaurs, and abstract pattern seems to take on a haunting and evocative quality which brings it much closer to more ordinary aesthetic responses.

Of all this Gordon Webber's show is of course a comparatively minor illustration: his pictures range from the rather feeble to the mildly interesting. Still, it is good to see some abstract painting in Canada: the only really modern art in Toronto is in the Museum, where it is labelled ancient.

6

Canadian and Colonial Painting

March 1941

From Canadian Forum, *20 (March 1941): 14. Reprinted in BG, 199–202. Frye's piece was inspired by an exhibition at the Art Gallery of Toronto, January 1941.*

The countries men live in feed their minds as much as their bodies: the bodily food they provide is absorbed in farms and cities: the mental, in religion and arts. In all communities this process of material and imaginative *digestion* goes on. Thus a large tract of vacant land may well affect the people living near it as too much cake does a small boy: an unknown but quite possibly horrible Something stares at them in the dark: hide under the bedclothes as long as they will, sooner or later they must stare back. Explorers, tormented by a sense of the unreality of the unseen, are first: pioneers and traders follow. But the land is still not imaginatively absorbed, and the incubus moves on to haunt the artists. It is a very real incubus. It glares through the sirens, gorgons, centaurs, griffins, cyclops, pygmies, and chimeras of the poems which followed the Greek colonies: there the historical defeat which left a world of mystery outside the Greek clearing increased the imaginative triumph. In our own day the exploration and settlement has been far more thorough and the artistic achievement proportionately less: the latter is typified in the novels of Conrad, which are so often concerned with finding a dreary commonplace at the centre of the unknown. All of which is an elaborate prologue to the fact that I propose to compare Tom Thomson with Horatio Walker, as suggested by a recent showing of them at the Art Gallery of Toronto; still, when in Canadian history the sphinx of the unknown land takes its riddle from Fraser and Mackenzie to Tom Thomson, no one can say that there has been an anticlimax.

Griffins and gorgons have no place in Thomson certainly, but the incubus is there, in the twisted stumps and sprawling rocks, the strident colouring, the scarecrow evergreens. In several pictures one has the feeling of something not quite emerging which is all the more sinister for its concealment. The metamorphic stratum is too old: the mind cannot contemplate the azoic without turning it into the monstrous. But that is of minor importance. What is essential in Thomson is the imaginative instability, the emotional unrest and dissatisfaction one feels about a country which has not been lived in: the tension between the mind and a surrounding not integrated with it. This is the key to both his colour and his design. His underlying "colour harmony" is not a concord but a minor ninth. Sumachs and red maples are conceived, quite correctly, as a *surcharge* of colour: flaming reds and yellows are squeezed straight out of the tube on to an already brilliant background: in softer light ambers and pinks and blue-greens carry on a subdued cats' chorus. This in itself is mere fidelity to the subject, but it is not all. Thomson has a marked preference for the transitional over the full season: he likes the delicate pink and green tints on the birches in early spring and the irresolute sifting of the first snow through the spruces; and his autumnal studies are sometimes a Shelleyan hectic decay in high winds and spinning leaves, sometimes a Keatsian opulence and glut. His sense of design, which, of course, is derived from the trail and the canoe, is the exact opposite of the academic "establishing of foreground." He is primarily a painter of linear distance. Snowed-over paths wind endlessly through trees, rivers reach nearly to the horizon before they bend and disappear, rocks sink inch by inch under water, and the longest stretch of mountains dips somewhere and reveals the sky beyond. What is furthest in distance is often nearest in intensity. Or else we peer through a curtain of trees to a pool and an opposite shore. Even when there is no vista a long tree-trunk will lean away from us and the whole picture will be shattered by a straining and pointing diagonal.

This focusing on the farthest distance makes the foreground, of course, a shadowy blur: a foreground tree—even the tree in *West Wind*—may be only a green blob to be looked past, not at. Foreground leaves and flowers, even when carefully painted, are usually thought of as obstructing the vision and the eye comes back to them with a start. Thomson looks on a flat area with a naive Rousseauish stare (see the "decorative panels"). In fact, of all important Canadian painters, only David Milne seems to have a consistent foreground focus, and even he is fond of the obstructive blur.

When the Canadian sphinx brought her riddle of unvisualized land to Thomson it did not occur to him to hide under the bedclothes, though she did not promise him money, fame, happiness, or even self-confidence, and when she was through with him she scattered his bones in the wilderness. Horatio Walker, one of those wise and prudent men from whom the greater knowledges are concealed, felt differently. It was safety and bedclothes for him. He looked round wildly for some spot in Canada that had been thoroughly lived in, that had no ugly riddles and plenty of picturesque clichés. He found it in the Ile d'Orléans. That was a Fortunate Isle with rainbows and full moons instead of stumps and rocks: it had been cosily inhabited for centuries, and suggested relaxed easy-going narratives rather than inhuman landscapes. Pictures here were ready-made. There was Honest Toil with the plough and the quaint Patient Oxen; there were pastoral epigrams of sheep-shearing and farmers trying to gather in hay before the storm broke; there was the note of Tender Humour supplied by small pigs and heraldic turkeys; there was the Simple Piety which bowed in Childlike Reverence before a roadside *calvaire*. Why, it was as good as Europe, and had novelty besides. And for all Canadians and Americans under the bedclothes who wanted, not new problems of form and outlines, but the predigested picturesque, who preferred dreamy association-responses to detached efforts of organized vision, and who found in a queasy and maudlin nostalgia the deepest appeal of art, Horatio Walker was just the thing. He sold and sold and sold.

7

Contemporary Verse

December 1941

Review of Contemporary Verse: A Canadian Quarterly, *1, no. 1. From* Canadian Forum, *21 (December 1941): 283.*

The first volume of this new magazine of verse contains nine poems by eight poets, some well known, others newcomers. Negatively, no poem is flat or bad, and all show considerable literary experience. Negatively, again, the quatrains of Leo Kennedy's *Carol for Two Swans* are very gracefully handled even if they hardly rise above facility: A.J.M. Smith's *The Face* is sharply conceived even if somewhat metallic in sound: Earle Birney's *Hands* is arrestingly beautiful in its imagery even if one or two prosaic construction lines have not been erased: Floris McLaren's *No Lock, No Light* is poignant even if too heavily accented, and so on.

Positively, if you buy this little pamphlet you will get wit:

> She thought intemperate and absurd
>   Her place among the constellations,
> And when his love soared like a bird,
>   Salted its tail with reservations   (Leo Kennedy[, *Carol for Two Swans*, 8])

satire:

>   ... back to the wrinkled
> Index weaving the virtuous sock, pointing the witch hunt
>   (Earle Birney[, *Hands*, 4])

music:

> At mothers in cool gowns who move about like moons
> Upon the eternal lawns . . .   (Dorothy Livesay[, *The Child Looks Out*, 10])

imagination:

> there,
> like a church-warden, like a stiff,
> turn-the-eye-inward, old man
> in a cut-away, in a mist,
> stands the crow   (P.K. Page[, *The Crow*, 14])

and where else can you get all that for two bits?

8

Canadian Chapbooks

December 1941

Review of Ebb Tide, *by Doris Ferne (Toronto: Ryerson Press, 1941);* The Artisan, *by Sara Carsley (Toronto: Ryerson Press, 1941); and* The Singing Gypsy, *by Mollie Morant (Toronto: Ryerson Press, 1941). From* Canadian Forum, *21 (December 1941): 283–4.*

These chapbooks are a real Canadian public service. They assume a large number of intelligent people writing occasional amateur verse for pleasure and expecting it to be read for pleasure, content with a restricted circulation confined largely to their friends. They assume also a large number of intelligent people ready to read poetry for pleasure, ready to pay fifty cents for a dozen poems even if they are not the greatest lyrics since Keats, and not consumed by a feverish itch to get published themselves. Every major poet is the apex of a pyramid of minor ones, and a contempt for minor poetry is more vulgar and more dangerous than the merely ignorant avoidance of all poetry. If Canadians ever get to buying verse as unself-consciously as they buy eggs or cigarettes, Dr. Pierce will deserve a monument of eternal bronze.[1]

All three of these poets have the ability to write smoothly and pleasantly. The kind of poetry they write depends entirely on honest and accurate observation and a fanatical adherence to the concrete and sharply outlined. This, however, takes harder work than they have always been willing to do, and good ideas are constantly being obscured by a haze of generalizing platitudes about war, life, and other large subjects. When Mollie Morant sticks closely to her impressions of fish boats and poplars she can achieve a touching simplicity: her singing gypsies and knights in gleaming armour are only poetic patter. When Sara Carsley speaks of

"The worm, unbeautifully long," she is writing poetry: when she says that man

> With teeming marvels of his brain
> Fills earth and air and sea   [*Conjuring Trick*]

she is writing doggerel. When Doris Ferne works hard to find just the right images for an authentic emotion, she can produce a beautiful poem, as the sonnet called *Memory* is: when she begins to worry about the war her mind wanders and her ear goes off duty:

> in the still caves of a great past
> where honour began and love
> and a vast capacity for self-sacrifice.   [*Sounding*]

The language of poetry has a complicated grammar of rhythm, cadence, epithet, and symbol, and there was a time when a poet could be called sincere and manly by simply refusing to learn it. That time is over: sincere emotion is still necessary to fine poetry, but sincerity no longer splutters.

9

Canadian Writing: *First Statement*

November 1942

Review of First Statement: A Magazine for Young Canadian Writers, 1, nos. 1–3, ed. John Sutherland. From Canadian Forum, 22 (November 1942): 253.

This little magazine comes out in mimeographed sheets, and, like *PM*,[1] which otherwise it does not resemble, it is stapled and carries no advertising. Brought out by five young Montreal people,[2] its editor says that, as Canadians pay very little attention to their literature, "a display of activity may symbolize a future, and plant a suggestion in someone's mind."[3] The magazine is to remind us that even when we are apparently least concerned with poetry, the purely creative spirit still survives in Canada, producing the odd sprig of edelweiss among the snows. Their main concern, therefore, is with literature as an end in itself. They consider that those who are concerned with it as a means, like many with strong political views, do not show a proper respect for craftsmanship, using words vaguely or messily to express a nonliterary meaning. "Every word," says one contributor, "contains what amounts nearly to a godhead."[4] This feeling that literature is primarily magical or evocative gives to the magazine a strongly imagist tone, reminiscent, in its way, of similar projects that appeared in the dying years of the last war.

No reviewer has any right to be patronizing, but there is something rather quaint and old-fashioned about this first statement, with its accent on youth, its earnest and rather pompous statement of ideals, its acute sense of the contrast of art and vulgarity, its opening plunge into a story without a single capital or punctuation mark. The poetry is much better than the prose: I liked *The Plight of the Revellers*, by Mary Miller. Its main defect is the kind of self-consciousness bred by this view of the associative impact of words. Too many phrases and images are deliberately striking, produced with the smugness of Little Jack Horner. Compare Mr. Creighton's remark about Bliss Carman in last month's *Canadian Forum*.[5] I find "a thigh smooth," "the poor soil lovely," "the green upspringing," "a breath spilling," in one short poem, which are inversions too many. I find "they all bend down swaying minds to listen to uncreated sounds crawling like caged animals inside the rock,"[6] "they" being obscure modern poets and the rock the one struck by Moses, which is overdone. I find

> And the blank litanies of sharp churches
> Formed fretworks to cage his soul,[7]

which is addled. But the magazine is pleasant to come upon, and if it keeps going for "at least a year," as promised, fine, and more power to it.

10

Canadian Poets: Earle Birney

December 1942

Review of David and Other Poems, *by Earle Birney (Toronto: Ryerson Press, 1942). From* Canadian Forum, *22 (December 1942): 278. Reprinted in* Earle Birney, *ed. Bruce Nesbitt (Toronto: McGraw-Hill Ryerson, 1974), 39–41.*

This is a book for those interested in Canadian poetry to buy and for those interested in complaining that we haven't got any to ignore. Anyone who follows Canadian verse at all closely will be very pleased to see Mr. Birney's fugitive pieces gathered into one little volume, and anyone who read the title poem when it first appeared in the *Forum* will be keenly interested in finding it again in a published book as part of a larger collection.

The people who are familiar with the conventions of modern poetry, who can grasp its difficult language and place its recondite allusions, now form a specialized cult largely confined to universities. *David* will get the full approval of this audience as being on its own merits a touching, beautiful, and sensitively written story. But a large reserve of intelligent readers, not in the cult but willing to listen to a poet who has a real story to tell and who tells it simply and honestly, will also like this poem. The more blasé will take a while to recover from their surprise at seeing, in a volume of contemporary verse, a straightforward narrative cut to fit the "common reader," without flounces of fake symbolism, gathers of atmosphere, tucks of philosophic rumination, or fullness of garrulous comment. But they will like it too. *David* is the best thing of its kind that I have seen in current poetry—and for some benighted reason its kind is rare.

The other poems are uneven, but frequently reach the high level of the title piece. As a lyrical poet, Mr. Birney is chiefly an artist in vignette, a sharp and humorous observer. His humour on the whole is best when least directly satiric: satire makes him relapse into an idiom more suitable to prose. But he utters "conceits," or deliberately strained images, with exactly the right kind of deadpan delivery, and his meticulous study of a slug, which should now be famous through its inclusion in Gustafson's Pelican anthology,[1] is a shimmering rich texture of poetic wit from beginning to end. This indicates that he is not, in spite of the simplicity of *David*, a naive poet, and there are some brilliant flashes of imagery, of the kind that come from short-circuiting associations, notably in the briefer lyrics, such as *Monody on a Century* and *European Nocturne*. A tendency to a rather facile animism, of the "grassy hair of old hobo ocean" variety, is the only weakness of an important virtue.

Quizzical and ironic imagery is frequent in North American poetry: the source of it is usually the fascinating stare of an indifferent Nature which was here long before man and could very well get along without him. In such a poet as Robinson Jeffers, whose Pacific symbolism Mr. Birney occasionally recalls, this develops into a philosophy of tragic nihilism: in such a poet as E.J. Pratt, the immense debauchery of Nature, its gigantic appetite for life and its incredible waste of it, is transmuted into strange visions of submarine souses, pliocene Armageddons, and maddened savages with a "viscous melanotic current" coursing through their blood. The former results in slick, portentous, stereotyped oratory; the richer humour and greater subtlety of the latter is a spiritual truancy (see elsewhere in these pages) which refuses to over-simplify the imagination. In searching for the basis of his own attitude, Mr. Birney gives us an example of each tendency. *Dusk on English Bay*, a vision of a spinning world at peace and at war, comes to a simple time-marches-on conclusion which seems to me rather frivolous: *Vancouver Lights*, ending in a tone of quiet resistance, is far more impressive.

The most obvious technical influence on Mr. Birney's work—he has gone somewhat out of his way to underline it—is the alliterative line and kenning of Old English. This is frequently claimed as an influence by modern poets, though many of them end up by producing imitations of Gerard Manley Hopkins, who, along with William Morris, started a vogue in the last century for bumping over offbeats, babbling bastard *Beowulf*. Here the influence is genuine, but the technique is difficult, and easily gets out of hand. It does so, for instance, when the alliteration becomes part of an over-elaborate pattern of repetition—the rhymes, for example, are sometimes harsh and insensitive—and it does so when the use of kennings and compound words makes the diction sound rather spiky and self-conscious. The rhythm also could sometimes be more fluent: there are too many run-on lines, especially in *David*, which have nowhere in particular to run to. I mention these details because this is not one of those impeccable and immaculate first volumes which "promise" nothing but more of the same. Just as a pregnant woman is in too interesting a condition to win a beauty contest, so the many and remarkable virtues of these poems are accompanied by faults which guarantee an increase in fertility. In case you didn't get the point the first time, for those who care about Canadian poetry this book is good enough to buy, not to borrow or get from a library.

11

Canada and Its Poetry

December 1943

A review of The Book of Canadian Poetry: A Critical and Historical Anthology, *ed. with introduction and notes by A.J.M. Smith (Chicago: University of Chicago Press; Toronto: Gage, 1943). From* Canadian Forum, *23 (December 1943): 207–10. Reprinted in BG, 129–43, in RCLI, 25–37, in ECLI, 23–36, in* The Making of Modern Poetry in Canada, *ed. Louis Dudek and Michael Gnarowski (Toronto: Ryerson Press, 1967), 86–97, and in* Towards a Canadian Literature: Essays, Editorials, and Manifestos, *ed. Douglas M. Daymond and Leslie G. Monkman (Ottawa: Tecumseh Press, 1985), 2:340–52. For a review of the 2nd ed., see no. 30.*

The appearance of Mr. A.J.M. Smith's new anthology is an important event in Canadian literature. For instead of confining his reading to previous compilations, as most anthologists do, he has made a first-hand study of the whole English field with unflagging industry and unfaltering taste. A straightforward research job is simple enough to do if one has the time: but Mr. Smith has done something far more difficult than research. He had to read through an enormous mass of poetry ranging from the lousy to the exquisite, the great bulk of which was that kind of placid mediocrity which is always good verse and just near enough to good poetry to need an expert to detect its flat ring. He had to pronounce on all this not only with a consistent judgment but also with historical sense. He had to remember that a modern poet may hold deeply and sincerely to the more enlightened political views and become so gnarled and cryptic an intellectual that he cannot even understand himself, and still be just as conventional a minor poet as the most twittering Victorian songbird. In dealing with many of the older writers, Campbell for instance, or Carman, he had to trace the thin gold vein of real imagination through a rocky mass of what can only be called a gift of metrical gab. He had to remember that occasionally a bad poem is of all the greater cultural significance for being bad, and therefore should go in. In judging his younger contemporaries he had to remember both that a flawed talent is better than a flawless lack of it and that still it is performance and not "promise" that makes the poet, of whatever age.

It is no easy job; but Mr. Smith has, on the whole, done it. Of course there are omissions, of which he is probably more acutely aware than his readers. In any case anthologies ought to have blank pages at the end on which the reader may copy his own neglected favourites. In my judgment, a few people are in who might well have been out, and a few out who might well have been in: some dull poems are included and many good ones are not; and one or two poets have been rather unfairly treated—including, I should say, one A.J.M. Smith. But no kind of book is easier to attack than an anthology; and in any case the importance of this one is not so much in the number or merits of the poems included as in the critical revaluations it makes. Mr. Smith's study of the pre-Confederation poets is the only one that has been made from anything like a modern point of view. In Charles Heavysege he has unearthed—the word will not be too strong for most of his readers—a genuine Canadian Beddoes, a poet of impressive power and originality: and he has given Isabella Crawford enough space to show that she is one of the subtlest poets that Canada has produced. The more famous writers of the so-called Maple Leaf school come down to a slightly more modest estimate, and, though Mr. Smith is scrupulously fair to them, he cannot and does not avoid saying that they talked too much and sang too little, or sang too much and thought too little. In any case the supremacy of Lampman over the whole group comes out very clearly. In the next period Pratt gets his deserved prominence, and the younger poets are generously represented. Here is, in short, what Canada can do: the reader who does not like this book simply does not like Canadian poetry, and will not be well advised to read further. Of course, as Mr. Smith says in his Preface, French Canadian poetry is a separate job—still to be done, I should think, for Fournier's *Anthologie des Poètes Canadiens* is, as its editor Asselin frankly admits, more a collection of poets than of poems. But we cannot leave the French out of our poetry any more than we can leave Morrice or Gagnon out of our painting, and one can only hope for some French-speaking philanthropist to produce a companion volume.

The thing that impresses me is the unity of tone which the book has, and to which nearly all the poets in various ways contribute. Of course any anthologist can produce a false illusion of unity by simply being a critic of limited sympathies, responding only to certain kinds of technique or subject matter. But Mr. Smith is obviously not that: his notes and introduction show a wide tolerance, and his selections, though bold and independent, are certainly not precious. No: the unity of tone must come from the material itself, and the anthology thus unconsciously proves the existence of a definable Canadian genius (I use this word in a general sense) which is neither British nor American but, for all its echoes and imitations and second-hand ideas, peculiarly our own.

Now admittedly a great deal of useless yammering has been concerned with the "truly Canadian" qualities of our literature, and one's first instinct is to avoid the whole question. Of course what is "peculiarly our own" is not what is accidentally our own, and a poet may talk forever about forests and prairies and snow and the Land of the North and not be any more Canadian than he will be Australian if he writes a sonnet on a kangaroo. One of F.R. Scott's poems included by Mr. Smith notes a tendency on the part of minor poets to "paint the native maple" [*The Canadian Authors Meet*, l. 23]. This is like saying that because the quintuplets are Canadian, producing children in litters is a Canadian characteristic. Nevertheless, no one who knows the country will deny that there is something, say an attitude of mind, distinctively Canadian, and while Canadian speech is American, there is a recognizable Canadian accent in the more highly organized speech of its poetry. Certainly if a Canadian poet consciously tries to avoid being Canadian, he will sound like nothing on earth. For whatever may be true of painting or music, poetry is not a citizen of the world: it is conditioned by language, and flourishes best within a national unit. "Humanity" is an abstract idea, not a poetic image. But whether Canada is really a national unit in any sense that has a meaning for culture I could not decide myself until I saw Mr. Smith's book; and even then one has misgivings. The patriotic avarice that claims every European as "Canadian" who stopped off at a Canadian station for a ham sandwich on his way to the States is, no doubt, ridiculous; but apart from that, does not any talk about Canadian poetry lead to some loss of perspective, some heavy spotlighting of rather pallid faces? Every Canadian has some feeling of sparseness when he compares, for example, Canada's fifth largest city, which I believe is Hamilton, with the fifth largest across the line, which I believe is Los

Angeles. And the same is true of poetry. Every issue of the *New Yorker* or *New Republic*, to say nothing of the magazines which really go in for poetry, contains at least one poem which is technically on a level with five-sixths of Mr. Smith's book. With so luxuriant a greenhouse next door, why bother to climb mountains to look for the odd bit of edelweiss? The only answer is, I suppose, that in what Canadian poets have tried to do there is an interest for Canadian readers much deeper than what the achievement in itself justifies.

The qualities of our poetry that appear from this book to be distinctively Canadian are not those that one readily thinks of: a fact which was an additional obstacle in Mr. Smith's path. For Canada is more than most countries a milieu in which certain preconceived literary stereotypes are likely to interpose between the imagination and the expression it achieves. What a poet's imagination actually can produce and what the poet thinks it ought to produce are often very different things. They never should be, but they sometimes are; and it is hard to judge accurately the work of a man who is a genuine poet but whose poetry only glints here and there out of a mass of verse on conventional themes he has persuaded himself he should be celebrating. If a poet is a patriot, for instance, there may be two natures within him, one scribbling ready-made patriotic doggerel and the other trying to communicate the real feelings his country inspires him with. If he is religious, the poet in him may reach God in very subtle ways; but the man in him who is not a poet may be a more commonplace person, shocked by his own poetic boldness. If he is revolutionary, the poet in him may have to argue with a Philistine materialist also in him who does not really see the point of poetry at all. This is at least one reason why so much patriotic, religious, and revolutionary verse is bad.

Now this creative schizophrenia is, we have said, common in Canada, and the most obvious reason for it is the fact that Canada is not only a nation but a colony in an empire. I have said that culture seems to flourish best in national units, which implies that the empire is too big and the province too small for major literature. I know of no poet, with the very dubious exception of Virgil, who has made great poetry out of what Shakespeare calls "the imperial theme" [*Macbeth*, 1.3.129]: in Kipling, for instance, this theme is largely a praise of machinery, and of the Robot tendencies within the human mind. The province or region, on the other hand, is usually a vestigial curiosity to be written up by some nostalgic tourist. The imperial and the regional are both inherently antipoetic environments, yet they go hand in hand; and together they make up what I call the colonial in Canadian life.

This colonial tendency has been sharpened by the French-English split, the English having tended to specialize in the imperial and the French in the regional aspects of it. The French are on the whole the worse off by this arrangement, which has made Quebec into a cute tourist resort full of ye quainte junke made by real peasants, all of whom go to church and say their prayers like the children they are, and love their land and tell folk tales and sing ballads just as the fashionable novelists in the cities say they do. True, I have never met a French Canadian who liked to be thought of as an animated antique, nor do I expect to: yet the sentimental haze in which the European author [Louis Hémon] of *Maria Chapdelaine* saw the country is still quite seriously accepted by Canadians, English and French alike, as authentic. A corresponding imperial preoccupation in English poets leads to much clearing of forests and planting of crops and tapping vast natural resources: a grim earnestness of expansion which seems almost more German than British. The more naive expressions of this do not get into Mr. Smith's book. Instead, he sets Isabella Crawford's song, *Bite Deep and Wide, O Axe, the Tree*, in its proper context, a viciously ironic one; and Anne Marriott's *The Wind Our Enemy* and Birney's *Anglosaxon Street* are also there to indicate that if we sow the wind of empire with too little forethought we shall reap a dusty whirlwind of arid squalor.

The colonial position of Canada is therefore a frostbite at the roots of the Canadian imagination, and it produces a disease for which I think the best name is prudery. By this I do not mean reticence in sexual matters: I mean the instinct to seek a conventional or commonplace expression of an idea. Prudery that keeps the orthodox poet from making a personal recreation of his orthodoxy: prudery that prevents the heretic from forming an articulate heresy that will shock: prudery that makes a radical stutter and gargle over all realities that are not physical: prudery that chokes off social criticism for fear some other group of Canadians will take advantage of it. One sees this perhaps most clearly in religion, because of the fact that the division of language and race is approximately one of religion also. Mr. Smith has included a religious poem called *Littlewit and Loftus* [by Pamelia Vining Yule], which, though in some respects a bad poem, is at any rate not a prudish one in the above sense: it ends with the authentic scream of the disembodied evangelical banshee who has cut herself loose from this world and who has the sense of release that goes with that, even if she is not wholly sure what world she is now in. It is a prickly cactus in a desert of bumbling platitude and the pouring of unctuous oil on untroubled waters; or else, as in Bliss Carman, prayers of a stentorian vagueness addressed to some kind of scholar-gipsy God.

I wish I could say that the tighter grip of religion on the French has improved matters there; but it has done nothing of the kind. In French poetry too one feels that the Church is often most vividly conceived not as catholic but as a local palladium to be defended for political reasons: as a part of the parochial intrigue which is given the title of "nationalism." The type of prudery appropriate to this is a facile and mawkish piety. In short, the imperial tendency may call itself "Protestant" and the regional one "Catholic"; but as long as both are colonial, both will be essentially sectarian. Similarly, the imperial tendency may call itself British and the regional one French; but as long as both are colonial, these words will have only a sectional meaning. It is an obvious paradox in Canadian life that the more colonial the English- or French-speaking Canadian is, and the more he distrusts the other half of his country, the more artificial his relation to the real Britain or France becomes. The French Canadian who translates "British Columbia" as "Colombie canadienne" and flies the tricolour of the French Revolution on holidays, and the English Canadian who holds that anything short of instant acquiescence in every decision of the British Foreign Office is treason, are the furthest of all Canadians from the culture of what they allege to be their mother countries.

But even when the Canadian poet has got rid of colonial cant, there are two North American dragons to slay. One is the parroted cliché that this is a "new" country and that we must spend centuries cutting forests and building roads before we can enjoy the by-products of settled leisure. But Canada is not "new" or "young": it is exactly the same age as any other country under a system of industrial capitalism; and even if it were, a reluctance to write poetry is not a sign of youth but of decadence. Savages have poetry: the Pilgrim Fathers, who really were pioneers, started writing almost as soon as they landed. It is only from the exhausted loins of the half-dead masses of people in modern cities that such weary ideas are born.

The other fallacy concerns the imaginative process itself, and may be called the Ferdinand the Bull theory of poetry. This theory talks about a first-hand contact with life as opposed to a second-hand contact with it through books, and assumes that the true poet will go into the fields and smell the flowers and not spoil the freshness of his vision by ruining his eyesight on books. However, practically all important poetry has been the fruit of endless study and reading, for poets as a class are and must be, as an Elizabethan critic said, "curious universal scholars."[1] There are exceptions to this rule, but they prove it; and it is silly to insist on them. In looking over Mr. Smith's book one is struck immediately by the predominance of university and professional people, and it is in the classical scholarship of Lampman, the encyclopedic erudition of Crémazie which is said to have included Sanskrit, and the patient research and documentation of Pratt's *Brébeuf* and sea narratives, that Canadian poetry has become most articulate. There is nothing especially Canadian about this, but one point may be noted. To an English poet, the tradition of his own country and language proceeds in a direct chronological line down to himself, and that in its turn is part of a gigantic funnel of tradition extending back to Homer and the Old Testament. But to a Canadian, broken off from this linear sequence and having none of his own, the traditions of Europe appear as a kaleidoscopic whirl with no definite shape or meaning, but with a profound irony lurking in its varied and conflicting patterns. The clearest statement of this is in that superb fantasy *The Witches' Brew*, Pratt's first major effort, a poem of which apparently I have a higher opinion than Mr. Smith. It is also to be found, I think, in the elaborate Rabbinical apparatus of Klein.

American even more than Canadian poetry has been deeply affected by the clash between two irreconcilable views of literature: the view that poets should be original and the view that they should be aboriginal. Originality is largely a matter of returning to origins, of studying and imitating the great poets of the past. But many fine American poets have been damaged and in some cases spoiled by a fetish of novelty: they have sought for the primitive and direct and have tried to avoid the consciously literary and speak the language of the common man. As the language of the common man is chiefly commonplace, the result has been for the most part disastrous. And here is one case where failing to achieve a virtue has really warded off a vice. There has on the whole been little Tarzanism in Canadian poetry. One is surprised to find how few really good Canadian poets have thought that getting out of cities into God's great outdoors really brings one closer to the sources of inspiration. One reason for this is that there has been no revolution in Canada and less sense of building up a new land into what the American Constitution calls a more perfect state. A certain abdication of political

Canada and Its Poetry

responsibility is sharply reflected in our poetry, and is by no means always harmful to it. We can see this clearly if we compare Bliss Carman with his American friend Hovey,[2] who sang not only of freedom and the open road but also of America's duty to occupy the Philippines and open up the Pacific. The Canadian likes to be objective about Americans, and likes to feel that he can see a bit of Sam Slick in every Yankee: as a North American, therefore, he has a good seat on the revolutionary sidelines, and his poetic tendencies, reflective, observant, humorous, critical, and quite frankly traditional, show it.

The closest analogy to Canadian poetry in American literature is, as one would expect, in the pre-1776 period: in Anne Bradstreet and Philip Freneau and the Hartford Wits. We have many excellent counterparts to these, and to the tradition that runs through Emerson, but few if any good counterparts to Whitman, Sandburg, Lindsay, Jeffers, or MacLeish. Early American poetry is traditional, but its tradition is a great one: and when the Americans gained maturity in government they lost some in poetry; for there is an assurance and subtlety in Bradstreet and Freneau that Longfellow and Whittier and many of those mentioned above do not possess. This is not to say that the best American poetry appeared before 1776, but as we seem to be stuck with at least some colonial characteristics, we may as well appreciate what virtues they have.

Nature in Canadian poetry, then, has little of the vagueness of great open spaces in it: that is very seldom material that the imagination can use. One finds rather an intent and closely focused vision, often on something in itself quite unimportant: in Birney's slug, Finch's station platform [*Train Window*], the clairvoyance of hatred in MacKay's *I Wish My Tongue Were a Quiver*, Hambleton's sharply etched picture of salmon fishing [*Sockeye Salmon*]. The first poet Mr. Smith includes, the Canadian Oliver Goldsmith, makes an accurate inventory of a country store,[3] and he sets a tone which the rest of the book bears out. The vocabulary and diction correspond: the snap and crackle of frosty words, some stiff with learning and others bright with concreteness, is heard wherever there is the mental excitement of real creation, though of course most obviously where the subject suggests it: in, for instance, Charles Bruce's *Immediates*:

> An ageless land and sea conspire
> To smooth the imperfect mould of birth;
> While freezing spray and drying fire
> Translate the inexplicit earth   [ll. 13–16]

or in P.K. Page's *[The] Stenographers*:

> In the felt of the morning, the calico minded,
> sufficiently starched, insert papers, hit keys,
> efficient and sure as their adding machines.   [ll. 30–32]

But, according to Mr. Smith's book, the outstanding achievement of Canadian poetry is in the evocation of stark terror. Not a coward's terror, of course; but a controlled vision of the causes of cowardice. The immediate source of this is obviously the frightening loneliness of a huge and thinly settled country. When all the intelligence, morality, reverence, and simian cunning of man confronts a sphinx-like riddle of the indefinite like the Canadian winter, the man seems as helpless as a trapped mink and as lonely as a loon. His thrifty little heaps of civilized values look pitiful beside nature's apparently meaningless power to waste and destroy on a superhuman scale, and such a nature suggests an equally ruthless and subconscious God, or else no God. In Wilfred Campbell, for instance, the Canadian winter expands into a kind of frozen hell of utter moral nihilism:

> Lands that loom like spectres, whited regions of winter,
>   Wastes of desolate woods, deserts of water and shore;
> A world of winter and death, within these regions who enter,
>   Lost to summer and life, go to return no more.   [*The Winter Lakes*, ll. 13–16]

And the winter is only one symbol, though a very obvious one, of the central theme of Canadian poetry: the riddle of what a character in Mair's *Tecumseh* calls "inexplicable life."[4] It is really a riddle of inexplicable death: the fact that life struggles and suffers in a nature which is blankly indifferent to it. Human beings set a high value on their own lives which is obviously not accepted in the world beyond their palisades. They may become hurt and whimper that nature is cruel to them; but the honest poet does not see cruelty: he sees only a stolid unconsciousness. The human demands that Patrick Anderson's Joe hurls at nature are answered by "a feast of No" [*Summer's Joe*, final line]; a negation with neither sympathy nor malice in it. In Birney's *David* a terrible tragedy of wasted life and blasted youth is enacted on a glacier, but there is no "pathetic fallacy" about the cruelty of the glacier or of whatever gods may be in charge of it. It is just a glacier. D.C. Scott's *Piper of Arll* is located in an elusive fairyland, but the riddle of inexplicable death is still at the heart of the poem. The same theme is of course clearer still in Pratt's sea narratives, especially the *Titanic*.

Sometimes this theme modulates into a wry and sardonic humour. In the laughter of that rare spirit Standish O'Grady, who in his picture of freezing Canadians huddling around "their simpering stove" [*The Emigrant*, l. 1719] has struck out one of the wittiest phrases in the book, something rather sharper sounds across the laughter:

> Here the rough Bear subsists his winter year,
> And licks his paw and finds *no better fare*.   [*The Emigrant*, ll. 1696–7]

In Drummond's finest poem, *The Wreck of the "Julie Plante,"* the grim humour of the ballad expresses the same tragedy of life destroyed by unconsciousness that we find in Pratt and Birney:

> For de win' she blow lak hurricane,
>   Bimeby she blow some more.   [ll. 5–6]

Tom MacInnes has the same kind of humour, though the context is often fantastic, and his *Zalinka* is a parody of Poe which somehow manages to convey the same kind of disturbing eeriness. But whether humorous or not, even in our most decorous poets there are likely to be the most startling flashes of menace and fear. A placid poem of Charles G.D. Roberts about mowing is suddenly punctured by the line, "The crying knives glide on; the green swath lies" [*The Mowing*, l. 9]. Archdeacon Scott writes a little poem on Easter Island statues which ends in a way that will lift your back hair.

But the poetic imagination cannot remain for long content with this faceless mask of unconsciousness. Nature is not all glacier and iceberg and hurricane; and while there is no conscious cruelty in it, there is certainly a suffering that we can interpret as cruelty. Hence the poet begins to animate nature with an evil or at least sinister power: night in Heavysege becomes a cacodemon [*Night*, l. 14], and spring in Dorothy Livesay a crouching monster [*Prelude for Spring*]. Mr. Smith's book is full of ghosts and unseen watchers and spiritual winds: a certain amount of this is faking, but not all: Lampman's *In November*, with its ghastly dead mullens and the wonderful danse macabre in which it closes, is no fake. The "crying in the dark" in Lampman's *Midnight*, the dead hunter in

Eustace Ross's *A Death*, the dead "lovely thing" in Neil Tracy's poem [*I Doubt a Lovely Thing Is Dead*], the married corpses in Leo Kennedy's *Epithalamium*: all these are visions, not only of a riddle of inexplicable death, but of a riddle of inexplicable evil. Sometimes, of course, this evil takes an easily recognized form: the Indians in Joseph Howe's spirited narrative and the drought wind in Anne Marriott have no spectral overtones. But it is obvious that man must be included in this aspect of the riddle, as it is merely fanciful to separate conscious malice from the human mind. Whatever sinister lurks in nature lurks also in us; and Tom MacInnes's "tiger of desire" and the praying mantis of a remarkable poem by Anne Dalton have been transformed into mental demons.

The unconscious horror of nature and the subconscious horrors of the mind thus coincide: this amalgamation is the basis of symbolism on which nearly all Pratt's poetry is founded. The fumbling and clumsy monsters of his "Pliocene Armageddon" [*The Great Feud*], who are simply incarnate wills to mutual destruction, are the same monsters that beget Naziism and inspire *The Fable of the Goats*; and in the fine *Silences*, which Mr. Smith includes, civilized life is seen geologically as merely one clock-tick in eons of ferocity. The waste of life in the death of the Cachalot and the waste of courage and sanctity in the killing of the Jesuit missionaries are tragedies of a unique kind in modern poetry: like the tragedy of Job, they seem to move upward to a vision of a monstrous Leviathan, a power of chaotic nihilism which is "king over all the children of pride" [Job 41:34]. I admit that Tom the Cat from Zanzibar in *The Witches' Brew* is good fun, but when Mr. Smith suggests that he is nothing more, I disagree.

In the creepy ambiguity of the first line of Malzah's song in Heavysege, "There was a devil and his name was I," the same association of ideas recurs, and it recurs again in what is perhaps the most completely articulate poem in the book, Lampman's *City of the End of Things*; which, though of course it has no room for the slow accumulation of despair that *The City of Dreadful Night* piles up, is an equally terrifying vision of humanity's Iron Age. In the younger writers the satire on war and exploitation is more conventional and anonymous, but as soon as they begin to speak with more authority they will undoubtedly take their places in the same tradition—Patrick Anderson especially.

To sum up. Canadian poetry is at its best a poetry of incubus and *cauchemar*, the source of which is the unusually exposed contact of the poet with nature which Canada provides. Nature is seen by the poet,

Canada and Its Poetry 37

first as unconsciousness, then as a kind of existence which is cruel and meaningless, then as the source of the cruelty and subconscious stampedings within the human mind. As compared with American poets, there has been comparatively little, outside Carman, of the cult of the rugged outdoor life which idealizes nature and tries to accept it. Nature is consistently sinister and menacing in Canadian poetry. And here and there we find glints of a vision beyond nature, a refusal to be bullied by space and time, an affirmation of the supremacy of intelligence and humanity over stupid power. One finds this in Kenneth Leslie:

> Rather than moulds invisible in the air
> into which petals pour selective milk
> I seem to sense a partnered agony
> of creature and creator in the rose.   [*Cobweb College*, ll. 125-8]

One finds it in Dorothy Livesay's apostrophe to the martyred Lorca:

> You dance. Explode
> Unchallenged through the door
> As bullets burst
> Long deaths ago, your breast.   [*For Federico Garcia Lorca*, ll. 62-5]

One finds it in Margaret Avison's very lovely *Maria Minor* and her struggle to divine "the meaning of the smashed moth" [*The Butterfly*, l. 17] in a poem which makes an excellent finale to the book. And one begins thereby to understand the real meaning of the martyrdom of Brébeuf, the theme of what with all its faults is the greatest single Canadian poem. Superficially, the man with the vision beyond nature is tied to the stake and destroyed by savages who are in the state of nature, and who represent its mindless barbarity. But there is a far profounder irony to that scene: the black-coated figure at the stake is also a terrifying devil to the savages, *Echon*, the evil one. However frantically they may try to beat him off, their way of savagery is doomed; it is doomed in their Nazi descendants; it is doomed even if it lasts to the end of time.

This is not, I hope, a pattern of thought I have arbitrarily forced upon Canadian poetry: judging from Mr. Smith's book and what other reading I have done this seems to be its underlying meaning, and the better the poem the more clearly it expresses it. Mr. Smith has brought out this inner unity quite unconsciously, because it is really there: just as in his

Ode on Yeats he has, again quite unconsciously, evoked a perfect image of the nature of poetic feeling in his own country:

> An old thorn tree in a stony place
> Where the mountain stream has run dry,
> Torn in the black wind under the race
> Of the icicle-sharp kaleidoscopic white sky,
>   Bursts into sudden flower.   [ll. 1–5]

12

A Little Anthology

February 1944

Review of A Little Anthology of Canadian Poets, *ed. Ralph Gustafson (Norfolk, Conn.: New Directions, 1943). From* Canadian Forum, *23 (February 1944): 263.*

It is very difficult to say much about an anthology unless there is some statement in it about why it was made, for whom it was made, and what literary principles were involved in making it.[1] Failing this, one can only say that Mr. Gustafson has produced a kind of supplement to his Pelican anthology[2] (though a few poems overlap). It has most of the essential younger people except Margaret Avison, and Finch's *Flight That Failed*, Anderson's *Drinker*, and a couple of beautiful Kleins are the most remarkable of those poems which are not so easily accessible elsewhere.[3]

13

Direction

March 1944

Review of Direction, *vol. 1. From* Canadian Forum, *23 (March 1944): 287.*

This, like its predecessors *Preview* and *First Statement*, is a new literary magazine, beginning very unpretentiously with stapled mimeographed sheets (unfortunately often physically unreadable, and befouled with some amazingly crude cartoons), and produced on an RCAF station by a group of young soldiers. The chief figure in the group seems to be the young poet, Raymond Souster. The contributions are mainly poems, and the leading themes are the sexual loneliness of army life and the ironic contrast between the certain fact of war and the vague hope of a better world after it. The writers are too readily content with a pinchbeck free verse which is really a series of flat prose statements, and are inclined to overestimate the poetic value of nostalgia. On the other hand, they are not afraid to make obvious protests against obvious evils, to look forward to a postwar period, not merely of reconstruction, but of general hell-raising with the "way of life" that blundered into the war, or to affirm with great earnestness that nearly all official Canadian literature is tripe. More power to them.

14

Water-Colour Annual

June 1944

From Canadian Art, *1 (June–July 1944): 187–89. Reprinted in* RW, *41–3. In* Canadian Art *the article was illustrated by three water-colours: Peter Haworth's* Repair Job, Canso, P.B.Y; *Julia Crawford's* Work and Relaxation (Our Wartime Square); *and David Milne's* Cedar Swamp.

A water-colour show is usually worth looking at in itself, and is even more so when it appears along with another show in oils. The exhibition of the Canadian Society of Painters in Water Colour at the Art Gallery of Toronto was accompanied by the Canadian Group of Painters (reviewed in the last issue of *Canadian Art* by Mrs. Housser),[1] and the conjunction of the two illustrated not only the range and variety of Canadian water-colour, but its relation to Canadian painting as a whole.

It seems as though in oil painting there is a constant and inevitable tendency to become conventionalized and academic. The academies themselves, with their endless repetition of Dutch and Victorian techniques, are the fossils which prove that this was true in vanished ages; but precisely similar trends are apparent even in the best current painting. When Canadian pictures are glibly spoken of as "posterish," what is meant is that there is in Canadian landscape, with its solidly massed clouds and its opulent barbaric colouring, or in its heavy lugubrious portraits, a latent tendency to relapse into ready-made formulas, either in design or in colour. When we see some of our best painters experimenting with abstraction, we see that they have recognized this tendency and are deliberately counteracting it. And it is here that water-colour painting takes on a peculiar significance, for I think a strong case could be made out for saying that one of the chief functions of water-colour is to keep painters interested in untried possibilities, whether in subject matter or in technique.

There are many reasons why this is so. Water-colour by its very nature is closer to the cultivated amateur than oil. And the cultivated amateur is not only the backbone of intelligent public appreciation of painting, he is not only a frequently interesting contributor to it himself (at least one amateur has contributed two delightful little studies to this exhibition), but he stands for a spirit no professional can do without: the spirit of painting for fun. Oil painting tends by itself to become exhibition painting, which in Canada means that it tends to centre in Toronto and Montreal. There is more opportunity for decentralization in water-colour, and one is not surprised to find Maritimers and Westerners making up so large a share of the contributions to this exhibition. Often, too, a painter, by the very fact that he is apt to take his water-colour less seriously than his big oils, will let himself go more, achieve more lightness and humour, get more space and air and light into his picture, sacrifice detail to carry through his rhythm, and in general preserve the vitality of the original sketch and avoid the self-conscious solemnity which is so often the mood of the big exhibition picture.

It is also the water-colour artist who is likely to be more attracted in the first place to the sort of subject that presents a challenge to the painter's power of organizing form. Even before the war, the grotesque twisted shapes of buoys, anchors, beached boats, fish nets, and lobster-pots were beginning to creep into Canadian painting; since the war, the immense pictorial possibilities of factories and war plants have reinforced them, and a whole new world of caulking, riveting, welding, marching men working in a confusion of smoke and noise and gantries and assembly belts and derricks and cartridge case plants has come into our pictures, one hopes for good.

This is in all our painting, but water-colour has probably taken the lead in exploring it, a fact which will be even more obvious when the war records now being done by Canadian artists in the armed forces are added to those on the home front. And the fact that such painting involves so many studies of people may eventually begin to wake up our portraiture. Perhaps, after so many sidelong glances at people engaged in their work, the Canadian painter may get in less of a panic at the sight of a human face, and less inclined to give it the blank unfocused stare of something out of the Douanier Rousseau.

The most obvious reason why water-colour is so continuously a fertilizing influence in painting is its great variety of techniques. In this show there is every kind of medium, from Fritz Brandtner's flaming dyes to Jack Humphrey's carefully balanced tempera, and every method of putting it on, from Milne's impressionistic wash on wet paper to the heavy opacity of Peter Haworth. All this tends in exactly the opposite direction from the conventionality noted above, and proves by illustration that painting may be as solid as the Florentines or as flat as the Chinese; that it may be all perspective or have no perspective; that it may catch the sweep of rain across a lake or the receding depths of Western mountains. Its only law is to be as lively and interesting as possible; and such exhibitions as this indicate that painting is in no danger of losing its place as the liveliest and most interesting of Canadian arts.

15

Unit of Five

May 1945

Review of Unit of Five, *ed. Ronald Hambleton (Toronto: Ryerson Press, 1944). From* Canadian Forum, *25 (May 1945): 48.*

This is a small collection of the work of five young (under thirty) Canadian poets: Louis Dudek, Ronald Hambleton, P.K. Page, Raymond Souster, and James Wreford. Three of these are in Smith's anthology, though represented there by earlier and less interesting work, and all five of them should be familiar to *Canadian Forum* readers. The title may mislead some into thinking that these poets all belong to one "school," and all are saying much the same thing, which would be an unfortunate error, there being at least as much variety as unity in the collection.

Dudek and Hambleton are both very good, often startlingly good. My preference for Dudek may be only a matter of personal taste: in Hambleton certain mannerisms which he shares with a group of post-Eliot English poets make his work sound more derivative. Chief among these are a highly developed faculty of allusion, a pleasure in digesting the long words which are difficult to digest in poetry (known in the trade as "aureate diction"), and an intellectual-colloquial sputter deriving ultimately from Donne. Dudek on the other hand is a good poet who does not remind us of better ones; his work has a novelty of cadence very seldom found in modern poetry except where it has become part of a formula. He is a fresh and attractive writer; he is not afraid to be naive; he does not, like Hambleton, bury his feelings in a conventional diction; his lines slide easily into the mind and do not easily slide out again. The imagery of both poets is frequently obscure, but for different reasons: Dudek because he sets the image down directly that seems to him to be the right one at that point, without worrying about its obvious relationship to the larger pattern of the poem; Hambleton because an intellectual interest guides the choice of images and often distorts them in doing so. Dudek's is an obscurity that will later disappear, for with practice the larger pattern will clarify along with the individual image. The one poem in which interest in the larger pattern runs away with him, the final long one called *The Sea*, is, with its self-consciously tight stanza, an exciting and promising failure. Hambleton's is the obscurity of modern poetry generally, and looks back to the immediate past, when the more thoughtful poets had to turn to private associations in symbolism because of the breakdown of conventional religious and romantic ones. Dudek's poetry, I hope, looks to the immediate future, to a wider and sounder appreciation of poetry, and to a corresponding increase of the poet's self-confidence.

In Miss Page's work there is a self-conscious and manipulative technique of description, a rather metallic glitter, which frequently takes the form of a series of imaginative wisecracks. This is, however, appropriate enough to the metropolitan setting of her poetry, and is unsatisfactory only when an irresponsible verbalism runs away with the feeling. Raymond Souster illustrates another familiar dilemma of the modern poet: he has strong and sound feelings about social injustice and war, and he expresses them with great sincerity, energy, and honesty. Now a socially minded poet may well become restless at seeing how greatly all other forms of human communication have been speeded up, while poetry remains as laborious and indirect as ever; so he may try to streamline his medium by bringing it down to the advertisement's level of automatic response, or by increasing the violence of his language so as to make that response less lethargic. Mr. Souster has chosen the latter method, and the integrity of his work is marred by an adolescent shrewishness. He is not so much a poet misled by the notion that poetry can become an effective social weapon, however, as a man of goodwill who has taken up poetry as an epigrammatic means of self-expression.

Mr. Wreford is "romantic" in the sense of accepting the validity of the immediate personal relation to life as opposed to the qualification of it by social or intellectual interests. His rhythm is more even and his vocabulary more traditional than that of the others, and his more limited technical objectives make his poetry seem more balanced and assured. There is, of course, the danger of facility in this, but in the meantime there are some very lovely poems. These vague and general comments will have to do in lieu of the exhaustive critical analysis which the tiny book well deserves, and which we have no space for: all I can say is that its eighty-seven pages are full of the real thing, and are entitled not only to the applause of those who get free copies, but the encouragement of those who buy.

16

Undemocratic Censorship

July 1946

From Canadian Forum, 26 (July 1946): 76. Reprinted in RW, 375–6.

One of the more undemocratic features of Canadian life is the censorship of current books and magazines according to an allegedly "moral" standard, the morality usually turning out to be the use by the author of one or more of half a dozen words which, though not in the dictionary, are well known to every Canadian citizen over the age of six. Canada does not suffer quite as much from this sort of thing as Boston, but runs Boston a close second.[1] Every once in a while a book that is being generally read in the United States disappears from circulation in this country, the latest victim being Edmund Wilson's series of sketches, *Memoirs of Hecate County*. A better-known example is, of course, James Joyce's *Ulysses*, which circulates freely in the United States and Britain, but is still not available here.[2]

The thing that is undemocratic about such censorship is not that it is against the wishes of the majority, who generally confine their reading to stuff that is censored or cooked in various ways all along the line of production. It is undemocratic because, in the case of a serious book like *Ulysses*, it compels the most intelligent and cultivated section of the public to break the law merely because it is the most intelligent and cultivated section of the public. And as long as such people are satisfied with running a brisk trade in highbrow smuggling, as they were after the last war, they have only themselves to blame. The whole question of who, if anyone, is officially appointed to do the censoring, what he is paid and what official status he has, to whom he is responsible and to whom he can be appealed from, whether he makes any reports to anyone, how his job is, if at all, tied up with political censorship, and, above all, what forms of lobbying and pressure he is subjected to, should be thoroughly aired in Parliament. The matter does not seem important now, but it is the sort of thing that can always become crucial, especially if, as often happens after a war, the public can be frightened into one of those superstitious tics often advertised as a "return to religion."

17

Canadian Authors Meet

August 1946

From Canadian Forum, *26 (August 1946): 101. Reprinted in* RW, *376–7. The occasion for the piece was the twenty-fifth anniversary of the Canadian Authors' Association.*

Everyone knows Mr. F.R. Scott's poem of this title, and for a long time meetings of Canadian authors have not altogether unjustly been associated with log-rolling, mutual admiration, clique-forming, claque-recruiting, lugubrious if somewhat inconsistent gripes about why there isn't a Canadian literature and why it isn't better known, and the like. But the twenty-fifth anniversary conference in Toronto, though of course it had all this, was a very different kind of meeting. Literature comes of age, not by improving its quality, but by adopting professional standards and ceasing to worry about its quality. Most Canadian literature is and always will be tripe for the simple reason that most literature of all countries in all ages is and always will be tripe. Any national group of authors will form a pyramid with a few serious writers on top and a broad base of pulp-scribblers at the bottom. No literary critic would say that these latter were even earning an honest living; but, commercially speaking, they sell their wares in the same market and are as much entitled to the name of author as Mr. Callaghan or Gabrielle Roy. An authors' association simply has to accept this fact, and, for the sake of its few serious writers, go ahead on trade union lines, working to get better publicity for its members, to equalize income tax so that it will be based on the average of several years instead of on the individual year, to standardize copyright laws, to arrange for pensions for elderly authors and scholarships or prizes for young ones, and so on. This last conference did begin to concern itself seriously with such matters, and the Canadian Authors' Association will be a valuable asset to Canadian culture in proportion to its advance in the direction of an authors' union. We should like to call its attention also to the question of censorship, mentioned last month, which with the banning of Farrell's latest novel has grown from a nuisance into a scandal.[1]

18

Green World

September 1946

Review of Green World, by Miriam Waddington (Montreal: First Statement Press, 1945). From Canadian Forum, 26 (September 1946): 141–2.

This is the third of a series of books of Canadian poetry which began with Irving Layton's *Here and Now* and Patrick Anderson's *A Tent for April*. Mrs. Waddington has a lyrical gift of great beauty and subtlety, and her work has a uniform level of excellence both in technique and expressive power. There are some peripheral poems: *In the Big City* and *Who Will Build Jerusalem* belong respectively to a type of allegory and of political comment that are not her long suits, and such poems as *Ballet* and *Cadenza* are decorative rather than evocative. But the volume as a whole is a striking and unexpectedly vivid personal communication—I say unexpectedly because a habitual reader of modern poetry gets accustomed to a colourless anonymity.

Like most lyrical poets, Mrs. Waddington has a song of innocence and a song of experience, knows that neither is unreal, and is perplexed by their contrast. The forcing bed, so to speak, of her lyrical genius is a "green world" of the mind, a kind of chrysalis or embryo of imaginative experience, represented by such symbols as a sleeping bird and a subterranean cavern, a soap-bubble world "where water images cling to the inside sphere" [*Green World*, l. 5], and where "green" has something of the symbolic meaning it has in the poetry of Marvell. Outside her is a world represented primarily by the "angled city" [*Morning until Night*, l. 16], a world of filth and selfishness and horror, where each person is imprisoned in "self's captivity" [*Who Will Build Jerusalem*, l. 26] and where even the symbols of the green world appear as lies:

> Under the dawn of city skies
> Moves the sun in presaged course
> Smoothing out the cunning lies
> That hide the evil at the source. [*The Bond*, ll. 9–12]

Or, in a bolder and finer imaginative flash:

> ... oh the blooded stars
> Roll down the world and bright as oranges
> They light the plundered groves. [*Dog Days*, ll. 16–18]

As this world of experience blocks up the present, the poet associates the green world with the past, either a personal past (as in *The Sleepers*) or a historical past (as in *Portrait*); hence it is constructed primarily out of memory and nostalgia. The bridges between the two worlds are not very secure or permanent—love is one, of course; human sympathy, of the kind that discovers one's common humanity with a Jewish whore in *The Bond*, is another; a settled will to remodel a world of misery is another:

> Because I love my past and hate yours
> Let us join hands and plunge into the future; [*Integration*, ll. 26–7]

and occasional flashes of vision like one in *Summer in the Street* is another. But the poet is most eloquent when she is describing their continuous conflict, as in the bitter and pathetic *Morning until Night* with which the book ends, or in *Circles*, which is possibly the finest of all her poems.

To Marvell in the seventeenth century, the green world was not a private possession to be carefully sheltered from a surrounding evil world, but itself the circumference of the evil world, an eternal permanence that not only antedates the evil world but has the power to destroy it. Mrs. Waddington has a symbol of a kind of solar energy radiating from the fingertips that suggests a similar idea, and she becomes still more explicit in a little poem called *Where*. If she pursues this line of thought she should have something very interesting to say as her work matures and becomes more complex and intellectualized.

19

Promising Novelist

October 1946

Review of Presently Tomorrow, *by Joyce Marshall (Boston: Little, Brown; Toronto: McClelland & Stewart, 1946). From* Canadian Forum, *26 (October 1946): 164.*

A celibate Anglican curate with a mild mother fixation attempts to run a church mission for Montreal's poor during the Depression, and finds that a concrete approach to the social problems involved is essential if he is to do any good. His rector calls this "materialism," his idea of spirituality being the putting of all the church's eggs into a reactionary middle-class basket. To punish the curate, the rector sends him to conduct a retreat held in a girls' school where four teenage girls are still left over from the end of the term. The curate runs foul of one of them, commits what the author makes him refer to as "the unpardonable sin," and is startled to find that the sin has given him the courage to tell a lot of people to go to hell, including his rector and the ghost of his mother. This is presented as an episode in the maturing of one of the girls (not the curate's ravisher), who discovers through it the impossibility of retaining the other three, almost the only people she knows, as friends, and who, like the curate, finds herself at the end of the book on the threshold of the new life indicated in the title.

We have on the one hand, then, a breezy and ribald tale, its satirical bite made all the sharper by its very unplausibility, of an apprehensive male virgin dragged from the horns of the altar and seduced by a schoolgirl practically in view of her three companions. On the other hand, we have the very stock theme of the enlightening of an adolescent mind, with its nostalgic memories of childhood, its shocks of disillusionment as it advances to maturity, its reveries over the strangeness of life, and so on, portrayed by a thoughtful, observant girl who plans to be a writer. This self-projecting apparatus simply acts as water-wings for a timid novelist, and Miss Marshall is good enough to do without her water-wings. Her use of a rather facile form of reflective analysis smothers her humour and spawns clichés all over her writing, so that one suspects at times that she does not know herself how funny her story really is, which seems unlikely. But she has the qualities of a real novelist, including a sense of construction (the little surprise in the plot is very deftly handled) and with a more dry and impersonal approach they should emerge in their full vigour.

20

The Narrative Tradition in English Canadian Poetry

Winter 1946

From BG, 145–55. Originally published in French as "La Tradition narrative dans la poésie canadienne-anglais," trans. Guy Sylvestre, Gants du Ciel, no. 11 (Winter 1946): 19–30. English text reprinted in RCLI, 39–49, in ECLI, 37–45, and in Canadian Anthology, ed. Carl F. Klinck and Reginald Watters (Toronto: Gage, 1966), rev. ed., 523–8, and 3rd ed., 605–8.

The Canadian poet cannot write in a distinctively Canadian language; he is compelled to take the language he was brought up to speak, whether French, English, or Icelandic, and attempt to adjust that language to an environment which is foreign to it, if not foreign to himself. Once he accepts a language, however, he joins the line of poets in the tradition of that language, at the point nearest to his immediate predecessors. A nineteenth-century Canadian poet writing in English will be emulating Keats and Tennyson; writing in French, he will be emulating Victor Hugo or Baudelaire. It may be thought that it would be a pure advantage to the Canadian poet to put an old tongue into a new face; that the mere fact of his being a Canadian would give him something distinctive to say, and enable him to be original without effort. But it is not as simple as that. His poetry cannot be "young," for it is written in a European language with a thousand years of disciplined utterance behind it, and any attempt to ignore that tradition can only lead to disaster. Nor is Canada a "young" country in the sense that its industrial conditions, its political issues, or the general level of its civilization are significantly different from contemporary Europe. Nevertheless, to the imaginative eye of the creative artist, whether painter or poet, certain aspects of Canada must, for a long time yet, make it appear young. Its landscape does not have, as that of Europe has, that indefinable quality which shows that it has been lived in by civilized human beings for millennia. Its villages do not "nestle"; they sprawl awkwardly into rectangular lines along roads and railways. Its buildings do not melt into their backgrounds; they stand out with a garish and tasteless defiance. It is full of human and natural ruins, of abandoned buildings and despoiled countrysides, such as are found only with the vigorous wastefulness of young countries. And, above all, it is a country in which nature makes a direct impression on the artist's mind, an impression of its primeval lawlessness and moral nihilism, its indifference to the supreme value placed on life within human society, its faceless, mindless unconsciousness, which fosters life without benevolence and destroys it without malice. There is, of course, much more to be said about nature than this, even by the Canadian artist, but this is an aspect of nature which the sensitive Canadian finds it impossible to avoid. It is all very well for a European poet to see nature in terms of a settled order which the mind can interpret, like Wordsworth, or even in terms of oracular hints and suggestions, like Baudelaire in *Correspondances*; but the Canadian poet receives all his initial impressions in the environment of Rimbaud's *Bateau Ivre*.

What the poet sees in Canada, therefore, is very different from what the politician or businessman sees, and different again from what his European contemporaries see. He may be a younger man than Yeats or Eliot, but he has to deal with a poetic and imaginative environment for which, to find any parallel in England, we should have to go back to a period earlier than Chaucer. In certain Old English poems, notably *The Wanderer* and *The Seafarer*, there is a feeling which seems to a modern reader more Canadian than English: a feeling of the melancholy of a thinly settled country under a bleak northern sky, of the terrible isolation of the creative mind in such a country, of resigning oneself to hardship and loneliness as the only means of attaining, if not serenity, at least a kind of rigid calm. It is a feeling which in later centuries becomes very rare, though there is something of it in some Romantic poems, such as Keats's *La Belle Dame Sans Merci*.

Now of course modern Canadian life is far less simple and homogeneous than Old English life. The Canadian poet, though he must try to express something of what the Old English poet felt, cannot afford to forget either that a highly sophisticated civilization is as much a part of Canadian life as deep snow and barren spaces. If we can imagine a contemporary of the *Beowulf* poet, with equal genius and an equally strong urge to write an archaic epic of the defeat of a monster of darkness by a hero of immense strength and endurance—a theme which should appeal powerfully to a Canadian—yet writing for the same public as Ovid and Catullus, and forced to adapt their sophisticated witticisms and emotional refinements to his own work, we shall begin to get some idea of what the Canadian poet is up against.

This is why nearly all good Canadian poets have much less simple poetic natures than they appear to have at first glance. The "framework" of Lampman, for instance, is that of a placid Romantic nature poet beating the track of Wordsworth and Keats. But there are also in Lampman many very different characteristics. He has, for instance, a spiritual loneliness, a repugnance to organized social life, which goes far beyond mere discontent with his provincial environment. This is a quality in Lampman which links him to the great Canadian explorers, the solitary adventurers among solitudes, and to the explorer-painters like Thomson and Emily Carr who followed them, with their eyes continually straining into the depths of nature. And in the terrible clairvoyance of *The City of the End of Things*, a vision of the Machine Age slowly freezing into idiocy and despair, something lives again of the spirit of the Old English Wanderer, who, trudging from castle to castle in the hope of finding food and shelter in exchange for his songs, turned to the great Roman ruins, the "eald enta geweorc" [l. 87] (the ancient work of giants), to brood over a greater oppression of man by nature than his own.

Similarly, the "framework" of Isabella Crawford is that of an intelligent and industrious female songbird of the kind who filled so many anthologies in the last century. Yet the "South Wind" passage from *Malcolm's Katie* is only the most famous example of the most remarkable mythopoeic imagination in Canadian poetry.[1] She puts her myth in an Indian form, which reminds us of the resemblance between white and Indian legendary heroes in the New World, between Paul Bunyan and Davy Crockett on the one hand and Glooscap on the other. The white myths are not necessarily imitated from the Indian ones, but they may have sprung from an unconscious feeling that the primitive myth expressed the imaginative impact of the country as more artificial literature could never do.

Some of the same affinities appear in those aspects of our literature that a poet would naturally be most interested in, though very few of them have received adequate poetic treatment. The martyrdom of the

Jesuit missionaries, the holding of the Long Sault against the Iroquois, the victories over incredible odds in the War of 1812, the desperate courage of the Indians who died with Tecumseh and Riel, the 1837 outbreak, the fight without gasmasks against gas at St. Julien, the spearheading of the plunge into Amiens, the forlorn hope at Dieppe—there is a certain family resemblance among all these events which makes each one somehow typical of Canadian history.[2] Is there not something in the character of such themes that recalls the earliest poetry of our mother countries, of the lost battle of Maldon where courage grew greater as the strength ebbed away, or of the reckless heroism at Roncesvalles which laid the cornerstone of French literature?[3] It is perhaps not an accident that the best known of all Canadian poems, *In Flanders Fields*, should express, in a tight, compressed, grim little rondeau, the same spirit of an inexorable ferocity which even death cannot relax, like the old Norse warrior whose head continued to gnash and bite the dust long after it had been severed from his body.

Hence it is at least possible that some of the poetic forms employed in the earlier centuries of English literature would have been more appropriate for the expression of Canadian themes and moods than the nineteenth-century Romantic lyric or its twentieth-century metaphysical successor. It is inevitable that Canadian poetry should have been cast in the conventional forms of our own day; but though the bulk of it is lyrical in form, a great deal of it is not lyrical in spirit, and when a Canadian poem has failed to achieve adequate expression, this may often be the reason. It has been remarked, for instance, that sexual passion is a theme that our poets have not treated very convincingly. This emotion is also lacking in Old English poetry, and perhaps for some of the same reasons. But sexual passion is one of the essential themes of the lyric: Canadian poetry is lyrical in form and Old English poetry is not, hence the failure to deal with sexual passion is felt as a lack in Canadian poetry but is not missed in Old English. On the other hand, it occasionally happens that a successful Canadian poem has owed its success to its coincidence, deliberate or otherwise, with one of the forms of pre-Chaucerian literature. Thus Drummond's best poem, *The Wreck of the "Julie Plante,"* is not merely a modern imitation of the ballad; it has the tough humour and syncopated narrative of the authentic ballad at its best. Consider too the subjects of many of D.C. Scott's finest poems, the lovers destroyed in a log jam, the lonely Indian murdered in the forest for his furs, the squaw who baits a fish hook with her own flesh to feed her children. These are ballad themes; and his longest poem *Dominique de Gourges*, a narrative filled with the sombre exultation of revenge, is curiously archaic in spirit for the author of a poem on Debussy. Something medieval has also crept in to the religious emotions of A.J.M. Smith and to Leo Kennedy's exercises in the macabre.

All this may help to explain a phenomenon of our poetry which must have puzzled many of its students. In looking over the best poems of our best poets, while of course the great majority are lyrical, we are surprised to find how often the narrative poem has been attempted, and attempted with uneven but frequently remarkable success. I say surprised, because good narratives are exceedingly rare in English poetry—except in the period that ended with the death of Chaucer. And this unusual prominence of the narrative is one of the things that makes Canadian poetry so hard to criticize with the right combination of sympathy and judgment. We tend to form our canons of criticism on carefully polished poetry, but such standards do not always apply to the narrative, for the test of the great narrative is its ability to give the flat prose statement a poetic value. And as there has been no connected tradition of narrative in English literature since 1400, the Canadian poet who attempts the form has to depend largely on his own originality, and no one except Pratt has worked hard enough and long enough at the form to discover its inherent genius. Hence among Canadian narratives there are many failures and many errors of taste and stretches of bad writing, but to anyone who cares about poetry there may be something more interesting in the failure than in a less ambitious success.

At the outset of Canadian literature we find many long poems, Goldsmith's *Rising Village*, O'Grady's brilliant but unfinished *Emigrant*, Howe's *Acadia*, also unfinished, and two dramatic poems by Duvar, *The Enamorado* and *De Roberval*, the last of which illustrate the fact that the Canadian narrative is frequently cast in the form of dialogue or literary drama. All of these follow well-established European conventions, and so do the first two productions of the clumsy but powerfully built genius of Heavysege. *Saul* belongs to the tradition of the Victorian leviathan, the discursive poem combining a Biblical subject with middle-class morality, represented by the better known Bailey's *Festus*. *Count Filippo*, too, is in the manner of nineteenth-century reactions to Jacobean drama and the Italian Renaissance, and might almost have served as the model for Max Beerbohm's *"Savonarola" Brown*. But *Jephthah's Daughter*, his third effort, strikes its roots deeply into Canada, and is the real commencement of a distinctively Canadian form of the narrative poem.

Heavysege begins by saying that the story of Jephthah's daughter is very similar to the story of Iphigenia, and that he has chosen the Hebrew legend because there is a spiritual loneliness about it which attracts him more profoundly. Iphigenia was sacrificed in the midst of great bustle and excitement, and was, as Samuel Johnson said of the victim at a public hanging, sustained by her audience:[4] Jephthah's daughter is destroyed by the mute anguish of uncomprehending superstition. To Heavysege, a man who, like Jephthah, worships a God who demands fulfilment of a rash vow of sacrifice even it if involves his own daughter, is really a man in the state of nature: he has identified his God, if not with nature, at any rate with a mindless force of inscrutable mystery like nature, and all Jephthah's questionings and searchings of spirit are the looks of intelligence directed at blankness, the attempts of a religious pioneer to find a spiritual portage through the heart of darkness. The passage in which Heavysege described this most clearly cannot be beaten in James Thomson for the sheer starkness of its mood, a grimness that is far deeper than any ghost-haunted horrors. Jephthah prays to be delivered from the blood of his daughter, and asks for a sign of divine mercy. There is a slight pause, then Jephthah hears:

> The hill-wolf howling on the neighbouring height,
> And bittern booming in the pool below.   [*Jephthah's Daughter*, ll. 389–90]

That is all the answer he gets.

In this poem Heavysege has put together certain essential ideas: the contrast of human and civilized values with nature's disregard of them in a primitive country, the tendency in the religion of such a country for God to disappear behind the mask of nature, and the symbolic significance, when that happens, of human sacrifice and the mutilation of the body (a theme already elaborated by Heavysege in the episode in *Saul* about the hewing of Agag in pieces).[5] Once one has carefully read this narrative, the essential meaning of many fine Canadian poems leaps out of its derivative and conventional context. Thus in Isabella Crawford's *Malcolm's Katie* there is a superbly ironic scene in which the hero sings of the irresistible advance of capitalist civilization and its conquest of nature, symbolized by the axe, and links his exuberant belief in the enduring power of the nation he is building with his belief in the enduring power of his love for the heroine. He is answered by the villain, in a passage of far greater eloquence, who points out the cyclic progress of all empires from rise to decline and the instability of woman's love.[6] As the hero turns indignantly to refute his slanders, the tree which he has not quite chopped down falls on him and crushes him. True, he recovers and marries the heroine and forgives the villain and lives happily ever after and love conquers all and nature is grand, but somehow the poem reaches an imaginative concentration in that scene which it never afterwards recaptures. In the same poem the heroine is caught in a log jam [pt. 3, ll. 198–217], and, though of course she is rescued, the sudden glimpse of the trap of nature, the endless resources it has for suddenly and unconsciously destroying a fragile and beautiful human life, is far more effective without the rescue, and is so developed in D.C. Scott's *At the Cedars*.

Mair's *Tecumseh* and Lampman's *At the Long Sault* apply the same pattern to Canadian history. The former has been charged with lack of unity, but the theme of the drama is the sacrifice of Tecumseh, to which everything else leads up, the various conflicts between his own fierce loyalties and the vacillations of his friends and enemies being merely the struggles of a doomed victim who now arouses and now disappoints our hopes for his escape. Lampman, too, seems most deeply impressed, not only by the sacrificial nature of what the Long Sault heroes did, which is obvious enough, but by its symbolic connection with, again, a state of nature in which the higher forms of life are so often destroyed by the lower. That is why he introduces the beautiful picture of the moose pulled down by wolves [ll. 47–60], the symbol of the exceptional and unblemished hero who falls a victim to the agents of a careless fate.

Pratt has studied the technique and resources of the narrative form more carefully than his predecessors, and so it is not surprising to find the themes we have been tracing much more explicitly set forth in his work. He delights in describing big and even monstrous things, and whenever he can he shows them exulting in their strength. In the antics of Tom the Cat from Zanzibar in *The Witches' Brew*, in the almost equally feline sense of relaxed power in *The 6000*, in the ferocious but somehow exuberant massacres in *The Great Feud*, there is more enthusiasm than in his other works, for naturally he greatly prefers the Othellos of this world to the Iagos, and hates to see the latter victorious. But the Canadian narrative demands a tragic resolution. *The Cachalot* is not perhaps a tragic poem, but is there really so much moral difference between the whale caught by men and the moose in Lampman pulled down by wolves? In *The Titanic* the mindlessness of the agent of destruction is the imaginative centre of the poem: the tragic theme of hubris, the punishment of man by fate for his presumption in defying it, is, though a very obvious and in fact ready-made aspect of the theme, deliberately played down. If *Dunkirk* seems less wholly convincing than some of his other narratives, it may well be because the absence of the theme of wasted life gives it a resolutely optimistic quality which seems rather forced, more the glossed and edited reporter's story than the poet's complete and tragic vision.

Brébeuf is not only the greatest but the most complete Canadian narrative, and brings together into a single pattern all the themes we have been tracing. Here the mutilation and destruction of the gigantic Brébeuf and the other missionaries is a sacrificial rite in which the Indians represent humanity in the state of nature and are agents of its unconscious barbarity. It is curious that, just as the poet minimizes the theme of hubris in *The Titanic*, so in *Brébeuf* he minimizes the awareness of the Indians, their feeling that they are disposing of a real enemy, a black-coated emissary of an unknown God and an unknown race that may soon wipe them out. In any case, Indians, even Iroquois, are not merely wolves; and while the conflict of mental and physical values is certainly present, there is a greater range of suggestiveness. In the first place, the scene is related to its universal archetype: Brébeuf is given the courage to endure the breaking of his body because the body of God was in a very similar way broken for him. Thus the essential tragedy of Jephthah's daughter, as a pointless and useless waste of life, ceases to exist. In the second place, the Indians represent the fact that the unconscious cruelty of nature is recreated by the partly conscious cruelties of ignorant and frightened men. This point is already implicit in *Jephthah's Daughter*; we have seen that Jephthah is really sacrificing his daughter to nature. But it is clearer here, and it is clear too that the monsters of *The Great Feud*, who are animated only by an impulse to mutual destruction, prefigure the stampeding and maniacal fury of Naziism as much as their descendants in *The Fable of the Goats* do.

In *Brébeuf* the poet makes a comment which may well be prophetic for the future of Canadian poetry:

> The wheel had come full circle with the visions
> In France of Brébeuf poured through the mould of St. Ignace. [ll. 2071–2]

For a wheel does come full circle here: a narrative tradition begotten in the nineteenth century, and heir to all the philosophical pessimism and moral nihilism of that century, reaches its culmination in *Brébeuf* and is hardly capable of much future development. True, Birney's *David* is a fine example of the same sort of tragedy that is in *At the Cedars* or even *The Titanic*, and in the phrase "the last of my youth" with which the poem ends there is even a faint suggestion of a sacrificial symbolism. And in Anne Marriott's *The Wind Our Enemy*, it is significant that the enemy is still the wind rather than the forces of economic breakdown that helped to create the wind. But neither of these poets seems likely to go on with this theme, and in such poems as *The Truant*, where man confronts the order of nature undismayed, it is evident that Pratt is abandoning it too. The poet's vision of Canada as a pioneer country in which man stands face to face with nature is bound to be superseded by a vision of Canada as a settled and civilized country, part of an international order, in which men confront the social and spiritual problems of men. That this development is now taking place and will greatly increase in future needs no detailed proof: but it is to be hoped that the poets who do deal with it will maintain an interest in the traditional narrative form. For the lyric, if cultivated too exclusively, tends to become too entangled with the printed page: in an age when new contacts between a poet and his public are opening up through radio, the narrative, as a form peculiarly well adapted for public reading, may play an important role in reawakening a public respect for and response to poetry. There are values in both tradition and experiment, and in both the narrative has important claims as Canadian poetry hesitates on the threshold of a new era.

21

Canadian Poet

September 1947

Review of Edwin J. Pratt *by Henry W. Wells and Carl F. Klinck (Toronto: Ryerson Press, 1947). From* Canadian Forum, *27 (September 1947): 140–1.*

This book contains a biographical study by C.F. Klinck of Waterloo College, followed by an "interpretation" by H.W. Wells of Columbia University. Mr. Wells relates each of Pratt's long poems to a classical model. Thus *The Titanic,* because tragic, is compared with *Agamemnon; The Witches' Brew,* because comic, with *The Frogs. The Song of Roland, Beowulf, Henry V, Reynard the Fox, Moby-Dick,* and others follow in demure procession. The idea is evidently not to suggest a comparison in merit with any of these biggies, much less with all of them at once, but to try to indicate both the variety of Pratt's achievement and the kind of traditions and standards to which his poems belong, and by which they should be judged. It is a curious method, and possibly a justifiable one, but the combination of an untried method and a still active poet may be confusing to the average reader, who could easily get a hazy impression that Mr. Wells thinks Pratt is all the great poets in the world rolled into one.

It seems to me that this does an unintentional disservice to Pratt, because Pratt is one of the most original poets now writing, if originality implies advancing the conquest of experience by art. And real originality usually springs up in unexpected quarters, catching all the critics off guard and with all their formulas useless. The subtilized lyric is now so conventional a means of poetic expression that there is practically no new variation of it that cannot be sympathetically examined. But then Pratt comes along with a series of exuberant narratives, plunging and floundering joyously about like a school of porpoises, and we discover that we have no standards ready for them. There have been very few good narratives in English poetry since the Middle Ages, and modern criticism is likely to be based on an unconscious identification of the poetical with the lyrical. But the most precise and subtle short-range critical equipment will get nowhere with a good narrative, where all the timing, phrasing, rhythm, and development of ideas are long-range.

I wish, then, that Mr. Wells had confined himself to a careful discussion of the problems and characteristics of the narrative form, referring to *The Song of Roland* and *Reynard the Fox* as much as he liked as examples of that form, and without dragging in Greek dramatists. And I wish that Mr. Klinck had been a little less folksy and anecdotal, and that he had prepared the way for his collaborator by showing how Pratt's work is linked historically to the striking predilection of Canadian poets for narrative. Most poets and critics believe that modern poetry should be more closely in touch with modern life, that it should have a more robust appetite for the phenomena of a mechanical and scientific age, that there should be more public respect for poetry, that poets should write for radio, for movies, even for government commissions. I know of no modern English poet except Pratt to whom all of these beliefs can be referred, and for that reason alone, apart from his merits, his work and his career deserve the systematic study which I feel that Messrs. Klinck and Wells have just missed making.

22

Canadian Accent

December 1947

Review of Canadian Accent: A Collection of Stories and Poems by Contemporary Writers from Canada, *ed. Ralph Gustafson (Harmondsworth: Penguin Books, 1944). From* Canadian Forum, *27 (December 1947): 214.*

This excellent little collection of contemporary Canadian poems, stories, and essays has only recently become available in Canada, but it has been out in England for some time, and seems to have been well received there. Even those who follow Canadian writing with some attention will find many pleasant surprises in the book, and those who do not will find that it is possible (with the aid of a good deal of intelligent editorial work on Mr. Gustafson's part) to obtain a book made up entirely of Canadian writing which is also a perfect weekend book in its own right. I do not describe it in detail, because it will betray its own secrets for thirty pieces of copper.

23

The Flowing Summer

December 1947

Review of The Flowing Summer, *by Charles Bruce (Toronto: Ryerson, 1947). From* Canadian Forum, *27 (December 1947): 215.*

The statement that this is a single narrative poem in blank verse sounds alarming. Actually, it is an account of a boy's vacation with a fisherman on the Atlantic coast, and with its black and white illustrations by Winifred Fox it makes a very pleasant book, almost like a child's book designed for adults.

24

Other Canadians

January 1948

Review of Other Canadians: An Anthology of the New Poetry in Canada, ed. John Sutherland (Montreal: First Statement Press, 1947). *From* Canadian Forum, 27 *(January 1948): 239.*

The poets chiefly featured here are or have been associated with *Preview*, *First Statement*, and the *Northern Review*, and include Patrick Anderson, Irving Layton, Kay Smith, and the "unit of five" (Dudek, Hambleton, Page, Souster, and Wreford). A good many of the poems first appeared in the *Canadian Forum*. Mr. Sutherland's title is explained by his preface, in which he attacks the genteel tradition in Canada which is fostered by the "Oedipus complex" of a vociferous colonialism, and the nervous prudery which goes with that. He claims that A.J.M. Smith's anthology has made this attitude intellectually respectable by interpreting Canadian poetry in terms of a Catholic-royalist-Classical dialectic derived from Eliot. He could have added that Mr. Smith has done his level best, and far more than anyone else, to bring these "other Canadians" also to public attention. On the positive side, however, Mr. Sutherland talks just like any other writer on Canadian poetry. "There are half a dozen poets writing in Canada today whose work compares favourably with English and American poetry, if it is not as good as that of the best English and American poets." That has the old familiar ring. Most of the poems are from published collections which have already been reviewed in these columns, and no critical revaluations are suggested by this anthology, which is nevertheless of value and interest as a guide to the younger Canadian poets.

25

Duncan Campbell Scott

February 1948

From Canadian Forum, 27 (February 1948): 244. Reprinted in RW, 381–2. Scott had died on 19 December 1947 in Ottawa.

The death of Duncan Campbell Scott ends one of the longest and most versatile careers in Canadian literature. Like most Canadian authors, he was a spare-time writer who never made enough money from writing to retire on it, though his real job, in the Civil Service at Ottawa, was done well enough to get him a CBE shortly after the last war. Nevertheless, he managed to make four considerable breaches into literature: as a biographer (of Simcoe), as an editor (of Lampman), as a short story writer, and as a poet. Critics rank him very near the Canadian top in both the last categories. And whatever a Canadian writer may be, there is no doubt that Scott had as varied and comprehensive a knowledge of Canada as any writer we have produced. This knowledge extended to the Indians and the French Canadians, as well as to his own Ontario background, and was in its turn the foundation of a general and very cosmopolitan culture.

As a poet, Scott is best known outside Canada for a lovely pre-Raphaelite fantasy, *The Piper of Arll*, which was acclaimed by Masefield and is still one of the best things of its period.[1] That was, so to speak, a carefully polished masterpiece designed for the export trade. His poetry, like his stories, is full of queer, grim, rather sardonic ballad themes, tales of lovers crushed in a log-jam, a solitary Indian murdered in the forest for his furs, a squaw baiting a fishhook with her own flesh to get food for her children. It is full too of quick apprehensions of a violent and unpredictable climate in which the most commonplace phrase, such as, "I think it will freeze tonight" [*In November*, l. 20], suddenly takes on sinister overtones. But it is also full of normal, even ready-made, religious, philosophical, and other reflections about God, the soul, the world, and nature as well as of an appreciation of the common heritage of modern civilization, like the poem on Debussy [*On the Death of Claude Debussy*] or the "Theme with Variations" series. His taste is far from faultless, and some of his best-known poems, notably *At the Cedars*, would hardly look out of place in *Sarah Binks*.[2] But the critic should not confine his appreciation to poets who were good only because they never had the nerve to write badly. Scott is good for much better reasons and is highly rewarding to read, not only for the Canadian who sees so much of his real and fictional environment reflected in him, but for the modern man who can see in his very unevenness of theme and achievement the typical modern poet singing, like the piper of Arll, of "the secret of his broken will" [l. 76].

26

David Milne: An Appreciation

May 1948

From Here and Now, *1, no. 2 (May 1948): 47–8 (illustrated). Reprinted in BG, 203–6. In* Here and Now, *the article was followed by reproductions of ten paintings by Milne*: Mist and Frost Pattern; Water-Fall and Easel; Red Church No. 3; Winter Rain; Noah and the Ark and Mount Ararat No. 4; Snow in Bethlehem; Outlet of the Pond; Water Lilies, Temagamy; Gulls and Lighthouse; *and* Palgrave 1932.

The problem of how to create while living in the world is always difficult, and in painting two extreme solutions of it are currently fashionable, perhaps because they are extreme. One is that of the primitive or "naive" painter who remains isolated from the world until the time comes for him to be dug out and patronized. The other is that of the "engaged" painter who is preoccupied with schools and movements and trends and isms, and whose painting is full of quotations. David Milne's solution is much nearer the mean that Aristotle would have recommended: he lives a very retired life, and works out all his pictorial problems by himself; but he is perfectly well aware of what is going on in modern painting, and all his pictures look unaffectedly contemporary.

Painting is a two-dimensional art, and one would normally expect it to adopt, as other arts do, the conditions of its medium, and present a two-dimensional view of reality. Yet since 1400 painting has been largely concerned with creating the illusion of three dimensions, using mechanical rules of perspective and lighting to help that illusion along. This implies that painting for the last five centuries has been from one point of view stunt-painting, an enormous refinement of the trick-perspective and peep-show pictures popular in the Renaissance. Our painting, still from this point of view, has been rather like what our music would have been if it had been all program music, confining itself to rearranging the sounds heard in nature. It seems odd to speak of such painting in such terms, but there is a real fact involved. Western painting, from Masaccio to Cézanne, has consistently illustrated the dogma of the externality of the world, a dogma which, as it has not obsessed the Orient to the same degree, has not been incorporated in its painting. Our painting normally recedes from the observer, and is often judged by critics in terms of whether it takes flight precipitately enough: whether it "goes back," as the phrase is.

At the same time nobody wants perfectly flat painting, which still gives one an external world, though stripped of one dimension and of all the seeing in depth which is half the pleasure of using one's eyes. That is the painting world of advertisements, posters, and other mentally invisible objects, and of those murals in which dead pasteboard figures glumly rehearse the progress of transportation from camel to jeep. Flat painting is tolerable only in genuinely childlike pictures, as the child's eye hardly seems to perceive in depth at all. But it is absurd to say that Oriental or medieval painting is flat in this sense, or that it has no perspective. The perspective is there all right, but it is a convex perspective which rolls up to the observer instead of running away from him. In some Oriental pictures the observer's eye seems to be at the circumference of the picture, so that it opens inward into the mind. Perspective in this kind of painting is not a mechanical handling of distance, but a proportioning of visual interest, which makes a man look smaller when further away because he is then pictorially less important.

It is an approach to perspective something like this which gives to those landscapes of Milne that depend on vista, such as *Palgrave* or the *Red Church*,[1] their extraordinary soap-bubble lightness. No emphasis is laid on the mass, volume, solidity, independence, or elusiveness of things "out there": all the shapes and forms are drawn toward the eye, as though the whole picture were floating in the air detached from its rectangular frame. Milne's whole aim is apparently to present a pure visual experience, detached from all the feelings which belong to the sense of separation from the object, feelings which are mainly tactile in origin.

The studies in still life, on the other hand, and the landscapes that are done inside a forest, or (as often happens) a house, are perhaps closer to Milne's immediate context in Canada. In temperament Milne is possibly

David Milne: An Appreciation 73

closer to Morrice than to any other Canadian painter (see especially *Winter Rain*), but he comes later on the Canadian scene and is more closely linked both with it and with the traditions of painting it than the friend of Matisse was. The Group of Seven felt that they were among the first to look at Canada directly, and much of their painting was based on the principle of confronting the eye with the landscape. This made a good deal of their work approach the flat and posterish, but that was a risk they were ready to take. Jackson, Lismer, and Harris all found this formula exhaustible, and have all developed away from it. Thomson and Emily Carr represent a more conscious penetration of the landscape: they seem to try to find a centre of rhythm deep within their subject and expand from there. Milne combines these techniques in a way that is apt to confuse people who look at him for the first time. The flatness in his painting is not a remote or external flatness, but an absorption of the painter's (and beholder's) eye in the subject. The beholder is at once well inside the picture, where he finds that everything is on much the same pictorial level. In other words, he finds a certain amount of camouflage or dazzle-painting (notice how hard it is to see the human figure in the untitled landscape study). Little allowance is made for the customary selective activity of the eye, and in a still life like the *Water Lilies*,[2] foreground and background seem to merge in an elaborate interlocking pattern, as substance and shadow do when trees are reflected in the *Outlet of the Pond*.

I happen to be personally more attracted by Milne's water-colours than by his oils, although his use of oil is very subtle and delicate, and in fact approximates his water-colour technique more closely than is usual with painters. (His drypoint etchings, which are of very great interest, have been discussed by himself in a recent issue of *Canadian Art*.)[3] He has painted what must surely be some of the wettest water-colours, both in technique and in subject-matter, ever done. In fact, rain, fog, snow, and mist (see *Mist and Frost Pattern* and *Winter Rain*) play an important role in his work: their function is not to blur the outlines but to soften them down so as to increase the sense of a purified visual pattern. Rain, which is very difficult to paint, has the paradoxical quality of bringing objects nearer by partly veiling them: it decreases the sunlight sense of hard objective fact, not by making things look unreal, but by making them seem less conventionalized. It often plays a similar role in Oriental painting.

In more recent years Milne has brought his painting to the point at which it has become the pictorial handwriting, so to speak, of a genuinely simple but highly civilized mind. This has enabled him to detach himself further than ever from the picturesque object and develop a free fantasy which may remind some of Chagall. One may see something of this even in the sea-gulls that flap like unwanted thoughts across the foreground of a picture where the focus of vision is on the skyline. It is more fully developed in the *Noah's Ark*, with its unforced humour that appeals to the child in the adult without being itself synthetically childlike. And in the very lovely *Snow over Bethlehem* the idea suggested, which we can take or leave alone, that every snowflake is a new star, and hence, if one likes, a new sign of the presence of God, floats so easily out of the picture because it is an inference from the picture and not its organizing idea. The organizing idea is simply the exploiting of the possibilities of a subject usually considered inaccessible to painting—the crystallization of snowflakes. This expansion of meaning from the desire to paint, rather than from a desire to say something with paint, is typical of the way that Milne's art works. Few if any contemporary painters, in or outside Canada, convey better than he does the sense of painting as an emancipation of visual experience, as a training of the intelligence to see the world in a spirit of leisure and urbanity.

27

Canadian Dreiser

September 1948

From Canadian Forum, *28 (September 1948): 121–2. Reprinted in* RW, *383–5, in* Frederick Philip Grove, *ed. Desmond Pacey (Toronto: Ryerson Press, 1970), 186–7, and (partially) in* Twentieth-Century Literary Criticism, *ed. Sharon K. Hall (Detroit: Gale Research, 1981), 4:135–6.*

Frederick Philip Grove was certainly the most serious of Canadian prose writers, and may well have been the most important one also. His first book was published in 1922, when he was fifty. If he had understood the mechanics of preparing manuscripts for publication, he might have been in print thirty years earlier, in which case he would have pioneered in realistic fiction along with Dreiser. He is best known for his novels, *The Yoke of Life, Settlers of the Marsh, Two Generations, Fruits of the Earth*, and, above all, *Our Daily Bread* and the comparatively recent *The Master of the Mill*. Next in importance come his autobiographical studies, *In Search of America* and *In Search of Myself*, then his narrative and descriptive essays, *Over Prairie Trails* and *The Turn of the Year*. There is a full-length critical study of him by Desmond Pacey.[1] Many of his books are out of print, and it is easy to pick up a hearsay impression that he wrote nothing but gloomy epics on the "no fun on the farm" theme. Those who read him, however, will find that he not only reads very well, but is full of surprising insights and an unflagging sincerity and power.

    Like many Canadian writers, he has a significance for Canadians that is difficult to share with other countries. Perhaps it is only to the Canadian reader that his faults seem to be, not only inseparable from his virtues, but curiously instructive in themselves. His life is a pitiful record of frustration and heartbreak, combined with a dogged insistence on writing as he felt without compromise. He is perhaps our only example of an artist who made his whole life a drama of the artist's fight for survival in an indifferent society. Yet one cannot help wondering how far his integrity merged with a self-conscious pose of integrity, how much of his frustration sprang out of an obscure but profound will to be frustrated. No one can answer such a question either about oneself or others, and the question would seem impudent if even the novels did not show a conflict between integrity and something else. A fine flash of ribald comedy may be smothered by a distrust of humour far deeper than prudery, or the logical development of a scene may be suddenly twisted into moralizing. There is something profoundly Canadian about this fear of letting oneself go, and Grove speaks for a whole era of Canadian literature when he says: "We (the artists) aim at creating that which will live beyond Christianity and in spite of whatever sublimation may take its place. We shall most certainly fail in that; for . . . this is not a time for the production of great art; but we are content to be the forerunners of such a time; and, to say it once more, we are not much concerned about our ultimate failure or success. Failure may be tragic; but we do not shrink from tragedy."[2] As Christianity would say, the time is at hand.

28

Editorial Statement

September 1948

From Canadian Forum, 28 *(September 1948): 123. Reprinted in* Canadian Forum, 35 *(October 1955): 161.*

The *Canadian Forum* has not for a long time issued a statement of editorial aims and policy to its readers, and it seems from some of the letters that have appeared recently in its columns that such a statement is timely.

The intelligent and critical reader has two main interests: the war of civilization and the peace of civilization. By the peace of civilization is meant the enjoyment of the best available cultural interests: books, movies, records, and the current trend of ideas. A Canadian reader will naturally have an additional interest in what is being done in Canada. So we try to provide as honest and well-informed criticism as we can along these lines, and also use some of our restricted space to provide an outlet for poetry, short stories, and critical essays.

By the war of civilization is meant in particular all the public activities which spring from the axiom that the price of liberty is eternal vigilance. Strong trade unions, well-organized social services, honest and efficient government, personal and social security, racial equality, are all objectives to be constantly fought for, and every inch of ground won or even held means endless patient, plodding work, sitting on committees, drafting constitutions, getting legal decisions, and organizing public opinion. We are trying to keep our readers in touch with as many aspects as we can cover of the fight to maintain and develop civilized life in Canada.

Such a fight involves action through political parties. We are interested in political parties, as we think all citizens of a democracy should be, but we are in no sense anybody's party organ, nor can we be one without becoming an entirely different kind of magazine. All political parties become involved in tactics: they have to adjust their objectives to election dates and the tempers of voters. Politicians sometimes get so absorbed in the exciting chess game of campaigning that their attention may be withdrawn from the actual social ends which are supposed to be served by it. We conceive it to be our job to keep the aims and objectives of social progress before our readers all the time, without regard to the immediate tactical requirements of any party. If a party is a genuinely progressive one, we can help it much more by doing this.

In Great Britain and the United States, with their large populations, there is a fairly sizeable minority of readers interested in the war and peace of civilization. Canada is smaller, and this body of readers is smaller. We think it is the function of the *Canadian Forum* to consolidate and develop this reading public. Besides being small, however, it is apt to be divided in temperament. There are many who work hard at the war of civilization: they are the salt of the earth, and we are proud to have them as readers. Some of them do not always enjoy the fruits of civilization as much as they might, and they write us letters saying that they can't understand a word of the poetry the *Canadian Forum* prints, no sir, not a single word. There are many who do like the poetry and criticism, and some of *them* write us letters asking us why we spoil a good critical review with a lot of ponderous statistics about labour disputes and social services. Both groups of critics may sometimes be right. But we are trying to help maintain the mental standard of living in Canada, and we feel that cannot be done in a small country either by a purely cultural magazine or a purely political one. So far as we can see, we are the only Canadian magazine devoted exclusively to both purposes. We make plenty of mistakes, and we need your constant criticism, but, as our ambitions are sincere enough, we think we have a right to ask also for your sympathy and your support.

29

Dean of Critics

November 1948

From Canadian Forum, *28 (November 1948): 169–70. Reprinted in RW, 385–6. Edgar had died on 7 October 1948.*

The death of Pelham Edgar removes from the scene the greatest public figure in Canadian literature. This seems the best title to give him, as he was so much more than a critic, even than the "dean of Canadian critics," as Mr. A.J.M. Smith calls him.[1] He certainly was a critic, and a very good one, in his own right. Many years before the present uproar over Henry James began, he produced a pioneering study of James described recently by an English reviewer as "still unrivalled for clarity."[2] But in Canada he was, besides a great teacher, a personal influence of a unique kind. This was partly because he brought a very cosmopolitan point of view to bear on Canadian literature—he knew French literature, which he originally taught, as well as English—but even more because he had a flair for discerning Canadian talent that at times verged on the uncanny.

For instance, one of his first acts as professor of English in Victoria College was to remove a young man named Pratt from psychology and take him into his department. Pratt had at that time written nothing, but his new chief thought he might some day. Later, he brought Marjorie Pickthall to the library; then he befriended Raymond Knister, who would have been one of Canada's best poets and novelists if he had lived longer. He also turned down an application for a job in the French department from Ezra Pound.

He belonged to the generation of Roberts, Carman, and D.C. Scott, and was an intimate friend of all of them, as well as providing critical standards for them. He was in a unique position to feel the maturing and developing of Canadian literature, and as he grew older in years he grew younger in spirit, because the people he helped got progressively younger than he. For a great teacher, retirement from active teaching often seems to wrench the king-pin out of life, and bring death in a few years. Not so with Pelham Edgar. "I have a naturally retiring disposition," he remarked demurely, and continued to organize the Canadian Authors' Association and raise money for indigent authors while holding down a very responsible job in the Censorship at Ottawa during the war. When he was born, Canadian literature was nothing much; today it's not bad. He had a lot to do with making the difference.

30

The Book of Canadian Poetry, Second Edition

November 1948

Review of The Book of Canadian Poetry: A Critical and Historical Anthology, *2nd ed., ed. A.J.M. Smith (Chicago: University of Chicago Press, 1948). From* Canadian Forum, *28 (November 1948): 188. For a review of the first edition, see no. 11.*

The word "anthology" meant originally a bouquet or nosegay of poems, a collection of lyric verse chosen solely on the basis of its immediate lyric appeal. Mr. Ralph Gustafson's Pelican anthology of Canadian verse is a true anthology in this sense: it collects poems and gives the minimum of information about their authors.[1] Mr. Smith's monumental work is of a very different kind, for which the word "chrestomathy" would be better, though it seems now a little obsolete. Though his standard admission is still literary merit, he presents his poems also as documents in the cultural history of Canada, relates them to the development of the country and to literary movements elsewhere, and in general attaches them to various parts of their surrounding environment.

For Mr. Smith's purpose it is necessary to collect the important poets and present a coherent piece of their life-work, rather than to seek out the random or occasional poetic surprise, however delightful in itself. The second edition of his book is much more solidly and intelligibly constructed along these lines. He has been greatly aided by the fact that since 1943, when the first edition appeared, many of the best younger people have published collected volumes of their verse, so that contemporary poetry is in a far less tentative state than it was then.

About ninety poems have been added, mainly though by no means exclusively in the later sections. Malcolm Lowry and Douglas LePan are among the best of the newcomers, and their contemporaries who appeared in the first edition are far better represented. The addition of Pratt's wonderful *Witches' Brew* and part of Patrick Anderson's *Poem on Canada*, which originally appeared in this magazine, are to be warmly welcomed, and they help also to illustrate a curious predilection of Canadian poets for narrative and descriptive verse which seems to be peculiar to Canada, and which the average anthology would give little hint of. The first edition of the book was lengthily reviewed in the *Canadian Forum* for December, 1943, and all that need be said of this edition is that it is a considerable improvement on what was already a sufficiently remarkable achievement.

31

The Varsity Story

November 1948

Review of The Varsity Story, *by Morley Callaghan (Toronto: Macmillan, 1948). From* Canadian Forum, *28 (November 1948): 189.*

This is a sort of intellectual guidebook to the University of Toronto, cast into the form of fiction. The warden of Hart House, a stranger from New Zealand named Tyndall, undertakes to find out just what it is that is distinctive about Toronto, and cruises about the campus interviewing professors and talking to students, getting the atmosphere and traditions of the various faculties and federated Arts colleges. His conclusion—possibly a more sardonic one than the author really intended—is that what is distinctive about Toronto is precisely a lack of interest in distinctiveness. Tyndall finds everywhere a self-deprecating anonymity which is peculiar to Canada in general and Toronto in particular, and yet seems typical too of a general tendency to transform universities into research factories and scholars and teachers into quacking robots.

The initiated reader will be confused by assuming to start with that Tyndall is a portrait of Mr. J.B. Bickersteth, who held the office of warden at the time of the story. It is clear, however, that Mr. Callaghan is not talking about Mr. Bickersteth at all, and that his warden is a purely fictional character assigned to that office because in it he would have special opportunities for carrying out such an investigation, and for meeting staff and students with equal freedom. Yet a fair proportion of the people Tyndall meets are real people, sometimes referred to by their real names and sometimes perfunctorily disguised. Thus the boundary between fact and fiction is difficult to find, perhaps more difficult for the insider than anyone else, and it is hard not to feel that the book falls between the stools of fiction writing and a straight reporting job. The latter would not necessarily have excluded the personal values which the use of fiction is designed to introduce. On the other hand, there is a great theme for a novel in the material of this book, and one would like to see a highly trained and experienced novelist like Mr. Callaghan write it. It is a pity to have one of his least important productions become, through the circumstances of its appearance, more widely publicized, read, and discussed than anything else he has written. At the same time the book is extremely readable, and is an experiment in a form and theme as yet untried in Canada.

The illustrations by Eric Aldwinckle are admirable.

32

The Pursuit of Form

25 December 1948

From Canadian Art, *6 (Christmas 1948): 54–7. Reprinted in* RW, *43–6. In* Canadian Art, *the article was accompanied by reproductions of three paintings by Harris*: Isolation Peak, Abstract Painting, *and* Lake Superior.

Most painters choose a certain genre of painting, which in Canada is generally landscape, and commit themselves to the genius of that genre. Their growth as painters is thus a growth in sensitive receptivity. In comparing early and late work of a typical landscape painter, such as Arthur Lismer, one can see a steady increase in the power of articulating what he sees. The early work generalizes colour and abstracts form; the late work brings out every possible detail of colour contrast and formal relationship with an almost primitive intensity. Emily Carr seems to go in the opposite direction, from the conventional to the conventionalized, from faithful detail to an equally intense abstraction. Yet there too the same growth in receptivity has taken place, the same power to express all the pictorial reality that she sees.

It is the peculiar quality of Lawren Harris's painting that it is partly an act of will. He does not surrender to nature and let it grow organically through his mind into art; he has a strongly intellectual mind which imposes pictorial form on nature. He explores and abandons one genre after another in a drive to articulate, not the pictorial genius of a subject, but the pictorial forms of his own mind which are projected on the subject. He is the type of painter who grows through states of metamorphosis, breaking his life into periods of experiment: the type represented by Turner and Picasso. This is the revolutionary type, and Harris is Canada's only important revolutionary painter.

In most exhibitions, as we follow the progression from early to late, we are brought back constantly to the same thing, which gets clearer all the time. But in a Harris exhibition we are following a trail. We pursue him northward from the early Ontario landscapes to the icebergs and bleak mountains of his middle period, and still further north to his abstractions, where he seems to be sitting on the North Pole in an inaccessible world of spinning globes and flashing aurora borealis. Nothing he paints ever seems to look at us. In the early landscapes, stiff with repainting and hard with Ontario sunlight, the main subject is usually a building or row of buildings, in which the ironic eye of a potentially abstract painter has caught, not the pictorial essence of the building, but, on the contrary, the sense of its pictorial incongruity. The buildings have proportions, but they are not very good proportions, so he leaves them imprisoned in their own angularity, so to speak, and goes to look for freer forms among the icebergs. In the two dreadful pictures of Maritime slums, which look a little like some of the nightmarish early Chiricos, this sense of human physical order as a parody of human mental order is at its sharpest. People sometimes appear in front of these buildings, but they are dream-figures, and in the amazing portraits of John Robins and Salem Bland, in which two very human and warm-blooded people are stylized into contemplative yogis, we again feel that the subject has been transmuted rather than evoked.

Harris is best known, of course, by his conventionalized Northern landscapes. They are not always liked for the right reasons: what with their blancmange colouring and their geometrical simplifications, they seem to be painted to a rather facile formula. But it is clear that Harris is the last man to relapse into a formula, and, going to these pictures from the earlier ones, one can only wonder at what he was willing to sacrifice in order to carry out his pursuit of form. What is most interesting in these pictures, perhaps, is the evidence of the strain and effort of will by which their deceptive serenity is achieved. In the gauntness of the dead trees, the staring inhumanity of the lonely mountain peaks, in the lowering mists along the skyline and the brooding confusions of colour in the foreground, one can see what Coleridge meant when he spoke of the poet as the tamer of chaos.[1]

When we enter the "abstract" room we are conscious first of all of a great release of power. The painter has come home: his forms have been emancipated, and the exuberance of their swirling and plunging lines takes one's breath away. One winces at the garishness of the colour, where the whole spectrum has sometimes been flung on the canvas with a kind of joyous vulgarity, but after a while one accepts even that as part of the mood of careless opulence. Here, for the first time, Harris really finds a third dimension, and we no longer have the flatness that makes some of the earlier ones look posterish. This flatness comes from a persistent feeling that the subject being painted is not the pictorial form, but is a natural obstacle blocking the view of the form, or, at best, a prison from which the form is struggling to escape. For such a feeling abstraction is the only possible release, and that is why Harris's abstractions have nothing in them of the self-conscious avoidance of narrative values which makes so many abstract paintings look like decorative doodles. Each one has been separately brought to birth: there is no longer even the suggestion of a formula.

The difference between nonobjective and abstract painting may be suggested by the difference between mathematics and music. Nonobjective painting does for painting what mathematics does for science: it sets up a logical system of pictorial relationships which may contain any number of possible "subjects." It produces not *a* picture, but a continuous series of pictorial suggestions and ideas. Abstract painting uses pictorial themes and motifs, and combines them so as to suggest a pictorial apprehension of reality which we all have but are hardly aware of. This apprehension comes out in the pictorial metaphors we use unconsciously: "a square deal," "a sphere of influence," "a line of action," and the like. It comes out in the dim feeling that the proportions of a good room or building are somehow "right," or that streamlining the design of a car gives a visual impression of speed. It comes out in the traditional occult philosophy, which stretches from Pythagoras and Plato to Blavatsky and Ouspensky, and which assigns to arithmetical number and geometrical form a critical place in the growth of mental comprehension. One can recognize the natural origin of many of Harris's motifs: the mountain and iceberg peaks, for instance, have blended with the pyramid and the cone, and one can "interpret" them indefinitely in terms of whatever meaning one may attach to them. But they are pictures and not cryptograms, and have no single explanation or key, just as music can suggest any number of emotions or ideas without being program music. With interpretation or without it, Lawren Harris's best abstractions are a unique and major contribution to Canadian painting.

33

Culture and the Cabinet

March 1949

From Canadian Forum, *28 (March 1949): 265–6. Frye was commenting on the speech from the throne given on behalf of Liberal prime minister Louis St. Laurent at the opening of Parliament, 26 January 1949. The commission proposed was to become the Royal Commission on National Development in the Arts, Letters, and Sciences (1949–51), also known as the Massey Commission.*

The speech from the throne contained the following paragraph:

> It is the view of my ministers that there should be an examination of the activities of agencies of the federal government relating to radio, films, television, the encouragement of arts and sciences, research, the preservation of our national records, a national library, museums, exhibitions, relations in these fields with international organizations, and activities generally which are designed to enrich our national life, and to increase our own consciousness of our national heritage and knowledge of Canada abroad. For this purpose, the government intends at an early date to establish a Royal Commission.

So much nonsense is talked about bringing together the two words "culture" and "Canadian" that many of us prefer to shy away from the subject altogether, and treat the whole subject as adolescent nationalism. It need be nothing of the kind: art and culture are produced neither in a vacuum nor in "society" in general, but by specific societies, and radiate from cultural capital cities. If there is no Canadian capital of literature, Canadian literature will find its capital in New York or London, and so be a branch of American or English literature. This actually is more or less true of Canadian literature. Canada has two arts which may be said to be distinctive: painting and radio drama. It so happens that we have a national art gallery and a national radio commission. At one time we had very distinctive documentary films and a national film board.[1] Whatever the relation between the art and the Ottawa department may be, it should be worth while trying a national theatre, to see whether Canadian literature and drama would take on more distinctive forms too.

Certainly the absence of a national library is a national disgrace. A library that would stock every book written or circulated in Canada would prevent many students from having to go to the States, perhaps for good, and save expense for others. There seems to be nowhere in Canada anything like a complete library of Canadiana. A national theatre at Ottawa is perhaps not too practicable for so huge a country, though the absence of a permanent legitimate stage in Ottawa has called forth many caustic comments from foreign diplomats there. But a national encouragement of regional theatres and some effort to break the movie monopoly in smaller towns is certainly needed.

Political parties have been most valuable to Canada when they had a specific federal job to do. The Conservative party took the lead in Confederation, and the Liberal party in the period of national consolidation in the first half of this century. Ahead of us, barring catastrophes, should be great developments in culture and the arts of peace. There is a great federal job for some future government. Not, it appears, the present one. To establish a Royal Commission to look into the possibility of doing something that should have been done fifty years ago is, perhaps, timely. There is nothing to show, however, that this will not be merely one more vast expenditure of brains and time and money and organization which will then gather dust in the Department of Procrastination. There is nothing to show either that the present government has the least interest in culture or any intention of promoting so unpromising a means of getting votes. A recent attempt to persuade the government to form a commission to organize a body that would work with UNESCO on cultural affairs got nowhere. The official attitude to literature is that authors' royalties, after the first year of publication, count as unearned income.

No, such a party would have to believe not only in culture for its own sake, but in federal planning, and say so. Mr. Drew's sustained piece of sniping at the radio and television clauses in the above paragraph was effective sniping,[2] because the government dares not say that it has outgrown and abandoned the principles on which his criticism was based. For sooner or later Canada must come to grips with a problem which, as yet, lies far over the horizon of practical politics. This is the problem of a federal policy on education, of some means of getting educational standards emancipated from the poverty, the disorganization, and the well-meaning ignorance of parochial school boards and provincial governments. If this happens in our time, it will be as important an event in the twentieth century as Confederation was in the nineteenth.

34
Letters in Canada: Poetry

April 1951–July 1960

These reviews of the poetry published in Canada during the preceding year were part of the annual survey of Canadian literature in each spring's issue of the University of Toronto Quarterly. *Book prices and number of pages given by Frye have been omitted. Those parts of the reviews that Frye did not include in his reprint in BG have been enclosed in braces ({}) in the present text.*

1. 1950

April 1951

From University of Toronto Quarterly, *20 (April 1951): 257–62. Reprinted (partially) in BG, 1–3. Frye's review was followed by a check-list of all volumes of poetry received, compiled by Francess Halpenny, assistant editor of the University of Toronto Press. This list is not reproduced here, but publication information from it has been inserted where necessary into the text to correspond with the* Quarterly's *practice in later years.*

Readers of Canadian poetry will often have seen the name of Mr. James Wreford, both in literary periodicals and in the fine little anthology of a few years back, *Unit of Five*. A collection of his verse, *Of Time and the Lover* (Toronto: McClelland & Stewart) makes the fourth volume in McClelland & Stewart's "Indian File" series. Mr. Wreford lives in Ottawa, and has several qualities in common with his predecessor Lampman, notably a tendency to be much more at ease with the vegetable than with the human world. He has, however, worked harder to reconcile his love of nature and his vision of the city of the end of things. His imagery turns on the antithesis of winter and spring: he associates winter with the contemporary world and spring with the promise, not only of better times, but of deliverance from the winter world through the infinity of the moment of love and faith in the Resurrection. The central theme that love's not time's fool thus applies to patriotic and religious as well as sexual love. A conventional frame of ideas, certainly, but a solid one to build on.

Mr. Wreford is a pensive and elegiac poet: his best phrases are usually embedded in long ruminating poems, and seem to need that kind of context. Sometimes, too, a sudden poignancy breaks out, as it were unawares, from a more commonplace setting:

> The little children of her hands
> run with the horses on the sands
> cry and are fastened into bands.   [*My Love*, ll. 10–12]

Metaphysical poetry is not a good influence on him: the echoes of Donne and Hopkins in his religious poetry merely add discord: some of his puns are striking ("To part, it is to die in part"); his verbal conceits and satiric rhymes are often laboured. He is not a poet who can absorb either the prose statement or the prosaic world; his social comment is generally querulous and preoccupied, and he is ill at ease with commercial clichés and technological images. He is best in straight couplet and quatrain and in a Housman-like baldness of statement:

> no strong men and no heroes,
> no brave, eternal youths,
> but only fiddling Neroes
> and purple, proud untruths.   [*Of Time and the Lover*, ll. 5–8]

This is from the title poem at the end, which is by far his finest work, and which shows many skilful variations in its octosyllabic metre:

> found pure when the snow is shadowed with
> the whiteness of a cloud of snow,
> how can you now destroy
> the host of your essential joy?   [ll. 41–4]

There are lapses of inspiration and of taste in Mr. Wreford's book, but there is also a dignified simplicity and a sincere eloquence.

Norman Levine's *The Tight-Rope Walker* (London, Eng.; Montreal: Totem Press) shows a high level of competence in what is so far a rather restricted range. Mr. Levine is an expatriate, or regards himself as one: he has left what he calls the land of "parchment summers and merchant eyes" [*Letter from England*, l. 19] for England, and many of his poems have a Cornish setting. His poems are also elegiac, even to the point of using a lamenting refrain, but he has more affinity with paradox and complex statement. *Cathedral by Sea* works out a fine contrast between the physical energy of the sea and the spiritual energy and physical stillness of the building. The title poem makes an oddly touching symbol out of its central theme:

> He was not lost. Only a little lonely
> He walked as a graveyard while around him
> Cities were no more than small lights
> Severed at the head by fog.

Airman and Seagull Killed by Water manages to reach an admirable final line, "What floats is dead," through some vigorous but tangled imagery.

{The invaluable and dauntless "Ryerson Poetry Chapbooks" series still goes on, with no fewer than six volumes this year, some in a simplified new format which I prefer to its predecessor. The best thing in them by far is Dorothy Livesay's radio play *Call My People Home* (Toronto: Ryerson), a story of the exile of the Japanese from British Columbia during the war. It is written with close sympathy and a dry, unlaboured irony, and in a taut, sinewy narrative style with no nonsense about it: it will pick up an image as it goes along, but it never stops for any synthetic beautifying. The lyrics which follow it are also highly readable, with a crackle of wit that sometimes throws smoke instead of a spark. Such cleverness as "pianoforte of sunlight / Fingering an adagio of heat" [*Invisible Sun*, ll. 7–8] should be left to inferior writers. Goodridge MacDonald's *Beggar Makes Music* also employs a narrative form, disengaged, easy, and conversational, for the title piece and for *Last Words*. The point of the latter poem is too obviously withheld until the end, but the insight it expresses has much intelligence and humour, and the same is even more true of *Beggar Makes Music*. Kathryn Munro's *Tanager Feather* consists mainly of passable descriptive verse made out of assembly-line images ("Fair is the dawn on these ancestral hills" [*Canadian Pastoral*, l. 1]) with one poem, *Retreat*, of a fresh and unhackneyed intensity. The setting of Geoffrey Drayton's *Three Meridians* is mainly the West

Indies, and there is a pleasantly exotic quality in the references to hibiscus and frangipani. The epigrammatic short poems are inconclusive; two longer ones, *The Sun-Worshippers* and *Letter from the Gatineau*, especially the latter, rise into a meditative eloquence. It is clear that for his best work he needs room to expand his ideas. Katherine Hale's *The Flute, and Other Poems* here and there catches a feeling of unexplained mystery, so that the total effect of *The Island* or *Arizona Desert Road* is more haunting than any lines quoted from them would indicate. Arthur Bourinot's *The Treasures of the Snow* affects a very short line which would be well adapted for bringing out rhythmical subtleties if there were more subtleties to bring out, and there is a trick of repetition which gives a certain feeling of incantation to *Haunted*.}

This is clearly not a banner year for Canadian poetry: the above practically exhausts the more sophisticated part of the output. In Canada, however, as elsewhere, there appears every year a fair quantity of naive or primitive verse, to use terms more familiar in the criticism of painting. There is no reason why all of this should be out of the range of critical interest: a good deal of Burns, of Wordsworth, of Kipling, even of Emily Dickinson, is naive poetry, and what Mr. Goodridge MacDonald calls "the truisms of popular song" [*Beggar Makes Music*, l. 9] are always well worth stating. One looks hopefully and constantly, in reading through this material, for some signs of an ability to express the simple rather than the commonplace emotion, to use traditional metres without unenterprising monotony, to make the art of writing a poem a fresh experience instead of a conditioned reflex of nostalgia. Occasionally one is rewarded, but self-consciousness and schoolmarmism hang cloudily in the poetic atmosphere. Of those in the check-list below, some achieve a certain uniform competence, {such as R.G. Lovell's *Peace and War*, Bertram Warr's *In Quest of Beauty* (both Carillon poetry chapbooks; Foleyet, Ont.: Crucible Press), and James A. Ross's (posthumous) *The Singer and His Song* (Ottawa: Tower Books),} but otherwise there is nothing for a reviewer to say except to hope that they will find their audience. The same may be said of the Poetry Books of Alberta and Saskatchewan.[1] The latter has a picture of a wildcat on its cover, but the poetry is unvaryingly gentle.

{On the other hand, Peter North's *Harshly the Rain Fell* (Toronto: n.p.) occasionally shows an active imagination coming sharply into focus:

> A black cat pads with purpose
> Down an alley of void.   [*Nocturnal Imagery*, ll. 15–16]

Grace Jacombe's *Chalk Dust* (Ottawa: Tower Books) sticks closely to school-teaching and its prevailing mood of exasperated affection, and her unforced humour can be very engaging. The title poem of Jenny O'Hara Pincock's (posthumous) *Hidden Springs* (Waterloo, Ont.: n.p.) is a narrative of pioneer life in Ontario, based on an experience of a type that is usually called telepathy. It is not a successful poem, but it is quite a striking one, with some vivid descriptive flashes. Hyman Edelstein's *Spirit of Israel* (Toronto: Ryerson) is considerably more pretentious, and therefore more disappointing. Mr. Edelstein knows a great deal about Jewish culture and ritual, and has included some useful notes on them: he is a Zionist and a Classical scholar, has lived in Ireland as well as Canada (a Dublin colleague contributes an urbane introduction) and shows the influence of a variety of poets, notably Heine. With all this learning and sophistication, one is chagrined to find that what he has to say never takes a poetic shape, but remains a noise without an echo. By nonpoetic standards, however, the book is interesting enough.}

2. 1951

April 1952

From University of Toronto Quarterly, *21 (April 1952): 252–8. Reprinted (partially) in* BG, *4–9. Material on Layton reprinted in* Irving Layton: The Poet and His Critics, *ed. Seymour Mayne (Toronto: McGraw-Hill Ryerson, 1978), 32–3. Frye's review was followed by a check-list of all volumes of poetry received, compiled by Francess Halpenny, assistant editor of the University of Toronto Press. This list is not reproduced here, but publication information from it has been inserted where necessary into the text to correspond with the* Quarterly's *practice in later years.*

The title poem of Philip Child's *The Victorian House and Other Poems* (Toronto: Ryerson) is a flashback narrative. The narrator has to sell his family home, and in throwing it open to a purchaser memories come back to him and build up a picture of his early life. As he muses, the contrast widens between the realized knowledge of love he has gained from his home and the externalized knowledge of hatred he has gained from watching the passage of wars and dictatorships. Gradually the impression of the reality of the former and the illusoriness of the latter increases until he gains a fleeting sense of an eternal home life in a single body of love. At that point the sharpest of all his memories, a friend dying in the confidence of resurrection, is illuminated for him. The theme of a death which no longer matters is summed up by the purchaser, who decides to tear the house down and use its bricks to build a new one.

In the narrative itself one regrets a rather self-deprecatory melancholy, a gentleness that often seems merely tentative, and, more technically, a mannerism of quoting too many tags from Shakespeare. It is in the interspersed lyrics where one best realizes how well practised a writer Mr. Child is. There his self-consciousness relaxes, and the poet in him speaks directly. In the first stanza of *Prometheus brings a pretty culture* and the sharp simplicity of *How still they lie, the dead* the narrative comes into a clear imaginative focus, and we do not feel, as we too often do in the body of a poem, that words are being used partly as a barrier between the poet and his reader. The lyrics which follow the title poem give, I think, a better impression of Mr. Child's variety and range as a poet than it does. Of these, there is the very impressive *Macrocosm*, with its precise but not over-neat conclusion:

> Beyond my sight the cloudless sky
> Is troubled with artillery

and *Descent for the Lost*, a poem on Judas Iscariot which returns to a theme that haunts the title poem also, that the redemptive power of Christ cannot rest until it has sought the lowest depth of human isolation.

Two first collections of poets already fairly well known to readers of Canadian poetry are issued by the First Statement Press of Montreal. Number 8 in the New Writers series is Anne Wilkinson's *Counterpoint to Sleep*. The title does not mean that the poems are a cure for insomnia: it means that Miss Wilkinson is essentially a dream-poet. At her best she has the significant vividness of the remembered dream, or nightmare; at her worst the confusions and obliquities of the forgotten one. Miss Wilkinson is clever: too clever for her own good, sometimes, when a self-conscious avoidance of the obvious leads to a rather wearying verbal dissection of her themes. There is some unsuccessful fantasy, and even the wit of *Winter Sketch* does not conceal the fact that it is bad metaphysical poetry to speak of a snowfall as

> Immaculate conception in a cloud
> Made big by polar ghost.

Letters in Canada: Poetry

But when the desire to say something breaks through the preoccupations of saying it a real poetic ability emerges. On this level we find the grisly variant of *Lord Randall* which so raised my hair when I first read it in *Contemporary Verse*, the teetering spiralling rhythm of *Tower Lullaby*, and the unsteady but genuine eloquence of *The Great Winds*.

Number 7 is Kay Smith's *Footnote to the Lord's Prayer and Other Poems*. The note on the back of the cover speaks of "her serious limitations, her crudities of music and structure," which is something new in publishers' blurbs. The revival of the medieval habit of paraphrasing the liturgy has its dangers, notably the danger of having the quotations provide all the impressiveness of the poem. This, I hasten to say, is not what has happened here: in fact I wish Miss Smith had refrained from quoting the clauses, as the poem would be less tied down without them, and its theme is clear enough. In her peroration, no doubt, one feels chiefly that Eliot does this kind of thing much better, but as a whole the poem is a distinctive meditation, with only one or two lapses into religiosity. I like the way she occasionally breaks from syntax to suggest a similar process in prayer, and the varieties of metrical organization show a better sense of structure than her publishers give her credit for. Of the other poems, *Conversations with a Mirror* seems to me an excellent design from a stock pattern; here again the subtitles, *The Girl Speaks* and the rest, are unnecessary, and make the poem look more naive than it is. On the whole, Miss Smith's high intelligence seems almost a disadvantage: such poems as *The Clown* and *When a Girl Looks Down*, which seem to be moving toward a poignant concreteness, dissolve at the end into a generalized and contemplative vision.

Of the more conservative offerings, I find Charles Bruce's *The Mulgrave Road* (Toronto: Macmillan) most consistently successful. His material is almost insistently unpretentious, confined to the simplest landscapes of farms and fishing villages in Guysborough County, Nova Scotia. One begins, probably, by feeling that nobody can make new poetry out of such material, then one reads:

> Slowly the days grow colder, the long nights fall;
> Plows turn the stubble, fires are tended, and apples
> Mellow in cellars; and under the roots of maples
> Mice are burrowing. And the high geese call.   [*Fall Grass*, ll. 13–16]

We are forced to recognize the measured authority of these elegiac cadences. We may say grumpily that anyway this *kind* of thing has often been done before. But repeating ready-made formulas is one thing; working within a convention is quite another. Mr. Bruce is quoted on the dust cover as saying that nostalgia is the silliest word in the language, and the remark is probably the key to his success. His themes have not really been exhausted by poetry; they have merely been exploited by nostalgia. The false notes induced by the latter, such as the "Wondering how they know" which puts a sentimental blur on the end of the otherwise flawless *Country Sunday*, are very rare, and hence noticeable. He turns his back on all the compulsions that so often go with the poetic impulse: he knows, he says, that

> gulls on waves of surging air
> Will never get me anywhere   [*Sketch for a Landscape*, ll. 29–30]

—which well evokes the immovable repose that one often senses in a Maritimer's mind.

Thomas Saunders is another regional poet, and his *Horizontal World* (Toronto: Ryerson) is Saskatchewan. Mr. Saunders may best be described, perhaps, as a metrical conversationalist: that is, he works in the idiom represented by Robert Frost, and is best when he is discursive, commenting on the life of the prairie and understating its harsh and obvious ironies. Too often, however, he fails to resist the temptation to underline his points and oversimplify his situations. I wish *Armand* had not gone on into a murder, not because such things never happen but because they are literary clichés when they do. Yet there is much that is readable in his book, and it is no small feat to put colloquial speech as authentic as this into blank verse:

> But now quick-growing wheats are ripe
> And harvested before July is out,
> Some places, or by middle-August at
> The most—with no big threshing-gangs, like in
> The steamer days, touring the country like
> A circus until after snow.   [*New-Fangled Ways*, ll. 19–24]

The poetry of social protest, during the 1930s, was attached to a number of powerful supports: it had a philosophy in Marxism, a program of action in the proletarian revolution, and a reading public among bourgeois intellectuals. It never achieved a really distinguished expression,

Letters in Canada: Poetry 99

but it spoke for a large and influential pressure group. *Nous avons changé tout cela*; the poet's heart is no longer so far on the left side, and the poetry of social protest has retreated into a disembodied anarchism, in some respects a reversion to the old artist-versus-society theme of earlier decades. One of the leaders in this anarchistic development is evidently Kenneth Patchen, whose merits are not yet entirely clear to me, though his mind certainly has some of the imaginative qualities of a great poet. The movement has a Canadian representative this year in Irving Layton's *The Black Huntsmen* (Montreal: n.p.)

The idea in Mr. Layton's poetry is to use an intensely personal imagination as an edged tool against a world cemented by smugness, hacking and chopping with a sharp image here, an acid comment there, trying to find holes and weak spots where the free mind can enroot and sprout. It is the misfortune of this technique that the successes are quiet and the faults raucous. There is a real poet buried in Mr. Layton, a gentle, wistful, lonely, and rather frightened poet who tells us how his childhood love for Tennyson grew into a defiant fear of a hostile and pursuing world:

> Now I look out for the evil retinue
> Making their sortie out of a forest of gold.   [*The Black Huntsman*, ll. 18–19]

But where the imagination is conceived as militant, there is apt to develop a split between what the poet can write and what he thinks he ought to write for his cause. Most of Mr. Layton's book is the work, not of the poet in him, but of a noisy hot-gospeller who has no real respect for poetry. The latter speaks in a violent rhetoric which is deliberately summoned up, an incantation that tries to make devils reveal themselves but succeeds only in nagging the air. The same lack of spontaneity in the imagery is betrayed by repetition. One can get as tired of buttocks in Mr. Layton as of buttercups in the *Canadian Poetry Magazine*; and a poet whose imagination is still fettered by a moral conscience, even an anticonventional one, gives the impression of being in the same state of bondage as the society he attacks.

Michael Hornyansky's *The Queen of Sheba* (Oxford: Basil Blackwell; Toronto: Copp Clark) won the Newdigate Prize for Poetry at Oxford, which is, if I remember correctly, awarded for the best poem on a set theme. Those who assigned the Queen of Sheba must have expected a good deal of paraphrase of the Song of Songs and a whole cargo of cassia, spikenard, aloes, frankincense, and other ingredients of the popular *orientale*. There is a certain amount of this in Mr. Hornyansky, but on the whole it is well subordinated to the main theme, the development in Solomon's mind from weariness through love to the resigned detachment expressed in Ecclesiastes. The poem is written in a sonorous five-line stanza rhyming *a b c b a, c d e d c*, etc. In the third and last part the somewhat too carefully modulated utterance begins to take on more warmth and life. It is an admirable practice piece, and it probably won by several lengths.

{Of the three Ryerson chapbooks, Theresa Thomson's *Silver Shadows* has the rather pallid elegance that its title suggests. Raymond Souster's *City Hall Street* is in his usual vein of satiric comment on the social scene. One feels that he has a prose mind and thinks immediately in prose rhythms, which are then forced consciously and somewhat impatiently into poetic form. The result is frequently a poem with a sententious moral attached at the end: this is true of the title poem, of *Riverdale Zoo*, and of *Court of General Sessions*. Yet there is a real pathos here and there, especially in *Speakers, Columbus Circle*, which survives some labouring of its point. Elizabeth Brewster's *East Coast* is another matter. Miss Brewster writes poetry because she thinks poetically; she is aware of the triviality in the love of mere poeticizing, "the poet baying the familiar moon," and her own images are sharp and crisp, her ideas wrapped around them with great dexterity and precision. One wishes there were more than a mere eight pages of an utterance so fresh and convincing as:

> Peace is what is found
> When the sailor sets his will
> To turn from a rough sea
> To a rougher still. [*Peace*, ll. 1-4]

But as it is, these eight pages are as good as any poetry produced in Canada in 1951 in a single volume.

I add this last because anyone seriously interested in what Canadian poetry is currently doing would be best advised to go first of all to two special issues of magazines. The dauntless *Contemporary Verse* produced its anniversary number (ten years—an extraordinary run for a magazine of poetry, even so good a one as this) in the fall of 1951, and an English periodical, *Poetry Commonwealth*, had a special Canadian number (unfortunately, but more typically, its last) in the spring of the same year.[2] Pratt, Birney, MacKay, F.R. Scott, and Floris McLaren are included in both, and half a dozen others equally well known can be found in each.

The rest of the year's product contains a good deal that merely beats the track of Sarah Binks,[3] but there is also a good deal of competent amateur verse, with much fluency, some humour, and a few glints of distinctive imaginative perception. It is, however, largely irrelevant to the present survey. The best of the Carillon Poetry Chapbooks (Foleyet, Ont.) is that of Edward A. Jameson, whose *Poems* show a variety of themes and considerable delicacy of treatment. Anthony Frisch's *Third Poems* (Hull: Ivy Publishing) is, as the title elliptically indicates, his third book of poems. Two are in German, and indicate a Germanic affinity for a simple utterance allied to folk song. In *The Maker of Umbrellas* and the second of the *Devil Poems* he has hit on themes of some originality. I.B. Ezra's *The Golden Kernel* (Toronto: Derby Publishing) has a poem called *On the Birth of a Child* which begins:

> A tragic being, toothless, blind, and gnarled,
> Came suddenly one day into my world—

but it doesn't go on like that.}

A selection of the poems of Duncan Campbell Scott (Toronto: Ryerson), with an introductory memoir, appeared last year as one of the posthumous works of Professor E.K. Brown, my predecessor in this survey, whose tact, skill, erudition, and comprehensiveness in making it I had long admired, and am now fully in a position to appreciate, if somewhat wryly. The memoir is supplementary to the essay on Scott in the same author's *On Canadian Poetry*.[4] Whatever one thinks of the total merit of Scott's very uneven output, he achieved the type of imaginative balance that is characteristic of so much of the best in Canadian culture down to the present generation, when altered social conditions are beginning to upset it. On one side he had the world of urbane and civilized values; on the other, the Quebec forest with its Indians and lonely trappers. He could write a poem on Debussy and a poem on a squaw feeding her child with her own flesh; he was at once primitive and pre-Raphaelite, a recluse of the study and a recluse of the forest. Not since Anglo-Saxon times, it seems to me, has there been the same uneasy conflict between elemental bleakness and the hectic flush of a late and weary civilization that there has been in Canadian poetry and painting of the period from Confederation to the Depression. It had to go as the country became more urbanized, and we may regret its passing only if nothing new comes to replace it.

3. 1952

April 1953

From University of Toronto Quarterly 22 *(April 1953): 269–80. Reprinted (partially) in* BG, *10–22, and in* Masks of Poetry: Canadian Critics on Canadian Verse, *ed. A.J.M. Smith (Toronto: McClelland & Stewart, 1962), 97–103. Material on Layton reprinted in* Irving Layton: The Poet and His Critics, *ed. Seymour Mayne (Toronto: McGraw-Hill Ryerson, 1978), 35.*

This year both of Canada's two leading poets have a new book to be discussed, and as one of them comes from Newfoundland and the other from British Columbia, there was never a neater opportunity of demonstrating the theory of cultural containment. I am inclined in any case to assert the existence of a Canadianism in Canadian poetry. Poets do not live on Mount Parnassus, but in their own environments, and Canada has made itself an environmental reality.

The United States is a symmetrical country: it presents a straight Atlantic coastline, and its culture was, up to about 1900, a culture of the Atlantic seaboard, with a north-south frontier that moved westward until it reached the Pacific. Canada has almost no Atlantic seaboard, and a ship coming here from Europe moves, like a tiny Jonah entering an enormous whale, into the Gulf of St. Lawrence, where it is surrounded by five Canadian provinces, all out of sight, and then drifts up a vast waterway that reaches back past Edmonton. There would be nothing distinctive in Canadian culture at all if there were not some feeling for the immense searching distance, with the lines of communication extended to the absolute limit, which is a primary geographical fact about Canada and has no real counterpart elsewhere. The best paintings of Thomson and the Group of Seven have a horizon-focused perspective, with a line of water or a break through the hills curving into the remotest background. In Emily Carr, too, the real focus of vision seems to be in the depth of the forest, *behind* the picture as it were. The same feeling for strained distance is in many Canadian poets and novelists—certainly in Grove—and it can hardly be an accident that the two most important

Canadian thinkers to date, Edward Sapir and Harold Innis, have both been largely concerned with problems of communication.

Most of the poetry of E.J. Pratt, including *Brébeuf*, has been a kind of summing up of the first phase of Canadian poetic imagination. In that phase Canada appeared in a flat Mercator projection with a nightmarish Greenland, as a country of isolation and terror, and of the overwhelming of human values by an indifferent and wasteful nature. It was a part of the development of poetic Darwinism from Tennyson and Melville (whom a Canadian critic was the first to appreciate,[5] and who has many links with Pratt) to Hardy and Conrad. Since *Brébeuf*, Pratt has shown an increasing interest in techniques of communication, an interest which may well go back to his early days as a student of psychology. In his fine poem *The Truant*, the David of human intelligibility confronts the stupid Goliath of nature, and in *Behind the Log* a network of wireless telegraphy, radar, and asdic contains the whole action of the poem. The theme of the epic act of communication in Canadian history, the linking of east and west by a great railway, was thus a logical one for Pratt to choose for his latest poem, *Towards the Last Spike* ([Toronto:] Macmillan).

But while the choice of theme may have been easy, the theme itself is fantastically difficult. The poem is in the epic tradition, without any of the advantages of epic to sustain it. No narrative suspense is possible where the ground has all been surveyed; no heroic action can be isolated in so concentrated an act of social will:

>   As individuals
> The men lost their identity; as groups,
> As gangs, they massed, divided, subdivided,
> Like numerals only.   [ll. 832–5]

The foresight and courage of Macdonald and Van Horne almost disappear in an intricate pattern of railway building, parliamentary strategy, industrial development, political unification, financing, and foreign and colonial policy. The real hero of the poem is a society's will to take intelligible form; the real quest is for physical and spiritual communication within that society. I have a notion that the technical problems involved in *Towards the Last Spike* are going to be central problems in the poetry of the future. And I think that the ingenuity with which these problems have been met would make the poem a historical landmark even for readers who disliked it as a poem.

In the first place, Pratt has here, as in *Behind the Log*, to give the sense of the energy of work as diffused through the whole action of the poem, with no real climax at the end. (Some younger writers mentioned below who are interested in the theory of "composition by field" may see an important aspect of it in this poem.) The driving of the last spike is technically a climax; imaginatively, it is an anticlimax. Strathcona has only one spike to drive in after the thousands that have preceded it, yet he fumbles it, and Van Horne has nothing to do but clear his throat and say "well done." The feeling of letdown after prodigious strain is part of the realization that men's work, like women's, is never done, and that the moment any act of social heroism is completed, it is absorbed into society and becomes part of new work.

In the second place, a poem of heroic action reminds us of the quest-poem, where a hero goes forth to kill a dragon. But here the real dragon to be killed is dead already: the obstacle is the torpor and inertia of unconscious nature, not an active or malignant enemy. Pratt's dragon,

> A hybrid that the myths might have conceived,
> But not delivered,   [ll. 871–2]

is a somnolent dragon, "asleep or dead," "too old for death, too old for life," who can resist only passively. The device of turning the azoic into the monstrous is, like all poetic devices that are any good, very old, and can be traced back at least to the *Odyssey*; but Pratt's carefully muted, unfaked description is profoundly contemporary, and has all the typically Canadian respect for geology in it. Like other dragons, this one guards a treasure hoard: there is again irony in the contrast between Macdonald's frantic efforts to get money out of the clutching fists of bankers and the riches revealed by every dynamite blast on the line—"nickel, copper, silver and fool's gold" [l. 1259]—and not only fool's gold either.

There would be much more to say about the poem if I had the space. There is the contrast between the desperate, quixotic, east-west reach from sea to sea which is the vision of Macdonald (Van Horne too, it is said, "loved to work on shadows"), and the practical, short-sighted vision of Blake, which sees the country realistically, as a divided series of northern extensions of the United States. (I don't know how true this is historically, but there is far too much accurate Canadian history now, and far too little accurate Canadian vision.) There is the portrait of

Strathcona as a Canadian culture-hero, a combination of Paul Bunyan and Sam Slick,

> ripping the stalactites
> From his red beard, thawing his feet, and wringing
> Salt water from his mitts; but most of all
> He learned the art of making change.   [ll. 641-4]

Above all, Pratt is a poet unusually aware of the traditional connection between poetry and oratory. The memory of 1940, when human freedom had practically nothing left to fight with except Churchill's prose style, is clearly fresh in his mind. A Communist magazine has criticized *Towards the Last Spike* for seeing the theme entirely in terms of the leadership of Van Horne and Macdonald, ignoring the workers. Pratt's point, however, is not that workers are the slaves of great leaders, but that leaders are the slaves of great words. Marlowe's Tamburlaine might have died unknown if he had not happened to hear the phrase "To ride in triumph through Persepolis." Similarly, it is only when Blake can think of a menacing phrase like "To build a road over that sea of mountains" that the fate of Canada is really in danger. Besides, all forms of communication are closely linked to poetry in imaginative appeal, and in this nomadic culture people who cannot write poetry are dependent on poets to express their inarticulate sense of the link. I remember, years ago, standing on an Oxford railway platform and hearing the guard say "The train for the north of England," and suddenly feeling as though my stomach had turned upside down. Pratt is one of the few poets I know who can understand such a feeling:

> Intercolonial, the Canadian Southern,
> Dominion-Atlantic, the Great Western—names
> That caught a continental note and tried
> To answer it.   [ll. 387-90]

Many readers of poetry today are brought up, whether they realize it or not, on Poe's dictum that a long poem is a contradiction in terms. For them, a Keats ode represents what poetry can do, and Shelley's *Revolt of Islam* what it cannot do. Hence they tend to examine poetry in terms of surface texture, and lose the faculty of appreciating the skill displayed in structure. Such an approach to *Towards the Last Spike*, where the surface is often as rough and forbidding as its theme, is much too myopic. An unfavourable judgment on such a line as "His personal pockets were not lined with pelf" [l. 447] should not set up an indicator of value in a poem which is so deliberately tough, gnarled, and cacophonous. With that warning, the reader may be safely left to discover for himself the unsuccessful images, the labouring of minor themes, the forced humour, and the dull stretches. The faults of the poem are obvious and commonplace; its virtues are subtle and remarkable.

What else is "distinctively Canadian"? Well, historically, a Canadian is an American who rejects the Revolution. Canada fought its civil war to establish its union first, and its wars of independence, which were fought against the United States and not Europe, came later. We should expect in Canada, therefore, a strong suspicion, not of the United States itself, but of the mercantilist Whiggery which won the Revolution and proceeded to squander the resources of a continent, being now engaged in squandering ours. There is in Canada, too, a traditional opposition to the two defects to which a revolutionary tradition is liable, a contempt for history and an impatience with law. The Canadian point of view is at once more conservative and more radical than Whiggery, closer both to aristocracy and to democracy than to oligarchy.

The title poem of Earle Birney's *Trial of a City and Other Verse* ([Toronto:] Ryerson) is described in its subtitle as "A Public Hearing into the Proposed Damnation of Vancouver." The time is the future, the setting the kind of pseudolegal kangaroo court which is the main instrument of McCarthyism, as packed and framed as a shipment of pictures, where everything is conducted on the crazy Alice-in-Wonderland principle of sentence first, verdict afterwards. The blowing up of Vancouver has already been decided upon by a mysterious "office of the future," represented by a lawyer named Gabriel Powers. As this name indicates, the setting has for its larger background the ancient theme of wrath and mercy, of man's perpetual failure to justify his existence in the sight of the gods by his merits, a failure now brought to a crisis by his new techniques of self-destruction. Powers, therefore, who seems to be a messenger of the gods, is actually a projection of man's own death-wish.

The only one to speak for the defence is a Mr. Legion, who represents the ordinary Vancouver citizen. He has, understandably, a strong prejudice against being annihilated, but it proves more difficult than he expected to refute the case of the prosecution. The city seems to Captain Vancouver only the pollution of the virginal nature he remembers. To an

Indian chief, who speaks for what is essentially an aristocratic point of view, the white man's city is an obscene disease that has devoured his own people. To Gassy Jack, a sailor and saloon-keeper of the early days, it represents a perversion of life far more sinister than his own relatively healthy vulgarity and vice. Finally William Langland, author of *Piers Plowman*, appears: in all English culture no better spokesman could have been found for the conservative-radical opposition to oligarchy mentioned above. He finds in Vancouver more or less what he found in medieval London: a society based on profiteering, or what he personified as Lady Meed.

The trouble with Legion is that he does not speak for the real Vancouver, but for the mercantilist Whiggery that has taken it over. His values and standards are precisely what is being condemned. He is the present as the inevitable consequence of the past, hence a future of annihilation is the inevitable consequence of *him*. At the crisis of the argument, he is suddenly pushed out of the way by a housewife. She stands for the real life of really free people, where the present is, at every moment, a new creation of meaning, of wonder, and of love. In such a conception of the present there is no causality, no inevitable future, no dead reckonings, and as she speaks the court begins to dissolve into unreality, even the imperious "Powers" being reduced to saying only "I'll have the skeleton."

I have emphasized the unity and seriousness of the theme because the brilliance of the writing may mislead one into regarding it only as a verbal stunt. It is true that for virtuosity of language there has never been anything like it in Canadian poetry. Gabriel Powers speaks in a *Finnegans Wake* doubletalk which, like *Finnegans Wake*, is both very funny and eerily haunting:

> From the ash of the fir springs the fire-weed;
> from the ask of his faring your fear.   [p. 22]

A professor of geology speaks in the archaic rhythms of Anglo-Saxon, and Legion in what the Germans call *knittelvers*. Langland's speech is, of course, a reproduction of Langland: such phrases as "an ego to an auto" [p. 36] may be a trifle too sophisticated for him, but

> Yea, then I moved west to my hill's margin
> and saw a soft middleclass swaddled in trees,
> in unfrequented churches and fears not a few   [p. 36]

has exactly the right balance between parody and recreation. The play's wit puts it in the same league as e.e. cummings and Auden; and as compared with Auden, it seems to me to have attained a crystalline transparency of thought. I imagine that the lines of the housewife, "By all the past we know our freedom is renewable each moment" [p. 45], or, "How could I know, without the threat of death, I lived?" [p. 47] would in Auden be sagging with the weight of Heidegger's *Augenblick* and Kierkegaard's *Angst*. Birney's seriousness is simple (to the verge, on the last page, of being sentimental); it is only his wit that is erudite.

Wit is also prominent in the other poems in the book: it is in a poem about Christmas which describes how a star appeared as a *"nova in Virgo"*; in satires on censorship, on signs reading "restricted," on an ill-fated Mr. Chubb of Minnesota, and in an account of a plane trip across Canada, where, in spite of some excellent passages, some of the boredom of the trip seems to have leaked into the poem. The other poems are largely concerned with the immense trees and sinister mountains of British Columbia landscape, whose moods the poet knows well how to convey. A few gingerbread conceits ("the pacifist firs," "revolver sun," "the pointless point of the peak") are unfunctional, but do not spoil them. There is also a cryptic but very attractive exercise in myth, *St. Valentine Is Past*.

It is good to see Mr. Alfred Bailey's poems collected in *Border River* (Toronto: McClelland & Stewart), and its appearance puts him into the first rank of Canadian poets. He writes usually in long assertive sentences, very close to prose in rhythm, but with the metrical features of the rhythm carefully marked. One gets the impression of a muttered crepitation of sound, a reticence of voice and thought that makes the reader strain for attention, as though the poet had his back turned. Professor Ross's remarks on the blurb mention the influences of Eliot and Dylan Thomas, which are there, but Eliot and Thomas are highly sensuous poets. Compared to them, reading Mr. Bailey is at first like walking over cinders. Accents stick spikily through the metrical feet; jarring rhythms and assonances turn up in the most disconcerting spots, and in two poems he pulls the last syllable of the line off its stem, like a child picking flowers. The forbidding landscape is not relieved by his fondness for the imagery of dry bones and dead trees, nor by a dense tangled diction that all too often makes the reader stop and wonder what the hell he is talking about.

However, dry bones can harm no one, as Eliot would say, and the difficulties created by intelligence and honesty are always worth attacking. We discover with Mr. Bailey what we discover with all good poets who look obscure at first but turn out to be rewarding. The difficulties are primarily his, and only incidentally ours. He speaks of the poet as pursuing his truth through the labyrinths of appearance and reality, and the river of his title poem grows into a symbol of poetic imagination. Its reefs and shoals are like the barriers that convention and dogma try to impose on the searching intelligence of the poet; it twists and zigzags and seems to lose its way in a wilderness, but always it is going toward an infinite sea. There are religious overtones, especially in the last of the three sections, but it is a religious feeling in which the central virtue is hope rather than faith:

> There will be no world there when we are there,
> and no one to know, even the lone hand
> at the wheel
> whose face is caught in a tanned and wrinkled dream
> [*Unreturning*, ll. 20–3]

and as we grow accustomed to the style, we become sensitive to the skill with which rhythm and speed alter to fit the curves of the thought:

> Tread silently lest someone wake
> to sense the peace that passeth here.
> Handle the creaking hinge with fear
> and into the yard tread softly
> over by the chicken coop
> dig us a hole, say five feet and a bit.   [*Plague Burial*, ll. 30–5]

I get very tired of the critical cliché that everything in poetry should be hard, concrete, and precise. That dogma was lugged in to rationalize the techniques of imagism thirty years ago, and it is time to realize that it is only one more formula, like the unities, designed to save critics the trouble of making independent judgments on poetry. It is quite possible to construct just as good poetry out of diffused, muzzy, and generalized language. Byron's *She walks in beauty like the night* is a very lovely poem, and it is a masterpiece of vagueness. Mr. Bailey's diction bristles with concreteness and precision, usually to its advantage, but I think he is equally good, and even more eloquent, when he relaxes into a more "Romantic" rhetoric:

> there to grow strength of body, faith of mind,
> accustomed to the water's way
> and understanding of its kind
> there
> in the green sea day.   [*Thanks for a Drowned Island*, ll. 18–22]

Of the shorter books, the best, I think, is Jay Macpherson's *Nineteen Poems* (Mallorca, Spain: Seizin Press). Miss Macpherson is, at least outwardly, a traditionalist: she writes in tight resonant stanzas, usually quatrains, with an adroit use of Classical mythology, and in a mood which is predominantly elegiac, though it can take in some fanciful humour too in the opening poem. It is a type of writing that has not been heard much in Canada since Louis MacKay forsook the chambers of the east. She seems to have the rhythmical structure of the whole poem clearly in her mind at the start, so that she can vary the length of the individual lines skilfully and subtly. In *The Comforted* two Classical images, the thread of life spun by the Fates and the clue through the Cretan labyrinth, are identified; *The Oracular Head* mingles memories of Cassandra and Friar Bacon; and *The Ill Wind* is a kind of distilled ballad:

> To reply, in face of a bad season,
> Pestilential cold, malignity,
> To the ill wind weeping on my shoulder:
> "Child, what have I to do with thee?"
>
> Is to deny the infant head
> And the voice complaining tirelessly:
> "Is there room for one only under your cloak,
> Mother, may I creep inside and see?
> Did you not know my wicked will
> When you summoned me?"

{Myra Lazechko-Haas is a new name to me, but she is obviously a practised writer, and *Viewpoint* ([Toronto:] Ryerson) is full of intelligence and a lively crackling humour. She is a visual poet; as long as there is something to catch her eye the imagery remains fresh-minted; but as soon as the context becomes more theoretical it droops into gray abstraction. This happens seldom, however, and the "Viewpoint" of her title poem is one of breezy confidence:

Letters in Canada: Poetry

>Granted the meek inherit earth,
>What would they do with it?

Mint and Willow ([Toronto:] Ryerson) by Ruth Cleaves Hazelton, and *A Few More Dawns* ([Toronto:] Copp Clark) by Vina Bruce Chilton, both maintain a level of competent poetizing, just good enough to keep one reading in the hope of finding something a little better. In the former a poem called *Persian Lesson* is the chief reward of the search; the latter is less interesting, but there are a few genuine phrases:

>Only sunpools on the lake
>Cause the battlements to shake.   [*Dust*, ll. 3-4]

It Was a Plane ([Toronto:] Ryerson), by Tom Farley, is concerned chiefly with the air force in wartime, and the poet's knowledge of his subject gives his writing concreteness and authority, both in description and in mood, in spite of some ready-made poetic diction and a few lapses of taste. The first stanza of *Radar Tower* is the best writing in this part of his work. Actually I like the other poems better: they seem to have more freedom of movement and directness. His vision of a narcissist middle-class female on a street-car ends with a most precise romantic parody:

>and she sleeps through the sunlight
>unshaken.
>She will never awaken,
>the lady with radiant hair.}   [*Street Car, Mid Morning*, ll. 19-22]

Louis Dudek's contributions this year are spread over three volumes, each showing a perceptibly different aspect of his style. *Twenty-Four Poems* (Toronto: Contact Press) evidently is a sequence of impressions, one for each hour of the day: at any rate the first poem is called *Dawn* and the twelfth *Noon*. They are strongly pictorial in mood, full of colour, and at times are merely decorative pattern. One continually thinks of paintings: so, rather unfortunately, does Mr. Dudek himself, as it seems to me that an over-explicit reference to Klee injures an otherwise fine sonnet. There is nothing startlingly good in the sequence, yet one is always just on the point of calling him facile and being brought up short by something like:

> Breath blown into a telephone:
> What ghosts are we
> to tell each other how alone
> lovers can be?   [*The Telephone*, ll. 1–4]

The Searching Image ([Toronto:] Ryerson), on the whole, contains more serious poetry, some of it, though disappointingly little, on a level with the best of his earlier work in *Unit of Five* and *East of the City*. *Theme with Variations* is a series of vivid sketches of sunrise in a city, in a long swinging oracular rhythm, and there is a delicately elaborated conceit in the opening poem, *The Bee of Words*. His favourite theme is the affinity between the creative powers of the mind and the vital energy that produces beautiful things in nature, particularly flowers:

> Yet love may tell one who grows a plant
> How a miraculous ignorance surrounds
> Each living thing. . . .   [*Flower Bulbs*, ll. 17–20]

He has more room to operate in *Cerberus* ([Toronto:] Contact Press), a collection of the work of three poets, Dudek, Irving Layton, and Raymond Souster, each of whom prefaces his poems with a manifesto. In deference to his colleagues, Mr. Dudek endeavours to recapture some of his earlier feeling for social problems, but it is clear from his manifesto that he is no longer in danger of confusing poetry with popular rhetoric. He realizes that the enemy of poetry is not social evil but slipshod language, the weasel words that betray the free mind: he realizes that to create requires an objective serenity beyond all intruding moral worries about atomic bombs and race prejudice. One sentence is particularly striking: "Actuality itself is a metaphor made of iron, the diseased poem which man has erected out of mass frustration, out of centuries of evil" [p. 14]. Of the poet he says:

> You will not learn from him of your danger,
> you must fear a more mean and mechanical murder.   [*Danger*, ll. 6–7]

As long as he preserves this austere detachment, he writes at his best, but his hold on it is uncertain: *A Drunk on the Sidewalk*, for instance, is a fine poem except for two silly lines at the end; *Suburban Prospect*, on the other hand, keeps a dry irony all through.

Mr. Dudek's ideas are more advanced than those of his two collaborators, and so it is not surprising that he writes with more authority than they do. Mr. Layton's work includes a number of epigrammatic squibs on other writers, the best of them, I blushingly report, being aimed at me [*The Excessively Quiet Groves*]. He speaks of "the holy trinity / Of sex revolution and poetry" [*Hymn to the Rising Sun*, ll. 31–2], and each of these is conceived as an explosion of creative energy against the inhibitions of prudery, exploitation, and philistinism respectively; a trinity more or less incarnate in Freud, Marx, and Whitman. The associating of the creative and the procreative functions, the tendency to talk about writing poetry instead of presenting it, and the conception of effective language as deriving from vocabulary rather than rhythm, are fallacies that get in the way of his militant writing. No other poem of his has anything like the quality of *To a Very Old Woman*, where he forgets his self-consciousness and his mission and simply studies his poetic subject:

> ... your face is a halo of praise
> That excludes nothing, not even Death.   [ll. 1–2]

Mr. Souster's vignettes of modern social life are done with much sincerity, and it would be a very hard-boiled critic who could read any poem of his without sympathy for what has been attempted. But in great poetry there is no difference between form and content, whereas one feels in Mr. Souster that though the content is interesting and valuable, it could have been expressed just as well in many different ways. His poems consequently sound moralizing and prosaic, attempting to express their subject by the energy of direct statement alone. When he writes *To an Antisemite* and says:

> All the filth of you and your kind, dark rats
> Of The Big Terrible City, sick, tormented, afraid,   [ll. 7–8]

one feels that anti-Semitism, approached in that way, is beyond the reach of poetic utterance, just as hell is beyond the reach of charity. Mr. Souster seems to me an introspective poet, better at entering his own or others' minds than at describing or commenting on the social scene.

Another poet with some Canadian connections who appears again this year is Robert W. Service, now nearly eighty, who has been living in Europe. *Rhymes of a Rebel* (New York: Dodd Mead; Toronto: McClelland

& Stewart) interests me chiefly because, since I began to make this survey, I have read so much verse in exactly the same idiom, and I wonder how far Mr. Service's earlier books may have influenced it. There was a time, fifty years ago, when Robert W. Service represented, with some accuracy, the general level of poetic experience in Canada, as far as the popular reader was concerned. The amount of good serious poetry produced in this country last year is evidence enough that, whatever querulous complaints may still be made about Canadian philistinism, there has been a prodigious, and, I should think, a permanent, change in public taste.

4. 1953

April 1954

From University of Toronto Quarterly, 23 (April 1954): 253–63. *Reprinted (partially) in* BG, 22–33.

The technical development of a modern lyrical poet is normally from obscurity to simplicity. As long as he is writing primarily for himself, his thought will be rooted in private associations, images which are linked to ideas through his own hidden and unique memory. This is not his fault: he can write only what takes shape in his mind. It is his job to keep on writing and not get stuck at that point, above all not to rationalize any failure to advance by asserting that one must write this way in an unpoetic age. It is the critic's job to tell him and the public that whatever his stuff means, it sounds genuine enough. Then he is likely to pass through a social, allegorical, or metaphysical phase, an awkward and painful phase for all concerned. Finally, a mysterious but unmistakable ring of authority begins to come into his writing, and simultaneously the texture simplifies, meaning and imagery become transparent, and the poetry becomes a pleasure instead of a duty to read. It takes a heroic supply of talent, practice, patience, and courage to get to that point. The process cannot of course be hurried by an act of will, but it can be affected by the environment. It was much easier to mature in England thirty years ago than to mature in America now, for example, no doubt because of all the adolescent fixations in American life. A glance at any American anthology reveals a series of poets who have progressed from

Letters in Canada: Poetry 115

gargle to Guggenheim in six easy volumes, and have still not seriously exploited their own resources. The number of such underdeveloped lyrical poets has created the illusion that the various stages of development are actually outposts. Every once in a while, however, we run across a poet who reminds us that when the lyrical impulse reaches maturity of expression, it is likely to be, as most lyrical poetry has always been, lilting in rhythm, pastoral in imagery, and uncomplicated in thought.

Patrick Anderson's *The Colour as Naked* ([Toronto:] McClelland & Stewart) is the work of a poet who is approaching maturity of expression, and who has shown himself to be, I think, essentially a poet in the pastoral tradition, the tradition of Wordsworth and of so many unpretentious but highly durable English poets of the previous generation. The influence of Auden has helped to give lightness and drive to his rhythm; the influence of Dylan Thomas ("my generation's genius," Mr. Anderson calls him, and certainly the greatest contemporary pastoral poet) has helped to give power and richness of feeling to his imagery. Bits of the cocoon of his apprenticeship cling to him here and there: he writes with conviction when he is the only person in his world, but the impact of "social significance" is usually disastrous. *The Lecturer as Prufrock* unites two of the most unnecessary ideas in literature, a parody of Eliot and a satire on the intellectual; *The Junior Class* is creaky and wooden; *Dialectics* belongs to that dreary metaphysical interregnum from which poetry now seems to be slowly recovering, and the closing *Ballad of a Young Man* is a fine and eloquent poem which deflates into bathos as soon as society appears over the horizon. Again, there is a telltale formula of "the adjective noun of noun" type, where the first noun is usually concrete and the second abstract, which most poets are unconscious of using (though many bad poets use practically nothing else), but which is very frequently the sign of undigested allegory, a perfunctory hitching of image to idea that marks incomplete craftsmanship. I find "their seas of risk," "the white horse of her bed," "the pretty architecture of our pleasure," "the columns of a cold and violent newspaper sky," "the firm and muscular body of faith," and (to make an end) "that island littoral of your eyes' bird brightened canopies," mostly in the less successful poems. But there is remarkably little fogged-up writing: even the words which seem to have a private significance for the poet, such as "long" and "green," obscure nothing in the meaning.

All of which prepares one to say that *The Colour as Naked* is delightful to read and is recommended without reservation. Over and over again, in the *Song of Intense Cold*, in *The Ball*, reminiscent of Rilke in both theme and rhythm, in *A Monkey in Malaya*, with its octosyllabic couplet that picks up the appropriate echoes of Vaughan and Marvell and with its Rousseau-like tropical stylization, in *The Strange Bird*, in the dazzling verbal patterns of the sestina and the six songs, and perhaps too in the lively narrative of the *Ode to Haydon*—in these and many other places we feel that the poet "brings it off." That is, the imagination has tamed fancy: conceits which would be only highbrow wisecracks in inferior writing have fused into a form that can only be called inevitable, the way it should be. The *Song of Intense Cold* begins:

> One night when the stars are exploding like nails
> comes Zero himself with his needle,
> an icicle full of the cold cocaine
> but as tall as the glittering steeple
> that pins us down in the town.

We recognize at once that if the phrase "exploding like nails" says nothing to common sense it says exactly the right thing to the poetic sense. Similarly with the drowsy blurring of images in *An Apple before Bedtime*:

> eating a last slow apple: Keep still, keep still,
> rose coal not fall from fire nor murmur
> dogs on their paws of dream nor ever
> lamp flare.... [ll. 29–32]

Many of the most effective poems are based on a quiet conversational tone—again I should call it a pastoral idiom— with a beautifully controlled melody that does not try too hard for ingenuity either in sound or in meaning. Sometimes, as in *A Seaside Fragment*, one feels that there are too many lines, certainly too many run-on lines, before we finally come to what we are waiting for:

> But suddenly there swells
> the sea's big muscle, suddenly the air
> darkens and it is later and strangely cold. [ll. 87–9]

Elsewhere we are conscious only of the kind of weight that good writing can achieve when the discipline of a great tradition gets behind it:

> The bitter rain is in the wind
> and something older than the rain, or cloud
> frayed from the night-packed West and closing down
> on the vast continent of fields, the wires
> of many fences and their moaning shreds
> and many eave-ends and their waving cries
> (low crying in the child's ear as his hair
> clips to his head—and then the flowers pour
> away from him, and the melancholy sheep
> stand in the wind with thistles in their curls
> and the water is affrighted). Then the tree
> comes in upon one, blows. [*The Pine: Christieville*, ll. 18–29]

Not all the book is on that level, but the point is that it *is* a level, a quality of writing and not a self-conscious rhetorical stunt. It compels us to admire, not Mr. Anderson's dexterity or skill or other such precarious qualities, but simply his actual achievement.

The poems in Douglas LePan's *The Net and the Sword* (Toronto: Clarke Irwin) are based on his experiences with the Canadian Army in Italy, and are, as one would expect, elegiac in tone. The title poem indicates a complex pattern of imagery—I should call it symbolism if that were not so restrictive a word—which runs through the whole book and ramifies and modulates into every poem. A fight between two gladiators, one armed with a sword and shield and the other with a net and trident, was a common feature in the Roman arena. Generally the net man won. In Mr. LePan's book the sword is the symbol of the young Canadian invader, with his smooth rifle-barrels and straight back, the "bronze rigidity" of his discipline showing a will not so much to conquer as to clean up the mess. He seeks the sun and the clear light, gorges on persimmons and the wine of the country, and preserves a vague hope that he is somehow part of a crusade. Against him is the net: first of all the net the technique of modern war forces on him, of "telephone wires, tank-traps, minefields," of camouflage and "the vehicles that sulked under leafy nettings," then the sinister entanglement of ruin and misery that war leaves behind it, and finally the sense of Italy itself as a huge stomach digesting, like a jungle, the havoc wrought by every invader whether he be "Visigoth or Canadian." What the sword is trying to cut through to is some vision of Paradisal peace and contentment which one gets fleeting glimpses of in Italy even in war, a vision identical with "Skating at Scarborough, summers at the Island" [*One of the Regiment*, l. 21], the corresponding vision of peace brought by the soldier with him from home:

> From untarnished lakes and rivers,
> Lakes of sweet water, skies of unsullied godhead.
>
> [*Elegy in the Romagna*, ll. 123–4]

Meanwhile the contrast between the soft Italian night and its "peacock train of stars" [*An Effect of Illumination*, l. 1] and the deadly illumination of shell-bursts is all that is so far apparent of the "fruition born of elected action" [*Lines for a Combatant*, l. 73]. The failure to achieve anything more than a dumb misery brings the poet back to the central image of his previous volume, the wounded body imprisoned in its own net, the labyrinth of nerves and bowels from which only a futile and wistful tenderness can emerge:

> Corrupted
> Our lungs breathe out a new heaven of pity and concern.
>
> [*Elegy in the Romagna*, ll. 237–8]

The larger implications of this imagery are suggested only by a small but remarkable tucked-in poem called *Idyll*: the main poems, *Tuscan Villa*, *Meditation after an Engagement*, *Field of Battle*, and *Elegy in the Romagna* deal with the foreground battle-symbols.

One obvious comment, that the horror of battle is somewhat strangled in fine writing, needs to be qualified by the fact that the muffling of shock and the numbing of pain in the midst of intense beauty form one of the poet's themes, and a part of his "net" imagery. In *An Incident*, for example, the dissolving of a shot soldier's body into a decorative landscape is precisely the irony the poet intends. Besides, the poems are not battlepieces but elegies, meditations on war recollected in tranquillity. Nevertheless one is at times baffled by the complications of the style: in *Meditation after an Engagement*, for instance, which ought to be, and to some extent is, emotionally a key poem, one becomes irritably aware of a barbed-wire entanglement of rhyme—more exactly, an eight-line stanza rhyming *a b b c a d d c*. (The next poem, *The Lost Crusader*, is in an elaborate canzone stanza rhyming, so help me, *a b c a d c d b c*.) However, the rhymes here are not disturbing in themselves, as they tend to be at the end of *One of the Regiment*, for instance, where "trumpet-tell" and "style" are two weak ones. One objects rather to a certain self-consciousness in the writing, marked by such phrases as "the white caesura that stripped down longings" or "eyelids that fleur-de-lis the dark," to forced inversions of the "castles builds" type, and to some difficulties with digesting the explicit statement, as at the end of *Reconnaissance in Early Light*, though the existence of such difficulties is a good sign, as it indicates that the poet has a genuine lyrical sense.

These lapses are noted only because the general level of the writing is good enough to make them show up. No poem in the book is bad, or even unsuccessful. The style as a whole is sonorous and eloquent; long lines vary easily with short ones; passages of pentameters are skilfully broken by short-line lyrics, and the variation of vowel-sounds and consonants is delicate and at times deeply moving. One experiences the thrill of response to authentic craftsmanship in the rhythm of:

> Delicately dawn will come with a garland of headlines—
> But not to sensitive retinas damaged;   [*An Effect of Illumination*, ll. 30–1]

or of:

> Cruel snows can hardly bear such lightness,
> Deftness;   [*In a Spring Night*, ll. 6–7]

or the dreamy melting of sounds and shapes in:

> For seas are skies and skies are seas, where float
> Cool swansdown clouds that sundown has subdued.
> Shadowed the snow about a swan's white throat;
> The daylight melts; slowly they drift and brood;
>   [*Interval with Halcyons*, ll. 14–17]

or the subtlety of:

> Till I wonder if it is they that please me, or the thought
> Of myself years on, remembering the light through the fig-tree,
>   [*Lines for a Combatant*, ll. 46–7]

where the strange working of the will to survive in the middle of the most lethal dangers is very accurately caught. The book is full of such pleasant surprises, but, as with Mr. Anderson, its more solid virtues are the important ones. The main impression one derives from it is produced by the poetry itself, not by the felicities it picks up in passing. One remembers its essence, the poetic assimilation of intense experience by a thoughtful and sensitive mind. The imaginative sword has cut its way through all the nets of verbal cleverness, heavy moralizing, and ready-made melodrama that beset the poet struggling with so oppressive a subject.

Ronald Hambleton's *Object and Event* ([Toronto:] Ryerson) begins with a series of vignettes of Canadian life, more particularly urban life. They are Audenesque in tone and technique, with light-verse stanzaic patterns and lively crackling rhymes. There is erudition as well as observation—the first poem is in the convention of disillusioned "answer" to Marlowe's *Come Live with Me*—and the author is equally good both at assonance and at the rhyme of monosyllable against suffix which has the effect of a disappointment-rhyme:

> This man knows history,
> And facts don't lie;
> He steps on graves now
> None too gently.   [*The Historian*, ll. 41–4]

The main theme is the contrast between the world of civilized "objects," geometrical, ugly, inhuman, and sterile, and the world of human "events," that pass away as soon as they come with all the pathos of time. The feeling expressed by the phrase "radar of indifference" [*That Strain Again*, l. 24], the sense of the city as full of eyes that stare but never see, is perhaps the most vividly conveyed mood. The style is epigrammatic, and in epigram the poet throws harpoons while the reader amiably pretends to be a pachyderm and tests them for sharpness. If they are not sharp, however, they fall with a dull thud, and are felt to be pointless because they should have a point. *The Criminal* and *At the Asylum* are pointless in this sense: we get a reporter's commonplaces instead of the distinctive poignancy that we look for in poetry. This is true even of the more elaborate *The Little Theatre*, as it takes more than puns to produce wit:

> We of the Land of the Third-Big-Week
>   Never know how to act;
> We welcome the fiction within our clique
>   But never the ugly fact. [ll. 53–6]

The second part of the book has less of the clarity of the first: nearly every poem has a fine phrase or image buried in mixed metaphors and didacticisms, as though the whole poem were only a pretext to communicate some crucial part. One approaches each poem like a berry-picker, extracting a bit of colour, beauty, and form from a thorny tangle of words. In *Ancient Priest*, for instance, we find:

> knowing as a hound that hobbles
> Droopingly doorward when an outward step fills
> His serviced ears . . . [ll. 3–5]

which is very lovely, though I get only a vague and diffused impression of the ancient priest himself. In the following stanza from *In Bed*,

> As if our duality
>   Had eclipsed my self,
> And by some agility
> Kept acres pressed
> For our interest
>   Into the sweet gulf
> Of your lips and breast [ll. 15–21]

the accuracy of the first two lines makes one try to believe, unsuccessfully, that the rest of the stanza is not the arid gibberish it seems to be. *Sockeye Salmon* has a theme as potentially moving as that of, say, Baudelaire's albatross, but it talks itself away into fuzziness. However, we judge a poet by his best things, and in the last two poems in the book, *After-Dinner Sleep* and *Nocturnal*, there is a consistent attempt to fill the whole poem with clarity and sincere feeling. One is based on Eliot's *Gerontion* and the other a poem of Donne's, but both are, probably for that very reason, thoroughly original. It is well worth struggling through pages of fugitive glimmers to get to something as articulate as the image of the gulls in the former poem, or, in the other, of:

> The nightingale, the breath of spring,
> The footsteps that in winter ring,
> Are bells that cry as sinners sing....
>
> In ether rolls the idle ball,
> Its firmness we doubt not at all,
> But if it fell, how far a fall! [ll. 10–12, 28–30]

There are not many other serious books of verse this year. *Love the Conqueror Worm*, by Irving Layton ([Toronto:] Contact Press), consists very largely of what one has come to recognize as Laytonese—forced language and flaccid rhythm—but at the beginning of the book there are a few poems with some freshness and originality. The reader is not only encouraged, but looks forward to seeing an even better book next year. *The Perverse Gulls* has wit rather than mere facetiousness; *Cemetery in August* and *A Vision* are genuine epigrams, and *The Death of Moishe Lazarovitch* has a poignancy that is sustained to its close:

> I do not know how they lifted him up
> Or held the vessel near their mourning silk,
> But their going was like a roar of flames
> And Matter sang in my ears like poured milk.

All My Brothers, by J.S. Wallace ([Toronto:] New Frontiers), illustrated with lino-cuts by Karl Rix, is verse in a familiar Communist idiom, sometimes laboured, especially in the Yanks-go-home passages, sometimes corny, especially in the concessions to such nonpolitical poetic themes as making love, but sometimes also crisp and precise. It derives much of its strength from the sheer intensity of the Marxist view of the capitalist world:

> Praise God from whom all blessings flow
> Provided it's the God we know
> Who sends us gushers fat with oil
> To keep our hands unspoilt by toil. [*I Saw a Star*, ll. 13–16]

Such poetry acquired illegitimate virtues twenty years ago from the masochism of bourgeois intellectuals; it acquires illegitimate obloquy now that the masochism has turned in a different direction. It is most important to keep the tone of genuine anger and contempt at hypocrisy alive in our poetry, no matter where it comes from or for what motives it is uttered.

{Two anthologies appeared last year: *Canadian Poems 1850–1952* ([Toronto:] Contact Press), by Dudek and Layton, and *Twentieth-Century Canadian Poetry* ([Toronto:] Ryerson), by Earle Birney. Both, with their explanatory notes and their cautious introductions, seem to be aimed at the high school trade. The former is the better book: the editors have obviously tried to avoid the hackneyed and yet to include nothing that they did not themselves believe to be reputable poetry. The result is a collection representing fresh insights and discoveries, well worth examining. The Birney anthology also has its virtues, but it seems deliberately oversimplified: it contains a number of poems that the editor could not possibly have believed to be very good, and must therefore have included because he thought his readers would think they were good.

Of the naive verse, the most ambitious effort is a narrative poem in fifteen cantos, *The House of Orseoli* (Manchester, Me.: Falmouth Publishing House), by Laurence Dakin. It tells the story of a dynasty of tenth-century Venetian doges, and is written in a six-line stanza with an unrhymed tetrameter in the middle. The idiom is that of the less introspective Romantic narratives of the *Revolt of Islam* type. Like most poems with ingenious stanzaic structures, the writing is full of metrical putty—doubled phrases and the like. The story is very evenly divided into parts of exactly the same length; a reviewer in another Canadian academic journal remarked that "the architectonics of the poem challenge comparison with the symmetrical structure of Dante's *Divine Comedy*."[6] In my opinion this is an overstatement.... There are two Ryerson chapbooks. Dr. Sherwood Fox offers a poetic paraphrase of Cicero's *De Amicitia* ([Toronto:] Ryerson) in quatrains of the *In Memoriam a b b a* type. It is an interesting idea, and one wishes that the poetic language employed had been less hackneyed, freshness of language being obviously necessary to rescue the platitudes in which, as Dr. Fox rightly says, Cicero mainly deals. R.E. Rashley's *Portrait and Other Poems* ([Toronto:] Ryerson) is in free verse, some of it rhymed, and exhibits the typical difficulty of free verse, which is that of giving a real spring to the rhythm of the sentence, so that the lines do not merely stumble awkwardly over a rocky path of subject, predicate, object, modifiers. *People* and *Hollow in the Wheat and Blackbirds* get away to some freedom of movement. Mr. Arthur Bourinot's *This Green Earth* ([Foleyet, Ont.:] Carillon Poetry Chapbooks) exhibits a good deal of Mr. Bourinot's trade mark, the very short line that ranges from a single syllable to three or four beats. In *Sun Flowers* there is some fresh imagery, in *Paul Bunyan* some rhythm, and in *Snow Anthology* there is a real idea, if somewhat attenuated in treatment. There is some genuine feeling in another green book, Gilean Douglas's *Now the Green Word* (Mill Valley, Calif.: Wings Press). The writing is commonplace but always carefully modulated, and there are a few phrases which, as is usual in this type of poetry, look better out of context:

> Morass flowers outshine the light;
> Moss is deeper than the night.   [*True Sight*, ll. 5–6]

A Morning Mood, by Lorene Frances Milliken ([Foleyet, Ont.: Carillon Poetry Chapbooks) contains a very curious poem called *Duomo*:

> Emit
>   Time's hours
> At moontide's noon
> With Elysium's melodies entuned
> Padrone.}

Most of the more technically competent naive verse produced every year is based on the theory that certain subjects or themes are inherently poetical: that the poet who aims at beauty should search in his memory for pleasurable experiences, and then use words as a charm to recall them. As the main function of the words is to stimulate the reader to remember a parallel experience of his own, the actual quality of the writing does not matter: it is enough for it to be cadenced in a familiar and unobtrusive way. This is the nostalgia theory of poetry, corresponding to the picturesque theory of painting. It is, of course, all wrong, but many people think it right, and this is a free country. It is often accompanied by a querulous sense of the disapproval of some reptilian intellectuals or moderns, who think beauty old-fashioned and want everything to be as bleak and obscure as possible. Often, too, its claims are endorsed by critics, including some who ought to know better, who classify it in a "conservative" or "romantic" school. It is, however, purely and simply the doggerel school, and one of its most skilful practitioners in Canada is Edna Jaques, whose *The Golden Road* ([Toronto:] Thomas Allen) appears in this year's production.

Letters in Canada: Poetry   125

I call Miss Jaques skilful because there is no nonsense about her, no queasy aspirations for all this and poetry too. The opening lines of her book indicate her mastery of the central technical device of nostalgic verse, a list of reminders or stimuli, vigorously checked off one after the other:

> The strong clean smell of yellow soap,
>   A farmer plowing with a team,
> The taste of huckleberry pie,
>   A pan of milk with wrinkled cream.   [*Down to Earth Things*, ll. 1–4]

Poem after poem exhibits a similar shopping-list sequence: *Mended Things, Keepsakes, Drug Store Smells*, occasionally varied by a phrase that shows a sharp awareness of what she is doing:

> There is a sweet nostalgic charm,
>   About an old Ontario farm,
> That pulls your heart strings all awry,
>   A clean breath taking sweep of sky
> An old grey barn built on a knoll . . .   [*Home Relish*, ll. 1–5]

and so on through another inventory. The tone of her writing is equally central to her approach. The psychologists have made us familiar with the disasters wrought by unpleasant and repressed memories; they have naturally said much less about the memories we select, the smoothly edited and censored transcript of wholesome food, happy children, simple virtues, and, of course, mother dear, which plays such a large part in keeping us adjusted. Miss Jaques's rule is never to stop flattering the selective memory:

> Beneath the fire's lovely light,
>   Faces take on a softer look,
> And little children from our street,
>   Look like gay pictures in a book. . . .
>
> To lift the dull and commonplace
> Into a realm of love and grace.   [*Bonfires*, ll. 19–22, 25–6]

No, if this kind of thing is worth writing, Miss Jaques is certainly the person who knows best how to write it, and all our poets who are ambitious of belonging to the "conservative" or "romantic" school should learn about nostalgia from her.

5. 1954

April 1955

From University of Toronto Quarterly, *24 (April 1955): 247–56. Reprinted (partially) in* BG, *33–44, and in* Masks of Poetry: Canadian Critics on Canadian Verse, *ed. A.J.M. Smith (Toronto: McClelland & Stewart, 1962), 103–5. Material on Layton reprinted in* Irving Layton: The Poet and His Critics, *ed. Seymour Mayne (Toronto: McGraw-Hill Ryerson, 1978), 38–9. Material on Carman reprinted in* Twentieth-Century Literary Criticism, *vol. 7, ed. Sharon K. Hall (Detroit: Gale Research, 1982), 147.*

The poetry of 1954 includes some reprinting of traditional poets as well as new work, and it may be simplest to deal with the serious verse in a roughly chronological order.

The impact of Lampman, Carman, Roberts, and D.C. Scott on Canadian poetry was very like the impact of Thomson and Group of Seven painting two decades later. Contemporary readers felt that whatever entity the word "Canada" might represent, at least the environment it described was being looked at directly. Like the later painters, these poets were lyrical in tone and romantic in attitude; like the painters, they sought for the most part uninhabited landscape. The lyrical response to landscape is by itself, however, a kind of emotional photography, and like other forms of photography is occasional and epigrammatic. Its variety is provided essentially by its subject-matter. Hence the lyric poet, after he has run his gamut of impressions, must die young, develop a more intellectualized attitude, or start repeating himself. Carman's meeting of this challenge was only partly successful, and it has long been a commonplace that he badly needs a skilful and sympathetic selection. This is provided in *The Selected Poems of Bliss Carman*, edited by Lorne Pierce ([Toronto:] McClelland & Stewart).

Carman should, of course, have edited himself. I have heard the late Pelham Edgar turn a poem of Carman's into a thing of unalloyed delight by leaving out a couple of bad lines, but what a public reader can do an editor cannot do. What the selection does bring out is that Carman's conscious mind and his poetic instinct were disastrously at odds. The first stage in the development of a Romantic poet's mind is normally a sense of the unity of that mind throughout its variety of impressions: this in turn is likely to be projected as some form of pantheism, which has its advantages if properly developed, as Wordsworth shows, but the disadvantage of adding vagueness to monotony if it is not. Carman's conscious mind stuck at a broken-down and corny version of Emersonian oversoulfulness: his editor, with a touch of distaste, speaks of "his elaborate theory of Unitrinianism— spirit-leading; mental guidance, physical fulfilment—the full revelation of the doctrine of Personal Harmonizing." I don't know what all this means, but it sounds in more than one sense too awful for words, and I note that most of the poetic results are omitted from this selection. On the other hand, Carman's poetic sense told him, as it told Isabella Crawford before him and Pratt after him, that the most obvious development of a Romantic landscape poet is towards the mythological, towards making his emotional impressions into a *dramatis personae* of forces at once human and natural. Carman's formative influences were late Victorian, and he follows Swinburne, Morris, and Rossetti in enamelling nature with primary colours and peopling it with the pagan gods of the turning year, "Our Lady of the Rain," the dying gods Adonis and Attis, nymphs and fauns. And while his conscious mind called for songs of the open road and getting in tune with the infinite, his real poetic imagination became increasingly brooding, lonely, and haunted:

> The windows of my room
> Are dark with bitter frost,
> The stillness aches with doom
> Of something loved and lost.
>
> Outside, the great blue star
> Burns in the ghostland pale,
> Where giant Algebar
> Holds on the endless trail.   [*A Northern Vigil*, ll. 37–44]

This is the kind of thing we remember from Carman, and we are grateful to Dr. Pierce for confining himself to the memorable work, completely ignoring the pseudo-Carman, with his stentorian hymns to the Great Beyond like *Lord of my heart's elation*, which are usually what get into anthologies.

A poet of the same generation as Carman is George Herbert Clarke, whose *Selected Poems* ([Toronto:] Ryerson) have been edited by George Whalley. Clarke was a university professor, and his poetic qualities are the typically scholarly ones, notably a tendency to identify the poetic impulse with melancholy moods and sonorous diction. Like most such poets, he loves the sonnet and the commemorative ode. The poems are academic in every sense, springing from a world in which everything from ideas to flowers has been ordered and disciplined, a world which would be almost paradisal if it were not just close enough to the working world to recollect its disorder in a meditative tranquillity. Death is for such a poet best understood in the funeral of George V, where it has the maximum of dignity; poverty and pain are best understood as things that may distract one from true knowledge:

> Perchance man may not climb
> Higher than Pisgah on the mountain road
> That twists and loops and narrows, for a load
> Of fear cumbers his heart, and sweat and grime
> Blind him. Benighted, he may mistake the trail. . . .
>   [*Hymn to the Spirit Eternal*, ll. 71–5]

The limitations of such poetry are obvious enough, but it is still a perfectly valid form of poetic experience, and it is good sometimes to be reminded of more leisurely days when poets wrote odes on the hundredth anniversary of Queen's or McMaster and could feel convinced that

> Man was born,
> To think eternal thoughts, yet to be torn
> Between the invisible world that looms sublime
> And this apparent, this ambiguous star.   [*Commemoration Ode*, ll. 68–71]

The {next} generation of poets{,} growing up in the twenties{, had} encountered more urban and intellectual poetic influences, and found in T.S. Eliot especially a technique for adapting the old mythological themes to a human as well as a natural environment, and to ironic as well as to

Romantic uses. The mythological impetus itself simply reinforced the Romantic heritage: Leo Kennedy's *Words for a Resurrection* is very close to Carman's *Resurgam*. This generation of poets is represented in the contributors to *New Provinces* (1936), two of whom, A.J.M. Smith and F.R. Scott, have issued new books of verse this year.

A.J.M. Smith has always been a careful and sparing writer, and *A Sort of Ecstasy* ([Toronto:] Ryerson) contains several poems which appeared in 1943 in *News of the Phoenix*, and were not new then. Even the passage from Santayana which gives him his title appeared in the earlier book. Mr. Smith has the reputation of being a metaphysical poet in the tradition of Donne: Professor Collin's essay on him in *The White Savannahs* uses his own phrase, "difficult, lonely music," to describe the quality of his work.[7] Certainly Mr. Smith is scholarly: we meet such phrases as "proud Romanticism" and "Apollonian energy," and part of the point about a poem on the H-bomb [*Fear as Normal, 1954*] turns on the ironic application to it of a phrase from Shakespeare about mercy and from Hopkins about the Holy Spirit. Every poet demands his own kind of erudition; we need some knowledge of the *Odyssey* to understand *The Plot against Proteus*, but we need much more Classical background than that to follow Carman's Sappho lyrics, and in both cases whatever obscurity there is is due to the reader's ignorance and not to the poet's wilfulness. Still, Mr. Smith's learning perhaps does interfere with his spontaneity. Too many of the poems seem to me to lack drive: the words do not develop rhythm but are fitted into a containing pattern. The poetry is intensely visual and conceptual; it slowly clarifies, but it does not dance. Sometimes, however, this slow clarification contains great emotional power, as in *The Bridegroom*, in which the social and sexual anxieties of modern man come into a nightmarish focus:

> Where slaves or workmen strained to twist huge gears
> That moved vast vents or fed the flues,
> And fell some
> Into the fire, of sheer fatigue, and fried.   [ll.39–42]

Looking at the new poems, one is surprised by the number of them that are Romantic landscape poems in the Carman tradition: *To Hold In a Poem* is a summary of Canadian Romantic themes. One wonders if the intellectualized irony of *Resurrection of Arp*, even of the remarkable *Universe into Stone*, is negative in direction, attacking the political and religious obstacles that prevent the poet from following a naturally Romantic bent. That would account for a lack of exuberance in the difficult lonely music, if I am right in finding the lack there:

> I would put away intellect and lust,
> Be but a red gleam in a crystal dish,
> But kin of the trembling ocean, not of the dust. [*The Sorcerer*, ll. 14–16]

Mr. Scott is a more fluent writer than Mr. Smith, and his *Events and Signals* ([Toronto:] Ryerson) gives the impression of highly cultivated metrical conversation. This does not mean that it is shallow, but that its sincerity is controlled by urbanity. Its main theme is the inability of events in the modern world to produce signals that are profoundly communicative. The poet stands in churches aware of, but untouched by, the symbols of communion; he reads newspapers which reveal a misery that he is powerless to affect; he goes through a day's duties realizing that

> Though all is available, nothing is taken
> that is not pre-selected, hence the unsubstantial
> is the practical, the theory all-important,
> and the routines, sub-conscious theories,
> wall up the doorways slowly, one by one. [*I Am Employed*, ll. 9–13]

It is part of the paradox of such an attitude that Mr. Scott's verse is least convincing when it is most explicit, and at its best when sardonically observant. He is one of our best writers of epigram and light verse, and sometimes a serious epigram, such as *The Bird*, hits a bull's-eye, but his fables are better without morals. In the first of the *Social Sonnets*, for instance, the octave sets up a satiric situation with great economy and brilliance, but the sestet, by commenting on it, merely weakens the point already made.

Students are often urged to use short words of Anglo-Saxon origin when possible—the polite ones, that is—but there are so many abstract and technical words in the language that the basis of conversational rhythm in modern English is polysyllabic, and a style founded on short Anglo-Saxon words is the most artificial of all styles. Mr. Scott has grasped this fact about conversational rhythm, and he has brought to a high level of technical competence a kind of meditative, musing poem through which the longer words of ordinary speech ripple with great colloquial freedom. *I Am Employed*, *My Amoeba Is Unaware*, and *Some Privy Counsel* are his best achievements in this vein. The same competence makes him extremely good at a kind of literary *collage*. *The Canadian Social Register* is based on an advertising prospectus, with all its fatuous phrases gripped in quotation marks like a pair of ice tongs. The very funny *Bonne Entente* I could quote, but I do not wish to save the reader the trouble of looking it up himself.

The next generation, growing up in a largely urbanized Canada, has two representatives this year. P.K. Page's *The Metal and the Flower* (Indian File Book, no. 7; [Toronto:] McClelland & Stewart) got the Governor-General's Medal, and deserved it, although my opinion of the practice of giving a medal to any poet over the age of ten is not high. But if there is such a thing as "pure poetry," this must be it: a lively mind seizing on almost any experience and turning it into witty verse. The taste is not faultless: sometimes a conceit is squeezed to a pulp, as in *Mystics Like Miners*, *Christmas Eve—Market Square*, and *Mineral*, or dragged in by a too restless ingenuity, like the unpearled barbiturates in *Subjective Eye* or the hydrocephalic idiot in *Sleeper*. The writing is less mannered than in *As Ten, as Twenty*, though she will still talk too much, in the sense that some of her points are made overconceptually, in undigested prose. This is true of *The Permanent Tourists*, for instance, where most of the impact is made by the first stanza. Although she is essentially an occasional poet, Miss Page has a symbolic language of her own that operates on three levels: a lower level of emotion and instinct, symbolized chiefly by the sea; an upper level of intelligence symbolized by angels and abstract patterns in white; and a middle level of metal and flower, rose garden, and barbed wire, where there is passion but little communion:

> Black and white at midnight glows
> this garden of barbed wire and roses.
> Doused with darkness roses burn
> coolly as a rainy moon;
> beneath a rainy moon or none
> silver the sheath on barb and thorn.   [*The Metal and the Flower*, ll. 14–19]

This lovely stanza needs to be read in its context, for Miss Page is very skilful at varying a stanzaic pattern throughout a poem—one of the most difficult techniques in modern lyric.

She seems interested in everything, from salt mines to ski tows, but resists the temptation to be merely decorative and looks for the human situations involved in what she sees. The salt mine poem has a deceptively casual development in perspective from beauty to horror. Only a few subjects (such as *Freak*) get outside her emotional range. Her studies of girls are perhaps the most obviously attractive of her poems: *Morning, Noon and Night*, *Sisters*, and *Probationer* are all highly successful, and the conclusion of *Young Girls*, in her lower-level key, is a most sensitive evocation of adolescent tremors:

> Too much weeping in them and unfamiliar blood
> has set them perilously afloat.
> Not divers these—but as if the water rose up in a flood
> making them partially amphibious
> and always drowning a little and hearing bells. . . .

She is also admirable in seeing a story within a scene, and *Man with One Small Hand*, *Portrait of Marina* (a spinster bullied by a sailor-father and "antlered with migraines" in consequence), and *Paranoid* are excellent little novelettes. More elaborate are the longer fantasies, *Images of Angels* and *Arras*, both very beautiful, the latter a somewhat elliptical treatment of the Alice-through-the-mirror theme. Miss Page's work has a competent elegance about it that makes even the undistinguished poems still satisfying to look at, and the book as a whole is as consistently successful in reaching its objectives as any book I have read since I began this survey.

Mr. Irving Layton, like Bliss Carman, is a poet whose conscious and creative minds are at odds, and the former has, up to now, effectively concealed the fact that he is not only a serious poet but an unusually gifted one. *The Long Pea-Shooter* ([Montreal:] Laocoon Press) is mainly satiric verse, the *double-entendre* in the title giving the general idea. The book takes what one might call, borrowing a term from architecture, a miserere view of humanity, but the ironic eye does not have free play; it is oppressed by a conscience-driven and resentful mind which sees modern society as a rock pile and the poet as under sentence of hard labour. When there is a core of detachment in satire, there may be a core of reality in its caricature, but most of the world of *The Long Pea-Shooter* is a depressingly unreal world. If the book stood alone, one would be inclined to say that here is a remarkable mind that has somehow missed its vocation. And yet, there is a personal test which every critic applies to poetry, the test of involuntary memorizing. If one remembers a poem, or part of a poem, without making a conscious effort to do so, one is probably dealing with a genuine poet. And the little pieces of phraseology that keep sticking in one's mind are surprisingly frequent:

> I saw a continent of railway tracks
> coiling about the sad Modigliani necks
> like disused tickertape, the streets
> exploding in the air
> with disaffected subway cars. [*How to Look at an Abstract*, ll. 2–6]

In any case, the question of whether Mr. Layton is a real poet or not is settled by *In the Midst of My Fever* (Majorca: Divers Press). An imaginative revolution is proclaimed all through this book: when he says that something "has taught me severity, exactness of speech" or "has given me a turn for sculptured stone," we see a new excitement and intensity in the process of writing. At last it is possible to see what kind of poet Mr. Layton is, and he proves to be not a satirist at all, but an erudite elegiac poet, whose technique turns on an aligning of the romantic and the ironic:

> Or hex me to see
> the great black-bearded Agamemnon
>   slain by a danceband leader
> bonged on the head on the polished floor. . . .
>   [*Lacquered Westmount Doll*, ll. 10–13]

The ridicule of the body, the sense that human genius grows out of human corruption, has always been a central theme in his work: here it becomes a co-ordinated vision of pity and terror:

> Life is horrifying, said Cezanne,
>   but this is not
>   what he meant who picked flowers blooming
>   in the slaughterhouse; he meant the slit throats,
> The bear traps smeared with blood, the iron goads, the frightened
>   servant-girl's Caesarian,
> And this planet dancing about Apollo,
>   the blood drying and shining in the sun. . . .
>   [*Seven O'Clock Lecture*, ll. 15–22]

One finds something of value on nearly every page of this book: vivid imagery in *Metzinger: Girl with a Bird*; quiet eloquence in *Paraclete*; well-paced narrative in *The Longest Journey*; and, in *The Birth of Tragedy*, this:

> A quiet madman, never far from tears,
> > I lie like a slain thing
> > under the green air the trees
> inhabit, or rest upon a chair
> > towards which the inflammable air
> tumbles on many robins' wings.... [ll. 23-8]

And whatever lapses in expression one may find are of little importance when one is so constantly in touch with a poetic mind of genuine dignity and power. The real poet is now strong enough to dispense with the bristly palisade of self-conscious satire which has obviously been protecting him, not against the world, but against his own fear of sentimentality.

A still younger generation of poets born during the twenties of this century is represented in *Trio* ([Toronto:] Contact Press), a selection of verse by Gael Turnbull, Phyllis Webb, and E.W. Mandel. Here finally one meets the responses of people reared in a fully modernized Canada who find the forest as strange as Lampman found the city (see Mr. Turnbull's *Lumber Camp Railway*), and who accept political malaise and existential dread as the most elementary poetical assumptions (see Mr. Turnbull's *Twentieth Century*, Miss Webb's *Earth Descending*, and all of Mr. Mandel's *Minotaur Poems*). In a way this acceptance has protected them, like an inoculation. Poets who reached maturity between 1930 and 1945 were affected by the world's hostility to creation: these poets take the hostility for granted, and have been driven back on poetry as the most solid basis for experience of anything they know.

None of them have as yet wholly distinguished the process of writing a poem from the process of finding a poetic subject and writing it up, and all of them are apt to take refuge in some kind of literary allusion when they approach the emotional crux of their poem. That there are influences and derivations, such as Marianne Moore in Miss Webb's *Standing*, goes without saying: one should not look at those, but past them. Mr. Turnbull's *Post-Mortem* treats a difficult subject with great simplicity and directness, and *A Landscape and a Kind of Man* well evokes that curious nostalgia for mean streets that is a trade mark of contemporary sensibility:

Letters in Canada: Poetry 135

> In some brick-infested town
> Where only the damp cobbles shine,
> And slate and soot and sameness blend,
> And smoke and cloud have no sure start or end,
> Crowded upon the margin of a garrulous sea. . . .   [ll. 20–4]

In Miss Webb another contemporary trade mark, the sense of apocalyptic parody, of the world soon coming to an end in after all a quite meaningless way, is what moves her to greatest eloquence:

> and, as a world tumbling shocks the theories of spheres,
> so this love is like falling glass shaking with stars
> the air which tomorrow, or even today, will be
> a slow, terrible movement of scars.   [*And in Our Time*, ll. 7–10]

The variety of tone and technique in her work makes it interesting but somewhat uncertain in direction: *The Color of the Light* perhaps indicates most clearly both her latent powers and the core of a more individual style.

Mr. Mandel is less superficially attractive, with his strident rhythm full of strong beats and spondees, and is much more difficult to follow, with his superimposed mythopoeic imagery. But these are signs of staying power, and to my mind he is the one of the three most likely to develop not only in technical skill but in depth and range of vision. He is preoccupied by the perennial technical problem of transmuting the substance of myth into the form of immediate experience. And just as Carman turned to Sappho and the Adonis lament to express the plangent melancholy of a late pagan Romanticism, so Mr. Mandel, born only a few years before Carman died, turns to the story of Theseus and the Minotaur to express our own sense of sinister initiation into some kind of fearful ordeal:

> It has been hours in these rooms,
> the opening to which, door or sash,
> I have lost. I have gone from room to room
> asking the janitors who were sweeping up
> the brains that lay on the floors,
> the bones shining in the wastebaskets,
> and once I asked a suit of clothes

>   that collapsed at my breath and bundled
>   and crawled on the floor like a coward.
>   Finally, after several stories,
>   in the staired and eyed hall,
>   I came upon a man with the face of a bull.   [Minotaur Poems, no. 1]

{Of the three Ryerson chapbooks, Elizabeth Brewster's *Lillooet* is a description of life in a small Canadian town, in tone a little like the Leacock Mariposa studies. It is very readable and in places quite skilful, though for someone of Miss Brewster's abilities it must have been rather easy to do. The second of the chapbooks, A.S. Bourinot's *Tom Thomson and Other Poems*, brings together half a dozen new pieces. Mr. Bourinot's verse has been praised by competent critics, and I wish I could feel that I was wrong in regarding the short-line rhythm of the title poem as only a kind of desiccated *Hiawatha*. On the other hand, the prose essays in *Five Canadian Poets* (Ottawa: n.p.), especially the last three, are recommended: they are on D.C. Scott, Lampman, Sangster, Cameron, and William Marshall, and will appeal to anyone interested in our earlier poets. The third of the chapbooks is Anthony Frisch's *Poems*, one or two of which appeared in previous collections; they are smooth tailor-made lyrics, mainly social vignettes, with relatively little freshness of insight. A mimeographed collection called *The Book of Sketches* contains much more interesting and uninhibited work. *The Machine* gives some new twists to a stock theme, in short oracular sentences expertly rhymed, and *Et Libera Me* deals with a bored God who wonders what he can make that will get away from his omniscience. The *Cancer Sonnets*, too, have an appealing simple intensity. Fred Cogswell's *The Stunted Strong* ([Fredericton:] Fiddlehead Poetry Books, University of New Brunswick) is a series of sixteen sonnets, in Spoon-River-Anthology vein, on the inhabitants of a rural Maritime community. Some real stories are told, and the sonnet-writing is fluent, though occasionally an imitation of colloquial speech gets caught up on a forced rhyme. The stories of Rose and Honour Logan seem to me to make the most direct impact, and to be freest of manipulation.

There is very little naive verse in the 1954 stack of song, and none of it gets its head above doggerel. One or two privately printed booklets are better held over for another year. *Canadian Poetry in English*, chosen by Bliss Carman, Lorne Pierce, and V.B. Rhodenizer ([Toronto:] Ryerson), is a disappointing continuation of a fine series of books on Canadian literature. In its present avatar this book, originally an admirable bilingual anthology, is an industrious but commonplace collection of the vacuum cleaner type, including something by everybody, good or bad. For readers who already know something about Canadian poetry it has considerable bibliographical value, but what an outsider would make of it I can hardly imagine. Of Mr. Rhodenizer's preposterous "introduction" and other critical comments the less said the better.}

6. 1955

April 1956

From University of Toronto Quarterly, *25 (April 1956): 290–304. Reprinted (partially) in* BG, *44–57, and in* Masks of Poetry: Canadian Critics on Canadian Verse, *ed. A.J.M. Smith (Toronto: McClelland & Stewart, 1962), 105–6. Material on Layton reprinted in* Irving Layton: The Poet and His Critics, *ed. Seymour Mayne (Toronto: McGraw-Hill Ryerson, 1978), 41–2. Material on Roberts reprinted in* Twentieth-Century Literary Criticism, *ed. Sharon K. Hall (Detroit: Gale Research, 1982), 8:319.*

Poetry, like painting, has two poles: the pole of content or subject-matter, the thing represented, and the pole of form, the conventional structure of the art. Painting may be very formal, as in geometrical ornament or abstraction, or it may be very representational, as in illusion-painting or *trompe l'oeil*. Poetry may be representational, as it is in reflective poetry where the poet describes a landscape, his emotions, his thoughts, or his society. When it is formal, the poet seeks metaphor, the language of pure identification that he shares with the lunatic and the lover; he seeks myth, the stories of gods whose actions are not limited by reality, and hence form abstract literary patterns; he is erudite and allusive, for the forms of poetry are conventions and grow out of other poems, and he seeks apocalyptic imagery, the vision of a universe which is humanly as well as divinely intelligible. The representational tendency in poetry is sophisticated and civilized: the formal tendency is primitive, oracular, close to the riddle and the spell. In our day, however, the primitive tendency has been reached through a further refinement of sophistication: "modern" poets use myth, metaphor, and apocalyptic imagery just as "modern" painters use abstract or stylized patterns. In Canada, the

Romantic nineteenth-century traditions are reflective and representational: "modern" poets have unconsciously bridged the cultural gap with the Indians, just as the painting of Emily Carr bridges the gap in British Columbia between a culture of totem poles and a culture of power plants.

Two volumes this year illustrate each of these tendencies in our tradition. *Sepass Poems* (mimeographed) is a collection of Okanagan Indian mythical poems recorded by a chief and translated by Mrs. Street. (They were apparently recorded in 1915 but not published because they conflicted with what scholars then thought they knew about the tribe's origin: an extraordinary reason, but that's what it says here.) They are myths of creation and flood, of the sun-god and his paradisal world, of the evil spirit, an Indian Ogopogo, at the bottom of a stormy lake; they are myths of metamorphosis, of how animals were shaped as they are; myths of Titans revolting against the sky-god and of a box of evils like Pandora's. In short, they are the same myths that we find in our European tradition. In spite of a slightly old-fashioned cast to the translation (the translator was born in 1857), the structural outlines and rhetorical devices of the original, notably repetition, obviously show through. They make fascinating and haunting reading.

The other tendency is illustrated in *The Selected Poems of Sir Charles G.D. Roberts* ([Toronto:] Ryerson), edited with a concise introduction by Desmond Pacey. This book is a companion volume to the selection of Carman by Lorne Pierce, reviewed here last year. Roberts is a subjective and descriptive poet, not a mythical one, and the organizing formal principles which give both intellectual and emotional unity to his work come out of his personal life. The formal basis of his poetry is chiefly in the recollections and associations of his Maritime childhood. Being a late Romantic, this means that his central emotional quality is nostalgia. From there he expands to descriptive landscape poetry, still usually with a nostalgic emotional core, and from there the next logical step would be to intellectualized poetry. Roberts tried hard to attain to this third stage, but had nothing intellectual in his mind, and Mr. Pacey has quite properly omitted the poetic results—still, the pattern of a representational poet is complete in him.

In 1955 there were four volumes of poetry of particular importance. Two, Wilfred Watson's *Friday's Child* and Anne Wilkinson's *The Hangman Ties the Holly*, are highly formalized poetry, making considerable use of relatively primitive forms, such as ballads and nursery rhymes.

Letters in Canada: Poetry   139

Miriam Waddington's *The Second Silence* and Irving Layton's *The Cold Green Element* are at once more subjective and more objective than the other two. They have very little in common with Roberts and his Romantic nostalgia, but their organizing associative patterns begin in personal experience, which in its turn shapes and colours a direct reaction to the world around them.

Wilfred Watson's *Friday's Child* ([London:] Faber & Faber) is typically formal poetry, mythical, metaphorical, and apocalyptic, using religious language because it is impossible to avoid religious language in poetry of this kind. The expected influences are present: Hopkins (notably in *I Praise God's Mankind*), Eliot, the later Yeats, and more particularly Dylan Thomas, the most exuberantly apocalyptic poet of our time. (There are two poems on Thomas, an *Admiration* and a *Contempt*: the latter seems to deny the apocalyptic element in him, which I find incomprehensible, in spite of the great eloquence of the poem itself.) Such themes and influences are by now familiar, and the familiarity is a challenge to the poet to "make it new," in Pound's phrase [*Canto 53*]. It is an impressive tribute to Mr. Watson's integrity as a poet that he meets this challenge by being simple rather than clever, and a tribute to his ability that he succeeds.

The framework of his ideas and imagery is conventional enough. There is a world that is "real," and another world that is intelligible. The real world is the world of nature, where life and death, love and lust, chase each other around in a closed circle. Its presiding genius is an "old woman crossing and breeding all creatures," the central figure of the haunting *Ballad of Mother and Son*. It is true that "the dead wave is pierced by the living reed," a phrase with overtones of Pascal[8] indicating that life is as powerful and as primeval as death. Yet one discovers

>   That love in its simple essence
>   Is death mourned to magnificence,   [*Love Song*, ll. 9–10]

and that the energy of passion is driven by the death-impulse: Tarquin the ravisher is "lit at death's white taper." In *In the Cemetery of the Sun* there is a wonderful evocation of the sense of life and death as simultaneously present: the city of Calgary is "a hill of tombstones" and the flapping clothes on Monday morning suggest the ghosts of the Crucifixion and Ezekiel's valley of dry bones.

The other, the intelligible world, is the world of divine presence revealed by Christ, and its first impact on the world of nature is one of total opposition, the light striking into the uncomprehending darkness, into a world protected from Paradise by "the hard mercy of the flaming sword" [*Love Song for Friday's Child*, l. 63]. The terror inspired by the "windy bishop"—presumably the Holy Spirit—"who'd preach our dust home" [*The Windy Bishop*, l. 56], is the terror of being confronted with something that threatens not death but annihilation—the same terror that made Eliot's Gerontion speak of "Christ the tiger." Yet there is a stage beyond this at which the world of light becomes simply the world of darkness illuminated, a new earth in a new heaven:

> ... the exigent
> Last moment, when the creature at last comes home
> To reason, order, proportion, doom. [*For Anne, Who Brought Tulips*, ll. 2–4]

The reconciliation of the two worlds and the awakening of life-in-death to life is the theme of the powerful *Canticle of Darkness*, typologically the key poem in the book, where we move from creation through the death and resurrection of Christ into a new creation.

Friday's Child is brought out by a well-known British publisher, and the blurb expresses a genuine admiration for the book, along with the faintest trace of polite surprise that lyrical tones more highly organized than a buffalo's mating call should come from the windy plains of Alberta. The present reviewer does not share the surprise, if it is there, but he fully concurs in the admiration. One gets very tired of poets who indicate an impressive subject and then walk quickly away from it, but Mr. Watson never starts anything he can't finish, even an apocalypse. He can describe Emily Carr in a way that reveals not what she painted but what she tried to paint, the vision she staked her life on. We feel that even a line as breath-taking as "When in her side my eyes were but blind seeds" [*And Should She Ask*, l. 10], or a phrase like "the tomb egg broken" [*Love Song for Friday's Child*, l. 12], is merely what fits the poem at that point: brilliant as the imagery is, there is no costume jewellery. A refrain, such as "Stand gentle in my words" in the *Canticle of Darkness*, steadily tightens the tension and concentrates the reader's awareness, where a merely facile refrain would put him to sleep. "Friday's child is loving and giving," and the book shows the upsurge of creative energy that obeys the command of the thunder in *The Waste Land* to give, sympathize, and control. How posterity will sort out and rank the poets of today I do not know, nor much care; but in such poems as *In the Cemetery of the Sun*, the *Canticle of Darkness*, and perhaps the title poem, one may catch a glimpse of the reasons why, in the course of time, what the poet has to say about his culture becomes so important and what everyone else has to say becomes so much less so.

Anne Wilkinson's *The Hangman Ties the Holly* ([Toronto:] Macmillan) is another book of mythical and metaphorical poetry which has many resemblances to *Friday's Child*. The resemblances would be startling to anyone unaware of the highly stylized nature of such poetry. A poem of Mr. Watson's puns on "gone" and Maud Gonne [*Yeats and Maud Gonne*]; a poem of Mrs. Wilkinson's, *Swimming Lesson*, a rather painful poem in spite of its crisp organization of narrative and description, speaks of "A good Seamaritan," "the warm gulf seam of love," and a girl who "did not holy believe." The subject of Mr. Watson's *O My Poor Darling* and of Mrs. Wilkinson's *The Pressure of Night*—very different and very remarkable poems—is the subject of beauty and the beast. Mr. Watson's *The White Bird* and Mrs. Wilkinson's *Dirge* are both based on the Cock Robin nursery rhyme, though Mr. Watson's bird connects with the Ancient Mariner's albatross and Mrs. Wilkinson's with the turtle-dove of marriage. The other nursery rhyme which gives Mr. Watson his title is quoted in Mrs. Wilkinson's *Once upon a Great Holiday*. Mr. Watson's *And Should She Ask* and Mrs. Wilkinson's *I Was Born a Boy* are both riddle-poems based on a conceit of reincarnation, like some of the early Welsh poems. Mrs. Wilkinson holds her own very well against this formidable competition—so well in fact that we must desert the comparative at once for the positive.

Mrs. Wilkinson's most obviously striking quality is a gift for sardonic parody. In brief we have the device of altering a stock phrase, a device that may again owe something to Dylan Thomas. Thus we have "new laid lovers," "a game they know by head," "one of those fly-by-days," and the like. In large we have the parody-poem, in most cases, including the title poem, *Dirge*, and parts of *Christmas Eve*, a folk song or nursery rhyme gone ingeniously sour. Virginia Woolf is described in the imagery of Ariel's sea song:

> From ivory pelvis spring
> Her strange sea changeling children;
> In sockets deep with six lost layers of sight
> The sea fans open.   [*Virginia Woolf*, ll. 5–8]

Not since Leo Kennedy has a Canadian poet done much with the macabre as a theme, but Mrs. Wilkinson is much possessed by death. It would be difficult to put the grotesque futility of our burial customs into fewer syllables than this:

> A miser's grace
> To fill with lead
> The breathing earth
> That gave us bread, [*Miser's Grace*, ll. 9–12]

or to make a more chillingly logical conclusion to the poet's conversation with two young lovers in a park:

> I moved
> To go but death sat down.
> His cunning hand
> Explored my skeleton. [*On a Bench in a Park*, ll. 35–8]

Mrs. Wilkinson sees nature in sharp outlines—it is significant that one of her favourite words is "lens"—and she has a liking for clear colours and conventionalizing forms (*Italian Primitive*). There is also a deeper prophetic sympathy with nature, of the kind that organizes the fine little poem *Tigers Know from Birth*, and flashes out a phrase like

> I put on my body and go forth
> To seek my blood. [*The Red and the Green*, ll. 3–4]

What she emphatically is not is apocalyptic: the death that recurs so often is the guarantee of man's identity with nature: human nature is her metaphor, and she has no use for the religious language that assumes the uniqueness of humanity. Hence what we have is a kind of parody-apocalypse, a union of life and death in nature, and the last image in the book is one of a falling man.

We turn now to the two less formal and more representational poets. In Miriam Waddington's *The Second Silence* ([Toronto:] Ryerson), there are no apocalypses or erudite parodies: just as her metaphors are rooted in her own life, so are her myths in the society around her:

> The wine we drink is bitter
> Compounded of the blood
> Of not one Christ but many
> Who gained no holihood.   [*The Bread We Eat*, ll. 25–8]

The central images of everyone's life are formed in childhood: the child's dream world is the world of the "second silence" in which creation begins. Mrs. Waddington's *Poems of Children* (the poems are arranged according to theme) move in the associative exuberance of the world of childhood, the world where everything is mysteriously linked with everything else. In sharp contrast to the brilliant clear outlines of the two previous poets, Mrs. Waddington's images break up into a kaleidoscopic impressionism:

> ... Lullabies from an old book
> Of apples and nutmegs and peacocks that flew
> Ceaselessly circling a golden sea.
> (It was dream, it was dream,
> Light echoed and keys were lost in the sea.)   [*Night in October*, ll. 9–13]

In adult life this associative world is driven underground into the subconscious, where the imagery of adult dreams, with all its guilt-ridden hauntings, collides or coincides with the outer world. This is the subject of the strikingly original *Morning until Night*:

> ... two black dogs dart out
> Swift as foxes to confound my eyes,
> And all the sudden wolves that had my dreams
> Revolving on fear startle me with their smiles....   [ll. 18–21]

Mrs. Waddington records both aspects of this conflict equally well. In *Poems of Love*, especially *Thou Didst Say Me*, the constant turning of the lover's individuality on its axis, so to speak, is expressed by an intense murmuring of repeated sound, and in *Poems of Work* the squalor that a social worker sees in a modern city is recorded with the kind of sympathy that comes from being emotionally involved in everybody else's fate. In the last section, *Poems of Living*, something of her earlier *Green World* imagery begins to creep back, like blades of grass rooting in pavement, particularly in the final poem, *Inward Look the Trees*, which brings the book to an impressive close. Where she is least successful, the failure is due to intellectual excess, not deficiency, as in the poems to a teacher and a pupil, where there is too much unorganized metrical talk. But she has her own distinctive quality: a gentle intimacy and an unmediated, though by no means naive, contact between herself and her world.

Irving Layton's *The Cold Green Element* ([Toronto:] Contact Press) is also polarized between personal association and a direct reaction to experience, though in a more explosive way than Mrs. Waddington's book. In such poems as *winter fantasy* (his titles are in lower case) and *me, the p.m., and the stars*, there is a subjective rearranging of images, of a kind that was called "surrealism" in the fashionable slang of twenty years back, dream poems a little like Chagall paintings. What many surrealists did not surrealize was that such techniques are of little point without their objective counterpart, the vision of a world which acts in as sex-goaded, as guilt-ridden, as arbitrarily foolish a way as the dream. Mr. Layton's fantasy is not irresponsible or a mere playing with verbal patterns, because the distortions of the poetic imagination are geared to the distortions of society. For this kind of writing a poet needs humour and technical competence, and Mr. Layton appears to have plenty of both. Sometimes the humour becomes sinister and Kafkaesque, as in *the executioner*, and sometimes self-mocking, as in the end of *the poet entertains several ladies*. In *me, the p.m., and the stars*, when the poet is rebuked by the Prime Minister for throwing a snowball through somebody's window, the poet explains that he has met a "sage"—presumably Zarathustra—who has given him a motive for doing so:

> He also said pity was loss of power.
>   Someone had to tell the people
> what was happening; it's indecent to let
> the death of the last god go by unnoticed.   [ll. 45–8]

The objective pole takes the form of social caricature—not satire or invective, for which Mr. Layton has no gift, but the mock-heroic, or, as in the lively *birds at daybreak*, the mock-mythical. In *Golfers* he says:

> And you see at a glance
> among sportsmen they are the metaphysicians,
> intent, untalkative, pursuing Unity . . .

And that no theory of pessimism is complete
which altogether ignores them.... [ll. 7–9, 11–12]

Exactly in the middle between the fantasy poems and the social poems comes the remarkable title poem, an ironic personal myth of the poet as a hanged god or nature spirit torn apart and distributed through the landscape. No quotation can do justice to the intricate unity of the poem, but we can see as soon as we read it that it presents the organizing image of the book. Again we note an odd coincidence: it is the same image as that of the central poem of Mrs. Wilkinson's book, *Carol*.

Of the poems mentioned, *Golfers* belongs to a second volume, *The Blue Propeller* (Contact Press), where there are two or three other poems, including *Portrait* and *Mute in the Wind*, that are witty and sharply pointed. Otherwise much of the book is an obstacle race for the sympathetic reader, a dark tunnel of noisy dullness. *The Cold Green Element* is infinitely better on all counts, and in it there are at least a half-dozen poems (including, besides those mentioned, the lilting *for Naomi* at the beginning) which have a rhythmical swing, an urbane humour and a technical finish guaranteed to make the reader's toes curl up in solid contentment.

II

Louis Dudek's *Europe* ([Toronto:] Laocoön [Contact] Press) is diary poetry: a sequence of ninety-nine short pieces recounting impressions of a trip to Europe, from England through France, Spain, Italy, and Greece, and ending with the discovery that what Europe, a shattered and demoralized civilization, really reveals to the North American is the virtues of his own culture. The century of meditation is a fatal idea for a facile poet, and although at his best Mr. Dudek escapes being merely facile, I find large stretches of the book unrewarding. In the first place, the influence of Pound is oppressive. Pound is everywhere: the rub-a-dub three- and four-accent line, the trick of snapped-up quotations and allusions, the harangues against usura, the toboggan-slide theory of the decline of Europe after the Middle Ages, and so on. In the second place, the conversational style brings the ideas into sharp relief, and the ideas are commonplace, prejudice reinforced by superficial tourism. To be told in rather pedestrian verse that the English are constrained by standards of what is and is not done hardly adds to the variety of one's poetic experience. Things improve however towards the end, where the rhythm firms up and begins to swing and lilt a bit, and where first-hand observation replaces second-hand theorizing. The eighty-first piece, a concise and ironic sketch of a Greek village, is an admirable vignette; and the ninety-fifth, on the sea, achieves the difficult feat of talking beautifully about beauty:

> Beauty is ordered in nature
> > as the wind and sea
> shape each other for pleasure; as the just
> know, who learn of happiness
> > from the report of their own actions.

Raymond Souster's *For What Time Slays* (mimeographed) shows a more distinctive and unified style than any previous collection of his. There are still too many expendable poems, based on a preoccupation with the process of writing, on a substituting of ready-made moralizing for observation and irony, and, most frequently, on an apparently unshakable conviction that the kind of sexual reverie indigenous to male boarding-houses is invariably poetic material. Such signs of immaturity are the result of too slavish an adherence to the conventions of his kind of poetry. In about every tenth poem he escapes these conventions and writes the kind of poem that only he can write. Usually it is an epigram based on observation unified by a single drop of emotional colouring: a type of epigram which for some reason has been more common in Chinese poetry than in our tradition:

> I fear this skull-capped priest.
>
> He tells his viewers
> Someone must have Authority,
>
> And clearly he is thinking of himself.   [*This Skull-Capped Priest*]

Two new series of collections of verse provide some very interesting work in small compass. Emblem Books are tiny little booklets put out by Jay Macpherson with covers by Laurence Hyde. There are three of them to date. Daryl Hine's *Five Poems* is a remarkable first volume, if one can call five poems a volume. Reading his long meditative lines is like watching heavy traffic at night: a brilliant series of phrases moves across a mysteriously dark background, the central driving force of the poem remaining elusive. It sounds condescending to speak of promise and a future, yet the sense of powerful gathering forces is stronger than any other reaction. The main line of development is probably indicated in such passages as this, from a dialogue of Theseus and the Minotaur (the Minotaur is speaking):

> I am Charon, and I wait
> beside this lightless river for my gold;
> my boat is paper; I am cold;
> the winds upon the water celebrate
>
> the soul's long shadow and the heart's
> red beacon; I perceive
> the wormy lover wearing on his sleeve
> funerals foreshadowed by his art. . . .
>
> [*A Glass House for Fallen Women*, ll. 47–54]

Jay Macpherson's *O Earth Return* is almost exactly the opposite in technique, using stanza forms, usually quatrains, with expertly varied timing, and with an interest in myth that classes her with the formal poets. The title indicates a Blakean influence, which is discernible, but the tradition is rather that of the Elizabethan lyric, where—as in Campion—the use of a mythical or conventional theme releases the emotion by detaching it from direct experience and containing it within the convention. Thus a poem that might seem at first glance to be only an allusive literary exercise becomes a kind of reservoir of feeling in which one's literary and personal associations mingle and are held in the kind of variable emotional contemplation that it is one of the primary functions of poetry to provide:

> Where is your god, Sibylla? where is he
> Who came in other days
> To lay his bright head on your knee
> And learn the secrets of Earth's ways?
>
> Silence: the bat-clogged cave
> Lacks breath to sigh.
> Sibylla, hung between earth and sky,
> Sways with the wind in her pendant grave.   [*Sibylla*, ll. 5–12]

There are fewer surprises in the third Emblem Book, Dorothy Livesay's *New Poems*, where the main impression is of a disciplined and experienced handling of modern poetic idioms. A sense of a lonely pessimism, of the shutting off of communication, of the inevitable victories of winter and darkness, gives the poems a plaintively muted quality: they seem to struggle against a conviction that they cannot say much:

> And deeper than flash
> Of fin in well
> Your thoughts dot, dash—
> But never tell.
>
> O when will you freeze
> Glassy, clear
> Frost-breathing image
> On polished air? [*Winter Song*, ll. 13–20]

{The same sense of accomplishment rather than mastery is present in the second Fiddlehead Poetry Book, G.V. Downes's *Lost Diver*. Slow monosyllables, and the kind of run-on line that pulls the rhythm around so that it moves out from a centre instead of pulsating, build up an introspective resonance which is consistently in good taste, but does not excite or give the sense of prefigured future developments. Thus:

> Minos' child
> a careless captive of the long day's gold
> she reached for the moon's bright platter, and her wild
> strong glittering young dolphins leapt and rolled
> to wallow lazy in the scrollèd sea. [*Minoan Room, Ashmolean*, ll. 5–9]

The last poem, *The Poet Is Discontent*, may promise a change of pace in her next volume, if not self-transformation.

There are seven Ryerson Chapbooks. Thecla Bradshaw's *Mobiles* is a lively little book. I have some prejudice against poems about poetry, but Miss Bradshaw talks about the place of the poet in society, his personal difficulties, and the technical problems of imagery in a machine age, with sparkling and sophisticated wit:

Letters in Canada: Poetry 149

>   Could you more easily endure this sprinkling of Chinese glass
>   if you knew that the colour, red, is casual blood;
>   that the scarlet is the shattered clittering, cluttering of warsmashed years?
>   [*These Space-Defying, Illustrated Jackets*, ll. 33–5]

Alfred Purdy's *Pressed on Sand* also has wit, and considerable expertise in metre, especially in quatrains with a final short line. *Seasonal Malady* reads like an ironic rewriting of Carman's *Make Me Over, Mother April*; *Onomatopoeic People*, on Indian names, succeeds where many poems on such subjects have failed, and *For the Record* is, except for a weak penultimate line, an admirably sinister little epigram. I like best, however, *Meander*, where the poet "would like to be a dirty, unkempt, old man" and protests that there is much poetry to be found in the experiences of such a life:

>   But someone has to write about the Indian dock
>   At Rupert, the dreamlike murmuring
>   Of lonesome waterclosets in a deserted hotel.   [ll. 14–16]

Myrtle Reynolds Adams' *Remember Together* deals mainly with the poetry of organic processes: there is some careful rhyming in *Hungry Mouths*, and *Hired Boy*, which I think is her best poem, sets an appealing human figure against her landscape. *Silver Light*, by Theresa E. and Don W. Thomson, is chiefly notable for *Tempest*, a vigorous poem about a global storm from the North Pole, the basis of a CBC radio play. Goodridge MacDonald's *Compass Reading* contains a series of colourful impressionistic sketches ranging from Ellesmere Land to Bermuda, and one philosophical poem, *Dialogue*, in which God tells his worshipper, like Ahab in *Moby-Dick*, that his right worship is defiance. Sutherland Groom's *Queens and Others* takes its title from poems on Elizabeth I and Lady Jane Grey, but most of the poems are on Biblical subjects. *Halfway to Emmaus* is a dialogue in a ponderous Victorian idiom, with some curious turns of diction. Robert Rogers' *The White Monument* also has religious poems and some based on war experiences: the central theme is thus the contrast between the life of God and the death of man. This comes into focus in a prophetic poem called *Omega*, a sonnet with the final couplet:

>   When all who really mattered had been killed
>   The meek took up the seats the mighty filled.

Pleasant Bay combines anapests with an alternation of feminine and masculine endings, in the manner of Roberts' *Tantramar Revisited*.

I.B. Ezra's *The Legend of the Four* (Philadelphia: Dorrance) provides stories, lyrics, and humour in cheerful doggerel verse. Arthur Bourinot's *Ten Narrative Poems* (privately printed) is a collection of his longer pieces. I like them best when, as in *Paul Bunyan*, the short line catches up the rhythmical elements in the syntax, with an occasional rhyme dropped in, or when, as in *The Indian*, an elegiac repetition gives some emotional unity to the poem. Eugenie Perry's *Green Timbers* ([Toronto:] Ryerson) is held together by some conversational liveliness in the style and some concreteness in vocabulary. The first section is entitled *Trees Are Such Lovely Things*, and one is pleasantly surprised, after preparing for the drivelling worst, to find the texture stiffening with a genuine interest in language:

> The slides shiver and straighten in the projector.
> The monitors force twin rainbows of water
> Against the placer bed, into the yawning sluice;
> Where the gravel hurdles the riffles,
> The tailings vanish in spray,
> And the residue is gold.   [*Where Gold Occurs*, ll. 5–10]

Possibly Pratt is an influence here: if so it is a healthy influence. There is also a great variety of subject, from historical and biographical sketches to reflective poems such as *Woman—What Do You Find?* which well evokes the dithers of a middle-class housewife with intellectual interests.}

This survey was originally bibliographical as well as critical, and it may well be thought that a review which mentions twenty-three separate items can have only a bibliographical interest. There is perhaps some point in explaining the critical principle. The ideal reader often visualized by founders of little mags, who is eager to read contemporary poetry but has no ambition to write it, barely exists. Practically everybody who habitually reads poetry habitually writes it as well. That is as it should be: there are many things wrong with the position of the poet in modern society, but this is not one of the wrong things. The cultivated amateur is the backbone of all the arts, especially poetry, as the professional poet who lives by his verse is usually a writer of newspaper doggerel. Criticism concerned primarily with measuring the distance between amateur verse and great poetry is essential, but there will never be any lack of it. Meanwhile, what with an indifferent public, the conscientiously contemptuous critics, and perhaps his own frustrated ambitions, the amateur poet has a hard time of it. Yet in Canada, where there is no sharp line between the regular and the occasional poet, it seems more appropriate to look at a year's output inclusively, as a total power of articulation, shading from a luminous centre to a pleasantly blurred periphery.

In every year in Canada, including 1955, most of the published verse shows the features of occasional amateur writing. Lines will be pumped up with adjectives; rhymes in a sonnet will clang like a typewriter bell; stodgy rhythms will be harried into movement by starting every line with a heavy accent; a sentence will begin in poetry and finish in vague prose; a failure in accurate expression will be concealed by an exclamation, and so on and so on. These faults also occur even in the best poetry, and many of the virtues of the best poetry reappear in the slighter books. Hence while much Canadian verse could be honestly described, by the highest standards of the best twentieth-century poets, as metrical doodling, it could also be described, just as honestly and perhaps more usefully, as the poetic conversation of cultivated people. After all, there are many who will read detective stories with pleasure even when they have the style of a riveting machine, the characterization of a tombstone, and the plot of a charade: perhaps poetry too might be approached with some tolerance for the convention as well as evaluation for the achievement.

7. 1956

April 1957

From University of Toronto Quarterly, *26 (April 1957): 296–311. Partially reprinted in* BG, *44–57. Material on Layton reprinted in* Irving Layton: The Poet and His Critics, *ed. Seymour Mayne (Toronto: McGraw-Hill Ryerson, 1978), 56–7.*

Poetry cannot be written by an act of will, and society cannot produce poets by an act of will. There is a strong desire in Canada to have fine poetry written in the country, but the will of society, as expressed in education, can be directed only towards building up a cultivated public for poetry, a public which would be able to recognize fine poetry if it saw it. Otherwise generous words about welcoming new poets will be accompanied by complaints that all the poets who have appeared so far are too "modern," and do not sound like poetry as the reader remembers it to have been when he stopped listening to it in grade 6. Young people should certainly be encouraged to write, for everyone can learn to write poetry up to a point—the point of discovering how difficult it is to write it unusually well. To get to that point is no mean achievement, as it is well past the substandard level of naive or doggerel verse which is the usual mode of amateur expression. But the main purpose of such encouragement is to breed a love of poetry, not to breed poets.

First Flowering ([Toronto:] Kingswood House), edited by Anthony Frisch, is a collection of poetry and prose in both languages written by young people (twelve to nineteen) in high schools all across Canada. Mr. Frisch has received warm praise, which he assuredly deserves, for the skill and energy with which he has carried out his task. The importance of what he has done is very considerable, though we should realize that the importance is educational and not literary in reference. The book is not an anthology of the Canadian writers of tomorrow: it is evidence of intelligence and cultivated taste among Canadian teenagers. I imagine that a comparable cross-section of any other age level in Canada would produce much the same literary result, though of course with less freshness and charm. I understand that Mr. Frisch is now busy with a similar anthology taken from an older professional group, which will do much to confirm or refute me on this point. Of the poems in *First Flowering*, we recognize all the familar conventions of poetry on that level. There is the nostalgic poem, the realistic poem, the didactic poem, the parody or comic poem, the poem of observed or remembered beauty, and so on. Here and there something less predictable emerges, as in Charles R. Eisener's delightful *The Planets*. But there is no reason to suppose that any of the contributors are about to start out on the lonely, uphill, flinty road of the professional poet. If there were any such, the book, for them, would be better entitled First Deflowering.

{Much the same reflections are generated by *New Voices*, subtitled "Canadian Writing of 1956" ([Toronto:] Dent), and selected by a committee of five. Here we meet for the most part the same conventions that we found in *First Flowering*, although they are handled with greater sophistication. The poems by Heather Spears and David Blostein's vision of *The Last Supper in King Edward Park* are perhaps the best in this category, except C.M. Chadwick's careful study of children watching a wounded sea-gull, where we have poetry which is as good as poetry can be before it crosses the boundary between cultivated poetic speech and specialized poetic expression. Two other contributors, Jay Macpherson and Daryl Hine, have already crossed it.

A much more deeply committed set of poets is to be found in *Poets 56* (Toronto: Contact Press), a mimeographed collection of the work of ten young writers (under thirty), most of them likely to devote a good deal of their future time and energy to writing. They are practising the particular conventions of contemporary poetry that they feel most at home with. Thus Avi Boxer works in the convention of abrupt or violent images set against an urban theme. He sees the traffic lights "hemorrhaging over the rain-wet asphalt" and comes home to a "gangrened banister"; places a stallion against a "tree-javelined sky" and "winds like fire-frightened pythons"; ridicules a pious friend who "takes the church to bed like an enormous nursing bottle," and appropriates jokes out of *Finnegans Wake* and parodies out of *Ulysses*. No poem is completely successful; none is without interest. Marya Fiamengo practises the convention of the decorative poem. There are reminiscences of a Yugoslavian background, with Moslem and Byzantine references; a poem on fabulous birds, a poem on queens and dwarfs, and the background is brilliant with lapis lazuli and peacocks with "feathered candelabra." William Fournier has a lively satire on Montreal financiers which uses a polysyllabic jargon appropriate to its theme. John Reeves and Peter Scott write with intelligence and fluency, though what they write I find less interesting; George Whipple is experimental, and shows an affinity with cummings which goes farther than the typographical appearance of his poems. As with cummings, the process of writing the poem becomes a part of the poem itself:

> aphonic, quote
> alliterative quiet. . . .

The last one, on a jazz saxophonist, is easiest to read without getting distracted by the cleverness of the devices. D.G. Jones contributes eleven carefully worked out lyrics: the rhythm and melody of *At Twilight in the*

Park is well sustained, and so is the conclusion of *Birches at R.M.C.*:

> They are an abstract of organic growth,
> The curve of an affair with wind and snow,
> The curve of a resistance to transparent time,
> Of earth's most candid passion for the sun.

Mortimer Schiff's meditative *Bird Nest with Young* also maintains a high level of intensity, and *Delia*, though more uneven, is still full of interest.

Daryl Hine's *Four Fabulary Satires* are free fantasies on well-known fables, as original in theme and treatment as anything that has appeared this year. His idiom is, in his own phrase, "as cerebral as Hades," and sometimes the reader simply has to pick up what he can of the meaning while a current of rhythm and sound flows by him. But his writing, however dense, carries its own authority. The second satire, based on *The Twa Corbies*, and like it an allegory of squalid vision, is the one that seems to me the best integrated; it concludes:

> O monuments of man's incomprehension!
> O permanent cadences of tales of August!
> The muse has carried off your blind bald knight
> to dive for refuse in her sluggish river;
> and the falcon rises in perpendicular flight
> like clever indications of a fever.

Jay Macpherson, the only completely articulate poet of the group, contributes some deceptively simple light verse: there is a lilting seventeenth-century-like melody in praise of a blue silk dress, a macabre epitaph on *The Gardeners* spoken by a complacently fertile corpse, and another epitaph on a dog:

> Lap-head led a dog's life: came when called,
> And often when not: would beg for smiles;
> At unkind treatment shrank appalled:
> Buried approval against colder whiles.
>
> But times are altered:
> None is left to scold,
> Nor comfort Lap-head
> Where he lies cold.

The sense of a fully realized maturity comes, not from the stricter character of her metres and rhymes, but from the skill and variety with which those metres and rhymes are handled. She is rather better represented in *New Voices* and in the first issue of *Tamarack Review*, and the three groups together make up perhaps as impressive a body of verse as was produced by anyone in Canada during 1956.

II

The usual place to look for the kind of poetry that we have described as the poetic conversation of cultivated people is in the Ryerson Chapbooks, of which there are five this year. One seldom finds any substandard writing in them, and they usually present an accomplished and fluent handling of late Romantic idioms deriving from the generation of Bliss Carman. In these conventions there are two main themes. One is the theme of the beauty of nature, producing descriptive poetry in which the poet is a kind of scarab of beauty, rolling all his strength and sweetness up into a ball; the other is a more sombre and moralizing theme of the transience of life, a theme handled less frequently but usually with more conviction. Nostalgia provides the motor energy of such poetry, and nostalgia expresses itself more clearly when it is alone with its own frustration than when it thinks it has found an objective correlative.

In Ruby Nichols' *Symphony* both themes are combined in the somewhat over-ambitious title poem, but the second theme gives a deeper eloquence to a sonnet on *Solitude*, and *Symphony* is also at its best in the same minor key:

> Knows only that it lives and hopes forever;
> Bows to the dust, and rises to the sun;
> Is Judas and the Christ, the thief and the giver,
> Defeated and triumphant, many and one.

In Freda Newton Bunner's *Orphan and Other Poems* there is fluent moralizing verse with some touches of humour, and in Marion Kathleen Henry's *Centaurs of the Wind*, along with some expendable "scented loveliness," there is again a more successful sombreness in *As Brown Birds*. Lenore Pratt's *Birch Light* is again mainly about natural beauty recollected in tranquillity, but is stiffened with a good deal of detailed knowledge about nature, and again the water-colour landscapes are most interesting when a modulation of mood brings up a darker tone than the prevailing placidity:

> We followed her
> Until our straining eyes could tell no longer
> The birch bark sails from a drift of foam.
> All the great ships in the world have vanished so
> To some last watcher.

Fred Cogswell's *The Haloed Tree* shows much the most interesting mind of the five, besides having the advantage of being written mainly in the more astringent, or dry Martini, tone. The opening poem, *Death Watch*, has a precision appropriate to its subject, but not matched in any of the other chapbooks:

> No thought or act of mine can twist
> The fate that ticks upon my wrist;
> Its sixty seconds deeper prod
> My body's stake towards the sod,
> And every pause becomes to me
> An ominous eternity.

The other poems do not quite meet this level, but contain a good deal of sharply etched epigrammatic writing. The shortest poems are usually the best, as a metaphysical conceit requires a shift of gear after a very few lines to avoid labouring. But *Two Fears* makes its point very neatly, and the assonance in the first stanza of *The Seed I Sowed* is delicate and skilful.

Hi, Sister, Hi Brother! ([Toronto:] New Frontiers), by Joe Wallace, a Communist poet, looks at first like naive verse, but a second glance indicates that a skilful and astute versifier is only pretending to write naive verse. There is a poem on Dr. Bethune, epigrams, ballads, and a rather striking poem on Burns, all of it fluent, some sharp and penetrating. Connoisseurs of irony will be interested to learn that the following poem called *Hungary* appeared in Canada in 1956:

> No more behind forbidden walls
> A secret blossom blows
> Its sacred incense hidden from
> The proletarian nose.

Letters in Canada: Poetry   157

> All walls are down, or open wide,
> And everything that grows
> Is there to seek and there to share
> And those who love her well may wear
> All Hungary as a rose.

The Serpent Ink ([Toronto:] Contact Press), by Henry Moscovitch, clearly a "first flowering," is a little tentative in grammar and no definite rhythmical patterns have yet established themselves, but all the poems in the book have a reason for existing: even when one feels that the poet has missed the point there has always been a point to miss. The images have a latent humour in them as well as intelligence, but the poet is too sincere to allow them to become wisecracks, and *Caught Fish* and *The Flight of the Crow* sustain a mood of genuine pathos as well as wit. From the *Introduction*, which catches the trochaic rhythm of the Introduction to Blake's *Songs of Innocence* and applies it to the world of experience, to the last poem, with its dog racing "to bite a bleeding Sun at the end of our journey," one feels that all the structural materials of poetry are continuously present.

Gael Turnbull's *Bjarni* ([Ashland, Mass.:] Origin Press) consists chiefly of adaptations of themes from the Icelandic Sagas, in unusual free-verse forms. It comes under the general heading of literary exercise, but in some poems at the end there are vivid phrases which have more in them than the shock of retrospection:

> The patience of the bricklayer
> is assumed in the dream of the architect.

Again, Beatrice Sforza in Piero's picture appears

> as obvious and secret
> as a peak on the horizon.

Contact Press is beginning a publishing venture well worth public support (not that their other ventures are not also worth it; the address is 28 Mayfield Avenue, Toronto): a mimeographed series of selections from French Canadian poets, with the original poem on one page and a poetic translation opposite. There are two volumes so far, one of Gilles Henault and the other of St.-Denys Garneau, and the translations are by Jean

Beaupré and Gael Turnbull. The translations are extremely close to the originals in rhythm as well as in meaning. The same press has also mimeographed a selection of early poems by W.W. Eustace Ross, partly in an effort to establish a tradition for the type of current poetry it is mainly concerned with. *Experiment 1923–29* brings to our attention "the first important modern Canadian poet writing in English." Whether the fact that he was influenced by Marianne Moore rather than by "Eliot, Yeats and others" really makes him less colonial than the contributors to *New Provinces*, as the editor suggests, at any rate most of the poems are straight Romantic lyrics, and very pleasant ones. *Spring Song* has a typographical break which gives it the effect of a two-part song, and in *Lions* a dissociation of language gives the poem a transparent childlike quality, as often in Gertrude Stein.}

Three Windows West, by Dick Diespecker ([Toronto:] Dent & Sons), is a strange mixture. Some of it is verse journalism of a type crisply described by W.H. Auden, in one of the better passages of *Under Which Lyre*, as designed "For recitation by the yard / In filibusters" [ll. 107–8]. A poem called *Prayer for Victory* was, the preface tells us, read to a million people in New York by Raymond Massey; it sold 35,000 copies on Canadian newsstands and 200,000 more copies were distributed by a bank during a Victory Loan drive; it has reached an estimated total of over half a billion people:

> Then, Dear God
> Make us worthy of Victory.
> Give us the strength
> To keep our pledges
> To make a better world ...
> So that never again
> Will there be a Hitler or a Mussolini,
> A Himmler or a Goebbels;
> Never again a blitzkrieg;
> Never again the bitter treachery
> Of Pearl Harbour ...

It is easier to turn on the mechanism of a conditioned reflex than to shut it off, and Mr. Diespecker has not escaped the fate of the sorcerer's apprentice. The sense of his formidable captive audience has given him a fatal fluency, which he employs in alternately addressing Dear God

Letters in Canada: Poetry 159

and summoning memories of the ol' swimmin' hole type:

> Betcha Mom's in the kitchen right this minute
> Making punkin pie.

If this were all his book contained, there would be no occasion for mentioning it in this survey. But here and there one finds, if not always genuine poetry, at least a genuine effort to write it, and a poem called *Return to Labour*, which would be good anywhere, is, in this context, shockingly good. The opening poem, with a South African setting, is also, in spite of a persistent misspelling of "its" and a somewhat discouraging first line ("A bok-ma-kerri scolds the lagging stars"), both honest and attractive. It is a disturbing thought that the writing of such stuff as *Prayer for Victory* and its congeners may have required the self-destruction of an authentic poet.

The Poetry of E.J. Pratt, by John Sutherland ([Toronto:] Ryerson), is one of the few pieces of sustained Canadian criticism that I have read slowly, marking passages with a pencil. Pratt is a genuinely popular poet, and hence a difficult subject for criticism: most of his readers read him for other values, and for many of the remainder, a poet with all those editions, honorary degrees, and medals (one could almost call him a gong-tormented poet) is too obfuscated by another kind of recognition. Mr. Sutherland's book is of importance, not only because it takes Pratt seriously, but because it takes poetry seriously, and accepts Pratt as a genuine and valid kind of poetic experience. It is important also as the only major work of a critic whose premature death has deprived the country of one of its most selfless and dedicated literary citizens.

Much of what he says about the relation of man to nature in Pratt, the ambivalence of Pratt's moral attitudes, and the point of identity between the slayer and the slain in his heroic narratives, is both new and sound. The symbolic expansion of Pratt's characters into Christian archetypes may not please every Pratt reader: granted the premises of this type of criticism, he does not falsify Pratt's meaning, but he does give the impression of straining his text. The reason for this may be that he seems to assume that Pratt is a poet who, through his background and also through some inner bent in poetry itself, absorbed a great deal of Christian symbolism more unconsciously than deliberately. I imagine that Christianity means something quite as positive to the poet as it does to his critic, and something rather more mature and complex. I feel that Mr. Sutherland misinterprets *The Truant*, which is the central poem in the Pratt canon as far as belief is concerned: the "great Panjandrum" in that poem is not God, and the attitude of the man to him is not "secular," otherwise he could hardly swear allegiance to the "rood" in the last line. But with these minor reservations the book is a fine and eloquent study, as worthy of its author as it is of its subject.

III

The editor of *The Selected Poems*, by Raymond Souster ([Toronto:] Contact Press), is Louis Dudek, and he has done a good job, perhaps intended, as the rather odd title suggests, to be definitive. Mr. Souster is revealed as a most prolific poet: ten collections of his work are in existence, of which I have seen only six, and the selections from the four I have not seen have given me a quite new idea of him. Mr. Souster is a genuine poet whose qualities are subtlety and humour, but he often spoils his subtlety with repetition and his humour with moralizing. Mr. Dudek's introduction approves of the moralist, but his critical taste does not, and his selection disentangles Mr. Souster's genuine poems from the straggly excelsior packed around them in the original collections. Subtlety and humour are also the qualities needed for epigram, and epigram is the genre to which the poet has, wisely, devoted himself. The effects of his epigrams are made chiefly by theme: verbal wit and metrical dexterity, the normal characteristics of epigram, are both rare. Occasionally there is a punch line, either conventionally at the end (*The Bourgeois Child*) or at the beginning, as in the study of the *Drummer Man* which flows easily out of its fine opening, "Sooner or later he was bound to put his sticks by." Mr. Dudek quotes Whitman on the "perfect candor" to which the poet is entitled,[9] but the essential, or creative, candour in Mr. Souster is that of the candid camera. For in the main his method is photographic, a sharply focused observation of life in the *fourmillante cité*, and his moralizing is akin to the photographer's sentimental caption.

There are still a few captions, but there is also a respectable body of serious and subtle verse. I like very much the snapshot of *Girls Playing Softball*:

> But it doesn't quite come off.
> The voices are a little too high, the ball
> Never seems to behave properly, the bats
> Heavy and awkward.

Letters in Canada: Poetry

There is a study of *Nice People*, in which a poet

> Sits gravely in the back kitchen, arguing with the negro maid
> (Almost an intellectual herself) the pros and cons
> Of sterilizing the family cat now curled in the centre of the floor.

There are some sombre but admirable hospital scenes, and *Old Man Leaning on a Fence* and *Bridge over the Don* catch another big-city vignette: the gloomy stare into darkness which seems to mean only a vacant mind but actually means that the will to live is ebbing:

> Haven't you seen
> The river before, don't you know it runs, smells like a sewer?

And there are some poems that are just good fun, like *The Opener* and the poem which concludes the book, *Flight of the Roller Coaster*.

In this kind of poetry all freshness and novelty come from the choice of subject: the whole creative energy is expended in looking for appropriate scenes and getting them into focus. Reflection and comment are left to habit, and habit produces only the commonplace: in Mr. Souster's poetry it produces mainly grousing. Mr. Dudek's poetry is a contrast in subject-matter, but the same general principle holds. Mr. Dudek is introverted and emotional: what takes fresh and novel shape in his poetry is a sensuous reaction. In *The Transparent Sea* ([Toronto:] Contact Press), a retrospective collection, the best pieces are songs conveying an immediate mood, such as the one beginning "A bird who sits over my door"; or studies in the movement and sound of words, like *Tree in a Snowstorm*; or ideas that suddenly twist round into paradoxes, like the admirable opening poem on the pineal gland, or his comparison of the universe to a watch which makes religion a search "for larger regions of clockwise justice"; or quick vivid sketches like *Late Winter* or *Lines for a Bamboo Stick*, the latter with an Oriental reference; or a study of swift movement, like his picture of a little girl skipping called *The Child*.

One of his favourite adjectives is "wet," and some of his best poems have the quality of the wet water-colour that is done quickly and makes its point all at once. Sometimes an image strikes him in a grotesque form, as in the astonishingly successful *Mouths*; sometimes as a muttering and brooding anxiety, as in the near-prose fantasy *The Dead*. One often feels that a poem is inconclusive, but then one often feels too that the inconclusiveness is part of the effect, as it is in a sketch. An example is one of the few photographic poems, *To an Unknown in a Restaurant*. In such poetry the ideas or comments have to be equally unpremeditated. When they are, they break out with the oracular tone appropriate to ideas that are not hooked on to others:

> What we call nature is nothing else than
> the triumph of life other than our own—

In short, I feel that when the poet says

> The world I see (this poem)
> I make out of the fragments of my pain
> and out of the pleasures of my trembling senses

he is telling us the exact truth about his poetic process.

It follows that he is working against his best qualities when he writes in a sequence, whether of description or thought. Here he is dependent on habit, and produces the clichés of habit. In the *Provincetown* sequence there is the same kind of maunderlust that filled so much of *Europe*. Sexual imagery is also a trap for him, for sex is something he feels self-conscious and explanatory about. At other times he is not satisfied with inconclusiveness, and some of the poems sag into platitude in an effort to round off, as in *On Sudden Death* and elsewhere. Yet, as the examples above have made clear, there is much to be grateful for in Mr. Dudek's book, and a great variety of pleasant and melodious writing.

Phyllis Webb's *Even Your Right Eye* ([Toronto:] McClelland & Stewart) in the Indian File series, is contemporary in technique: one senses Marianne Moore and Wallace Stevens respectively in a pair of poems called *Poetry* and *In Situ*, though of course this may be general idiom rather than actual derivation. But it is not the technique but the combination of decorative elegance in the diction and melancholy in the mood that marks her affinities. Such poems as *Standing* and *Double Entendre* are almost a kind of verbal embroidery, making one wonder about the role of the typewriter carriage in the twentieth-century poetic process, or, as she says:

> shapes fall in a torrent of design
> and over the violent space
> assume a convention. . . .

Letters in Canada: Poetry 163

The attitude which corresponds to such diction is one of amused detachment. She has a talent, not fully exploited, for sophisticated light verse, and the concluding *Earth Descending*, which appeared in *Trio* two years ago and is like an adult version of the *Planets* poem in *First Flowering*, is still perhaps her best single poem. But the general principle holds that her most sharply realized writing comes in moods of doubt, loneliness, and unhappiness. When such writing occurs, the reader feels that he is no longer listening in on an educated monologue, but being directly spoken to:

> where does it dwell, that virtuous land
> where one can die without a second birth?

There are some uncertainties in the style. Strained is the syntax in "sensed is the green grape pulse" and *Sprouts the Bitter Grain*, and the latter poem, for all its eloquence, has not quite sifted the allegorical ash from the metaphorical flame. On the other hand, *The Second Hand* seems to me successful all through, and *Sacrament of Spring*, based on an April-is-the-cruellest-month theme, is something more than successful, with its haunting refrain and its line "The flower and the whip are wed." *Incidental*, with its admirable final couplet, is brief enough to quote in full:

> In that indelible year
> when the soldiers came
> and the dogs and harpies visited churches
> the creatures of my infant dreams
> rose up in agony and fear
> and splayed the air with foetal screams
> and left the year uncompromised.
>
> The year then knew its form and fled
> into the cities of the dead.

A Window on the North, by R.A.D. Ford ([Toronto:] Ryerson), is the work of a poet who has been in the diplomatic service in Brazil and in Russia. The poems include two translated from Brazilian poets, one, *Confidences of an Itabirano*, being a remarkable poem which makes one wish for more such translations. Six poems are translated or adapted from modern Russian poets. Four of them are from Sergei Yessenin, who, like Mayakovsky, committed suicide in the early years of the Communist regime. The implied contrast in imagery between the brilliant and turbulent South and the grey mechanized North enters the Canadian poems too, and is brought into focus in the long concluding poem, *Luis Medias Pontual in Red Square*. This poem depicts the hollow ache in the soul of a disillusioned Spanish refugee in Moscow, who notes that Russia and Spain have both been touched by the Orient, and are alien to both East and West.

I have seldom read a book of poems so uniformly bleak and desolate in their imagery, yet bleakness, especially to a reader brought up in Canada, is a very appealing imaginative mood. Mr. Ford is in the tradition of Carman, Campbell, D.C. Scott, and others who have communicated the sense of the lonely winter afternoons, the struggling sun, the lynx and wolf lurking in the black woods, the long white expanses of fields, and the resulting fear in the mind of the beholder who feels, so to speak, spiritually responsible for the landscape, stretching as it does "to the Arctic ends of the earth." It is essential that the mind should set itself against such a world, otherwise the world will move in and reduce the mind to its own level of merciless terror and death. This has already happened in a grim poem called *Roadside near Moscow*, where the poet sees, but dares not look too closely at:

> the almost human-like
> Column of prisoners, waiting for the snow
> To fill in their tracks.

His favourite pattern is an extension of his South-and-North imagery, the contrast between the brilliant reds and yellows of autumn and the black and white winter. The symbol of the hunter, pursuing death in his red coat across the stubble fields, seems to reflect the world of the middle twentieth century, fading from its past heritage into its future dispossession. Sometimes a symbolism of fertile valley and bare hill is used instead, with the same meaning. In *A Delusion of Reference* the "delusion" is an instant of pattern or design, perceived a moment before "the universe / Settles into its usual disarray." Mr. Ford's style is lucid and sober, qualities especially valuable in translators: it can be dull but is thoughtful and not sloppy, and his cosmopolitan influences and settings give his book unusual claims on our attention.

Leonard Cohen's *Let Us Compare Mythologies* (McGill Poetry Series;

[Toronto:] Contact Press) is the first in a series of books featuring McGill poets, which we owe, as we owe so much, to the generous enthusiasm of Louis Dudek. The poems are of very unequal merit, but the book as a whole is a remarkable production. The erotic poems follow the usual convention of stacking up thighs like a Rockette chorus line, and for them Mr. Cohen's own phrase, "obligations, the formalities of passion," is comment enough. But it is an excess of energy rather than a deficiency of it that is his main technical obstacle. Sometimes moods and images get tangled up with each other and fail to come through to the reader, or allusions to books or paintings distract the attention and muffle the climax, as in *Jingle*. In short, this book has the normal characteristics of a good first volume.

To come to his positive qualities, his chief interest, as indicated in his title, is mythopoeic. The mythologies are Jewish, Christian, and Hellenistic. The Christian myth is seen as an extension of the Jewish one, its central hanged god in the tradition of the martyred Jew ("Saviors"), and Hellenism is the alien society which Christianity has come to terms with and Judaism has not. The mythical patterns of the Bible provide some of the paradigms of his imagery:

> The sun is tangled
>   in black branches
> raving like Absalom
>   between sky and water,
> struggling through the dark terebinth
> to commit its daily suicide.

Other mythical figures, such as the femme fatale at the centre of *Letter*, *Story*, and *Song of Patience*, and the dying god of *Elegy*, are of white-goddess and golden-bough provenance. Mr. Cohen's outstanding poetic quality, so far, is a gift for macabre ballad reminding one of Auden, but thoroughly original, in which the chronicles of tabloids are celebrated in the limpid rhythms of folk song. The grisly *Halloween Poem*, with its muttering prose glosses, is perhaps the most striking of these, but there is also a fine mythopoeic *Ballad* beginning "My lady was found mutilated," which starts with a loose free verse idiom and at the end suddenly concentrates into quatrains. The song beginning *My Lover Peterson* is simpler but equally effective, and so is another disturbing news item called *Warning*. In *Lovers* he achieves the improbable feat of making a fine dry sardonic ballad out of the theme of a pogrom. No other Canadian poet known to me is doing anything like this, and I hope to see more of it—from Mr. Cohen, that is.

The year 1956 is certainly Irving Layton's year, as far as English Canadian poetry is concerned. Three collections of his work have appeared. *The Improved Binoculars* ([Highlands, N.C.:] Jonathan Williams) is a selection of his poems, mainly from the collections of the last three years, with an introduction by William Carlos Williams. Dr. Williams writes with commendable enthusiasm, and I find only his epithet "backwoodsman" difficult—perhaps that is how Montreal looks from the perspective of Paterson, N.J. The collection is strongly recommended to those who are becoming curious about this poet, and who have missed the individual volumes from which it has been made. This is also the third year that Mr. Layton has issued two books of verse, one containing most of his more serious poems, the other devoted chiefly to expressions of his poetic personality. The latter group comprise *The Long Pea-Shooter*, *The Blue Propeller*, and now *Music on a Kazoo* ([Toronto:] Contact Press). Mr. Layton's poetic personality is entertaining enough, but is altogether a more stereotyped and predictable character than the actual poet. *Music on a Kazoo* is chiefly remarkable for *The Dwarf*, a Kafkaesque murder trial which brings out such evidence as this:

> The manufacturer excused
> himself, saying he had loved her, that he was
> not a sentimental philistine but a poet: he
> had provided the money.

There is perhaps nothing of major importance in *The Bull Calf and Other Poems* (Contact Press), at least nothing with the excitement of the title poem of *The Cold Green Element* or the better poems in *In the Midst of My Fever*. But there are some excellent poems, which emphasize the growing serenity and precision in Mr. Layton's best work and his power of telling the whole disinterested imaginative truth about his subject, free of both querulousness and posing. These are qualities which the more self-advertising poems give little hint of. Mr. Layton has spoken of the influence of D.H. Lawrence, and there are certainly signs of that influence. There is the same sacramental conception of sex in *The Dark Nest*, *Sacrament by the Water*, and elsewhere, and the same ability to humanize the animal world in the title poem (about a newborn bull calf killed because he is unprofitable), and in a poem about a mosquito

> with a queer sort
> of dignity clinging to its inert legs.

There may be some Lawrence, too, in his sacrificial symbolism, which enters the bull calf poem and crops up elsewhere, as in a poem about chokecherries where the caterpillar-ridden leaves are a sacrifice for the cherries. But he has, for one thing, a sense of ethical reality that Lawrence lacked. He notes the "stale melodrama of guilt" in the brooding resentments of the inner mind; he notes the curious parody of self-sacrifice which will make a man deliberately undercut himself in order to maintain his good opinion of himself; he notes the alliance of morality and desire in sexual relations when he advises a seducer to make a wife feel that she is lying with her husband. This shrewd insight into the self-satisfactions of evil brings him closer to Kafka, even to Eliot, particularly in an extraordinary "hollow men" poem called *Letter from a Straw Man* and another called *Halos at Lac Marie Louise*, where the skilful use of assonance-rhyme indicates an unobtrusive mastery of technique:

> It was a white skeleton
>   Of a tree ominously gnarled;
> And around the singular crow
> The stark crows whirled.

In short, Mr. Layton appears to be gathering together the powers and range of what is certainly the most considerable Canadian poet of his generation, and may soon become something more.

8. 1957

July 1958

From University of Toronto Quarterly, *27 (July 1958): 434–50. Partially reprinted in* BG, *70–87.*

This is an unusually thin year: one good book, two promising ones, and a miscellaneous assortment of what the Elizabethans might politely have called a paradise of dainty devices, though it would be more accurate to speak of an amusement park of rhythmical gadgets. Some of these latter are pleasant and readable enough: with others, one is strongly tempted to take the plangent tone of a couplet which appears on the opening page of one of the year's few published volumes:

> Last of the mighty oaks nurtured in freedom!
> Brambles and briars now supersede treedom.

However, here goes. The good book, of course, as the Governor-General's committee has this time recognized, is Jay Macpherson's *The Boatman* ([Toronto:] Oxford).[10] The book itself is one of the few physically attractive objects on my Canadian poetry shelves, and the fact is an appropriate tribute to its contents, for *The Boatman* is the most carefully planned and unified book of poems that has yet appeared in these surveys. It is divided into six parts. The first, *Poor Child*, contains poems that appeared in a small pamphlet reviewed here some years ago:[11] they form a series of tentative explorations of poetic experience, ranging in tone from the macabre *The Ill Wind* to the plaintive *The Third Eye*. The next two sections are called *O Earth Return* and *The Plowman in Darkness*. The titles come from two poems of Blake that deal with "Earth" as the whole of fallen nature in female form, and the subjects are chiefly the more common mythical figures connected with this "Earth," including Eve, Eurynome, the Cumaean Sibyl, Mary Magdalene, and the bride of the Song of Songs, identified with the Queen of Sheba. Hence the subtitle, *A Speculum for Fallen Women*. The two parts are, like Blake's lyrics, matched by contrast against each other, the relation often being marked by identical titles. The contrast is not so much Blake's innocence and experience, though related to it, as a contrast between a theme idealized by a kind of aesthetic distance and the same theme made colloquial and familiar. *Sibylla*, whose fate is described in the motto to Eliot's *The Waste Land*, appears in *O Earth Return* thus:

> Silence: the bat-clogged cave
> Lacks breath to sigh.
> Sibylla, hung between earth and sky,
> Sways with the wind in her pendant grave   [ll. 9–12]

and in *The Plowman in Darkness* thus:

Letters in Canada: Poetry   169

> I'm mercifully rid of youth,
> No callers plague me ever:
> I'm virtuous, I tell the truth—
> And you can see I'm clever!   [ll. 17–20]

In the last two sections the corresponding male figures appear. *The Sleepers*, intensely pastoral in tone, is focused on Endymion and his moon-loved daze, with overtones of Adonis and Adam. Then the figures of Noah and his ark emerge, expanding until they become identified with God and his creation respectively. The creation is inside its creator, and the ark similarly attempts to explain to Noah, in a series of epigrams in double quatrains, that it is really inside him, as Eve was once inside Adam:

> When the four quarters shall
> Turn in and make one whole,
> Then I who wall your body,
> Which is to me a soul,
>
> Shall swim circled by you
> And cradled on your tide,
> Who was not even, not ever,
> Taken from your side.   [*Ark Overwhelmed*]

As the ark expands into the flooded world, the body of the Biblical leviathan, and the order of nature, the design of the whole book begins to take shape. *The Boatman* begins with a poem called *Ordinary People in the Last Days*, a wistful poem about an apocalypse that happens to everyone except the poet, and ends with a vision of a *Fisherman* who, more enterprising than Eliot's gloomy and luckless shore-sitter,[12] catches "myriad forms," eats them, drinks the lake they are in, and is caught in his turn by God.

Such myths as the flood and the apocalypse appear less for religious than for poetic reasons: the book moves from a "poor child" at the centre of a hostile and mysterious world to an adult child who has regained the paradisal innocent vision and is at the circumference of a world of identical forms. In the title poem the reader is urged to follow this process as best he may:

> Then you take the tender creature
> —You remember, that's the reader—
> And you pull him through his navel inside out.   [ll. 10–12]

The wonderland of this Noah's ark inside Noah, where the phoenix and the abominable snowman have equal rights with books and eggs and the sun and moon, is explored in the final section: *The Fisherman: A Book of Riddles*. The riddles are not difficult, the solutions being thoughtfully provided in the title, and, like so many of the Anglo-Saxon riddles, they are circumferential rather than simply elliptical descriptions, hence the riddle on *Egg* symbolizes the poet's relation to her reader as well:

> Reader, in your hand you hold
> A silver case, a box of gold.
> I have no door, however small,
> Unless you pierce my tender wall.
> And there's no skill in healing then
> Shall ever make me whole again.
> Show pity, Reader, for my plight:
> Let be, or else consume me quite.

Miss Macpherson chooses strict metres and small frames: she is, as the blurb says, melodious, but her melody is of that shaped and epigrammatic quality which in music is called tune. Within her self-imposed limits there is an extraordinary tonal variety, from the delicate *ritardando* of *The Caverned Woman* to the punning *knittelvers* of *The Boatman*, and from the whispered *pianissimo* of *Aiaia* (the island of Circe) to the alliterative thundering of *Storm*. She can—a noticeable feat in Canada—write a sexual poem without breaking into adolescent pimples and cackles; she can deal with religious themes without making any reed-organ wheezes about the dilemma of modern man; she has a wit and an erudition that are free of wisecracks and pedantry; she can modulate in eight lines from "Philomel's unmeasured grief" to the human jay who

> Chatters, gabbles, all the day,
> Raises both Cain and Babel.   [*While Philomel's unmeasured grief*..., ll. 7–8]

The elegiac poems are the most resonant, and they make the strongest initial impression, though the lighter ones have equal staying power.

Letters in Canada: Poetry

There are few dying falls: usually a poem ends with a quiet authority that has a ring of finality about it, leaving the reader nothing to do but accept the poem—"Reader, take," as the riddle on *Book* says.

There is little use looking for bad lines or lapses in taste: *The Boatman* is completely successful within the conventions it adopts, and anyone dissatisfied with the book must quarrel with the conventions. Among these are the use of a great variety of echoes, some of them direct quotations from other poems, and an interest in myth, both Biblical and Classical, that may make some readers wonder uneasily if they should not be reading it with a mythological handbook.

One should notice in the first place that the echoes are almost invariably from the simplest and most popular types of poetry. They include Elizabethan lyrics (*While Philomel's unmeasured grief* sounds like the opening of a madrigal); the lyrics of Blake; hymns (*Take not that Spirit from me*); Anglo-Saxon riddles; Christmas carols (*The Natural Mother*); nursery rhymes (*Sheba*); ballads and newspaper verse (*Mary of Egypt* and the second *Sibylla*). The use made of these echoes is to create a kind of timeless style, in which everything from the tags of medieval ballad to modern slang can fit. One has a sense of rereading as well as reading, of meeting new poems with a recognition that is integrally and specifically linked with the rest of one's poetic experience. The echoes also enable the poet to achieve the most transparent simplicity of diction. There is little of the "density" of more intellectualized poetry, and ambiguities and ironies are carried very lightly:

> In a far-off former time
> And a green and gentle clime,
> Mamma was a lively lass,
> Liked to watch the tall ships pass,
> Loved to hear the sailors sing
> Of sun and wind and voyaging,
> Felt a wild desire to be
> On the bleak and unplowed sea.   [*Mary of Egypt*, ll. 5–12]

The flat conventional phrases here, including the Homeric tag in the last line, would seem commonplace or affected if their context had not been so skilfully worked out for them. It is true that for many readers there is nothing so baffling as simplicity, but Miss Macpherson's simplicity is uncompromising.

As for mythology, that is one of poetry's indispensable languages: most of the major English poets, including the best poets of today, demand and expect a considerable knowledge of myth, and although Douglas LePan calls Canada a country without a mythology,[13] the same thing is increasingly true even of Canadian poets. Miss Macpherson's myths, like her allusions, flow into the poems: the poems do not point to them. Knowing who Adam and Eve and Noah are will get one through most of the book, and although a glance at the opening page of Robert Graves's Penguin book on Greek myth might help with Eurynome,[14] I find no poem that has the key to its meaning outside itself.

> Oh wake him not until he please,
> Lest he should rise to weep:
> For flocks and birds and streams and trees
> Are golden in his silver sleep.   [*The Sleeping Shepherd*, ll. 5–8]

For thousands of years poetry has been ringing the changes on a sleeper whom it is dangerous to waken, and the myths of Endymion, of the bridegroom in the Song of Songs, of Adam, of Blake's Albion, of Joyce's Finnegan, are a few of the by-products. Such myths in the background enrich the suggestiveness of the above four lines, but the lines are not dependent on the echoes, either for their meaning or for their poetic value. Or again:

> The woman meanwhile sits apart and weaves
> Red rosy garlands to dress her joy and fear.
> But all to no purpose; for petals and leaves
> Fall everlastingly, and the small swords stand clear.   [*The Martyrs*, ll. 9–12]

The reader who remembers his Milton, however vaguely, will see how the fall of sex from love to lust belongs in a complex which includes the first efforts at clothing, the appearance of thorns on the rose, the coming of winter after fall, the angelic swords over Paradise, and the aggressive use of sex which the phallic image of "small swords" suggests. But none of this would have any point if the quatrain itself did not carry its own meaning.

I have glanced at the critical issues raised by *The Boatman* because it seems to me a conspicuous example of a tendency that I have seen growing since I began this survey eight years ago. With the proviso that "professional" in this context has nothing to do with earning a living, the younger Canadian poets have become steadily more professional in the last few years, more concerned with poetry as a craft with its own traditions and discipline. The babble of unshaped free verse and the obscurities of private association are inseparable from amateurish poetry, but they are emphatically not "modern" qualities: serious modern poets in Canada struggle hard for clarity of expression and tightness of structure. The second volumes of Douglas LePan, P.K. Page, and James Reaney (of whom more next year) show this markedly, as do the first volumes of Wilfred Watson and Anne Wilkinson, and all the volumes of Irving Layton since *In the Midst of My Fever*. It is consistent with this that the more amateurish approach which tries to write up emotional experiences as they arise in life or memory has given way to an emphasis on the formal elements of poetry, on myth, metaphor, symbol, image, even metrics. The development is precisely parallel to the development in Canadian painting from deliberately naive landscape to abstraction and concentration on pictorial form. As in 1890 with the Scott-Lampman-Roberts group, and again in the *New Provinces* generation, there seems to be once more in Canadian poetry, on a much bigger scale, a "school" in its proper sense of a number of poets united only by a common respect for poetry.

The title of Daryl Hine's *The Carnal and the Crane* (McGill Poetry Series, n.p.) comes from a ballad in which two birds (carnal in this context means *corneille*, crow) discuss the Incarnation. The *double entendre* in the word "carnal" suggests the theme of the dialogue of soul and body as well, and in connection with "crane" one very astute critic, Mr. Milton Wilson, has murmured the name of Hart Crane.[15] Abandoning speculation, we find *The Carnal and the Crane* also a carefully planned book, leading up to and moving away from a central poem called *The Return from Unlikeness*, a group of three dialogues on the Nativity. I take it that "unlikeness" is here used in its Augustinian sense of remoteness from God, by way of the conclusion of Auden's *For the Time Being*, so that a return from it, which the Incarnation makes possible, would be the achieving of a total identity, a universal homecoming in which everyone, including Judas Iscariot, goes to his own place.

We begin with the three kings, representing the three aspects of wisdom: wonder, trust in love, and distrust of unaided reason, confronting Herod. Herod agrees on the importance of finding

> ... the silent centre of private wars
> of blindmen who can't imagine all the stars.   [pt. 1, ll. 75–6]

But for himself he himself occupies that centre and cannot move out: in other words he is spiritual pride, the demonic centre in Everyman whose vision is despair. The second part deals with the shepherds, who by a most ingenious modulation are identified with the Corydon and Alexis of Virgil's *Second Eclogue*. Virgil is traditionally a prophet of the Incarnation, but it is a very different eclogue that has made him so. Corydon and Alexis are also associated with Cain and Abel, destructive passion and its shepherd victim, and with the warning "armed head" of the witches' vision in *Macbeth*, which we remember was followed by a bloody child and a crowned one. The third dialogue deals with the Annunciation and the jealousy of Joseph. Against the invisible appearance of the Child is set the collapse of earthly power, symbolized by the recent assassination of Caesar, a theme developed later in a fine series of sonnets called *At Pompey's Statua*.

The climax of the book is a series of three poems, of which the first two concern a "fat boy," a poet, seen first from the outside by his friends who bury him, and then from the inside as an unconscious denizen of Eden. The poet dies

> declaring that the universe was tandem,
> not single, quod erat demonstrandum.
>
> [*An Apology for the Burial of the Fat Boy*, ll. 20–1]

Tandem means among other things fallen, and we hear a great deal about the "January apple," the twisting of love into lust, the fatality of the "father," and similar *topoi*. Mr. Hine's fallen world is an underworld of death and rebirth, many of its features derived from the sixth book of the *Aeneid*. It is associated with autumn and winter, the hunting season and "The air grown perilous with falconry," when Orion, the hunter and the winter constellation, lover of Aurora and type of cyclical rebirth opposed to the dialectic of resurrection, presides over both love and death. It is the world of *Avernus*, where Aeneas, in one of the most eloquent poems in the book, wanders talking to the shadow of the silent Dido, and where sex is represented by the wound of Adonis. It is a world full of ferocious birds and beasts of prey, a "flood of animals" like those Dante fled from, including the wolf who "is time," and which in the aggregate are Cerberus, the watchdog of death, whom the friends of the fat boy assume to have swallowed him. We reach this world by being ferried over the Styx by Charon, who also haunted Mr. Hine's earlier *Five Poems*. But a more

Letters in Canada: Poetry 175

concentrated look shows that Avernus is really a water-world *under* the Styx, the world that has never recovered from the deluge. In *The Boat* and *The Lake* (a frozen lake, modulating the water symbol to ice) this water-world expands into what Mr. D.G. Jones, of whom more in a moment, calls the more frequented and practical pool of Narcissus.[16]

This world, then, *is* the pool of Narcissus: what goes on in it is the dreamy reflection of reality into which Adam fell, the hypnotized imitation of life by the ego. Marriage, for instance (see *Epithalamium*, one of the most equivocal poems in that genre I have ever read), introduces lovers to an Elysium which is the reflection of Eden, but full of serpents and bitter fruits. What the flood did the fire shall overthrow, and the redemption of this world by Christ is usually symbolized by fire, the fiery furnace and the burning bush that burn without destroying, and in which reflections find their own true forms: "Lent's end in Easter, water's in ice that shone."

There are great inequalities in the success with which Mr. Hine expresses all this. *The Return from Unlikeness* seems to me a poetic exercise, not a realized poem, and I have no hesitation in calling *The Entombment* a positively bad poem, because no mediocre poet can be positively bad. I doubt if any Canadian poet has potentially greater talents than Mr. Hine, and few in recent years have struck out more vivid and haunting lines, lines that can become part of one's permanent reading. As we eavesdrop on the murmuring dialogues going on in the poet's mind, every so often a voice speaks, like Friar Bacon's head, with oracular simplicity and power. But these lines are often embedded, like Jack Horner's plums, in a context of rather soggy verbiage. Thus:

> ... hero turns
> to Christmas Eve where Southwell's infant burns—
> heat as continence! fire as innocence!
> and the offended eye goes dark in marvels,
> while the heart asks of its thorns
> the sort of alchemy that transfigures peril.   [*Poem for Palm Sunday*, ll. 12–17]

The reference to Southwell's *Burning Babe* is creaky but passable; the next line is a fine comment on it; the third line is superb; the fourth and fifth are blither. One still, in speaking of *The Carnal and the Crane*, has to speak of expendable poems, of great advance, of promise and future achievement. These are not, to be sure, small things to speak of.

It is disturbing to find that, after the "fat boy" poems have reached some kind of synthesis, the final poem, *The Farewell*, is still musclebound and squirming, and one feels the truth of the poet's remark:

> Only gargoyles leaning out of dogma,
> elements of doubt in faith's alloy,
> deny the gravitation of belief,
> defy the forts and pass the last frontiers. [*The Gift*, ll. 19–22]

But it is not the gravitation of belief that is the difficulty of using religion as metaphors for poetry: it is rather (apart, of course, from the superficial temptation to easy resonance) the rigidity of the construct from which the gargoyles lean. Christianity is held together by doctrine, compelling the poet to the struggle of digesting abstractions. One feels that the decentralized mythology in Miss Macpherson (to whom *The Carnal and the Crane* is dedicated) at any rate permits of a more relaxed and spontaneous poetic process. However, that is a technical obstacle only, and one that Mr. Hine is well equipped to surmount. More important, the modern religious poet is apt to confuse inspiration with a state of grace, and feel that it is safer to renounce the full authority of poetry and keep ironically swimming around with all us other poor fish. See Eliot and Auden, more or less *passim*. *Facilis descensus Averno*, and Mr. Hine clearly has no interest in being facile. He has a grotesque wit, of a kind that takes the stock example of vulgarity, the replica of the Venus of Milo with a clock in her stomach, and expands it into "Venus big with time," and we may look forward to a poetry of released powers and flying gargoyles.

D.G. Jones's *Frost on the Sun* ([Toronto:] Contact Press) shows a talent of considerable force emerging from some undistinguished competence. There are a few rather laboured conceits, like *Public Figure*, *Death of a Hornet*, and *Clothesline*; the rare allusions to myth, in striking contrast to the two previous poets, are not made with much conviction, and an occasional flash of wit, like the description of a *Faculty Party* as "a matter of oral adventure," does not always prevent a poem from sagging into commonplace. These peripheral points noted, what remains is for the most part an intensely pictorial poetry, with reference to Marin, Klee, Hokusai, and the Chinese, the favourite subject being birds, which Canadian poetry seems to be strongly for this year. "Do poems too have backbones?" the poet asks in a poem called *John Marin*, and he clearly

Letters in Canada: Poetry

knows the answer. In *A Problem of Space* he speaks of the power that a poem, like a picture, can gain by sketching in the essentials only, "Leaving all the rest to space." Poetry of course has the problem of rhythm in addition to that of pattern, and I think Mr. Jones succeeds most completely in his economical and disinterested ambitions when he is less preoccupied with visual design and lets his rhythm work itself out. In *Request* and *Soliloquy* a lilting variable rhythm sustains itself to the end— a notable achievement in free verse, which is so apt to cripple itself by cutting off its feet, like the dancer in Andersen's fairy tale.[17] In *The Phoebe* the rhythm follows the fluttering movements of the bird, and in *The Time of the Fictitious "I"* it follows the subject:

> Sometimes we are shattered. The
>   coherence gone, the planets of our brain
>   sail loosely in their microcosmic air.
> Sometimes we can
>   pick up nothing, start nothing;
>   poise lost, stance lost,
>   neither in the wind nor out of it
> we must wait, on choppy seas,
>   till the wind turn,
>   till the moon come round,
> and wind and tide, again, draw on.

To write like this a poet has to be indifferent to his own cleverness, and achieve the kind of higher detachment in which genuine sympathy and insight become possible. There are deeper tones in the book, in *Desire Is Not Lust*, in *Strange Characters for Christmas*, in *At Twilight in the Park*, which make one hope that eventually such words as serenity and wisdom may be appropriate for this poet. *Strange Characters for Christmas* has a fine haunting phrase about "the silent bleeding of small human lives," and is written in quatrains in which the first and third lines rhyme and the second and fourth do not, giving the effect of a precise twist:

> And remember now the falling night
> And the years of the darkening Lord of Love
> And the illusive April of Platonic Light
> And the fiery winter of mechanic power. [ll. 9–12]

At Twilight in the Park shows that it is possible to be delicate without being sentimental, and *November, Gananoque*, despite a bad line or two, that it is possible to make something out of ugliness and boredom—no poet in this century can avoid that technical problem—without being cute.

Alfred W. Purdy's *Emu, Remember!* (Fredericton: Fiddlehead Poetry Books) is conversational lyrical verse, less formally precise than his earlier work. It is quite skilful in the use of slant rhymes in *Poem* and *Elegy for a Grandfather*, if more hampered by stock phrases of the "forest of always Sunday" type. The tone is strongly personal, as the poet tends to see nature as a wilderness of self-reflecting mirrors, whether it presents "halls of trembling glass" on shipboard or "vectors of light" at sunrise. In this situation one is in danger of going backward into the pure narcissism of nostalgia. The poet's distrust of this is marked in the phrase:

> ... time is a wound
> Delivered when new things can't strike flame
> [*News Item: "Ice-boats nearly extinct in eastern Canada,"* ll. 4–5]

and in the self-discoveries of *Cantos* and *Contraband*. The forward direction is the subject of two of the best poems, *Post Script* and *The Cave Painters*. The cave painters, we are told:

> Having discovered an ache in the loins,
> A clarity of colour, shores beyond their shores,
> Become inhabitants of loneliness and applicants
> To leave the mind-prison, be dissolved
> In the myth's creation and absorbed.   [ll. 27–31]

We may assume that this indicates the direction that Mr. Purdy's future writing will take, perhaps in fiction, as the biographical note suggests, where he will have a chance to recapture the more objective and dramatic qualities of his earlier work that are largely missing from this collection.

Three Dozen Poems, by R.G. Everson (Montreal: Cambridge Press), illustrated by Colin Haworth, with drawings "done with lamp black and a dry hog's hair brush," is amateur verse at its best—limited in its objectives, amused and amusing, unfailingly urbane, and with the primary aim of being pleasant to a reader. All the poems are brief epigrams in a cultivated speech in which life and literature meet on equal terms. Thus a vision of *Lovers under Parliament Hill*, ending with the reflection that "lovers possess the world while overthrown," suggests Themistocles and Landor by contrast. Sometimes the wit increases to brilliance:

> In a dark house that they passed
> A telephone hunted with magical empty sounds,
>
> [*Winter Evening after the Theatre*, ll. 7–8]

the context of this being a crowd leaving a theatre after a performance of *The Tempest*. More deeply disturbing tones than this do occur, as in *Comical Sun*, but they are rare. There is a conventional but nicely turned irony in *Coming Home in Winter* and *The Fishermen*, and vigorously sketched imagery in *Late-August Breeze*:

> A belly-low wolf breeze
> pursued a thistledown whose untied hair
> and white face curved above the cattle-bellowing
> lawn chairs. The leaves like fishes
> turned death-white undersides. We later found
> nothing was hurt except the feel of Summer.   [ll. 4–9]

{There are eight Ryerson chapbooks this year, which is perhaps a few too many. I find little to say about *Myth and Monument*, by Theresa E. and Don W. Thomson: the title poem seems to be founded on a West Coast Indian legend, but not much of a story gets told. *Of Diverse Things*, by Mary Elizabeth Bayer, has two poems in a dialect I don't recognize, though it seems consistent and well sustained; there is an appealing simplicity in *Remember*, and touches of a greater breadth of vision in *Song of the Stranger*. Joan Finnigan's *Through the Glass, Darkly* deals mainly with ironies inherent in the sexual relationship. Her observation comes out in bits and pieces, and one wishes that English had more of the capacity of Oriental languages for isolating the core of a poetic experience. *The Substitute*, for example, has over thirty lines which merely paraphrase the first two:

> I did not love him,
> But the grass was there.

The Arrow-Maker's Daughter and Other Haida Chants, by Hermia Harris Fraser, contains a number of poems that have been around for quite a while, but are still very arresting. The title poem is an extraordinary *mélange* of the tragic, the ghostly, and the ironic. We can hardly get too much of this kind of thing: in spite of the complete cultural break between Indian and white culture, there are affinities among poets in the same environment that cannot be argued about, and I think Indian poetry can still do much to shape the imagination of Canadian poets. Fred Cogswell's *Testament of Cresseid* is a modernization of Henryson's fifteenth-century poem, which tells how Cressida was punished for her infidelity by the God of Love with leprosy, became a beggar, and received alms from Troilus, who did not recognize her at the time. The poem is a melodrama, not high tragedy, and it is a parish church to Chaucer's cathedral, providing a simple moral issue for readers baffled by the sombre complexities of Chaucer's gigantic poem. Mr. Cogswell does a good job of preserving the archaic feeling while removing the difficulties of Middle Scots.

Dazzle, by Dorothy Roberts is, I think, the best of the eight chapbooks. *Cold* brings Canadian pioneer life into a brilliant focus: the physical energy and toughness, the strenuous distrust of comfort, the sense of the healthiness of a low temperature that permits no relaxation, and the Puritanism which expresses all this in religion, are there, but something more is there too: the imaginative power of containing opposites which is one of the things we read poetry for:

> They lived in cold
> And were seasoned by it and preached it
> And knew that it blazed
> In the burning bush of antiquity
> With starry flowers.   [*Cold*, ll. 13–17]

She is not always as successful as this, but it is still a remarkable mind that has not quite fused the imagery in:

> We on the turnpike going fast see signs
> Two miles before the act—obey, obey
> As in the land of the Bible.   [*Turnpike*, ll. 1–3]

The Farm is full of wit, ending with a vision of "The broken horses with their bits of gold"; *Veranda Spinsters* well evokes the sense of the inscrutability of the commonplace; *Old Japanese Prints* has the accuracy of observation that the subject suggests, and ends with a most perceptive comment:

> The figures follow the centuries in a simple order,
> There are changes enough from within when the trees flower.

Elizabeth Brewster's *Roads and Other Poems* is partly meditative like the earlier *East Coast*, and partly in the narrative and fictional idiom of *Lillooet*. The present collection lacks the freshness of the earlier books: the poems are written with intelligence and discipline, but remain derivative—that is, self-derivative. Of the narratives, *Canon Bradley* has the most distinctive outline, and there are some well-turned epigrams in double quatrains:

> The medalled heroes die,
> The shouting millions pass,
> And on their sunken graves there grows
> The mute, tenacious grass.   [*Only the subtle things*, ll. 5–8]

There is nothing wrong with this, but there is not the sense of immediate emotional awareness that marked the best passages of *East Coast*.

Goodridge MacDonald's *Recent Poems* show a sophisticated intelligence and a good deal of wit, occasionally strained. His settings are mainly urban, and his technique is well adapted to the sense of myriad glitterings from hard shiny surfaces that is the chief visual effect of a modern city:

> Ribbons of river, fragment of estuary, miniature
> channel; splintered steel, and mirror shard.   [*From the Lookout*, ll. 4–5]

The sense of the identity of the organic and the mechanical is another aspect of the urban nightmare that comes out in *Tree Sculpture*, *Sacrament*, and in the very precise conclusion of *Proclamation of a Plant*:

> foiled lips wither and waste;
> green tongues tumble, innocent of word.

Two other Ryerson books are in harder covers; I don't know why. Harry Amoss's *Churchill and Other Poems* is mainly doggerel about teaching, with a sympathetic eye for children which makes *Two Prison Camps* almost a poem. Gordon LeClaire's *Carpenter's Apprentice and Other Poems* has a lot of doggerel too, of a more sophisticated kind. There are some sonnets with obtrusive rhymes and jammed-up metres, and a poem about a Hawaiian lover contracting leprosy, which could have been poignant but gets smothered in pretentious writing. The best poems are brief epigrams with some sharp simplicity of phrasing, such as *Paradox*, part of *Song after Sleet*, and, the best in the book, *Nostalgia*, which turns on an ingenious conceit:

> Her grief had run full circle
>   while she yearned
> back toward the past; a bead
>   of saltfire burned
> along her cheek. Prisoned within
>   its opal light,
> the ghost of Sodom's pillar
>   glimmered white.

Two new magazines of verse have appeared, both quarterlies issued in Montreal. *Yes* is edited by Glen Siebrasse and others; *Delta* by Louis Dudek. The addresses are respectively 5616 McAlear Ave., Côte-St-Luc, Montreal 29, and 1143 Sixth Avenue, Montreal 19; yearly subscriptions of both, $1.00 a year. It must be the influence of the soap companies that prescribes the convention of a single word for the title of a poetry magazine: I wonder what would happen to one called Poems on Several Occasions. Both carry names familiar to readers of these pages, along with younger and less-known ones. Canadian poetry magazines have the dilemma of either imposing what seems a small-minded protective tariff on Canadian writing, or running the risk of becoming a dumping ground for otherwise unpublishable American stuff. This dilemma is most strongly marked in *Fiddlehead*, which has been going longer than the others. My own editorial experience, for what it is worth, has convinced me that there is something to be said for the protective tariff, however indefensible in theory.}

The other publications of the year are retrospective. *The Blasted Pine: An Anthology of Satire, Invective and Disrespectful Verse* ([Toronto:]

Macmillan) is edited by F.R. Scott and A.J.M. Smith. It is no surprise to readers of Canadian poetry that so unusually large a proportion of it should be satire and light verse. Canada's place on the revolutionary sidelines of the United States, and its status as a small nation between huge empires, determined that bent in our genius long ago. But still it took very expert scholarship and critical judgment to produce a book like this, which not only features such regular satirists as McLachlan, Glendinning, O'Grady, Leacock, and Hiebert, and such largely satiric poets of our day as Birney, Louis MacKay, Souster, Layton, Dudek, and Klein, but also isolates a most lively element from Pratt, Lampman, Wilson MacDonald, and many others, including of course the two editors. A few non-Canadian poems are included, notably Samuel Butler's *A Psalm of Montreal*. Some questions suggest themselves. Are there no satiric folk songs? No poetic wits born of political controversy in the newspapers, especially in the previous century? Why is the religious satire exclusively Protestant: don't Canadian Catholics ever laugh at themselves? Is it editorial predilection or Canadian poetry that admits so little right-wing satire? Where is Pamela Vining Yule, that engaging discovery of the first edition of Mr. Smith's anthology? Meanwhile the book we have is delightful.

The Eye of the Needle ([Toronto:] Contact Press) is a collection of F.R. Scott's "satires, sorties and sundries," i.e., the light verse of one of our best light verse writers. There are a few new poems, but the majority are well known to readers of Canadian poetry. It is good to have them together. Many of them were inspired by the Depression and allied events, and, appearing now in the full tide of the capitalist counterreformation, with the political principles they support obviously heading for the limbo that swallows all political principle on this continent, they have an oddly desperate air. But they are not, as the poet himself notes, out of date: rather they remind us of all the things that we are zealously trying to forget: unemployment, exploitation, social and cultural snobbery, the unscrupulousness of the press, the middle-class hypocrisy that asserts that only striking workers are being selfish, the helplessness of the intellectual, and the fact that most of the guardians of our destinies are exactly as stupid and ill-informed as they appear to be.

Dorothy Livesay is a poet who has remained within a single convention, though with modulations. *Selected Poems 1926–1956* ([Toronto:] Ryerson) is a retrospective exhibition of Miss Livesay's five volumes of verse, with an introduction by Professor Pacey. The book is really her collected poems, with some omissions: I do not know, for example, why the epilogue to *The Outriders* is simply called *Epilogue*. Miss Livesay is an imagist who started off, in *Green Pitcher* (1929), in the Amy Lowell idiom:

> I remember long veils of green rain
> Feathered like the shawl of my grandmother—
> Green from the half-green of the spring trees
> Waving in the valley. [*Green Rain*, ll. 1–4]

The virtues of this idiom are not those of sharp observation and precise rhythm that the imagists thought they were producing: its virtues are those of gentle reverie and a relaxed circling movement. With *Day and Night* (1944) a social passion begins to fuse the diction, tighten the rhythm, and concentrate the imagery:

> Day and night rising and falling
> Night and day shift gears and slip rattling
> Down the runway, shot into storerooms
> Where only eyes and a notebook remember
> The record of evil, the sum of commitments. [*Day and Night*, ll. 31–5]

From *Prelude for Spring* on, the original imagist texture gradually returns, and is fully re-established by the end of the book:

> I dream of California, never seen:
> Gold globes of oranges, lantern lemons,
> Grapefruit moving in slow moons,
> Saucers of roundness
> Catapulting colour. [*Genii*, ll. 4–8]

Imagism tends to descriptive or landscape poetry, on which the moods of the poet are projected, either directly or by contrast. The basis of Miss Livesay's imagery is the association between winter and the human death-impulse and between spring and the human capacity for life. Cutting across this is the irony of the fact that spring tends to obliterate the memory of winter, whereas human beings enjoying love and peace retain an uneasy sense of the horrors of hatred and war. That man cannot and should not forget his dark past as easily as nature I take to be the theme of *London Revisited*, and it is expressed more explicitly in *Of Mourners*:

Not on the lovely body of the world
But on man's building heart, his shaping soul.
Mourn, with me, the intolerant, hater of sun:
Child's mind maimed before he learns to run.

The dangers of imagism are facility and slackness, and one reads through this book with mixed feelings. But it is one of the few rewards of writing poetry that the poet takes his ranking from his best work. Miss Livesay's most distinctive quality, I think, is her power of observing how other people observe, especially children. Too often her own observation goes out of focus, making the love poems elusive and the descriptive ones prolix, but in the gentle humour of *The Traveller*, in *The Child Looks Out*, in *On Seeing*, in the nursery-rhyme rhythm of *Abracadabra*, and in many other places, we can see what Professor Pacey means by "a voice we delight to hear."

The Selected Poems of Marjorie Pickthall ([Toronto:] McClelland & Stewart) has an introduction by Dr. Lorne Pierce. The introduction is written with much sympathy, but tends to confirm the usual view of this poet as a diaphanous late Romantic whose tradition died with her. "With Marjorie Pickthall the old poetic tradition in Canada may be said to have come to its foreordained end. It came to its end at Victoria College. With a young student, E.J. Pratt, who borrowed books from the Library where Marjorie Pickthall was assistant, the new tradition began." Dr. Pierce knows far more about Marjorie Pickthall than I do, but still I have some reservations about this. She died at thirty-nine: if Yeats had died at the same age, in 1904, we should have had an overwhelming impression of the end of a road to Miltown that we now realize would have been pretty inadequate. Marjorie Pickthall was, of course, no Yeats, but her Biblical-Oriental pastiches were not so unlike the kind of thing that Ezra Pound was producing at about the same time, and there are many signs of undeveloped possibilities in this book. For some reason I had not read her little play, *The Wood Carver's Wife*, before, and I expected to find it Celtic twilight with a lot of early Yeats in it. It turned out to be a violent, almost brutal melodrama with a lot of Browning in it. Also, it is an example of a very common type of critical fallacy which ascribes to vagueness in her theoretical grasp of religion what is really, at worst, second-hand Swinburne, and, at best, the requirements of her genre. When she writes of Père Lalemant she is subtle and elusive, not because her religion was fuzzy, but because she was writing lyric; when Pratt writes of Brébeuf he is dry and hard, not because his religion is dogmatic, but because he is writing narrative. Anyway, I think she handed rather more over to Pratt, besides library books, than simply her own resignation.

9. 1958

July 1959

From University of Toronto Quarterly, *28 (July 1959): 345–65. Partially reprinted in* BG, *87–107. Material on Layton reprinted in* Irving Layton: The Poet and His Critics, *ed. Seymour Mayne (Toronto: McGraw-Hill Ryerson, 1978), 62–4.*

James Reaney's *A Suit of Nettles* ([Toronto:] Macmillan) is a series of twelve pastoral eclogues, one for each month of the year, modelled on Spenser's *Shepherd's Calendar*. The speakers are geese, and the tone is that of satire: there is a prelude addressed to the muse of satire. The themes are also reminiscent of Spenser: we have love songs (February), elegies (June and October), singing-matches (April and August), dialogues (January and July), fables (March), fabliaux (May), and a *danse macabre* (December). We begin in January with a Yeatsian dialogue between two geese, Mopsus and Branwell, in which the former, after making a fine caricature of the contrast between sacred and profane love, advocates forsaking both Elijah and Jezebel and adopting a calm rational view of the world, as white and sterile as the winter landscape. Branwell however protests that he wants "offspring summerson autumnman wintersage," and so the theme of fertility and sterility, the main theme of the poem, is announced. Sterility is symbolized in May by two lady experts in contraception who insist on tying up their husbands in "sheets of tight / Glass, beaten gold, cork, rubber, netting, stoppers, sand," but who get pregnant in spite of it. In July it is represented by a progressive education maniac, with his hatred for mental order and for the learning habits that build it up. August introduces a third emasculate, a literary critic who has mastered the easy trick of giving the illusion of raising his standards by limiting his sympathies. The theme of fertility appears in the two spring songs of April, with a contrast of white-goddess and sleeping-beauty myths. The names of the singers, Raymond and Valancy, suggest an oblique commentary on the symbolism of two earlier Canadian poets, Knister and Isabella Crawford.

The first experience awaiting Branwell as he plunges into the cycle of the year is to be crossed in love, an experience that produces the melancholy songs of June and October, and is apparently the reason for his wearing a suit of nettles, which seems to represent life in the world of Eros or natural love, a mixture of stimulation and discomfort. At the end of the year is Christmas, to which the geese are ruthlessly sacrificed: this approaching debacle hangs over the whole book, and gives it a larger human dimension. One can hardly call this allegory, as no one expects such a poem to be an uncomplicated story about geese. A religious theme is developed through the March fable, indicating that religion, like art and love, is a weapon of consciousness against death. This theme comes into focus in November, where, after three birds sing of the natural cycle from the perspective of winter, spring, and autumn respectively, Mopsus, the rationalist of January, introduces the symbolism of Christmas, which has to go here in view of the theme of the December eclogue:

> At the winter sunstill some say
> He dared be born; on darkest day
> A babe of seven hours
> He crushed the four proud and great directions
> Into the four corners of his small cradle.
> He made it what time of year he pleased, changed
> Snow into grass and gave to all such powers.   [ll. 46–52]

The climax of the book comes in the extraordinary firework show of September, a description of *Mome Fair*. In Spenser mome means bumpkin and in Lewis Carroll it means away from home, but this is an ordinary small town fair in Ontario with its sideshows, ferris wheels, prize animals, freaks, and merry-go-rounds. The ferris wheel is here associated with a series of images from *The Golden Bough*, to which *A Suit of Nettles*, a story of a cycle of the year ending in a sacrifice, has obvious affinities. The merry-go-round illustrates the progress of human thought as it goes around its circle from Parmenides to Heidegger and so back again: this episode indicates a strong influence of the "vicous cicle" of *Finnegans Wake* on Mr. Reaney's book. The "funhouse" is "an attempt to compress Canadian history and geography into a single horrific scenic railway ride," as the author puts it ["To the Reader," p. viii], and is a series of emblematic riddles. Thus "an old Indian's skin is turned into horsewhips and shoelaces" refers to the death of Tecumseh, and "The train comes to grief in a drift of flourdough" to the Titanic. At this point we become aware of the many links between the story of the geese and the story of Canada, the geese's Christmas being paralleled by the appalling massacres of Canadians which result from the quarrels of Europeans. A drunken preacher sums it all up with a brief sermon on the two hanged victims, Jesus and Judas Iscariot.

Spenser intended his *Shepherd's Calendar* to be something of a stunt, a display of professional competence in a field which at that time was largely monopolized by easy-going amateurs. Similarly Mr. Reaney puts on an amazing technical show. The metres include a long ten-line stanza with four rhymes and an Alexandrine at the end in the first three months; a sestina in February; octosyllabic couplets in March; a variety of poulterer's measure, with strong rhymes against weak ones, in May; dialogue prose in July; alliterative verse and catalogue prose (which is really a form of verse) in September, blank verse in December, and of course every variety of lyrical stanza, from the quatrains of May, June, and October to the complicated songs of April and August. Spenser got a friend to edit his book and provide an introduction and annotations: Mr. Reaney does his own editing, but invites commentary, not because he is pedantic or obscure, but because he has so much of the quality that is the opposite of pedantry, intellectual exuberance. Spenser's was a courageous effort, and met with a good deal of opposition from poets who complained that he "writ no language." Mr. Reaney's book will no doubt seem to many readers to have only too apt a title, to be bristly, forbidding, and irresponsibly inwrapped; or, in the words of his own goose-critic:

> No real emotion, no language of the people,
> Immoral in its basic avoidance of simplicity.   [*August*, ll. 99–100]

But at a time when most poets write, however unconsciously, with one eye on the anthologist, it takes a good deal of courage to work out a scheme like this—a Stratfordian courage, of the kind that took *Tamburlaine* to Broadway.[18]

Courage, however, is often the only virtue of failure, and *A Suit of Nettles* is a remarkable success. Just how remarkable it is too early yet

Letters in Canada: Poetry

to say. Anyone familiar with the puckish humour and twisted fantasy of Mr. Reaney's earlier volume *The Red Heart* might expect to find long passages in *A Suit of Nettles* where the poet is only playing around. The more one rereads the book the more one is convinced that there are no such passages. In February, for instance, we wonder why the tricks of inverted constructions and final spondees are used so persistently, until we see what fidelity they give to the fluttering movements of a bat:

> He hangs from beam in winter upside down
> But in the spring he right side up lets go
> And flutters here and there zigzagly flown
> Till up the chimney of the house quick-slow
> He pendulum-spirals out in light low
> Of sunset swinging out above the lawns.... [ll. 41-6]

Similarly with the lovingly meticulous description of a cow in the alliterative verse of September. And while the line of narrative is easy enough to follow, a little study of the imagery will soon reveal a Joycean complexity of cross-reference and interlocking symbolism.

I have no space, with a dozen books still ahead of me, to dwell on the innumerable felicities of the writing. I will say only that I have never read a book of Canadian poetry with so little "dissociation of sensibility" in it, where there was less separating of emotion and intellect, of the directly visualized and the erudite. There are breath-taking flashes of wit, like the sexual image in January, "This stake and heart-of-vampire sexual eye of ooze"; there are moments of poignant beauty like the conclusion of June or the winter song in November; there are farce, fantasy, religion, criticism, satire, all held together in a single controlling form. Mr. Reaney has not tried to grapple with contemporary life in the raw, but merely to perfect his poem. And—such is the perverse morality of art—he has succeeded, as I think no poet has so succeeded before, in bringing southern Ontario, surely one of the most inarticulate communities in human culture, into a brilliant imaginative focus.

The core of John Glassco's *The Deficit Made Flesh* (Indian File Books, no. 9, [Toronto:] McClelland & Stewart) is a series of poems about rural life in that northern spur of New England known as the Eastern Townships. One might expect such a poet to sound like a Canadian Robert Frost, but Mr. Glassco doesn't, and I mention Frost only for contrast. Mr. Glassco's ground bass, so to speak, is the driving human energy that settles down to wrest a living from this harsh land, where

> while the eternal mountains stand,
> Immortal stones come up beneath the plough. [*Gentleman's Farm*, ll. 55–6]

Under the grinding pressure of work in such a country the farmer is reduced to "rotten fenceposts and old mortgages," which is "No way of living, but a mode of life." Such a mode of life is based on necessity, but behind the necessity is what the poet calls "The structural mania of the human heart," the lunatic compulsion to take thought for the morrow and keep rebuilding the Tower of Babel. There are several images of an exhausting uphill journey that gets one nowhere in particular and of dying coals blown into renewed heat by an alien power. We see how a feverish vision of a paradise of conquered nature forces generations to wear themselves out to construct and maintain a *Gentleman's Farm* or a *White Mansion*. The latter, as the poet describes it, takes on something of the malignancy of a white goddess:

> Two hearts, two bodies clove, knew nothing more.
> Ere I was done I tore them asunder. Singly
> They fled my ruin and the ruin of love.
> I am she who is stronger than love. [ll. 33–6]

Against this blinkered will to power are set those who have refused to be propelled by it. There is the "deficit made flesh" who gives the book its title, an old bum left on the hands of a town council meeting, whose helplessness inspires them with what the poet sardonically calls "The rainbow-vision of a lethal chamber." In *Deserted Buildings*, the poet meditates on the problem of the picturesque, the emotional response we give to ruined or deserted buildings like the "falling tower" of another poem which is the timing-tower of a race track. Perhaps our affection for such things has something to do with our sense of the latent irony in the illusions that drive a man to follow "his blind will to its end in nature." In *Stud Groom* the irony sharpens: the stud groom has renounced all ambition to live beyond the round of "another race, Another show," and as a consequence has given up everything that the world considers morally valuable for the sake of

… an instant that lasts forever, and does no harm

Except to the altar-fated passion it robs,
The children it cheats of their uniforms and wars,
And the fathomless future of the underdog
It negates—shrugs off like the fate of a foundered mare.   [ll. 60-4]

Mr. Glassco is technically a very able poet, who can manage anything from villanelles to blank verse which, in *The White Mansion*, he makes into stanzas by repeating the cadence of a line. The dactylic hexameter, for all its Classical glory, seems in English to be good only for the most pastel kinds of romantic nostalgia, as in *Evangeline*, and it was an accurate sense of parody that chose it for *The Burden of Junk*. The finest poem in the book, I think, is *Gentleman's Farm*, where the alternating long and short lines of the stanza give a heavy thrust-and-relax rhythm, supported by the alternating of short words in description and longer ones in comment, and develop a most impressive cumulative power.

In some other poems of the book we move from the Eastern Townships into the mythical and religious archetypes that the poet has found embodied there. The white mansion thus expands into Penelope and her web in *The Web*, and the structural mania of the human heart is illustrated in two sonnets called *Utrillo's World*: I don't care for the second, but the first is a moving and eloquent poem. The driving force of life is connected with the Freudian imago or admiration of the father, which is projected in religion as *Nobodaddy* (Mr. Glassco adopts Blake's term for the sulky bewhiskered sky-god of popular piety). This father-figure is explored psychologically in *The Whole Hog*, and in *The Entailed Farm* the poet speaks of the adjustment of maturity reached by those

Who composed our quarrel early and in good season
Buried the hatchet in our father's brain.   [ll. 47-8]

In *Shake Dancer* we have a fine conceit in which the figure of the dancer is gradually transformed into the outline of her dance, the "man of air" that complements her erotic movements.

I do not find Mr. Glassco's book uniformly satisfying: the echoes of Donne in *A Devotion* bother me and I have so far missed the point of the ballad on the death of Thomas Pepys. But on the whole *The Deficit Made Flesh* exhibits a most unusual poetic intelligence and talent.

The title of Ronald Everson's *A Lattice for Momos* ([Toronto:] Contact Press) is a reference to the legend that Momos, unaware of the function of poetry, criticized the human body for its lack of a window that would reveal thoughts and emotions. This is Mr. Everson's second volume, and we learn that he has returned to writing poetry after an abstinence of a quarter-century. It is perhaps a consequence of this that his writing shows so much freshness, with a highly sophisticated naivete, as though such things as metaphor and metre were being discovered for the first time. In *L'Abbé Lemaitre's Universe* he spins a delicate web of seven quatrains around three rhymes; there are skilful slant rhymes in *One-Night Expensive Hotel* and initial rhymes in *Winter at Lac des Deux Montagnes*; *Fish in a Store-Window Tank* has the first quatrain and the sestet of a regular sonnet that isn't a regular sonnet, and he has a feeling of the primitive mystery of the sound and sense of words that comes out in the very lovely *Christening* at the end of the book.

He is similarly able to exploit the fact that anything goes in metaphor: in three poems he is dead and takes a corpse-eye view of life; in another he is the waves on a shore; in *June 21* he says:

> I laugh while huge reality,
> a mindless lout, summersaults for my pleasure.   [ll. 10–11]

There is a reminiscence of Wallace Stevens in his bright intellectual precision, and, like Stevens, he has the knack of making the title of a poem a part of the poem itself, as in the fine quatrain which bears the title *To the Works Superintendent on His Retirement*. Often an epithet or two will give an ordinary poetic conceit a new dimension of significance, like *Letter from Underground*, which tells how young colts are shocked by an electric fence that "underprivileged beetles" crawl under undisturbed. Sometimes we get irony through the honesty of a simple description:

> A conformist
> in bluejeans-crewcut plays bold pioneer
> with a capgun.   ["*All Wars Are Boyish and Are Fought by Boys*," ll. 4–6]

His main theme is that of the innocent vision, the "original sin of childhood rapture," which in adult life operates as love. Love is an irrational emotion that makes more and more sense as the world that is supposed to be sensible is gradually distorted into the illusions of fear and the anxieties of a desperate ritual:

> A large wild animal
> prowls outside my office.
> I chant Audograph incantations
> and, bowing, drum the typewriter.   [*Working Late*, ll. 1–4]

Similarly, the certainties of immediate experience and the "pleasure-principle," the feeling that one is the centre of the universe and the conductor of a universal orchestra (see *Corduroy Road through the Marsh*), build up in proportion as time and space dissolve into relativity. In *Fall of the City* the fall of Rome and of our own civilization are simultaneous; in *Fish in a Store-Window Tank* the poet is contemporary with his caveman ancestors; elsewhere we read of "darting slowpoke swallows" and of an aeroplane travelling "childhood-slow." Such themes are common enough among poets, but are not often handled with such unfailing good humour and intelligence. The book is also illustrated with drawings by Colin Haworth. The illustrations are said only to "match the moods" of the poems, but in most cases they do illustrate them, and very pleasantly.

Irving Layton's *A Laughter in the Mind*, published by Jonathan Williams, Highlands, North Carolina, in 1958, was reissued, with twenty additional poems, in February 1959, by the Editions d'Orphée of Montreal. This enlarged version is the one reviewed here. There is, as usual, an astonishing variety of themes and techniques, and it is difficult to make a generalization about the place of this book in the author's development. There is perhaps more consistent interest in strict metres—witness the blank verse of *Cain*, the nine-syllable line of *Climbing*, the irregular couplets of *A Roman Jew to Ovid* and *Laurentian Rhapsody*, the lucidly simple stanzas of *Two Songs for Sweet Voices* and the curious Heine-like *Rain*, and the easy lilt of *Dance, My Little One* and the third stanza of *Poem for the Year 2058*:

> This is the house the jacks built
> Out of hemlock and gilt:
> The saints and lovers are dead
> And all is common as bread.
> Now none believe in greatness,
> The dwarfs possess the bridges.

The central themes of Mr. Layton's poetry are here too. Apart from the personal poems and satires, which are of more ephemeral interest, there is the sympathy with animals which makes their suffering, or even their physical expression, a mirror of human guilt, as in *Garter Snake*, *Sheep*, *Cat Dying in Autumn*, and *Cain*—this last on the shooting of a frog. There is a delicate vein of fantasy in two of the best poems in the book, *Venetian Blinds* and *Paging Mr. Superman*. The latter tells us of the magic effect of this name even when pronounced in a dreary hotel lobby by a pageboy more familiar with comic strips than with Nietzsche or Shaw:

> This was the cocktail hour when love
> Is poured over ice-cubes and executives
> Lay their shrewdest plans for the birth of twins
> With silver spoons.... [ll. 44–7]

The general point of view in the book is Nietzschean: the conception of the "outsider," however vulgarized it may have been recently, is still a real conception, and to Mr. Layton the poetic imagination leads one outside society, where one can turn back and see the world writhing in its own hell of selfishness and malice:

> How the loonies hate each other
> How they jeer & grunt & swear,
> Their sullen faces happy
> When another's wound they tear.   [*Captives*, ll. 21–4]

The way of *Jesus and Buddha*, whose symbol is the "leprosarium," is to return to this world and work in it; the way of the poet is to keep clear of it, at least imaginatively. The reward of keeping clear of it is joy, the result of accepting life without a death-wish in it. Joy is not created by merely releasing one's sexual inhibitions, as the irony of *Obit* and *Enigma* warns us; and it is something very different from pleasure. It is what the poet calls, in the Yeatsian *Parting*:

> A laughter in the mind
> For the interlocking grass
> The winds part as they pass;
> Or fallen on each other,
> Leaf and uprooted flower.

"I must bone up on Parmenides," the poet says: in the meantime his imagery is Heraclitean. Fire and dry light are the symbols of the laughter of the mind, watching the world burn up its rubbish; mist and damp are the symbols of the dying and life-hating world. Thus in *Love Is an Irrefutable Fire* we have the contrasting images of moon and cloud, street-lamp and black air. The two symbols come together in the fine opening poem, where the mist is the poet's mortality, like the waves that reminded Canute of the limits of his power. In this poem the poet is a clown, buffoon, or starving minstrel, for in Mr. Layton genuine dignity is closely allied to the ridiculous.

Raymond Souster's *Crêpe-Hanger's Carnival: Selected Poems, 1955–58* ([Toronto:] Contact Press) is a mimeographed collection of poems in his usual epigram form. As compared with his earlier collections, the rhythm is tighter, and there are fewer poems that read like prose *collage*; the imagery is more accurate and objective, a little poem called *The Cobra* being evidence of Mr. Souster's awareness that his chief virtue is in objectivity. It is still true that the most emphatic poems are also the most perfunctory ones, and there is still a good deal of the moral exasperation that paralyses every comment except the most obvious one. But, as the title suggests, there are a good many poems about death, some of them, especially *The Deaths*, very eloquent, and they help to deepen and give seriousness to the book. On the other hand, *The Grey Cup, Cat on the Back Fence*, and *The Goat Island Poetry Conference* show a gift for sardonic fantasy that Mr. Souster does not indulge in nearly often enough, and many sparks and crackles in the imagery suggest that for this poet the act of writing has become less of a relief and more fun:

> Why, he treated that hound
> Better than his wife,
> Or so she tells me. [*My Father-in-Law*, ll. 4–6]

Occasionally, as in *The American in Montreal*, or *Two Pictures of Bay Street*, a brief sketch has emotional ripples that spread into a much larger area of significance, as has a curious little poem called *The Switch*, depicting a Utopia in which the *parents* have to search for eggs on Easter morning. There are also—rare in Mr. Souster—flashes of verbal wit, like his reference to the spear thrust into the side of Christ *For Auld Lang Synne*. He will even desert his social conscience long enough for an occasional metaphysical conceit, as in *Summer Evening*, or *That Shape in the Fog*, which is apparently the fog itself.

However, the main impact of the book is to be found in Mr. Souster's study of the dereliction in a modern city: old men muttering to themselves or snatching cigarette butts from snow-cleaning machines, drunks, suicides, patients in hospitals, a blind beggar on a street corner "Watching the darkness flash by," prostitutes, neglected children. They are nearly always inarticulate or silent, for they live in a world of submerged consciousness which they share not only with animals but with trees, buildings, and litter like the old tin kettle which has, the poet says:

> ... that discarded look which moves me to pity
> In people, animals, things.   [*The Old Tin Kettle*, ll. 10–11]

Such a conceit might seem faked, but in Mr. Souster's world, where human beings are on so rudimentary a level of consciousness, it is more plausible that subhuman life, or human artefacts like wrecked buildings, should express a good deal of human feeling. Hence such poems as *Sucker Run*, *The Wreckers*, *The Tree*, and *Shea's Coming Down*.

Louis Dudek's *En Mexico* ([Toronto:] Contact Press) is a long fragmented poem, less ambitious than *Europe*, but in my opinion more successful and better unified. It gets away to a slow start: the impact of a new country, like nostalgia, can often be a ready-made substitute for genuine poetic feeling, and, again like nostalgia, may produce only a facile reminder of experience, like a colourful label plastered on a suitcase. The comments about life and death which intervene are not much more rewarding, for Mr. Dudek has little to add to the eternal verities. But he soon picks up his main theme:

> How the temple came out of the heart of cruelty
> and out of the jungle the singing birds!   [p. 23]

Nature is an organic process out of which man evolves, and the process itself is full of unconscious art:

> Study the way of breaking waves
> for the shape of ferns,
>   fire and wind
> for whatever blows or burns.   [p. 68]

Man's life forms a history, which "Begins from the place we're in," out of which his art evolves. Art is therefore, for man, the key to reality, for "Form is the visible part of being." The whole poem leads up to this recognition of art in the final pages, and the observations on the jungle, the Aztec temples, Christianity with its man of sorrows, the modern class-conscious students of Mexico, the frogs and crabs and snakes and "all the gentle mechanical creatures that we kill" fall into place as integral parts of the total vision. In the middle is the simple human act, the routine work on which all history turns, symbolized by women washing laundry in a stream. In this poem Mr. Dudek has matured his technique of indented lines and parenthetical rhythms, and the gentle rocking sway of this meditative poem is full of a contemplative charm.

Mr. Dudek's other book, *Laughing Stalks* (Contact), is a collection of light verse. Some of the poems are about nothing except the poet's own self-consciousness: these are expendable, even though some of them proclaim the virtues of expendability. The reflections on scholarship and criticism illustrate a highly confused state of mind that may be called pseudo-anti-intellectualism. But when Mr. Dudek is not pretending to be a simple soul, and is his natural complex self, he can be witty and amusing. He has some good parodies of other Canadian poets, the best of them being a *Composite Poem by Six Leading Canadian Poets*, a pastiche of thefts from Eliot and Thomas. There is also a vigorous explosion in Skeltonics called *Sunday Promenade*, a nightmarish vision of a crowd of children. There are some free-verse political poems in the manner of F.R. Scott, but Mr. Dudek in a satiric mood seems, unlike Mr. Scott, to be more at ease in a strict satiric metre:

> The Farmby Program fills the soul,
> Telling the folks how many cows
> Were burned last night while chewing chows,
> Who had a birthday, who ate hash
> And died of piles in St. Eustache.   [*Tar and Feathers*, ll. 38–42]

There are sharp images of a bird returning to his cage and "the fictions defining life and its limits," of radio commentators "looking through glass at the sad Sardou comedy"; there are well-turned epigrams in *The Cure, Make It New, Good Literature Teaches,* and *Reality*. The third of these poems explains very clearly how the conception "beauty," if used in its proper sense as an attribute of good art, has nothing whatever to do with the conception "attractive subject-matter," in spite of the fact that most people, including most of the cultivated Canadian public, are firmly convinced that it has. This opposition of beauty to sentimentality is a central issue in Mr. Dudek's poetry, and is what gives most of the real bite to his lighter verse.

Miriam Waddington's *The Season's Lovers* ([Toronto:] Ryerson Press) continues with the subjects and qualities of her earlier collection *The Second Silence*. Much of it is concerned, like Mr. Souster's book, with dereliction in the city, but in the more direct context of social work the derelicts are less inarticulate, and consequently less pathetic. We hear their splutters of self-justification, their whimpering screen memories, and all the rhetoric of human nature under duress. Naturally such sounds are not confined to the unfortunate or criminal, and we hear them also from old women in Toronto scheming to get a best room or chair, and from the crowds on Montreal street-cars who form the family background of the city's thieves and prostitutes:

> From the same parish, aunts in hats,
> Green and painted loud as parrots,
> Have issued forth to board the buses;
> Between their words, small cries, and fusses,
> I've heard their false teeth click and clamor
> And answered with my English stammer. [*The Thief*, ll. 15–20]

Not that the poet is merely amused by all this: there is a fine flash of sympathy in her comment on the lonely woman who has "nothing to buy that's personal to her," and there is a good deal of old-fashioned moralizing: one poem is entitled *My Lessons in the Jail*.

The main theme of the book is the sense of the difficulty of communication, with its accompanying sense that on deeper levels of the mind, including some of the areas gingerly explored in analysis, there is far less isolation. In the love poems, which become more frequent towards the end of the book, this theme tightens up both in irony and intensity. Sometimes the irony predominates, as in the encounter with the young poet who comes to tea and finds that

>   he has come too early
> to dine on answers, and I, ill-served by fate,
> dug up from scullery, have come too late. [*The Young Poet and Me*, ll. 22–4]

Sometimes, as in *No Earthly Lover*, there is rather the feeling that in love the sense of identity, or union in one flesh, may be something more than a metaphor. Occasionally winter symbolizes the isolation of ordinary human contacts, and spring the unity underlying them. In the title poem at the end we finally meet the "season's lovers," the poet's version of Adam and Eve, united in their hidden paradise, with an ironic echo of Milton in "He clung to self, and she to him."

Mrs. Waddington's two gifts, one for spontaneous lyricism and one for precise observation, are better integrated here than in *The Second Silence*, but are still not completely fused. In such poems as *Semblances* there is a kind of lilting melody that springs over the diction, which in itself would hardly bear too sustained analysis. But one pauses with pleasure over better realized passages in *Jonathan Travels*, in the song beginning *Paint me a bird upon your wrist*, and in *An Elegy for John Sutherland*.

Marya Fiamengo's *The Quality of Halves* (Vancouver: Klanak Press) is by a British Columbia writer who appeared in *Poets 56* two years ago, but is essentially a newcomer. The quality of halves, we are told, is expressed by the muted sound of the vowel in the word "dusk." Miss Fiamengo is a mythopoeic poet, and to her the world of myth is a night world (or sometimes, as in *At the Lake*, a world of mist), full of symbols of aristocracy: imprisoned queens, peacocks, swans, and jewels. This world is opposed to the "republican and sane" daylight of a more tedious reality, which needs the mythical night to complement itself. A strong Yeatsian influence on this mythology is acknowledged in the title poem. There are lapses of taste, especially in *These Faces Seen*, and some muddy writing in *Song for Sunday*, where it is difficult to sort out all the mandalas and pieces of angels. But she manages her sonorous elegiac rhythm very well; the particular kind of decorative loveliness she aims at she often succeeds in getting, and one finds some tense organization of sound here and there:

> A liquid whorl of lostness as when ducks
> Make suctions when they seek the sea.
>
> [*As Birds in Their Mute Perishability*, ll. 6–7]

The most consistently successful poem, I think, is *In the Absence of Children*, where, in spite of an elaborate symbolic construct, a bit more of the republican daylight is allowed into the poem than usual.

Peter Miller's *Meditation at Noon* ([Toronto:] Contact) is an extremely interesting, if uneven, collection, with three translations at the end that indicate an unusually thorough knowledge of contemporary poetry in other languages. The usual level is that of poetic rhetoric rather than fully realized poetry, although the rhetoric is that of a lively and sharp mind—some of his own poems read rather like translations too, where the form has been abstracted from the content. Poems are often brilliant in conception but less satisfying in execution, as in *Photographer in Town*, or well started and finished only by repetition, as in *Samson of the Arts*. Most of the poems are in free verse, and in a rhythm that is well handled, though the title poem and one or two others have a more strongly accented beat. Formal metrical schemes, as in *Total War* and *Christmastide at the Pornographers*, tend to lead to forced rhymes, though even those are sometimes appropriate, as in *Resignation*.

Mr. Miller generally tends to be metaphysical, his conceits varying from the pendantry of *Tangential Girl* to the witty and ingenious *Abstraction*. In the latter the versatility of behaviour shown by human character is compared with the capacity of an abstract painting to be a reservoir of subjects instead of a single one. The general mood is that of a good-humoured detachment, sharpening to intellectual satire in *Sensationalist*, *Synthetic You* (a poem that might well have been called *History of Canadian Poetry*), and *The Eyes*, this last dealing with the effect of executive staring on intellectual diffidence. The title poem shows a strong interest in the theme of the mental landscape, which reappears in three other poems, all among his best, *The Open Season*, *The City, Then*, and *A City Refound*. These are based on the theme of a mental or ideal city as contrasted with an actual one: a concrete abstract, so to speak, as compared with the abstract concrete of Yonge Street or Manhattan.

{George Ellenbogen's *Winds of Unreason* (McGill Poetry Series, [Toronto:] Contact) is the third in the series of McGill Poetry Books edited by Louis Dudek, and is illustrated with drawings by Peter Daglish. The poems are in a relentless free verse in which a long sentence is chopped irregularly into two-beat, three-beat, four-beat lines, giving something of the effect of a memorized and badly delivered speech. The result is that they slide over the mind without taking a grip anywhere, as though what the poet calls "the flat rhythms of a dull dishonest age" had infected what he also calls his "weary songs." All the poems are short enough to go on a single page, and the best way to read them is *en bloc*, for the theme rather than for the quality of the writing. There is a good deal of variety of theme, but only in the final section of the book do we find anything much more distinctive, in *The Falling Leaves*, with its melancholy cadences, in *Just Another Whisper*, and in *Through a Greyhound Skylight*, which ends with a more sharply pointed irony:

> Yet as the wheels indiscriminately
> crush the bodies of stray dogs
> who will tell the other passengers
> to keep looking at the scenery?

Other volumes which contain much pleasant and melodious verse, but need no extended critical comment in a survey of this kind, are: H.J.T. Coleman's *The Far Hills and Other Poems* ([Toronto:] Ryerson), Nan Emerson's *Wind Song and Other Verse* (Winnipeg, privately printed), Mary (Davidson) Bishop's *In Heaven's View* (Hounslow: Cedar Press {Toronto: Ryerson}), a memorial volume, and R.A. Parsons' *Reflections, Books I and II* (Ryerson), a double volume of verse by a Newfoundland poet, with introductions by Monsignor Dinn and President Gushue.[19] Wallace Havelock Robb's *Tecumtha* ([Kingston:] Abbey Dawn Press) is more difficult to characterize. It is a long prose poem, with verse interludes, on the figure better known as Tecumseh, who is treated not historically but mythically, as (I quote the subtitle): *Revelation of the True Shawano Tecumtha; Dreamer of Amity; Lonely Redman Monarch and Mighty Mentor of the Forest; Leaping Panther Frustrated and Shooting Star Betrayed; Gigantic Genius and Magnificent Mystic among the Gods*. It is said to have taken thirty years of research, and is a remarkable conception, however grotesque in execution.

II

There are five Ryerson chapbooks. There is little to say about the four poems in *Samson in Hades* by Ella Julia Reynolds, except that they are rather long for the points they make, and while they have a good deal of fluency in rhythm and diction, they have a disconcerting tendency to collapse into cliché in moments of stress. Myrtle Reynolds Adams' *Morning on My Street* has some lively bouncing imagery in the title poem, and a more sombre search for a past identity in *Gift to the Years* and *This I*. In the last poem, *Shallow to Deep*, the two themes come together with some genuine feeling and eloquence. In Fred Swayze's *And See Penelope Plain* there is some lively satire: what with this book and Reaney, Souster, Dudek, and Layton, the anthology *The Blasted Pine*, reviewed here last year, already needs a second edition. The *Penelope* of the title poem is the wife of a well-to-do Canadian who, uprooted from all her interests ("societies, mainly missionary") to make the regulation conspicuous-consumption pilgrimage to Florida, works off her boredom in incessant knitting. *Caedmon, Sing Me Something of the National Potential* threatens us with

> A terza rima on Chalk River and Hiroshima,
> A lyric on Social Credit, a panegyric
> On wages in bargain basements, a squib for sages
> Who serve on Royal Commissions and deserve
> What they get.   [ll. 14–8]

Toronto has some demure echoes of Sandburg ("They tell me you want to be loved, and I believe them") and *Education Is a Race* puts the irony of that subject into a compact nutshell. I think however that the more serious *The Drowning* is the best-integrated poem in the book, although *Spring Song*, except for the single bit of metrical putty in the phrase "Wholeheartedly pagan," ought to have a leading place in any collection of Canadian spring songs.}

Thomas Saunders's sober unpretentious studies of rural life in Saskatchewan are always welcome, and I like *Something of a Young World's Dying* better than his two previous chapbooks. Here the comparison with Robert Frost would have more point than it would for Mr. Glassco, yet here too the differences are more important. The poems, which look like blank verse at first glance, are actually in surprisingly elaborate rhyme schemes, and the rhymes have a harsh obtrusiveness that distresses the ear and yet seems curiously appropriate. Mr. Saunders gives us a Wordsworthian illusion of the language of real life by coming close to doggerel and yet skilfully avoiding it. The main theme of the book, too, as expressed in the title, is quite different from Frost, being purely Western. Mr. Saunders is fascinated by the curiously uneasy relationship between man and nature on the prairie. In *Coyote's Howl*, a very simple, even obvious poem, yet a haunting and effective one, a farmer, as his wife is dying in childbirth, hears in the howl of a coyote the latent hostility of the land to him and his life. *The Mill* (a title which makes one look twice at the poem) tells of an early pioneer who remains on the prairie because he has never known any other home, and yet does not really feel at home there. *Poplar Hollow*, from which the book's title is quoted, describes a ghost town, struck with a kind of precocious senility, "growth in its first decay." *Sandy Bowles* and *Empty House* deal with the desperate effort to maintain a continuum of identity in this flat world where "No third dimension rises but the dreams / Of man," and *Adjustment* and *An Old Man and the Land* with the spirit of resignation that up to a point succeeds in achieving it.

John Heath's *Aphrodite* is a posthumous collection of poems by a writer who was killed in Korea at the age of thirty-four. There is a foreword by Henry Kreisel, who is apparently the editor of the collection. The effect of these poems is like that of a good jazz pianist, who treats his piano purely as an instrument of percussion, whose rhythm has little variety but whose harmonies are striking and ingenious. There is a group of poems in quatrains, split in two by the syntax, where most of the protective grease of articles and conjunctions is removed and subject, predicate, object, grind on each other and throw out metaphorical sparks:

> Red razor dawn shears shadow beard
> Along jawline of head turned earth
> The seaweed dream stalks desiccate
> As mind tides back to daylight berth.   [*The Sun, Mine Executioner*, ll. 13–16]

The vigour and liveliness of the style have all the characteristics of light verse: polysyllabic diction in *Sleep* and *The Season*, rollicking rhymes in *Superscriptions*, and a limerick-like stanza in *Burdens*. In *Northern Spring* the sound is more carefully organized:

> The outspace looking, stark, star bitten
> Pole slopes back into the sun,
> The white owl haunted, gray wolf daunted
> Winter world hears rivers run.   [ll. 1–4]

In several poems one feels that the poet has no real theme: he is observing and describing with great wit, but does not know where to *take* all his cleverness, and hence the poem sags after a promising beginning. I think this happens for instance in *Fun Fair*, a curious anticipation of Mr. Reaney's September eclogue. In the title poem, on the other hand, there is a real theme: Aphrodite's complacent reflection that as long as the cycle of nature continues to turn on copulation she will be "still queen":

> I have outlasted them,
> Poor peacock Hera petulant at Zeus
> And Attica's longnose divinity
> And some young moonfaced chit of Bethlehem
> Bouncing a second Eros on her knee. [ll. 8–12]

This poem in particular indicates what we have lost by the poet's death.

Jay Macpherson's Emblem Books series continues with two more chapbooks this year. Violet Anderson's *The Ledge* (n.p.) is at its best in close description and observation of *Poet's Minutiae*, the title of one of her poems. *The Well*, *Sea Piece*, and *Under the Juniper* have a good deal of charm, with a murmuring pleasant rhythm and sound as well as careful imagery. Mrs. Anderson is most successful when she is not *saying* anything: when she states her theme before drawing a moral or making reflective comments. *Collectivist World* is an example of this: it sags into talk, but only after an excellent image, which is really the whole poem, of:

> the shape of a committee meeting
> varnished about the circumference
> with the usual chairs,
> and cloudy at the core
> with the jargon of cigarette smoke.
> The windows stick. [ll. 4–9]

Heather Spears's *Asylum Poems and Others* are much more ambitious, and have a strident power in them which does not depend on their success, though I hasten to add that it does not depend either on the automatic shock of the subject-matter. The percussive vocabulary and wrenched syntax, the pounding and clanging of monosyllables, the use of such phrases as "on bed to lie me" that suggest a dissociation of personality, have all been deliberately adopted to give the sense of a mind at breaking point. A strong Hopkins influence comes into view in an extraordinary *Sonnet*, where there are only three rhymes for the whole fourteen lines, and even those repeated in inner rhymes. Miss Spears makes it clear that while an asylum may well be as close to hell as we can ordinarily get on earth, that is so partly because the madman's self-created hell demands an objective counterpart:

> They took him back, when he could walk
> To his own bed which he did not know
> And left him drowsy and numb for a cure.
> How bound and blasted week after week
> He was, how watched—and now
> He is building against them again, and is still obscure.
> <div style="text-align: right">[<i>My Love behind Walls</i>, ll. 43–8]</div>

The title speaks of "other" poems, but we never get very far from the asylum, and even the religious poems still talk of severed minds, dragging chains, and screaming, only reaching some kind of troubled serenity at the very end. A most disconcerting and haunting little book.

A third chapbook series, Fiddlehead Poetry Books, contributes Alden A. Nowlan's *The Rose and the Puritan* ([Fredericton:] University of New Brunswick). These are mainly vignettes of childhood on a farm, and are full of the sufferings of animals, which seem so much a part of the order of nature on farms as elsewhere. It is curious how often the themes of Mr. Reaney's book recur in the other verse of the year. All the poems are well written, pleasant, and carefully worked out. The low-keyed sensibility and lucid diction are a model of what at least most chapbook writing should be. The purely human subjects treated in *The Brothers and the Village* and *All Down the Morning* are a bit on the hackneyed side, and such themes as *The Egotist* are much more deeply felt and distinctive:

> A gushing carrousel, the cock
> Revolved around the axeman's block.
>
> Sweet Christ, he kicked his severed head
> And drenched the summer where he bled.
>
> And terrible with pain, the scream
> Of blood engulfed his desperate dream—
>
> He knew (and knowing could not die)
> That dawn depended on his cry.

The title poem is considerably more complex, and suggests that the gentle pastoral sympathy of the other poems is by no means Mr. Nowlan's only poetic quality.

{A number of students, mainly undergraduates at University College, have shown a good deal of poetic activity this year. Most conspicuous among them is John Robert Colombo, who has had four chapbooks attractively printed by the Hawkshead Press in Kitchener. *Fragments* is a collection of epigrams, in a blinding typography, which perhaps need a little more wit to bring them off; *This Studied Self* has more variety as well as greater intensity. *angry young man* (the titles are in lower case), an ingenious circular structure, and *palm leaf*, on the Cumaean Sibyl, are the most notable poems here, along with *nightfall*:

> When the last of the summer sun
> Bright casement of an ancient church
> Cracks in the distant chaos of trees
>
> As dark clouds merge to knit once more
> In the wake of the parting birds
> And shadows shroud a once-wake world
>
> Then there will die in heart and head
> That stunning sun, that gilded gaze
> That demon woman earth

Variation contains some vignettes of city life somewhat in the manner of Mr. Souster, though the elegiac tone in *Eveningfall* and the reflective mood of *Thinking Function* are I think better managed. *In the Streets*, by Ruta Ginsberg (still Mr. Colombo, apparently), is a broadside (privately printed) with an amusing poem about a lion in the Riverdale Zoo who was born in captivity and is consequently as Canadian as his visitors. *This Citadel in Time* is more ambitious, and in my opinion more successful. Mr. Colombo is a serious poet who has not yet squeezed the prose out of his style, and these are religious poems in a very long meditative line which allows him the fullest scope for his abilities, which are at present on the plane of rhetorical eloquence rather than poetic form. The citadel is the Church, and the poems deal with various aspects of the conception of the Church, *The Apostles of Night* being perhaps the best sustained.

Another broadside of four poems "for the Missile Age" by Kenneth McRobbie, *Jupiter C* ([Toronto:] Contact Press), deals with the theme indicated in the title, the poet taking over the functions of the warning prophet after religion has become futile. Of the four poems, which are untitled, the fourth is perhaps most successful in its fusion of mechanical, erotic, and parody-religious imagery:

> No mere sign will do now unless it be
> the haloed breast of a Japanese woman
> turned to steam in her baby's mouth
>   and radiant surely over
> all the world's sites its thin ash of piteous religion.

The annual poetry edition of the University College *Gargoyle* contains twenty-six poems by Mr. Colombo, Christopher Priestley, Gerry Vise (whose two religious poems stand out sharply), E.A. Lacey, and others. Most of the contributors show the conservatism of their generation: the main effort is to clarify and round out a clearly conceived metrical form. A certain impatience with more self-communing types of poetry would be consistent with this: thus Alexander Leggatt in *Poetry 1958*:

> The lyre's strings are tied in knots
> The flute is stuffed with plasticine
> The Muse has laryngitis now
> Whose voice had once been crisp and clean.

Three other chapbooks, *Scales*, by Jack Winter (n.p.), *Daydreams*, by Dora P. Fortner ([Foleyet, Ont.:] Carillon Poetry Chapbooks), and *Canada for Man and Other Poems*, by V.B. Rhodenizer (Wolfville, N.S.: privately printed), call for no particular comment.

I am not sure whether *Poems* by Martin Gray (Edinburgh: Serif Books Ltd.; Toronto: Contact Press) belongs in this survey or not. Mr. Gray is an erudite poet of considerable expertise, with a well-modulated meditative style, though the trick of ending a sentence oracularly in the middle of a line is somewhat overdone. Some of the poems are in oddly old-fashioned idioms, like the Tennysonian *Telemachus* and *Pastoral Conversation A.D. 33*, which discusses the Crucifixion. In some of the poems the style is so clear and correct that the limitations of the poet's mind become visible, as in the poems on Venice and Port Royal and the Spenglerian

Speculation, where reflection has little to add to description. I like best the drifting descriptive poems, *Belle Isle*, *Across the Continent*, and *Caribbean*, with their gentle stanzas spaced out like the whorls of a canoe-paddle. The poet also has a special affection for insects that gives unusual intensity to *Notes on Ants*, and, if one may say so, a sharp bite to *Flea.*

[NOTE: *The Collected Poems of E.J. Pratt*, second edition, edited with an introduction by the present writer ([Toronto:] Macmillan), will be reviewed in a future issue by Dr. F. W. Watt.]}

10. 1959

July 1960

From University of Toronto Quarterly, 29 *(July 1960): 440–60. Partially reprinted in* BG, *107–27, and in* Masks of Poetry, *ed. A.J.M. Smith, 106–9. Material on Layton reprinted in* Irving Layton: The Poet and His Critics, *ed. Seymour Mayne (Toronto: McGraw-Hill Ryerson, 1978), 99–101.*

There is nothing particularly "modern" about the gap between poetry and its reading public, or about the charge that poets are wilfully obscure, a charge levelled with great enthusiasm against (for example) Keats's *Endymion*. In every age the envious readers—a large group of every writer's contemporaries—have resented the humility that close attention requires, and poetry has never been popular except when it provided some kind of middle distance, by telling stories or crystallizing into proverbs and slogans. But there are, perhaps, some additional hazards about our own age. Most people nowadays are accustomed to the double talk of journalism, and it is not the difficulty of poetry that they find baffling, but its simplicity. Vivid imagery and concrete language are too sharp for readers accustomed to the murkiness of dead words, and make them wince and look away. A recent Canadian book of verse was reviewed in an American journal devoted entirely to poetry, by a reviewer who kept protesting that he couldn't understand a word of it.[20] The writing could not have been clearer or simpler; but that was the trouble. Again, lyrical poetry cannot be read quickly: it has no donkey's carrot like a whodunit, and the developing of "reading skills," which enable the reader to come to terms with his own sense of panic, has no relation to the reading of poetry. The reading of poetry is a leisurely occupation, and is possible only for that small minority which believes in leisure.

George Johnston's *The Cruising Auk* ([Toronto:] Oxford) should appeal to a wider audience than most books of poems surveyed in these reviews. Even the envious reader should be disarmed by the simplicity, which may make him feel that he could do as well if he set his mind to it, or that here at last is a "light" verse which "doesn't take itself too seriously," the favourite cliché of the culturally submerged. The critic, however, has to explain that the substance of Mr. Johnston's poetry is not at all the image of the ordinary reader that is reflected from its polished surface. He must explain that seriousness is not the opposite of lightness, but of portentousness, and that genuine simplicity is always a technical *tour de force*. In short, he must insist that Mr. Johnston's most pellucid lyrics have to be read as carefully as the most baffling paper chase of e. e. cummings.

The difference between the simple and the insipid, in poetry, is that while simplicity uses much the same words, it puts them together in a way that keeps them echoing and reverberating with infinite associations, rippling away into the furthest reaches of imaginative thought. It is difficult for a critic to demonstrate the contrast between the simplicity that keeps him awake at night and the mediocrity that puts him to sleep in the day. In *The Cruising Auk*, however, there is one major clue to the simplicity. Like Mr. Reaney and Miss Macpherson before him, Mr. Johnston has produced a beautifully unified book, the apparently casual poems carrying the reader along from the first poem to the last in a voyage of self-discovery. We begin with a Narcissus image, a boy gazing into a pool and feeling an identity with "the abyss he gazes on," and we end with *O Earth, Turn!* (the echo of Miss Macpherson can hardly be an accident) where the abyss opens up again inside the adult:

> I love the slightly flattened sphere,
> Its restless, wrinkled crust's my here,
> Its slightly wobbling spin's my now
> But not my why and not my how:
> My why and how are me.   [ll. 6–10]

Between these two points, a state of innocence and a state in which all paradise is lost except a residual intuition, Mr. Johnston surveys the ages of man. He first explores the "pool" or pond, life or the objective side of existence, which remains the controlling image of the book. In *In the Pond* the poet lies beneath it; in *In It* he sails over it in a boat; in *The Queen of Lop* it enters a girl's dreams as a death symbol; in *Poor Edward* it forms the basis for a beautifully cadenced death-by-water poem of suicide; in *Wet* the death symbol modulates into rain. Human life is thus looked at as symbolically under water, hence the watching fish in *Rapture* and *Life from a Goldfish Bowl*, and the fine *Eating Fish*, where the fish disappears into the man, a quizzical analogue to Miss Macpherson's fisherman. The poet first discovers that the innocence of childhood is not self-contained but rebellious, a battle with invisible gods revealed in the noise of a small boy:

> Grievous energies of growth,
> Storms of pride and tides of sloth
> Sweep across his giant soul
> Against the gods, the small and whole.   [*Rest Hour*, ll. 9–12]

As one gets older one comes to terms with experience, and the age of anxiety settles more or less contentedly into

> ... this excellent street-scattered city,
> This home, this network, this great roof of pity.   [*Love of the City*, ll. 13–14]

The cosiness of domestic life among family and friends occupies much of Mr. Johnston's foreground: he depicts it without rancour and without insisting, like so many more obsessed intellectuals, that only a damned soul can remain absorbed in it:

> My pleasures, how discreet they are!
> A little booze, a little car,
> Two little children and a wife
> Living a small suburban life.   [*War on the Periphery*, ll. 5–8]

For if one can be deeply moved (in *Cathleen Sweeping*) by a three-year-old daughter struggling with a broom, one can appreciate that a small suburban life, even as lived by adults, may have something equally pathetic and dauntless about it. Thus Mr. Murple's mother, who gets a bottle of gin from her son on Mother's Day but defiantly buys her own flower:

Letters in Canada: Poetry

> "A nice red rose to show I'm still alive:
> Fifty cents they asked me for it, thieves!
> Yellow to show you're dead is fifty-five
> All done up in ferny things and leaves." [*Life from a Goldfish Bowl*, ll. 13–16]

In fact Mr. Johnston has a Dickensian sense of the violence of the life force in drab or even squalid surroundings, a sense not many modern poets show, apart from Thomas's *Under Milk Wood*. He admires his gigantic aunts and the vast pregnancy of Bridget, and wonders why Eternity should be too stuffy for the "bugs and bottles and hairpins" of Mrs. McWhirter's highly unsanitary existence and should reduce her instead to a more impersonal dust.

Yet it is still the age of anxiety: the clock, a recurring image, keeps placidly ticking away the moments of life; the "spider's small eye" is watching and waiting, and all around is a sinister and conspiratorial darkness, of a kind that scares Edward reading *Light Literature* and eventually pulls him into it, and that forms the background of the very lovely *A Little Light*. Actual ghosts appear in *A Happy Ghost* and the demure parody of Yeats's *All Souls' Night*. Part of this world is a cheerfully murderous nature: a cat stalking a squirrel reminds us that

> Life is exquisite when it's just
> > Out of reach by a bound
> Of filigree jaws and delicate paws [*Cats*, ll. 19–21]

and Miss Beleek is visited by "Moments almost too bright to bear" when she thinks of shooting the children who trample over her garden. A darker ferocity appears on the horizon in *War on the Periphery*, in the marching of

> The violent, obedient ones
> Guarding my family with guns. [ll. 15–16]

Part of it again is the sense of a submerged communion in nature, like the dogs reconnoitering at posts in *Noctambule*, or the "ecstatic edge of pain" in *After Thunder*. Part of it is the hidden private world that everyone retires into in sleep, the world so prominent in sexual love, with its hard narcissist core of self-absorption represented by *Elaine in a Bikini*, by the Lorelei figure in *Music on the Water*, and by the woman in *Home Again* who returns from a night on the tiles with this inner core almost, but not quite, violated:

> Now I am a bent doll, I shed my silky stuff
> And soon I'll be a sleeping heart. The gods got enough.   [ll. 5–6]

Even altruism may be expressed by the same kind of ego, like the contracting heart of Boom the "saint," or the pity that the poet feels for his other friend Goom.

And as we go on we feel less reassured by "the savoir faire of doom" and by the poet's insistence, sailing his crowded boat on the sea of life, that "Important people are in it as well." Life is not going anywhere except into death, and its minor pleasures of beer and love and sleep are all rehearsals for death. In *Smilers* something of the bewilderment of Willy Loman appears in the successful extrovert surrounded by what he is beginning to realize are fixed and glassy grins:

> After all, I made some dough,
> By and by I made some more;
> Anywhere I like to go
> Friends, my goodness, friends galore!   [ll. 9–12]

And eventually one begins to see that the "pond" has a bottom, familiarly known as death and hell, and that perhaps the "airborne" career of the cruising auk, an absurd and extinct bird that nevertheless manages somehow to get above himself, may have something to be said for it. At any rate it, or something like it, inspires Mrs. McGonigle into the stratosphere, frightens Mr. Smith, her protégé, into a coffin-like telephone booth, and sends Mr. Murple into a tree, where, in the curious Orpheus poem at the end of the second part, he sits charming the local frogs and bugs (in contrast to the crow at the end of the first part, who can only choose "Empty tree for empty tree"). Even a much rarer event, the "apocalyptic squawk" of the great dufuflu bird, does not pass wholly unheeded.

If I have not demonstrated how simplicity reverberates, at any rate I have shown that Mr. Johnston is an irresistibly readable and quotable poet. His finest technical achievement, I think, apart from his faultless sense of timing, is his ability to incorporate the language of the suburbs into his own diction. He does not write in the actual vulgate, but he manages to suggest with great subtlety the emotional confusions behind the pretentious diction and vague syntax of ordinary speech:

> Mrs. Belaney has a son
>   —Had, I should say, perhaps—
> Who deeds of gallantry has done,
>   Him and some other chaps.   [*The Hero's Kitchen*, ll. 5–8]

Or the elusiveness of large ideas as their shadows pass over an inarticulate mind:

> And as it happened we agreed
> On many things, but on the need
> Especially of mental strife
> And of a whole new source of life.   [*A Saint*, ll. 5–8]

It is this controlled portrayal of the ineffectual that gives Mr. Johnston his unique bittersweet flavour, and a "disconsolate" tone, to use one of his favourite words, that would be merely coy if it were less detached, or merely brittle if it were more so.

Ronald Bates's *The Wandering World* ([Toronto:] Macmillan) is another voyage of discovery, this time of Canada. We begin with a section called *Histories*, dealing with early voyages of exploration, with the sense of vast spaces in front and the illusion of some ineffably glamorous Cathay in the distance that has given its name to Lachine. In *Parallels in a Circle of Sand* the poet describes how the oppressiveness of the lack of tradition, the feeling of time cut off at the roots, pulls the Canadian back into Europe, only to make him realize how his real traditions are those of the explorers, and that the mutilation of time in his experience is hereditary. The next section, *Myths*, deals with the huge mythological figures in which an imagination first tries to conquer a new land, some of them assimilated to modern life, like *Overheard in the Garden*, very Audenesque in its linking of the immemorial lost garden symbol to a detective story. Next are the *Interiors*, where the themes are drawn from ordinary civilized life, and the *Landscapes*, the corresponding images of nature outside. Finally we come to *Constructions*, where the poet reaches the end of his journey in his own mind, the one fixed point of the wandering world, not only the world of space but of time also:

> Each man must come at last upon that point,
> Where all roads meet, all currents cross,
> Where past and future are valid,
> And now. [*The Wandering World*, ll. 14–17]

Thus we go from the open world of endless space to the contained world of the mind, and from exploration to self-knowledge.

As this brief summary indicates, an extraordinary variety of themes, moods, and techniques are attempted in the book. The histories employ what might be called a documentary style, much of it in unrhymed verse, which imitates historical narrative:

> What one cannot remember
> Concerning the customary rites,
> Prayers, plans, and polymorphous
> Duties, can be improvised.
> Some died of scurvy, the first winter,
> Some were tried for theft and shot. [*Founder's Day Speech*, ll. 25–30]

In the *Landscapes* there are more lyrical measures, stanzas in fairly strict metrical patterns; the *Interiors* are longish descriptive poems in an irregular meditative rhythm approximating blank verse. I find the poems in the tighter stanzaic patterns more consistently successful. Mr. Bates seems to me a Romantic poet, in the sense that he often uses abstract and unvisualized language but is keenly sensitive to evocative sound. Thus the forsaken god Pan whispers in his sleep:

> Chill as the night air is
> In the garden
> Still I will not be their guardian
> Still. [*After Pan Died*, ll. 9–12]

Mr. Bates's Canadian landscapes are mainly of winter, and he is eloquent about the delicate cruelty of winter, the feelings of menace it can arouse in a child which are "not of cold or fear," and the way that it seems to make visible the hidden death-world of primary qualities, where colour and warmth are gone and only the measurable remains. Winter also seems to symbolize for him both the source of imaginative energy in Canada and that curious offbeat rhythm of modern life where

Letters in Canada: Poetry

sterility has priority, so that one somehow never seems to have time for the important experiences, like love. In the fine *Ornithomachy* both of these are symbolized by the swan-song:

> But far away where the swans belong,
> In fields of iridescent snow,
> The songs of flesh and blood are blown
> Like leaves about the cold, the shrill
> Throat where all the singing starts.   [ll. 10–14]

In *The Fall of Seasons* the same association of winter and a failure of experience recurs in the life of a married couple, studied under the imagery of the seasons. Courtship comes in the springtime, where "Nobody came to bother them"; summer brings an oscillation of love and routine worries, the former growing increasingly furtive as the latter take over the mind, and an ironic refrain recurs in the autumn of old age:

> They stand together in dusty photo albums,
> The last repository of dreams.
> But nobody bothers to look at them.
> Nobody bothers at all.   [ll. 123–6]

There is nowhere in *The Wandering World* that we do not feel a contact with a richly suggestive intelligence. It sometimes happens that a poem succeeds by the interest of its controlling idea even when the texture of writing is unsatisfactory: I am thinking in particular of *I Skjaergaarden III*. I find, especially in the histories and myths, a good deal of talk, and too ready a satisfaction with such phrases as "all and sundry," "meticulous care," "fall from grace," or "absolutely certain." There are inorganic adjectives, like the "chthonic" and "powerful" which make *After Pan Died* more pedantic than it should be; bleak allegory in *Industrious Revolutions*, where the fly-wheel of pride meshes with the cog-wheel of man; vague words like the "pawn" which weakens the otherwise lovely *Bestiary*; and rhymes like those in *The Unimaginable Zoo* which seem to be dictating the thought. But there is much to return to, from the meditation on memory as a cable laid along "The ancient mountain ranges of the sea" near the beginning to the poet building himself a tower, like Yeats, and feeling that he can "put my hand on my hand's hidden power" near the end. In a first volume we can have all this and promise too.

Irving Layton's *A Red Carpet for the Sun* ([Toronto:] McClelland & Stewart) is a collection, according to the author, of "all the poems I wrote between 1942 and 1958 that I wish to preserve." As such, it is, of course, a volume of great importance, and if it is not examined in detail here, that is because the poems in it have been commented on before. It needs a full-length separate review and another reviewer. The introduction, in the first place, is Mr. Layton's first articulate statement in prose, and shows that, although he still admires the energy of his own reaction to modern life, he has become more detached from it. Hence his refusal to be content with the merely poetic, to make aesthetic pearls out of his irritations, has not landed him outside poetry but into the realization that "all poetry . . . is about poetry itself."

All Layton is here: there is the satire based, like Swift's, on the conception of man as characterized less by reason than by an ability to rationalize ferocity which makes him the only really cruel animal (*Paraclete, Abel Cain*). There are the recurring symbols of this cruelty: the tormenting and massacring of animals (*Cain, The Bull Calf, The Mosquito*), the desire for castration of those with more life (*Mr. Ther-Apis, Letter to a Librarian, The Puma's Tooth*), the refined efforts to ignore the democracy of the body (*Seven O'Clock Lecture, Imperial, Anti-Romantic*), the passion for envy and backbiting and every form of murder that cannot be punished (*The Toy Gun, Now That I'm Older, The Improved Binoculars*). There are the "atheistic" reflections on those who hope for eternal life but have never come alive (*Rose Lemay, Two Ladies at Traymore's*), the refusals to make the compromises of pity and gregarious love (*New Tables, Family Portrait, For Mao Tse-Tung*), and the sense of the interpenetration of love and death (*Orpheus, Thanatos and Eros*). There are the images of the Heraclitean fire that will burn up all the human rubbish of the world (*Love Is an Irrefutable Fire, The Poet Entertains Several Ladies*), and of the sensuous and relaxing water that will drown it (*The Swimmer, The Cold Green Element, Thoughts in the Water, Sacrament by the Water*). There is the figure of poet, outcast (*The Black Huntsmen*), madman (*The Birth of Tragedy, I Would for Your Sake Be Gentle*), "Jewboy" (*Gothic Landscape, The Statuettes of Ezekiel and Jeremiah*), Chaplinesque clown (*Whatever Else Poetry Is Freedom*), yet with the prophet's lion voice (*Woman, Rain at La Minerve*), who occasionally disappears into a strange world where all the expected associations come loose and get reassembled (*It's All in the Manner, The Poetic Process, Winter Fantasy*). It is all here, and a great deal more, and as rich an experience as ever.

Yet Mr. Layton seems tired of his present achievement, and one wonders if there is anything in his work so far that a reader might tire of too. In all genuine poetry we can hear the voice of a distinctive personality; but this is the poetic personality, not the ordinary one—nobody's ordinary personality can write a poem. Neither is it the deliberately assumed stage personality with which one meets the public. Mr. Layton's stage personality has recently been embalmed in the clichés of the *Star Weekly*, which carefully refrains from quoting anything from him except *obiter dicta* of the "sex is here to stay" variety. This stage personality has much the same relation to the poet that the begorra-and-bejabers stage Irishman has to Synge or O'Casey, and Mr. Layton clearly takes this view of it himself, as anyone may see who compares the poems in this collection with what has been rejected from the twelve volumes out of which it was made. Some writers have to kill themselves with drink and apoplexy before those who cannot read poetry will believe that anyone is writing it: Mr. Layton has been more ingenious. He has satisfied the public with an image of its own notion of what a genius should be like, and has thereby set himself free for his serious work.

But if one's stage personality is separable, the poetic personality may be too. Minor poets have only one voice; major ones speak with the gift of tongues, the multitudinous voices of sea and forest and swarming city. If one tires of anything in Mr. Layton's book, it is, perhaps, the sense of too insistent a speaking voice, and of being never out of listening range of it. One is grateful for such poems as *Song for Naomi*, where the poet is talking to someone else and the reader has only to eavesdrop. There is great variety of theme and imagery and mood, always touched with distinction, but little variety of tone. I imagine that Mr. Layton's future work will show a greater impersonality, which means a larger stock of poetic *personae*, as he becomes less afraid of not being sincere and less distrustful of the merely poetic.

Fred Cogswell's *Descent from Eden* ([Toronto:] Ryerson) contains, in the first place, a good many vignettes of New Brunswick life of the type that he has done hitherto. He has an excellent eye for this genre, and one wishes that his ear always matched it. I don't see why they all have to be clumping sonnets with rhymes like typewriter bells, and the two in a freer form, *In These Fall Woods* and *Lefty*, I like better, as the form gives him more scope to tell his story. But he catches very well the prurient wistfulness of a small community for whom the beautiful, the sinful, and the ridiculous are so closely linked that every pretty girl ill-advised enough to grow up in it has to run away and go into burlesque, like *Rose* and the mother of *Lefty*, or else remain and take it, like *Beth* with her miscarriage, whom the poet compares to an angleworm squirming "As some one shoves a fish-hook up her gut."

Of the epigrams and satires, there is a pungent *Ode to Fredericton*, and a quatrain which ends:

> A poem is a watch designed
> To tick forever in the mind.   [*A Poem*, ll. 3–4]

There are also two ballads, plaintive and melodious, *The Ballad of John Armstrong* being the odyssey of a sailor who has a response of indifference in every port. In mood the theme has some resemblance to Patrick Anderson's *Summer's Joe*. There is a lively fantasy called *The Jacks of History*, too well integrated to quote from, and as well realized a poem as any in the book. There are several fine lyrics turning on well worked out conceits, including *The Water and the Rock* and *Displaced*.

The title poem and a few others that go with it add a new mythopoeic dimension to Mr. Cogswell's poetry. Eden is presented as the life in the trees enjoyed by our simian ancestors before famine forced them on the ground to become "the scourge and terror of the earth," and which still survives as a kind of social memory of a paradisal tree "With fruit and innocence among its boughs." *The Dragon Tree* continues this theme of the lost garden which children can still enter but which a dragon guards against adults, and in *The Idiot Angel* and *The Fool* we are brought closer to the perversity of mind that makes us lose it. A most eloquent poem, *The Winter of the Tree*, sets up the opposing symbol of a tree dying in winter "Caught in the body of its death." This last is a Biblical phrase, and links the poem with a number of religious poems (*The Web: For Easter*, *A Christmas Carol*, and *For Good Friday*) which associate the dead tree with the cross as a central image of the post-paradisal world. So far the versatility of Mr. Cogswell's talents has been more in evidence than their concentration, but the present volume is a remarkable achievement, and the general impression is one of slow and rich growth.

The title poem of Peter Miller's *Sonata for Frog and Man* ([Toronto:] Contact) contrasts the bullfrog's spontaneity of song with the curse laid upon "man, greedy for meaning," which makes him "seek the symbolism of nightbirds." I find it hard to understand why one should look for sermons in stones when the inability to preach is so attractive a feature of

Letters in Canada: Poetry

stones. But there are bullfrogs who loaf and invite their souls with Whitman, and men like Emerson who explain that they are not really wasting time picking flowers because every one "Goes home loaded with a thought."[21] Mr. Miller is on the side of Emerson in this matter. For a poet, he seems curiously insensitive to the sound and movement of words: poem after poem bogs down in shapeless free verse and gabbling polysyllables. His poetic interest is mainly in allegory, and most of the poems are fables, based on conceits of comparison like *The Thaw* or *Railroad Perspective*, or on moralized emblems like *Past President* or *The Bracelet*. When the conceit is good and consistently worked out, the poem makes its point. *People Are 8 Parts Deep* compares the visible part of an iceberg to the eyes which focus the consciousness in the body; *Private Eye* reflects on the smugness inspired by the thrillers that identify one with the hunter instead of the victim, and *Lemmings*, of course, comments on the human analogies to the death-march of those lugubrious rodents.

Mr. Miller appears to have travelled widely, and many of the poems with Mexican, Continental, and Levantine settings are full of sharp observation, as are some of the Ontario countryside. I find, however, the more reflective poems like *Passage to Thule* more arresting, and *The Prevention of Stacy Miller*, based on a theme like Lamb's *Dream Children*, is, to me, much the most moving poem in the book. But *The Capture of Edwin Alonzo Boyd* is a skilful adaptation of the idiom of the naive ballad, and in some of the later poems, such as *Your Gifts*, the rhythm picks up and the lines start to swing. *Hour in the Warren* is based on a sharp contrast of semantic and metrical rhythms, a little like Marianne Moore, and the third *Murder Jury* poem reaches a carefully muted conclusion:

> From this turret, vision is vast,
> all heaviness lifts at the last
> and certainty, as an aerial thing,
> takes wing.

George Walton's *The Wayward Queen* ([Toronto:] Contact) is light but highly cultivated verse, much of it in an idiom of familiar address rare in Canadian poetry. It is a retrospective collection, some of the poems being dated as far back as 1919. The poems are least successful when adhering to certain literary stereotypes, as in the Falstaff poems, and occasionally, as in *Prairie Village*, a poem talks all around a theme without finding the central words. They are most successful when the poet realizes that the lightness of light verse is a matter of rhythm and diction and not of content. Thus in the title poem:

> The Queen of Cilicia slept with Cyrus—
> Xenophon says they said,
> now, dust is Xenophon, scattered Cyrus,
> the wayward Queen is dead.   [*Ancient Gossip*, ll. 6–9]

The content is deliberately commonplace, which, when the rhythmical lilt is so attractive, is a positive virtue: one gets the feeling of popular song, as one often does in Housman, whom Mr. Walton seems to be echoing in *Isolt the Queen*. Similarly the poems with refrains or repetitive sound patterns, like *Madrigal* or the opening *Security*, which begins with the jingle "No noise annoys an oyster," often give an effect of rising from talk into singing. Such increased intensity gives a well-rounded conclusion to an otherwise less interesting *Borrowed Themes*.

Mr. Walton is a well-read poet, who delicately calls a politician a jackass by means of a reference to Apuleius, and gets Panurge into a poem about the female sexual appetite. Once in a while he exploits the opportunities of light verse for a casual treatment of solemn themes, as in *Dies Irae*, which tells how "Through the clear aether Gabriel flew horning," and, more frequently, its ability to express anger or contempt, as in *November II*. But on the whole his range is more domestic and familiar: whether satire or love song, the tone is quiet and controlled. Thus *For My Daughters* ends with the mixture of truth and detachment from truth that such a poem requires:

> Disregard advance, accept
> not the proffered rose—
> there's a door he'd open
> Time will never close.

("He" is Love.) Similarly *Miranda's Mirror* ends with an irony which has enough sympathy in it to keep clear of glibness, and *Where I Go*, again close to popular song, has the emotional resonance that an unresolved situation often produces when abandoned at the right point.

Anerca ([Toronto:] Dent) is a collection of Eskimo poems edited by Edmund Carpenter, and illustrated with delightful little drawings by

Enooesweetok, an otherwise unknown Eskimo artist whose work was preserved by the late Robert Flaherty. Mr. Carpenter has collected the poems from a variety of sources, and has added a few bits of prose comment which have the same kind of expectancy about them that the printed introductions to Flaherty's silent documentaries had. For one poem Mr. Carpenter supplies the Eskimo text, which indicates that the originals are intensely repetitive in sound, and have a kind of murmuring magical charm about them that no translator could reasonably be asked to recapture.

It is difficult for us to imagine a life in which the fight to keep alive is so intense, in which the will to live is as constant and palpable as the heartbeat. One ghoulish story in prose tells how a party comes upon a starving hag who has eaten her husband and children, most of her clothes, and finally, as she confesses, "I have eaten your fellow-singer from the feasting." The response is only "You had the will to live, therefore you live." The same will is strong enough to make an old man hurl defiance at the Eskimo Cerberus who comes for him on his deathbed:

> Who comes?
> Is it the hound of death approaching?
> Away!
> Or I will harness you to my team.

What is still more difficult to imagine is that when life is reduced to the barest essentials of survival, poetry should turn out to be one of those essentials. "Anerca," Mr. Carpenter tells us, means both "to make poetry" and "to breathe." Its primitive rhythm, which we interpret as "magic," is part of the physical energy with which the living man maintains his life as he seeks for his food:

> Beast of the Sea,
> Come and offer yourself in the dear early morning!
> Beast of the Plain!
> Come and offer yourself in the dear early morning!

Nature cannot exterminate such a people: only civilization, with its high-powered death-wish, can do that. It is very comfortable in the settled parts of Canada, and hard to hear such things as the screams of trapped animals, much less the thin delicate cry, faint as a wisp of snow and yet as piercing as the revelation by word itself, that comes to us in this—a song to ensure fine weather, Mr. Carpenter says:

> Poor it is: this land,
> Poor it is: this ice,
> Poor it is: this air,
> Poor it is: this sea,
> Poor it is.

{With the exception of *Songs from Kawartha*, by Florrie Baxter Young (New York: Vantage; Toronto: Foulsham), a collection mainly of children's verse, and outside the scope of a survey of this kind, the remaining volumes are chapbooks, ten of them Ryerson's. No particular comment is necessary on Arthur S. Bourinot's *A Gathering: Poems, 1959* (Ottawa: n.p.), or on *River and Realm*, by Teresa E. and Don W. Thomson (Ryerson Chapbook no. 185), a collection of poems about rivers in an amiable downstream rhythm. In *Faces of Love*, by Mary Elizabeth Bayer (Ryerson Chapbook no. 181), there is some genuine poetry in bits and pieces of sharp imagery to be picked out of a talkier context, like the jury image in *Jealousy* or this in *Mother and Child*:

> This is the My love, the grim maternal,
> Careless of sire and ready for the fight. [ll. 13–14]

In *Ad Astra* and *The Message* there is some distinctiveness of theme and a compact and varied rhythmical organization. *In Her Mind Carrying*, by Verna Loveday Harden (Ryerson Chapbook no. 183), begins with an appropriately laboured comparison of poetry-writing to pregnancy, but picks up in *Saint John Harbour* and *Resurgence*, where the repeated patterns of sound unify the poem. *Poems* (Ryerson Chapbook no. 188) by Florence Wyle, better known as a sculptor, with an introduction by Ira Dilworth, has the merit of concentrating on emotion and sensation, so that while we have poems as nakedly subjective as *The Dark Valley*, or as objective as *April Snow*, we do not get the kind of sententious filler that is such a nuisance in most of these chapbooks. *Lost* has an interesting theme well worked out, and in *Spring Comes Up the Land* and *Normandy Orchards* there is some tense accurate timing and organization of sound:

> Stark gnarled trees with branches cut
> Stand guard over springing grain,
> While grey old houses soundly sleep
> Through sun and rain.   [*Normandy Orchards*, ll. 5-8]

The natural compensation for sculpture is the colour and flatness of painting, and the poetry in this book shows a strong pictorial interest.

Douglas Lochhead's *The Heart Is Fire* (Ryerson Chapbook no. 184), apart from a longish poem about the jealousy of Joseph that doesn't seem to me to get anywhere, is closely observed poetry with a Maritime setting. *Birth of a Legend* is admirable in the irony of its balance between what really happened and the point of legendary birth; *What Stirs a Bird* is a spring poem in which the poet, unlike ground-hogs and most spring poets, manages to see a bit more than his own shadow. *The Recruit* is the most concise of several interesting war poems, with a fine closing stanza:

> You will pray when no one is looking.
> You will curl in fear, in the womb
>   of your pounding blood,
>   in your private bed of whittled thorns.

Nova Scotia Fishermen ends by reducing the perilous struggle of fishermen's lives to an eloquent abstraction:

> Wild crying from their drunken nights
> Dull oblivion in Sunday suits
> Along the blue-road of white rocks,
> Along their eastern sea.

R.E. Rashley's *Moon Lake and Other Poems* (Ryerson Chapbook no. 187) shows considerable fluency and charm in organizing some longish poems with variable rhythms and rhymes. A mind of unusual interest is revealed in the linking of eoliths and satellites in *Satellite*, and in the reconciling, in the same poem, of the moon of lovers and poets with the stony sun-mirror of science. The poet is most successful in rendering the tranquillity of moonlight and snowfall, with the snow

> Building with infinite care
> On telephone wires and posts.   [*Snowfall*, ll. 3-4]

But there is a more ironic tranquillity in his observation of *Marianne*, whose preoccupation with a caged bird develops into identity with it, and in *At Forty*, which juxtaposes a retarded spring and a full-blown suburban matron insensible to rebirth.

Alfred Purdy's *The Crafte So Longe to Lerne* (Ryerson Chapbook no. 186) contains some woodenly self-conscious satire and a villanelle on the theme "Embrace, my verse, the language of the age," which he approaches in the general spirit of Flaubert's St. Julian. Of other poems, such as *Driftwood Logs*, one feels that there is something "in" them, that they are not poems so much as prosodic frameworks that contain a good deal of poetry. The first stanza of *If Birds Look In* is admirable, but the second shows a restless pursuit of conceits that almost breaks down into free association. A much more interesting poem, *After the Rats*, is one of those chilling poems that talk quietly and reasonably on an insane subject, as the poet wonders what the rats do with all the parts of his body that they gnaw off and carry away. *Where the Moment Is* is quieter, but there is still much point in such lines as

> I can pre-determine you or
> Taste your becoming in my mouth.   [ll. 18–19]

There is a lively poem about a cat called, I regret to say, *For Oedi-Puss*, and *From the Chin P'ing Mei* catches very well the mood of meditative plaintiveness that seems to get into all poetic chinoiserie. *Passport*, a tribute to the late Alec Crawley, is much the most deeply felt poem in the book.

Poems by Michael Collie (Ryerson Chapbook no. 182) are written mainly in that equal balance of metrical and semantic rhythms which gives the effect of deep thought, where a slowly unfolding meditative sentence is regularly punctuated by slightly enjambed rhymes. Mr. Collie's handling of this rhythm is still mainly on the level of poetic exercise, though the exercises show a good deal of originality, such as *At Clearwater*, quite interesting in its accentuation, with the caesura hitting the middle like a putt-putt, and *In Time of Aerial Warfare*, which is something genuinely new in sonnets. There are many indications too that the practice is developing into a more realized skill. *An Assertion* has a theme like that of Henry James's *Jolly Corner*; a sonnet speaks of girls in a foreign city

> Whose voices are anonymous delight
> sung to the pattern of a silent care   [*Six Sonnets*, ll. 73–4]

Letters in Canada: Poetry   225

and *The Candle* has a fine contrasting image:

> It distracts and teases the mind
> already on guard for facile sentiment,
> as a bandaged soldier who fears he will be blind.   [ll. 9–11]

The poet's eye is caught by patterns of light and movement in fireworks, falling water, and the flight of birds, and *The Pembina Highway by Night*, the most successful of several poems on the relation of art, nature, and mechanisms, works out an intricate conceit concluding:

> the highway is man's brash courageous flare
> to catch chromatic fancies in cold light,
> create his own perspective, and to fear
> no specious artifice behind delight.

Two other chapbooks, *The Varsity Chapbook*, edited by John Robert Colombo, and *The McGill Chapbook*, edited by Leslie L. Kaye (both [Toronto:] Ryerson), are collections of poetry by younger writers who are or have recently been connected with those universities. Not everybody can fill up a whole chapbook without thin spaces, but there are a good many cultivated people who can make one or two admirable contributions to an anthology, and both these chapbooks are recommended unreservedly. In the McGill book I noticed particularly the mellow conversational tone of Morty Schiff's *Winter in Paris*, D.G. Jones's *Like One of Botticelli's Daughters*, with its final "O angels, what has heaven lost!," Daryl Hine's *Trompe l'Oeil*, with its intoxicating couplet rhythm, Mike Gnarowski's lively and good-humoured *Transition as a Sharp Musical Note*, and Phyllis Webb's *The Galaxy*, one of a group of four poems by her of greater seriousness than anything in *Even Your Right Eye*. The Toronto one is less exciting, but there are James Reaney's macabre *The Man Hunter*, Frances Wheeler's *Proserpina Unfallen*, with its anapestic lilt, Francis Sparshott's vigorous sonnet *Tankerton*, E.A. Lacey's *The Butterfly*, with its repetitions building up an impressive sound-pattern, Jay Macpherson's *The Wound*, three beautifully precise quatrains, and Christopher Priestley's *The Gorgon*, on an Ozymandias theme, and technically a skilful handling of a difficult metre. However, these are somewhat random likings in two most rewarding little books.

Lamplight Poems ([Toronto:] Hawkshead) is a broadside containing three poems: *Anthropos in Transit*, by Gerry Vise, on a Cynic philosopher; a poem by E.A. Lacey on a fugitive lover; and *Don Panza, Sancho Quixote*, by Peter Miller, which would have been one of the best poems in *Sonata for Frog and Man* if it had been included there. Pretty good value for a dime, which is its marked price.}

Perhaps the most distinguished of all this year's chapbooks is Dorothy Roberts's *In Star and Stalk* ([Toronto:] Emblem Books). This is poetry in a sombre and heavily churning rhythm, showing a unified imagination of unusual power. It is an imagination for which the spoiled word "mystical" still has some relevance. In the background of her imagery are the free-wheeling rhythms of nature, the spinning earth and the setting sun, the stream of time that carries away the childhood memories of grandparents, the violence of storm and the fragility of birth. In the foreground is the image of the "shell," the home occupied by the lonely and uncertain self in the "almighty sea" of nature. Its products are the body itself, the house, and the stone buildings of civilization, the bus clinging to the white line of the highway, the memories of the past, and finally the gravestones of a cemetery. What matters, of course, is the intensity with which these images are realized. In *Our Shells* the birth of a child is set against the two backgrounds at once, making what is perhaps the most impressive and memorable poem of the group:

> In this pattern of silent homes and heavenly bodies
> The walls have been pushed out to a vast wandering—
> How many stars to lead me to this child?
>
> Only the constellations house with fables
> Like brilliant parables upon church windows,
> Making of night a high roof for the spirit.   [ll. 7–12]

With this review I complete a decade of observing Canadian poetry, and retire from the scene. The fifties have been a rich and fruitful time: no other decade in our history has seen such variety of originality. *Towards the Last Spike, Trial of a City, In the Midst of My Fever, The Boatman, A Suit of Nettles, The Cruising Auk*: this is an extraordinary range of new discoveries in technique and sensibility, created at every age level from the veteran to the newcomer. *Victorian House, The Colour as Naked, The Net and the Sword, Friday's Child, The Selected Poems* (Souster), *The Transparent Sea*, and many others represent what may be called the resonance of tradition. This does not mean that they follow after the other group, necessarily: in literature it is the traditional book that pioneers, the new settler who has his roots elsewhere. There are also a number of poets—I think particularly of Eli Mandel and Margaret Avison—who have not received their due of attention only because no published volume has been available to the present writer.

The reviewer knows that he will be read by the poets, but he is not addressing them, except indirectly. It is no part of the reviewer's task to tell the poet how to write or how he should have written. The one kind of criticism that the poet himself, qua poet, engages in—the technical self-criticism which leads to revision and improvement—is a criticism with which the reviewer has nothing to do. Nor is it his task to encourage or discourage poets. To encourage a genuine poet is impertinence, and to encourage a mediocre one is condescension. Discouragement is an even more dubious practice. To say that no one should write poetry except good poets is nearly as silly as saying that no one should read it except teachers of English. There are some who write poetry not because they care about poetry but for more devious reasons, but such people can be discouraged only by implication, by showing from the real poets that an ignorant or anti-intellectual mind can never be good enough.

The reviewer's audience is the community of actual and potential readers of poetry. His task is to show what is available in poetic experience, to suggest that reading current poetry is an essential cultural activity, at least as important as keeping up with current plays or concerts or fiction. He has the special problem, too, of bridging the gap between poetry and its public, already mentioned. I have spent a great deal of my space in trying to explain as clearly as I can what the poet is saying, and what is characteristic about his handwriting, so to speak, in imagery and rhythm. I have felt that it is well worth insulting the intelligence of some readers if one can do anything to breach the barriers of panic and prejudice in others.

The ordinary reader of poetry may exercise a preference. He may have a special feeling for religious poetry or landscape poetry or satire and light verse or narrative; he may like poetry that expresses involvement in society, or poetry written in certain technical forms, or poetry that is dense in texture, or poetry that is loose in texture. The reviewer must take poetry as he finds it, must constantly struggle for the standards of good and bad in all types of poetry, must always remember that a preference for any one kind of poetry over another kind is, for him, laziness and incompetence. The poets themselves are sometimes eager to tell him that if he thinks less of their poetry than they do, it is because he underestimates the importance of their kind of poetry, being too Philistine or modern or bourgeois or academic or intellectual or prudish—I list only a few of the things I have been called myself. Assuming a certain amount of technical competence, the reviewer can be satisfied with his efforts only if he feels that he has tried to be honest: no batting average of hits and errors is either attainable or relevant.

Finally, the community that I have been addressing is the Canadian community. As Canada is a small country, that fact raises the problem: do you estimate Canadian poets in Canadian proportions or in world proportions? I have considered this question carefully, and my decision, while it may have been wrong, was deliberate. I have for the most part discussed Canadian poets as though no other contemporary poetry were available for Canadian readers. The reviewer is not concerned with the vague relativities of "greatness," but with the positive merits of what is before him. And every genuine poet is entitled to be read with the maximum sympathy and concentration. When he is, an astonishing amount of imaginative richness may be obtained from him, and without reading into him what is not there. Shakespeare is doubtless an infinitely "greater" poet, but there is a limit to what a limited mind can get out of Shakespeare, and if one continually tries to break through one's limitations in reading one's contemporaries, one may also achieve a clearer vision of greatness. In the context of their importance for English-reading posterity as a whole, many poets may have been considerably over-praised in these reviews. But I am not writing for an invisible posterity anxious to reduce the bulk of its required reading. The better poets of every age seem all the same size to contemporaries: it takes many years before the comparative standards become clear, and contemporary critics may as well accept the myopia which their near-sighted perspective forces on them. Then again, poetry is of major importance in the culture, and therefore in the history, of a country, especially of a country that is still struggling for articulateness. The appearance of a fine new book of poems in Canada is a historical event, and its readers should be aware that they are participating in history. To develop such awareness it is an advantage to have a relatively limited cultural horizon. *Ubi bene, ibi patria*: the centre of reality is wherever one happens to be, and its circumference is whatever one's imagination can make sense of.

The last ten reviews have recorded what T.S. Eliot calls the horror, the boredom, and the glory of their subject:[22] writing them has been of immense profit to me, and some, I hope, to my readers. But if I could go on doing such a job indefinitely it would not have been worth doing in the first place. At a certain point diminishing returns set in for both reviewer and reader. No poet has written more good poetry in Canada in the last decade than Irving Layton, yet Mr. Layton has just announced that he is dead, and that a new Mr. Layton is to rise from his ashes. If so, new critics should welcome him, as well as other newcomers, should find different reasons for helping established poets to defend their establishments, should respond to new currents in imaginative life and to new needs in society. The critic to whom falls the enviable task of studying Canadian poetry in the sixties will, I trust, be dealing with a fully matured culture, no longer preoccupied with the empty unpoetics of Canadianism, but with the genuine tasks of creative power. For the poets of the next decade will have the immense advantage of the tradition set up by the poets of the last one, whose imaginative feats, as far as this critic is concerned, have been, like the less destructive efforts of Milton's Samson, "not without wonder or delight beheld."[23]

35

Pelham Edgar

1952

Editor's introduction to Pelham Edgar, Across My Path *(Toronto: Ryerson Press, 1952), vii-xi.*

During the last few years of his life, Dr. Pelham Edgar was engaged in preparing an autobiography of a somewhat unusual kind. In addition to the standard reminiscent and anecdotal material of the ordinary autobiography, he was anxious to cast his recollections of the people of public interest he had met into a series of informal essays, partly an impression of them as personalities and partly a critical estimate of their work. In a "Proem" to this autobiography he speaks of the interest shown in it by the publisher of the present volume, and remarks, "He is surely well aware that a certain fell sergeant is 'strict in his arrest.'" This was unluckily prophetic, for the thrombosis referred to in his letter to me proved fatal, and the chapter he was then working on is apparently unfinished, as he obviously intended a fourth section on Professor E.K. Brown's study of Matthew Arnold,[1] and a fifth on the work of another pupil he was most proud of, Professor Douglas Bush, now of Harvard. The present book began as an effort to give what remained of his original task at the time of his death. This comprises the first part, which consists of five sections of his manuscript, and the first chapter of the second part. Most of the second part was published elsewhere, but designed to be incorporated in the autobiography. The third part consists of essays on Yeats and Hardy. The whole book constitutes, it is hoped, some of the best of his critical writing, apart from his two full-length studies, *Henry James, Man and Author* (Toronto[: Macmillan], 1927), and *The Art of the Novel [from 1700 to the Present Time]* (New York[: Macmillan], 1933), his chapter on Canadian literature contributed to *The Cambridge History of English Literature*, and two fine essays on Matthew Arnold regretfully excluded from this volume.[2] My own embarrassment at finding myself the editor of a book in which I am featured with all the author's typical generosity is something that has had to give way to other considerations. One can hardly take advantage of his death to omit material which he would have used—besides, in the record of my personal debt to him the reader may see the kind of influence he could be in a younger man's life.

Dr. Edgar has left no connected account, except by implication, of the long career, centred at Victoria College as professor first of French and then of English, which made him so uniquely important a figure in Canadian letters. He was in the first place a close and lifelong friend of the leading poets of his generation, Carman, Roberts, and D.C. Scott. Then came his association with E.J. Pratt and J.D. Robins on his own English staff at Victoria, and then, as the age gap slowly increased between him and the newer writers, a long period of helping, encouraging, and publicizing Canadian literary talent from Marjorie Pickthall and Raymond Knister to many who have hardly yet reached their prime. With all this, he was one of Canada's great English teachers, and he retired from teaching only to devote himself with all the more energy to the Canadian Authors' Association and the Canadian Writers' Foundation, two of the many literary societies which, in his own words, he "helped either to found or to fold up." It is natural, therefore, to think of him as having had largely a personal importance in Canadian literature, and before this tradition hardens, it may be as well to enter the present volume in the evidence. His writing was so occasional, and spread over so many magazines, several of them now defunct, that no one would realize, without Miss Ray's help, how much of it he actually did, apart altogether from his extensive correspondence.[3]

His strong and constant interest in the contemporary was part of his feeling—derived partly from Arnold, as his essays on Arnold show—that literature helps to create the standards and values of life, and that consequently the appearance of a new good poem or novel is a significant historical fact. John Donne in his *Litanie* prays to be delivered "from light affecting, in religion, news"—if this means that undervaluing the contemporary event is a sin of presumption, Dr. Edgar was free of it. The poets of the nineties are the theme of essays written when he had barely come of age, and while his interest in drama never equalled his interest in poetry and fiction, he was reporting to Canadians on Ibsen and the

Irish theatre at the turn of the century. By 1904 he was discussing the perennial Canadian question, "Have we a National Literature?" The answer, as it always is, is in effect no, but wait a while. One of the most remarkable things about his study of Henry James is its date—1927, some years before the present uproar over James began.[4] His intellectual curiosity took him into a great variety of subjects. He was, as has been said, originally a professor of French, and he wrote several fine essays on French topics which I wish I had room for. Even Professor Infeld's fictional biography of the mathematical prodigy Galois, *Whom the Gods Love*, was anticipated by Dr. Edgar in an article on Galois in the *Ottawa Journal*.

Dr. Edgar refers in his essay on Yeats to Yeats's conception of the mask or anti-self, the theory that an artist's creative personality is as different from his ordinary one as it can possibly be.[5] His discovery of Shelley, recorded in the second chapter of this book, seems at first a good example of the theory. He was reared in the colonial aristocracy of Upper Canada and trained in all the exacting rituals of its self-conscious grand style; yet it was the callow revolutionary ardours of Shelley that woke him up to the imaginative life. Dr. Edgar lived to see the destruction of that society, not only in Ontario but over the whole world; he saw two wars destroy many things far less superficial than it was; he saw the poet dwindle from the "unacknowledged legislator" of the nineteenth century to the "bourgeois intellectual" of the twentieth; he saw the professor transformed from the guardian of leisure-class wisdom into a harried employee of a culture-processing factory. He saw all this without ever following Shelley in his exuberant repudiation of the values of the public school and the squirearchy. But the temperamental link between him and Shelley is there none the less. As he makes clear, it was the candid simplicity of Shelley's mind that attracted him, the obviousness of the questions he asked and the objections he raised. And it was a kindred simplicity which gave Dr. Edgar his place in Canadian life as a scholar, teacher, and critic.

Reading through his essays and reviews, and remembering his teaching, one is struck by the frequency with which he is willing merely to quote his author or say the obvious thing about him. He brings nothing of the historian or the philosopher to his criticism; he gazes at the poem or the novel with a quiet, untroubled stare, content to let it speak for itself whenever it can. His study of Henry James was described by an English critic, writing in the year of his death, as "still unrivalled for clarity"—no mean tribute considering the nature of its subject. As a teacher, however magnetic he might be to those who were willing to listen, he puzzled and annoyed students who wanted examination cribs instead of poetic experience, who expected their teachers, not to read poetry to them (which Dr. Edgar did well, and frequently), but to roll all a poet's sweetness up into one ball, in the manner of crammers and dung-beetles. His criticism, in short, was as far as possible "uncritical," in the narrower sense, and this is why it is so closely bound up, as the present volume shows, with his personal relationships. As a critic he had the quality that marks the devoted friend in ordinary life. He assumed that his poet was most truly himself when he was at his best, and neither approved of nor denounced his failings. His criticism of Roberts and Carman went infallibly to the sincere and unpretentious lyrical feeling at the heart of them both, ignoring all the ready-made forms of metrical excelsior which insulated it. The posing and the awe-inspiring gullibility of Yeats is passed over in the word "enigma." The prissiness of Arnold is politely overlooked—this in spite of Arnold's reflection, in his essay "Equality," that Goldwin Smith's "long winter evenings in Toronto" (spent no doubt in the society of such fellow-Grits as the Edgars), would give him abundant experience of a dismal and illiberal life.[6]

Naturally Dr. Edgar was a critic of his own generation. The great Romantics took the primary hold on his affections, and they coloured his appreciation of all other poetry. He formed his prose style in the age of Pater, and never lost the feeling that persuasiveness of sense was mysteriously involved with elegance of rhythm. Criticism for him was the *causerie* of his critical idol Sainte-Beuve, the man of taste demonstrating how literature is to be absorbed into society. The limits of his sympathies were mainly chronological limits. He was baffled by Joyce, bored by Eliot, never became reconciled to the later Yeats, and an unfortunate article entitled "The Changing Aspects of Poetry" on Auden, Spender, and their contemporaries contains the only crotchety passages I have found in his writing. But even there we have his old candid vision in a remark: "A poet should never think how his mind works, but in the emotional urge that launches the poem he should be grateful that it works at all."[7] It was not the superficial difficulty of this later writing that repelled him, for he was very patient with the involutions of Henry James and the murkiness of Meredith, and three or four years before this essay he had written a sympathetic review of Virginia Woolf's most elusive novel, *The Waves*.[8] It was rather that he sensed in it, whether rightly or wrongly, a decline of the old Shelleyan belief in the social value of creative power.

He learned from Sainte-Beuve that great culture is cosmopolitan, that the standards of the classic have no reference to time or space, to language or conditions of life. He learned from Shelley (I am thinking of the Preface to *Prometheus Unbound*) that great culture is also completely provincial, that it is as racy of the soil as a fine wine, and can only grow where there is a powerful sense of locality. Whatever verbal contradiction there may be between these two statements does not prevent them from being equally and simultaneously true. Dr. Edgar worked hard for Canadian literature without forgetting that good writing is no better for being Canadian; he studied the classics of two literatures, taught them, and maintained the standards implied by them, without losing touch with his own community. To deserve the great titles of scholar and teacher one must do much more than merely hold down a certain kind of white-collar job. Some of the evidence of Dr. Edgar's right to these titles will be found in the following pages; some more is in his writing which is not included here; but much of it is still, and happily will be for many years yet, in the affectionate memories of those who came "across his path."

36

New Liberties for Old

December 1952

From Canadian Forum, 32 *(December 1952): 195–6. Reprinted in* RW, *401–2. This editorial was written shortly after the sale of Consolidated Press, the owner of the magazine* Saturday Night, *to entrepreneur and baseball club owner Jack Kent Cooke. The change of ownership was followed by the resignation of editor emeritus B.K. Sandwell, current editor Robert Farquharson, and two other writers.*

Saturday Night, which recently changed its face, has now changed hands as well. It is a paper for which the *Canadian Forum* has always had the greatest respect and affection, and some editorials in it encourage us to believe that these feelings are in some measure reciprocal. Of late years, *Saturday Night* has been increasingly preoccupied with the relation of private enterprise to individual freedom, and with the authoritarian dangers in all bureaucratic control. We, on the other hand, believe that any social tendency becomes pernicious whenever it is carried through to its logical conclusion without opposition. Private enterprise may, in some circumstances, be a safeguard of individual freedom. It may also, given unchecked power, turn into its exact opposite: a development of engrossing monopolies in which journals of independent opinion can be bought up like cigarettes and pulped into mass-circulation tabloids.

It is very hard to believe that any such fate can be in store for *Saturday Night*, particularly when its new owner has repeatedly declared that he has no such plans. The trouble is that the debasing of a paper's standards cannot be prevented by anybody's good intentions, even an owner's: it can only be prevented by good journalists. And the recently announced resignations of four journalists of unquestioned ability and integrity from the staff of *Saturday Night* is, to say the least, disconcerting.

37

John D. Robins

January 1953

From Canadian Forum, *32 (January 1953): 218. Reprinted in* RW, *402–3. Robins had died on 18 December 1952.*

The *Canadian Forum* regrets very much to go into a new year looking as though it had lost one of its best friends, but unfortunately that is precisely what has happened.

John D. Robins, Professor of English at Victoria College, Toronto, was one of the most active contributors both to the *Forum* itself and to its predecessor the *Rebel*, in the years immediately following the First World War. He wrote stories, sketches, and humorous parodies, but as he was modest about his own works to the point of self-deprecation, he made no attempt to publish them. Even when he edited, with Margaret Ray, the anthology of Canadian humour that was published a year ago,[1] it did not occur to him to reprint anything of his own. The *Canadian Forum* took a different view, and reprinted "The Golfic Mysteries" as a supplement to his collection. Two years ago he gave a series of talks over the CBC on the history of the *Forum* which showed how longstanding his interest in us had been.

Many readers of this magazine have been students of his, many more will have known him through his radio work and through his two widely read and well-loved books, *The Incomplete Anglers* and *Cottage Cheese*. Still others will remember him as a close friend and warm supporter of many of Canada's best painters. However he is remembered, it is no exaggeration to say that he was a central figure in the cultural history of Canada. His academic training was in German philology and the Teutonic languages, including Old and Middle English, and, being a scholar and not a pedant, he grasped the close connection in mood between that period and his own. To find anything analogous to the Canadian culture of the early twentieth century, with its uneasy mingling of the sophisticated and the primitive, one has to go back to the Europe of the great migrations. And John Robins, a highly civilized scholar and teacher, was at the same time a kind of modern minstrel. Everyone who came in contact with him knew of his vast fund of stories, folk tales, ballads, songs, and of his encyclopedic knowledge of primitive and popular literature. But it would be a mistake to think of him simply as a great entertainer. His anthology, *A Pocketful of Canada*, for all its unpretentiousness, is actually a powerful analysis of the cultural development of the country: he saw, perhaps more clearly than anyone else has seen, the shaping and growth of Canadian writing and painting out of the conditions of Canadian life. Of the sense of personal loss this is perhaps not the place to speak, and those of our readers who knew him, in the flesh or through books, will not require that anything should be said.

38

Turning New Leaves: *Folk Songs of Canada*

July 1954

A review of Folk Songs of Canada, *ed. Edith Fulton Fowke and Richard Johnston (Waterloo, Ontario: Waterloo Music Company, 1954). From* Canadian Forum, *34 (July 1954): 89, 91. Reprinted in BG, 157-62.*

This is the first collection of Canadian folk songs which attempts to cover the whole country and is designed for the general public. To have produced such a book at all is a public service; to produce it with such competence is a feat that leaves a reviewer (unless he has the special knowledge of the field that the present one has not) little to say that is not better said in the two introductions.

To come at it from the outside, the book is an attractive physical object, illustrated with drawings and end papers by Elizabeth Wilkes Hoey which are cheerful without being cute. The printing of both words and music is clear, and the editor's comments, printed in a box at the end, tell you exactly what you want to know. Mrs. Fowke's knowledge of her subject is almost as complete as the average Canadian's ignorance of it, yet her scholarship is quiet and unobtrusive. She has humour but no condescension; she is appreciative but never writes advertising copy. Dr. Johnston's settings are simple and unpretentious, partly because he has the guitar as well as the piano in mind. The piano scores nearly always contain the tune, so that the reader can try them out on a piano without having to struggle with three lines of music. The French songs are given both in the French and in English translations, the latter being better than most of the translations we know, especially when Mrs. Fowke does them. The book deserves a long career in Canadian schools and homes,

Turning New Leaves: *Folk Songs of Canada*

and future editions can improve it in the way that it can best be improved, by enlarging it.

The term "folk song" in the title has been most hospitably interpreted. Drummond's *Wreck of the "Julie Plante,"* Tom Moore's *Canadian Boat Song*, and the *Huron Carol* are all included, quite properly, because the ordinary reader would expect to find them there.[1] The silly and pedantic cliché that all true folk songs must be anonymous has been ignored. The cliché itself is based on a conception of ballads and folk songs as "communal" compositions which has been defunct for half a century. (One leading Canadian authority on the ballad who repudiated this view of it was Dr. John D. Robins, to whom the book is dedicated.) As Mrs. Fowke says, Canada affords an admirable opportunity to watch the folk song going through its various stages, from original composition to pure oral transmission.

So we have in this book variants of the canon of great ballads, traditional tunes set to new words, traditional themes reshaped on a new historical event, such as a shipwreck or the death of a lumberjack, individual contributions to the folk song idiom (several songs from Newfoundland by identified authors, such as *The Squid-Jiggin' Ground*,[2] are included), broadsides and naive newspaper verse (*The Badger Drive*), commercial songs that have stuck in the popular memory, intellectuals' parodies of folk themes (*The Day Columbus Landed Here, Unfortunate Miss Bailey*)—in short, the real unselected complex of genuine popular song. The tunes are equally various—the tight, precise little French tunes, hardly moving out of a major third in range, the lovely modal melodies like the mixolydian *The Blooming Bright Star of Belle Isle* and the swinging dorian *Lumber Camp Song*, the six-eight Irish jig tunes from Newfoundland, the Western patter songs, and the more stretchy and lugubrious nineteenth-century tunes of the *Heart Songs* persuasion (*The Red River Valley*, and *Bury Me Not on the Lone Prairie*).

Naturally the book is based on the systematic collections of folk songs that have already been made. It is regrettable that the three thousand transcribed Indian and Eskimo tunes are so sparsely represented here, though one can see the reason for it in a book designed for the general public. Elsewhere, the collecting of ballads has been confined to Newfoundland, Nova Scotia, and French Canada. "No systematic collecting of songs from any region west of Quebec has yet been undertaken," says Mrs. Fowke, but her book indicates a surprising richness in the Ontario field, chiefly in the northern lumber camps. The Western songs, as she also says, are largely American imports, though some of her specimens are still uncollected in the States (*Smoky Mountain Bill*, for instance, can only have come from the Smokies in Tennessee).

It is not easy to see any "distinctively Canadian" quality to the Canadian folk song, particularly as the most distinctive thing about the folk song is its ability to travel over all cultural, and even linguistic, barriers. (One is startled to learn that an American authority assigns *The Jam on Gerry's Rock* to Canada on the ground that it portrays lumberjacks as unwilling to break a log jam on Sunday.) Newfoundland and Nova Scotia have preserved many fine variants of the standard English ballads (see *The False Young Man* and an excellent version of the Riddle Song in this book), and occasionally an ancient ballad has survived only in Canada (three of these, *The Bonny Banks of Virgie O*, *The Morning Dew*, and *She's Like the Swallow* are worth the price of admission in themselves to anyone seriously interested in ballads). The whole colonial phase of Canada's history, its invasion by English and French cultures, is of course fully represented in its folk song. One wonders how many Canadians know the *Brave Wolfe* song, with its delicate romantic theme and its lovely aeolian tune that sounds almost Hebridean. The War of 1812, the Rebellion of 1837, Confederation (from an unreconstructed Newfoundland point of view), the Negro slave refugees, and various tales of logging, shipping, fishing, and ranching are all included. Another important aspect of our history is here too: Canadian life and climate as they appeared to disgruntled outsiders. In our poetry we have Standish O'Grady; in our prose Susanna Moodie; in our folk song (we may call it ours by reversion) we have:

> And now the winter's over, it's homeward we are bound,
> And in this cursed country we'll never more be found.
> Go back to your wives and sweethearts, tell others not to go
> To that God-forsaken country called Canaday-I-O.

Presumably those who remained were of sterner stuff, and we are not surprised to find so much tough humour and realism. The reason for this is partly that folk song is essentially a public and dramatic genre: the most subjective emotion it admits is sexual love. Here the unpredictable genius of oral transmission occasionally turns into a breath-taking beauty, as in the last line of:

Turning New Leaves: *Folk Songs of Canada*

> She's like the swallow that flies so high,
> She's like the river that never runs dry,
> She's like the sunshine on the lee shore,
> I love my love and my love is no more.

But this kind of felicity is very rare, and the sense of isolation and loneliness, the feeling of the waste and indifference of nature, which is so marked in the more urban poetry, is largely absent from the folk song. There is tragedy, heroism, and pathos, but what loneliness there is arises simply from want of company (as in *The Little Old Sod Shanty*), or from rejected love (as in the Housman-like *The Stormy Scenes of Winter*) or from premature death (as in *Peter Amberley*)—all socially directed feelings. The most notable poetic feature is a kind of grim irony that falls just short of satire.

This takes various forms—it is simplest, of course, in the sagas of the bucked-off Western tenderfoot and the unfortunate bumpkin José Blais (in *Le Bal Chez Boulé*). Occasionally, though not often in this deadpan northern country, it turns into fantasy or riddle, and it would be interesting to know what a future historian would make of this:

> Were you ever in Quebec
> Stowing timber on the deck,
> Where there's a king with a golden crown,
>   Riding on a donkey?

But the real basis of the irony is something that we rarely have in the poetry that is published in books, as books form part of a money economy. Newfoundland, Nova Scotia, and French Canada are food-producing communities where money is an alien, sinister, intrusive thing, controlled by crafty foreigners with a vicious knack of making more of it for themselves and less of everything for everybody else. We meet this situation in the very first song in the book:

> "Marchand, marchand, combien ton blé?"
> "Trois francs l'avoin', six francs le blé."
> "C'est bien trop cher d'un bonn' moitié."

We meet it again in a delightful bit that could only have come from one place in the world, southeastern Newfoundland:

"Oh, mother dear, I wants a sack
With beads and buttons down the back . . .
Me boot is broke, me frock is tore,
But Georgie Snooks I do adore . . .
Oh, fish is low and flour is high,
So Georgie Snooks he can't have I."

And hence even love is expressed in ironic terms. There is no Sehnsucht or Leidenschaft or Weltschmerz in this, but there is something much more permanent:

Oh, had I but a flask of gin
   With sugar here for two,
And a great big bowl for to mix it in,
   I'd pour a drink for you, my dear, Mary Ann!

Now that the log-jam has been broken, so to speak, by the efforts of Mrs. Fowke and Dr. Johnston, one looks for an increase in public interest in Canadian folk song, and hence, not only for other popular collections, but for further editions of this one that will not be restricted to seventy-seven titles. There are still quantities of wonderful stuff in the Creighton, Greenleaf, and Barbeau collections, as no one knows better than these editors.[3] It is particularly in the French section that the present book shows a tendency to stick to somewhat hackneyed favourites—though again a collection for the general public could not leave out *A la Claire Fontaine* or *En Roulant Ma Boule*, to say nothing of *Alouette*. Again, there is an enormous amount of work still to be done in the field, and to foster public interest is the best way of insuring that it will be done. Meanwhile, when the blurb calls this book "a major contribution to Canadian culture," one can only agree.

39

English Canadian Literature, 1929–1954

Summer 1955

From Books Abroad, *29 (Summer 1955): 270–4. Reprinted in* Canadian Library Association Bulletin, *13 (1956): 107–12, and in* World Literature Today, *63 (Spring 1989): 246–9.*

Canada is such a huge and sprawling country that only a tremendous effort of will has made and kept it a single environmental unit. It has a prodigious interior but almost no coast line, and hence has had nothing to correspond to the Atlantic seaboard culture of the United States. It has the handicap of two languages; it has an almost uninhabited wilderness in Northern Ontario separating the East from the West; and it exists in practically one dimension, like a bigger Chile. With all this, its primary problems of communication have long overshadowed the secondary ones connected with culture and literary expression. Up to the First World War, English Canada was a scattered series of British colonies, of which only those close to Toronto and Montreal could get far enough above the cultural subsistence level to keep a literary output going. After 1918 the colonial phase gave way to a more distinctive growth, in which the pioneering art was landscape painting. American influences slowly began to appear beside British ones, and both in the prosperity of the 1920s and the Depression of the 1930s English Canadian culture began to assume the appearance of northern spurs of the United States—the Maritimes of New England, Ontario of the Great Lakes region, the Canadian West and Pacific coast of their American counterparts.

With the Second World War a tremendous growth of industry, the rise of air transport, and the exploiting of natural resources deep in the North brought about a further change in the Canadian spirit. Since 1812, the most dangerous enemy of Canada has not been a foreign invader but its own geography, and with the overcoming of this the feeling of expectancy about Canadian culture has been given a new concreteness and immediacy. Canadian intellectuals have always been, for the most part, cultural nationalists, fostering a Messianic hope that something of major importance is just about to happen to Canada, but they never have been more so than at present.

The foregoing may help to explain a fact that might otherwise puzzle an outsider. During the past twenty-five years the most impressive literary achievements in English Canada have not been in the imaginative fields, but in scholarship. The bulk of this scholarship has been Canadian in reference. Canadian history, and the new techniques of study provided by the social sciences, constitute a scholarly basic industry in Canada, paralleling the rise of "American civilization" studies across the border. Similarly, Canadian critics no longer contribute essays to small periodicals under the title "Is There a Canadian Literature?" The question itself may be as relevant as ever, but, whatever the answer, Canadian poems and short stories are anthologized and literary histories and bibliographies are appearing, along with some critical monographs. The best of the latter are E.K. Brown's *On Canadian Poetry* (1943) and W.E. Collin's *The White Savannahs* (1936); the most recent history of Canadian literature is Desmond Pacey's *Creative Writing in Canada* (1952); an exhaustive annual survey, including French and other languages, has been provided by "Letters in Canada," in the April issue of the *University of Toronto Quarterly*, since 1935. Tentative beginnings toward Canadian literature courses have been made in universities. As yet, all this activity is largely sociological: Canadian culture is studied because it is the actual cultural environment, not because it presents cultural phenomena of world-wide importance. But if such phenomena do appear—and the argument that a country with such pulpwood resources must produce a great literature sooner or later is probably quite a sound one—a critical and scholarly apparatus has been set up which is ready to receive it.

English Canadian poetry up to 1929 was dominated by what had then become the clichés of English Romantic and Victorian poetry. Apart from Whitman, there was little American influence, and the American poetic renaissance that began around 1912 was unfelt in Canada for a long time. The most strikingly original of Canadian poets, E.J. Pratt, began his productive career in the 1920s, somewhat late in life. A

Newfoundlander by birth, he chose the unfashionable heroic narrative for his medium and tales of shipwreck, whale hunts, and extravagant maritime fantasy for his themes. The narrative has always been a favourite form of expression in Canada, but Pratt gave it zest and bounce, a humour and a hyperbole that were all his own. In a series of poems climaxed by *The Titanic* (1935) and *Brébeuf and His Brethren* (1940), he established himself as the dominating personality in Canadian poetry, and as almost the only important connecting link between the old school and the newer writers. His *Collected Poems* appeared in the United States and Canada in 1944, and little that is essentially new in his work has succeeded it. His later position as a sort of unofficial Canadian poet laureate, devoting himself mainly to themes of national heroism, has not been an unmixed blessing for his purely poetic reputation. But in few parts of the world today can we find a poet so genuinely popular, in the classical and uncondescending sense of the word, as Pratt is in Canada.

In the year 1936 a small and somewhat belated publication entitled *New Provinces* indicated the rise of a new group of poets, representing more international influences, and showing less of the poetry of facile romantic and patriotic formulas that had come to be called the "maple leaf school." The contributors to this volume included Pratt himself, in a new, quieter, and more subtle lyrical vein, Leo Kennedy, A.J.M. Smith, A.M. Klein, F.R. Scott, and Robert Finch. Leo Kennedy, whose *The Shrouding* (1932) was one of the most remarkable volumes of poetry in the period, gave an original turn to the waste-land and death-and-resurrection themes popularized by Eliot, but has unfortunately written little poetry in recent years. A.J.M. Smith, who also has published very little since his *News of the Phoenix* (1943), showed the influence of metaphysical poets, the later Yeats, and an attraction to what he called, in a phrase his critics were quick to seize on, "difficult, lonely music."[1] Abraham Klein has been declared to be the finest Jewish poet of the century, and his *Hath Not a Jew* (1940) and *Hitleriad* (1944) are full of the Rabbinical spirit of erudition, humour, kindliness, and charity under pathological and meaningless hatred. He refused, however, to settle into his ethnical mould, and *The Rocking Chair* (1948) is full of brilliant and sympathetic studies of French Canada, some of them written in a curious bilingual vocabulary which is one of the liveliest poetic experiments yet made in the country. F.R. Scott, whose *Overture* appeared in 1945, is more politically minded; his poems combine a sharp social awareness with a kind of intellectual austerity that is difficult to characterize. Robert Finch, a professor of French, has brought some of the discipline of *symbolisme* to his *Poems* (1946) and *The Strength of the Hills* (1948). All of the above except Kennedy, and including Pratt, are university professors, mainly at Toronto and McGill, and are actively engaged in criticism as well. A.J.M. Smith's *Book of Canadian Poetry* (1943) is the best and most scholarly anthology of Canadian poetry. Klein has published a strange symbolic novel called *The Second Scroll* (1951), a tale of modern Zionism, and is now engaged in what seems a definitive critique of Joyce's *Ulysses*.

Of those who belong to the *New Provinces* generation, though not to their group, the most notable are two British Columbia poets, Dorothy Livesay and Earle Birney. The former was, during the 1930s, the Canadian poet most deeply touched by the moral and political challenges presented by the rise of Fascism and the Spanish Civil War. The latter has in some respects followed the Pratt tradition, both in his frequent use of the narrative genre, as in his remarkable poem *David* (1942), and in his attraction to national themes, though he makes much more use of satire than Pratt. *Now Is Time* (1945), *The Strait of Anian* (1948), and *Trial of a City* (1952) are his later volumes of poetry; he has also published a novel, a war satire in the picaresque tradition, called *Turvey* (1949). Louis Mackay, who has also lived in British Columbia, has, in his *Viper's Bugloss* (1938) and *The Ill-Tempered Lover* (1948), produced some of the best verse satire and some of the most beautiful "anthology pieces" in Canadian poetry.

In a still later group, Patrick Anderson has shown, in *The White Centre* (1946) and *The Colour as Naked* (1953), a gift for pastoral lyric somewhat akin to that of Dylan Thomas, who has, of course, influenced him. In Douglas LePan's *The Wounded Prince* (1948) and *The Net and the Sword* (1953) the tone is more romantic and elegiac, and the chief influence Eliot; the earlier book deals with the Canadian landscape and the later one with the Italian campaign, in which the poet served. Louis Dudek is the centre of an active Montreal group of poets whose main interests are social and realistic, though his *East of the City* (1946) still represents his best work. The most gifted, subtle, and technically expert of all the younger Canadian poets, Margaret Avison, has appeared in *Poetry* and elsewhere, but her work has not yet been published in a single volume.

In drama there is less to report; there has been an extraordinary amount of dramatic activity, but the number of good, indigenous stage dramatists is very small. In the earlier period the most serious dramatist was Gwen Pharis, who lives in Alberta and whose plays, the best of which are perhaps *Still Stands the House* (1938), *Dark Harvest* (1939), and *Stampede* (1946), usually have a Western setting. More recently Robertson Davies, an Ontario essayist and newspaper editor, has given us in *Fortune My Foe* (1948), *Eros at Breakfast* (1949), and *At My Heart's Core* (1950), the last on the 1837 Rebellion, a series of lively topical plays with unusually literate and urbane dialogue. John Coulter is perhaps more an Irish than a Canadian dramatist, except for a play on the Riel Rebellion (1950), which may well be his best work.

Every aspect of Canadian culture has been affected by the enormously beneficent influence of the Canadian Broadcasting Corporation. However one may criticize the CBC in detail, there is no reasonable doubt that without the steady employment it has given to writers, actors, musicians, and composers, and without its consistent efforts to guide as well as to reflect popular taste, Canadian culture would be in a desperate state. American influences are frequently decried in Canada: this is not the result of any chauvinistic or anti-American feeling, but arises from the simple perception that Canada's position is such that it gets, culturally, all the disadvantages of being so close to the United States without sharing in the important compensations. The CBC is one of the major defences behind which a Canadian culture can survive. And nowhere has the radio been so important as in the field of drama. Len Peterson, Lister Sinclair, Tommy Tweed, Bernie Braden, Joseph Schull, Graham Ferguson are a few whose names are household words in Canada, and who have provided a consistently superior brand of radio drama in every genre.[2] Dorothy Livesay's *Call My People Home* (1950) and Earle Birney's brilliant fantasy *Trial of a City* (1952) are poetic dramas written for radio. The radio has exploited and publicized the narrative talents of Pratt also, and, through its poetry readings, it has not only increased the audience of younger poets, but encouraged them to think in less involuted terms than they might do if their communication were confined to the printed page.

In the field of fiction, the short stories represent, on the whole, a higher level of competence than the novel. Here again we have to recognize the influence of the radio as a medium for reading stories aloud. Two good collections are Desmond Pacey's *A Book of Canadian Short Stories* (1949) and *Canadian Short Stories* edited by Robert Weaver and Helen James (1952). The former is historical and comprehensive, but most of the stories belong to the last twenty-five years; the editors of the latter are CBC producers, and the stories in their book were written for radio.

The Canadian novelist who is perhaps best known outside Canada is Mazo de la Roche, whose long "Jalna" series of stories began in 1927. The formidable family with which these books deal is well representative of the colonial phase of Canadian development, and of the ability of well-to-do families during that phase to live apart from, and almost in defiance of, the real life of the nation around them. There are not many other good popular novelists. There is in Canada, as elsewhere, a voluminous romance factory turning out historical tales of all sorts and periods: tales of the French and Indian wars, of the early days in Quebec, of pioneer life in Ontario, of adventure in the far North, of the intricate relationships between Canadian fauna and the nature-faker. Occasionally a historical novel of genuine literary merit turns up—an example is Thomas Raddall's *His Majesty's Yankees* (1942)—but the bulk of such work consists of antiquarian information on filing cards interspersed with erotic stimuli. The serious novel in Canada is therefore frequently marked by a militant realism, an emphatic underlining of the contemporary relevance of the theme.

The most impressive figure in Canadian fiction before 1929 was Frederick Philip Grove, who produced some extraordinary descriptive writing and some rather more maladroit fiction, mostly with a Western setting. His fame was obscured by an innocence of the world which bordered on perversity—it is said that he would have been the pioneer of naturalistic fiction, antedating even Dreiser, if he had understood the prejudice of publishers against huge manuscripts handwritten on both sides of the page. After 1929 he lived in Ontario, and his novel *Two Generations* (1939) has an Ontario setting. His last work was the awkward, unsuccessful, yet hauntingly powerful allegorical fantasy, *The Master of the Mill* (1944).

Fiction of the prairies has manifested a number of lively and readable variations on what used to be profanely called the "no fun on the farm" formula. Frederick Niven, a writer of brilliant promise, used both Canadian and Scottish settings; his *Story of Their Days* (1939) is one of his best works. Edward McCourt's *Music at the Close* (1947) and *Home Is the Stranger* (1950) and W.O. Mitchell's remarkable *Who Has Seen the Wind* (1947) also belong to the West, as does Henry Kreisel's *The Rich Man,* which has a Viennese setting, and is generically an expertly turned German *Novelle* written in English. In British Columbia, Ethel Wilson, by virtue of *Hetty Dorval* (1947), *The Innocent Traveller* (1949), and *The Equations of Love* (1952), is the leading fiction-writer. She is less a "Canadian novelist" than a very good writer who happens to live in Canada, and is better known outside the country than in it. Roderick Haig-Brown's *On the Highest Hill* (1949) records an unusually sensitive and intimate communion with nature, and the famous British Columbia painter Emily Carr produced in *Klee Wyck* (1941) the best collection of essays and descriptive pieces that appeared in Canada during the period under review.

In the East, Morley Callaghan had by 1929 established himself as perhaps the best short-story writer in Canadian fiction; a collection of his stories, under the title *Now That April's Here* (1936), is still representative of his best work. He has been less consistently successful in the novel, although *Such Is My Beloved* (1934), *They Shall Inherit the Earth* (1935), and *More Joy in Heaven* (1937) are head and shoulders above everything contemporary with them in Canadian writing. After a long silence, Callaghan returned to the novel in a half-symbolic, half-realistic tale of mean streets in Montreal, *The Loved and the Lost* (1951), a work of impressive if not wholly realized strength. Hugh MacLennan, a Maritimer, began his career with a lively story of the Halifax explosion, *Barometer Rising* (1941), and followed it with a more ambitious study of religious and cultural conflicts between English and French in Quebec, *Two Solitudes* (1945), one of the most deeply interesting of Canadian novels for Canadian readers. A similar conflict between Jew and Gentile in Montreal forms the theme of Gwethalyn Graham's *Earth and High Heaven* (1944), and the conflict of white and half-breed the theme of Christine van der Mark's *In Due Season* (1947). Other excellent one-shot novels are Selwyn Dewdney's *Wind without Rain* (1946), a story of the totalitarian trends in education that masquerade as progressive, and Ernest Buckler's violent and sombre tale of Nova Scotia, *The Mountain and the Valley* (1953). Of war novels, among the best are Ralph Allen's *Home Made Banners* (1946) and Hugh Garner's *Storm Below* (1949). The latter's *The Yellow Sweater* is perhaps the most distinguished one-man collection of short stories since the Callaghan book referred to above.

As the above catalogue implies, there is much eloquent and intelligent writing going on in Canada, without anything as yet having achieved the kind of greatness that would raise a different set of standards altogether. English Canada offers the writer a restricted market, but a maximum of recognition within it, along with the opportunity to expand into the whole English-reading world. Canada's possessive attitude to its literature is frankly provincial, but the assumption that such provincialism is always and everywhere wrong is merely an assumption based on a different kind of provincialism. It would be wrong if it tried to limit the variety of Canadian writing to a few acceptable formulas, and there is something of this in Canada, but the philistine resistance to imaginative literature seems to be gradually weakening. The result is a body of work which is partly a miscellany with no definite characteristics, except that it happens to be Canadian by one definition or another of that word, and partly the expression of a recognizable type of English literature which is steadily growing in articulateness and power.

40

Introduction to *I Brought the Ages Home*

October 1956

"Introduction," in Charles Trick Currelly, I Brought the Ages Home (Toronto: Ryerson Press, 1956, 1958, 1967), vii-x. *Currelly was the founder and first director of the Royal Ontario Museum.*

For several years the author of this book used to go, for his lunch, across the street to the Senior Common Room of Victoria College, the college of which he was a graduate, for which he had originally intended the museum, and which he was still serving as a member of the Board of Regents. It was in the Senior Common Room that I, along with many of my colleagues, first heard some of the reminiscences set down in the book that you are about to read. The remarks made afterward, in his absence, included two almost invariable points. First, he certainly should write his memoirs, as his story was one of the most amazing ever to come out of Ontario. Second, but, of course, it wouldn't be the same without his accomplished raconteur's skill. "If he wrote it all down," I remember someone saying, "it would just be Currelly without Currelly."

As you will see in a few moments, we reckoned without his versatility. When this manuscript came to me for editing, it was immediately clear that my editorial duties were to be of the most unobtrusive kind. They have been confined to minor rearrangements and to some smoothing of the reader's path. The lively narrative style, the humour, the expert dove-tailing of one story into another, the continuity, the concreteness and wealth of detail, are all evidence that the raconteur's skill was quite equal to the demands of the full-length book.

A graduate of Victoria College in a generation when so many of its most brilliant graduates became missionaries, Dr. Currelly was a cultural missionary. His converts were Canadians and his gospel was preached by all the world. There cannot be many museum collections, of an excellence comparable to Toronto's, so dependent on the energy and foresight of a single man. If he had been backed by unlimited funds, his shrewdness in buying and the breadth of his range would still be impressive enough. As it was, and as the book describes it, he had to be his own salesman, to pile up mountains of debt in the hope that some benefactor would clear them off, to struggle with myopic politicians and apathetic committees. As the book very briefly hints, he spent endless time giving illustrated lectures in towns and villages all over Ontario. As the book does not say at all, he was a great teacher. There must be several hundred people in Ontario who in their student days encountered him in his museum and were never the same again. The transition from books to life, from theoretical knowledge to the wisdom of experience, is a most difficult one to make—many "practical" people only make it by ignoring what is in books. Dr. Currelly had an extraordinary knack of persuading people, including children, to look with their own eyes, and with their eyes to bring the dreamlike pageants of history and geography into life.

The book's story begins in the days when the complex of ideas revolving around the word "evolution" was profoundly affecting the evangelical Protestantism in which Dr. Currelly was brought up. What was really at work was a reawakened sense of history. It seemed that the Bible was perhaps not a completely middle-class and Anglo-Saxon document after all, and that there were limits to the process of making it one: that it was the product of a specific culture and way of life, alien to ours in many essential respects. To bolder minds, Dr. Currelly's among them, this came with the force of an emancipating vision. We can see, from his account of W.E.H. Massey, how closely his interest in archaeology was connected with his interest in the church. For one of his upbringing, anything that helped to illuminate the significance of any part of the Bible was of absorbing fascination. My mind goes back to the Senior Common Room and a remark made by Dr. Currelly to a clergyman: "How many of you parsons in this city ever tell your congregations that we've got one of Nebuchadnezzar's lions here in Toronto? Nebuchadnezzar's in the Bible, isn't he?" The clergyman, who had obviously never mentioned Nebuchadnezzar in any context, and could hardly have cared less whether he was in the Bible or not, had no answer to this. Here Dr. Currelly's was the more evangelical mind of the two, in secular as well as Biblical matters. For, just as the original foreignness of the Bible makes its meaning more catholic, so the strangeness of foreign art makes the world smaller. Dr. Currelly remarks that Canadians need to know something of Oriental art because the Far Eastern nations are now our neighbours, in a world where indifference to other cultures is not only morally wrong and aesthetically barren but politically dangerous.

Now that archaeology is one of the world's major sciences, it is hard to realize how new it is. We can see in the book how the idea of "evolution" was transformed, in archaeology, into the idea of continuity. In excavation this replaced the mere digging for buried treasure with the careful observing and comparing of strata. In collecting it replaced the notion of "great periods" with the conception of all periods as being of equal primary interest. Nothing in this book is more remarkable than its record of the author's steady resistance to the tyranny of the "great period," and its accompanying notion that only certain things in Greek or Chinese or Egyptian art were really "worth" having, usually at fabulous expense. Such notions, as he explains very clearly, are matters not of taste but of fashion or craze, and they follow the manic-depressive cycle of fashion from contemptuous neglect to hysterical adulation, dragging of course the market prices with them. The principle that no aesthetic judgment is worth anything that is not founded on an impartial survey of an entire field is fundamental to this book. The author arrived at it fifty years ago out of clear-headedness and a good deal of moral courage. There are many brilliant workers in my own field of literary criticism who have not learned it yet.

It is only when we have made the effort to understand other ways of life that we can come to see our own as a specific culture too, and our own artefacts and traditions as equally worthy of preservation. It is a natural human tendency, said to be abnormally developed among Canadians, to undervalue whatever one has oneself. It goes without saying that Dr. Currelly put much of his effort into securing a representative Canadian collection, from British Columbia totem poles to French Canadian church carvings. I am thinking at the moment, however, of his remark to me that he had never taken a pleasure trip, although of course he had travelled widely over four continents. He made no journey that was without reference to the Ontario community he served so long and faithfully. No one can talk to him without realizing that his ambition for a fine Provincial museum was only a part of his deep love for Ontario. He has always taken the keenest interest in good farming, in the saving of threatened woodlots, in the preserving of genuine community life in rural areas, in any measure that will help to make the trees grow again and the dried-up rivers run again. He has never ceased to encourage his literary friends to interpret their own country and look directly at its people. Something of this aspect of his personality has impressed itself on his museum, where every day people of every age and interest come in crowds to look at the treasures he brought, as the title has it, "home." It is part of the greatness of such an achievement that so much of Crete and Mexico and China should now be "ours," not in the sense of possession, but in the sense of shared experience.

I am deeply obliged to Dr. Homer Thompson,[1] whose distinguished career has included personal experience of the Toronto museum and of Dr. Currelly, for introducing this book to a wider public.

41

Preface to an Uncollected Anthology

June 1956

From Studia Varia: Royal Society of Canada, Literary and Scientific Papers, *ed. E.G.D. Murray (Toronto: University of Toronto Press, 1957), 21–36. Reprinted in* BG, *163–79, in* RCLI, *49–64, in* ECLI, *47–62, and in* Contexts of Canadian Criticism, *ed. Eli Mandel (Toronto: University of Toronto Press, 1971), 181–97. Reprinted in abridged form in* Canadian Anthology, *ed. Carl F. Klinck and Reginald E. Watters (Toronto: Gage, 1966), 515–23, and subsequent editions. This talk was presented to section 2 of the Royal Society of Canada in a session on Canadian literature. It was preceded by the following explanation: "the author imagines that he has collected his ideal anthology of English Canadian poetry, with no difficulties about permissions, publishers, or expense, and is writing his preface."*

Certain critical principles are essential for dealing with Canadian poetry which in the study of English literature as such are seldom raised. Unless the critic is aware of the importance of these principles, he may, in turning to Canadian poets, find himself unexpectedly incompetent, like a giraffe trying to eat off the ground. The first of these principles is the fact that the cultivated Canadian has the same kind of interest in Canadian poetry that he has in Canadian history or politics. Whatever its merits, it is the poetry of his own country, and it gives him an understanding of that country which nothing else can give him. The critic of Canadian literature has to settle uneasily somewhere between the Canadian historian or social scientist, who has no comparative value judgments to worry about, and the ordinary literary critic, who has nothing else. The qualities in Canadian poetry which help to make Canada more imaginatively articulate for the Canadian reader are genuine literary values, whether they coincide with other literary values or not. And while the reason for collecting an anthology can only be the merit of the individual poems, still, having made such a collection, one may legitimately look at the proportioning of interests, at the pattern of the themes that seem to make Canadian poets eloquent.

It is not a nation but an environment that makes an impact on poets, and poetry can deal only with the imaginative aspect of that environment. A country with almost no Atlantic seaboard, which for most of its history has existed in practically one dimension; a country divided by two languages and great stretches of wilderness, so that its frontier is a circumference rather than a boundary; a country with huge rivers and islands that most of its natives have never seen; a country that has made a nation out of the stops on two of the world's longest railway lines: this is the environment that Canadian poets have to grapple with, and many of the imaginative problems it presents have no counterpart in the United States, or anywhere else.

In older countries the works of man and of nature, the city and the garden of civilization, have usually reached some kind of imaginative harmony. But the land of the Rockies and the Precambrian Shield impresses painter and poet alike by its raw colours and angular rhythms, its profoundly unhumanized isolation. It is still *The Lonely Land* to A.J.M. Smith, still *A Country without a Mythology* to Douglas LePan. The works of man are even more imaginatively undigested. A Canadian village, unlike an English one, does not "nestle": it sprawls awkwardly along a highway or railway line, less an inhabited centre than an episode of communication. Its buildings express an arrogant defiance of the landscape; its roads and telephone wires and machinery twist and strangle and loop. Irving Layton says, looking at an abstract picture,

> When I got the hang of it
> I saw a continent of railway tracks
> coiling about the sad Modigliani necks
> like disused tickertape, the streets
> exploding in the air
> with disaffected subway cars. [*How to Look at an Abstract*, ll. 1–6]

The Wordsworth who saw nature as exquisitely fitted to the human mind would be lost in Canada, where what the poets see is a violent collision of two forces, both monstrous. Earle Birney describes the bulldozers of a logging camp as "iron brontosaurs"; Klein compares grain elevators to leviathans.[1]

Poets are a fastidious race, and in Canadian poetry we have to give some place, at least at the beginning, to the anti-Canadian, the poet who has taken one horrified look at the country and fled. Thus Standish O'Grady, writing of *The Emigrant*:

> Here forests crowd, unprofitable lumber,
> O'er fruitless lands indefinite as number;
> Where birds scarce light, and with the north winds veer
> On wings of wind, and quickly disappear,
> Here the rough Bear subsists his winter year,
> And licks his paw and finds *no better fare*. . . .
> The lank Canadian eager trims his fire,
> And all around their simpering stoves retire;
> With fur clad friends their progenies abound,
> And thus regale their buffaloes around;
> Unlettered race, how few the number tells,
> Their only pride a cariole and bells. . . .
> Perchance they revel; still around they creep,
> And talk, and smoke, and spit, and drink, and sleep!   [ll. 1692 ff.]

There is a great deal of polished wit in these couplets of the modern ambiguous kind: the word "lumber," for example, has both its Canadian meaning of wood and its English meaning of junk. We notice that "Canadian" in this poem means French Canadian habitant: O'Grady no more thinks of himself as Canadian than an Anglo-Indian colonel would think of himself as Hindu. Here is an American opinion, the close of a folk song about a construction gang that spent a winter in Three Rivers:

> And now the winter's over, it's homeward we are bound,
> And in this cursed country we'll never more be found.
> Go back to your wives and sweethearts, tell others not to go
> To that God-forsaken country called Canaday-I-O.[2]

Thanks to the efforts of those who remained, this particular theme is now obsolete, although Norman Levine in 1950 spoke of leaving the land of "parchment summers and merchant eyes" for "the loveliest of fogs," meaning England.[3] Still, it will serve as an introduction to two central themes in Canadian poetry: one a primarily comic theme of satire and exuberance, the other a primarily tragic theme of loneliness and terror.

It is often said that a pioneering country is interested in material rather than spiritual or cultural values. This is a cliché, and it has become a cliché because it is not really true, as seventeenth-century Massachusetts indicates. What is true is that the imaginative energy of an expanding economy is likely to be mainly technological. As a rule it is the oppressed or beleaguered peoples, like the Celts and the Hebrews, whose culture makes the greatest imaginative efforts: successful nations usually express a restraint or a matter-of-fact realism in their culture and keep their exuberance for their engineering. If we are looking for imaginative exuberance in American life, we shall find it not in its fiction but in its advertising; not in Broadway drama but in Broadway skyscrapers; not in the good movies but in the vista-visioned and technicoloured silly ones. The extension of this life into Canada is described by Frank Scott in *Saturday Sundae*, by James Reaney in *Klaxon*, a fantasy of automobiles wandering over the highways without drivers, "Limousines covered with pink slime / Of children's blood," and by many other poets.

The poet dealing with the strident shallowness of much Canadian life is naturally aware that there is no imaginative change when we cross the American border in either direction. Yet there is, I think, a more distinctive attitude in Canadian poetry than in Canadian life, a more withdrawn and detached view of that life which may go back to the central fact of Canadian history: the rejection of the American Revolution. What won the American Revolution was the spirit of entrepreneur capitalism, an enthusiastic plundering of the natural resources of a continent and an unrestricted energy of manufacturing and exchanging them. In *A Search for America*, which is quite a profound book if we take the precaution of reading it as a work of fiction, Grove speaks of there being two Americas, an ideal one that has something to do with the philosophy of Thoreau and the personality of Lincoln, and an actual one that made the narrator a parasitic salesman of superfluous goods and finally a hobo. At the end of the book he remarks in a footnote that his ideal America has been preserved better in Canada than in the United States. The truth of this statement is not my concern, but some features of my anthology seem to reflect similar attitudes.

In the United States, with its more intensively indoctrinated educational system, there has been much rugged prophecy in praise of the common man, a tradition that runs from Whitman through Sandburg and peters out in the lugubrious inspirationalism of the Norman Corwin school.[4] Its chief characteristics are the praise of the uncritical life and a manly contempt of prosody. One might call it the Whitmanic-depressive tradition, in view of the fact that it contains Robinson Jeffers. It seems to me significant that this tradition has had so little influence in Canada. I find in my anthology a much higher proportion of humour than I expected when I began: a humour of a quiet, reflective, observant type, usually in a fairly strict metre, and clearly coming from a country with a ringside seat on the revolutionary sidelines.

A song from a poem by Alexander McLachlan called, like O'Grady's, *The Emigrant*, will illustrate what I mean:

> I love my own country and race,
> > Nor lightly I fled from them both,
> Yet who would remain in a place
> > Where there's too many spoons for the broth.
>
> The squire's preserving his game.
> > He says that God gave it to him,
> And he'll banish the poor without shame,
> > For touching a feather or limb. . . .
>
> The Bishop he preaches and prays,
> > And talks of a heavenly birth,
> But somehow, for all that he says,
> > He grabs a good share of the earth.

In this poem there is nothing of the typically American identification of freedom with national independence: the poet is still preoccupied with the old land and thinks of himself as still within its tradition. There is even less of the American sense of economic competition as the antidote to social inequality. The spirit in McLachlan's poem is that of a tough British radicalism, the radicalism of the Glasgow dock worker or the Lancashire coal miner, the background of the Tom Paine who has never quite fitted the American way of life.

We may find something similar in a totally different context: an episode in the *Malcolm's Katie* of that very shrewd woman Isabella Crawford [pt. 4, ll. 40 ff.]. The hero is engaged in cutting down a tree and singing the praises of the axe as the agent of progress. He is interrupted by the villain, who is something of a Spenglerian and who speaks of the eventual downfall of all cycles of civilization. The hero turns indignantly to refute this unhealthy pessimism, whereupon the tree, which he has forgotten about, falls over and flattens him. The irony of the scene is all the more striking for being somewhat out of key with the general romantic tone, as of course the hero gets up again, and his simple-minded view of life eventually baffles the villain and annexes the heroine. If we are to read Canadian poetry sympathetically we must often keep an eye out for such disturbers of poetic convention.

It is not surprising to find a good deal of satiric light verse in this imaginative resistance to industrial expansion and the gum-chewing way of life. Frank Scott we have mentioned: his *Canadian Social Register* is a ferocious paraphrase of an advertising prospectus, and his *Social Notes* are also something un-American, social poems with an unmistakably socialist moral. The observations of Toronto by Raymond Souster and of Montreal by Louis Dudek, Miriam Waddington, and Irving Layton have much to the same effect: of golfers Layton remarks "that no theory of pessimism is complete / Which altogether ignores them" [*Golfers*, ll. 11–12]. But of course it is easy for the same satiric tone to turn bitter and nightmarish. Lampman's terrible poem, *The City of the End of Things*, is not only social but psychological, and warns of the dangers not simply of exploiting labour but of washing our own brains. There are other sinister visions in A.J.M. Smith's *The Bridegroom*, in Dudek's *East of the City*, in Dorothy Livesay's *Day and Night*, in P.K. Page's *The Stenographers*, and elsewhere. Canadian poems of depression and drought, like Dorothy Livesay's *Outrider* or Anne Marriott's *The Wind Our Enemy*, often have in them the protest of a food-producing community cheated out of its labour not simply by hail and grasshoppers but by some mysterious financial finagling at the other end of the country, reminding us of the man in Balzac's parable who could make his fortune by killing somebody in China.[5] The same feeling comes out in a poignant folk song that could have come from only one part of the world, southeastern Newfoundland:

> "Oh, mother dear, I wants a sack
> With beads and buttons down the back....
> Me boot is broke, me frock is tore,
> But Georgie Snooks I do adore....
> Oh, fish is low and flour is high,
> So Georgie Snooks he can't have I."[6]

Preface to an Uncollected Anthology   261

There are of course more positive aspects of industrial expansion. In Canada the enormous difficulties and the central importance of communication and transport, the tremendous energy that developed the fur trade routes, the empire of the St. Lawrence, the transcontinental railways, and the northwest police patrols have given it the dominating role in the Canadian imagination. E.J. Pratt is the poet who has best grasped this fact, and his *Towards the Last Spike* expresses the central comic theme of Canadian life, using the term "comic" in its literary sense as concerned with the successful accomplishing of a human act.

The imagery of technology and primary communication is usually either avoided by poets or employed out of a sense of duty: its easy and unforced appearance in Pratt is part of the reason why Pratt is one of the few good popular poets of our time. Technology appears all through his work, not only in the poems whose subjects demand it, but in other and more unexpected contexts. Thus in *Come Away, Death*:

> We heard the tick-tock on the shelf,
> And the leak of valves in our hearts.   [ll. 43–4]

In *The Prize Cat*, where a cat pounces on a bird and reminds the poet of the deliberately summoned-up brutality of the Fascist conquest of Ethiopia, the two themes are brought together by the inspired flash of a technical word:

> Behind the leap so furtive-wild
> Was such ignition in the gleam,
> I thought an Abyssinian child
> Had cried out in the whitethroat's scream.   [ll. 17–20]

As a student of psychology, before he wrote poetry at all, he was preoccupied with the problems of sensory response to signals, and the interest still lingers in the wireless messages of *The Titanic*, the radar and asdic of *Behind the Log*, and the amiable joggle of *The 6000*, one of the liveliest of all railway poems:

> A lantern flashed out a command,
> A bell was ringing as a hand
> Clutched at a throttle, and the bull,
> At once obedient to the pull,
> Began with bellowing throat to lead

> By slow accelerating speed
> Six thousand tons of caravan
> Out to the spaces—there to toss
> The blizzard from his path across
> The prairies of Saskatchewan. [conclusion]

In *Behind the Log*, Canadians undertake a mission of war in much the spirit of an exploration: there is a long journey full of perils, many members of the expedition drop off, and those that reach the goal feel nothing but a numb relief. Nothing could be less like the charge of the Light Brigade. Yet perhaps in this poem we may find a clue to the fact that Canada, a country that has never found much virtue in war and has certainly never started one, has in its military history a long list of ferocious conflicts against desperate odds. The Canadian poem best known outside Canada, MacCrae's *In Flanders Fields*, breathes a spirit like that of the Viking warrior whose head continued to gnaw the dust after it had been cut from his body; and it comes from the country of the Long Sault, Crysler's Farm, St. Julien, and Dieppe.[7] Douglas LePan's *The Net and the Sword*, the title poem of a book dealing with the Italian campaign of the Second World War, mentions something similar:

> In this sandy arena, littered
> And looped with telephone wires, tank-traps, mine-fields,
> Twined about the embittered
> Debris of history, the people whom he shields
> Would quail before a stranger if they could see
> His smooth as silk ferocity.

LePan finds the source of the ferocity in the simplicity of the Canadian soldier's vision: "Skating at Scarborough, summers at the Island," but perhaps it is also a by-product of engineering exuberance. We notice that the looped litter of telephone wires and the like belongs here to Europe, not to Canada, and the same kind of energy is employed to deal with it.

The tragic themes of Canadian poetry have much the same origin as the comic ones. The cold winter may suggest tragedy, but it may equally well suggest other moods, and does so in Lampman's sonnet *Winter Evening*, in Patrick Anderson's *Song of Intense Cold*, in Roberts' *The Brook in February*, in Klein's *Winter Night: Mount Royal*, and elsewhere. Other seasons too have their sinister aspects: none of Lampman's landscape poems is finer than his wonderful Hallowe'en vision of *In November*, where a harmless pasture full of dead mullein stalks rises and seizes the poet with the spirit of an eerie witches' sabbath:

> And I, too, standing idly there,
> With muffled hands in the chill air
> Felt the warm glow about my feet,
> And shuddering betwixt cold and heat,
> Drew my thoughts closer, like a cloak,
> While something in my blood awoke,
> A nameless and unnatural cheer,
> A pleasure secret and austere. [In November (2), ll. 47–54]

Still, the winter, with its long shadows and its abstract black and white pattern, does reinforce themes of desolation and loneliness, and, more particularly, of the indifference of nature to human values, which I should say was the central Canadian tragic theme. The first poet who really came to grips with this theme was, as we should expect, Charles Heavysege. Heavysege's first two long poems, *Saul* and *Count Filippo*, are Victorian dinosaurs in the usual idiom: *Count Filippo*, in particular, like the Albert Memorial, achieves a curious perverted beauty by the integrity of its ugliness. His third poem, *Jephthah's Daughter*, seems to me to reflect more directly the influence of his Canadian environment.

He tells us in the introduction that he decided on Jephthah's daughter rather than Iphigeneia because Iphigeneia was, as Samuel Johnson said of the victim of a public hanging, sustained by her audience;[8] the Biblical theme had a solitary bleakness about it that was nearer to what he wanted. During the action Jephthah goes out in the darkness to pray for release from his vow, asking for some sign of that release. He listens a moment and then hears:

> The hill wolf howling on the neighbouring height,
> And bittern booming in the pool below. [ll. 389–90]

He gets of course no other answer, and it is clear that what Jephthah is really sacrificing his daughter to is nature, nature as a mystery of mindless power, with endless resources for killing man but with nothing to respond to his moral or intellectual feelings. The evolutionary pessimism of the nineteenth century awoke an unusual number of echoes in Canada, many of them of course incidental. In a well-known passage from Charles Mair's *Tecumseh*, Lefroy is describing the West to Brock, and Brock comments: "What charming solitudes! And life was there!" and Lefroy answers: "Yes, life was there! inexplicable life, / Still wasted by inexorable death";[9] and the sombre Tennysonian vision of nature red in tooth and claw blots out the sentimental Rousseauist fantasy of the charming solitudes.

In the next generation the tragic theme has all the more eloquence for being somewhat unwanted, interfering with the resolutely cheerful praise of the newborn giant of the North. Roberts, Wilfred Campbell, Wilson MacDonald, and Bliss Carman are all Romantics whose ordinary tone is nostalgic, but who seem most deeply convincing when they are darkest in tone, most preoccupied with pain, loss, loneliness, or waste. We notice this in the poems which would go immediately into anyone's anthology, such as Campbell's *The Winter Lakes*, Wilson Macdonald's *Exit*, Carman's *Low Tide on Grand Pré*. It is even more striking when Carman or Roberts writes a long metrical gabble that occasionally drops into poetry, like Silas Wegg, as it is almost invariably this mood that it drops into. Thus in Roberts' *The Great and the Little Weavers*:

> The cloud-rose dies into shadow,
> The earth-rose dies into dust.

The "great gray shape with the palaeolithic face" of Pratt's *Titanic* and the glacier of Birney's *David* are in much the same tradition as the gloomy and unresponsive nature of *Jephthah's Daughter*. In fact the tragic features in Pratt mainly derive from his more complex view of the situation of Heavysege's poem. Man is also a child of nature, in whom the mindlessness of the animal has developed into cruelty and malice. He sees two men glare in hatred at one another on the street, and his mind goes

> Away back before the emergence of fur or feather, back to the unvocal sea and down deep where the darkness spills its wash on the threshold of light, where the lids never close upon the eyes, where the inhabitants slay in silence and are as silently slain. [*Silences*, l. 35]

From the very beginning, in *Newfoundland Verse*, Pratt was fascinated by the relentless pounding of waves on the rocks, a movement which strangely seems to combine a purpose with a lack of it. This rhythm recurs several times in Pratt's work: in the charge of the swordfish in *The Witches' Brew*; in the "queries rained upon the iron plate" of *The Iron Door*; in the torpedo launched from *The Submarine*; in the sinking of the *Titanic* itself, this disaster being caused by a vainglorious hubris which in a sense deliberately aimed at the iceberg. In *Brébeuf* the same theme comes into focus as the half-mindless, half-demonic curiosity which drives the Iroquois on through torture after torture to find the secret of a spiritual reality that keeps eluding them.

It is Pratt who has expressed in *Towards the Last Spike* the central comic theme, and in *Brébeuf* the central tragic theme, of the Canadian imagination, and it is Pratt who combines the two in *The Truant*, which is in my anthology because it is the greatest poem in Canadian literature. In it the representative of mankind confronts a "great Panjandrum," a demon of the mathematical order of nature of a type often confused with God. In the dialectic of their conflict it becomes clear that the great Panjandrum of nature is fundamentally death, and that the intelligence that fights him, comprehends him, harnesses him, and yet finally yields to his power is the ultimate principle of life, and capable of the comedy of achievement only because capable also of the tragedy of enduring him:

> "We who have learned to clench
> Our fists and raise our lightless sockets
> To morning skies after the midnight raids,
> Yet cocked our ears to bugles on the barricades,
> And in cathedral rubble found a way to quench
> A dying thirst within a Galilean valley—
> No! by the Rood, we will not join your ballet."

We spoke at the beginning of certain principles that become important in the study of Canadian poetry. One of these is the fact that while literature may have life, reality, experience, nature, or what you will for its content, the forms of literature cannot exist outside literature, just as the forms of sonata and fugue cannot exist outside music. When a poet is confronted by a new life or environment, the new life may suggest a new content, but obviously cannot provide him with a new form. The forms of poetry can be derived only from other poems, the forms of novels from other novels. The imaginative content of Canadian poetry, which is often primitive, frequently makes extraordinary demands on forms derived from Romantic or later traditions. Duncan Campbell Scott, for instance, lived in Ottawa as a civil servant in the Department of Indian Affairs, between a modern city and the Ungava wilderness. He has a poem on the music of Debussy, and he has a poem on a starving squaw trying to catch fish for her child and having nothing but her own flesh to bait the hook with. To find anything like such incongruity in English life we have to go clear back to Anglo-Saxon times. If we think of an Old English poet, with his head full of ancient battles and myths of dragon-fights, in the position of having to write for the sophisticated audience of Rome and Byzantium, we shall have some parallel to the technical problems faced by a Lampman or a Scott who had only the elaborate conventions of Tennysonian Romanticism to contain his imaginative experience. Pratt's attempt to introduce the imagery of dragon-killing into a poem about the Canadian Pacific Railway is another good example; and I have much sympathy for the student who informed me in the examinations last May that Pratt had written a poem called Beowulf and his Brothers.

I think it is partly an obscure feeling for more primitive forms that accounts for the large number of narratives in Canadian poetry. I am aware, of course, that the narrative was a favourite Romantic form, but the themes of Canadian narrative, the sacrifice of Jephthah's daughter, the catching of Isabella Crawford's Max in a log jam, Dominique de Gourges' quest for vengeance in D.C. Scott, the death of Birney's David on the glacier, have a primeval grimness about them that is not Romantic or even modern fashion. Pratt has also turned to older and more primitive types of narrative: Chaucerian beast-fable in the *Pliocene Armageddon* and *The Fable of the Goats*, saint's legend in *Brébeuf*, heroic rescue in *The Roosevelt and the Antinoe*.

It is more common for a Canadian poet to solve his problem of form by some kind of erudite parody, using that term, as many critics now do, to mean adaptation in general rather than simply a lampoon, although adaptation usually has humorous overtones. In Charles Mair's *Winter* some wisps of Shakespearean song are delicately echoed in a new context, and Drummond's best poem, *The Wreck of the "Julie Plante,"* is an admirable parody of the ballad, with its tough oblique narration, its moralizing conclusion, and its use of what is called incremental repetition:

> For de win' she blow lak' hurricane,
>   Bimeby she blow some more.

According to his own account, Pratt, after his college studies in theology, psychology, literature, and the natural sciences, put everything he knew into his first major poetic effort, an epic named *Clay*, which he promptly burnt. Soon afterwards all this erudition went into reverse and came out as the fantasy of *The Witches' Brew*, in which parody has a central place. Since then, we have parody in Anne Wilkinson and Wilfred Watson, who use nursery rhymes and ballads as a basis; Birney's *Trial of a City* is among other things a fine collection of parodied styles; and Klein's devotion to one of the world's greatest parodists, James Joyce, has produced his brilliant bilingual panegyric on Montreal

> Grand port of navigations, multiple
> The lexicons uncargo'd at your quays,
> Sonnant though strange to me; but chiefest, I,
> Auditor of your music, cherish the
> Joined double-melodied vocabulaire
> Where English vocable and roll Ecossic,
> Mollified by the parle of French
> Bilinguefact your air!   [*Montreal*, ll. 25–32]

Much of Canada's best poetry is now written by professors or others in close contact with universities. There are disadvantages in this, but one of the advantages is the diversifying of the literary tradition by a number of scholarly interests. Earle Birney's *Anglosaxon Street* reminds us that its author is a professor of Anglo-Saxon. Louis Mackay, professor of Classics, confronts an unmistakably Canadian landscape with a myth of Eros derived from Catullus:

> The hard rock was his mother; he retains
> Only her kind, nor answers any sire.
> His hand is the black basalt, and his veins
> Are rocky veins, ablaze with gold and fire.   [*Nunc scio, quid sit amor*, ll. 5–8]

Robert Finch, professor of French, carries on the tradition of Mallarmé and other *symbolistes*; one of his most successful poems, *The Peacock and the Nightingale*, goes back to the older tradition of the medieval *débat*. Klein, of course, has brought echoes from the Talmud, the Old Testament, and the whole range of Jewish thought and history; and the erudition necessary to read Roy Daniells and Alfred Bailey with full appreciation is little short of formidable. It may be said, however, that echoes and influences are not a virtue in Canadian poetry, but one of its major weaknesses. Canadian poetry may echo Hopkins or Auden today as it echoed Tom Moore a century ago, but in every age Echo is merely the discarded mistress of Narcissus. This question brings up the most hackneyed subject in Canadian literature, which I have left for that reason to the end.

Political and economic units tend to expand as history goes on; cultural units tend to remain decentralized. Culture, like wine, seems to need a specific locality, and no major poet has been inspired by an empire, Virgil being, as the *Georgics* show, an exception that proves the rule. In this age of world-states we have two extreme forms of the relationship between culture and politics. When cultural developments follow political ones, we get an anonymous international art, such as we have in many aspects of modern architecture, abstract painting, and twelve-tone music. When a cultural development acquires a political aspect, we frequently get that curious modern phenomenon of the political language, where a minor language normally headed for extinction is deliberately revived for political purposes. Examples are Irish, Norwegian, Hebrew, and Afrikaans, and there are parallel tendencies elsewhere. I understand that there is a school of Australian poets dedicated to putting as many aboriginal words into their poems as possible.[10] As the emotional attachments to political languages are very violent, I shall say here only that this problem has affected the French but not the English part of Canadian culture. As we all know, however, English Canada has escaped the political language only to become involved in a unique problem of self-identification, vis-à-vis the British and American poets writing in the same tongue. Hence in every generation there has been the feeling that whether poetry itself needs any defence or manifesto, Canadian poetry certainly does.

The main result of this has been that Canadian poets have been urged in every generation to search for appropriate themes, in other words to look for content. The themes have been characterized as national, international, traditional, experimental, iconic, iconoclastic: in short, as whatever the propounder of them would like to write if he were a poet, or to read if he were a critic. But the poet's quest is for form, not content. The poet who tries to make content the informing principle of his poetry can write only versified rhetoric, and versified rhetoric has a moral but not an imaginative significance: its place is on the social periphery of poetry, not in its articulate centre. The rhetorician, Quintilian tells us, ought to be a learned and good man, but the critic is concerned only with poets.[11]

By form I do not of course mean external form, such as the use of a standard metre or convention. A sonnet has form only if it really is fourteen lines long: a ten-line sonnet padded out to fourteen is still a part of chaos, waiting for the creative word. I mean by form the shaping principle of the individual poem, which is derived from the shaping principles of poetry itself. Of these latter the most important is metaphor, and metaphor, in its radical form, is a statement of identity: this is that, A is B. Metaphor is at its purest and most primitive in myth, where we have immediate and total identifications. Primitive poetry, being mythical, tends to be erudite and allusive, and to the extent that modern poetry takes on the same qualities it becomes primitive too. Here is a poem by Lampman, written in 1894:

> So it is with us all; we have our friends
> > Who keep the outer chambers, and guard well
> Our common path; but there their service ends,
> > For far within us lies an iron cell
> Soundless and secret, where we laugh or moan
> > Beyond all succour, terribly alone.   [*Loneliness*]

And here is a poem by E.W. Mandel, published in 1954:

> It has been hours in these rooms,
> the opening to which, door or sash,
> I have lost. I have gone from room to room
> asking the janitors who were sweeping up
> the brains that lay on the floors,
> the bones shining in the wastebaskets,
> and once I asked a suit of clothes
> that collapsed at my breath and bundled
> and crawled on the floor like a coward.
> Finally, after several stories,
> in the staired and eyed hall,
> I came upon a man with the face of a bull.   [*Minotaur Poems*, no. 1]

Lampman's poem is certainly simpler, closer to prose and to the direct statement of emotion. All these are characteristics of a highly developed and sophisticated literary tradition. If we ask which is the more primitive, the answer is certainly the second poem, as we can see by turning to the opening pages of the anthology to see what primitive poetry is really like. Here is a Haida song translated by Hermia Fraser:

> I cannot stay, I cannot stay!
> I must take my canoe and fight the waves,
> For the Wanderer spirit is seeking me.
>
> The beating of great, black wings on the sun,
> The Raven has stolen the ball of the sun,
> From the Kingdom of Light he has stolen the sun . . . .
>
> The Slave Wife born from the first clam shell
> Is in love with the boy who was stolen away,
> The lovers have taken the Raven's fire.   [*Song to the Wanderer*, stanzas 1, 2, 4]

When we look for the qualities in Canadian poetry that illustrate the poet's response to the specific environment that we call approximately Canada, we are really looking for the mythopoeic qualities in that poetry. This is easiest to see, of course, when the poetry is mythical in content as well as form. In the long mythopoeic passage from Isabella Crawford's *Malcolm's Katie*, beginning "The South Wind laid his moccasins aside,"[12] we see how the poet is, first, taming the landscape imaginatively, as settlement tames it physically, by animating the lifeless scene with humanized figures, and, second, integrating the literary tradition of the country by deliberately re-establishing the broken cultural link with Indian civilization:

>   . . . for a man
> To stand amid the cloudy roll and moil,
> The phantom waters breaking overhead,
> Shades of vex'd billows bursting on his breast,
> Torn caves of mist wall'd with a sudden gold,
> Reseal'd as swift as seen—broad, shaggy fronts,
> Fire-ey'd and tossing on impatient horns
> The wave impalpable—was but to think
> A dream of phantoms held him as he stood.

Preface to an Uncollected Anthology 271

And in the mythical figures of Pratt, the snorting iron horses of the railways, the lumbering dinosaurs of *The Great Feud*, the dragon of *Towards the Last Spike*, and above all Tom the Cat from Zanzibar, the Canadian cousin of Roy Campbell's flaming terrapin, we clearly have other denizens of the monstrous zoo that produced Paul Bunyan's ox Babe, Paul Bunyan himself being perhaps a descendant of the giants who roamed the French countryside and were recorded by the great contemporary of Jacques Cartier, Rabelais.

We are concerned here, however, not so much with mythopoeic poetry as with myth as a shaping principle of poetry. Every good lyrical poet has a certain structure of imagery as typical of him as his handwriting, held together by certain recurring metaphors, and sooner or later he will produce one or more poems that seem to be at the centre of that structure. These poems are in the formal sense his mythical poems, and they are for the critic the imaginative keys to his work. The poet himself often recognizes such a poem by making it the title poem of a collection. They are not necessarily his best poems, but they often are, and in a Canadian poet they display those distinctive themes we have been looking for which reveal his reaction to his natural and social environment. Nobody but a genuine poet ever produces such a poem, and they cannot be faked or imitated or voluntarily constructed. My anthology is largely held together by such poems: they start approximately with D.C. Scott's *Piper of Arll*, and continue in increasing numbers to our own day. I note among others Leo Kennedy's *Words for a Resurrection*, Margaret Avison's *Neverness*, Irving Layton's *Cold Green Element*, Douglas LePan's *Idyll*, Wilfred Watson's *Canticle of Darkness*, P.K. Page's *Metal and the Flower*, and similar poems forming among a younger group that includes James Reaney, Jay Macpherson, and Daryl Hine. Such poems enrich not only our poetic experience but our cultural knowledge as well, and as time goes on they become increasingly the only form of knowledge that does not date and continues to hold its interest for future generations.

42

Culture and the National Will

17 May 1957

From the booklet Convocation Address at Carleton University, 17 May 1957 *(Ottawa: Carleton University for the Institute of Canadian Studies, 1957). Partially reprinted as "The Writer and the University" in DG, 118–24. A typescript is in NFF, 1988, box 1, file f. Frye addressed Convocation on the occasion of receiving an honorary LL.D. from Carleton. The cultural context of his talk is the creation of the Canada Council by a bill of 28 March 1957. The Council, which was the result of the Massey Commission announced in no. 33, was given a $50 million endowment for programs supporting the arts, humanities, and social sciences, as well as a $50 million capital grants fund for university buildings.*

I am, of course, deeply appreciative of the honour that Carleton University has done me. It is particularly an honour to receive this degree in the company of Mr. A.Y. Jackson, as well as a great pleasure, because Mr. Jackson is an old friend. May I congratulate also those of you who are receiving your degrees, and who are leaving the real world of the university and going out to the confused illusions of the world outside. Here you are in contact with reality at every point: this is the engine room; this is where the great ideas and forces and symbols that shape human behaviour take their start. Soon you will be in the ivory towers of business, in the escapist retreats of the suburbs, in the charmless magic of teaching, or in the schizophrenic fantasies of government. Wherever you are, you will be in a labyrinth, and only your four years at Carleton will give you a clue to it.

I should like also to congratulate President Bissell and everyone else concerned on the graduating of Carleton College itself into Carleton

University.¹ A graduate school usually means, in practice, that the teaching staff has to do twice as much work for the same money: but teachers are curious people, and they seem to thrive on such arrangements.

Carleton University has some of the advantages that often go with being the youngest in a large family. It began its history when Canada was developing an entirely new attitude toward its universities. The Canadian public didn't realize how important universities were until it was clear that we couldn't win a war without them. That gave us a sense of urgency about them: we began to realize that a nation has to take care of its universities or disappear from the modern world. Not long after Canadian universities started receiving federal grants. Now federal grants can never be the sole or even the main financial support of any university, but the fact that they exist sets up two essential principles in Canadian life. In the first place, universities are far too important to the country not to be recognized as essential non-profit industries like the postal service, for which the state is to some degree responsible.

In the second place, universities in a democracy must remain universities, and that means academic freedom, the unrestricted pursuit of undiscovered truth, and not the repeating of the truths that the different pressure groups in society think they already have. All pressure groups in society are anti-educational, no matter what they are pressing for. In Wilkie Collins's detective story *The Moonstone* there's an unpleasant nosy female who speaks of "the blessed prospect of interfering,"² and there are people like that in every country. But the more remote and diverse the financial support of a university is, the less easy it is for them to get inspired by that prospect.

Now, with the Canada Council Act, federal aid for universities is linked with federal aid for culture. The principles involved for culture are precisely the same. Federal aid cannot be the sole or even the main financial support of Canadian culture, but having it establishes the same double recognition of its necessity and its freedom: it has to be there, and it has to be left alone. It is logical to link the university and culture: in fact it could almost be said that the university today is to culture what the church is to religion: the social institution that makes it possible. It teaches the culture of the past, and it tries to build up an educated public for the culture of the present.

In the Soviet Union, as I understand it, culture is regarded as a function of the state, and hence all culture comes directly under political criticism. I dare say a great deal of lively discussion results, which may often be quite free in its own context, or even help the artist from a Marxist point of view. Still, the principle involved strikes us here in the democracies as pernicious. Yet it seems to me that a good deal of public thinking about culture here is still stuck in the laissez-faire economics of a century ago. For us the writer is still a small retailer, who has to be subsidized to compete with the mass media. This makes the writer an economic absurdity. A few novelists, most of them bad ones, may eke out a small living by writing, or even hit a best-seller jackpot; but a poet would have to be spectacularly bad before he could live on his poetry. The writer, unlike the painter, has nothing to sell that becomes the exclusive property of the buyer. Speaking of literature, which is the aspect of culture I know most about, I should say that the writer as such really has no economic position at all, and depends for his living on various official and semi-official devices.

One obvious place for the writer to work in is the university, and most serious writers are now university employees, at least in the summer. Of course there is no reason why a university should employ writers who are not scholars or teachers, and not all good writers are. Still, if it does employ a good writer, it also recognizes his social importance, and it covers his freedom with its own academic freedom.

A writer who does not feel that he is developing as well as reflecting public taste will lose his self-respect very quickly. In the mass media of radio and television, as everywhere else, the democratic way is a middle way between rigid control and the anarchy of laissez-faire. This applies also to the grants for writers through wealthy foundations which help them to devote a certain amount of free time to writing. Such assistance only goes so far, but here is still another way of recognizing the importance of the writer without trying to control what he says. Sometimes it may be a very moderate talent that is being encouraged, but you never know: if such a grant had been made to Keats in the summer of 1819 the whole sensibility of the modern world might have been very different. In all these fields democracy has to follow its own trial-and-error, inductive, illogical, and well-meaning way. It will not solve large problems by this method, but it will do a great deal of piecemeal good. And as with the Canada Council Act we enter a new era in the recognition of culture by society, we may keep in mind the shrewd advice of William Blake:

> He who would do good to another must do it in Minute Particulars;
> General Good is the plea of the scoundrel, hypocrite and flatterer.[3]

Children in Canadian schools study Canadian geography, not because it is better than the geography of other nations, but because it is theirs; and similarly with Canadian history and politics. Canadian writing, too, has a value for Canadians independent of its international value. It tells us how Canadian imaginations have reacted to their environment, and therefore it tells us something about Canada that nothing else can tell us. Even if it were not very good in itself, still a Canadian who did not know something of his own literature would be as handicapped as if he had heard of Paris and Rome but never of Ottawa. The study of Canadian literature is not a painful patriotic duty like voting, but a simple necessity of getting one's bearings.

It is reasonable to assume that most Canadian literature would be roughly Canadian in subject-matter, not because it ought to be, but because a serious writer finds it easier to write if he knows what he is talking about. It is often assumed that there is something unique, or at least distinctive, about the Canadian environment or character, and that it is the duty of our writers to interpret those distinctive qualities. Well, this is, of course, the most hackneyed problem in Canadian culture: all our intellectuals are thoroughly tired of it, and very suspicious of attempts to revive it. But they would not feel tired or suspicious if it were or ever had been a genuine problem. The question is put the wrong way round. Writers don't interpret national characters; they create them. But what they create is a series of individual things, characters in novels, images in poems, landscapes in pictures. Types and distinctive qualities are second-hand conventions. If you see what you think is a typical Englishman, it's a hundred to one that you've got your notion of a typical Englishman from your second-hand reading. It is only in satire that types are properly used: a typical Englishman can exist only in such figures as Low's Colonel Blimp.[4] If you look at Mr. Jackson's paintings, you will see a most impressive pictorial survey of Canada: pictures of Georgian Bay and Lake Superior, pictures of the Quebec Laurentians, pictures of Great Bear Lake and the Mackenzie River. What you will not see is a typically Canadian landscape: no such place exists. In fiction too, there is nothing typically Canadian, and Canada would not be a very interesting place to live in if there were. Only the outsider to a country finds characters or patterns of behaviour that are seriously typical. *Maria Chapdelaine* has something of this typifying quality, but then *Maria Chapdelaine* is a tourist's novel.

I insist on this point because it's a special case of widespread misunderstanding about literature. It is often believed that a new environment is a creative influence: that because we have a lot of new things and experiences in Canada, we ought to have a new literature too. So we ought, except that novelty relates to content, not to form or technique. Form and technique don't exist outside literature, and a writer's technical power will depend, not on new experience or new feelings, but only on how well he can absorb what he reads. A hundred years ago Canada was a much newer experience than it is now, and critics were predicting that new *Iliad*s and heroic sagas would emerge from the virgin forests. But what the poets produced was faint echoes of Tom Moore and a few bits of Byron and Wordsworth, because that was what they had absorbed from their reading. That is why the ultimate standards of Canadian literature have to be international ones. The forms in which Canadian writers must write are established in the literary world as a whole, chiefly in Great Britain and the United States for writers in English. The independent value of Canadian culture for Canadians that I just spoke of doesn't excuse the Canadian writer from being judged by world standards. So a good deal of serious Canadian writing is likely to seem like second-hand echoes of American or British writers, who are not only remote from the Canadian scene but often seem to be unreasonably difficult in themselves. Many people in that case would be apt to feel that if the Canada Council encourages the sort of culture that only a small minority can understand, or if it only helps Canadians to imitate writers who have nothing to do with Canada, it can only widen the gap between the Canadian writer and his public. I am not speaking of the Yahoos who sound off about feeding arty bums at the public trough and so forth; I am speaking of what a responsible citizen might reasonably feel.

This raises the question of how far a serious Canadian literature can also be popular, in the sense of being a genuine possession of its people. There are several kinds of popular literature. One kind is the commercial or best-seller type of popular book, usually fiction: its popularity depends on its news value, and when that dies the book dies too. Or it depends on sexual stimulation, which is equally short-lived, as most of you have already discovered. Then there is the kind of book that appeals to the eternal bourgeois in the heart of man, the book that tells him how to get ahead in life and supplies him with inspiring slogans and proverbial philosophy. Books on the power of positive thinking and on winning friends and influencing people have been popular since the days of ancient Egypt: an eighteenth-century example was called *The Way to Be*

Rich and Respectable, which is as good a title as any. Devotees of these books attach an exaggerated importance to such poems as Kipling's *If* or Longfellow's *Psalm of Life*, which represents the same kind of thing in poetry. There seems to be an inner law that prevents this proverbial philosophy from getting beyond a certain point of literary merit. I once heard a speaker recommending Shakespeare as a poet who said profound things about life, but this was the kind of poetry he liked, and I couldn't help noticing that all his quotations were from Polonius and Iago.

But there is another kind of popular literature which is more important. This comes into the reading and listening of the child, in the songs and stories, the history and the wisdom, which are central in our cultural tradition. Whatever literature we learn early, from pre-school nursery rhymes to high-school Shakespeare and beyond, provides us with the keys to nearly all the imaginative experience that it is possible for us to have in life. The central part of this training consists of the Bible, the Classics, and the great heritage of our mother tongue. Such education includes genuinely popular literature: that is, literature which provides a simple and direct form of imaginative experience. In America this would include Rip van Winkle and Huckleberry Finn, the songs of Foster, the tall tales of the West and the comic strips that develop similar folklore cycles in the Tennessee hills and the Florida swamps. We have very little of it in Canada independent of its North American context. The popular in this sense is the contemporary primitive, what in previous ages was folk song and folk tale. Much of it is rubbish, and it includes the cheap fiction and comic books that the enormous maw and the ostrich digestion of a ten-year-old reader assimilates after school hours.

What is popular, in the sense of being permanently and genuinely well loved, is a by-product of education, and as one's education improves, the quality of what one likes improves too, until we reach the fully mature level at which the Bible and Shakespeare and the other staples of culture are popular. A good deal of the worry over the ten-year-old's comic books would be far better expended on making sure that the central educational structure is a sound one. I recently heard of a grade 8 teacher in an expensive regressive school in New York, welcoming a boy who had been away with some joke about the prodigal's return, and gradually realizing that no one in her class had heard the story of the prodigal son. Now a grade 8 student who does not know that story has not simply missed out on a piece of information that can be supplied at any time. He has been deprived of one of the keys to the whole imagination and thought of Western culture, no less than if he had been deprived of the multiplication table. An educational theory which does not recognize this is not just a mistaken theory: it is criminally negligent.

If his elementary education is sound, no student will find contemporary literature remote from him. On the contrary, he will realize that T.S. Eliot and William Faulkner and Dylan Thomas have far more in common with popular literature, as I have defined it, than any positive thinker could ever have. But by this time he is beginning to feel something of the weight and power of the forces at work in society that are trying to prevent him from getting educated. Contemporary culture is very obviously about us, and it talks to us in a fully mature way. Society consists largely of adolescents and arrested adolescents, and departments of education who have to arrange high-school curricula are well aware of the fact. As a rule a student has to get to university before he can make contact with the culture of his own time.

This suggests that much of what is now central in our cultural tradition was in its day equally disturbing in its impact, and still can be. The earliest of the prophets of Israel, we are told, was Amos, and the Book of Amos includes a few of the agonized squeals of his contemporaries: "the land is not able to bear all his words," they said [7:10]. That has been the history of great culture ever since. When Wordsworth said:

> We must be free or die, who speak the tongue
> That Shakespeare spake; the faith and morals hold
> Which Milton held[5]

he meant what he said and he was telling the truth. But school texts of Shakespeare continue to be expurgated, for this fair land is still unable to bear all Shakespeare's words; the faith and morals of Milton are as violently resented today as they ever were. If we subsidize our culture properly, we are certain to encourage a good deal that will be described by a good many people as everything from longhair to filthy. If you think that society has outgrown such narrow-mindedness, I would call your attention to the fact that Canada, like all other countries, has laws of book censorship that no serious student of literature can possibly have the slightest respect for. Or you might ask Mr. Jackson about some of the early reviews of Group of Seven exhibitions.

This is where the class of 1957 at Carleton University comes in. As

John Stuart Mill proved a century ago, the basis of all freedom is academic freedom of thought and discussion. You have had that here, because you are responsible for carrying it into society. I know the staff of Carleton fairly well, and I know that none of them would try to adjust you or integrate you with your society. They have done all they could to detach you from it, to wean you from the maternal bosom of *Good Housekeeping* and the *Reader's Digest*, the pneumatic bliss of the North American way of life. They have tried to teach you to compare your society's ideas with Plato's, its language with Shakespeare's, its calculations with Newton's, its love with the love of the saints. Being dissatisfied with society is the price we pay for being free men and women. And that should help you to understand the Canadian writer better, because he's so often forced to say most loudly what his audience least wants to hear. If people are morally smug, they will think their writers blasphemous; if they are sodden with integration and adjustment, they will think their writers neurotic; if they accept a way of life, they will think their writers subversive. Sometimes, of course, they will be right, but their rightness is not important, and poems which are immoral or hopelessly obscure today may be babbled happily from infant lips tomorrow. Whatever people do, most of their best writers will be doing the opposite. And if the worst of all came upon us, if we had to fight to the last ditch for our freedom, with our brothers killed and our cities in smoking ruins, our poets would still stand over against us, and break out in hymns to the glory of God and in praise of his beautiful world.

43

Poetry

1958

From The Arts in Canada: A Stocktaking at Mid-Century, *ed. Malcolm Ross (Toronto: Macmillan, 1958), 84–90.*

Literary dates coincide only approximately with political ones, and the date which marks the political appearance of the entity we know as "Canada," 1867, precedes by several years the development of a poetry in which the sense of "Canada" as a genuine imaginative environment can be discerned. The new literary age is signalized by the appearance of Charles G.D. Roberts' *Orion and Other Poems* in 1880, when the poet was twenty. Lampman's first volume, *Among the Millet*, partly inspired by the example of Roberts, appeared in 1888; Carman's *Low Tide on Grand Pré* and Duncan Campbell Scott's *The Magic House* in 1893. The work of these four poets is the cornerstone of Canadian poetry, and many readers of Canadian anthologies feel that only with Roberts does the quality of writing leap from clumsy amateurishness into professional competence. All four are Romantic and subjective poets, at best when confronting nature in solitude, in moods of nostalgia, reverie, observation, or extra-sensory awareness. Their sensibility is emotional in origin, and they attain conceptual precision by means of emotional precision. Lampman, who had the keenest mind of the group, often does this; Carman and Roberts, trying with emotional sensibility to reach something beyond it, are apt to let their sensibility go out of focus into a woozy inspirationalism. This subjective and lyrical sensibility, sharp and clear in its emotional foreground but inclined to get vague around its conceptual fringes, is deeply rooted in the Canadian tradition. Most of its characteristics reappear in the Group of Seven painters, in Tom Thomson

Poetry

and Emily Carr, with their odd mixture of *art nouveau* and cosmic consciousness.

The Canadianism of Canadian poetry is of course not a merit in it, but only a quality in it: it may be revealed as clearly in false notes as in true ones, and may be a source of bad taste as well as of inspiration. The Canadian reader of Canadian poetry, however, may legitimately be concerned not only with poetic merit but with the imaginative articulateness of his own country. If so, he may find much to interest him in poetry of less limited objectives than the Romantic lyric, poetry which attempts more and has greater flaws, or is more impressive in conception and theme than in achievement. Some literary values may emerge from an intense struggle between a poetic imagination and the Canadian environment even if the former is defeated. It is a somewhat narrow view of criticism, and in Canada an impossibly pedantic one, that excludes all sympathy for poets who have tried something big with only a little success.

Romanticism was almost incidentally a lyrical development: the bulk of it consisted of narrative, didactic, or dramatic poems, the last group seldom intended for acting. As the exotic is, so to speak, indigenous to Romanticism, a North American setting is not uncommon even in European Romantic poems, as in Chateaubriand. This largely neglected, almost forgotten Romantic tradition produced Longfellow's *Hiawatha* and *Evangeline*, and it flourished in Canada side by side with the lyrical poetry. Isabella Crawford's *Malcolm's Katie* appeared in 1884, Mair's *Tecumseh* in 1886, Duvar's *De Roberval* in 1888. The four lyrical poets attempted longer forms too, and D.C. Scott has a narrative poem on Dominique de Gourges, a subject also considered by Wordsworth as a possible epic theme.

If we look back at the pre-Confederation poets, we see at once that this narrative tradition is more deeply rooted than the lyrical one. There are very few good pre-Confederation lyrics, but there are several quite interesting longer poems: Sangster's *The St. Lawrence and the Saguenay* (1856), a Canadian echo of Tom Moore's series of poems on his travels in North America; O'Grady's *The Emigrant* (1841); Heavysege's *Jephthah's Daughter* (1865), which is Canadian in feeling if not in theme; Howe's *Acadia* [1874]. It looks as though Canadian poets have always felt that a longer form than a lyric was needed to convey the central imaginative impact of a huge, primitive, and sparsely settled country. Such poems can hardly be exported: they are primarily for sympathetic and historically minded

Canadian readers. Perhaps it could also be said that such poems are evidence of a healthier public attitude to poetry than we now have, when stories or disquisitions in verse could be read without the feeling that a poem must justify itself by being strikingly poetic in every line. Certainly we must abandon, in reading them, our modern prejudice that density of poetic texture is always a primary virtue. It is in certain forms, but a narrative often achieves its emotional climax with the driest and baldest of statements. Here is the martyrdom of Père Lalemant in the lyrical context of Marjorie Pickthall, where the texture is appropriately elusive and indirect:

> My hour of rest is done;
> On the smooth ripple lifts the long canoe;
> The hemlocks murmur sadly as the sun
> Slants his dim arrows through.
> Whither I go I know not, nor the way,
> Dark with strange passions, vexed with heathen charms,
> Holding I know not what of life or death . . .   [*Père Lalemant*, ll. 41–7]

and here it is in Pratt's *Brébeuf*, where the virtues are the very different virtues of narrative:

> The wheel had come full circle with the visions
> In France of Brébeuf poured through the mould of St. Ignace.
> Lalemant died in the morning at nine, in the flame
> Of the pitch belts. Flushed with the sight of the bodies, the foes
> Gathered their clans and moved back to the north and west
> To join in the fight against the tribes of the Petuns.   [ll. 2071–6]

This prelude is necessary to explain why certain phenomena of contemporary Canadian poetry are as they are, and in particular why Pratt is still its dominating figure. Pratt's poetic instincts took him back to the narrative rather than the lyrical tradition, although he has written some fine lyrics. One can no more get him into anthologies than one could get his whales and dinosaurs into a circus parade: he has to be read by himself or not at all. There is much in his work that recalls the earlier narrative poems mentioned above, with their sense of the loneliness of man facing the huge untamed Canadian landscape and pitting his forlorn moral and civilized standards against nature's vast indifference to them. But in striking contrast to the earlier Romantics, Pratt's poetry is intensely social, even gregarious: there are no wanderers in his poems, only hunters, fighters, builders, and missionaries. He has written of railways and shipping with a genuine love of technological language: his poetry rings with the noise of the machinery that has grappled with the country, and he makes himself and his reader participators rather than spectators of the heroic actions he celebrates. In relation to what has gone before him, he has clarified and brought into focus a distinctively Canadian kind of imaginative consciousness. As a result he has achieved a popularity in his own country which is a genuine and healthy popularity, not the false popularity of the Service school, with its lurking anti-intellectual bias. As part of the same result, he has had a very limited recognition in Great Britain and the United States. Pratt's achievement has been too individual to leave an integrated tradition behind, but indirectly he has influenced Canadian poetry a great deal by loosening and informalizing it, encouraging poets to think in less introverted and page-bound categories. Here his influence has partly coincided with that of the CBC, which has also done a great deal to make poets realize the importance of oral reading and a listening audience.

We may take 1943–44 as the year marking the beginning of contemporary Canadian poetry. Pratt's collected poems appeared in 1944, and though he has written some of his best poetry since (*Behind the Log*, 1947; *Towards the Last Spike*, 1952), the collection indicates the general range and tone of his work. At almost the same time (1943) there appeared E.K. Brown's *On Canadian Poetry*, a rather casual historical survey with a more detailed consideration of Pratt, Lampman, and D.C. Scott. Its opening pages, however, clearly state, in its contemporary context, the perennial dilemma of the English Canadian poet: the fact that he is involved in a unique problem of self-identification, torn between a centrifugal impulse to ignore his environment and compete on equal terms with his British and American contemporaries, and a centripetal impulse to give an imaginative voice to his own surroundings. The centrifugal poet lacks a community, and if we look at the proportion of recent poetry in Britain, for instance, that has been produced by Irishmen, Welshmen, and home-rule Scotsmen, we can see how important a restricted community is. Besides, Canada is not a bad arena for poets as such things go: a few Canadian publishers are generous to them; a surprising proportion of the poetry bought in Canada is Canadian poetry; Canadian journals give space for reviews and discussion which enable the poet in Canada to achieve an amount of recognition that he could hardly attain in the larger countries; Canadian radio and television disseminate his work and exhibit his personality. But of course there is the opposite danger of being too easily satisfied with provincial standards, when today the real standards of poetry are set in the world as a whole. Some of our best poets have been confused by a tendency, conscious or unconscious, to develop either the centripetal or the centrifugal impulse into a moral principle.

The first edition of A.J.M. Smith's *A Book of Canadian Poetry*, the most impressive piece of historical and critical stock-taking yet made in Canadian poetry, also appeared in 1943. This anthology represented a thorough first-hand revaluation of Canadian poetry up to that time, in the light of liberal and intelligently applied critical canons. The picture of Canadian literary history presented by it has remained in the foreground of Canadian criticism ever since. Those poets who did not appear in Mr. Smith's book, such as Wilson MacDonald, were, whether their omission was deliberate or involuntary, almost obliterated from the serious discussions of Canadian poetry that followed it. Mr. Smith discovered or re-emphasized neglected merits in the pre-Confederation poets; he gave the next or Romantic generation a more modest rating, indicating that in all of them except Lampman the proportion of chaff to grain was high. He then dramatized the conflict of centripetal and centrifugal impulses by dividing his "modern" poets into a "native" and a "cosmopolitan" group, with Pratt at the head of one and Frank R. Scott at the head of the other. This division was dropped in the second edition of 1948, and probably should have been, as it represents a division of mind within each poet, not a division between two groups of poets. Nevertheless, the older scheme does correspond, if accidentally, to the facts of the contemporary situation in Canadian poetry, where Pratt and F.R. Scott are certainly the chief personal influences.

A survey of Canadian poetry since 1943 has certain inherent difficulties. It is only where there is great genius that the critic is provided with a ready-made construct, for the life of a great genius is, as Keats said, a continuous allegory,[1] however tragic or truncated his life. In Canada the critic must set up a more or less plausible construct of his own, made out of trends and schools and groupings, which every poet of unusual talent bursts out of. Further, Canada naturally has no full-time poets: every poet writes in what time he can spare from some exacting profession, usually the academic one. Hence many poets have to be slow and thrifty writers, eking out every volume of new poems with reprinted older

Poetry

ones. Canadian anthologies are even more confined to stock repertory than anthologies elsewhere. Again, a cultural lag of approximately a decade keeps dogging publication dates. Death-and-resurrection poems with Waste-Land overtones were being written during the twenties, but did not reach the public until Leo Kennedy's *The Shrouding* (1933) and the collection *New Provinces* (1936), of which more in a moment. A glance at some of the books that appeared at the end of the war, such as Dorothy Livesay's *Day and Night* (1944), F.R. Scott's *Overture* (1945), and Louis Dudek's *East of the City* (1946), would convince one that the country was in a state of social ferment, but the main inspiration is of the previous Depression decade. Finally, some poets, notably George Johnston and Margaret Avison, are in too unpublished a state as yet to be dealt with here, although they may well be of greater interest to posterity than many who are mentioned.

The primary channels for the publication of Canadian poetry are of course precarious "little magazines," which, in Canada as elsewhere, bloom and vanish like a display of fireworks. Most important of these is the indomitable *Canadian Forum*, founded in 1920 and still going on, which, though never primarily a literary magazine, has done more than any other single periodical for Canadian poetry. *Contemporary Verse*, in British Columbia, edited by Alan Crawley, survived for over ten years, and *Fiddlehead*, in New Brunswick, is still active. *Preview* (1942) in Montreal expired when the group that founded it disintegrated; *First Statement* (1945) was reborn as the *Northern Review*, edited by John Sutherland, which, though it eventually tended to become something of a catechist's manual, represented great editorial energy and devotion. In the last year or so some of the best current poetry has appeared in the *Tamarack Review*, but of the subsidized magazines, only *Queen's Quarterly* pays much serious attention to poetry. The Contact Press in Toronto, under the management of Raymond Souster, has sponsored an extraordinary variety of poetic ventures, many of them mimeographed. The Ryerson Press, besides publishing several books of verse every year, also issues a series of "chapbooks" in paper covers, in which a great number of both permanent and transient talents have appeared. McClelland & Stewart's "Indian File" series, as its name indicates, averages one volume a year. Readings of poetry are featured by the CBC, chiefly on its "Anthology" program. This list is not intended to be exhaustive, but apart from it the catalogue of accessible Canadian poetry would be, like some Anglo-Saxon elegies, simple, brief, and bleak.

A little book called *New Provinces* (1936) contained new poems by Pratt and by a group of younger poets born between 1900 and 1910, all of whom except Leo Kennedy have continued productive. A.J.M. Smith's *News of the Phoenix* appeared in 1943 and *A Sort of Ecstasy* in 1955. Along with Kennedy, though in a much solider way, he shows the increasing influence of metaphysical poets and the contemporary impact of Eliot and the later Yeats. In this and in his critical and scholarly approach to poetry—he is a professor of English—he is typical of what we may call the academic tradition in Canadian poetry, which was largely established by the poets of his generation. In Robert Finch (*Poem*, 1946; *The Strength of the Hills*, 1948), who also appeared in *New Provinces*, in Roy Daniells (*Deeper into the Forest*, 1948), in Alfred Bailey (*Border River*, 1952), in Louis MacKay (*The Ill-Tempered Lover*, 1948), professors respectively of French, English, History, and Classics, we find a great variety and range of the normal characteristics of academic poetry. Echoes abound from the great tradition of poetry, from Virgil in MacKay to Mallarmé in Finch; shadows of Frazer, Jung, Freud, Spengler, and Toynbee lurk around the margins; the symbols and rites of religion inform the themes.

As long as these influences were new to Canada, an impression grew up that this "difficult, lonely music"[2] was an intellectual reaction to the emotional facility of the earlier Romantics, or, with the hazier-minded, that some erudite and esoteric group was seizing control of Canadian poetry, taking it away from the people, and retreating from direct experience. The causes of the fact that nearly all the best Canadian poetry today is academic poetry, and will be in the foreseeable future, lie deep in the nature of poetry itself and of twentieth-century society: it is not its causes but its effects that concern us here. With the passing of time it has become more apparent that much of the poetry of the academic generation shows the tradition of the Romantic lyric continuing with a slight change of idiom and literary taste. The path is direct from Bliss Carman's *Resurgam* to Leo Kennedy's *Words for a Resurrection*, and from Lampman's *City of the End of Things* to Smith's *The Bridegroom*. But there is another element in academic poetry that needs more careful analysis.

If we look back at the narrative poems of the nineteenth century with twentieth-century eyes, we find ourselves less interested in the story being told than in what seem the imaginative reasons for telling it: the attempt to dramatize certain themes or situations that have for the poet a symbolic or mythical importance. Poe's "poetic principle" that long poems are actually fragments of vision stuck together with prose is a principle that works fairly well for Canadian narrative poetry. What we remember of *Malcolm's Katie* or *Jephthah's Daughter* are the bits like the "south wind" passage from the former or Jephthah calling to his blind god for release from his vow and hearing only the hill wolf and the bittern.[3] Here something looms out of the poet's environment with the mysterious urgency of a myth, a symbol, an epiphanic moment, an evocative mood, or whatever we like to call the sudden fusing of subject and object. These moments of fusion seem to us the *raison d'être* of such poems. And if we look at John Sutherland's study of Pratt, we can see what younger poets mainly read Pratt for: they read him less for the story than for the mythical or symbolic significance of his characters and themes. The poetry of what we have called the academic school is overwhelmingly mythopoeic. The hills and forest and river of Finch and Daniells and Bailey are partly landscape and partly the landscape of the more mysterious parts of the mind. Hence what the academic tradition represents in Canadian poetry is a fragmenting of the narrative tradition, a concentrating on the significant moods and symbols in which poet and environment are identified. The Romantic lyrical poets are normally detached from their environment: they observe and describe what they see, and they observe and describe the emotions with which they see it. Thus Lampman:

> And yet to me not this or that
> Is always sharp or always sweet;
> In the sloped shadow of my hat
> I lean at rest, and drain the heat;
> Nay more, I think some blessed power
> Hath brought me wandering idly here:
> In the full furnace of this hour
> My thoughts grow keen and clear.   [*Heat*, ll. 41–8]

The "modern" poet strives to break down this mutually aggressive barrier between the mind and its environment; he seeks some enveloping myth in which mind and nature become the same thing. Thus Irving Layton:

> But the furies clear a path for me to the worm
> who sang for an hour in the throat of a robin,
> and misled by the cries of young boys
>   I am again
> a breathless swimmer in that cold green element.
>   [*The Cold Green Element*, ll. 36–40]

And when Layton so writes he is writing in the mythopoeic tradition of Isabella Crawford when she comes to an imaginative focus in her narrative:

> The pulseless forest, lock'd and interlock'd
> So closely, bough with bough, and leaf with leaf,
> So surf'd by its own wealth, that while from high
> The moons of summer kiss'd its green-gloss'd locks;
> And round its knees the merry West Wind danc'd;
> And round its ring, compacted emerald;
> The south wind crept on moccasins of flame.

Further, poetry is a world of its own: it does not reflect life but contains it in its own form, and hence what is most profoundly evocative in poetry is, nine times out of ten, not an evocation of life but of other parts of one's literary experience. When Louis MacKay calls one of his poems *Nunc Scio, Quid Sit Amor*, he is not echoing Virgil because he is lazy or lacking in originality, but because his mood evokes specifically this echo, not a general series of associations. The erudition in academic poetry is neither ostentation nor an accident of the poet's profession, but a precise guidance of the reader's emotional reactions.

Earle Birney belongs, chronologically and by profession, to the academic group. His scholarly competence in Old and Middle English is reflected in *Anglosaxon Street* and elsewhere. But *David* (1942), the poem that established his reputation, is an admirable, and unfragmented, later product of the narrative tradition. The impact of the war on Birney diversified a talent for satire with a sense of comradeship, perhaps more genuine in feeling than successful as poetry. In *Trial of a City* (1952) there is a theme (a proposed destruction of Vancouver) fitted to bring out the best of his powers: erudition, satire, parody, and a sense of the irresistible power of ordinary humanity as against pedantic officialdom. The relation of this radio play to the Canadian tradition of narrative and dramatic poetry is clear enough, and indicates that that tradition, even in its continuous form, may still have a long development ahead of it.

Abraham M. Klein, also one of the *New Provinces* group, is perhaps the most distinguished single poet of the generation following Pratt, though none of his poetry equals the passion and fire of his prose romance *The Second Scroll*, which for sheer intensity has little if anything to rival it in

Canadian fiction. Klein's earlier poetry (*Hath Not a Jew*, 1940) is steeped in Jewish life and culture, and reminds us that of all groups in English-speaking Canada, the Jews are in a most favourable position to deal with the environmental dilemma mentioned above. They form a close Canadian community which is immediately linked to other parts of the world, and the advantages of belonging to such a community have been exploited by both Jewish poets and novelists, especially novelists. Klein, however, was not content merely to exploit the special knowledge and sensitivity which his religious and ethnical affinities gave him. In *The Rocking Chair* (1948) there are brilliant vignettes of French Canadian life that show how understanding of one community may develop an understanding of another; there are lively linguistic experiments stimulated by a profound study of Joyce; and, in *Portrait of the Poet as Landscape* there is one of the most searching studies of the modern poet in Canadian literature.

The last of the *New Provinces* group is F.R. Scott, whose *Overture* appeared in 1945 and *Events and Signals* in 1955. A penchant for political and social satire is more conspicuous in him than in most of his contemporaries, but by no means peculiar to him: a recent anthology of light verse compiled by him and A.J.M. Smith, *The Blasted Pine*, shows how deep-rooted the sense of irreverence in Canadian poets is, and has been from the beginning. His satires, however, are not shots at random targets, but part of a consistent social attitude, intensely Canadian in reference. We notice that he is not at all a mythopoeic or symbolic poet, but a poet of detached comment: the Romantic duality of mind and environment reappears in him. He is in fact a neo-Romantic, a product of an age in which the centre of Canadian social gravity has finally shifted to the urban, the industrial, and the political.

Scott has been a major personal influence in encouraging a neo-Romantic movement in Canadian poetry, a descriptive and nostalgic commentary on the *fourmillante cité*. This movement is, of course, often rationalized as a rediscovery of reality. Thus the magazine *Preview*, founded mainly by Patrick Anderson, P.K. Page, and Scott himself in 1942, wished to "look forward, perhaps optimistically, to a possible fusion between the lyric and didactic elements in modern verse, a combination of vivid, arresting imagery and the capacity to 'sing' with social content and criticism." Patrick Anderson's *The White Centre* and P.K. Page's *As Ten, As Twenty* (1946) are full of sharp glances at landladies, stenographers, hospitals, and of course the war. As in the previous Romantic movement, the emotional reaction is clear and the intellectual one fuzzy: whenever lyric and didactic impulses fail to fuse, this is usually the reason for it. In their second volumes these poets have moved over into the academic camp. Anderson's *The Colour as Naked* (1953) is, at its best, pastoral poetry, and Miss Page's *The Metal and the Flower* (1954) has absorbed its sharpness of perception into an elaborate and quite recognizably mythical framework of expression.

The Romantic tradition is now carried on by Raymond Souster and Louis Dudek. The former, whose *Selected Poems* appeared in 1956, has finally developed a form of epigram, the theme almost invariably urban life, which at its rare best is a type of poetic experience as immediate and sharply pointed as anything in Canadian poetry. Louis Dudek has never quite fulfilled the promise of his earlier *East of the City* (1946), but he has produced a great deal of original and striking poetry, which appears to be forceful by conviction and delicate and haunting by instinct. His retrospective collection *The Transparent Sea* (1956) gives a good idea of the range of his powers.

Irving Layton has been closely associated with this group, and much at least of his earlier poetry is indistinguishable from it. But beginning with *In the Midst of My Fever* (1954) he began to turn his enormously prolific talents in other directions. One aspect of him, represented by *The Long Pea-Shooter* (1954) and *The Blue Propeller* (1955), is the dramatizing of a poetic personality not unlike that favoured by the "jam session" schools of New York City and California. The other aspect is consolidated in *The Improved Binoculars* (1956), a collection of his work which is perhaps the most important single volume of Canadian poetry since the Pratt collection of 1944.

It is difficult to do justice in a sentence or two to the variety and exuberance of Layton's best work. The sensuality which seems its most obvious characteristic is rather an intense awareness of physical and bodily reality, which imposes it own laws on the intellect even when the intellect is trying to snub and despise it. The mind continually feels betrayed by the body, and its resulting embarrassments are a rich source of ribald humour. Yet the body in the long run is closer to spirit than the intellect is: it suffers where the intellect is cruel; it experiences where the intellect excludes. Hence a poetry which at first glance looks anti-intellectual is actually trying to express a gentler and subtler kind of cultivation than the intellect alone can reach. Thus Layton is, in the expanded sense in which the term is used in this article, an academic rather than a Romantic poet, though one of his own highly individual kind.

Out of the great number of contemporary Canadian poets who have some valid claims on our attention, we may make a more or less arbitrary choice of six: Douglas LePan (*The Wounded Prince*, 1948; *The Net and the Sword*, 1953); Wilfred Watson (*Friday's Child*, 1955); Anne Wilkinson (*The Hangman Ties the Holly*, 1955); James Reaney (*The Red Heart*, 1949); Jay Macpherson (*The Boatman*, 1957), and (perhaps as yet more potentially than actually) Daryl Hine (*The Carnal and the Crane*, 1957). All of these represent the academic tradition in its second generation. In them the use of myth and metaphor has become instinctive, and allusions to other poems, including nursery rhymes, are unforced and unself-conscious. Such characteristics are, as we have tried to show, not superficial, but signs of a habit of poetic thought. LePan is the most conspicuous figure of this group: *The Net and the Sword* deals with the poet's experiences in the Italian campaign, and shows very clearly how what in the previous century would probably have been a continuous narrative has become fragmented into brief moments of intense apprehension. Wilfred Watson, whose book was published by Faber & Faber, uses a good deal of sacramental religious language, but his central vision, a kind of *Sartor Resartus* contrast between the world as we see it and the same world in its naked apocalyptic form, does not depend on such language. Anne Wilkinson has some curious accidental resemblances to Watson, though in her the religious language turns into sardonic parody. James Reaney showed in *The Red Heart* (1949) a puckish humour and a gift for disconcerting fantasy that has developed into the extraordinary and erudite satire of *A Suit of Nettles* (1958). Daryl Hine has also shown very little of the full range of his developing abilities as yet, though one feels that his power will be considerable when it turns from self-communing into direct communication. At present (1957), the Canadian poetic scene is dominated by Jay Macpherson's *The Boatman*, a book of very lovely lyrics ranging in tone from light verse to elegy, and which is not simply a collection of poems, but one of the most carefully and exquisitely constructed books in Canadian poetry.

In the best of contemporary Canadian poets one senses an extraordinary sureness of direction. They work in the midst of a society which is largely indifferent to them, not because it is stupid or vulgar or materialistic, but because it is obsessed by the importance of putting ideas into words, and cannot bring itself to understand that putting words into patterns is a much more profound and fundamental reshaping of thought. They give little sign of wanting either to fight this indifference or to compromise with it, and hence they are not simply an indication of the quality of Canadian civilization today, but one of the few guarantees of its permanence.

44

Preface and Introduction to Pratt's Poetry

September 1958

Editor's Preface and Introduction, from The Collected Poems of E.J. Pratt, *2nd ed. (Toronto: Macmillan, 1958), xii–xxviii. Reprinted in* Canada: A Guide to the Peaceable Kingdom, *ed. William Kilbourn (Toronto: Macmillan, 1970), 299–303. Introduction translated into French by Claudette Laprise and published in* Ellipse, *41 (1989): 92–103.*

Preface

This second edition of the *Collected Poems* of E.J. Pratt comprises all the poems that the author is willing to reprint, along with *Behind the Log, Towards the Last Spike,* and a group classified as "Later Poems," which have been written since the appearance of the first edition in 1944. As compared with the first edition, *Carlo* and *A Dirge,* from *Newfoundland Verse, Putting Winter to Bed* from *Many Moods,* and *The Mirage* and *The Illusion* (formerly called *The Drowning*) from *The Fable of the Goats and Other Poems* have been added. *A Reverie on a Dog* and *The Fable of the Goats,* not included here, may be found in the first edition.

If the reader is wondering, as he easily may, why this poet should need either an editor or an introduction, I should explain that my very simple editorial duties have been assumed purely as an act of personal homage to the poet in his seventy-fifth year.

Introduction

The purpose of this introduction is not to speak for a poet who can speak quite well for himself. Its purpose is to encourage the reader to commit himself to the poet. If he is unfamiliar with Pratt, this is the right book for him to start with. Pratt cannot be sampled in anthologies: he must be read in bulk or not at all. If he is familiar with only part of Pratt's work, this book will give him the poet's whole scope and range. If he has certain preconceived ideas about Pratt, he will be able to compare them with the poems. If he knows Pratt thoroughly, he still has a rich and complex poetic experience awaiting him. Pratt has genuine simplicity, but, as William Blake wrote, there is a wide gulf between the simple and the insipid.[1] Simplicity is difficult, not easy; it destroys laziness and prejudice, it does not confirm them.

Pratt's life has been outwardly quiet, but he has been one of those creators Henry James spoke of, who do not need to search for experience because they are the kind of people on whom nothing is lost.[2] Born in Newfoundland in 1883, his first impressions were of Newfoundland fishing villages, where, in the words of one of their folk songs, "fish is low and flour is high," and where men fought for their food at the risk of their lives. More than once his father, who was a clergyman, had to inform a fisherman's wife that her husband would not return from the sea. Newfoundland was followed by Victoria College, where he was graduated in 1911, and by graduate work in theology and psychology. In Methodism at that time the battle of "higher criticism" had been won, Biblical archaeology (see *The Epigrapher*) was opening up, there was general enthusiasm for such new world-pictures as "evolution," *Angst* and *Existenz* were unheard of, and there was no difficulty—certainly the poet has never found any—in being Christian and liberal at the same time. Psychology was concerned largely with experiments in sensory response to signals, with colour wheels that turned grey when revolved, an apparatus that made the poet long for a more entertaining type of spinner:

> Fled was the class-room's puny space—
> His eye saw but a whirling disk.   (*In Absentia* [, ll. 13–14])

Finally he became a teacher of English literature at Victoria College, and remained there until his retirement as Professor Emeritus in 1953. Each of these strata of experience can be easily traced in his work. As a student of literature he struck his roots directly into Shakespeare and the major Romantics—poets great enough to allow him to find his own mode of poetic speech for himself. He has never followed or started any particular "trend" in poetry, never learned or imposed any particular mannerisms of expression. The record of the rest of his life, from *Newfoundland Verse* in 1923 onwards, is the substance of this book.

It is interesting to compare the original *Newfoundland Verse* with what the author has been willing to reprint of it here. Always contemptuous of what he calls "O thouing," he has tried to cut away two things: the intrusion of the poet on his reader, and the detachment of the poet from his surroundings. He is already well aware that writing narrative poetry is no job for an egocentric poet. For narrative, the poet must have a story worth telling, and then get out of its way. Thus, in the final quatrain of *The Ice-Floes*:

> Of twenty thousand seals that were killed
>   To help to lower the price of bread;
> Of the muffled beat ... of a drum ... that filled
>   A nave ... at our count of sixty dead.   [ll. 145–8]

The dots are not put there just to look impressive; they are there to slow down the end of a beautifully paced narrative. There is no attempt to pack in Higher Significance, no bluster about red-blooded heroes, no underlining of the irony, no comment on the tragedy. The poet knows that a good story cannot be pumped up by fine writing, and that a fable that is any good contains its own moral.

It is a law of poetic creation that the poet who is willing to lose his personality in his work finds it again. Out of his self-effacing concern with the poetic object, Pratt developed a flexible, unpretentious speaking style which is amazingly versatile, yet always unmistakably his. A slight turn in one direction, and this style goes into broad burlesque, with comic rhymes and anticlimaxes in the tradition of *Hudibras* and *Don Juan*:

> A walrus' heart and pancreas,
> A blind Auk from the coast of Java,
> A bull moose that had died from gas
> While eating toadstools near Ungava.   (*The Witches' Brew*[, ll. 128–31])

A slight turn in another direction, and it becomes delicate and fanciful, as in this description of Cassiopeia:

> For high above the table head
> Shall sway a candelabrum where,
> According to the legend, dwelt a
> Lady seated in a chair
> With Alpha, Beta, Gamma, Delta,
> Busy braiding up her hair.   (*The Depression Ends*[, ll. 97–102])

It can dramatize a poker game or a whale hunt, summarize history or expound science, swivel easily from the colloquial to the eloquent. In a tragic context, the same style can achieve the peculiar virtue of narrative, of being able to communicate the most deeply impressive moments in a bald, flat statement, as in the account of Lalemant's martyrdom in *Brébeuf*:

> Lalemant died in the morning at nine, in the flame
> Of the pitch-belts.   [ll. 2073–4]

"Ther is namore to seye," as Chaucer, who ought to have known something about narrative, so often remarks.

The patient scholarship and research that has gone into the major poems is another self-effacing quality that has made for distinctiveness. One would expect such research in *Brébeuf* or *Towards the Last Spike*, but the poet also understands that aspect of erudition which is irresistibly comic. In fact, he did not really find himself as a narrative poet until the knowledge painfully acquired in a decade of study began to strike him as having a funny side. Before *The Witches' Brew*, according to his own account, he had composed and burnt a portentous epic named *Clay*, which apparently contained a good deal of metrically organized information. The wit and exuberance of *The Great Feud* depend on the plethora of unusual technical terms, and *The Witches' Brew* itself, in the energy of its defiance of an environment of Methodism and prohibition, sweeps in an encyclopedic survey of brands of liquor, to the great confusion of its original reviewers.

In all his poetry Pratt's language bristles with the concrete and the definite. He has always understood that the imagination has to realize its whole area, not bits and pieces of it, and he has the swift selective eye—or rather ear—for the relevant detail that distinguishes the scholar from the pedant. In search of a monosyllable that would convey the hardness of rock, he ransacked a department of geology until he extracted the word "schist." While he was working on *Behind the Log*, anyone in a naval uniform he met would be backed into a corner and forced to reveal what he knew (or, much more frequently, did not know) about the anatomy of a ship. For the band in *The Titanic*, he asked me for a term in music denoting a moderate rate of speed—four syllables, main accent on the third. I gave him his choice of andantino, moderato, and allegretto. He chose andantino, but as the line "The allegretto strains in human tears" occurs in a poem published many years later [*Autopsy on a Sadist*, l. 11], he had clearly not forgotten the alternatives.

Another feature already present in *Newfoundland Verse* is the unifying of the poet with his society, and of that society with nature. The rhythm that drives the sea against the rocks drives the blood through the human body; even when in bed inside a cottage the spirit is aware of its kinship with the wind outside. It is against this background of identity that man fights nature in his tiny open boats, his work gangs, his hunting and clearing of land. The struggle for life is an enmity which has a kind of innocence about it, because it is an enmity without hatred:

> The hour had called for argument more rife
> With the gambler's sacrificial bids for life,
> The final manner native to the breed
> Of men forging decision into deed—
> Of getting down again into the sea,
> And testing rowlocks in an open boat,
> Of grappling with the storm-king bodily,
> And placing Northern fingers on his throat.
> (*The Roosevelt and the Antinoe*[, ll. 776–83])

The reader will notice that Pratt's moral standards have few surprises: he is much more of a spokesman than a critic of public opinion and generally accepted social reactions. The reason—or one reason—is that he is almost always dealing with a society in a state of emergency: a Newfoundland fishing village depending on the next catch; a nation at war anxiously scanning the headlines; a band of missionaries surrounded by hostile Indians; sailors or railway workers trying to finish a dangerous quest on schedule. Such societies are engaged, and those who go out to meet the engagement are quite obviously heroes: there is no time to analyse motives or question values.

The conception of heroism in Pratt is of the kind that belongs to our age, and to an industrial democracy. It is the whole group engaged in the quest that is the hero. When Pratt names an individual hero, like Brébeuf, he thinks of the heroism as like that of a soldier who has received a medal for valour—as representative rather than isolated. The cowards and slackers who desert the quest are usually ignored. In the story of the *Titanic* there are many obvious things to consider: the "hap" or mysterious fate that attracted Hardy, the outrage at the incompetence of those in charge that brought some blistering essays from Conrad,[3] the vainglorious confidence that the ship was unsinkable which seems, in retrospect, to have almost deliberately aimed at the iceberg. But Pratt pays little attention to any of this. His chief interest is in the society of the first-class lounge, with the luxurious food, the music, the gossip, and the brilliantly described poker game. It is a brittle society, without much human point to it—until disaster strikes. Then it becomes the beleaguered group that the poet so well understands, and its genuine humanity suddenly becomes the focus of the poem, and the key to its meaning.

Not only is the individual hero apt to be anonymous, but, especially in the later narratives, even the crucial heroic *act* is not definitely pointed out: it is merely diffused through the poem. Nothing is truer to the spirit of modern heroism than the story told in *Behind the Log*: but where is the thrilling moment, the wild death-defying charge, the cops-and-robbers race, the cliff-hanging suspense? The genuine heroic act takes place unconsciously, in the midst of preoccupation; it has been done before even the doer is aware of having done it. Further, it takes place in time, and an instant later has vanished forever into the dark. What the group as a whole accomplishes—the railway, the martyr's shrine, the terms of a victorious peace—may last longer, but that too is temporal. The story of the *Titanic* is only one of several studies in Pratt (see *The Ritual, The Sea-Cathedral, A Prairie Sunset*) of a tremendous glittering achievement that does nothing but disappear.

In this world of unconscious or preoccupied action, communication takes place very largely on unconscious levels too. The communication of loyalty and comradeship which makes heroism possible is mostly unconscious; the communication of enmity is even more primitive, like the squid's awareness of the whale in *The Cachalot* as:

> . . . a deep consonant that rides
> Below the measured beat of tides
> With that vast, undulating rhythm
> A sounding sperm whale carries with him.   [ll. 150–3]

Such unconscious communication takes many forms. There is correspondence, the feeling in *The Ground Swell* of the identity of man and nature, already mentioned. There is the answering sign, as when in *Come Away, Death* modern man looks into the face of death with the same "hieroglyph" of horror as his caveman ancestor. There is repetition on different levels, as when in *Erosion* the sea carves the rocks, then, after wrecking a boat, carves the lines of agony on a widow's face. On a conscious level Pratt is fascinated by the intricate machinery of signals and response, of radar and asdic in *Behind the Log*, of wireless messages in *The Titanic*, of electric charges bounced off an unresponsive whale or an unromantic moon.

Of all conscious signals the most important is the human word, especially the word of command that starts the social achievement going. But what is the origin of the word of command? Pratt observed how in the Second World War the cause of tyranny depended on Hitler's screaming *Baritone*, and the cause of freedom on the measured cadences of Churchill. His sense of the immense moral force in rhetoric can be seen all through the later poems. In *Towards the Last Spike* he takes the anonymity of heroism for granted, to an extent that startled some of his readers:

> As individuals
> The men lost their identity; as groups,
> As gangs, they massed, divided, subdivided,
> Like numerals only.   [ll. 832–5]

"Where are the coolies in your poem, Ned?" protests another poet, F.R. Scott. Twenty years earlier there would probably have been more about the coolies. At this stage the poet is interested rather in the power of the word, and in the source of its power. He finds it in the Parliamentary debates, with Macdonald's "from sea to sea" countering Blake's "to build a road over that sea of mountains."[4] Both phrases are Biblical, with Biblical promises lurking in one and Biblical warnings in the other. The source of the word of command, as far as this poem is concerned, is a battle of metaphors, a conflict of rival visions. And if rhetoric is so important in controlling the movement of society, poetry is by implication even more so. In *Myth and Fact* the poet shows us how much of our life is involved in realizing and giving substance to the dreams of childhood, and the myths which are the dreams of man's childhood.

The sense of the identity of man and nature, and of man as a rebellious child of nature, led Pratt naturally to the theme of evolution, the sense of the eons of ferocity that lie behind human hatred and warfare. This is the theme of some of his best-known poems, of *Silences*, of *The Prize Cat*, of *From Stone to Steel*:

> The snarl Neanderthal is worn
> Close to the smiling Aryan lips,
> The civil polish of the horn
> Gleams from our praying finger tips. [*From Stone to Steel*, ll. 5–8]

This is normally a pessimistic conception, but the pessimism for Pratt has an important qualification. When we look from the outside on one of Pratt's heroic exploits, we see people suffering, dying, and finally vanishing into the awful annihilation of the past. When we look from the outside at evolution, we see only an endless struggle to survive which has been practically all pain and cruelty. But when we shift the view to the inside, we see an exuberant, unquenchable force of life, which fights to maintain itself certainly, but can find its fulfilment also in defeat and death. Sometimes this shift to the inside in Pratt is unexpectedly literal, as when he takes us on that wonderful voyage through the interior of the cachalot whale, or places us within a Scotchman's stomach to watch the metamorphosis of oatmeal into obstinacy. But it is this transfer of attention from the external nature, red in tooth and claw, to the internal life force, swarming and exulting and devouring itself in other forms, that gives to that magnificent fantasy *The Great Feud* its logical coherence.

It is consistent with his interest in evolving life that the poet should admire size, health, strength, and energy. His sympathies are normally on the side of *The Big Fellow*. "Breed" is a favourite word of his: it has no racial connotations, but means that the poet likes things to be fully developed examples of what they are. It pleases him when a rock is hard, when a whale is huge, when a Scotchman is named Sandy MacTavish. But "evolution" is much too simplified a picture of reality by itself. There is a pull of inertia backwards as well as development forwards. The ferocity of Tom the Cat from Zanzibar, in *The Witches' Brew*, is explained by such a retrograde movement:

> His stock were traitors to the sea,
> Had somehow learned the ways of earth,
> The need of air, the mystery
> Of things warm-blooded, and of birth. [ll. 465–8]

In a more serious context in *The Highway*, brief but one of Pratt's definitive poems, he speaks of the development of life from the star through the rose to, not man, but to Christ as the fulfilment of man. In the last stanza he speaks of the misstep or falling away which is so much older a conception than evolution, and still seems an essential one:

> But what made *our* feet miss the road that brought
> The world to such a golden trove,
> In our so brief a span?
> How may we grasp again the hand that wrought
> Such light, such fragrance, and such love,
> O star! O rose! O Son of Man?   [ll. 19–24]

The first great product of the evolutionary force is mechanism, the intricate machinery of the revolving stars, the automatic movements of matter, the wonderful complex precision of animal bodies. Pratt recurs over and over to the analogy between the machine and the animal: in *The Submarine*, in *The Dying Eagle*, in *The Man and the Machine*:

> The man whose hands were on the wheel
> Could trace his kinship through her steel,
> Between his body warped and bent
> In every bone and ligament,
> And this "eight-cylinder" stream-lined,
> The finest model yet designed.   [*The Man and the Machine*, ll. 3–8]

Several poets, including Hart Crane, have asserted that the modern poet ought to be able to make an unforced and spontaneous use of mechanical imagery:[5] Pratt is one of the few poets who have done so. It is particularly in warfare that he notices the reappearance of mechanical forms and rhythms in human life, of how insect forms, like the locusts in the Apocalypse, take on the outlines of conscious malignity:

> It is these that the rearguards are facing—
> Creatures of conveyer belts,
> Of precision tools and schedules.
> They breathe through carburetted lungs;
> If pierced, they do not feel the cut,
> And if they die, they do not suffer death.   (*Dunkirk*, [ll. 264–9])

The Tartars and Mongols who swept over Asia, the Nazis who polluted modern Europe, the Iroquois who tortured Brébeuf, all derive their ferocity from the mechanical energy of life, like the bonitoes and barracudas in *Silences*. But they are evil, not innocent, because they are also actively resisting the pull forward of their real human nature into love. *The Highway* of the human race is a path that "lies through Gethsemane." In the dialectic of love and ferocity the reason may take either side: if it chooses ferocity we have that strange phenomenon of the modern age, the reasoning mechanism, the destroying angel that the pitiful rabble of free men at Dunkirk wrestled with and held until daybreak:

> No tolerance befogged the reason—
> The *reason* with its clear-swept halls,
> Its brilliant corridors . . .
> The straightedge ruled out errors,
> The tremors in the sensory nerves,
> Pity and the wayward impulses,
> The liberal imbecilities. [*Dunkirk*, ll. 34–6, 39–42]

If the reason joins forces with love, on the other hand, it can see, to return to the last stanza of *The Highway*, that the Son of Man is identical with the star and the rose, and includes them, and that the divinity of man is not an ideal to be reached in the future, but a presence confronting him now.

Pratt's religious views are never obtrusive, but they organize all his poetry. Considering that he has a degree in theology, it is not surprising that they should be consciously held—he can hardly have acquired his Christian archetypes in the way that a sleeping camper acquires mosquito bites, involuntarily and in the dark. They come out most clearly in two extraordinary poems, *The Truant* and *The Depression Ends*, modestly included with the "Extravaganzas" in the first edition of this book.

The Truant presents us with the figure of a "Great Panjandrum," a prince of the power of the air, who talks as though he were God, who obviously thinks he is God, but who is no more God than Blake's Urizen, Shelley's Jupiter, Byron's Arimanes, or Hardy's President of the Immortals. He is the mechanical power of the universe: he controls the stars, the movement of matter, the automatic instincts of living things, even reason and consciousness. It infuriates him that something in the human soul should elude him, and as he screams at man in the "shrillest tenor" [l. 63] which is the voice of tyranny, he gradually takes on the outlines of Satan the accuser. What he has to accuse man of is his mortality. As far as we can see, everything man does, however heroic, vanishes and leaves not a rack behind. The Panjandrum should know, for he was in the "grey shape with the palaeolithic face" [l. 1032] that sank the *Titanic*, in the mechanical mantrap sprung at Dunkirk, even in the "leopards full of okra pods" [l. 571] in *The Great Feud*. He was certainly in the Iroquois torturing Brébeuf, knowing that they could kill anything that could die, driven by a demonic curiosity to find somewhere in Brébeuf's body the source of his strength, the origin of the word of command that had driven him into the wilderness. Brébeuf represented a more advanced civilization than the Iroquois, but that was not why he was there: his origin was not in France

>   But in the sound of invisible trumpets blowing
>   Around two slabs of board, right-angled, hammered
>   By Roman nails and hung on a Jewish hill. [ll. 2068–70]

Similarly the "genus homo" in *The Truant* taunts the Panjandrum with his lack of real intelligence, but the real source of his strength is his knowledge that for him there can be no God who has not also been a human being, suffered with the beleaguered society which is Pratt's hero, yielded to the power of death, and yet conquered it too. His language toward the Panjandrum is humorous, erudite, arrogant, but behind all his brilliance is his awareness of "A dying thirst within a Galilean valley" [l. 189].

The Depression Ends is the poem that most vividly summons up, for those who know him, the personality of Ned Pratt: his kindness and his genius for friendship, his epic generosity and hospitality. No one who has ever encountered his limitless good will can doubt that he would, if he could, give an "apocalyptic dinner" [l. 12]. But as the poem goes on, the significance of this adjective begins to sink in. This is no stag party: this is Pratt's beleaguered society on the march. All the oppressed and hungry and neglected in human history, all the lame and halt and blind, all the slaves and the poor, all the invisible proletariat who are the people of God, are shuffling raggedly and dazedly into a splendid feasting-hall. The hall turns out to be the starry heavens, their original birthright and their dwelling-place, as the emptiness of outer space and the empty inner spaces of hungry stomachs are simultaneously filled. At one pole of human life is a cross, at the other is a last supper; and these two poles give position and meaning to everything that occurs between them.

The prevailing idiom in Canadian poetry when Pratt began to write was that of the Romantic lyric as practised by Carman, Roberts, D.C. Scott, and Marjorie Pickthall. It was an idiom that was most successful in evocative nostalgia, as in Carman's *Low Tide on Grand Pré*, in fairylike fantasy, as in Scott's *Piper of Arll*, in wistful charm, as in Marjorie Pickthall's *Little Sister of the Prophet*. The noises that exploded in *Newfoundland Verse*, the pounding of surf, the screaming of wind, the crash of ships on rocks, rudely shattered these moods. Yet if we look back to earlier Canadian poetry, we can see that the effort to convey something of the size and variety of the country through narrative, often realistic narrative, was much more deeply rooted in Canadian literature. There are no Canadian lyrics of any account before about 1880, but there are several quite striking nineteenth-century experiments in narrative, which in their various moods and themes—bleakness in Heavysege, fantasy in Duvar, mythopoeia in Isabella Crawford—not only anticipate Pratt but indicate how sure Pratt's technical instincts were.

It is because his imagination has been so concrete, so devoted to realizing the Canadian environment directly in front of him, that Pratt's career has been so odd a mixture of the popular and the unfashionable. When everybody was writing subtle and complex lyrics, Pratt developed a technique of straightforward narrative; when everybody was experimenting with free verse, Pratt was finding new possibilities in blank verse and octosyllabic couplets. He had the typical mark of originality: the power to make something poetic out of what everybody had just decided could no longer be poetic material. He worked unperturbed while the bright young men of the 1920s, the scolding young men of the '30s, the funky young men of the '40s, and the angry young men of the '50s, were, like Leacock's famous hero, riding off rapidly in all directions.[6] Meanwhile he was reaching an increasingly large public in Canada, and by 1940, when *Brébeuf* appeared, he was established in Canada as one of the few good popular poets of the twentieth century. He has never been afraid to be topical, is in fact rather impatient with poets of "still life," and he has accepted both the responsibilities and the risks that go with being a kind of unofficial laureate.

Many popular poets are either deliberately bad poets, or, if good ones like Burns or Kipling, are admired for bad reasons, as anti-intellectual rallying-points. Pratt has never been what we ordinarily think of as an "intellectual." He is not a poet of verbal jig-saw puzzles, of ambiguities or dense textures or erudite allusions, nor has he ever built himself a religio-political Eiffel Tower from which to look down on the human situation. His moral and social values are where those of most sensible people are, and where the heart usually is in the body, a little left of centre. But he has never been anti-intellectual either, a feat which requires a good deal of integrity in this age. He is a scholar and university teacher, with graduate degrees in several disciplines, who works with the whole weight of poetic tradition behind him, and has never talked as though he undervalued culture or intelligence. Yet he has been able to introduce poetry to thousands of readers, including high-school children, with little if any previous experience of it. Meanwhile the cycle of fashion has come full circle, and Pratt looks much more modern and contemporary, if that is a virtue, in 1958 than he did in 1938.

His work now, of course, has a stature and an authority that reaches beyond Canada. But he will always have a special place in the affections of Canadian readers (I am speaking by synecdoche of English Canada). His work began with Newfoundland, and his latest major narrative ends in British Columbia. On his seventy-fifth birthday the CBC recorded tributes to him from all over Canada, some of the most eloquent being from the province of the ice-floes and from the province of the last spike. It was a sign that the work he had helped to do had been, not of course done, but well begun. In defiance of every geographical and economic law, Canada has made itself not simply a nation but an environment. It is only now emerging from its beginning as a shambling, awkward, absurd country, groping and thrusting its way through incredible distances into the West and North, plundered by profiteers, interrupted by European wars, divided by language, and bedevilled by climate, yet slowly and inexorably bringing a culture to life. And as long as that culture can remember its origin, there will be a central place in its memory for the poet in whom it found its tongue.

45

Introduction to *The Stepsure Letters*

1960

Introduction to Thomas McCulloch, The Stepsure Letters *(Toronto: McClelland & Stewart, 1960), iii–ix. Typescripts are in NFF, 1988, box 1, file m, and NFF, 1991, box 38, file 4. These letters were first published in the* Acadian Recorder, *1821–23, as* The Letters of Mephibosheth Stepsure. *Page references in the text are to the McClelland & Stewart edition.*

As soon as a certain type of middle class comes into social prominence, there arises the parable of the idle apprentice, along with that of his duller but inseparable partner, the industrious apprentice. Everybody, however restricted his reading otherwise, has read some kind of story about one or the other. The industrious apprentice works hard, attends to business, saves his money, never gets into debt, and does not attempt to reach any position in society above what he can afford. His moral principles are based on his social ones: he does not drink, gamble, or wench because those activities waste time and money. As a result he becomes a "self-made man," and attains his two major ambitions, independence and respectability. If the industrious apprentice is female, she usually marries someone of higher social status than her own. In contrast, we have the idle apprentice, who usually begins with more advantages, but ends, owing to a corresponding perseverance in all the corresponding vices, in a debtor's prison, a madhouse, or a pauper's grave.

This tale first becomes important in Elizabethan times, in the fiction of Deloney and in such plays as *Eastward Ho!* which catered to an audience of apprentices. By Defoe's time, when the class it represented had risen to supreme power, it moved into the centre of literature. Pope's *Moral*

Essays, with their contrasting pictures of Sir Balaam and the Man of Ross, incorporate it; much of Hogarth's work, including *The Rake's Progress* and *The Harlot's Progress*, is based on it; Defoe's *Moll Flanders* and Richardson's *Pamela* provide female examples of it; in Victorian times all the best fiction of the period is full of it, and it also struck its roots deep into the popular literature that has always been its natural habitat, the most famous example being *Self Help*, by Samuel Smiles.

But it was in North America, where there was no aristocracy to suggest an alternative type of social prestige, that the tale flourished in its fullest vigour. In the *Autobiography* of Benjamin Franklin we see how closely life can imitate literature, as Franklin devotes himself to the character type of the industrious apprentice. When he sets out to be a printer, someone comments: "The industry of that Franklin is superior to anything I ever saw of the kind; I see him still at work when I go home from club, and he is at work again before his neighbours are out of bed."[1] Here we see how self-help and social reputation proceed hand in hand. In the nineteenth century the doctrine of self-reliance, however refined, is still the basis of the thinking of Emerson and Thoreau. Thoreau's account in *Walden* of the miserable and half-starving John Field contains a social philosophy strikingly similar to Stepsure's: "as he began with tea, and coffee, and butter, and milk, and beef, he had to work hard to pay for them, and when he had worked hard he had to eat hard again to repair the waste of his system."[2] Thorstein Veblen's famous satire, *The Theory of the Leisure Class*, draws a picture of society as one in which the idle apprentice has become the "gentleman," or the person who has nothing to do but waste money.

Many people still alive can remember Horatio Alger from their childhood. In Alger there was invariably a boy as hero who started with nothing but the industrious-apprentice virtues, and wound up at the end of the story in a steady job earning five dollars a week with a good chance of a raise. Sometimes, if the not very resourceful Alger were hard up for a plot, he attained this by sheer luck, but it was understood that luck comes to the deserving, not to the lucky. Yet already in Alger we are beginning to realize that such fiction can hardly survive the class that produced it, and that that class is on its way out. The kind of entrepreneur capitalism that it helped to rationalize was dead by the First World War, and the fiction died with it. It lingered in the 1920s in the infantilism of Henry Ford and the kind of popular fiction represented by the *Saturday Evening Post*, and in such moral stampedes as the one that passed the Eighteenth Amendment.[3] But of course the fact that it survived only in such ways showed that it had disappeared into what literary critics call a pastoral myth. Even yet, whenever some people get to the point of emotional confusion at which the feeling "things are not as good as they ought to be" turns into "things are not as good as they used to be," back comes this fictional image of thrift, hard work, simple living, manly independence, and the like, as the real values of democracy that we have lost and must recapture if, etc.—the rest of the sentence depends on whatever is alarming the writer most at the moment.

The Stepsure Letters have a minor place in the development of this convention, but their place is strategic for anyone interested in the origins and traditions of what is now Canadian culture. The conception of society which underlies them is a simple one, but it embraces a simple society. Nova Scotia, as McCulloch saw it, was a country rich in natural resources, and designed mainly for mixed farming. Those who cleared land, developed their farms, and lived on them were the real producers; those who tried to make quicker incomes by trading or by seeking some form of government patronage were parasites. Mephibosheth Stepsure represents the genuine workers. He is lame, and the moral of his lameness is that it is only deformities of which one is unconscious that are ridiculous. He starts with nothing, an orphan sold at public auction under an extraordinary Nova Scotian law which reappears in Haliburton's blistering paper "The White Nigger."[4] What saves Stepsure from priggishness is his good taste, which in his society is a major moral principle, as it includes simplicity, economy, cleanliness, and comfort. Even the shape of his dumpy wife Dorothy is functional rather than fashionable. McCulloch makes it clear that by simple living he does not mean poverty, still less a mode of life that excludes the cultivating of the mind. Like the man in Robert Frost, Stepsure believes that good fences make good neighbours, although there are references to his willingness to help such neighbours as are not mere spongers. His lameness acts as a kind of lightning rod to deflect the envy of others—one juvenile delinquent, we learn, would otherwise have beaten him up merely out of exasperation at his serenity. Stepsure, with his conventional, old-fashioned, homespun virtues, is the kind of character that satirists have used for a norm ever since satire has been written.

On Stepsure's side are Parson Drone and the ferocious Scantocreesh: on the other side is a remarkably varied gallery of comic figures, their "humours" or defining characteristics indicated in their names. In Trot,

Introduction to *The Stepsure Letters*

who rides around the countryside to tell his neighbours about the shortness of summer and the length of winter, we recognize a close relative of Rip van Winkle; in the devotion of the young lady Pumpkins to the New England custom of "bundling," we learn that McCulloch regarded this practice as being quite as morally equivocal as it sounds. These comic figures represent every type of folly from the relatively harmless to the more genuinely vicious; but nearly all of them are held, like Stephano and Trinculo in *The Tempest*, by the false glitter of fine clothes and of what goes with them: city manners, possession of luxuries on credit buying, and the thrill of getting above themselves socially by some kind of money-making ruse. They try to evade the rule of hard work imposed on Adam by being "cute" (a word which then meant crafty and has now become a female expletive, much as "quaint" did earlier and as "tricky" is doing now). As a result they fall, by a law of social gravitation, into the hands of the sheriff, or else drag out their lives in a self-imposed misery. McCulloch keeps his touch light, and the harsher legal penalties awaiting them are referred to only parenthetically.

The attitude of encouraging a farming population to stay at home (we notice that "home" is already becoming a magic word in McCulloch), if necessary by imposing tolls, is the traditional attitude of clerical paternalism in both Protestant and Catholic parts of Canada, and so it is fittingly expounded by the local parson, Mr. Drone. There is also a parson called Drone in Leacock's *Sunshine Sketches*, but the name in McCulloch refers only to elocution, whereas in Leacock it may refer also to industry. McCulloch stresses the hard work Drone does, because in his workers' society the professional man is in an ambiguous position, most lawyers and many clergymen being parasites. (Nothing is said about doctors: one gathers that Stepsure's neighbours got little medical attention beyond poultices of cowdung and the like prescribed by the local wise women.) It is interesting that, although McCulloch spent much of his life in controversy with Roman Catholics and Anglicans, the only religious attitude he ridicules in these letters is the evangelical. We hear of a Reverend Shadrach Howl, who, "being tired of chopping down trees, converted himself into a preacher of the gospel, [and] affirms that our calamities are a judgment upon the town for rejecting his doctrines" [25]. We hear of Mrs. Whinge, who, understanding from St. Paul that a woman should not uncover her head, wore unwashed mobcaps until she became spectacularly lousy. And there is the scene in which Mr. Scantocreesh, one of McCulloch's genuine workers, is visited by two converters. He tells them off very adequately, but before doing so he gets them out of his house, where he is still the host, on the pretext that their type of conversion requires a good deal of "tumbling and roaring" [81], for which the front lawn would be more appropriate.

The kind of religious culture that McCulloch assumes in his readers appears by implication. Mephibosheth, according to the second book of Samuel [4:4], was a son of King Saul who was lame in both feet. Whether such a name as Mephibosheth Stepsure would be a funny name and a catchy title for a book would clearly depend on how well the reader knew the second book of Samuel. McCulloch expected his readers to react instantly to this and to such names as "Tubal Thump" for a blacksmith, and his readers were people for whom it was, if humorous, still not too impossibly far-fetched that Mr. Scantocreesh should be reminded by his neighbour's carriages of those Israelites who "trust in chariots and in horses, and go down to Egypt for help, and at last get themselves drowned in the Red Sea" [cf. 116]—this last being, as we are told in a final wriggle of mental agility, a sea of red ink. And of course McCulloch's whole satiric social attitude is embedded in a Biblical context. His motto could well be the verse from the first chapter of Proverbs [1:26], to which he directs our special attention: "I will laugh at your calamity; I will mock when your fear cometh."

Haliburton's much more famous Sam Slick papers came along about fifteen years later than McCulloch's.[5] There is little doubt that Haliburton knew McCulloch's work well enough to draw the whole framework of his satire on Bluenose society from it. Professor Victor Chittick, Haliburton's best biographer and critic, gives a brilliant summary of Haliburton's debt to McCulloch, and concludes that Haliburton "but followed the lead of one who for subtlety and skill in the good-natured indictment of popular error was easily his master."[6] It was, of course, inevitable that Haliburton's more brilliant and highly coloured satire should have pushed McCulloch's into obscurity. The characterization of Sam Slick, stage American though he may be, was a considerable imaginative feat, for Sam Slick is not a wound-up mechanical toy, like most of his kind, but a genuinely likable human being. A vein of grotesque and rugged poetry runs through his speech, as when he boasts that he can spit through a keyhole and never wet the wards,[7] or when he compares the moon on a murky night to a dose of castor oil in a glass of cider. Yet McCulloch grows on one, in a way that Haliburton does not. Haliburton was a more naive Tory than McCulloch, yet he was fascinated by his own shrewd, hard-trading, sharp-eyed and utterly Whiggish mouthpiece. He believed that Nova Scotia should learn economically from the United States, while rejecting its political ideology, and Sam Slick expounds a gospel of go-ahead and hustle which is foreign to McCulloch's way of thinking. McCulloch throws his main emphasis, not on raising the standard of living, but on making sure that it is a standard.

Further, the very quality that makes Haliburton so readable, his exuberant wit, has a somewhat dehumanizing tendency. He says the things that those who are comfortably sedentary love to say about manual workers, and he discovered, long before the automobile, what fun it was to ride through the countryside criticizing the way that farmers run their farms. The criticism is sharp and well pointed, but we do not see people behind it. McCulloch studies his people more carefully: if he tells us that a man is a drunk, he gives us a credible account of how he came to be a drunk. Again he shows himself the better conservative, and indicates how many nineteenth-century conservatives, Cobbett for example, could, because of their concrete sense of human living conditions, be radical in a way that more doctrinaire believers in laissez-faire often were not. There is, in short, some genuine charity in McCulloch, and charity is always radical.

Haliburton adopts the proverbial style of Benjamin Franklin's *Poor Richard's Almanac*, and emphasizes his proverbs: whenever Sam Slick says anything that his creator thinks particularly good he prints it in italics. Stepsure's letters are written in the formal, almost stilted, literary prose of the age of Scott and, like Scott, they unfold at a maddeningly deliberate pace. Yet this style has its own point. The passages of slapstick, like the battle of Captain Shootem and the pigs [103–4], are all the funnier for being recounted in so leisurely a syntax. McCulloch has little of Haliburton's very unusual sense of the vulgarity of prudery (as when the Lowell factory girl tells Sam Slick, with many blushes, that her brother is a "rooster swain" in the navy),[8] but still he can be mildly ribald, and in his account of Hodge's broken-winded "apology" [126–7], the delicacy of the language is essential to the humour. The same is true of the demure guileless way in which Stepsure conveys the mental processes of his characters by simply recounting their remarks in the right order. On the other hand, the same style gives the authority of a documentary film to the terrifying description of the filth and squalor of Loopy and Mrs. Whinge [71, 94].

Above all, McCulloch, in striking contrast to Haliburton, specializes in the "throwaway" line, the parenthetical proverb, and an almost furtive irony. Thus, on the progress of a courting: "Whether his present wife had taken a fancy for him, I cannot say; but when some mischievous boy slipt a hornet's nest into Job's trowsers, there was no end to her dissatisfaction, that providence should allow such doings" [89]. Or, again: "Miss Clippit, though formerly a miserable sinner, is now, as she says herself, a very religious young woman" [116]. Or this lethal comment about aging: "Amidst the infirmities of age, it is a great comfort to old folks, that, whatever destruction time works in their memory, they never find it affecting their judgment" [57]. And again, in a passage where the literary principle involved is that often nothing can be sharper satire than the obvious truth: "There is not one of my neighbours who would not kick mightily at the name of rogue; and among us, were any person to take a penny from the pocket of another, the whole town would cry out against such a sinful and shameful operation; but cheating the whole community at once, was so far from being considered as either sin or shame, that Deacon Scruple, who allowed nothing to be sung in his vessel but hymns, was the greatest smuggler of the whole" [27]. Such sentences have to be read slowly, if only to understand what place leisure has in McCulloch's values. And leisurely reading often discovers an unexpected allusiveness in the style, as when Stepsure remarks of his neighbours' cattle that "after looking at the fence of my orchard, they always went away abusing the trees for being as sour as crabs" [73–4].

McCulloch is the founder of genuine Canadian humour: that is, of the humour which is based on a vision of society and is not merely a series of wisecracks on a single theme. The tone of his humour, quiet, observant, deeply conservative in a human sense, has been the prevailing tone of Canadian humour ever since. There are two main values to be derived from the study of our cultural traditions. One is that what writers write and readers respond to instinctively, by virtue of their context in space and time, they do with greater skill and pleasure, respectively, if they know more about that context. The other is that such study helps to distinguish for us what is past from what is permanent. The idle and industrious apprentice are no longer central types of vice and virtue except for those who are living in myth rather than fact. But vice and virtue are still what they always were. The society McCulloch depicts is gone: it is gone even in the Maritimes, where sheriffs' sales and writs of capias were, as late as the 1930s, almost as conspicuous a feature of life as they are in *The Stepsure Letters*. But if it is not here now, it was there then, and our own society is continuous with it.

46

John George Diefenbaker

21 September 1961

From the typescript in NFF, 1988, box 1, file d. The occasion was Victoria University's awarding of the honorary degree of D.Litt. to Mr. Diefenbaker, Conservative prime minister of Canada 1957–63.

The Prime Minister of Canada is, as most of you know, a graduate of the University of Saskatchewan, and holds the earned degrees of Master of Arts and Bachelor of Laws from that university. His career began in law, when he was called to the Bar of Saskatchewan in 1919, after his service in the First World War. His political activity, which has been mainly associated with the constituency of Prince Albert, began in 1925 and in 1940 moved from the provincial to the federal area. In December, 1956, he was chosen federal leader of the Progressive Conservative Party, and since the election of June, 1957, his career has formed part of the history of the country.

Naturally a great variety of distinctions has come his way. I understand that he is occasionally alluded to as Dief the Chief, and it would in fact be correct to address him, if one had a working knowledge of Cree, Sioux, or Kainai, as Chief Eagle, Chief Walking Buffalo, or Chief Many Spotted Horses. But the majority of his honours are academic ones. They include an honorary fellowship in the Royal Society of Canada and in several other learned societies. According to my information, this is the nineteenth honorary degree that he has received from a Canadian university, and his twenty-eighth altogether.

There is a significance in this which is not wholly accounted for either by Mr. Diefenbaker's personal qualities or by his high office. Since the

Second World War, government and university have discovered a principle which is not in Euclid, but is quite as demonstrable as if it were. Government and university are both essential to the same society, and things which are essential to the same thing are essential to one another. Canadians, with a relatively small population, are perhaps less timid of experiment than a great power would be. And just as Canadians discovered, long before our neighbours did, that it was possible to elect a Roman Catholic to the highest office without becoming annexed to the Vatican, so we have discovered that it is possible for universities to receive federal aid without having to teach their courses from government directives. Mr. Diefenbaker's government is committed to the financial support of universities, to the encouragement, through the Council, of such enterprises as the building of the Victoria College Library,[1] and to the respecting of the university's autonomy and of academic freedom. Such responsibility is likely to become increasingly a two-way traffic, as the university comes to put more and more of its knowledge and expertise at the service of government. Mr. Diefenbaker himself is aware of the importance, not merely of knowledge, but of an intellectual framework to the modern conception of democracy. He realizes what a disadvantage democracy labours under in not having the clear vision of its goals and ideals that the revolutionary philosophy of Marxism possesses, and he has stressed—most notably in a recent address to the University of Toronto—the need for a greater intellectual awareness on our part.

It is a sign of an immature society when politicians are contemptuous of eggheads. It is equally a sign of an immature society when the university is contemptuous of politics, when it congratulates itself unduly on its clean hands and its pure heart. There is a natural tension between university and government. Government is based on majority rule; the universities are one of the most effective instruments of minority right. The university seeks truth at all cost; the government must seek compromise at all cost. The university, like a totalitarian state, is exclusive, and holds annual purges to remove those who do not support it with sufficient energy. The government, in a democracy, must deal with all the people, and Mr. Diefenbaker was no less representing the people of Canada when he was Leader of the Opposition than he does now. The university tries to abolish conflicting opinion by facts and evidence; the government must reconcile conflicting opinion in an area where all facts and evidence come too late. What the university stands for demands admiration and respect from government; what the government stands for demands admiration and sympathy from the university. It is this equal pact that is symbolized by the honour which the Prime Minister has done us in accepting our degree, and by our desire to honour him in offering it.

47

Haliburton: Mask and Ego

December 1962

From Alphabet, *no. 5 (December 1962): 58–63. Reprinted in* On Thomas Chandler Haliburton, *ed. Richard A. Davies (Ottawa: Tecumseh Press, 1979), 211–15, and in* Beginnings, *vol. 2 of* The Canadian Novel, *ed. John Moss (Toronto: New Canada Publications, 1980), 40–4.*

Haliburton would never have called himself a Canadian. He was a Nova Scotian, a Bluenose, and died two years before Confederation. He was born and brought up in Windsor, and represented Annapolis in the legislature. There he did good work in fighting the Family Compact, and became the friend of an even more brilliant man than himself, Joseph Howe. It was in Howe's paper that he began the series of sketches later known as *The Clockmaker*: the sayings and doings of Sam Slick of Slickville, Onion County, Connecticut. The Sam Slick books extend from 1835 to 1860, there are eight of them,[1] and they take in nearly everything Haliburton wrote that we still read, except for some sketches of Nova Scotia called *The Old Judge*.

After his first skirmishes as a Liberal, Haliburton became a judge, a judge like the one in Stephen Leacock's *Sunshine Sketches*, who says he has no politics because he's on the bench, but—and then we get a belligerent Tory speech. To call Haliburton a Tory would be an understatement. He fought responsible government; he fought the Durham Report;[2] and until toward the end of his life he fought Confederation. He didn't want Great Britain either to give Nova Scotia self-government or run it from London; but to appoint Nova Scotians to the government. In other words, he wanted patronage on a grand scale. As for the kind of person who should be appointed—well, there are several hints, sometimes not very subtle hints, about one in particular who has deserved well of his country.

Later Haliburton moved to England and was elected to the British Parliament. He was, naturally, a Conservative member; he said he thought the Conservatives must be the right party because the Tories supported them, but he thought most Conservatives were Tory renegades. The truth was, of course, that the kind of Toryism he stood for had been extinct in Great Britain for a hundred years. Not that it made any more sense in Nova Scotia. Personally Haliburton must have had great charm, as he kept the friendship of Joseph Howe, who fought for self-government. But as a political thinker and writer he's a strange figure, half pathetic and half absurd, grumpy, tactless, and hopelessly romantic.

The poet Yeats has a theory that a writer's personality is the exact opposite of his normal personality.[3] It would certainly be hard to find anything much further from the political Haliburton than a breezy, shrewd, detached, and realistic Yankee peddler. Anyone who knew Haliburton's background and had never read him would probably expect him to make fun of Americans, and to dump on Sam Slick all the cheap, stale sneers about American brag and vulgarity and dollar-snatching. Anybody who expects that will get the shock of his life when he opens *The Clockmaker*. The more we read about Sam Slick the better we like him. He brags about himself, but nearly everything he says he can do he can do. I say nearly everything, because I have some doubts about his ability to spit through a keyhole and never wet the wards.[4] He's kindly, humane, and courteous; he puts himself out a great deal for other people; he's a dangerous man in a fight but he never starts one; he's a sharp operator but he's right when he says he never really cheats anybody; he just doesn't interfere with people who are determined to cheat themselves. It's clear that Haliburton himself despises anti-American prejudice, and he makes fun of people who write books on the States after a two-week visit.

Naturally there are a lot of things in the American way of life that Haliburton himself disapproves of. He's strongly attached to the Church of England establishment, and he says that the separating of Church and State will eventually make the United States a Roman Catholic country. He says that Americans are too much subject to mass rule and hysteria, and he predicts, in 1835, that there will be a bloody civil war before long. But it gives him no pleasure to predict this, and his treatment of America is both sympathetic and affectionate.

Still, of course, Sam Slick is a comic, or stage-American, type. He always refers to Americans as "our free and enlightened citizens";[5] he speaks of the Fourth of July as "fifteen millions of free men and three millions of slaves a-celebratin' the birthday of liberty";[6] he is convinced that the British Empire is done for: "Their glory has departed across the Atlantic to fix her everlastin' abode in the United States."[7] Haliburton's biographer is a brilliant critic and scholar, Victor Chittick of the University of Washington, and Professor Chittick tells us that Sam Slick, as a literary type, comes from two main sources. One is the shrewd Yankee peddler, already popular on the stage; the other is the Western blowhard, the "ring-tailed roarer" of the Davy Crockett stories, which Haliburton had carefully studied.[8] The combination has made Sam Slick something unique.

His talk is full of proverbs, and whenever Haliburton feels that his hero has said something particularly wise he prints it in italics. But proverbs are apt to fade into platitudes with the passing of time, and it's not so much Sam's wisdom as his wit that keeps him alive today. The wit is a queer mixture of exaggeration, epigram, and poetry embedded in prose. The stars on a clear summer night remind him of "our national flag," and that reminds him of "the great American Eagle on its perch, balancing itself for a start on the broad expanse of blue sky, afeared of nothin' of its kind, and president of all it surveys."[9] A moon on a murky night, on the other hand, reminds him of "a dose of castor oil in a glass of cider."

His language, too, is mostly stage-American language, the way British readers expect a Yankee to talk—although I think Haliburton did have a real ear for the spoken word. Most of Sam's vulgar pronunciations, like Huckleberry Finn's forty years later, are survivals of correct eighteenth-century speech, such as "varmint" for "vermin" and "nater" for "nature." When Sam Slick speaks of the bowels of the earth, Haliburton puts two e's in front of the o in bowels. In other words, the Americans have already begun to pronounce words like house, cow and about as though they were lyrical poems composed by an amorous tomcat.

Like most popular comic writers of his day, Haliburton expected to be read mainly by men, which is one reason why his humour is sometimes of the type that Victorian critics called coarse. He is in fact very unusual for his time in realizing that prudery is both vulgar and funny. There's his story of the factory girl in Lowell who tells Sam Slick, with many blushes, that her brother is a "rooster swain" in the American navy.[10]

And there is Sam Slick's own account of his trip to Italy to buy religious pictures: "I bought two Madonnas, I think they call them—beautiful little pictur's they were too; but the child's legs were so naked and ondecent, that to please the Governor and his factory gals, I had an artist to paint trousers and a pair of lace boots on him, and they look quite genteel now."[11]

Haliburton's real aim was not to make fun of Americans but to make fun of his own people, the Bluenoses. Nova Scotia, he felt, had nothing to learn politically from the States, but it had a lot to learn economically. The Americans had succeeded, not because independence is better than colonial status, but because they had developed their own resources with so much drive and energy. So, if the Bluenoses would stop trying to tinker with their political machinery and expect magical results to follow from changing it, and get busy developing their natural resources, they'd really go places. We read a good deal about how lazy the Bluenose farmers and fishermen are, how they waste money on frills and expect free handouts from the government, and all the other things that sedentary people love to say about manual workers. Then, too, long before the automobile Sam Slick gets a big kick out of driving through the country and criticizing the way the farmers run their farms. Here's one of his inventories: "Them old geese and vet'ran fowls, that are so poor the foxes won't steal 'em for fear o' hurtin' their teeth: that little yaller, lantern-jaw'd, long-legg'd, rabbit-eared runt of a pig, that's so weak it can't curl its tail up; that old frame of a cow, a-standin' there with her eyes shot to, a-contemplatin' of her latter eend; and that varmint-lookin' horse, with his hocks swelled bigger than his belly, that looks as if he had come to her funeral, is all his stock, I guess."[12]

Haliburton is a Maritimer, and for the true Maritimer the universal and the local are much on a level. A Bluenose is interested about equally in the existence of God, the nature of man, the destiny of nations, and whether the road from Shubenacadie to Musquodoboit should be paved or left in gravel. Sam Slick is at his best when he's describing the country and its customs, and he's at his best often enough to bring Nova Scotia in the 1830s really to life. That doesn't make *The Clockmaker* provincial or antiquated; it makes it concrete. Next to the Bluenoses, the British are scolded for not realizing what assets their colonies could be and for filling up colonial administration with party hacks at home. Haliburton uses Sam Slick's anti-British prejudices to make some tart comments on the English as seen by colonials. One passage reads like a song from

Pinafore: "The *Eye*talian is too lazy, the French too smirky, the Spaniard too banditti, the Dutch too smoky, the German too dreamy, the Scotch too itchy, the Irish too popey, and the Yankee too tricky: all low, all ignorant, all poor. He thinks the noblest work of God an *Englishman*. He is on considerable good tarms with himself, too, is John Bull."[13]

The whole success of Haliburton's scheme depends on keeping Sam Slick a character in his own right. As we go on through the eight volumes, Sam Slick becomes more and more just a mouthpiece for Haliburton's own political harangues, and then everything falls to pieces. That isn't because Haliburton was perverse and wrong-headed—many great writers have been that—but because Sam Slick is a shrewd and humorous Yankee, proud of his own country, who looks at Nova Scotia as an outsider; and when he begins to sound like a cranky Nova Scotian Tory who wants a bigger job from the British Government, scolding everybody else for wanting the same thing, he isn't Sam Slick any more. Then he makes us feel that we're listening, not to Sam Slick or even to the real Judge Haliburton, but only to Haliburton's ego, and nobody's ego is worth listening to. Still, in spite of all that is dull or forced or silly, one's first feeling on rereading *The Clockmaker* sketches is the feeling of how extraordinarily good they are, and it's more sensible to appreciate the good writer we have than to regret the great writer we might possibly have had. And it's only fair to give Sam Slick the last word on what he thinks he accomplished as a social and political commentator: "Now, I have held the mirror up to these fellows to see themselves in, and it has scared them so they have shaved slick up, and made themselves look decent. I won't say I made all the changes myself, . . . [but] the blisters I have put on their vanity, stung 'em so they jumped high enough to see the right road, and the way they travel ahead now is a caution to snails."[14]

48

Governor-General's Awards (I)

29 March 1963

Address to Governor-General's Committee Awards Dinner, from the typescript in NFF, 1988, box 1, file q. The winners of the Governor-General's literary awards for 1962 were Kildare Dobbs, Running to Paradise *(English fiction); Jacques Ferron,* Contes du pays incertain *(French fiction); Marshall McLuhan,* The Gutenberg Galaxy *(English non-fiction); Gilles Marcotte,* Une littérature qui se fait *(French non-fiction); James Reaney,* Twelve Letters to a Small Town *and* The Killdeer and Other Plays *(English poetry and drama); Jacques Languirand,* Les insolites et les violons de l'automne *(French drama).*

The Governor-General's Committee is delighted to add its congratulations and best wishes to the winners of the 1962 awards. This is their night, and my chief duty is simply to point to them. If I refer to ourselves on the judging committee also, it is only because the question has occurred to many, and may occur to you: what kind of motivation could drive seven very busy people to read so many books for such a purpose? All of us must consider ourselves to have some critical ability, but is trying to pick the best books in six different categories a genuinely critical procedure? One of my former colleagues on the committee, in fact, remarked that there was an insoluble dilemma about everything we did. If a decision is easy, the inference to be drawn is a very depressing one; if it is hard, someone has been done an injustice. Even the question of what authors are sufficiently Canadian, in any practical sense, to be eligible for such awards is full of pitfalls, and a committee's decision on such points is often ungracious and may be arbitrary. Establishing the proper categories, even, may be a matter of some delicacy. How is it possible to give Mr. Dobbs an award in the fiction division without appearing to reflect on his veracity? If we have two writers widely dissimilar in attitude and style and outlook, on what basis does one compare them? Real poets, said William Blake, "have no competition: none are greatest in the Kingdom of Heaven; it is so in poetry."[1] And if this is true even of poets and novelists, how much more true is it of writers in the third category of *autres genres littéraires* (there is no English equivalent for this except the absurd "non-fiction"), who may be writing on any subject whatever, and in the style appropriate to that subject?

The relevant question is not how we try to surmount these obstacles, but why we think it worth while to try to surmount them. Our primary reason for being willing to serve on this committee is that we think literature an exceedingly important matter to Canada, and that some public recognition of its importance is a good thing in itself. We resign ourselves to the fact that some of the interest these awards stir up is negative. An obvious choice may always look timid, and a less obvious one erratic. To others, again, a committee with so august a name attached to it represents an Establishment, to be attacked for that reason alone; to still others, or more commonly the same ones, our choices appear to symbolize some official approval of the types or schools of writing to which they belong. It has even been argued that we ought to give our awards to bad books, on the ground that the Canadian public would then read them with greater interest. This we are ready for; and we make no claim to have successfully compared the incomparable. In nearly all the six categories there were other strong contenders, and when that is true, our choice does not mean: "this book is better than all those books." It means: "seeing that we have to choose one, this is the one we choose."

Our real judgments, therefore, are positive, not comparative or superlative. One rule that we have rigidly kept to is never to make an award to a book that dissatisfied us, and was merely the best available in its category. This is, I think, the first time since this committee was established in its present form that we have given all six of the possible awards. The six award winners, therefore, are here tonight because they have written good books. They have provided coral islands of wit and imagination, of intelligence and beauty, that were worth swimming through oceans of print to reach. On the eve of this election Canada presents a somewhat demoralized appearance,[2] and one would expect its literature to be entirely, in a sense unintended by M. Ferron, *contes d'un pays incertain*. But a small and divided nation that can produce, in one year, the powerful and yet delicate fantasy of M. Languirand and Mr. Reaney, the sharp wit and satire of Mr. Dobbs and M. Ferron, the encyclopedic speculative range of Mr. McLuhan and the incisive critical powers of M. Marcotte is a nation that has more sense of identity than its political leaders always give it credit for. The title of M. Marcotte's book, *Une littérature qui se fait*, represents what we all hope for in Canada and what our six award winners have done so much to help achieve.

Our committee owes a great debt of gratitude to the devoted labours of the Canadian Authors' Association, who maintained an unvarying standard for these awards which enabled them to be regarded with respect and prestige for over a quarter of a century. We owe a different kind of debt to the Canada Council for fulfilling the proper function of a patron of letters. It has provided your committee with food and shelter while in Ottawa, and with abundance of reading matter while at home; and now it rewards our prize winners according to its abilities, which are, of course, considerably less than their merits or its own good will.

49

Governor-General's Awards (II)

24 April 1964

Address to Governor-General's Committee Awards Dinner, from the typescript in NFF, 1988, box 1, file t. The winners of the Governor-General's literary awards for 1963 were Hugh Garner, Hugh Garner's Best Stories *(English fiction); J.M.S. Careless,* Brown of the Globe *(English non-fiction); Gustave Lanctot,* Histoire du Canada *(French non-fiction); Gatien Lapointe,* Ode au Saint-Laurent *(French poetry).*

The primary reason for this dinner is to honour the four winners of the awards, to congratulate them, and to thank them for the distinction they have brought to Canadian letters. All the awards this year are won by men, and in front of the successful male writer there is usually a wife, keeping, if not the wolf from the door, at any rate the magazine salesman, the milkman, the census taker, the questionnaire filler, the Girl Guide cookies, the cancer society subscriptions, and other interruptions of the flowing rhythms of verse and prose. So the wives are to be honoured too. Then again, a serious published book means a publisher willing to publish a serious book. Such a publisher deserves a good dinner, though he seldom needs one, as the less serious books on his list can usually provide for his sustenance. But still he is an honoured guest. The presence of seven judges can be explained more simply by the exuberant hospitality of the Canada Council.

As General Chairman I have received a good many letters beginning: "I have just written a poem: how do I enter it in your contest?" I have always answered that there is no contest, and I repeat that statement. In a real contest, like a horse race, we can see the horses that also ran. But these awards make no mention of the other contenders, of the strong

Governor-General's Awards (II)

support they had and the heated arguments they caused. We have, we think, read everything there was to read and tried to judge it fairly; but we can offer no proof of this. Then again, contests are among comparable things. No one can really compare one book with another which is totally different. We have chosen these four books because they seemed to us books of enduring worth, not because they symbolized values or attitudes that we preferred to others. And the sense of the award is not comparative but positive: it means an *ouvrage couronnée*. I have nothing to add to what I said on this point last year: our choice does not mean "this book is better than all those books," it means "seeing that we have to choose one, this is the one we choose."

Canada is a divided and inarticulate country, and Canadian culture, for Canadians, is a kind of propaganda in reverse: we need it, not to present our image to others, but to present it to ourselves. Our poets and novelists and scholars are therefore of immense importance in giving us the kind of knowledge that we can get only from a creative mind. Perhaps we ask more from our culture than it can well give. Canadian intellectuals, whether French or English, are apt to be fierce cultural nationalists. Yet it is the destiny of man to unite rather than to divide, and our real loyalties are to unities much larger than Canada, or North America, or even Western civilization. The epigraph to M. Lapointe's book reads "Tous les hommes portent le même nom." Nor is this merely external, for in the fine ode that gives the book its title he begins by saying how deeply rooted he is in his own country ("Je suis né de ce paysage"), and yet how through that very fact it is the universal and not the immediate that he finds:

> Je découvre ma première blessure
> Je plante dans le sol ma première espérance.

Mr. Garner's vision is more extroverted, as is natural to a story-teller, yet the life he studies is an aspect of Canada that is identical with almost any part of the modern world. As for Mr. Careless and M. Lanctot, their work is concentrated on very specific sections of Canadian history, but the universality of all history, however specialized, is the axiom of historical scholarship and the guarantee of its value.

The normal political instinct is to rule by dividing; the cultural instinct is to unite by reflecting. It has often been pointed out that one may oppose or attack an argument, but not a song or a story. In our world we are trying to outgrow the political instinct, to escape from the intrigue of ruling and dividing. We must outgrow this or disappear from history. Ahead of us is a greater ideal, the road to which is pointed out by imaginative writers and objective scholars. It is the presence of this ideal in our community that makes the kind of work that M. Lanctot, M. Lapointe, Mr. Careless, and Mr. Garner have done so important, and that makes the honouring of their work appropriate. We are not conferring a distinction on them; we are merely pointing out the distinction they themselves have achieved.

I feel particularly happy in being able to leave the Governor-General's Committee in the competent hands of M. Roger Duhamel, who will be General Chairman next year. Nobody can work with M. Duhamel, as I have done for many years, without being deeply impressed by his encyclopedic knowledge, the fairness and human warmth of his judgments, and his unselfishness in undertaking a public service of this kind. Under him the committee will gain greatly in prestige and importance.

50

Ned Pratt: The Personal Legend

Summer 1964

From Canadian Literature, *21 (Summer 1964): 6-9. Prat had died on 26 April, 1964.*

Ned Pratt is the only figure in Canadian literature, so far, who was great enough to establish a personal legend. The legend was simpler than the man, or, more accurately, it was cruder, because the man himself had the genuine simplicity that is so rare and so difficult. Poets and professors are supposed to be absent-minded, and people delighted in telling stories of Ned's absent-mindedness. They are also supposed to be unpractical, and the fact that he was easily baffled by mechanical contrivances also pleased them. But Ned always remembered a great deal more than he forgot. He carried for many years a teaching, speaking, and social schedule that nobody in business or politics would attempt without a secretary. I remember many graphic stories he could tell of how his lecturing and visiting arrangements got fouled up, but I remember too that it was generally other people's dim-wittedness that was responsible and not his. When I first began to try to write myself, the only really sensible and well-informed advice about publishers and contracts I got came from Ned. And while it was true that he always counted the left turns he had to make before setting out anywhere with a car, I know of no contemporary poet who has used technological and mechanical languages with such easy assurance.

In my fourth year as an undergraduate I was editor of the college magazine, and had to administer a prize of ten dollars for the best poem contributed. The poems came in, and I took them to Ned. Ned didn't recommend an award. What he did was to put his finger on one poem and say, "Now this one—it has some feeling, some sensitivity, some sense of structure. But—well, damn it all, it isn't worth *money*." I have never had a profounder insight into literary values, and I was lucky to have it so early. As a graduate student I was his assistant when he became the first editor of the *Canadian Poetry Magazine*. I am not saying that what was printed in those opening issues was imperishable, but it was certainly the best of what we got. What impressed me was the number of people (it was the Depression, and the magazine paid a dollar or two) who tried to get themselves or their friends in by assuming that Ned was a soft touch. In some ways he was, but he was not compromising the standards of poetry to be so: poetry was something he took too seriously. And, as I realized more clearly later, friendship was also something he took too seriously to compromise. People who thought him a soft touch were never his friends. He could be impulsively, even quixotically, generous to bums and down-and-outs, and I think I understand why. His good will was not benevolence, not a matter of being a sixty-year-old smiling public man.[1] It was rather an enthusiasm that one was alive, rooted in a sense of childlike wonder at human existence and the variety of personality. This feeling was so genuine and so deep in him that I think he felt rather guilty when approached by someone towards whom he was actually indifferent.

His hospitality and his love of parties was the central part of the Pratt personal legend. The chair at the end of the Senior Common Room table in Victoria College was always left vacant for him, for Ned Pratt could not sit anywhere but at the head of the table. (It remained vacant for several months after it was clear that he would never return to that table.) Yet those who attended his parties realized how passionate his concern was for the genuine symposium, the exchange of ideas. He wanted good stories and picturesque language, most of which he contributed himself. Not many of his guests are apt to forget such things as the huge salmon hooked by the Governor of Newfoundland, who poured an entire bottle of Newfoundland screech down its throat and then released it, only to have it circle the boat on its tail singing Rule Britannia. But he was quickly bored if the conversation ran down in gossip or trivialities. The personnel at his parties naturally changed over the course of years, but from Bertram Brooker and Wilson Knight in the 1930s to Marshall McLuhan and Douglas Grant in the 1960s, he never wavered in his affection for friends who could talk, and talk with spirit, content, and something to say.

His entire poetic career was spent as a full-time member of the teaching staff of Victoria College. He never made a song and dance about being "creative," and he never felt the need of compensating for the way he earned his living by issuing anti-academic pronouncements. The college took unobtrusive measures to make it easier for him to get on with his work, but it could not have helped beyond a certain point. His reputation as absent-minded and as a complete duffer in practical affairs was carefully staged by himself, in order to stay clear of the enormous complication of committees and similar substitutes for thought and action that are such a bane of university life. He taught students, and worked harder to get to know them than anyone else on the staff. (Even after his retirement he gave luncheon parties for the students in the classes he had previously taught.) He worked with colleagues, to such effect that one came to recognize a special kind of affectionate smile that preceded any reference to Ned. But he stuck to the essentials of university work, to teaching and his own writing, and as a result it was hardly noticed that he was an academic poet.

He was also a Canadian writer, without either trying to be one or trying not to be one. Not many Canadian writers would really be content to be popular inside the country and largely unknown outside it. I am not saying that he was wholly content with this either—nor am I. But he did realize that he was addressing a specific community, and he showed extraordinary integrity in addressing also the general reader in that community, instead of writing for other poets. He was never in fashion, and he never tried to be out of fashion, and as a result he has introduced hundreds of Canadians to poetic experience who would not otherwise have got it, or who would have tried to get it from some phoney anti-intellectual doggerelist. There are many popular features in his work, some of them obvious, such as the preoccupation with physical courage and heroic action, and some of them less obvious, such as the absence of bad language, even when dealing with the grousing of sailors in *Behind the Log*. Yet there is a tough conceptual skeleton behind all his writing: his supposed incompetence in the two disciplines he tried before he tried English, theology and psychology, was part of his own campaign to persuade others that he was too simple-minded to have his time wasted in their interests.

So although he was never anti-intellectual, and never undervalued or deprecated what the university stood for, he still avoided the pitfalls that beset intellectuals in modern society. Of these, one of the most striking is the fascination with the logical extreme, as opposed to the illogical golden mean. To write and to teach in Ned's generation meant defending the values of the imagination through a depression and a war, and this took courage of a kind that he not only celebrated but, very unostentatiously, possessed. Some of us grew up in that generation and tried to hold on to the kind of liberal values that are not simply the values of the left as against the right, but are the values of human dignity as opposed to stupidity and hysteria. We remember many lost leaders in that period, some temporarily and some permanently lost, who deserted wisdom for paradox. The sense of outrage and betrayal that I felt when I first opened [T.S. Eliot's] *After Strange Gods* is something I hope never to feel again. But during the war, at an evening in Earle Birney's apartment in Toronto, I heard Ned read *The Truant*, and felt, not simply that I had heard the greatest of all Canadian poems, but that the voice of humanity had spoken once more, with the kind of authority it reserves for such moments as the bombing of London, when the powers of darkness test the soul and find once more that "The stuff is not amenable to fire" [l. 31].

51

Silence upon the Earth

August 1964

From Canadian Poetry Magazine, 27 (August 1964): 71–3.

It is hardly possible for anyone who knew him to write impersonally of Ned Pratt. I remember a struggling little magazine of poetry, many years ago, which he had helped by contributing a poem to its first issue. Under Notes on Contributors it said, "E.J. Pratt is the best poet and the kindest man in Canada." It is difficult to improve on the economy of that statement, and few men can have left behind them a more uniform impression of good will. Like other great men, he created a legend, and the legend, as legends are so apt to be, was much simpler than the man. Poets and professors are supposed to be absent-minded, and many stories are told of his forgetfulness. But he always remembered far more than he forgot, and through his active career he carried a teaching, speaking, and social schedule that few men would have attempted without a secretary. Now that practically every university has a resident poet, or other such symbol of its interest in a continuing creative process, it is worth recalling that Ned's entire poetic career was spent as a full-time member of the teaching staff. So far from pulling rank as a poet, he made more effort to get to know students than anyone else on the staff, as many generations of students for whom he carved hams will testify. Even after his retirement he took out to lunch all the students in the third year drama and fourth year modern poetry courses that he had taught for so many years.

His hospitality and his love of parties were of course a central part of the legend. The chair at the end of the Senior Common Room table in Victoria College was always left vacant for him: obviously Ned Pratt could not sit anywhere but at the head of the table. Yet those who attended his parties realized how passionate was his concern for the exchange of ideas; how eagerly he entered into a serious discussion, and, for all his rich fund of good stories and flow of picturesque language, how bored he became if the conversation ran down in gossip or trivialities. The spirit that animated his parties was not one of mere gregariousness, but the spirit of the symposium which, according to Plato, is the central symbol of civilization.

In his relations with people, his good will had nothing in it of the kind of benevolence that goes with being a public figure, or what Yeats calls a sixty-year-old smiling public man.[1] It was rather an enthusiasm that one was alive, rooted in a sense of childlike wonder at human existence and at the variety of personality. A friend of his could hardly encounter this, even on the street, without feeling that perhaps he had underestimated his own qualities, that life had more meaning than he had thought, and that the weather had taken a turn for the better. Of course once in a while someone would assume that because he was kindly he must also be gullible and a soft touch. Such people did not get very far. Friendship and poetry were two things he took seriously, and he refused to debase the currency of either.

In his poetry his favourite theme was courage, and no man can have understood courage so well except by possessing it himself. In a quiet teaching and writing life at Victoria College one would assume that courage was a virtue seldom called for. But there are many forms of courage besides those evoked by shipwreck or martyrdom or warfare. To write and to teach as Ned did, to defend the values of the imagination through a depression and a war, to be a focus of a community of students and colleagues—this requires a serenity of spirit which is impossible without courage of a rare and subtle kind. Only occasionally did one realize this. In the years preceding the war, I had a strong sense of the betrayal of liberal values I had been brought up in, by many of the writers and poets I most admired, as one after another of them became complacent reactionaries in both religion and politics. For me it was one of the turning points of my life to hear Ned read, at an evening in Earle Birney's apartment, the poem called *The Truant*, to me the greatest of all Canadian poems, and to realize that the poet I most loved was still in there fighting:

> "We who have met
> With stubborn calm the dawn's hot fusillades;

Who have seen the forehead sweat
Under the tug of pulleys on the joints,
Under the liquidating tally
Of the cat-and-truncheon bastinades;
Who have taught our souls to rally
To mountain horns and the sea's rockets
When the needle ran demented through the points;
Who have learned to clench
Our fists and raise our lightless sockets
To morning skies after the midnight raids,
Yet cocked our ears to bugles on the barricades,
And in cathedral rubble found a way to quench
A dying thirst within a Galilean valley—
No! by the Rood, we will not join your ballet." [Conclusion]

What he did for me he has already done for several generations of Canadian students who have learned about poetry through his work. For him, poetry was the most concrete expression of that unrelenting conflict with an indifferent and unconscious nature, armed with all the powers of death, in which the courage and intelligence of man struggle to achieve some human form of the city and the garden of God. And because he was great enough to understand this, he discovered once more what every poet since Homer has known, that the central theme of poetry is heroism. It is not in the rarefied and subtle experiences of the intellect (though he never undervalued these experiences) but in the simplest forms of work and suffering, that man reveals most clearly his divine inheritance and his ultimate destiny:

The hour had called for argument more rife
With the gambler's sacrificial bids for life,
The final manner native to the breed
Of men forging decision into deed—
Of getting down again into the sea,
And testing rowlocks in an open boat,
Of grappling with the storm-king bodily,
And placing Northern fingers on his throat.
[*The Roosevelt and the Antinoe*, ll. 776–83]

52

Opening Ceremonies of the
E.J. Pratt Memorial Room

15 October 1964

From a tape in the CBC archives and E.J. Pratt Library, transcribed by Monika Lee. Frye's talk, given on the 128th anniversary of the founding of Victoria University, opened the E.J. Pratt Room of Contemporary Poetry in the new Victoria library, which had been erected in 1961. As President A.B.B. Moore explained in his introductory remarks, the room was to be a "lively and stimulating centre" housing Victoria's large collection of Pratt manuscripts, printed books, and records, and a collection of contemporary poetry. The nucleus of the latter had been donated by Principal Frye, supplemented by a gift from the class of 1926, of which Pratt had been the honorary president. In spite of what Frye said in his opening remarks, the library as a whole was renamed the E.J. Pratt Library in 1967, and shortly afterwards the Pratt Room was closed.

It is, of course, difficult to know what to select in speaking of Ned Pratt. There is so much to say about him, and it is easy to take great pride in him as a product of the college. But I would prefer to think of the college as, in some degree, a product of him and as reflecting, in a permanent way, the impress of his personality. When we built our library, it would have been very easy to call it the Pratt Library, but a building, however beautiful and functional, always has something monolithic about it and there was nothing monolithic about Ned Pratt. One hesitated to enshrine his name in silent stone. We thought rather of something that would start in a small way, that would be simple, as he was, that would be unpretentious, as he was, and yet would somehow contain a kind of vital and human spirit. Something too which would unite the three aspects of his genius—the scholarly, the poetic, and the social.

He had a legendary reputation as a hospitable man, who loved giving parties and whose parties his guests will never forget, and, at those parties, he loved a flow of good stories and of picturesque language to which he contributed most himself. Not very many of his guests are ever likely to forget such epics as the account of the Governor of Newfoundland who hooked a huge salmon, greatly to his surprise, poured an entire bottle of Newfoundland screech down its throat, and then released it, whereupon for the rest of the day the salmon circled the boat on his tail singing Rule Britannia. But it was easy to see too that what Ned loved in his parties was the exchange of ideas. What he wanted was a genuine symposium. He became very quickly bored if the conversation ran down in gossip or trivialities, and he never wavered in his affection for the people who could talk with spirit and content and something to say.

As a poet, he spent his entire career on the full-time staff of Victoria College. The college made unobtrusive steps from time to time to lighten his teaching schedule to make it easier for him to get on with his work. It could not have helped beyond a certain point, but Ned was never a resident poet and he was never set aside under a sort of hermetically sealed tube as a creative spirit kidnapped by a university. He worked with students and with colleagues. He worked harder to get to know his students than I think anyone else on the staff. After he had finally retired and one of his undergraduate courses came into my hands, I was summoned by Ned with a note to say that he wanted to take the class of students in this course, that he had taught for so many years, out to lunch. They were not his students any more, but he was still interested in them as people, and his poetry has also an unobtrusive scholarship. He was an academic poet of the very best kind. The patient research and documentation that went into all his works is something that he wore as lightly as he took the job itself seriously.

A university is a community, and I remember, as an undergraduate, how deeply impressed I was at meeting that formidable trio of English teachers, Pelham Edgar, Ned Pratt, and John Robins. I say that I was impressed, because, at the age of seventeen, I was not easy to impress. I knew the answers to a great many more questions than I know now. But I do feel that the merits of each of those three men had a great deal to do with the presence of the other two. They all had in common a sense of the contemporary which, I think, was extraordinary. All over Canada and the United States, students were being placidly informed in classrooms that many of the contemporary writers, such as D.H. Lawrence or James Joyce or T.S. Eliot, were either obscure or obscene, and that, in a properly regulated society, they would be either in jail or in a madhouse. But this imperturbable Methodist institution, in the persons of Edgar and Pratt and Robins, informed their students that these people were serious writers who should be investigated. And they all had in common too an extraordinary sense of the vitality and promise of Canadian literature. Pelham Edgar would interrupt a class on Shakespeare to tell us about Raymond Knister or about Audrey Alexander Brown or Duncan Campbell Scott. I'm going back in time, but that was a long way back, and Robins and Ned did the same thing. Robins with his encyclopedic knowledge of the oral tradition, the ballad and folk song, rounded out this sense of the contemporary and the immediate.

Ned was less of a discoverer of genius, I think, than Pelham Edgar. He tended rather to be a self-contained standard. People brought their work to him and they knew that he was a touchstone to bring it to. In my fourth year as an undergraduate I was the editor of the college magazine and I had to administer a ten dollar prize for the best poem. The poems came in and I took them to Ned. Ned did not recommend an award. What he did was to put his finger on one of the poems and say, "Now this one, it has some feeling, some sensitivity, some sense of structure, but, well, damn it all, it isn't worth *money*." I have seldom had a profounder insight into literary values and I was fortunate to have it so early.

As a graduate student, I assisted him in selecting work on a poetry magazine, and, there again, I was impressed by the inflexibility of his standards and realized that poetry, like friendship, was something he took too seriously to compromise. I remember an argument in his office between himself and another distinguished poet, whose literary judgment was apt to be affected by the sex of the authors of poems, and I remember this man trying to persuade Dr. Pratt to put in a poem, which he had rejected with the greatest enthusiasm. And I remember the first line of the poem. It read, "Ah, are you singing on my breast?" The other distinguished poet said, "That's one of the most exquisite things you will ever have a chance to print," because the author was a protégée of his. Ned said, "That poem is bilge and you know it," and this left the other distinguished poet without much to say, because, of course, he did know it. And I remember a young poet, again consulting Ned, who was known to be one of the kindest men in Canada, who was enormously proud of everybody who achieved any distinction whatever in any creative field and who would go to any lengths to help and encourage. This, however, was a young man who had mistaken his vocation and I remember Ned's voice pleading with him saying, "Can't you see what appalling drivel this is?"

It always seemed to me in being warmed, as I so constantly was, by Ned's personal kindliness, that his kindliness was the product of a kind of hidden strength. His personal relations took their cue from his utter honesty and integrity as a craftsman and, because that standard was so securely kept, he could afford to be what he was once described as being in a small magazine, as not only the best poet but the kindest man in Canada. When you met him on the street you were incorporated in a moment of a pure, present experience. His eye never sailed past your shoulder in search of the next person, nor did he give the impression that he was on his way to another appointment. He was able to live in a present moment in a way which requires a great integrity, a great simplicity, and a quality which is certainly allied to, if it is not identical with, a quality of sanctity.

I remember too, during the Depression and the Second World War, having cause to reflect that to teach English through that period and to write poetry through that period was something that took the qualities which Ned was particularly anxious to celebrate in his poetry, the qualities of courage, the long fight against the most desperate odds. The motto of Ned's life, perhaps, was the very unobtrusive passage in the poem on the shipwreck, *The Roosevelt and the Antinoe*, where the captain is asked, near the beginning of the poem, "Do you wish to abandon?" and he answers, "Not just yet," and then goes on to say what resources he still has. During the 1930s and '40s, I was conscious too that many intellectual leaders whom I most admired were deserting wisdom for paradox, were falling in love with authoritarian standards and values, whether of the extreme right or the extreme left, and that the main danger of the intellectual in modern society is perhaps a fascination with the logical extreme instead of with the illogical golden mean. I remember a sense of betrayal by several writers and thinkers of that period whom I most admired, and consequently it was a turning point in my life when, at an evening in Earle Birney's apartment in Hazelton Avenue, I heard Ned read his poem, *The Truant*.

The Truant, to my mind, is not only the greatest of Canadian poems, but one of the almost definitive poetic statements of our time, and its theme is the confrontation of the force of nature with the force of humanity. In one passage in this poem, Pratt is outlining the sheer blank pessimism which one is bound to feel when one looks at the world as infinite space and infinite time with no future except what the scientists call entropy, a gradual running down and an eventual extinction:

> "No final tableau of desire,
> No causes won or lost, no free
> Adventure at the outposts—only
> The degradation of your energy
> When at some late
> Slow number of your dance your sergeant-major Fate
> Will catch you blind and groping and will send
> You reeling on that long and lonely
> Lockstep of your wave-lengths towards your end." [ll. 166–74]

It takes a good deal of courage, I think, to face the pessimistic view of life so fully and so uncompromisingly, as he does just before the great affirmation at the end of the poem, where the human being confronting this power of nature says, "No! by the Rood, we will not join your ballet" [105].

There is also the poem called *The Depression Ends*, which begins in a way which anyone who ever knew Ned Pratt will recognize at once:

> If I could take within my hand
> The rod of Prospero for an hour,
> With space and speed at my command,
> And astro-physics in my power,
> Having no reason for my scheme
> Beyond the logic of a dream
> To change a world predestinate
> From the eternal loom of fate,
> I'd realize my mad chimera
> By smashing distaff and the spinner,
> And usher in the golden era
> With an apocalyptic dinner. [ll. 1–12]

And there you have perhaps the two poles within which Ned accomplished his poetic vision, the bleakness and the pessimism of life as it would be if it had no faith, and, of course, every poem is an act of faith, and, on the other hand, something compounded of fantasy and unreality and a limitless good will, which is somehow greater and somehow survives after the vision of silence and the dark is no more.

53

Conclusion to the First Edition of *Literary History of Canada*

1965

From Literary History of Canada: Canadian Literature in English, *ed. Carl F. Klinck, Alfred G. Bailey, Claude Bissell, Roy Daniells, Northrop Frye, and Desmond Pacey (Toronto: University of Toronto Press, 1965), 821–49, reprinted in 2nd ed. (1976), 2:231–61. Also in the French version,* Histoire littéraire du Canada: Littérature canadienne de langue anglaise, *trans. Maurice Lebel (Quebec: Les Presses de l'Université Laval, 1970), 971–1005. Reprinted in edited form in BG, 213–51, in RCLI, 65–99, in ECLI, 63–95, in* An Anthology of Canadian Literature, *ed. Russell Brown and Donna Bennett (Toronto: Oxford University Press, 1982), 1:536–65, and in* Towards a Canadian Literature: Essays, Editorials, and Manifestos, *ed. Douglas M. Daymond and Leslie G. Monkman (Ottawa: Tecumseh Press, 1985), 2:460–93. Printed in an edited version in StS, 279–312 (the source of the notes labelled [NF]), and (in part) in* Canadian Writing Today, *ed. Mordecai Richler (Baltimore: Penguin, 1970), 312–22. For the new conclusion Frye wrote for the second edition, see no. 68.*

The scholars Frye refers to and the chapters they wrote are as follows: David Galloway, University of New Brunswick, "The Voyagers"; William H. Kilbourn, York University, "The Writing of Canadian History"; Kenneth Windsor, Trent University, "Historical Writing in Canada (to 1920)"; Matthew Scargill, University of Victoria, "The Growth of Canadian English"; Carl F. Klinck, Middlesex College, University of Western Ontario, two essays on literary activity in the Canadas, 1812–80; Alfred Bailey, University of New Brunswick, "Overture to Nationhood"; Elizabeth Waterston, Middlesex College, two essays on travel books; Michael Tait, Ryerson Polytechnical Institute, "Drama and Theatre"; Fred Cogswell, University of New Brunswick, "Haliburton"; Desmond Pacey, University of New Brunswick, "The Writer and His Public"; John Irving, Victoria College, University of Toronto, "The Achievement of G.S. Brett";

Victor G. Hopwood, University of British Columbia, two essays on explorers; Millar MacLure, Victoria College, University of Toronto, "Literary Scholarship"; James S. Thomson, McGill University, "Religious and Theological Writings"; Frank Watt, University College, University of Toronto, "Literature of Protest"; Edith Fowke, Canadian Folk Music Society, "Folktales and Folk Songs"; Hugo McPherson, University College, University of Toronto, "Fiction (1940–1960)"; Gordon Roper, Trinity College, University of Toronto, three essays on fiction, 1880–1920; Alec Lucas, McGill University, "Nature Writers and the Animal Story"; and Marjorie McDowell, City of Saint John, "Children's Books."

I

It is now several years since the group of editors listed on the title-page met, under Carl Klinck's leadership, to draw up the first tentative plans for this book. What we then dreamed of is substantially what we have got, changed very little in essentials. I expressed at the time the hope that such a book would help to broaden the inductive basis on which some writers on Canadian literature were making generalizations that bordered on guesswork. By "some writers" I meant primarily myself. I find, however, that this book tends to confirm me in most of my intuitions on the subject: the advantage for me is that this attempt at conclusion and summary can involve some self-plagiarism.

The book is a tribute to the maturity of Canadian literary scholarship and criticism, whatever one thinks of the literature. Its authors have completely outgrown the view that evaluation is the end of criticism, instead of its incidental by-product. Had evaluation been their guiding principle, this book would, if written at all, have been only a huge debunking project, leaving Canadian literature a poor naked *alouette* plucked of every feather of decency and dignity. True, the book gives evidence, on practically every one of its eight hundred odd pages, that what is really remarkable is not how little but how much good writing has been produced in Canada. But this would not affect the rigorous evaluator. The evaluative view is based on the conception of criticism as concerned mainly to define and canonize the genuine classics of literature. And Canada has produced no author who is a classic in the sense of possessing a vision greater in kind than that of his best readers (Canadians themselves might argue about one or two, but in the perspective of the world at large the statement is true). There is no Canadian writer of

Conclusion to the First Edition of *Literary History of Canada* 341

whom we can say what we can say of the world's major writers, that their readers can grow up inside their work without ever being aware of a circumference. Thus the metaphor of the critic as "judge" holds for the Canadian critic, who is never dealing with the kind of writer who judges him.

This fact about Canadian literature, so widely deplored by Canadians, has one advantage. It is much easier to see what literature is trying to do when we are studying a literature that has not quite done it. If no Canadian author pulls us away from the Canadian context toward the centre of literary experience itself, then at every point we remain aware of his social and historical setting. The conception of what is literary has to be greatly broadened for such a literature. The literary, in Canada, is often only an incidental quality of writings which, like those of many of the early explorers, are as innocent of literary intention as a mating loon. Even when it is literature in its orthodox genres of poetry and fiction, it is more significantly studied as a part of Canadian life than as a part of an autonomous world of literature.

So far from merely admitting or conceding this, the editors have gone out of their way to emphasize it. We have asked for chapters on political, historical, religious, scholarly, philosophical, scientific, and other non-literary writing, to show how the verbal imagination operates as a ferment in all cultural life. We have included the writings of foreigners, of travellers, of immigrants, of emigrants—even of emigrants whose most articulate literary emotion was their thankfulness at getting the hell out of Canada. The reader of this book, even if he is not Canadian or much interested in Canadian literature as such, may still learn a good deal about the literary imagination as a force and function of life generally. For here another often deplored fact also becomes an advantage: that many Canadian cultural phenomena are not peculiarly Canadian at all, but are typical of their wider North American and Western contexts.

This book is a collection of essays in cultural history, and of the general principles of cultural history we still know relatively little. It is, of course, closely related to political and to economic history, but it is a separate and definable subject in itself. Like other kinds of history, it has its own themes of exploration, settlement, and development, but these themes relate to a social *imagination* that explores and settles and develops, and the imagination has its own rhythms of growth as well as its own modes of expression. It is obvious that Canadian literature, whatever its inherent merits, is an indispensable aid to the knowledge of Canada. It records what the Canadian imagination has reacted to, and it tells us things about this environment that nothing else will tell us. By examining this imagination as the authors of this book have tried to do, as an ingredient in Canadian verbal culture generally, a relatively small and low-lying cultural development is studied in all its dimensions. There is far too much Canadian writing for this book not to become, in places, something of a catalogue; but the outlines of the structure are clear. Fortunately, the bulk of Canadian nonliterary writing, even today, has not yet declined into the state of sodden specialization in which the readable has become the impure.

I stress our ignorance of the laws and conditions of cultural history for an obvious reason. The question, Why has there been no Canadian writer of classic proportions? may naturally be asked. At any rate it often has been. Our authors realize that it is better to deal with what is there than to raise speculations about why something else is not there. But it is clear that the question haunts their minds. And we know so little about cultural history that we not only cannot answer such a question, but we do not even know whether or not it is a real question. The notion, doubtless of Romantic origin, that "genius" is a certain quantum that an individual is born with, as he might be born with red hair, is still around, but mainly as a folk-tale motif in fiction, like the story of Finch in the Jalna books.[1] "Genius" is as much, and as essentially, a matter of social context as it is of individual character. We do not know what the social conditions are that produce great literature, or even whether there is any causal relation at all. If there is, there is no reason to suppose that they are good conditions, or conditions that we should try to reproduce. The notion that the literature one admires must have been nourished by something admirable in the social environment is persistent, but has never been justified by evidence. One can still find books on Shakespeare that profess to make his achievement more plausible by talking about a "background" of social euphoria produced by the defeat of the Armada, the discovery of America a century before, and the conviction that Queen Elizabeth was a wonderful woman. There is a general sense of filler about such speculations, and when similar arguments are given in a negative form to explain the absence of a Shakespeare in Canada they are no more convincing. Puritan inhibitions, pioneer life, "an age too late, cold climate, or years"[2]—these may be important as factors or conditions of Canadian culture, helping us to characterize its qualities. To suggest that any of them is a negative cause of its merit is to say much more than anyone knows.

One theme which runs all through this book is the obvious and unquenchable desire of the Canadian cultural public to identify itself through its literature. Canada is not a bad environment for the author, as far as recognition goes: in fact the recognition may even hamper his development by making him prematurely self-conscious. Scholarships, prizes, university posts, await the dedicated writer: there are so many medals offered for literary achievement that a modern Canadian Dryden might well be moved to write a satire on medals, except that if he did he would promptly be awarded the medal for satire and humour. Publishers take an active responsibility for native literature, even poetry; a fair proportion of the books bought by Canadian readers are by Canadian writers; the CBC and other media help to employ some writers and publicize others. The efforts made at intervals to boost or hard-sell Canadian literature, by asserting that it is much better than it actually is, may look silly enough in retrospect, but they were also, in part, efforts to create a cultural community, and the aim deserves more sympathy than the means. Canada has two languages and two literatures, and every statement made in a book like this about "Canadian literature" employs the figure of speech known as synecdoche, putting a part for the whole. Every such statement implies a parallel or contrasting statement about French Canadian literature. The advantages of having a national culture based on two languages are in some respects very great, but of course they are for the most part potential. The difficulties, if more superficial, are also more actual and more obvious.

Some of the seminal facts about the origins of Canadian culture are set down with great clarity near the beginning of this book. Canada began, says Mr. Galloway, as an obstacle, blocking the way to the treasures of the East, to be explored only in the hope of finding a passage through it. English Canada continued to be that long after what is now the United States had become a defined part of the Western world. One reason for this is obvious from the map. American culture was, down to about 1900, mainly a culture of the Atlantic seaboard, with a western frontier that moved irregularly but steadily back until it reached the other coast. The Revolution did not essentially change the cultural unity of the English-speaking community of the North Atlantic that had London and Edinburgh on one side of it and Boston and Philadelphia on the other. But Canada has, for all practical purposes, no Atlantic seaboard. The traveller from Europe edges into it like a tiny Jonah entering an inconceivably large whale, slipping past the Straits of Belle Isle into the Gulf of St. Lawrence, where five Canadian provinces surround him, for the most part invisible. Then he goes up the St. Lawrence and the inhabited country comes into view, mainly a French-speaking country, with its own cultural traditions. To enter the United States is a matter of crossing an ocean; to enter Canada is a matter of being silently swallowed by an alien continent.

It is an unforgettable and intimidating experience to enter Canada in this way. But the experience initiates one into that gigantic east to west thrust which, as Mr. Kilbourn notes, historians regard as the axis of Canadian development, the "Laurentian" movement that makes the growth of Canada geographically credible. This drive to the West has attracted to itself nearly everything that is heroic and romantic in the Canadian tradition. The original impetus begins in Europe, for English Canada in the British Isles, hence though adventurous it is also a conservative force, and naturally tends to preserve its colonial link with its starting point. Once the Canadian has settled down in the country, however, he then becomes aware of the longitudinal dimension, the southward pull toward the richer and more glamorous American cities, some of which, such as Boston for the Maritimes and Minneapolis for the eastern prairies, are almost Canadian capitals. This is the axis of another kind of Canadian mentality, more critical and analytic, more inclined to see Canada as an unnatural and politically quixotic aggregate of disparate northern extensions of American culture—"seven fishing-rods tied together by the ends," as Goldwin Smith, quoted by Mr. Windsor, puts it.[3] Mr. Kilbourn illustrates the contrast in his account of the styles, attitudes, and literary genres of Creighton and Underhill.

The simultaneous influence of two larger nations speaking the same language has been practically beneficial to English Canada, but theoretically confusing. It is often suggested that Canada's identity is to be found in some *via media*, or *via mediocris*, between the other two. This has the disadvantage that the British and American cultures have to be defined as extremes. Haliburton seems to have believed that the ideal for Nova Scotia would be a combination of American energy and British social structure, but such a chimera, or synthetic monster, is hard to achieve in practice. It is simpler merely to notice the alternating current in the Canadian mind, as reflected in its writing, between two moods, one romantic, traditional, and idealistic, the other shrewd, observant, and humorous. Canada in its attitude to Britain tends to be more royalist than the Queen, in the sense that it is more attracted to it as a symbol of tradition than as a fellow nation. The Canadian attitude to the United

States is typically that of a smaller country to a much bigger neighbour, sharing in its material civilization but anxious to keep clear of the huge mass movements that drive a great imperial power. The United States, being founded on a revolution and a written constitution, has introduced a deductive or *a priori* pattern into its cultural life that tends to define an American way of life and mark it off from anti-American heresies. Canada, having a seat on the sidelines of the American Revolution, adheres more to the inductive and the expedient. The Canadian genius for compromise is reflected in the existence of Canada itself.

The most obvious tension in the Canadian literary situation is in the use of language. Here, first of all, a traditional standard English collides with the need for a North American vocabulary and phrasing. Mr. Scargill and Mr. Klinck have studied this in the work of Mrs. Moodie and Mrs. Traill. As long as the North American speaker feels that he belongs in a minority, the European speech will impose a standard of correctness. This is to a considerable extent still true of French in Canada, with its campaigns against "joual" and the like. But as Americans began to outnumber the British, Canada tended in practice to fall in with the American developments, though a good deal of Canadian theory is still Anglophile. A much more complicated cultural tension arises from the impact of the sophisticated on the primitive, and vice versa. The most dramatic example, and one I have given elsewhere,[4] is that of Duncan Campbell Scott, working in the Department of Indian Affairs in Ottawa. He writes of a starving squaw baiting a fish-hook with her own flesh, and he writes of the music of Debussy and the poetry of Henry Vaughan. In English literature we have to go back to Anglo-Saxon times to encounter so incongruous a collision of cultures.

Cultural history, we said, has its own rhythms. It is possible that one of these rhythms is very like an organic rhythm: that there must be a period, of a certain magnitude, as Aristotle would say, in which a social imagination can take root and establish a tradition. American literature had this period, in the northeastern part of the country, between the Revolution and the Civil War. Canada has never had it. English Canada was first a part of the wilderness, then a part of North America and the British Empire, then a part of the world. But it has gone through these revolutions too quickly for a tradition of writing to be founded on any one of them. Canadian writers are, even now, still trying to assimilate a Canadian environment at a time when new techniques of communication, many of which, like television, constitute a verbal market, are annihilating the boundaries of that environment. This foreshortening of Canadian history, if it really does have any relevance to Canadian culture, would account for many features of it: its fixation on its own past, its penchant for old-fashioned literary techniques, its preoccupation with the theme of strangled articulateness. It seems to me that Canadian sensibility has been profoundly disturbed, not so much by our famous problem of identity, important as that is, as by a series of paradoxes in what confronts that identity. It is less perplexed by the question, "Who am I?" than by some such riddle as, "Where is here?"

Mr. Bailey, writing of the early Maritimes, warns us not to read the "mystique of Canadianism" back into the pre-Confederation period. Haliburton, for instance, was a Nova Scotian, a Bluenose: the word "Canadian" to him would have summoned up the figure of someone who spoke mainly French and whose enthusiasm for Haliburton's own political ideals would have been extremely tepid. The mystique of Canadianism was, as several chapters in this book make clear, specifically the cultural accompaniment of Confederation and the imperialistic mood that followed it. But it came so suddenly after the pioneer period that it was still full of wilderness. To feel "Canadian" was to feel part of a no-man's-land with huge rivers, lakes, and islands that very few Canadians had ever seen. "From sea to sea, and from the river unto the ends of the earth"—if Canada is not an island, the phrasing is still in the etymological sense isolating.[5] One wonders if any other national consciousness has had so large an amount of the unknown, the unrealized, the humanly undigested, so built into it. Rupert Brooke, quoted by Mrs. Waterston, speaks of the "unseizable virginity" of the Canadian landscape.[6] What is important here, for our purposes, is the position of the frontier in the Canadian imagination. In the United States one could choose to move out to the frontier or to retreat from it back to the seaboard. The tensions built up by such migrations have fascinated many American novelists and historians. In the Canadas, even in the Maritimes, the frontier was all around one, a part and a condition of one's whole imaginative being. The frontier was primarily what separated the Canadian, physically or mentally, from Great Britain, from the United States, and, even more important, from other Canadian communities. Such a frontier was the immediate datum of his imagination, the thing that had to be dealt with first.

After the Northwest Passage failed to materialize, Canada became a colony in the mercantilist sense, treated by others less like a society than as a place to look for things. French, English, Americans plunged into it to carry off its supplies of furs, minerals, and pulpwood, aware only of their immediate objectives. From time to time recruiting officers searched the farms and villages to carry young men off to death in a European dynastic quarrel. The travellers reviewed by Mrs. Waterston visit Canada much as they would visit a zoo: even when their eyes momentarily focus on the natives they are still thinking primarily of how their own sensibility is going to react to what it sees. Mrs. Waterston speaks of a feature of Canadian life that has been noted by writers from Susanna Moodie onward: "the paradox of vast empty spaces plus lack of privacy," without defences against the prying or avaricious eye. The resentment expressed against this in Canada seems to have taken political rather than literary forms: this may be partly because Canadians have learned from their imaginative experience to look at each other in much the same way: "as objects, even ultimately as obstacles," to quote Miss Macpherson on a Canadian autobiography.[7]

It is not much wonder if Canada developed with the bewilderment of a neglected child, preoccupied with trying to define its own identity, alternately bumptious and diffident about its own achievements. Adolescent dreams of glory haunt the Canadian consciousness (and unconsciousness), some naive and some sophisticated. In the naive area are the predictions that the twentieth century belongs to Canada,[8] that our cities will become much bigger than they ought to be, or, like Edmonton and Vancouver, "gateways" to somewhere else, reconstructed Northwest passages. The more sophisticated usually take the form of a Messianic complex about Canadian culture, for Canadian culture, no less than Alberta, has always been "next year country."[9] The myth of the hero brought up in the forest retreat, awaiting the moment when his giant strength will be fully grown and he can emerge into the world, informs a good deal of Canadian criticism down to our own time.

Certain features of life in a new country that are bound to handicap its writers are obvious enough. The difficulties of drama, which depends on a theatre and consequently on a highly organized urban life, are set out by Mr. Tait. Here the foreshortening of historical development has been particularly cruel, as drama was strangled by the movie just as it was getting started as a popular medium. Other literary genres have similar difficulties. Culture is born in leisure and an awareness of standards, and pioneer conditions tend to make energetic and uncritical work an end in itself, to preach a gospel of social unconsciousness, which lingers long after the pioneer conditions have disappeared. The impressive achievements of such a society are likely to be technological. It is in the inarticulate part of communication, railways and bridges and canals and highways, that Canada, one of whose symbols is the taciturn beaver, has shown its real strength. Again, Canadian culture, and literature in particular, has felt the force of what may be called Emerson's law. Emerson remarks in his journals that in a provincial society it is extremely easy to reach the highest level of cultivation, extremely difficult to take one step beyond that.[10] In surveying Canadian poetry and fiction, we feel constantly that all the energy has been absorbed in meeting a standard, a self-defeating enterprise because real standards can only be established, not met. Such writing is academic in the pejorative sense of that term, an imitation of a prescribed model, second-rate in conception, not merely in execution. It is natural that academic writing of this kind should develop where literature is a social prestige symbol, as Mr. Cogswell says. However, it is not the handicaps of Canadian writers but the distinctive features that appear in spite of them which are the main concern of this book, and so of its conclusion.

II

The sense of probing into the distance, of fixing the eyes on the skyline, is something that Canadian sensibility has inherited from the *voyageurs*. It comes into Canadian painting a good deal, in Thomson whose focus is so often farthest back in the picture, where a river or a gorge in the hills twists elusively out of sight, in Emily Carr whose vision is always, in the title of a compatriot's book of poems, "deeper into the forest."[11] Even in the Maritimes, where the feeling of linear distance is less urgent, Roberts contemplates the Tantramar marshes in the same way, the refrain of "miles on miles" having clearly some incantatory power for him.[12] It would be interesting to know how many Canadian novels associate nobility of character with a faraway look, or base their perorations on a long-range perspective.[13] This might be only a cliché, except that it is often found in sharply observed and distinctively written books. Here, as a random example, is the last sentence of W.O. Mitchell's *Who Has Seen the Wind*: "The wind turns in silent frenzy upon itself, whirling into a smoking funnel, breathing up top soil and tumbleweed skeletons to carry them on its spinning way over the prairie, out and out to the far line of the sky." Mr. Pacey quotes the similarly long-sighted conclusion of *Such Is My Beloved*.

A vast country sparsely inhabited naturally depends on its modes of transportation, whether canoe, railway, or the driving and riding "circuits" of the judge, the Methodist preacher, or the Yankee peddler. The feeling of nomadic movement over great distances persists even into the age of the airplane, in a country where writers can hardly meet one another without a social organization that provides travel grants. Pratt's poetry is full of his fascination with means of communication, not simply the physical means of great ships and locomotives, though he is one of the best of all poets on such subjects, but with communication as message, with radar and asdic and wireless signals, and, in his war poems, with the power of rhetoric over fighting men. What is perhaps the most comprehensive structure of ideas yet made by a Canadian thinker, the structure embodied in Innis's *Bias of Communication*, is concerned with the same theme, and a disciple of Innis, Marshall McLuhan, continues to emphasize the unity of communication, as a complex containing both verbal and non-verbal factors, and warns us against making unreal divisions within it. Perhaps it is not too fanciful to see this need for continuity in the Canadian attitude to time as well as space, in its preoccupation with its own history (the motto of the Province of Quebec is *je me souviens*) and its relentless cultural stock-takings and self-inventories. The Burke sense of society as a continuum—consistent with the pragmatic and conservative outlook of Canadians—is strong and begins early. Mr. Irving quotes an expression of it in McCulloch, and another quotation shows that it was one of the most deeply held ideas of Brett.[14] As I write, the centennial of Confederation in 1967 looms up before the country with the moral urgency of a Day of Atonement: I use a Jewish metaphor because there is something Hebraic about the Canadian tendency to read its conquest of a promised land, its Maccabean victories of 1812, its struggle for the central fortress on the hill at Quebec, as oracles of a future. It is doubtless only an accident that the theme of one of the most passionate and intense of all Canadian novels, A.M. Klein's *The Second Scroll*, is Zionism.

Civilization in Canada, as elsewhere, has advanced geometrically across the country, throwing down the long parallel lines of the railways, dividing up the farm lands into chessboards of square-mile sections and concession-line roads. There is little adaptation to nature: in both architecture and arrangement, Canadian cities and villages express rather an arrogant abstraction, the conquest of nature by an intelligence that does not love it. The word conquest suggests something military, as it should— one thinks of General Braddock, preferring to have his army annihilated rather than fight the natural man on his own asymmetrical ground.[15] There are some features of this generally North American phenomenon that have a particular emphasis in Canada. It has been remarked—Mr. Kilbourn quotes Creighton on the subject—that Canadian expansion westward had a tight grip of authority over it that American expansion, with its outlaws and sheriffs and vigilantes and the like, did not have in the same measure. America moved from the back country to the wild West; Canada moved from a New France held down by British military occupation to a Northwest patrolled by mounted police. Canada has not had, strictly speaking, an Indian war: there has been much less of the "another redskin bit the dust" feeling in our historical imagination, and only Riel remains to haunt the later period of it, though he is a formidable figure enough, rather like what a combination of John Brown and Vanzetti would be in the American conscience. Otherwise, the conquest, for the last two centuries, has been mainly of the unconscious forces of nature, personified by the dragon of the Lake Superior rocks in Pratt's *Towards the Last Spike*:

> On the North Shore a reptile lay asleep—
> A hybrid that the myths might have conceived,
> But not delivered.   [ll. 870–2]

Yet the conquest of nature has its own perils for the imagination, in a country where the winters are so cold and where conditions of life have so often been bleak and comfortless, where even the mosquitoes have been described, Mr. Klinck tells us, as "mementoes of the fall." I have long been impressed in Canadian poetry by a tone of deep terror in regard to nature, a theme to which we shall return. It is not a terror of the dangers or discomforts or even the mysteries of nature, but a terror of the soul at something that these things manifest. The human mind has nothing but human and moral values to cling to if it is to preserve its integrity or even its sanity, yet the vast unconsciousness of nature in front of it seems an unanswerable denial of those values. I notice that a sharp-witted Methodist preacher quoted by Mr. Cogswell speaks of the "shutting out of the whole moral creation" in the loneliness of the forests.

If we put together a few of these impressions, we may get some approach to characterizing the way in which the Canadian imagination has developed in its literature. Small and isolated communities surrounded with a physical or psychological "frontier," separated from one another and from their American and British cultural sources: communities that provide all that their members have in the way of distinctively human values, and that are compelled to feel a great respect for the law and order that holds them together, yet confronted with a huge, unthinking, menacing, and formidable physical setting—such communities are bound to develop what we may provisionally call a garrison mentality. In the earliest maps of the country the only inhabited centres are forts, and that remains true of the cultural maps for a much later time. Frances Brooke, in her eighteenth-century *Emily Montague*, wrote of what was literally a garrison; novelists of our day studying the impact of Montreal on Westmount write of a psychological one.

A garrison is a closely knit and beleaguered society, and its moral and social values are unquestionable. In a perilous enterprise ones does not discuss causes or motives: one is either a fighter or a deserter. Here again we may turn to Pratt, with his infallible instinct for what is central in the Canadian imagination. The societies in Pratt's poems are always tense and tight groups engaged in war, rescue, martyrdom, or crisis, and the moral values expressed are simply those of that group. In such a society the terror is not for the common enemy, even when the enemy is or seems victorious, as in the extermination of the Jesuit missionaries or the crew of Franklin[16] (a great Canadian theme, well described in this book by Mr. Hopwood, that Pratt pondered but never completed). The real terror comes when the individual feels himself becoming an individual, pulling away from the group, losing the sense of driving power that the group gives him, aware of a conflict within himself far subtler than the struggle of morality against evil. It is much easier to multiply garrisons, and when that happens, something anticultural comes into Canadian life, a dominating herd-mind in which nothing original can grow. The intensity of the sectarian divisiveness in Canadian towns, both religious and political, is an example: what such groups represent, of course, vis-à-vis one another, is "two solitudes,"[17] the death of communication and dialogue. Separatism, whether English or French, is culturally the most sterile of all creeds. But at present I am concerned rather with a more creative side of the garrison mentality, one that has had positive effects on our intellectual life.

They were so certain of their moral values, says Mr. Cogswell, a little sadly, speaking of the early Maritime writers. Right was white, wrong black, and nothing else counted or even existed. He goes on to point out that such certainty invariably produces a sub-literary rhetoric. Or, as Yeats would say, we make rhetoric out of quarrels with one another, poetry out of the quarrel with ourselves.[18] To use words, for any other purpose than straight description or command, is a form of play, a manifestation of *homo ludens*. But there are two forms of play, the contest and the construct. The editorial writer attacking the Family Compact, the preacher demolishing imaginary atheists with the argument of design, are using words aggressively, in theses that imply antitheses. Ideas are weapons; one seeks the verbal *coup de grâce*, the irrefutable refutation. Such a use of words is congenial enough to the earlier Canadian community: all the evidence, including the evidence of this book, points to a highly articulate and argumentative society in nineteenth-century Canada. Mr. MacLure remarks on the fact that scholarship in Canada has so often been written with more conviction and authority, and has attracted wider recognition, than the literature itself. There are historical reasons for this, apart from the fact, which will become clearer as we go on, that scholarly writing is more easily attached to its central tradition.

Leacock has a story which I often turn to because the particular aspect of Canadian culture it reflects has never been more accurately caught. He tells us of the rivalry in an Ontario town between two preachers, one Anglican and the other Presbyterian. The latter taught ethics in the local college on weekdays—without salary—and preached on Sundays. He gave his students, says Leacock, three parts Hegel and two parts St. Paul, and on Sunday he reversed the dose and gave his parishioners three parts St. Paul and two parts Hegel.[19] Religion has been a major—perhaps the major—cultural force in Canada, at least down to the last generation or two. The names of two Methodist publishers, William Briggs and Lorne Pierce, recur more than once in this book, and illustrate the fact that the churches not only influenced the cultural climate but took an active part in the production of poetry and fiction, as the popularity of Ralph Connor reminds us. But the effective religious factors in Canada were doctrinal and evangelical, those that stressed the arguments of religion at the expense of its imagery.

Such a reliance on the arguing intellect was encouraged by the philosophers, who in the nineteenth century, as Mr. Irving shows, were invariably idealists with a strong religious bias. Mr. Irving quotes George as saying that civilization consists "in the conscience and intellect" of a cultivated people, and Watson as asserting that "we are capable of knowing Reality as it actually is.... Reality when so known is absolutely rational."[20] An even higher point may have been reached by that triumphant theologian cited by Mr. Thomson, whose book I have not read but whose title I greatly admire: *The Riddle of the Universe Solved*.[21] Naturally sophisticated intelligence of this kind was the normal means of contact with literature. Mr. MacLure tells us that James Cappon judged poetry according to whether it had a "rationalized concept" or not—this would have been a very common critical assumption. Sara Jeannette Duncan shows us a clergyman borrowing a copy of Browning's *Sordello*, no easy reading, and returning it with original suggestions for interpretation.[22] Such an interest in ideas is not merely cultivated but exuberant.

But using language as one would use an axe, formulating arguments with sharp cutting edges that will help to clarify one's view of the landscape, remains a rhetorical and not a poetic achievement. To quote Yeats again, one can refute Hegel (perhaps even St. Paul) but not the *Song of Sixpence*.[23] To create a disinterested structure of words, in poetry or in fiction, is a very different achievement, and it is clear that an intelligent and able rhetorician finds it particularly hard to understand how different it is. A rhetorician practising poetry is apt to express himself in spectral arguments, generalizations that escape the feeling of possible refutation only by being vast enough to contain it, or vaporous enough to elude it. The mystique of Canadianism was accompanied by an intellectual tendency of this kind, as Mr. Daniells indicates. Worldviews that avoided dialectic, of a theosophical or transcendentalist cast, became popular among the Canadian poets of that time, Roberts and Carman particularly, and later among painters, as the reminiscences of the Group of Seven make clear. Bucke's *Cosmic Consciousness*, though not mentioned by any of our authors so far as I remember, is an influential Canadian book in this area. When minor rhetorically minded poets sought what Samuel Johnson calls, though in a very different context, the "grandeur of generality,"[24] the result is what is so well described by Mr. Beattie as "jejune chatter about infinity," and the like.

Mr. Watt's very important chapter on the literature of protest isolates another rhetorical tradition. In the nineteenth century the common assumption that nature had revealed the truth of progress, and that it was the duty of reason to accommodate that truth to mankind, could be either a conservative or a radical view. But in either case it was a revolutionary doctrine, introducing the conception of change as the key to the social process. In those whom Mr. Watt calls proletarian social Darwinists, and who represented "the unholy fusion of secularism, science and social discontent," there was a strong tendency to regard literature as a product and a symbol of a ruling-class mentality, with, as we have tried to indicate, some justification. Hence radicals tended either to hope that "the literature of the future will be the powerful ally of Democracy and Labour Reform," or to assume that serious thought and action would bypass the creative writer entirely, building a scientific socialism and leaving him to his Utopian dreams.

The radicalism of the period up to the Russian Revolution was, from a later point of view, largely undifferentiated. A labour magazine could regard Ignatius Donnelly, with his anti-Semitic and other crank views, as an advanced thinker equally with William Morris and Edward Bellamy.[25] Similarly, even today, in western Canadian elections, a protest vote may go Social Credit or NDP without much regard to the difference in political philosophy between these parties. The Depression introduced a dialectic into Canadian social thought which profoundly affected its literature. In Mr. Watt's striking phrase, "the Depression was like an intense magnetic field that deflected the courses of all the poets who went through it." In this period there were, of course, the inevitable Marxist manifestos, assuring the writer that only social significance, as understood by Marxism, would bring vitality to his work. The *New Frontier*, a far-left journal of that period referred to several times in this book, shows an uneasy sense on the part of its contributors that this literary elixir of youth might have to be mixed with various other potions, not all favourable to the creative process: attending endless meetings, organizing, agitating, marching, demonstrating, or joining the Spanish Loyalists. It is easy for the critic to point out the fallacy of judging the merit of literature by its subject matter, but these arguments over the role of "propaganda" were genuine and serious moral conflicts. Besides helping to shape the argument of such novels as Grove's *The Master of the Mill* and Callaghan's *They Shall Inherit the Earth*, they raised the fundamental issue of the role of the creative mind in society, and by doing so helped to give a maturity and depth to Canadian writing which are a permanent part of its heritage.

It is not surprising, given this background, that the belief in the inspiration of literature by social significance continued to be an active force long after it had ceased to be attached to any specifically Marxist or other political programs. It is still strong in the *Preview* group in the 1940s, and in their immediate successors, though the best of them have developed in different directions. The theme of social realism is at its most attractive, and least theoretical, in the poetry of Souster. The existentialist movement, with its emphasis on the self-determination of social attitudes, seems to have had very little direct influence in Canada: Mr. Beattie's comment on the absence of the existential in Pratt suggests that this lack of influence may be significant.

During the last decade or so a kind of social Freudianism has been taking shape, mainly in the United States, as a democratic counterpart of Marxism. Here society is seen as controlled by certain anxieties, real or imaginary, which are designed to repress or sublimate human impulses toward a greater freedom. These impulses include the creative and the sexual, which are closely linked. The enemy of the poet is not the capitalist but the "square," or representative of repressive morality. The advantage of this attitude is that it preserves the position of rebellion against society for the poet, without imposing on him any specific social obligations. This movement has had a rather limited development in Canada, somewhat surprisingly considering how easy a target the square is in Canada: it has influenced Layton and many younger Montreal poets, but has not affected fiction to any great degree, though there may be something of it in Richler. It ignores the old political alignments: the Communists are usually regarded as Puritanic and repressive equally with the bourgeoisie, and a recent poem of Layton's contrasts the social hypocrisy in Canada with contemporary Spain. Thus it represents to some extent a return to the undifferentiated radicalism of a century before, though no longer in a political context.

As the centre of Canadian life moves from the fortress to the metropolis, the garrison mentality changes correspondingly. It begins as an expression of the moral values generally accepted in the group as a whole, and then, as society gets more complicated and more in control of its environment, it becomes more of a revolutionary garrison within a metropolitan society. But though it changes from a defence of to an attack on what society accepts as conventional standards, the literature it produces, at every stage, tends to be rhetorical, an illustration or allegory of certain social attitudes. These attitudes help to unify the mind of the writer by externalizing his enemy, the enemy being the anticreative elements in life as he sees life. To approach these elements in a less rhetorical way would introduce the theme of self-conflict, a more perilous but ultimately more rewarding theme. The conflict involved is between the poetic impulse to construct and the rhetorical impulse to assert, and the victory of the former is the sign of the maturing of the writer.

III

There is of course nothing in all this that differentiates Canadian from other related cultural developments. The nineteenth-century Canadian reliance on the conceptual was not different in kind from that of the Victorian readers described by Douglas Bush, who thought they were reading poetry when they were really only looking for Great Thoughts.[26] But if the tendency was not different in kind, it was more intense in degree. Here we need another seminal fact in this book, one that we have stumbled over already: Mr. Hopwood's remark that the Canadian literary mind, beginning as it did so late in the cultural history of the West, was established on a basis, not of myth, but of history. The conceptual emphasis in Canadian culture we have been speaking of is a consequence, and an essential part, of this historical bias.

Canada, of course, or the place where Canada is, can supply distinctive settings and props to a writer who is looking for local colour. Tourist-writing has its own importance (e.g., *Maria Chapdelaine*), as has the use of Canadian history for purposes of romance, of which more later. But it would be an obvious fallacy to claim that the setting provided anything more than novelty. When Canadian writers are urged to use distinctively Canadian themes, the fallacy is less obvious, but still there. The forms of literature are autonomous: they exist within literature itself, and cannot be derived from any experience outside literature. What the Canadian writer finds in his experience and environment may be new, but it will be new only as content: the form of his expression of it can take shape only from what he has read, not from what he has experienced. The great technical experiments of Joyce and Proust in fiction, of Eliot and Hopkins in poetry, have resulted partly from profound literary scholarship, from seeing the formal possibilities inherent in the literature they have studied. A writer who is or who feels removed from his literary tradition tends rather to take over forms already in existence. We notice how often the surveyors of Canadian fiction in this book have occasion to remark that a novel contains a good deal of sincere feeling and accurate observation, but that it is spoiled by an unconvincing plot, usually one too violent or dependent on coincidence for such material. What has happened is that the author felt he could make a novel out of his knowledge and observation, but had no story in particular to tell. His material did not come to him in the form of a story, but as a consolidated chunk of experience, reflection, and sensibility. He had to invent a plot to put this material in causal shape (for writing, as Kafka says, is an art of causality),[27] to pour the new wine of content into the old bottles of form. Even Grove works in this way, though Grove, by sheer dogged persistence, does get his action powerfully if ponderously moving.

This brings us nearer the centre of Mr. Hopwood's observation. Literature is conscious mythology: as society develops, its mythical stories become structural principles of story-telling, its mythical concepts, sun-gods and the like, become habits of metaphorical thought. In a fully mature literary tradition the writer enters into a structure of traditional stories and images. He often has the feeling, and says so, that he is not actively shaping his material at all, but is rather a place where a verbal structure is taking its own shape. If a novelist, he starts with a story-telling impetus; if a poet, with a metaphor-crystallizing impetus. Down to the beginning of the twentieth century at least, the Canadian who wanted to write started with a feeling of detachment from his literary tradition, which existed for him mainly in his school books. He had probably, as said above, been educated in a way that heavily stressed the conceptual and argumentative use of language. Mrs. Fowke shows us how the Indians began with a mythology which included all the main elements of our own. It was, of course, impossible for Canadians to establish any real continuity with it: Indians, like the rest of the country, were seen as nineteenth-century literary conventions. Certain elements in Canadian culture, too, such as the Protestant revolutionary view of history, may have minimized the importance of the oral tradition in ballad and folk song, which seems to have survived best in Catholic communities. In Canada the mythical was simply the "prehistoric" (this word, we are told, is a Canadian coinage),[28] and the writer had to attach himself to his literary tradition deliberately and voluntarily. And though this may be no longer true or necessary, attitudes surviving from an earlier period of isolation still have their influence.

The separation of subject and object is the primary fact of consciousness, for anyone so situated and so educated. Writing for him does not start with a rhythmical movement,[29] or an impetus caught from or encouraged by a group of contemporaries: it starts with reportage, a single mind reacting to what is set over against it. Such a writer does not naturally think metaphorically but descriptively; it seems obvious to him that writing is a form of self-expression dependent on the gathering of a certain amount of experience, granted some inborn sensitivity toward that experience. We note (as does Mr. McPherson) how many Canadian novelists have written only one novel, or only one good novel, how many Canadian poets have written only one good book of poems, generally their first. Even the dream of "the great Canadian novel," the feeling that somebody some day will write a Canadian fictional classic, assumes that whoever does it will do it only once. This is a characteristic of writers dominated by the conception of writing up experiences or observations: nobody has enough experience to keep on writing about it, unless his writing is an incidental commentary on a nonliterary career.

The Canadian writers who have overcome these difficulties and have found their way back to the real headwaters of inspiration are heroic explorers. There are a good many of them, and the evidence of this book is that the Canadian imagination has passed the stage of exploration and has embarked on that of settlement. But it is of course full of the failures as well as the successes of exploration, imaginative voyages to Golconda that froze in the ice, and we can learn something from them too. Why do Canadians write so many historical romances, of what Mr. McPherson calls the rut and thrust variety? One can understand it in Mr. Roper's period: the tendency to melodrama in romance makes it part of a central convention of that time, as Mr. Roper's discerning paragraph on the subject shows. But romances are still going strong in Mr. Pacey's period, and if anything even stronger in Mr. McPherson's. They get a little sexier and more violent as they go on, but the formula remains much the same: so much love-making, so much "research" about antiquities and costume copied off filing cards, more love-making, more filing cards. There is clearly a steady market for this, but the number of writers engaged in it suggests other answers. There is also a related fact, the unusually large number of Canadian popular best-selling fiction writers, from Agnes Fleming through Gilbert Parker to Mazo de la Roche.

In Mr. Roper's chronicle not all the fiction is romance, but nearly all of it is formula-writing. In the books he mentions that I have read I remember much honest and competent work. Some of them did a good deal to form my own infantile imagination, and I could well have fared worse. What there is not, of course, is a recreated view of life, or anything to detach the mind from its customary attitudes. In Mr. Pacey's period we begin to notice a more consistent distinction between the romancer, who stays with established values and usually chooses a subject remote in time from himself, and the realist, who deals with contemporary life, and therefore—it appears to be a therefore—is more serious in intention, more concerned to unsettle a stock response. One tendency culminates in Mazo de la Roche, the other in Morley Callaghan, both professional writers and born story-tellers, though of very different kinds. By Mr. McPherson's period the two tendencies have more widely diverged. One is mainly romance dealing with Canada's past, the other is contemporary realism dealing with what is common to Canada and the rest of the world, like antique and modern furniture stores. One can see something similar in the poetry, a contrast between a romantic tradition closely associated with patriotic and idealistic themes, and a more intellectualized one with a more cosmopolitan bias. This contrast is prominently featured in the first edition of A.J.M. Smith's anthology, *A Book of Canadian Poetry* (1943).

This contrast of the romantic and the realistic, the latter having a moral dignity that the former lacks, reflects the social and conceptual approach to literature already mentioned. Here we are looking at the same question from a different point of view. Literature, we said, is conscious mythology: it creates an autonomous world that gives us an imaginative perspective on the actual one. But there is another kind of mythology, one produced by society itself, the object of which is to persuade us to accept existing social values. "Popular" literature, the kind that is read for relaxation and the quieting of the mind, expresses this social mythology. We all feel a general difference between serious and soothing literature, though I know of no critical rule for distinguishing them, nor is there likely to be one. The same work may belong to both mythologies at once, and in fact the separation between them is largely a perspective of our own revolutionary age.

In many popular novels, especially in the nineteenth century, we feel how strong the desire is on the part of the author to work out his situation within a framework of established social values. Mr. Roper notes that in the success-story formula frequent in such fiction the success is usually "emotional," i.e., the individual fulfils himself within his community. There is nothing hypocritical or cynical about this: the author usually believes very deeply in his values. Moral earnestness and the posing of serious problems are by no means excluded from popular literature, any more than serious literature is excused from the necessity of being entertaining. The difference is in the position of the reader's mind at the end, in whether he is being encouraged to remain within his habitual social responses or whether he is being prodded into making the steep and lonely climb into the imaginative world. This distinction in itself is familiar enough, and all I am suggesting here is that what I have called the garrison mentality is highly favourable to the growth of popular literature in this sense. The role of romance and melodrama in consolidating a social mythology is also not hard to see. In romance the characters tend to be psychological projections, heroes, heroines, villains, father-figures, comic-relief caricatures. The popular romance operates on Freudian principles, releasing sexual and power fantasies without disturbing the anxieties of the superego. The language of melodrama, at once violent and morally conventional, is the appropriate language for this. A subliminal sense of the erotic release in romance may have inspired some of the distrust of novels in nineteenth-century pietistic homes. But even those who preferred stories of real life did not want "realism": that, we learn, was denounced on all sides during the nineteenth century as nasty, prurient, morbid, and foreign. The garrison mentality is that of its officers: it can tolerate only the conservative idealism of its ruling class, which for Canada means the moral and propertied middle class.

The total effect of Canadian popular fiction, whatever incidental merits in it there may be, is that of a murmuring and echoing literary collective unconscious, the rippling of a watery Narcissus world reflecting the imaginative patterns above it. Robertson Davies's *Tempest-Tost* is a sardonic study of the triumph of a social mythology over the imaginative one symbolized by Shakespeare's play. Maturity and individualization, in such a body of writing, are almost the same process. Occasionally a writer is individualized by accident. Thus Susanna Moodie in the Peterborough bush, surrounded by a half-comic, half-sinister rabble that she thinks of indifferently as Yankee, Irish, native, republican, and lower class, is a British army of occupation in herself, a one-woman garrison. We often find too, as in Leacock, a spirit of criticism, even of satire, that is the complementary half of a strong attachment to the mores that provoke the satire. That is, a good deal of what goes on in Mariposa may look ridiculous, but the norms or standards against which it looks ridiculous are provided by Mariposa itself. In Sara Jeannette Duncan there is something else again, as she watches the garrison parade to church in a small Ontario town: "The repressed magnetic excitement in gatherings of familiar faces, fellow-beings bound by the same convention to the same kind of behaviour, is precious in communities where the human interest is still thin and sparse."[30] Here is a voice of genuine detachment, sympathetic but not defensive either of the group or of herself, concerned primarily to understand and to make the reader see. The social group is becoming external to the writer, but not in a way that isolates her from it.

This razor's edge of detachment is naturally rare in Canadian writing, even in this author [Duncan], but as the twentieth century advances and Canadian society takes a firmer grip of its environment, it becomes easier to assume the role of an individual separated in standards and attitudes from the community. When this happens, an ironic or realistic literature becomes fully possible. This new kind of detachment of course often means only that the split between subject and object has become identified with a split between the individual and society. This is particularly likely to happen when the separated individual's point of view is also that of the author, as in the stories of misunderstood genius with which many minor authors are fascinated. According to Mr. Tait this convention was frequent in the plays put on in Hart House during the twenties; it certainly was so in fiction. But some of the most powerful of Canadian novels have been those in which this conflict has been portrayed objectively. Buckler's *The Mountain and the Valley* is a Maritime example, and Sinclair Ross's *As for Me and My House* one from the prairies.

Mr. Conron quotes B.K. Sandwell as saying: "I follow it [society] at a respectful distance . . . far enough away to make it clear that I do not belong to it." It is clear that this is not necessarily any advance on the expression of conventional social values in popular romance. The feeling of detachment from society means only that society has become more complex, and inner tensions have developed in it. We have traced this process already. The question that arises is: once society, along with physical nature, becomes external to the writer, what does he then feel a part of? For rhetorical or assertive writers it is generally a smaller society, the group that agrees with them. But the imaginative writer, though he often begins as a member of a school or group, normally pulls away from it as he develops.

If our general line of thought is sound, the imaginative writer is finding his identity within the world of literature itself. He is withdrawing from what Douglas LePan calls a country without a mythology into the country of mythology, ending where the Indians began. Mr. Tait quotes John Coulter's comment on his play, or libretto, *Deirdre of the Sorrows*: "The art of a Canadian remains . . . the art of the country of his forebears and the old world heritage of myth and legend remains his heritage . . . though the desk on which he writes be Canadian." But the progress may not be a simple matter of forsaking the Canadian for the international, the province for the capital. It may be that when the Canadian writer attaches himself to the world of literature, he discovers, or rediscovers, by doing so, something in his Canadian environment which is more vital and articulate than a desk.

IV

At the heart of all social mythology lies what may be called, because it usually is called, a pastoral myth, the vision of a social ideal. The pastoral myth in its most common form is associated with childhood, or with some earlier social condition—pioneer life, the small town, the *habitant* rooted to his land—that can be identified with childhood. The nostalgia for a world of peace and protection, with a spontaneous response to the nature around it, with a leisure and composure not to be found today, is particularly strong in Canada. It is overpowering in our popular literature, from *Anne of Green Gables* to Leacock's Mariposa, and from *Maria Chapdelaine* to *Jake and the Kid*. It is present in all the fiction that deals with small towns as collections of characters in search of an author. Its influence is strong in the most serious writers: one thinks of Gabrielle Roy, following her *Bonheur d'occasion* with *La petite poule d'eau*. It is the theme of all the essayists who write of fishing and other forms of the simpler life, especially as lived in the past. Mr. Conron quotes MacMechan: "golden days in memory for the enrichment of less happier times to come." It even comes into our official documents—the Massey Report begins, almost as a matter of course, with an idyllic picture of the Canada of fifty years ago, as a point of departure for its investigations.[31] Mr. Bailey speaks of the eighteenth-century Loyalists as looking "to a past that had never existed for comfort and illumination," which suggests that the pastoral myth has been around for some time.

The Indians have not figured so largely in the myth as one might expect, though in some early fiction and drama the noble savage takes the role, as he does to some extent even in the Gothic hero Wacousta. The popularity of Pauline Johnson and Grey Owl, however, shows that the kind of rapport with nature which the Indian symbolizes is central to it. Another form of pastoral myth is the evocation of an earlier period of history which is made romantic by having a more uninhibited expression of passion or virtue or courage attached to it. This of course links the pastoral myth with the vision of vanished grandeur that comes into the novels about the *ancien régime*. In *The Golden Dog* and *The Seats of the Mighty* the forlorn little fortress of seventeenth-century Quebec, sitting in the middle of what Madame de Pompadour called "a few arpents of snow," acquires a theatrical glamour that would do credit to Renaissance Florence.[32] Mr. Klinck gives a most concise summary of the earlier literary romanticizing of this period, and Mr. Pacey studies its later aspects. The two forms of the myth collide on the Plains of Abraham, on the one side a marquis, on the other a Hanoverian commoner tearing himself reluctantly from the pages of Gray's *Elegy*.[33]

Close to the centre of the pastoral myth is the sense of kinship with the animal and vegetable world, which is so prominent a part of the Canadian frontier. I think of an image in Mazo de la Roche's *Delight*, which I am encouraged to revert to because I see that it has also caught Mr. Pacey's eye. Delight Mainprize—I leave it to the connoisseurs of ambiguity to explore the overtones of that name—is said by her creator to be "not much more developed intellectually than the soft-eyed Jersey in the byre." It must be very rarely that a novelist—a wide awake and astute novelist—can call her heroine a cow with such affection, even admiration. But it is consistent with what Mr. Pacey calls her belief in the "superiority of the primitive and the instinctive over the civilized and conventional." The prevalence in Canada of animal stories, in which animals are closely assimilated to human behaviour and emotions, has been noted by Mr. Lucas and Miss McDowell particularly. Conversely, the killing of an animal, as a tragic or ironic symbol, has a peculiar resonance in Canadian poetry, from the moose in Lampman's Long Sault poem to the Christmas slaughter of geese which is the informing theme of James Reaney's *A Suit of Nettles*. More complicated pastoral motifs are conspicuous in Morley Callaghan, who turns continually to the theme of betrayed or victorious innocence—the former in *The Loved and the Lost*, the latter in *Such Is My Beloved*. The Peggy of *The Loved and the Lost*, whose spontaneous affection for Negroes is inspired by a childhood experience and symbolized by a child's toy, is particularly close to our theme.

The theme of Grove's *A Search for America* is the narrator's search for a North American pastoral myth in its genuinely imaginative form, as distinct from its sentimental or socially stereotyped form. The narrator, adrift in the New World without means of support, has a few grotesque collisions with the hustling mercantilism of American life—selling encyclopedias and the like—and gets badly bruised in spirit. He becomes convinced that this America is a false social development which has grown over and concealed the real American social ideal, and tries to grasp the form of this buried society. He wants to become, to reverse Mr. Lucas's clever phrase, a Rousseau and not a Crusoe of his new world. In our terms, he is trying to grasp something of the myth of America, the essential imaginative idea it embodies. He meets, but irritably brushes away, the tawdry and sentimentalized versions of this myth—the cottage away from it all, happy days on the farm, the great open spaces of the west. He goes straight to the really powerful and effective versions: Thoreau's *Walden*, the personality of Lincoln, Huckleberry Finn drifting down the great river. The America that he searches for, he feels, has something to do with these things, though it is not defined much more closely than this.

Grove drops a hint in a footnote near the end that what his narrator is looking for has been abandoned in the United States but perhaps not yet in Canada. This is not our present moral: pastoral myths, even in their genuine forms, do not exist as places. They exist rather in such things as the loving delicacy of perception in Grove's own *Over Prairie Trails* and *The Turn of the Year*. Still, the remark has some importance because it indicates that the conception "Canada" can also become a pastoral myth in certain circumstances. Mr. Daniells, speaking of the nineteenth-century mystique of Canadianism, says, "A world is created, its centre in the Canadian home, its middle distance the loved landscape of Canada, its protecting wall the circle of British institutions . . . a world as centripetal as that of Sherlock Holmes and as little liable to be shaken by irruptions of evil." The myth suggested here is somewhat Virgilian in shape, pastoral serenity serving as a prologue to the swelling act of the imperial theme. Nobody who saw it in that way was a Virgil, however, and it has been of minor literary significance.

We have said that literature creates a detached and autonomous mythology, and that society itself produces a corresponding mythology, to which a good deal of literature belongs. We have found the pastoral myth, in its popular and sentimental social form, to be an idealization of memory, especially childhood memory. But we have also suggested that the same myth exists in a genuinely imaginative form, and have found its influence in some of the best Canadian writers. Our present problem is to see if we can take a step beyond Grove and attempt some characterization of the myth he was looking for, a myth which would naturally have an American context but a particular reference to Canada. The sentimental or nostalgic pastoral myth increases the feeling of separation between subject and object by withdrawing the subject into a fantasy world. The genuine myth, then, would result from reversing this process. Myth starts with the identifying of subject and object, the primary imaginative act of literary creation. It is therefore the most explicitly mythopoeic aspect of Canadian literature that we have to turn to, and we shall find this centred in the poetry rather than the fiction. There are many reasons for this: one is that in poetry there is no mass market to encourage the writer to seek refuge in conventional social formulas.

A striking fact about Canadian poetry is the number of poets who have turned to narrative forms (including closet drama) rather than lyrical ones. The anthologist who confines himself wholly to the lyric will give the impression that Canadian poetry really began with Roberts's *Orion* in 1880. Actually there was a tradition of narrative poetry well established before that (Sangster, Heavysege, Howe, and several others), which continues into the post-Confederation period (Mair, Isabella Crawford, Duvar, besides important narrative works by Lampman and D.C. Scott). It is clear that Pratt's devotion to the narrative represents a deep affinity with the Canadian tradition, although so far as I know (and I think I do know) the affinity was entirely unconscious on his part. I have written about the importance of narrative poetry in Canada elsewhere,[34] and have little new to add here. It has two characteristics that account for its being especially important in Canadian literature. In the first place, it is impersonal. The bald and dry statement is the most effective medium for its treatment of action, and the author, as in the folk song and ballad, is able to keep out of sight or speak as one of a group. In the second place, the natural affinities of poetic narrative are with tragic and ironic themes, not with the more manipulated comic and romantic formulas of prose fiction. Consistently with its impersonal form, tragedy and irony are expressed in the action of the poem rather than in its moods or in the poet's own comment.

We hardly expect the earlier narratives to be successful all through, but if we read them with sympathy and historical imagination, we can see how the Canadian environment has exerted its influence on the poet. The environment, in nineteenth-century Canada, is terrifyingly cold, empty, and vast, where the obvious and immediate sense of nature is the late Romantic one, increasingly affected by Darwinism, of nature red in tooth and claw. We notice the recurrence of such episodes as shipwreck,

Indian massacres, human sacrifices, lumbermen mangled in log-jams, mountain climbers crippled on glaciers, animals screaming in traps, the agonies of starvation and solitude—in short, the "shutting out of the whole moral creation."[35] Human suffering, in such an environment, is a by-product of a massive indifference which, whatever else it may be, is not morally explicable. What confronts the poet is a moral silence deeper than any physical silence, though the latter frequently symbolizes the former, as in the poem of Pratt that is explicitly called *Silences*.

The nineteenth-century Canadian poet can hardly help being preoccupied with physical nature; the nature confronting him presents him with the riddle of unconsciousness, and the riddle of unconsciousness in nature is the riddle of death in man. Hence his central emotional reaction is bound to be elegiac and sombre, full of loneliness and fear, or at least wistful and nostalgic, hugging, like Roberts, a "darling illusion" [*Tantramar Revisited*, l. 63]. In Carman, Roberts, and D.C. Scott there is a rhetorical strain that speaks in a confident, radio-announcer's voice about the destiny of Canada, the call of the open road, or the onward and upward march of progress. As none of their memorable poetry was written in this voice, we may suspect that they turned to it partly for reassurance. Mr. Daniells remarks of D.C. Scott: "The imprecision of his views is in part the result of having nothing specific to oppose." The riddle of unconsciousness in nature is one that no moralizing or intellectualizing can answer. More important, it is one that irony cannot answer:

> The gray shape with the paleolithic face
> Was still the master of the longitudes.

The conclusion of Pratt's *Titanic* is almost documentary: it is as stripped of irony as it is of moralizing. The elimination of irony from the poet's view of nature makes that view pastoral—a cold pastoral, but still a pastoral. We have only physical nature and a rudimentary human society, not strong enough yet to impose the human forms of tragedy and irony on experience.

The same elegiac and lonely tone continues to haunt the later poetry. Those who in the twenties showed the influence of the death-and-resurrection myth of Eliot, notably Leo Kennedy and A.J.M. Smith, were also keeping to the centre of a native tradition. The use of the Eliot myth was sometimes regarded as a discovery of myth, as Mr. Beattie notes, but of course the earlier poets had not only used the same myth, but were equally aware of its origins in Classical poetry, as Carman's *Sappho* indicates. The riddle of the unconscious may be expressed by a symbol such as the agonies of a dying animal, or it may be treated simply as an irreducible fact of existence. But it meets us everywhere: I pick up Margaret Avison and there it is, in a poem called *Identity*:

> But on this sheet of beryl, this high sea,
> Scalded by the white unremembering glaze,
> No wisps disperse. This is the icy pole.
> The presence here is single, worse than soul,
> Pried loose forever out of nights and days
> And birth and death
> And all the covering wings.

In such an environment, we may well wonder how the sentimental pastoral myth ever developed at all. But of course there are the summer months, and a growing settlement of the country that eventually began to absorb at least eastern Canada into the north temperate zone. Pratt's Newfoundland background helped to keep his centre of gravity in the elegiac, but when he began to write the feeling of the mindless hostility of nature had largely retreated to the prairies, where, as Mr. Pacey shows, a fictional realism developed, closely related to this feeling in mood and imagery. The Wordsworthian sense of nature as a teacher is apparent as early as Mrs. Traill, in whom Mr. Lucas notes a somewhat selective approach to the subject reminiscent of Miss Muffet. As the sentimental pastoral myth takes shape, its imaginative counterpart takes shape too, the other, gentler, more idyllic half of the myth that has made the pastoral itself a central literary convention. In this version nature, though still full of awfulness and mystery, is the visible representative of an order that man has violated, a spiritual unity that the intellect murders to dissect. This form of the myth is more characteristic of the second phase of Canadian social development, when the conflict of man and nature is expanding into a triangular conflict of nature, society, and individual. Here the individual tends to ally himself with nature against society. A very direct and haunting statement of this attitude occurs in John Robins's *Incomplete Anglers*: "I can approach a solitary tree with pleasure, a cluster of trees with joy, and a forest with rapture; I must approach a solitary man with caution, a group of men with trepidation, and a nation of men with terror."[36] The same theme also forms part of the final cadences of Hugh MacLennan's *The Watch That Ends the Night*: "In the early October of that year, in the cathedral hush of a Quebec

Indian summer with the lake drawing into its mirror the fire of the maples, it came to me that to be able to love the mystery surrounding us is the final and only sanction of human existence."

It is the appearance of this theme in D.C. Scott which moves Mr. Daniells to call Scott one of the "ancestral voices" of the Canadian imagination. It is much stronger and more continuous in Lampman, who talks less than his contemporaries and strives harder for the uniting of subject and object in the imaginative experience. This union takes place in the contact of individual poet and a landscape uninhabited except for Wordsworth's "huge and mighty forms" that are manifested by the union:

> Nay more, I think some blessed power
> Hath brought me wandering idly here.   [*Heat*, ll. 45–6]

Again as in Wordsworth, this uniting of individual mind and nature is an experience from which human society, as such, is excluded. Thus when the poet finds a "blessed power" in nature it is the society he leaves behind that tends to become the God-forsaken wilderness. Usually this society is merely trivial or boring; once, in the unforgettable *City of the End of Things*, it becomes demonic.

The two aspects of the pastoral tradition we have been tracing are not inconsistent with each other; they are rather complementary. At one pole of experience there is a fusion of human life and the life in nature; at the opposite pole is the identity of the sinister and terrible elements in nature with the death-wish in man. In Pratt's *The Truant* the "genus *homo*" confronts the "great Panjandrum" of nature who is also his own death-wish: the great Panjandrum is the destructive force in the Nazis and in the Indians who martyred Brébeuf, the capacity in man that enables him to be deliberately cruel. Irving Layton shows us not only the cruelty but the vulgarity of the death-wish consciousness: as it has no innocence, it cannot suffer with dignity, as animals can; it loses its own imaginary soul by despising the body:

> Listen: for all his careful fuss,
> Will this cold one ever deceive us?
>   Self-hating, he rivets a glittering wall;
> Impairs it by a single pebble
> And loves himself for that concession.   [*Maurer: Twin Heads*, ll. 6–10]

Conclusion to the First Edition of Literary History of Canada

We spoke earlier of a civilization conquering the landscape and imposing an alien and abstract pattern on it. As this process goes on, the writers, the poets especially, tend increasingly to see much of this process as something that is human but still dehumanized, leaving man's real humanity a part of the nature that he continually violates but is still inviolate.

Reading through any good collection of modern Canadian poems or stories, we find every variety of tone, mood, attitude, technique, and setting. But there is a certain unity of impression one gets from it, an impression of gentleness and reasonableness, seldom difficult or greatly daring in its imaginative flights, the passion, whether of love or anger, held in check by something meditative. It is not easy to put the feeling in words, but if we turn to the issue of the *Tamarack Review* that was devoted to West Indian literature [no. 14], or to the Hungarian poems translated by Canadians in the collection *The Plough and the Pen*,[37] we can see by contrast something of both the strength and the limitations of the Canadian writers. They too have lived, if not in Arcadia, at any rate in a land where empty space and the pervasiveness of physical nature have impressed a pastoral quality on their minds. From the deer and fish in Isabella Crawford's *The Canoe* to the frogs and toads in Layton, from the white narcissus of Knister to the night-blooming cereus of Reaney, everything that is central in Canadian writing seems to be marked by the imminence of the natural world. The sense of this imminence organizes the mythology of Jay Macpherson; it is the sign in which Canadian soldiers conquer Italy in Douglas LePan's *The Net and the Sword*; it may be in the foreground, as in Alden Nowlan, or in the background, as in Birney; but it is always there.

To go on with this absorbing subject would take us into another book: *A Literary Criticism of Canada*, let us say. Here we can only refer the reader to Mr. Beattie's able guidance and sum up the present argument emblematically, with two famous primitive American paintings. One is *Historical Monument of the American Republic*, by Erastus Salisbury Field. Painted in 1876 for the centennial of the Revolution, it is an encyclopedic portrayal of events in American history, against a background of soaring towers, with clouds around their spires, and connected by railway bridges. It is a prophetic vision of the skyscraper cities of the future, of the tremendous technological will to power of our time and the civilization it has built, a civilization now gradually imposing a uniformity of culture and habits of life all over the globe. Because the United States is the most powerful centre of this civilization, we often say, when referring to its uniformity, that the world is becoming Americanized. But of course America itself is being Americanized in this sense, and the uniformity imposed on New Delhi and Singapore, or on Toronto and Vancouver, is no greater than that imposed on New Orleans or Baltimore. A nation so huge and so productive, however, is deeply committed to this growing technological uniformity, even though many tendencies may pull in other directions. Canada has participated to the full in the wars, economic expansions, technological achievements, and internal stresses of the modern world. Canadians seem well adjusted to the new world of technology and very efficient at handling it. Yet in the Canadian imagination there are deep reservations to this world as an end of life in itself, and the political separation of Canada has helped to emphasize these reservations in its literature.

English Canada began with the influx of defeated Tories after the American Revolution, and so, in its literature, with a strong antirevolutionary bias. The Canadian radicalism that developed in opposition to Loyalism was not a revival of the American revolutionary spirit, but a quite different movement, which had something in common with the Toryism it opposed: one thinks of the Tory and radical elements in the social vision of William Cobbett, who also finds a place in the Canadian record. A revolutionary tradition is liable to two defects: to an undervaluing of history and an impatience with law, and we have seen how unusually strong the Canadian attachment to law and history has been. The attitude to things American represented by Haliburton is not, on the whole, hostile: it would be better described as noncommittal, as when Sam Slick speaks of a Fourth of July as "a splendid spectacle; fifteen millions of freemen and three millions of slaves a-celebratin' the birthday of liberty."[38] The strong romantic tradition in Canadian literature has much to do with its original conservatism. When more radical expressions begin to creep into Canadian writing, as in the poetry of Alexander McLachlan, there is still much less of the assumption that freedom and national independence are the same thing, or that the mercantilist Whiggery which won the American Revolution is necessarily the only emancipating force in the world. In some Canadian writers of our own time—I think particularly of Earle Birney's *Trial of a City* and the poetry of F.R. Scott—there is an opposition, not to the democratic but to the oligarchic tendencies in North American civilization, not to liberal but to laissez-faire political doctrine. Perhaps it is a little easier to see these distinctions from the vantage-point of a smaller country, even one which has, in its material culture, made the "American way of life" its own.

The other painting is the much earlier *The Peaceable Kingdom*, by Edward Hicks, painted around 1830. Here, in the background, is a treaty between the Indians and the Quaker settlers under Penn. In the foreground is a group of animals, lions, tigers, bears, oxen, illustrating the prophecy of Isaiah about the recovery of innocence in nature [11:6–9]. Like the animals of the Douanier Rousseau, they stare past us with a serenity that transcends consciousness. It is a pictorial emblem of what Grove's narrator was trying to find under the surface of America: the reconciliation of man with man and of man with nature: the mood of Thoreau's Walden retreat, of Emily Dickinson's garden, of Huckleberry Finn's raft, of the elegies of Whitman, whose reaction to Canada is also recorded in this book. This mood is closer to the haunting vision of a serenity that is both human and natural which we have been struggling to identify in the Canadian tradition. If we had to characterize a distinctive emphasis in that tradition, we might call it a quest for the peaceable kingdom.

The writers of the last decade, at least, have begun to write in a world which is post-Canadian, as it is post-American, post-British, and post everything except the world itself. There are no provinces in the empire of airplane and television, and no physical separation from the centres of culture, such as they are. Sensibility is no longer dependent on a specific environment or even on sense experience itself. A remark of Mr. Beattie's about Robert Finch illustrates a tendency which is affecting literature as well as painting: "the interplay of sense impressions is so complicated, and so exhilarating, that the reader receives no sense impression at all." Marshall McLuhan speaks of the world as reduced to a single gigantic primitive village, where everything has the same kind of immediacy. He speaks of the fears that so many intellectuals have of such a world, and remarks amiably: "Terror is the normal state of any oral society, for in it everything affects everything all the time."[39] The Canadian spirit, to personify it as a single being dwelling in the country from the early voyages to the present, might well, reading this sentence, feel that this was where he came in. In other words, new conditions give the old ones a new importance, as what vanishes in one form reappears in another. The moment that the peaceable kingdom has been completely obliterated by its rival is the moment when it comes into the foreground again, as the eternal frontier, the first thing that the writer's imagination must deal with. Pratt's *The Truant*, already referred to, foreshadows the poetry of the future, when physical nature has retreated to outer space and only individual and society are left as effective factors in the imagination. But the central conflict, and the moods in which it is fought out, are still unchanged.

One gets very tired, in old-fashioned biographies, of the dubious embryology that examines a poet's ancestry and wonders if a tendency to fantasy in him could be the result of an Irish great-grandmother. A reader may feel the same unreality in efforts to attach Canadian writers to a tradition made up of earlier writers whom they may not have read or greatly admired. I have felt this myself whenever I have written about Canadian literature. Yet I keep coming back to the feeling that there does seem to be such a thing as an imaginative continuum, and that writers are conditioned in their attitudes by their predecessors, or by the cultural climate of their predecessors, whether there is conscious influence or not. Again, nothing can give a writer's experience and sensitivity any form except the study of literature itself. In this study the great classics, "monuments of its own magnificence,"[40] and the best contemporaries have an obvious priority. The more such monuments or such contemporaries there are in a writer's particular cultural traditions, the more fortunate he is; but he needs those traditions in any case. He needs them most of all when what faces him seems so new as to threaten his identity. For present and future writers in Canada and their readers, what is important in Canadian literature, beyond the merits of the individual works in it, is the inheritance of the entire enterprise. The writers featured in this book have identified the habits and attitudes of the country, as Fraser and Mackenzie have identified its rivers. They have also left an imaginative legacy of dignity and of high courage.

54

Foreword to *The Prospect of Change*

1965

From The Prospect of Change: Proposals for Canada's Future, *ed. Abraham Rotstein (Toronto: McGraw-Hill, 1965), xiii–xv. This book is a collection of essays by professors at the University of Toronto who met regularly, as the University League for Social Reform, to suggest new approaches to the social and economic problems of Canada. The essays Frye refers to are as follows: David P. Gauthier, Department of Philosophy, "Alignment for Peace"; Ramsay Cook, Department of History, "Quebec: The Ideology of Survival"; Joseph E. Laycock, School of Social Work, "New Directions for Social Welfare Policy"; Melville H. Watkins, Department of Political Economy, "Canadian Economic Policy: A Proposal"; Hugo McPherson, Department of English, University College, "Gilding the Muses: The Canada Council"; and Ian Drummond, Department of Political Economy, "Some Economic Issues in Educational Expansion."*

This book comes at a strategic time, when Canadians, like everyone else, are faced with immanent and unescapable changes in the habits of their lives. These changes are so revolutionary that they force us into re-examining the assumptions underlying those habits, or, as I tend to say, being a literary critic, to re-examine the myths which make up our customary vision of life. In such a world it is irresponsible to call oneself *a* conservative or *a* liberal—that is, a person devoted to a specific aspect of life—for every responsible citizen has to be both at once. He must be concerned with finding means of adaptation to change, and therefore he must also be concerned with finding the pattern of continuity at the centre of change. The old metaphors of "left" and "right," though still used, are becoming dangerously misleading. A generation ago, the "intellectual" got himself a bad name as a social critic, because at that time some intellectuals, living in a simplified Euclidean world remote from responsibility, advocated extreme "left" or "right" positions. Their motives were masochistic, as such positions required the leadership of profoundly anti-intellectual people. In our day there is wider recognition of the fact that such a leader as Barry Goldwater, who is said to represent a consistently "conservative" position and to present voters with a "real choice," is only a nuisance.

That is, he is a nuisance on the presidential level. Nowadays consistent political lines are becoming increasingly parochial, at most a pressure group within a larger unit. The more important the statesman's position, the more exclusively he is devoted to reconciliation, to containing conflict within and lessening tension without. The American electorate's rejection of Goldwater, as of Wallace earlier,[1] was not a rejection of right or left policies, but of the conception of the militant leader. The genuine leader of our time is what the United Church calls a "moderator," whether his position in the colour spectrum of personality is at the Khrushchev or at the Eisenhower end. Pope John is the most impressive example of this contemporary type of irenic leader.[2] British politics are said to be more dialectical than ours, but this statement becomes less true with every British election, while the reverse process, despite NDP hopes, is not occurring at all. And, as Mr. Gauthier argues, the only creative international role for Canada is a moderating one, gathering to a greatness as the ooze of oil, to misquote Hopkins,[3] greasing the wheels of the greater powers to keep them from grinding directly on each other.

The authors of this book are intellectuals of a new generation, actively concerned with the specific problems of continuity and change, which they see as a single process. They are aware of the dangers in the two extremes of flight from these problems: the introverted effort to retain identity and resist change, and the tendency to dissolve identity into a lonely crowd, where all lines of action are prompted by conformity or rumour. If we visit a great city with a long history, say London, we find it a mere mass of people and buildings sprawled over most of southeast England. But at its heart in the City there are a few traces, and place names ending in "gate," which remind us that it was once a small, clearly defined, walled town. Those who are fond of London or feel identified with it usually build a mental wall around a relatively small part of it. All identity has a boundary, whether we call it Canada or the individual, and our social mythology keeps this walled and bounded unit as its central structure.

Mr. Cook shows how some nineteenth-century French Canadian intellectuals, inspired by literary clichés and religious anxieties, adopted the extreme introverted motto, "emparons-nous du sol," a metaphor from vegetation which for mobile animals suggests rather the fable of the ostrich, and so left their successors unprepared for the social revolution that came upon them. The statements of the more extreme separatists today are a cultural lag from the intellectuals of the last generation who urged that Fascism was the wave of the future because it subordinated all change to a nationalistic identity. What the present book lacks, it seems to me, is a corresponding study of the ideology of survival in English Canada, the heritage of nineteenth-century myths that obstruct the contemporary English Canadian outlook. The ideology itself meets us everywhere. Thus, as Mr. Laycock shows, we tend to meet social welfare questions with a myth of a working and beleaguered "pioneer" society, where the minimum care should be taken of the handicapped or unfortunate, but where any effort to give the unemployed a genuine first-class citizenship inspires panic and uneasiness. The "average Canadian" whose arguments are demolished by Mr. Watkins and his economist colleagues assumes the necessity of a protecting tariff wall around the identity of "Canada" as the only thing that will prevent its dissolution into the United States. The same "pioneering" myth of a small society of primary producers establishes, as Mr. McPherson shows, unconscious priorities in our minds in which the creative arts and the more disinterested forms of scholarship occupy the place of peripheral frills. We meet educational changes, Mr. Drummond shows, by transferring the pioneering-society myth to the conception of a small group of professional students who will form the elite corps of our "mental resources." And so on. If I were reviewing the book, I could carry this point much further, but my task here is merely to point out how important and useful a book it is and then get out of its way.

It is possible that what we think of as the centenary of Confederation may turn out to be our genuine Confederation, a period of spiritual rebirth in response to the central social fact of our time: that man must unite, not divide, because he simply will not survive in a state of radical disunity. Technology of course helps to unite the world: we cannot take off in a jet plane and expect a wholly different way of life in the place where the plane lands. But technology in itself does not distinguish unity from uniformity. This distinction is the great mental achievement that democracy has created for the modern world: the realization that identity cannot be preserved either by cutting oneself off from others or by dissolving oneself in others, but only by the flexibility of a larger group where there are great variations of character, and sharp differences of opinion and emphasis, yet all contained within the sense of a common heritage and a common destiny.

55

A Poet and a Legend

June 1965

From Varsity Graduate, *11 (June 1965): 65–9. Reprinted in* Vic Report, *7 (Summer 1979): 6–7. The* Graduate *was belatedly noting the opening of the E.J. Pratt memorial room (see no. 52) "early this academic year."*

Everybody who knew Ned Pratt misses him greatly now he is gone, and it is natural to feel that his passing is the end of an era. But there was no era: there was only Ned: a kind of force of nature that could have existed at any time, though it can only exist once. Everybody knew, or thought he knew, who Ned was: a genial, rather simple soul who loved giving parties, who was incompetent at all practical affairs, from car-driving to committee-sitting, who was as absent-minded as poets and professors are supposed to be, who never failed to respond to a bum with a hard-luck story, who had an endless appetite for good stories and wrote a good many poems that were good stories too.

Well, he was like this in some ways, but one could describe him very differently and still be accurate. He was a scholar who had reached an impressive level of competence in three disciplines: theology, psychology, and English literature. He wrote a book on St. Paul which included an exhaustive analysis of Paul's language;[1] he was a demonstrator in psychology who brought Wundtian and Jamesian conceptions into his poetry[2] (one of the many things to regret about the recent sudden death of Professor Irving was that he never completed an illuminating essay that he had in mind on Pratt's use of psychological conceptions).[3] He was an erudite student of literature, and literary echoes and allusions came effortlessly from him. Each of his major poems was also a work of scholarship, carefully documented by research both theoretical and practical. His themes and moods, too, were often lonely, brooding, bitter ones, full of the pointless cruelty of both man and nature, of man's capacity for suffering and endurance, of the agonized questionings that shatter the comfortable words of religion, of the great achievements of man that vanish into the past with no trace left of them.

How does one put these two Pratts together? Yeats has a theory that poets adopt a "mask," and write poetry that is as different from their ordinary personalities as it can be.[4] And to some extent there was, in Ned's life at Victoria College, a dramatic reversal of his earlier life in Newfoundland, where his poetic imagination had taken shape. In the fishing villages of Newfoundland men fought for their food at the risk of their lives; they spent winters eating monotonously and not enough; anything in the way of gracious living was a prohibitive luxury. I am unlikely to forget the moment when, in the first year of our marriage, Ned encountered my wife and me on the street and said, with his blue eyes gleaming: "I'm going to buy you a great big steak!" Nobody but Ned, with a background of Newfoundland life and many years of living on very little to get through college, would have expressed so much affection so directly in terms of food. Ned dramatized, for all his friends and for the whole university, the conception of the symposium, the intimate party where food and drink served the interests of jokes and good stories, and where, much more important, jokes and good stories served the interests of the lively but serious talk, the flow of ideas, which was what he really wanted from his parties. In Newfoundland he was filled with the sense of the purposelessness of nature: the sea endlessly beating and wearing down the rocks, the great icebergs floating down from the Arctic and melting into the water, the storms that destroyed human life without either malice or pity. Something of this gave him the capacity to live in a pure present moment: to meet him, however casually, was to be accepted completely for that moment. His eyes never strayed over one's shoulder to look for someone else more interesting or important; and his occasional absent-mindedness was the result of the fact that his mind, unlike most of ours, was not continually revolving around his watch.

There were some contrivances in Ned's life, perhaps. I think he was willing to caricature himself, to give people the impression that he was much more simple-minded than he actually was, in order to carry on his own work undisturbed. One has to resort to such devices, in a modern university, if one is to concentrate on the primary work of teaching and

A Poet and a Legend

writing, avoiding the mazes and meanders that practical sense is apt to wander in. In the year of his retirement he turned up unexpectedly at a meeting of the Graduate Department of English (he hated graduate teaching), and sat through three hours and a half of petitions and what not, and then, under "further business," announced that this was undoubtedly his last meeting of the Graduate Department, and therefore—at which point he produced a bottle of rye. It was a typical gesture, but he was also reminding us of a certain sense of proportion. Of course no one can maintain such an attitude consistently without having it become a part of oneself. Ned's innocence was as genuine as anything could be, and he was the most uncalculating of men, yet a hidden and deeply calculating wisdom inside him deliberately chose that innocence. I suppose I am saying only that he could have been a great many other things if he had wanted to be.

There was a mask, then: there was a poet and there was a personality, and they were a contrast. But there was only one man, a man of such complete and obvious integrity that it never occurred to anybody to ask why the author of *The Witches' Brew* should have spent his entire career teaching in a Methodist college. The point at which the personality turned into the poet was the point at which the sincerity of his kindliness and good will suddenly became sincerity of craftsmanship. Nobody ever confused him about the difference: that is, nobody ever took a bad poem to Ned and got it called a good poem because he liked the poet. Ned himself had been discovered by Pelham Edgar, who, if somewhat aloof in his social manner, was constantly looking for and helping out impoverished literary talent. Ned would help, but he was not a discoverer of others' talents: he set a standard, and others came to him. I remember him almost pleading with an undergraduate: "But can't you *see* what awful drivel this is?" Well, he couldn't, but if he had he might have understood how the two halves of Ned fitted together. Ned Pratt is the only figure in Canadian literature, so far, great enough to establish a personal legend. And the legend was unique, because it had the poet behind it. There have been, on this campus and elsewhere, many genial hosts and absent-minded and lovable professors, but only one in whom the light of that kind of genius shone through.

56

Edwin John Pratt

June 1965

Presented at the Royal Society of Canada's meeting of June 1965. From Proceedings of the Royal Society of Canada, 4th series, 3 (1965): 161–5.

Edwin John Pratt, C.M.G., M.A., B.D., Ph.D., LL.D., D.C.L., D.Litt., F.R.S.C., Professor Emeritus of English at Victoria College in the University of Toronto, and distinguished poet, died after a protracted illness on April 26, 1964.

Pratt was born at Western Bay, Newfoundland, on February 4, 1882 (this is the correct date, although on his authority it was often given as 1883). His preparatory education was obtained in St. John's, and after a few years of teaching he entered Victoria College in the Class of 1911, as a church student. After he was graduated, he was ordained in the Methodist Church in 1913, and did graduate work in theology. His thesis, which according to the rules then obtaining was published at his own expense, was on the eschatology of St. Paul,[1] though it is less remarkable for its treatment of eschatology than for its sensitive analysis of the Pauline vocabulary, the evidence of a poet's interest. He then turned his attention to psychology, and was a lecturer in the Department of Psychology in the University of Toronto from 1913 to 1919. In 1920 he was appointed, through the influence of Dr. Pelham Edgar, to the Department of English at Victoria College. He remained with that department until his retirement in 1952, when he became professor emeritus. He was married in 1918 to Viola Whitney, and his daughter, Claire, was included with his wife in the dedication to his *Collected Poems*.

It will be seen from this that his apprenticeship was a lengthy one: he was over forty when *Newfoundland Verse* appeared in 1923. Although he wrote many fine lyrics, he was primarily a narrative poet, and chose themes that required a good deal of scholarly research, not only into historical sources but also into vocabulary and phrasing. With *The Witches' Brew* (1926) he developed both his sense of narrative structure and the broad humour that made it easy for him to swing from light to serious verse with no essential change of style. *Titans* (1926), perhaps his best-known work, consists of two narrative poems, *The Cachalot*, a fine description of a whale hunt, and *The Great Feud*, a fantasy in a vein that would now be called science fiction. *The Iron Door* (1927), commemorating the death of his mother, recaptured his earlier religious interest, and *The Roosevelt and the Antinoe* (1930) and *The Titanic* (1935) were stories of shipwreck that brought out his expert knowledge of the sea and seafaring, and his sombre preoccupation with the destructive indifference of nature pitted against the courage of man. *Fable of the Goats* (1937), not reprinted in the second edition of his collected works, shows fantasy expanding into political satire, which became more and more prominent in his work after the rise of Hitler. *Many Moods* (1932) and *Still Life* (1943) contain most of his best lyrics. *Brébeuf and His Brethren* (1940) is the story of the martyrdom of Jesuit missionaries at the hands of the Iroquois, and established Pratt as not simply Canada's leading poet, which he had been ever since *Newfoundland Verse*, but as her most popular poet and as a kind of unofficial poet laureate. *Dunkirk* (1941) was evidence of his willingness to accept the responsibilities of being a public poet, responding to and interpreting contemporary events, in contrast to the poets of "still life," who avoid such themes. The first edition of his *Collected Poems* appeared in 1944; the American edition (1945) included an admiring preface by William Rose Benet. *Behind the Log* (1947) told the story of a Canadian convoy running a gauntlet of enemy submarine action on its way to Murmansk during the war, and *Towards the Last Spike* (1952) returned to Canadian history and dealt with the building of the Canadian Pacific Railway. The second edition of his *Collected Poems* appeared in 1958. Around the time of the first edition there began the long series of honours that were showered on him, including the degrees listed above, three Governor-General's awards, the Canada Council Medal, and the Royal Society's Lorne Pierce Medal in 1940.

Pratt is generally acknowledged to be Canada's greatest poet in English, and is extremely popular in his own country: he has been extensively prescribed for high school reading and has thus introduced a great number of young people to their first poetic experience. At the same time he is still not well known outside Canada. This is partly the result of his fondness for narrative and for his relatively unfashionable use of conventional metres, such as octosyllabic couplets and blank verse. But it is also true that he is in a peculiar way an interpreter of the Canadian imagination, and is most readily intelligible within his own context. He deals with such themes as the closely knit and beleaguered social group engaged in shipwreck or labour construction or rescue, with the immense size and strength of nature and its amoral relation to human society, and with those primordial human virtues that are in the near vicinity of heroism. These themes are those appropriate to an imagination growing up in a huge, thinly settled country and a formidable climate. He is a "Dionysian" poet, concerned with energy, courage, exuberance, unquenchable life, even, by way of parody, drunkenness, and belongs to a nation more remarkable for the energy of its conquest of its environment than for the discipline of its culture. Yet there is a breadth of scope and perspective, much of it derived from the religious strain in his development, which prevents his themes from becoming merely historical. In such poems as *The Truant*, *The Depression Ends*, and *The Highway*, we can see that the sense of the indifference of nature never cheapens into pessimism, nor his sense of the indomitable courage and endurance of man into cliché. He may be popular but he is never, as some popular poets are, anti-intellectual, and he stands for the mental as well as the physical exuberance of Canadian life.

He is also the only figure in Canadian literature in English, so far, great enough to establish a personal legend. The legend was one of boundless generosity and kindliness, of a love for parties and *bonhomie* that was famous beyond his personal orbit. He did love giving parties, but not for their own sake: his friends felt that they belonged to a special society that he had done much to create. And his generosity was not simply that, but the expression of something infinitely rarer: a genuine enthusiasm for human life and personality, and a sense of the reality of love.

57

Silence in the Sea

1 March 1968

From the booklet Silence in the Sea *(St. John's: Memorial University of Newfoundland, 1969). Reprinted in BG, 181–97, and in* E.J. Pratt, *ed. David G. Pitt (Toronto: Ryerson, 1969), 124–38; a few portions reprinted in* Modern Commonwealth Literature, *ed. John H. Ferres and Martin Tucker (New York: Ungar, 1977), 333–4. A typescript is in NFF, 1988, box 2, file bb. This was the first in an annual series of Pratt Lectures founded by Memorial University in 1968 to honour Pratt, the subject each year to be some aspect of modern poetry.*

I

It is a genuine pleasure, and of course a great privilege, to inaugurate this series of annual lectures in honour of E.J. Pratt. As I understand that it is intended to devote the series to modern poetry in general, it seems logical to speak in this opening lecture about Pratt, but about Pratt in the context of modern poetry, and in the further context of the relation of modern poetry to modern civilization.

Pratt's life, like an ellipse, revolved around two centres. One centre was where I am, in Victoria College in the University and city of Toronto. The other centre was of course where you are, in southeastern Newfoundland. I shall start with my centre, and then try to establish the connection with yours.

The fact that so many important modern poets are professional men as well—Eliot a banker and publisher, Williams a doctor, Stevens an insurance executive—suggests that the ability to write poetry often goes with an unusual ability to organize one's time and social schedule. Similarly

Pratt was in a university, not as a "writer in residence," but as a full-time teacher and scholar, with the same load of graduate and undergraduate teaching as any other colleague of his seniority, and he had come into English after completing graduate degrees in theology and psychology. It is true that his erudition, his love of technical language, and the careful research he did for each of his long narratives, are presented in a humorous and sometimes deprecating way. The lumbering polysyllables of *The Great Feud* remind us of Wyndham Lewis's remark that writers, unless they are bluffing, use their full vocabularies only for comic purposes. Nevertheless he is one of our scholarly poets. It is also true that Pratt diligently cultivated an image of himself as an incompetent and hopelessly absent-minded duffer. This is what poets and professors are popularly supposed to be, and so the image was accepted by those who did not notice that he was for years carrying on, quite without secretarial assistance, a formidable teaching, speaking, and social schedule, in addition to his writing. The reason for the duffer image was that it enabled him to escape the vast accumulation of committee and paper work (or pseudo-work) which causes the real fatigue in the modern university. In the background of Victoria was the city of Toronto itself, where he carried on his legendary parties and golf games. And Toronto, according to Morley Callaghan, who should know, is a good place for a writer to work: he can have all the friends he likes, but there is something in the Canadian reserve that allows him to write without feeling that anyone is breathing down his neck.

I have often been asked why I went into English teaching, with a second half of the question, "when there were better things you might have done," sometimes being obviously suppressed. But no one who knew the teachers I had at Victoria: Pelham Edgar, Pratt himself, and J.D. Robins, would be in the least surprised at any student's wanting to pursue the careers they were so brilliant an advertisement for. This extraordinary trio had two qualities in common. One was an unusually fresh and detached interest in the contemporary literary scene. I say unusually, because such an interest could by no means be taken for granted among English professors in the nineteen-twenties. As few contemporary writers were on any course, this often meant digression and self-interruption in order to mention them at all, which is good testimony to the genuineness of the interest. But Robins would interrupt a lecture on the ballad to read us a story by Hemingway—not a household word among Canadian undergraduates in 1929—and Edgar would digress from Shakespeare to tell us something about the narrative techniques of Virginia Woolf. Pratt was a more conventional teacher, but any interested student could get vast stores of information about contemporary poetry out of him. And I say detached, because at a time when many professors were still telling their students that Joyce and D.H. Lawrence were degenerates wallowing in muck, these three would discuss them seriously and (considering that Joyce and Lawrence were by no means favourite authors of theirs) sympathetically. What they also had in common was a keen and generous (often very practically generous, as many could testify) interest in younger Canadian writers, and a desire to do what they could to foster the creative talent around them.

What they did not have in common was a set of scholarly interests that complemented one another in a way very profitable for their students, Pratt's knowledge of modern poetry being rounded out by Edgar's knowledge of modern fiction. I doubt if I should really have got to appreciate Pratt properly if it had not been for Robins. Robins' special fields were the ballad and oral literature, along with folk tales and popular literature in that orbit, and Old English. This combination of interests was not an accident: through him I began to understand something of the curious affinity between the spirit of Canadian poetry, up to and including Pratt, and the spirit of Anglo-Saxon culture. In both the incongruity between a highly sophisticated imported culture and a bleakly primitive physical environment is expressed by familiar, even ready-made, moral and religious formulas which raise more questions than they answer. And what I think would have fascinated me in Pratt's poetry, even if I had never known him, is the way in which, unlike any other modern poet I know, he takes on so many of the characteristics of the poet of an oral and preliterate society, of the kind that lies immediately behind the earliest English poetry. There was no reason for Pratt to be this kind of poet except the peculiar influence of his Newfoundland and Canadian environment on him: I am quite sure that he was unconscious of this aspect of his work.

In an oral culture, which has to depend so much on memory, the poet is the teacher, the one who remembers. (I am speaking here of the professional oral poet; there are of course other kinds.) It is he who knows the traditions of his people, its great heroic legends, the names of its kings, its proverbial philosophy, its rudimentary sciences in which there is still a great deal of magic, the stories and myths of its gods, the details of correct ritual in religious and social life, the calendar with its lucky and unlucky days, the mysteries of taboo and the complexities of family and class relationships. The poet knows these things because verse, by which I mean poetry with a relatively simple metrical or alliterative structure, is the obvious way of organizing words so that verbal information can be easily remembered. The fact that names of Anglo-Saxon kings so often begin with the same letter has, or had originally, much to do with Old English alliterative verse. Such a poet is a profoundly impersonal poet. He does not write love poetry or cultivate his private emotions; he hardly thinks of himself as a personality separate from his public. Homer, and the surviving poems of the heroic age of the North, give us some notion of what the vast corpus of oral poetry, lost because not written down, must have been like. The name of Homer, along with more legendary names, survived for centuries as symbols of a remote past in which the poet had a central social function from which he has since been dispossessed.

As time goes on, and literature assumes different functions, we may come to feel rather condescending about this early function of poetry; but poets and readers alike impoverish their literary experience if they underestimate it. W.H. Auden remarks that if we really *like* lists and catalogues in poetry, such as the roll-call of ships in the second book of the *Iliad*, that liking is probably the sign of a serious interest in poetry.[1] This principle, which so obviously applies to, for instance, Whitman, could also be applied to such catalogue features in Pratt as the brands of liquor in *The Witches' Brew*. Similarly, Pratt has a primitive sense of the responsibility of the poet for telling the great stories of his people. At first his stories are typical stories, like *The Roosevelt and the Antinoe* or *The Cachalot*; then they become such central stories as the martyrdom of the Jesuits and the building of the Canadian Pacific Railway, to which, most unfortunately, the story of the Franklin expedition was never added. It is in *Brébeuf* particularly that Pratt shows his affinity to the oral poets in his respect for his sources. He does not use the Jesuit Relations as a basis for fine writing: his whole effort is to let the Relations tell their own story through his poem. His genre is the narrative poem, and the narrative has a unique power of dry impersonal statement which makes sophisticated or clever writing look ridiculous.

A preliterate culture is a highly ritualized one, where doing things decently and in order is one of the most essential of all social and moral principles. The care that Pratt expends on a sequence of physical movements meets us everywhere in his work: in the throwing of the harpoon in *The Cachalot*, in the getting out of the lifeboats in *The Roosevelt and the Antinoe*, in the manoeuvring of ships in *Behind the Log* that forms so ironic a contrast to the bland strategic directives at the beginning. Such delight in sequential detail shows his sense of a mode of life where safety, or even survival, depends, not simply on activity, but on the right ordering of activity. At the other extreme are the first-class passengers on the Titanic, who have, literally, nothing to do, and so ritualize their lives by a poker game. In religion, we notice how clearly Pratt, himself a Nonconformist Protestant, understands the immense importance, for a Catholic, of the unbroken repetition of the mass at Ville Marie, which he makes the conclusion of his poem on Brébeuf. And certainly no poet without so intensely ritualistic a feeling would have symbolized the end of the "depression" (i.e., human history) by an "apocalyptic dinner." There is also the beautiful evocation of the sense of ritual surrounding death, some of it the sacrament of extreme unction, some of it going back to pre-Christian times, but in every age assimilating the dramatic moments of life to the recurring rhythm that gives a sense of spaciousness and dignity to the individual consciousness:

> There was a time he came in formal dress,
> Announced by Silence tapping at the panels
> In deep apology.
> A touch of chivalry in his approach,
> He offered sacramental wine,
> And with acanthus leaf
> And petals of the hyacinth
> He took the fever from the temples
> And closed the eyelids,
> Then led the way to his cool longitudes
> In the dignity of the candles.   [*Come Away, Death*, ll. 8–18]

I spoke of the poetry of an oral culture as simple in rhythmical structure, however subtle the effects of which it is capable. Verse is a much simpler and more obvious way of conventionalizing ordinary speech than prose is, which accounts for the cultural priority of verse to prose. It is consistent with Pratt's general attitude to poetry, not merely that he should be conservative in his diction, which never plays any syntactical tricks, and in his standard metres, but that his poetry should reflect the pleasure of linear movement, whether directly physical, as in *The 6000*, or subtilized into following the swift pace of a story-teller's narrative. It is normally only the standard metres (especially, perhaps, Pratt's beloved octosyllabic couplet) that can convey this particular kind of poetic pleasure, one of the most ancient that poetry can give. Even some of the poems that are technically in free verse, such as *Newfoundland* and *Silences*, express something of the recurring wash of the sea on rocks. Another ancient and primitive pleasure of poetry is the sententious utterance that gives epigrammatic form to a familiar but deeply held idea, and the tight stanzaic patterns of Pratt's lyrics are well adapted to give this too.

When the poet has so central a relation to his society, there is no break between him and his audience: he speaks for, as much as to, his audience, and his values are their values. Even if a professional poet, he is popular in the sense that he is the voice of his community. Shakespeare, who is still essentially an oral poet, shows a similar identification with the assumptions of his audience. It is particularly this empathy between poet and listening audience that is broken by the rise of a writing culture. In a writing culture, philosophy develops from proverb and oracle into systematic concept and logical argument; religion develops from mythology into theology; magic fades out and is absorbed into science. All these speak the language of prose, which now becomes fully developed, and capable of a conceptual kind of utterance that poetry resists. It is the discursive writer or thinker who is assumed to have the primary verbal keys to reality; the norms of meaning become the norms of a prose sense external to poetry. As a result the poet becomes increasingly isolated in spirit from much of the thought of his time, even though he continues, as a rule, to be a scholarly and erudite person, aware of what is going on in the rational disciplines. As the structures of philosophy and science become more complete, the poet retreats from large-scale cosmological and epic themes summing up the learning of his time, and partakes of a growing fragmentation of experience. He tends more and more to convey his meaning indirectly, through imagery and metaphor, and the surface of explicit statement that he shares with other writers becomes increasingly opaque. He is sometimes difficult to read—Eliot even suggests that difficulty is a moral necessity for writers of his time[2]—and above all, originality, saying things in one's own way instead of simply saying them in the way that they have always been said, becomes accepted as part of the convention of serious literature.

This means that the serious poet is likely to have a restricted audience of cultivated people—"fit audience find, though few," as Milton said of *Paradise Lost* [bk. 7, l. 31]—and that the importance of his social function is not widely recognized or understood. Shelley called the poet an "unacknowledged legislator," in a *Defence of Poetry* which was an answer to a brilliant and paradoxical essay of his friend Peacock, in which Peacock had noted a primitive, even an atavistic, quality in the poet's mind, and its affinity with an earlier type of civilization. The poet, Peacock remarked, had had for his chief social function the flattering of barbarians, whom he called "heroes," and such a person was utterly lost in a developed society.[3] Peacock's essay points, among other things, to the growing estrangement of the poet from the values of a conformist and materialistic society which a great majority of important modern poets share, however great the variety of kinds of opposition they may display.

Pratt was a Romantic poet in the Romantic tradition, and, like his older colleague Pelham Edgar, had a particular affection for Shelley. It was seldom that he admitted to a specific influence, but he did tell me once of how he had been haunted by Shelley's *Julian and Maddalo*, that strange, wonderful poem in which two poets discuss the reasons for the continuing captivity of human intelligence, while that intelligence itself is symbolized by a madman unable to escape from the fixations of broken love. Yet Pratt certainly did not follow Shelley in the latter's repudiation of the religious and political organizations of his time, although he understood and sympathized with Shelley's attitude. Pratt's relation to the Romantics indicates a different and somewhat contradictory tendency in Romanticism from the one we have been discussing.

For Romanticism also featured the revival of oral poetry and the ballad. One would expect, then, some revival in the popularity of the poet: one would think that some poets might become, once again, spokesmen for their communities, their tales and proverbial philosophies becoming a part of ordinary verbal culture. Burns became such a poet for one group, though for somewhat exceptional reasons: Wordsworth, across the border, and writing quite as simply and intelligibly, hardly did. But in the next century the few popular poets with more than a documentary interest, such as Longfellow or Kipling, make it obvious that, paradoxical as it sounds, the popular tradition from Romantic times on has been mainly a submerged tradition. The intense desire of a community to have a poet of its own as a cultural possession cannot be doubted; neither can the desire of many poets to achieve this kind of relation to a community. Pratt has been, in Canada, a kind of unofficial poet laureate; this was an office that Whitman would have been delighted to hold for America, and that Tennyson, who did hold it in Great Britain, worked hard to maintain in dignity. With the twentieth century the tension between the desire to be popular and the necessity to be restricted in audience takes some grotesque forms. One thinks of Eliot, ending his *Waste Land* with a quotation in Sanskrit, yet speaking of the advantage, for a dramatist, of an audience that could not read or write;[4] or of Yeats trying to bring drama to communities that often could hardly read or write, yet filling his poems with recondite Kabbalism. But the idioms of popular and serious poetry remain inexorably distinct. Popular poems tend to preserve a surface of explicit statement: they are often sententious and proverbial, like Kipling's *If* or Longfellow's *Psalm of Life* or Burns's *For A' That*, or they deal with what for their readers are conventionally poetic themes, like the pastoral themes of James Whitcomb Riley or the adventurous themes of Robert W. Service. Affection for such poets is apt to be anti-intellectual, accompanied by a strong resistance to the poetry that the more restricted audience I spoke of finds interesting.

One of the chief barriers to the appreciation of Pratt in many quarters is the tendency in him to be a popular poet. Like Kipling, and like Longfellow in a different way, he writes in a style that steers close to the perilous shallows of light verse. He is ready to linger over rather self-indulgent nostalgic or whimsical themes, as in *Reverie on a Dog* (not reprinted in his second edition), or in *Magic in Everything*, or in *Putting Winter to Bed*. Again, he tends to accept the values of his society without much questioning. His assumptions about the Second World War, the Jesuit-Iroquois conflict, the relation of officers to men in war and of bosses to workers in peace, are those of an ordinary conservative citizen who reads the morning paper and believes, on the whole, what it says. In his poetry, as in his personal life, Pratt is someone who quite frankly wants to be liked, and liked immediately, not after a generation or two. To some extent he has succeeded: his readiness to disarm the suspicions of the ordinary reader has gained him an unusually large number of ordinary readers, at least in Canada. But he has raised other suspicions in other readers, not accustomed to poets who expect them to be complaisant, and who consequently feel that *this* poet must be simple-minded in a way that, say, Ezra Pound is not.

Perhaps this means only that, like the seventeenth-century British poets who wrote in Latin instead of English, Pratt has had his reward of recognition in his life, and is likely to be neglected in future for having backed the wrong horse. I think there are other factors to be considered, however. When I edited Pratt's poems in 1958, I remarked that, if to be "modern" is a virtue, Pratt looked more modern and up to date in 1958 than he did in 1938.[5] I was thinking then mainly of the growing tendency to write in more conventional metres and to provide a more explicit surface of direct statement. I now feel that it is possible to update the remark to 1968, though for somewhat different reasons. In the last few years there has been a startling social development which makes all my talk about oral and preliterate poets much more relevant both to Pratt and to the contemporary scene. The rise of communications media other than the book has brought back some of the characteristics of oral culture, such as the reading of poetry to a listening public, often with some musical accompaniment, the employing of topical themes, the tendency to the direct statement of a social attitude which the audience is expected to share, and many other features of oral literature that have not been genuinely popular for centuries. True, most of such poetry is associated with a dissenting or protesting social attitude, and from its point of view Pratt's poetry would look like a defence of establishment values. But the dissenting values of today are the establishment values of tomorrow, and perhaps Pratt will come into an even clearer focus in 1978.

II

Many modern poets seem to strike their roots in a small and restricted locality. Thus Frost is a poet of northern New England, Stevens of southern New England, Yeats of Sligo, Eliot of the City of London (it has even been asserted that all Eliot's London allusions are within a single postal district), Dylan Thomas of Southern Wales, Jeffers of the Monterey and Carmel region of California. They may live in and write poetry about many other places, but the relation to a specific environment is still there. And Pratt's fundamental environment was the Avalon peninsula, the area of St. John's and the outports adjoining it. Like all poetic environments, his was a mixture of memory and literary convention, and many of you might not recognize it as the place that you actually live in. But it would certainly never have existed without this actual place.

Pratt's immediate contact with this community was through religion, as exemplified in his father's profession, which he followed. Perhaps his training as a preacher, which certainly influenced his admiration for the rhetoric of Spurgeon,[6] and, later, of Churchill, also had something to do with his attitude to poetry as a kind of rhetorical friendly persuasion, the winning over of an audience. In any case the rigours of the life in the Newfoundland outports, the hard fight to survive and the frequency of violent death, threw into strong relief a fundamental cleavage in Christianity which runs all through his work and is the theme of his profoundest poem, *The Truant*.

Christianity has always been both a revolutionary and an institutionalized religion: subversive and repressive social movements have both appealed to its principles. The revolutionary core of Christianity is its identifying of God with a suffering, persecuted, and enduring man. It was in the sign of the cross, a ridiculous and shameful emblem, that an outcast religion conquered the world's greatest empire. But the conquest itself began to shift the attention of Christianity to an establishment God, one who created and governed the order of nature. What Pratt's poetic vision first seized on was the contrast, in the life he saw around him, between the human heroism and endurance, in which the divine inheritance and destiny of man was so clearly reflected, and the moral unconsciousness of nature. Whatever the source of the latter, it is there, and there is little point in trying to see it as somehow reflecting a will or providence or intelligence that has planned it all quite coherently and has foreseen all difficulties. Such a Supreme Arranger of order and authority may be called God or Nature—it makes little difference which—but invoking it affects us as a complacent denial of the reality of human feeling:

>   The doctor spoke
> Of things like balance, purpose—balance? Yes,
> We got that from a dory in a gale,
> From weights and springs and piling rock in holds
> Through lack of cargo. Purpose? Faith—we knew that;
> Assumed it in the meshes of a net,
> Or else denied it when a child was drowned.
> But these were matters past the doctor's mind—
> "Sharks too had purpose for the sea would rot
> Without them." This too strong a dose for us . . .
>   [*The Doctor in the Boat*, ll. 21–30]

Many arguments of the "what are sharks good for?" type were in Pratt's cultural background, the efforts of intellectual conservatism to fit the facts of its existence into some prearranged scheme. Such conservatives would often have taken a religious line, but the man who, like the man in an unreprinted poem in *Newfoundland Verse*, "sticks by Moses" is more likely to be sticking by some kind of Stoic universal governor imported into Christianity to rationalize its adherence to established authority. For the Stoic is the most impressive example of the man who tries to find some kind of moral order behind nature, and so tries to keep neutral in the struggle of human heroism and natural indifference: a neutrality always dubious and in the twentieth century entirely impossible:

> What are the Stoic answers
> To those who flag us at the danger curves
> Along the quivering labyrinth of nerves?   [*The Stoics*, ll. 27–9]

We notice how it is the enduring, resisting, and suffering Christ of *Gethsemane* who is at the centre of Pratt's religion. Over against him is the dead God of fatality, the mindless, pointless world of the wheeling stars and the crashing seas. In *The Highway* the poet speaks of nature in terms of an evolutionary scheme which seems to indicate some kind of purpose, even if a very slow-moving one; but we cannot accept this scheme without the feeling expressed by the myth of the fall of man, glanced at in the last stanza. Man's essential heritage is spiritual rather than natural: he is cut off from nature by his own consciousness, and has to turn for his loyalties to an ideal which (or rather who: the "Son of Man") is human and yet qualitatively different from human life as we know it. Such an ideal is not in nature, where visions of apocalyptic human cities like the one in *The Mirage* are only illusions destroyed by "the darker irony of light," and where the struggle to survive knows no more of ultimate purpose than a coral insect knows of a coral island, developing as it did

> Away back before the emergence of fur or feather, back to the unvocal sea and down deep where the darkness spills its wash on the threshold of light, where the lids never close upon the eyes, where the inhabitants slay in silence and are as silently slain.   [*Silences*, l. 35]

Students of the submarine world tell us that the sea is not silent, and that its creatures manage to make a fair amount of noise in spite of the impediment of water. But the silence in this poem is the symbolic silence of a moral chaos in which the creative word has not yet been spoken, the word of the conscious mind able to detach itself from a life wholly engaged in predatory aggression and see and judge of what it is doing. The door of the cottage closed against the storm in *The Weather Glass, The Lee-Shore,* and elsewhere is a simple but very central image of separation between conscious and mindless worlds.

But of course human life itself, as the *Silences* that we have just quoted from shows, exhibits the conflict between the spirit and the nature of man, between the unspoken ferocity which makes man the devil of nature, infinitely more evil than Tom the Cat from Zanzibar, and the speaking of the word, which, even if a word of enmity, may still be the basis of community. The demonic in human life expresses itself in a peculiar form of mechanism: in the developing of a technology which symbolizes a will to merge human life into a vast destructive machine. The reason asks questions to which, as in quadratic equations, there are two answers. One answer is the fatalism which makes the total commitment to death in modern warfare consistent with the reason, one logical consequence of the relation of nature and man, and absurd only to the rebellious free spirit:

> Seven millions on the roads in France,
> Set to a pattern of chaos
> Fashioned through years for this hour.
> Inside the brain of the planner
> No tolerance befogged the reason.   [*Dunkirk*, ll. 30–4]

There is another answer, less narrowly logical, and this takes us back to our discussion of the social function of the poet.

I have spoken of the primitive function of the oral poet as the teacher of his society, which sounds as though he were a mere repository of facts, an ambulatory Larousse. But, of course, the oral poet does not deal in facts at all, as such: what he deals in are myths, that is, stories of gods, historical reminiscences, and concepts founded on metaphors. Such myths are neither true nor false, because they are not verifiable. Myths are expressions of concern, of man's care for his own destiny and heritage, his sense of the supreme importance of preserving his community, his constant interest in questions about his ultimate coming and going. The poet who shapes the myth is thus entrusted with the speaking of the word of concern, which, even though in early times it may often have been a word of hostility and a celebrating of war and conquest, is still the basis of social action. Primitive myths are conservative because primitive societies are conservative, and last a long time without much change. But the myth-making impulse is recreated in each generation, as the wonder which Samuel Johnson called the effect of novelty upon ignorance awakens in every child:[7]

> We showed them pictures in a book and smiled
> At red-shawled wolves and chasing bruins—
> Was not the race just an incarnate child
> That sat at wells and haunted ruins?   [*Myth and Fact*, ll. 9–12]

With Romanticism, when the poet's sense of isolation from society reached an extreme and began to turn back again, poetry once more became mythopoeic. The new myths that came in with Romanticism, however, were often revolutionary, expressing hopes for greater freedom than man had hitherto had. At the centre of these revolutionary myths is Shelley's hero Prometheus, who is also the hero of many of Pratt's poems, including *Fire*. Prometheus is the symbol of the technology which is developed by man in the interests of his own concern for a fuller human life. This is the technology which so fascinates Pratt and which he has celebrated in his work more eloquently, perhaps, than any other poet of his time. At the centre of this imaginative technology is the signal, the scientific extension of the human word, and around the signal all genuine science, science as a form of human life and achievement rather than as a death-wish, takes shape:

> He had an instrument in his control
> Attested by the highest signatures of science . . .
> And here, his head-phones on, this operator,
> Sleeve-rolled mechanic to the theorists,
> Was holding in his personal trust, come life,
> Come death, their cumulative handiwork.
> Occasionally a higher note might hit
> The ear-drum like a drill, bristle the chin,
> Involving everything from brain to kidneys,
> Only to be dismissed as issuing
> From the submerged foundations of an iceberg,
> Or classified as "mutual interference."   [*Behind the Log*, ll. 484–5, 493–502]

The operator gets only puzzling answers from nature, but there is an answer from nature none the less. As soon as man splits his life-impulse off from his death-impulse, and stops thinking of his technology as primarily a way of making war, the nature around him also takes on a twofold aspect. The death-impulse is answered by the ferocity and destructiveness of nature, but the life-impulse is answered by the energy and the inner exuberance in nature—much the same phenomena, but seen from the inside as a living process rather than from the outside as something completed by death. The energy of life is nature's response to human concern: this is the reason for that curious identity between the pursuer and the pursued which John Sutherland has noted in his study of Pratt.[8] Man being what he is, he often tries to dominate nature in ways that choke the life out of it, even if he is not actually engaged in war. The poet of Newfoundland, with its sparse soil, knows that the life of *The Good Earth* is precious, and that nature, being a part of man too, always makes the appropriate response, whether to love or to contempt:

> Hold that synthetic seed, for underneath
> Deep down she'll answer to your horticulture:
> She has a way of germinating teeth
> And yielding crops of carrion for the vulture. [ll. 21–4]

The attitude I have been trying to trace in Pratt and associate with his Newfoundland origin is most clearly expressed, naturally, in the poem called *Newfoundland* which stands first in his collected poems. As the poet watches the sea beating on the Newfoundland shores, a possible ironic or fatalistic vision is dismissed and the vision of the unquenchable energy and the limitless endurance which unite the real man with real nature takes its place:

> Here the tides flow,
> And here they ebb;
> Not with that dull, unsinewed tread of waters
> Held under bonds to move
> Around unpeopled shores—
> Moon-driven through a timeless circuit
> Of invasion and retreat;
> But with a lusty stroke of life
> Pounding at stubborn gates,
> That they might run
> Within the sluices of men's hearts. [ll. 1–11]

And just as the closed door separates the world of consciousness and feeling from the blind fury of storms, so the open door unites man and his world in a common vision. Even the "iron door" of death opens a crack to enable the poet to catch a fleeting glimpse

> Of life with high auroras and the flow
> Of wide majestic spaces   [*The Iron Door*, ll. 282–3]

but fortunately it was to be a long time before that wider life claimed him. In this life he took his place at the centre of society where the great myths are formed, the new myths where the hero is man the worker rather than man the conqueror, and where the poet who shapes those myths is shaping also a human reality which is greater than the whole objective world, with all its light-years of space, because it includes the infinity of human desire. This greater universe is revealed to us in whatever poetry is founded on the vision expressed in the closing lines of *Newfoundland*, a vision

> *Of dreams that survive the night*
> *Of doors held ajar in storms.*

58

Lawren Harris

1969

"Introduction," from Lawren Harris, ed. Bess Harris and R.G.P. Colgrove (Toronto: Macmillan, 1969), ix–xii. Reprinted in BG, 181–97. The typescript is in NFF, 1988, box 2, file ww.

As a rule, when associations are formed by youthful artists, they break up as the styles of the artists composing them become more individual. But the Group of Seven, who did so much to revitalize Canadian painting in the '20s and later of this century, still retain some of the characteristics of a group. Seven is a sacred number, and the identity of the seventh, like the light of the seventh star of the Pleiades, has fluctuated somewhat, attached to different painters at different times. But the permanent six, of whom four are still with us, have many qualities in common, both as painters and in fields outside painting. For one thing, they are, for painters, unusually articulate in words. J.E.H. MacDonald and Lawren Harris wrote poetry; Harris, as this book shows, wrote also a great deal of critical prose; A.Y. Jackson produced a most entertaining autobiography; Arthur Lismer, through his work as educator and lecturer, would still be one of the greatest names in the history of Canadian art even if he had never painted a canvas. For another, they shared certain intellectual interests. They felt themselves part of the movement towards the direct imaginative confrontation with the North American landscape which, for them, began in literature with Thoreau and Whitman. Out of this developed an interest for which the word theosophical would not be too misleading if understood, not in any sectarian sense, but as meaning a commitment to painting as a way of life, or, perhaps better, as a sacramental activity expressing a faith, and so analogous to the practising of a religion. This is a Romantic view, following the tradition that begins in English poetry with Wordsworth. While the Group of Seven were most active, Romanticism was going out of fashion elsewhere. But the nineteen-sixties is once again a Romantic period, in fact almost oppressively so, so it seems a good time to see such an achievement as that of Lawren Harris in better perspective.

This remarkable book presents a fine selection of Lawren Harris's paintings in the context of the various speeches, essays, poems, letters, notebook jottings, and drafts of books by which he tried to express his conception of art as an activity of life, and not something separable from it. What he says forms the context of the paintings, and the paintings form the context of what he says. Much of what he says might seem over-general or lacking in applicability if we did not see it, with the expert and patient help of the editors, as specifically illustrated by the painting. An example is the placing of his painting *The Bridge* beside a number of statements about art as various forms of a bridge. Even so he has some difficulty in saying in words what he says so eloquently in the pictures. One reason for this is that our language is naturally Cartesian, based on a dualism in which the split between perceiving subject and perceived object is the primary fact of experience. For the artist, whatever may be true of the scientist, the real world is not the objective world. As Shelley, another Romantic, insisted, it is only out of laziness or cowardice that we take the objective world to be the real one. The attempt to produce a "realism" which is only an illusion of our ordinary objectifying sense leads to insincere painting, technique divorced from intelligence. But, says Harris, art is not caprice either. The artist, unlike the psychedelic, does not confuse the creative consciousness with the subjective or introverted consciousness. Fantasy-painting becomes insincere also whenever it evades the struggle with the material which is the painter's immediate task. The genuine artist, Harris is saying, finds reality in a point of identity between subject and object, a point at which the created world and the world that is really there become the same thing.

In Harris's earlier works, the paintings of houses and streets in Toronto and the Maritimes and that extraordinary piece of Canadian Gothic, the portrait of Salem Bland, we are struck at once by the contemplative quality of the painting, by the intensity with which the painter's whole mind is concentrated on his object—or, as the curious vagaries of language have it, his "subject." Because of this meditative intensity, the painting is representational. But it is very far from what is often called photographic realism, although what this phrase usually refers to is just as bad in photography as it is in painting. The sombre, brooding miners' cottages and the bizarre lights and shadows of a Toronto street, with their unpredictable splashes of colour (deftly illustrated by the editors in placing one of the painter's poems beside a similar picture), stare at us with an emotional intensity which ordinary eyesight cannot give us. This intensity is, of course, the kind of thing we turn to pictures for. But neither do we have the feeling that this emotional power is simply there as a reflection of what the painter felt and was already determined to impose on whatever he saw. Such paintings are the painter's inventions, a word which means both something made and something found. There is tension and struggle between the act of seeing and the resistance of the thing seen: we who see the picture participate in the struggle, and so make our own effort to cross the *pons asinorum* of art, the "bridge" between the ordinary subject and the ordinary object.

Lawren Harris makes it clear that what drove him and his colleagues out to the northern part of Canada was their distrust of the "picturesque," that is, the pictorial subject which suggests a facile or conventional pictorial response. His paintings of Lake Superior and the Rockies are as much of an exploration as the literal or physical explorations of La Vérendrye or Mackenzie. Harris remarks on the "austerity" of nature: she does not tell the artist what to do; she speaks in riddles and oracles, and the painter is an Oedipus confronting a sphinx. He also insists on how necessary it was for him, as for his associates, to seek a three-dimensional grasp of what MacDonald called the "solemn land,"[1] to avoid the merely decorative as he avoided all other forms of pictorial narcissism, the landscape which is merely in front, looked at but not possessed. A picture has to suggest three dimensions before it can suggest four, before the object can become a higher reality by becoming also an event, a moment suspended in time.

It has been said of some Canadian painters, notably Thomson, that their sketches are often more convincing than the worked-up picture. The former gives more of a sense of painting in process, as an event in time, as a recording of the act of vision, and the final picture, it is said, sometimes becomes monumental at the expense of vitality and immediacy. The editors have juxtaposed some paintings with their preparatory sketches so that the reader can judge for himself as regards Lawren Harris. But there is no doubt that this painter felt the tension between process and product of painting, and that his logical development from stylized landscape to abstraction was his way of escaping from it.

Lawren Harris

In the abstract paintings the rudiments of representation are still there, with triangle and circle replacing mountain and horizon; but the stylizing and simplifying of outline have been carried a step—perhaps one should say a dimension—further. The more dependent a picture is on representation, the more epigrammatic it is, and the more it stresses the immediate context, in space and time, of a particular sense experience. The effect of stylizing and simplifying is to bring out more clearly, not what the painter sees, but what he experiences in his seeing. Abstraction sets the painter free from the particular experience, and enables him to paint the essence of his pictorial vision, with each picture representing an infinite number of possible experiences. The units of the picture have become symbols rather than objects, and have become universal without ceasing to be particular.

Traditionally, the metaphor of the magician has often been used for the artist: the Orpheus whose music moved trees, the Prospero whose fancies are enacted by spirits. The kernel of truth in the metaphor is that the artist's mind seeks a responding spirit in nature. Harris speaks of "informing cosmic powers" in his landscapes. This responding spirit is not a ghost or a god or an elf like Puck, but the elemental spirit of *design*, the quality in nature which for the artist, as for the scientist in a different way, contains what can be identified with the searching intelligence. Such design is often quasi-geometrical in form—the "books" of Prospero that Caliban so feared and hated would have been, being magic books, full of geometrical and kabbalistic designs. This geometrical magic has always been an informing principle of painting, though it was probably Cézanne who was most influential in stressing its importance for the modern painter. There are many kinds of abstract painting: those that are clear and sharp in outline emphasize the rigorous control of the object by the consciousness; others express rather a sense of the inner power of nature, the exploding energy that creates form. Both kinds are prominent in, for instance, Kandinsky. Most of Lawren Harris's abstractions reflect a strict conscious control of experience, as one would expect from the clarity of outline in the landscapes that preceded them. But in the two remarkable 1967 paintings reproduced near the end of the book [*Abstraction* and *The Rising Sun*], there is a sense of a relaxation of control, as though the informing cosmic powers themselves were taking over from the painter.

After the conservative stock responses to the Group of Seven ("hot mush school" and the like) were over, there followed radical and left-wing stock responses which accused them of the decadent bourgeois vice of introversion, turning their backs on society and its problems to develop their own souls in the solitudes of the North. I even remember a Communist magazine which asserted that to find the true revolutionary tradition in Canadian painting we should go back to the Victorian anecdotal painters. One thing that will strike the reader of this book at once is the painter's social concern, a concern which actually increases as he goes further into abstract techniques. The first and most important of his "bridges" is the bridge between the artist and his society. He is missionary as well as explorer: not a missionary who wants to destroy all faith that differs from his own, but a missionary who wants to make his own faith real to others. Just as a new country cannot become a civilization without explorers and pioneers going out into the loneliness of a deserted land, so no social imagination can develop except through those who have followed their own vision beyond its inevitable loneliness to its final resting place in the tradition of art. The record of an imaginative journey of remarkable integrity and discipline is what is commemorated in this book.

59

America: True or False?

1969

From Notes for a Native Land: A New Encounter with Canada, *ed. Andy Wainwright (Canada: Oberon Press, 1969), 52–5. Reprinted in RW, 334–6. Two typescripts are in NFF, 1988, box 2, file ww. Frye wrote at the height of the social unrest associated with the Vietnam War.*

I gather that one theme of this book is the perpetual identity crisis that Canadians, especially English-speaking Canadians of British origin, find themselves in. I myself am, for example, a Wasp: white and Anglo-Saxon by the accident of birth, and though born a Protestant too, I have remained one by conviction. But it seems a strange conviction if it separates me, as it does, from others who call themselves Protestant, like the Rev. Dr. Paisley and the Prime Minister of South Africa, much more widely than it does from others who would care nothing for my views. And I do not think of my hereditary affinities as attaching me to an establishment: I simply belong to the one sizeable social group whom it is entirely safe to ridicule. There are French-speaking separatists who can apparently take some satisfaction in a maudlin colonialism in regard to France, to the extent of picketing a cabinet minister when he announces that in his opinion a French-made airplane is inferior to an American one. A similar colonialism afflicted a good many British Canadians a century ago, but their descendants have outgrown such stereotypes, and so, of course, has Great Britain.

As for the U.S.A., there is a political separation from that country which a Canadian feels as soon as he goes outside Canada. Politically, Canada ought to be one of the small, observant countries in a new world of continental powers, much as, say, Switzerland has been in Europe. A

Canadian going to the United States to teach in a university there is often asked by his American students if he notices any difference. They expect the answer to be no, and nine-tenths of the time it is no, but the tenth time there is some point of discussion that suddenly makes him feel like a Finn in Russia or a Dane in Germany. His students have been conditioned from infancy to be citizens of a vast imperial power; he has been conditioned to watch, to take sides in decisions made elsewhere.

But what does political separation matter when economically and culturally there seems to be no difference at all? The great producing machine of North American capitalism knows nothing of an undefended border: it spews its consumer goods all over us, pollutes our air and water and earth, turns our landscapes into a strangling nightmare of highways, tears the guts out of our cities and strews them along "ribbon developments," cuts down our forests and digs up our mines, bellows and mimes a mixture of advertising and propaganda into our eyes and ears all day long. In short, everything that happens in the United States happens in Canada too, except that most of it is crossing a border and invading another country. But is that any real exception? Canadians seem to be quite willing to go along with this process: no political leader dares resist it for fear of "lowering the standard of living." If our identity is to consist only of a querulous and pointless anti-Americanism, it is hardly worth holding on to.

The economic development of America has been intensely competitive, and so has developed in an oligarchic direction, taking advantage of everything that increases social inequality, like racism. Exclusiveness breeds hysteria, because of the constant fear of revolt from "below," and the hysteria is increased by an economy that depends on advertising, and so tries to create a gullible and uncritical public. Advertising absorbs propaganda as the economic expansion goes beyond the limits of America and turns imperialist, and the two merge into the category of "public relations," where one throws oneself into a dramatic role, and says, not what one means, but what the tactics of the situation are supposed to demand. In so insane a context the question of whether or not murdering a prominent figure or planting a bomb would be good publicity for one's cause becomes almost a rational question. Hysteria breeds counter-hysteria, racism counter-racism, and American capitalism is now facing various opposed forces who may turn out to be stronger than it is, because they fight with the same weapons but believe in them more intensely. On both sides the social unit is the organized mob. An appalling crash in the near future seems to be at least a possibility for American society, and Canada could no more avoid such a conflict than Belgium could avoid a war between Germany and France. We look round for a third force, but the best organized one seems to be the criminals, who profit from both.

And yet everyone realizes that there are two Americas, and that underneath this gigantic parasite on the American way of life there is quite a different America, tough, shrewd, humorous, deeply committed to a belief in democracy, with a genuine hatred of violence and unreason, anxious to reduce, even try to eliminate, poverty and social discrimination in its own country and to keep out of trouble with other nations. It may be sentimental and easily misled, but it is very far from being inarticulate or powerless. It is potentially in control of the political structure, which may often be, in practice, the executive committee of the economic structure, but does not have to be: the Constitution which is its basis aims at democracy, not at oligarchy, and it is still a powerful revolutionary force.

I do not see how America can find its identity, much less avoid chaos, unless a massive citizens' resistance develops which is opposed to exploitation and imperialism on the one hand, and to jack-booted radicalism on the other. It would not be a new movement, but simply the will of the people, the people as a genuine society strong enough to contain and dissolve all mobs. It would be based on a conception of freedom as the social expression of tolerance, and on the understanding that violence and lying cannot produce anything except more violence and more lies. It would be politically active, because democracy has to do with majority rule and not merely with enduring the tyranny of organized minorities. It would not be conservative or radical in its direction, but both at once.

What is true of American identity is *a fortiori* true of Canadian identity. Our political independence, such as it is, is the chance that enables us to make common cause with the genuine America that Thoreau and Jefferson and Mark Twain and even Ezra Pound were talking about. This all sounds very vague, but that doesn't worry me: this is a statement of belief, not a program of action. It also sounds very unlikely, but hope is said to be a major virtue.

60

Dialogue on Translation

1970

"Foreword" from Dialogue sur la traduction à propos du "Tombeau des rois," *by Anne Hébert, author of the French poem, and Frank R. Scott, who translated it into English (Montreal: Éditions HMH, 1970). The page references in the text are to this edition. Frye's words appear in English, 9–14, and in French, 15–21 (trans. Jean Simard). Jeanne Lapointe of Laval University was the moderator.*

In the course of this fascinating dialogue Mr. Scott quotes Robert Frost as saying that "the poetry" is what is lost in translation, adding that he does not think this the whole truth [55]. As a result of reading what follows, I have become convinced that it is the opposite of the truth, and that "the poetry" is precisely what, given exceptionably favourable conditions like these, can be translated. What cannot be translated are the linguistic accidents, such as the sound patterns that a language makes or the nuances of meaning peculiar to it, like the difference between *rêve* and *songe* in French which has no counterpart in English. Even the sound pattern, as Mme Lapointe points out [28], may vary from one reader to another within the same language: consider, for example, the difference between a British and a North American reading of this line from Spenser's *The Faerie Queene*:

> The willow worn of forlorn paramours.

Meaning is derived from context, and there are two contexts for verbal meaning: the context of literature and the context of ordinary explicit or intentional discourse. When we first read a concentrated and difficult poem, we first try to grasp its explicit meaning, or the prose sense of what it says. We often call this the "literal" meaning, but actually it is a translation of the poem into a different verbal context, and is not what the poem really means at all. Gerard Manley Hopkins draws a distinction between the poet's "overthought" or explicit meaning, and his "underthought," or the meaning given by the progression of images and metaphors.[1] But it is the "underthought" that is the real poetic meaning, and the explicit meaning must conform to it. Mr. Scott went directly to the real meaning, the imagistic and metaphorical meaning, of what he was translating: this caused Mlle Hébert to think long and deeply about the real meaning of her poem, and so the whole conversation is carried on within the proper context of meaning. There have been many arguments over whether a translation should be slavishly literal or faithful only to the general spirit of the original, but these arguments are usually based on the wrong kind of meaning. Of course the translation of any poem worth translating should be as literal as the language will allow, but it should be a literal rendering of the real and not of the superficial meaning. Every one of Mr. Scott's improvements is a step toward a more literal rendering in this sense. Further, Mr. Scott's original version was not the result of any lack of understanding of French: a French reader too might very well read "j'ai mon coeur au poing" with the image of "I hold my heart in my clenched hand" in his mind. We thus see that a translation, when thorough enough, may be a critical elucidation of its original as well as a translation.

We hear much less than we used to do about the wilful obscurity of modern poets and their lack of concern to make their meaning plain to the ordinary reader. This is, of course, also an assumption based on ignorance of what genuine poetic meaning is. In what follows we see how a fine poet struggles to make her meaning precise and lucid to the last syllable, first on the largely instinctive level of her poetic skill, and then on a more conscious level as she confronts the translation. Mr. Scott consolidates the result into English, and it is clear that without the stimulus of the other language, Mlle Hébert would never have discovered so much about her own meaning. Translation here becomes a creative achievement in communication, not merely a necessary evil or a removal of barriers. One can hardly learn more in less compass about the kind of craftsmanship that goes into the making of poetry than is given in these few pages.

61

Rear-View Crystal Ball

April–May 1970

From Canadian Forum, 50 (April-May 1970): 54–5. Reprinted in RW, 337–40. *The typescript is in NFF, 1988, box 3, file cd. This was one of a number of recollections published in the fiftieth anniversary issue of the* Forum.

I have no interest in what is alleged to be the world of fifty years hence. I shall not be around to see it, and therefore, according to the only philosophical principle I ever thought I understood, it will not exist. But I have seen fifty years of future turn into fifty years of past, and have been reading the *Canadian Forum* for nearly forty of those years. Marshall McLuhan has a phrase about reactionaries who don't get with it as people driving by a rear-view mirror.[1] This assumes the monumental fallacy that we move forward in time as well as in space, whereas actually, of course, we face the past, and the rear-view mirror of that direction is the shape of things to come. Perhaps the *Canadian Forum* is such a rear-view mirror, with its fifty years of history. Those who reject the past have no defence against the future, for the future is nothing but the analogy of the past.

What is surprising about the last fifty years is how little of what has happened is really surprising. It was already obvious in 1920 that Fascism and Communism were going to cause a lot of trouble, that capitalism would have to be modified and become less laissez-faire, that Canada would soon become a satellite of the United States, that our natural resources were being recklessly plundered and wasted, that radio would develop both itself and eventually a visual brother, that separatist agitation in Quebec would continue, that colonies would want and eventually take independence, that the influence of middle-class religion would decline, that man's capacity to injure himself would increase, not merely in wars but in the growth of cities and industries. Nearly all these issues are discussed repeatedly in the early issues of the *Forum* and its predecessor the *Rebel*, discussed in every tone from hope to fear, and with that uneasy sense of a future looking over one's shoulder which is so characteristic of twentieth-century prose style and yet so hard to characterize. Similarly, it is possible that nothing will be happening in 2020 except what is obvious now: the future that may be technically feasible is not the future that society can actually assimilate.

The *Forum* was a by-product of a cultural exhilaration that hit Toronto in particular during the early twenties. It was brilliantly recalled by the late J.D. Robins in some talks he gave over the CBC at the time of the twenty-fifth anniversary. There was a new and exciting movement in painting around the Group of Seven, very articulately championed by Barker Fairley; there were new developments in drama centring on Hart House Theatre; it was the great days of the Arts and Letters Club, and in general civilized life in Canada seemed to be on the march. In those days one obvious response to such a mood of exhilaration was to found a magazine devoted to both political and cultural matters. The *Forum*, however, unlike most of its kind, has never consistently been a political journal with cultural affairs and book reviews in its cellar: it often devotes its leading article to something in literature or the arts, and its highly individual slant on what it considers to be news is one of its most endearing qualities.

The next decade brought the Depression and a much more radical political atmosphere. When I began to contribute to the *Forum* it had passed through a Liberal phase and a League for Social Reconstruction phase, and was in a mainly CCF phase. The editor was Eleanor Godfrey, now Graham, then, as I remember, about nineteen years old. The late Herbert Davis, Earle Birney, Frank Underhill, Carl McNaught, and the two Classical scholars George Grube and Eric Havelock were some of the people then and later associated with it. One of the editors had Trotskyite sympathies; consequently the local Stalinist squad denounced the *Forum* as a "hive of Trotskyism," which caused my bewildered wife, then art editor, to look into some Trotskyite pamphlets to see what she was supposed to be. The next decade brought the war, some strong differences of opinion over Canada's role in that war, and finally, a few years after the war, when I was managing editor, a separation from the CCF, when the *Forum* became the "independent journal of opinion" that it still is. And always, of course, there were Lou and Kay Morris (along with, for many years, Alan Creighton), working day and night, issue after issue, keeping the presses turning, the bills paid, ads solicited, proof-readers organized, editorial meetings assembled, and performing continuous artificial respiration on the gasping subscription list. There has to be one reason in particular for a magazine's lasting fifty years, and the Morrises are that particular reason.

I once asked an early editor, a university professor, how much time he spent on the *Forum* back in the twenties. He thought about half of his time. Those were days of leisure, not in the sense of having nothing to do, but in the sense of being able to choose what one did. The growth of graduate work in particular has made this proportioning of time impossible, but as we become busier our lives become more introverted: we tend to beat a path from home to office without looking up. This is part of the general growth of introversion during the last fifty years, for nearly all our technological developments—the automobile, the passenger airplane, the high-rise apartment, the television set, even the cocktail party—make for increased introversion, and our traditional communities, the school, the home, the university, the church, the labour temple, the corner store, disintegrate in direct proportion. In such an atmosphere the journal of opinion becomes obsolete. "No ideas but in things," says W.C. Williams:[2] he is speaking of poetry, but in social life we may say: "no ideas but in events." The university as a community, the debating society, the supremacy of Parliament, and the journal of opinion discussing the "issues" of the day form a consistent social pattern. The university as an intellectual factory, students demonstrating and confronting, the circumventing of Parliament, and the forming of opinion by immediate response to announcement and newscast also form a consistent social pattern.

Fifty years ago, the little magazine was the means of creating what is now called "dialogue," the opposite voice in the thunder of advertising propaganda, platitude, and bumbling rhetoric. Today, we are preoccupied with the feeling that communication has to become a two-way street if mankind is to stay sane. The voices that bellow and wheedle and plead through our television sets have become intolerable, and apathy is no defence. Some take to drugs; some to rock music, wrapping themselves up in an impermeable cloak of noise; some loot and smash and scream obscenities—anything to hit back at that unceasing roar of sound. In the age of the global village the strongest political force is separatism.

Whatever else happens in the next fifty years, some righting of the communication balance, some loosening of the stranglehold of introversion, is bound to happen, and we may find, like Elijah, that the quiet voice is more audible than the earthquake and fire. A journal of independent opinion, a monthly, trying to live on subscriptions, not paying for contributions, seems as far out of the contemporary world as a coelacanth. But history has an odd way of coming back to the same point. Perhaps the obsolete creature is, just because it is that, a portent of the future; and perhaps its unquenched vitality is a sign that we may after all have a future.

62

Preface to *The Bush Garden*

1971

From The Bush Garden: Essays on the Canadian Imagination *(Toronto: Anansi, 1971), i–x. Reprinted in* The Oxford Anthology of Canadian Literature, *ed. Robert Weaver and William Toye (Toronto: Oxford University Press, 1973), 126–44, and 2nd ed., 107–14, and in* Vic Report, *4 (June 1976): 6–7, 13. Partially reprinted as "In Quest of Identity and Unity,"* Globe Magazine, *20 (February 1971): 8–9, 12. Two typescripts are in NFF, box 3, file cj, and box 24, file 2. In* The Bush Garden *are reprinted ten of Frye's essays on Canadian culture (nos. 34, 11, 20, 38, 41, 57, 6, 26, 58, and 53 in the present volume), whose context Frye discusses in the concluding pages of the preface.*

What follows is a retrospective collection of some of my writings on Canadian culture, mainly literature, extending over a period of nearly thirty years. It will perhaps be easiest to introduce them personally, as episodes in a writing career which has been mainly concerned with world literature and has addressed an international reading public, and yet has always been rooted in Canada and has drawn its essential characteristics from there.

The famous Canadian problem of identity may seem a rationalized, self-pitying, or made-up problem to those who have never had to meet it, or have never understood that it was there to be met. But it is with human beings as with birds: the creative instinct has a great deal to do with the assertion of territorial rights. The question of identity is primarily a cultural and imaginative question, and there is always something vegetable about the imagination, something sharply limited in range. American writers are, as writers, not American: they are New Englanders, Mississippians, Middle Westerners, expatriates, and the like. Even in the much smaller British Isles we find few writers who are simply British: Hardy belongs to "Wessex," Dylan Thomas to South Wales, Beckett to the Dublin-Paris axis, and so on. Painters and composers deal with arts capable of a higher degree of abstraction, but even they are likely to have their roots in some very restricted coterie in Paris or New York.

Similarly, the question of Canadian identity, so far as it affects the creative imagination, is not a "Canadian" question at all, but a regional question. An environment turned outward to the sea, like so much of Newfoundland, and one turned towards inland seas, like so much of the Maritimes, are an imaginative contrast: anyone who has been conditioned by one in his earliest years can hardly become conditioned by the other in the same way. Anyone brought up on the urban plain of southern Ontario or the gentle *pays* farmland along the south shore of the St. Lawrence may become fascinated by the great sprawling wilderness of Northern Ontario or Ungava, may move there and live with its people and become accepted as one of them, but if he paints or writes about it he will paint or write as an imaginative foreigner. And what can there be in common between an imagination nurtured on the prairies, where it is a centre of consciousness diffusing itself over a vast flat expanse stretching to the remote horizon, and one nurtured in British Columbia, where it is in the midst of gigantic trees and mountains leaping into the sky all around it, and obliterating the horizon everywhere?

Thus when the CBC is instructed by Parliament to do what it can to promote Canadian unity and identity, it is not always realized that unity and identity are quite different things to be promoting, and that in Canada they are perhaps more different than they are anywhere else. Identity is local and regional, rooted in the imagination and in works of culture; unity is national in reference, international in perspective, and rooted in a political feeling. There are, of course, containing imaginative forms which are common to the whole country, even if not peculiar to Canada. I remember seeing an exhibition of undergraduate painting, mostly of landscapes, at a Maritime university. The students had come from all over Canada, and one was from Ghana. The Ghana student had imaginative qualities that the Canadians did not have, but they had something that he did not have, and it puzzled me to place it. I finally realized what it was: he had lived, in his impressionable years, in a world where colour was a constant datum: he had never seen colour as a cycle that got born in spring, matured in a burst of autumn flame, and then died out into a largely abstract, black and white world. But that is a factor of latitude rather than region, and most of the imaginative factors common to the country as a whole are negative influences.

Negative, because in our world the sense of a specific environment as something that provides a circumference for an imagination has to contend with a global civilization of jet planes, international hotels, and disappearing landmarks—that is, an obliterated environment. The obliterated environment produces an imaginative dystrophy that one sees all over the world, most dramatically perhaps in architecture and town planning (as it is ironically called), but in the other arts as well. Canada, with its empty spaces, its largely unknown lakes and rivers and islands, its division of language, its dependence on immense railways to hold it physically together, has had this peculiar problem of an obliterated environment throughout most of its history. The effects of this are clear in the curiously abortive cultural developments of Canada, as is said later in this book. They are shown even more clearly in its present lack of will to resist its own disintegration, in the fact that it is practically the only country left in the world which is a pure colony, colonial in psychology as well as in mercantile economics.

The essential element in the national sense of unity is the east-west feeling, developed historically along the St. Lawrence–Great Lakes axis, and expressed in the national motto, *a mari usque ad mare* [from sea unto sea]. The tension between this political sense of unity and the imaginative sense of locality is the essence of whatever the word "Canadian" means. Once the tension is given up, and the two elements of unity and identity are confused or assimilated to each other, we get the two endemic diseases of Canadian life. Assimilating identity to unity produces the empty gestures of cultural nationalism; assimilating unity to identity produces the kind of provincial isolation which is now called separatism.

The imaginative Canadian stance, so to speak, facing east and west, has on one side one of the most powerful nations in the world; on the other there is the vast hinterland of the North, with its sense of mystery and fear of the unknown, and the curious guilt feelings that its uninhabited loneliness seems to inspire in this exploiting age. If the Canadian faces south, he becomes either hypnotized or repelled by the United States: either he tries to think up unconvincing reasons for being different and somehow superior to Americans, or he accepts being "swallowed up by" the United States as inevitable. What is resented in Canada about annexation to the United States is not annexation itself, but the feeling that Canada would disappear into a larger entity without having

Preface to *The Bush Garden* 415

anything of any real distinctiveness to contribute to that entity: that, in short, if the United States did annex Canada it would notice nothing except an increase in natural resources. If we face north, much the same result evidently occurs: this happened to the Diefenbaker campaign of 1956, which has been chronicled in books with such words as "lament" and "renegade" in their titles.[1]

Whenever the east-west context of the Canadian outlook begins to weaken, separatism, which is always there, emerges as a political force. Every part of Canada has strong separatist feelings: there is a separatism of the Pacific coast, of the prairies, of the Maritimes, of Newfoundland, as well as of Quebec. Ontario, of course, began with a separatist movement from the American Revolution. But since the rise of the great ideological revolutionary movements of our time, whether Communist, fascist, imperialist, Islamic or what not, separatism has been an almost wholly destructive force. The successful separatings, like that of Norway and Sweden in 1905, took place before the rise of these movements. In India and Pakistan, in the Arab-Jewish world, and in many other centres divided by language, colour, or religion, separatism has seldom if ever stabilized the prejudices which gave rise to it, but has steadily increased them. Even where there is no political affiliation, the separation of Cuba from the American sphere of influence, or of Yugoslavia from the Russian one, cannot be a politically neutral act. Quebec in particular has gone through an exhilarating and, for the most part, emancipating social revolution. Separatism is the reactionary side of this revolution: what it really aims at is a return to the introverted malaise in which it began, when Quebec's motto was *je me souviens* and its symbols were those of the habitant rooted to his land with his mother church over his head, and all the rest of the blood-and-soil bit. One cannot go back to the past historically, but the squalid neo-Fascism of the FLQ terrorists indicates that one can always do so psychologically.[2]

What has just been said may seem inconsistent with some of what is said later on in this book; but the essays cover a period of thirty years, and naturally conditions in Canada itself have changed a good deal in that time. At the same time the changes have occurred within an intelligible pattern of repetition. The most striking changes are in French Canada, but some of those changes recapitulate earlier developments in English Canada. Thus the admiration for France, which on one occasion took the form of picketing a cabinet minister for saying that a French-made airplane was not as good as an English-made one, indicates a phase of colonialism now obsolete in the other culture. Similarly, separatism in the Atlantic or prairie provinces is often based on a feeling that Ontario regards itself as an Israel or Promised Land with the outlying provinces in the role of desert wanderers: this is much the same as the attitude that Quebec separatism explicitly adopts toward the Francophone Canadians in New Brunswick or Manitoba. There may be a clue here to the immediate future prospects of the country worth investigating, and the following essays, with all their repetitions and dated allusions, may provide some useful historical perspective.

I grew up in two towns, Sherbrooke and Moncton, where the population was half English and half French, divided by language, education, and religion, and living in a state of more or less amiable Apartheid. In the Eastern Townships the English-speaking group formed a northern spur of New England, and had at a much earlier time almost annexed themselves to New England, feeling much more akin to it than to Quebec. The English-speaking Maritimers, also, had most of their cultural and economic ties with New England, but their political connection was with New France, so that culturally, from their point of view, Canada stopped at Fredericton and started again at Westmount. There were also a good many Maritime French families whose native language was English, and so had the same cultural dislocation in reverse.

As a student going to the University of Toronto, I would take the train to Montreal, sitting up overnight in the coach, and looking forward to the moment in the early morning when the train came into Lévis, on the south side of the St. Lawrence, and the great fortress of Quebec loomed out of the bleak dawn mists. I knew that much of the panorama was created by a modern railway hotel, but distance and fog lent enchantment even to that. Here was one of the imaginative and emotional centres of my own country and my own people, yet a people with whom I found it difficult to identify, what was different being not so much language as cultural memory. But the effort of making the identification was crucial: it helped me to see that a sense of unity is the opposite of a sense of uniformity. Uniformity, where everyone "belongs," uses the same clichés, thinks alike and behaves alike, produces a society which seems comfortable at first but is totally lacking in human dignity. Real unity tolerates dissent and rejoices in variety of outlook and tradition, recognizes that it is man's destiny to unite and not divide, and understands that creating proletariats and scapegoats and second-class citizens is a mean and contemptible activity. Unity, so understood, is the extra dimension that raises the sense of belonging into genuine human life. Nobody of any intelligence has any business being loyal to an ideal of uniformity: what one owes one's loyalty to is an ideal of unity, and a distrust of such a loyalty is rooted in a distrust of life itself.

In the last essay in this book [no. 53] I speak of the alternating rhythm in Canadian life between opposed tendencies, one romantic, exploratory, and idealistic, the other reflective, observant, and pastoral. These are aspects of the tension of unity and identity already mentioned. The former is emotionally linked to Confederation and Canadianism; the latter is more regional and more inclined to think of the country as a series of longitudinal sections. They are the attitudes that Pratt symbolizes in *Towards the Last Spike* by Macdonald and Blake, and in fact they did at one time have analogues in our political philosophies. I first became aware of this polarization of mood through Canadian painting, which is why I include three short pieces on painting here. The romantic and exploratory tendency was represented for me by Thomson, the Group of Seven (especially Harris, Jackson, and Lismer), and Emily Carr; the pastoral tendency by most of the better painters before Thomson and by David Milne later. "Canadian and Colonial Painting" was contributed to the *Canadian Forum*, whose good-natured hospitality has helped so many Canadians to learn to write. The piece is polemical and immature, but I think it got hold of a genuine theme. The tribute to Milne appeared in the second issue of *Here and Now*, accompanied by illustrations which the imaginative reader should have little difficulty in reconstructing. The Lawren Harris essay was the preface to the book of his writings and paintings edited by my classmate R.G. Colgrove and published in 1969: it is therefore recent, but its attitude is very close to another article on Harris written many years earlier.

I joined the Department of English at Victoria College, and there became exposed to the three personal influences described in "Silence in the Sea." This lecture inaugurated a series established in honour of Pratt by Memorial University in 1968. When I was still a junior instructor, the first edition of A.J.M. Smith's *Book of Canadian Poetry* appeared (1943), and my review of it in the *Canadian Forum* was perhaps my first critical article of any lasting importance. It is hard to overstate my debt to Mr. Smith's book, which brought my interest in Canadian poetry into focus and gave it direction. What it did for me it did for a great many others: the Canadian conception of Canadian poetry has been largely formed by Mr. Smith, and in fact it is hardly too much to say that he brought that conception into being. The article on the narrative tradition resulted from a lead given me by the same book: this article was translated by Guy Sylvestre and appeared in an issue of his magazine *Gants du ciel* which was devoted to English Canadian poetry. The "Preface to an Uncollected Anthology," a paper read to the Royal Society in Montreal in 1956, follows the same general line—in the original there was some deliberate overlapping with the narrative tradition article, as the latter was available only in French and in a periodical that had ceased publication. Towards the end it touches on the question of popular culture, which is also glanced at in the review of Edith Fowke's collection of folk songs, also from the *Canadian Forum*.

At the time that I reviewed Mr. Smith's anthology, I was struggling with my own book on the symbolism of William Blake (*Fearful Symmetry*, 1947). In the last chapter of that book the conception emerges of three great mythopoeic periods of English literature: one around 1600, the age of Spenser, Shakespeare, and the early Milton; one around 1800, the age of Blake and the great Romantics; and one around the period 1920–1950. I thought at first of writing my second book on Spenser, but the pull of contemporary literature was too strong and the theory of literature too chaotic, and I was drawn to a more general and theoretical approach which ultimately became the *Anatomy of Criticism* (1957). When I had got started on this, in 1950, during a year I had off on a Guggenheim Fellowship, I was asked by my colleague J.R. MacGillivray, then editor of the *University of Toronto Quarterly*, to take over the annual survey of Canadian poetry in its "Letters in Canada" issue which had been made by the late E.K. Brown from the beginning of the survey nearly up to the time of his death. Reviews from the ten essays I wrote through the decade of the 1950s form the bulk of the present book.

These reviews are too far in the past to do the poets they deal with any good or any harm, not that they did much of either even at the time. In any case the estimates of value implied in them are expendable, as estimates of value always are. They may be read as a record of poetic production in English Canada during one of its crucial periods, or as an example of the way poetry educates a consistent reader of it, or as many other things, some of them no doubt most unflattering to the writer. For me, they were an essential piece of "field work" to be carried on while I was working out a comprehensive critical theory. I was fascinated to see how the echoes and ripples of the great mythopoeic age kept moving through Canada, and taking a form there that they could not have taken

Preface to *The Bush Garden*

elsewhere. The better the poet, the more clearly and precisely he showed this, but the same tendencies could be seen even as far down as some of the doggerel, or what I called the naive verse.

By myth I meant, not an accidental characteristic of poetry which can be acquired as an ornament or through an allusion or by writing in a certain way, but the structural principle of the poem itself. Myth in this sense is the key to a poem's real meaning, not the explicit meaning that a prose paraphrase would give, but the integral meaning presented by its metaphors, images, and symbols. Naturally before this view had established itself it was widely misunderstood, and I became for a time, in Mr. Dudek's phrase, the great white whale of Canadian criticism.[3] That is, I was thought—still am in some quarters, evidently—to be advocating or encouraging a specific "mythological school" of academic, erudite, repressed, and Puritanical poetry, in contrast to another kind whose characteristics were undefined but which was assumed to be much more warm-hearted, spontaneous, and soul brother to the sexual instinct. Such notions came mainly not from other critics but from poets making critical *obiter dicta*. It does no great harm, however, for poets to be confused about the principles of criticism as long as some of the critics are not.

I was still engaged in this survey when I was approached by my friend Carl Klinck of [the University of] Western Ontario, with his project for a history of English Canadian literature, and I joined his committee. The conclusion which I wrote for this history repeats a good many conceptions worked out earlier during the poetry reviews, but it is closely related to the rest of the book in which it first appeared, and is heavily dependent on the other contributors for data, conceptions, and often phrasing. I emphasize this because I have edited the text, to save the reader the distraction of being continually referred to another book, and the editing has concealed my debts.

For a long time it has been conventional for Canadian criticism to end on a bright major chord of optimism about the immediate future. This tone is in a curious contrast to the pervading tone of Canadian economists, historians, political theorists, and social scientists. Some observers of the Canadian scene, including Professors Donald Creighton and George Grant, feel that there has been too long and too unchecked a domination of the longitudinal mentality in Canada, and that the tension between region and nation has finally snapped. Certainly a century after the American Civil War, the true North strong and free often looks more like a sham South weak and occupied—sham because there has been no war with this confederacy and no deliberate occupation. The national emphasis is a conservative one, in the lower-case sense of preserving the continuity of political existence, and it is typical of the confusions of identity in Canada that the one genuinely conservative Canadian party of the twentieth century, the CCF, expired without recognizing itself to be that. However, what seems to reason and experience to be perpetually coming apart at the seams may seem to the imagination something on the point of being put together again, as the imagination is occupationally disposed to synthesis. Perhaps that is part of the real function of the imagination in every community, and of the poets who articulate that imagination. In any case, there are many titles from many of the best-known Canadian poets, *Resurgam, Words for a Resurrection, News from the Phoenix, The Depression Ends, Poem for the Next Century, O Earth Return, Home Free, Apocalyptics,* for the Canadian critic to murmur in his troubled sleep.

The title of the book has been pilfered from Margaret Atwood's *Journals of Susanna Moodie,* a book unusually rich in suggestive phrases defining a Canadian sensibility.

63

Canadian Scene: Explorers and Observers

1973

Prefatory essay to R.H. Hubbard's catalogue, Canadian Landscape Painting 1670–1930 *(Madison: University of Wisconsin, Elvehjem Art Center, 1973), 1–4. Reprinted in* Art News, *72 (April 1973): 68–9, and in RW, 57–61. Typescripts are in NFF, 1988, box 4, files l-m. Frye's remarks were written for the exhibition "The Artist and the Land: Canadian Landscape Painting, 1670–1930," which opened at the Elvehjem Art Center at the University of Wisconsin on 11 April 1973.*

Naturally, many of the developments in Canadian painting reflect similar developments in the United States. But an exhibition like this is very far from being merely a provincial aspect of American painting. Canada's experience in both time and space has been very different from that of its neighbour, and the visual imaginations of Canadian painters are bound to show the differences.

In time, the United States had a revolutionary war first, a struggle against European domination, and a civil war afterwards, a purely domestic affair. Canada had its civil war first, a struggle of two European powers on its soil, and a war of independence afterwards, which curtailed a thrust of aggression coming from this continent. At least, that was the point of the War of 1812 for Canada, so far as that incredibly bungling and inept collision in the dark had any point.

One result of this difference in historical development is that, while the United States has made a "melting pot" of its immigrants, and has constantly struggled to become a more homogeneous country, Canada developed under the sign of Gemini, the twins, and has consequently made much less effort to assimilate its other ethnical groups. To show

how this is reflected in Canadian painting would take a more comprehensive exhibition than this, but one can see here that the differences between, say, Quebec and Ontario painting are often closer to being national than merely regional differences. We speak of a British "conquest" of Canada, but the French Canadian was never really conquered. The British army climbed the heights of Quebec in 1759 and defeated the French army outside the city: the French, following an "equal time" policy which has been observed in elections ever since, climbed up the heights the next year and defeated the British army. The conquest had to become a compromise, in which a good deal of French law, the French language, and the religion of the great majority of the French population were left without interference. As Canada expanded, it presented the appearance of "seven fishing-rods tied together by the ends," as Goldwin Smith put it,[1] and separatism has been a very vocal sentiment ever since, not only in Quebec, but in every part of Canada.

The development of Canada in space is equally distinctive. The United States is a relatively symmetrical country, and has grown from the Atlantic seaboard westward, pushing a frontier ahead of it until it reached the other coast. The Revolutionary War was carried through by a group of states extending from north to south. Canada, as a glance at the map will show, has no north-south coastline: the axis of its development has been a tremendous east-west thrust into its interior, down the St. Lawrence, through the Great Lakes, across the Prairies, and down to the Pacific coast. One wonders how Marcuse would have worked out his thesis of "one-dimensional man" if he had to live in a one-dimensional country, a country which for most of its history has been longer and narrower than Chile. This thrust into the interior modulated from canoe to rail, and its economic motives from furs to timber and minerals. The imaginative movement that followed it forms the bulk of what is shown here.

That is, the primary rhythm of English Canadian painting has been a forward-thrusting rhythm, a drive which has its origin in Europe, and is therefore conservative and romantic in feeling, strongly attached to the British connection but "federal" in its attitude to Canada, much possessed by the vision of the national motto, *a mari usque ad mare*. It starts with the documentary painters who, like Paul Kane, have provided such lively and varied glimpses of so many vanished aspects of the country, especially of Indian life. A second wave began with Tom Thomson, continued through the Group of Seven, and has a British Columbia counterpart in Emily Carr. (The romantic side of the movement is reflected in the name "Group of Seven" itself: there were never really more than six, in fact there were effectively only five, but seven is a sacred number, and the group had a strong theosophical bent.) One notices in these paintings how the perspective is so frequently a twisting and scanning perspective, a canoeman's eye peering around the corner to see what comes next. Thomson in particular uses the conventions of *art nouveau* to throw up in front of the canvas a fringe of foreground which is rather blurred, because the eye is meant to look past it. It is a perspective which reminds us how much Canada developed as a passage or gateway to somewhere else, being merely an obstruction in itself. Further, a new world is being discovered. There is an immense difference in feeling between north and south Canada, but as north Canada is practically uninhabited, it exists in Canadian painting only through southern eyes. In those eyes it is a "solemn land" as frightening and fantastic as the moon.

For those who settle in the country, there is no frontier on the West: the frontier is all around, and the loneliest and most frightening part of it is the part that is within the eye and mind of the settler. Except in some parts of Quebec, there is very little in Canada to compare with the grafting of a European culture in seventeenth-century New England, New York, or Virginia, which then develops with its own traditions, so that the feeling of settlement is always there as a part of one's being. In the earlier poetry of Canada, much more than in the painting, there is the sense of being completely surrounded by an indifference or a hostility that may take the form of human enemies, predatory animals, or of a desperately cold winter.

Along with the documentary painters came other painters who were reconstructing the landscape in front of them into forms of vision which had been made in Europe. These painters were mainly looking for the picturesque, the novel subject that could be presented in relatively familiar conventions. They correspond to the many examples in Canadian literature of a new life in a new world being transmitted through metrical and imaginative patterns derived from Campbell, Tom Moore, and the more solemn side of Byron. Some of them, notably Krieghoff, had a sufficiently fresh eye to be able to combine the picturesque subject with the documentary outlook. But in general the picturesque eye was an idealizing one, assimilating past experience in Europe to a future when the new world would look more like the old one.

After settlement had been accomplished, a different aspect of Canadian imagination developed, north-south in direction, and accompanied by a sense of strong dislocation, as the Canadian began to feel that he was on the fringes of a continent whose centre is in the United States. This feeling turns into something shrewd, humorous, observant, the attitude of a country which is on the sidelines of history. The consciousness of being part of a vast imperial power, oppressed by the responsibility that goes with that, which the American has from birth, the Canadian does not have at all. The result is something cooler in the Canadian temperament, in which such things as the American sense of malaise and moral failure in the 1960s necessarily take a more muted and toned-down form. Politically, this consciousness is longitudinal, a feeling that Canada is split into a number of northern extensions of the United States. As Quebec will not fit into this conception, it eventually becomes as isolated from it as from the more romantic and federal attitude.

Nevertheless, it is Quebec that has taken the lead in developing a pictorial consciousness which is cool, detached, urbane, and limited in objectives. There are many examples in this exhibition: the most important is the painting of Morrice, who turned the Impressionist and Fauvist techniques he had learned in Paris to very different uses from those we find in the Group of Seven. Later on, David Milne, and LeMoine FitzGerald, give us something of the same kind of feeling in English Canada. The Quebec tradition expresses itself also in some extraordinary variations of primitive painting that cannot be represented here, and it turned, more easily than English Canadian painting did, to the more abstract and post-Kandinsky structures which are also out of our present range.

For landscape, which was the backbone of Canadian painting for so long, has largely gone now, in favour of more international developments with few local features left, although in some more recent painters, notably Riopelle, I can see what I think is a powerful sense of sublimated landscape. Great imaginative developments seem to begin much as God does in the Bible, with a sense of the contrast between creation and chaos. As they subside, social conditions become more disturbed, and eventually the arts come to be preoccupied, first with reflecting the chaos about them, and then with becoming identified with it. This is happening in Canada as elsewhere, at a time when the future existence of Canada itself is still a matter of some doubt. It is a curious irony that, just as technology, with the jet plane, was beginning to make sense of the country, the political imagination, which always lumbers along in ox-carts many decades behind the world it is actually in, has become more divisive than ever. A sour little joke was circulating in Canada during the centennial year of Confederation (1967), to the effect that when Canada was formed, it was hoped to make it a combination of British political institutions, American economic buoyancy, and French culture; and that what it now appears to have, a century later, is French politics, British economic buoyancy, and American culture. However, there are always more hopeful signs, and a study of the energy and precision of the Canadian pictorial imagination will lead us to one of them.

64

Lester Bowles Pearson, 1897–1972

31 January 1973

Speech at a memorial service in the Victoria College Chapel. From the typescript in NFF, 1988, box 4, file cc. An earlier typescript is in file dd. Pearson, who died on 27 December 1972, was Liberal prime minister of Canada 1963–68.

A college has very few graduates whose names are well known to all its other graduates, and Lester Pearson may be the only graduate of Victoria of whom that is true. He arrived on the Victoria campus in the fall of 1913: Burwash Hall had just been opened, and he was one of the first residents of Gate House. The Dean of Residence was Vincent Massey, recently back from Oxford, and trying valiantly, if not very successfully, to bring Burwash nearer to the ideal represented by Balliol College. Mr. Pearson's ancestral roots were deeply Victorian. In those days the senior executive of the college was called the Chancellor, and the new Chancellor was R.P. Bowles, a cousin of the student whose full name was Lester Bowles Pearson. His father and grandfather were Methodist ministers and Victoria graduates also. There is a legend—I don't vouch for its truth—that his grandfather, an old-line Tory, had withdrawn his father from Victoria, at the time when Victoria was moving from Cobourg to Toronto, on the ground that he didn't want his son to associate with all those Toronto Grits.

Mr. Pearson broke off his undergraduate studies to join up during the First World War, and in the next few years he saw enough of war to make him prefer peace. After his return he was graduated in the class of 1919, and began an academic career in Modern History, being a don in Middle House until his marriage. His wife was a student of his, and a graduate of Victoria in the class of 1924.[1] He reached the rank of assistant

Lester Bowles Pearson, 1897–1972

professor before he left for Ottawa in 1929 to join the Department of External Affairs. Canada had only very recently acquired autonomy in foreign policy, and this was a new and exciting field. I hardly need to chronicle all the steps of his brilliant career: he remained in the Civil Service until 1948, when he entered Parliament and became Minister of External Affairs. His work with the United Nations and NATO attracted the admiration of the entire world, and he was awarded the Nobel Peace Prize in 1957. From 1963 to 1968 he was, of course, Prime Minister of Canada.

In the 1930s Victoria changed its pattern of administration, so that the senior executive became known as President and Vice-Chancellor, leaving the Chancellorship as a more or less honorary post. Mr. Pearson was the second of three Chancellors whom we have had on that basis, and served from 1951 to 1958. He was, I understand, advised against accepting it in some quarters, as it was thought that it might prejudice his career to emphasize his own background and origins. But his loyalty to Victoria easily triumphed over all such small-minded fears, and he was inaugurated in Convocation Hall in February, 1952. In his very eloquent speech there were two sentences that particularly struck me at the time. "History," he said, "is full of turbulence and terror. But throughout the ages wise and brave men have been able to find within themselves the resources to keep that terror at arm's length, and the courage to keep their spirits unclouded and their integrity intact." He would have been horrified to think that others might regard this as an unconscious characterization of himself, but it was, and because it was, he was one of the most universally respected figures in politics. When we opened the new library the ceremonies included giving an honorary degree to the Prime Minister of that day, Mr. John Diefenbaker.[2] On entering the building, Mr. Diefenbaker noticed that Gate House had broken out a large sign reading "Welcome Mike Pearson." He remarked that he quite understood Victoria's affection for its famous alumnus, and that whatever political differences there might be did not alter his high personal regard for his opponent.

I do not think of Mr. Pearson as a great man: I think of him as one of the best products of a society which is gradually outgrowing the conception of the great man. He was a good man, trying to do a good job; a man of exceptional abilities who used those abilities for public service and not for private profit. If I read the Gospels correctly, this is a more impressive achievement than what is usually meant by greatness. The great man is typically in the position of a military commander, giving orders that others carry out. Mr. Pearson's career was an unending process of negotiation and bargaining, with all the illogical anomalies, conflicting pressure groups, compromises, and inevitable carping that go with democracy and diplomacy. I can hardly imagine a better training ground for such a career than Canada. Canada never gave him a clear mandate as Prime Minister, yet he managed to get through an extraordinary amount of legislation. His ambition for Canada was founded on his experience in external affairs: he wanted it to be, in the international scene at least, a quiet and sensible country, with no interest in fighting or aggression, devoting itself to discouraging fighting and aggression among its more powerful neighbours. We honour his memory today, not merely as a graduate of Victoria who achieved unique fame and admiration, but primarily as the faithful servant of a Master who, as far as the political world is concerned, reserves his blessing for the peacemakers.

65

Cold Green Element

1974

"*Introduction to* Il Freddo Verde Elemento *(1974),*" *in* Irving Layton: The Poet and His Critics, *ed. Seymour Mayne (Toronto: McGraw-Hill Ryerson, 1978), 251–4. The text appeared originally in Italian as the introduction to Amleto Lorenzini's translation of Irving Layton's* Cold Green Element, Il freddo verde elemento *(Turin: Einaudi, 1974), v–viii. Typescripts are in NFF, box 4, files r–s.*

It is a genuine pleasure to introduce the work of Irving Layton to the Italian reading public. Layton's output has been impressive in quantity as well as quality, and shows a size and range, as well as an intensity, that make him perhaps the most outstanding poetic personality in contemporary Canada. He is not easily anthologized: the present collection is representative of his best work, but does not include all of his best work by any means. But if not easily anthologized he seems to me to be eminently translatable. He is not an obscure poet; his meaning is always straightforward: he has a solid structure of imagery rooted in concrete nouns and simple verbs, and he makes relatively little use of complex patterns of the accidents of language, rhyme, alliteration, assonance, and the like, which cannot be translated into another language except by other accidents. Reading through this collection, it occurs to me that if Layton's native language had been Italian, his lyrical mood would probably have been gentler and more delicate, his satirical mood less dependent on heavily accented monosyllables, of which there are so many in English. The last stanza of *The Birth of Tragedy*, for example, has a fluttering and dissolving movement in the Italian that is not there in the original, though it fits the context admirably. To survive translation is one of the crucial tests of a poet's genuineness, and the reader may be assured that in this book he is hearing the authentic voice of the poet.

Layton grew up in Montreal, the child of a Romanian Jewish family, in an environment full of strong partisan feelings, French, English, Jewish, Catholic, Protestant. There have always been two aspects in his poetry, those of the satirist and of the lyricist. The satirist made his reputation in Canada partly as a "shocking" poet, using an explicit sexual imagery and vocabulary of a type normally omitted from poetry up to a generation ago. Those who were preoccupied with this side of him, however, often overlooked the moral seriousness behind it. The satirist in Layton speaks for a kind of imaginative proletariat, a minority not concerned with social rank or position but with the compassion of genuine human relationships, creative but well aware that creation is part of a cycle that emerges out of corruption, the honeycomb in the dead lion as Yeats would say,[1] and is at all times linked to the democracy of the body, with all its sexual and excretory functions. Opposed to this is the type of bourgeois whose religion is, whatever he says it is, always the religion of self-justification. Such a person sees his own body as a hierarchy; he tries to be idealistic and ignore or subordinate what is below his navel, and he takes the same view of society, which he sees as another hierarchy, with people like himself on the better levels. He is cerebral without being intelligent; he cannot love because he can only use sex as an instrument of aggression or sadism, a buzzing and spineless insect with a head and sting in the tail, but without either vision or love:

> I and modern tyrants know
> The petit-bourgeois is hollow;
> Unable to think or feel
> He clutches at an ideal,
> Some abstraction that is bright
> To illumine his soul's night. [*Reply to a Rhyming Notary*, ll. 13–18]

There are a good many poets who are spokesmen for this kind of culture, including, for Layton, T.S. Eliot, and a good many religions devoted to rationalizing it. Layton sees many examples of these religions, not only in the English and Protestant minority in Montreal but in the curiously ferocious piety that, up to a short time ago, often characterized the French-speaking Catholic. What is significant about such religion is not that its God is dead, but that its God is death. It cannot mask the self-absorption which is really a death-wish, a denial of life that subordinates everything to calculation ("no money in bull calves") or the pseudo-logic of war and persecution:

> It is life itself offends this queer beast
> And fills him with mysterious unease;
> Consequently only half-movements
> Delight him—writhings, tortured spasms... [*Paraclete*, ll. 9–12]

There is an intense eloquence in his poems about the deaths of animals, where (as in *Cain*) the rifle becomes the erotic organ of the death-wish, and an intense bitterness in his ridicule of those who wish to castrate everybody with more love of life than they have, who make refined efforts to ignore their own bodies and so can only try to possess the bodies of others, who use their reason only to rationalize cruelty, who have carried self-love to the point at which it is indistinguishable from self-hatred.

Marxism, in its propaganda, accepts this view of bourgeois man and has tried to turn it to its own account. But Layton sees in the "totalitarian" societies merely a further development of the bourgeois death-wish. We have Hitler murdering six million Jews to settle the "Jewish question," which would never have been a question for anyone capable of living a human life, and Hitler is followed by Stalin, who massacres even larger numbers in the same frenzy of pseudo-logical calculation. What is wrong is essentially the attitude of consciousness, the sense of separation from nature with its cycle of life and death which makes man the "darling pervert" of nature.

The moral that Layton draws from this is a Nietzschean one: the way of Jesus and Buddha, whose symbol is the leprosarium, which attempts to work with the world in its own diseased condition, is not his way. The poet keeps clear of the world, at least imaginatively; he will have no relations with others that are not genuine ones. In the background there is a vision of a "superman" who may come to surpass the all-too-human man, and of a Heraclitean fire that will burn up all the human rubbish of the world. The poet who records the world as it is is by turns prophet, madman, outcast, clown, for genuine dignity is inseparable from the ridiculous, just as genuine seriousness is from humour. One does not have to "agree" with poets, and Layton himself is generous enough to admire the emotional honesty of Ezra Pound, whom he could hardly agree with. But one may always recognize the integrity of a poet who sees poetry steadily as an expression of whatever is humane in a creature who behaves so much of the time like a psychotic ape.

There is much in Layton's attitude that may remind the reader of D.H. Lawrence, though Layton is less possessed by death, more capable of humour and fantasy, and, in his later work particularly, less querulously personal. The other side of Layton, the more lyrical side, sees nature as a symphony of life, of which death is a necessary part, and which man must join if he is to be human. The image of the swimmer appears as the symbol of an imagination which has abandoned the separating consciousness which stands on the shore and contemplates the life before him as an alien thing:

> For sun throbs with sexual energy;
> The meadows bathe in it, each tall tree.
> The sweet dark graves give up their dead.
> Love buries the stale fish in their stead.
>
> [*I Know the Dark and Hovering Moth*, ll. 21–4]

Nature knows nothing of pity, for pity, as Blake says, "divides the soul";[2] she cares nothing either for the isolated individual or for the gregarious herd. But she speaks deeply to the creative impulse in the poet, because she is absorbed in making more and more life, and occasionally, after long efforts, making it better.

66

Douglas Duncan

1974

A tribute under the heading "Northrop Frye," in Douglas Duncan: A Memorial Portrait, *ed. Alan Jarvis (Toronto: University of Toronto Press, 1974), 14–15. Duncan was a Toronto bookbinder, art collector, founder of the Picture Loan Society (1936), and supporter of Canadian artists, notably David Milne. He had died in 1968.*

The opening page of Evelyn Waugh's *The Loved One* introduces an Englishman, exiled in California, who is trying to make sense of an article in *Horizon* on Scottie Wilson. Scottie Wilson was, of course, one of that very large group of painters whose careers owed much of their success to a friendly push from Douglas Duncan at a crucial stage. The *Horizon* article speaks of Douglas as "a refined and charming man." The author of the article obviously did not know him, and the phrase is oddly out of keeping with the general tone of the article. It looks as though the phrase had been supplied by Scottie Wilson himself, or perhaps that he had insisted on some such phrase being inserted.[1]

If this is true, as it may well not be, it would be a good example of the way in which those who were fond of or grateful to Douglas might struggle for phrases to describe him, only to have the right one elude them. Of course he was a refined and charming man, but so have a lot of other people been who never got anywhere near being Douglas Duncan. The phrase suggests something of a dilettante, which he was far from being. My own association with him professionally was through Victoria College, where my wife was for years chairman of the Art Committee. The year's activity usually began by getting hold of Douglas. When suggestions for exhibitions did not come from him, they almost always referred to painters he knew about and had done something to help. Whenever he spoke, his encyclopedic knowledge came out in a context of complete simplicity and candour. He seemed to be a still centre in the swirling egotisms and aggressions and intrigues which characterize the art world in all cities, and his critical judgments had the kind of impartiality that only a genuine sympathy can produce.

We all tend to like what is like ourselves: if we try to be objective, we may eventually come to like what is like our best self. Canadian history and politics have always been polarized between two tendencies: one aggressive, exploratory, and romantic; the other reflective, observant, and pastoral. The same polarization occurs in Canadian literature and painting. In painting the aggressive and romantic tendency is represented by Thomson, the Group of Seven, and Emily Carr; in the second group I think particularly of David Milne and LeMoine Fitzgerald. Tolerant and catholic as Douglas's tastes were, he had a strong temperamental affinity with the second group, and he had an extraordinary genius for discovering painters of crisp, delicate, and precise drawing and colouring, whose work was close to a kind of pictorial calligraphy.

I never go into Alumni Hall in Victoria College, where he had arranged so many exhibitions, without thinking of him, in the centre of a great mass of paintings, with his little piece of green felt for twisting the screws, hanging the pictures, arranging them, disregarding the very considerable pain that his disc trouble often gave him. It is a picture of extraordinary selflessness: hard, conscientious, and almost anonymous work done so that the artist would have another exhibition to chalk up on his record and Victoria students would have pictures to look at. Paradoxically, the memory of him is far more vivid than the memory of even the finest of the pictures.

67

Canada: New World without Revolution

7 October 1975

Address to the Royal Society of Canada, from Preserving the Canadian Heritage/La préservation du patrimoine canadien, *ed. Keith J. Laidler (Ottawa: Royal Society of Canada, 1975), 15–25. Reprinted partially as "The Root of the Problem" in* Heritage Canada, *5 (May 1979): 33, and in* DG, *167–80. Typescripts are in NFF, 1988, box 5, files g–h, and NFF, 1993, box 2, file 4. Frye's address was part of a symposium on preserving the Canadian heritage held in Ottawa in association with Heritage Canada.*

This conference, as I understand it, is concerned mainly with practical, even with administrative, problems, and an introduction like this can hardly do more than suggest some perspective on those problems. Canada, with four million square miles and only four centuries of documented history, has naturally been a country more preoccupied with space than with time, with environment rather than tradition. The older generation, to which I have finally become assigned, was brought up to think of Canada as a land of unlimited natural resources, an unloving but rich earth-mother bulging with endless supplies of nickel and asbestos, or, in her softer parts, with the kind of soil that would allow of huge grain and lumber surpluses. The result of such assumptions is that many of our major social problems are those of ecology, the extinction of animal species, the plundering of forests and mines, the pollution of water, as the hundreds of millions of years that nature took to build up our supplies of coal and oil are cancelled out in a generation or two. The archaeologists who explore royal tombs in Egypt and Mesopotamia find that they are almost always anticipated by grave robbers, people who got there first because they had better reasons for doing so than the acquisition of knowledge. We are the grave robbers of our own resources, and posterity will not be grateful to us. There is, however, a growing understanding that our situation is not simply one of people against planes, or whatever the current issue may be, but of soil and trees and water against concrete and tarmac.

These spatial and environmental problems have a temporal dimension as well. Our history began in the seventeenth century, the age of Baroque expansion in Europe, where the countries advancing most rapidly into the future were those on the Atlantic seaboard. Rapid advance is usually followed either by rapid decline or by a rapid change in some other direction: even by then Spain and Portugal had passed their meridian of growth, and France soon turned back to its European preoccupations. If the French had held Canada they might well have sold it, as they did Louisiana. What is important is not nationality but cultural assumptions. The Baroque age was an age of intense belief in the supremacy of human consciousness over nature. It had discovered something of the technological potential of mathematics, once mathematics had become attached to a powerful social organization. It was not an age of individualism, as is often said, but an age of relatively enlightened despotism, and in some ways very like the dawn of civilization in the Near East, when the pyramids of Egypt and the ziggurats of Babylon emerged as dramatic witness to what men could do when united under a sufficiently strong social will. Both then and in the Baroque period mathematics, and the appearance of geometrical patterns in the human environment, was a symbol of aggressiveness or imperialistic domination. We can see the results all over our country, in the grid patterns of our cities, the concession lines that divide up the farmland into squares, the railways and highways that emphasize direction through the landscape rather than accommodation to it. Improvement in such communications always means a wider and straighter path through nature, and a corresponding decline of interest in it. With the coming of the airplane, even the sense of passing through a natural environment disappears. Our attitude to nature is reflected in our social environment, the kind we build ourselves. Washington was a city designed for automobiles rather than pedestrians long before there were any automobiles: Los Angeles, a city never designed at all, seems to have broken through the control even of the automobile. It was, after all, named after angels, who traditionally do not travel through space but simply manifest themselves elsewhere.

The religion that the British and French brought to the New World was not a natural monotheism, like the Algonquin worship of a Great Spirit, nor an imperial monotheism like that of the Stoics, but a revolutionary monotheism, with a God who took an active and partisan role in history; and like all revolutionary movements, including Marxism in our time, it equipped itself with a canon of sacred books and a dialectical habit of mind, a mental attitude in which the neighbouring heresy is much more bitterly hated than the total rejection of the faith. The dialectical habit of mind produced the conception of the false god, a conception hardly intelligible to an educated pagan. All false gods, in the Christian view, were idols, and all idolatry came ultimately from the belief that there was something numinous in nature. The Christian teaching was that there were no gods in nature; that nature was a fellow creature of man, and that all the gods that had been discovered in it were devils. We have derived many benefits from this attitude, but it had a more sinister side: it tended to assume that nature, not being inhabited or protected by gods or potentially dangerous spirits, was simply something available for human exploitation. Everywhere we look today, we see the conquest of nature by an intelligence that does not love it, that feels no part of it, that splits its own consciousness off from it and looks at it as an object. The sense of the absolute and unquestionable rightness of man's conquest over nature extended to other cultures regarded as being in a "state of nature." The primary principle of white settlement in this country, in practice if not always in theory, was that the indigenous cultures should be destroyed, not preserved or continued or even set apart.

The spokesman for the Baroque phase of this attitude is Descartes, whose fundamental axiom, "I think, therefore I am,"[1] rested on a desire to derive human existence from human consciousness, and to see that consciousness as being in a different world from the nature which for Descartes was pure extension in space. This attitude, in itself a logical development from the traditional Christian view of nature, got so far away from idolatry that it became a kind of idolatry in reverse, the idol this time being human consciousness itself, separated from nature. We live today in a social environment which is a triumph of Cartesian consciousness: an abstract and autonomous world of interlocking co-ordinates, in which most of our imagination is focused not on nature but on the geometrical shapes that we have imposed on nature. My own few childhood memories of big cities are full of a kind of genial clutter: crowds of people on streets, shops with their doors open, theatres with glittering lights; and certainly the exhilaration of this had much to do with the attractiveness of cities for those in smaller centres a generation or two ago. Much of it of course remains, but it is becoming clearer that each advance of technology is accompanied by an advance in introversion, and less sense of public use. Many of the streets now in these same cities, with their deserted sidewalks and cars whizzing up and down the road past scowling fortress-like buildings, show us the kind of anti-community symbolized for me by University Avenue in Toronto and by the areas in Los Angeles where pedestrians are regarded as vagrants. The amount of mental distress caused by living in an environment which expresses indifference or contempt for the perspectives of the human body is very little studied: one might call it proportion pollution.

My own university is in the middle of a big industrial city: this means great masses of box-lunch students, who commute in and out from distant suburbs and take their courses with little experience of a real university community, of the kind that Cardinal Newman regarded as the "idea" of the university. The surrounding streets keep steadily turning into anonymous masses of buildings that look eyeless in spite of being practically all windows. Many of them seem to have had no architect, but appear to have sprung out of their excavations like vast toadstools. City planners speak of the law of conserving the plan, meaning that Bloor Street in Toronto or Sherbrooke Street in Montreal are still where those streets originally were even though there has been a total metamorphosis of the buildings on them. But even this law, which seems at first sight like a concession to a sense of tradition, is really a means of confining change to the inorganic. And as we shuttle from a pigeon-hole in a high-rise apartment to another pigeon-hole in an office, a sense of futility and humiliation takes possession of us that we can now perhaps see in its historical dimension.

As civilization has "progressed" from axe to bulldozer, the growing withdrawal from nature paralyses something natural in ourselves. A friend of my wife's, an interior decorator, remarked that she had a group of neurotic clients whom it seemed impossible either to please or to get rid of, and she suddenly realized that they had something in common: they all lived in high-rise apartments at a level above the trees. A withdrawal from nature extends into a growing withdrawal from human society itself. I mentioned the increasing introversion that technology brings with it: the airplane is more introverted than the train; the superhighway, where there is a danger of falling asleep, more introverted than the most unfrequented country road. The international airport, completely insulated even from the country it is in, is perhaps the most eloquent symbol of this, and is parodied in Stanley Kubrick's movie *2001*, where the hero lands on the moon, dependent on human processing even for the air he breathes, and finds nothing to do there except to phone his wife back on earth, who is out.

A revolutionary habit of mind, being founded on the sense of a crucial break in time at some point, the Exodus from Egypt, the Incarnation of Christ, the flight of Mohammed, the October Revolution in Russia, has a hostility to continuous tradition built into it. In Moslem countries everything that happened before Mohammed's time is part of the age of ignorance. Guides in developing countries, especially Marxist ones, want to show tourists the achievements of their own regime, and often get angry or contemptuous when the tourists want to see the cultural products of the old exploiting days. Similarly with our own culture. The Puritans in Massachusetts were in communion with the Puritans in Norwich who petitioned the Cromwellian government to pull down a useless and cumbersome cathedral which was a mere relic of superstition. Even the Jesuit missionaries, for all their zeal and devotion, still assumed that the Indians, so long as they were heathen, were a part of subconscious nature, and that only Christianity could incorporate them into a fully human society. A cultural sense thus got started which was still operative until quite recently. My late friend Charles Currelly, the founder of the Archaeological Museum in Toronto, was horrified by the indifference with which the authorities of his day regarded the British Columbia totem poles, and by the eagerness with which they were ready to sell them off to anyone who they thought would be fool enough to want them. What we are now beginning to see is that an original belief in the rightness of destroying or ignoring a so-called "savage" culture develops toward a contempt for our own. In Margaret Atwood's very ironic novel *Surfacing*, the heroine, trying to get back to an original identity represented by the Quebec forest, finds that she has to destroy everything cultural that she possesses, or, as she says: "everything from history must be eliminated."[2]

The revolutionary aspect of white settlement extended from religion into economics, as entrepreneur capitalism developed. Every technological change brought with it a large-scale shift in population centres. The skyline of Toronto sixty years ago was dominated by the spires of the great churches: now the churches are points of depression within the skyline. My moral is not the shift of interest from spiritual to financial administration: my moral is rather that the churches themselves are now largely without parishes, the population, at least the church-going part of it, having moved elsewhere. Similarly Canada is a land of ruins to an extent that the less spacious countries of Europe would not dare to be: ghost towns at exhausted mines or the divisional points of old railways remind us how quickly our economy can scrap not merely a building but an entire city. As Earle Birney remarks, the country is haunted by its lack of ghosts, for a ghost town has no ghosts;[3] it is only one of the rubbish heaps that spring up in an economy of waste. We may remember Sam Slick on the beauties of Niagara Falls:

> "It would be a grand speck to get up a jint stock company for factory purposes, for such another place for mills ain't to be found atween the poles. Oh dear!" said I, "only think of the cardin' mills, fullin' mills, cotton mills, grain mills, saw mills, plaster mills, and gracious knows what sort o' mills might be put up there . . . and yet them goneys the British let all run away to waste."[4]

For Sam Slick the ideal thriving mill town of this sort was Lowell in Massachusetts, where my father started in business, and it was a sad day for both of us when I took him there as an old man, after all the mills had been moved to the South, and he saw only the empty shell of the town he once knew. One question that such events raise is obviously: what can or should be preserved of what is no longer functional, and has little interest in itself apart from being a part of our past?

Whatever the answer, our social environment is a revolutionary one in which the main forces are indiscriminately destructive. This has to some extent always been true. Once there was a great city called Nineveh, so great that, according to the Book of Jonah, it took three days to journey across it. Then, quite suddenly, Nineveh disappeared under the sand, where it remained for nearly three thousand years. This kind of destruction, from enemy action without, is a greater danger now as hydrogen bombs would leave nothing for the sand to preserve; but along with it is the even more insidious sense of destruction from within, destruction that proceeds from the very nature of technology itself, not impossibly inspired by some death-wish in ourselves. The only possible economic alternative to capitalism, we feel, is socialism, but if capitalism is a destroyer, socialism is even more of one, because more committed to technology. In ancient Egypt one of the first things a new Pharaoh often did was to deface his predecessor's monuments: this is still our rhythm of life, but it is largely an unconscious one, except when rationalized as progress.

The violence of our almost unmanageable cities is bringing about another great population shift, as people move out of them and back to smaller centres. We are beginning to see a very large cycle of history turning here, and with this is slowly growing another social vision. Ecology, the sense of the need for conserving natural resources, is not a matter of letting the environment go back to the wilderness, but of finding some kind of working balance between man and nature founded on a respect for nature and its inner economies. As part of natural ecology, we are also developing some sense of the need for a kind of human ecology, of conserving not only our natural but our cultural and imaginative resources. Again, this is not simply a matter of leaving alone everything that is old: it is a way of life that grows out of a sense of balance between our present and our past. In relation to the natural environment, there are two kinds of people: those who think that nature is simply there to be used by man, and those who realize that man is himself a part of nature, and will destroy himself if he destroys it. In relation to time and human history, there are also two kinds of people: those who think that the past is dead, and those who realize that the past is still alive in us. A dead past left to bury its dead ends in a dead present, a society of sleepwalkers, and a society without a memory is as senile as an individual in the same plight.

The very word "preservation" reflects some of the panic that goes with the sense of imminent destruction. Some time ago Eric Arthur produced a book on Toronto called *No Mean City*, full of photographs of its older architecture. If we count the number of buildings that have been destroyed, many of them before the book appeared, we can see that there is something else in the city which is, if not mean, at least reckless and out of control, something that needs strong organizing to resist it. According to John Stuart Mill, there is a liberal and a conservative question to be asked about everything: what good is it? and why is it there?[5] If these questions are asked about public, cultural, or historical monuments, the prevailing answer in our day to the question, what good is it? is, no good unless useful to the present owner of the property it stands on; and the answer to the question, why is it there? is, because it is not yet worth anyone's while to remove it. Clearly we need more intelligible answers to both questions. What is called future shock is simply a by-product of the destructiveness of technology: it represents a genuine social problem, and it produces such mental diseases as the conviction among educators (noted by Bernie Hodgetts in his trenchant survey of the teaching of Canadian history, *What Culture? What Heritage?*) that it doesn't matter what we teach, because society is so transient that all one's skills and assumptions will soon be out of date anyway. This is a lethal state of mind to get into. Trying to sharpen one's sense of the future is useless, as the future has no existence; trying to see the present as an interim in which anything may go at any time merely adds to the mood of destruction. Not everything that can happen will happen: we have to understand what kind of people we are before we can begin to guess what we shall do. What kind of people we are is perhaps determined, and certainly conditioned, by what we realize of our past, and sharpening our sense of the past is the only way of meeting the future. Preserving our heritage is a central part of that realization and that sharpened sense.

In the Book of Jeremiah [36:20–3] there is an episode that I often return to, in which Jeremiah's secretary is reading, to the King of Judah, the prophecy which consists so largely of denunciations of the royal policy. A fire, we are told, was burning in the room, and every so often the infuriated king would cut off part of the scroll being read with a knife and throw it on the fire. This must have been a papyrus scroll, and what fascinates me is that the king's palace disappeared totally in a few years, and not the slightest trace of it remains, whereas the Book of Jeremiah, entrusted to the most fragile and combustible substance produced in the ancient world, is still with us, and still in good shape. The inference, or at least the human inference, appears to be that what is easiest to preserve is what has the power of reproduction. Literature has always survived much better than the visual arts for this reason, and now, with recorded music, photography, and tape, an immense amount of cultural material has become preservable. From the Avalon peninsula to the Queen Charlotte Islands, scholars have been collecting ballads, folk songs, folk tales, and whatever a tape recorder can preserve of vanishing attitudes and ways of life. Sometimes the collector arrives too late for the crucial things to be preserved, but what is done is better than nothing, and our archives and libraries are growing in cultural importance accordingly. One of the most rewarding of the W[orks] P[rogress] A[dministration] projects of forty years ago was the Index of American Design, an inventory of the conventions of the popular visual arts, a project which extended into

Canada, and this kind of record is still one of our most useful allies in the fight against oblivion.

As a part of this development, the contempt for primitive or popular art that so distressed Currelly a half-century ago has largely disappeared: in fact we set so high a value now on such art that we have almost transformed the Eskimos into a nation of sculptors, at least with one hand, even though we may be destroying the sources of their creativeness with the other. Some of our attitude to this, perhaps, can be discounted as a patronizing sense of what used to be called the "picturesque," something which appeals to us because we think it comes just under our own standard of sophistication. But this is a minor and expendable attitude: what really attracts us in what we so misleadingly call "primitive" art is rather the recognition of a powerful convention at work within it. Such a convention is in the visual arts something of a parallel to what the ability to reproduce is in literature: it indicates, if it does not guarantee, a continuing vitality in the tradition that will make possible a steady production of high quality. Similar conventions operate, or should operate, in the area generally called handicraft, but the one-sided competition with mass-produced goods has largely reduced this to a boutique culture, or what I think of as the ashtray syndrome. In the past, everything from buildings to clothes and household objects went through a certain cycle of taste: first they were in fashion; then they fell out of fashion and became ridiculous; then they settled into the softer lighting of "quaint," and cultivated people became interested in them again; and finally they began to take on some of the archaic dignity of the primitive. Nowadays, the expanding of the antique market and the growing sense of the possible commercial value of whatever is no longer being produced has considerably shortened this process. The sojourn in a period of unfashionable limbo has to be very brief when an "antique" can be an object twenty years old. Similarly, immigrants from Europe or Asia often reject their own cultural heritage in an effort to adapt to the new country, so that it takes another generation before they turn toward their own origins again, but that cycle is also shortening.

This levelling out of cultural interest is in itself healthy: the wild fluctuations of taste and fashion in the past have done nothing but harm, and any philosophy of preservation has to avoid the value judgments which are really nothing but rationalizings of a destructive impulse. I think of the Italian Director of Antiquities in Thornton Wilder's *The Cabala*, whose reputation was based on his eagerness to destroy a Baroque church in order to expose a thirteenth-century door. Our attitude to the past needs more of the impartiality of the archaeologist who excavates all layers and cultural periods of his site with equal care. One would be very deficient in imagination and curiosity not to have some interest in relics of the Hopewell culture or in the Norse remains, if that is what they are, at L'Anse aux Meadows in Newfoundland. But the industrial archaeology that uncovers the pottery, glass, and brick factories of nineteenth-century Ontario has its importance too, as we need more tangible reminders of our immediate past than the mere fact that many place-names end in "mills."

Despite the best efforts of reproduction it remains true that any physical artefact is subject to decay, especially if it is an outdoor object in any climate that at all resembles ours. Restoration is an often disastrous solution: tourists in English cathedrals hear a good deal about the vandalism of Cromwell's soldiers, but the devastation wrought by Victorian restorers has been often far worse, however much better the motive. The kind of preservation that we have in Williamsburg and similar large-scale open museums is in a sense almost antihistorical: it shows us, not life in time as a continuous process, but life arrested at a certain point, in a sort of semi-permanent drama. There is nothing wrong with this, but it gives us a cross-section of history, a world confronting us rather than preceding us. Something similar is true of the building which is a historical allusion or quotation, like collegiate Gothic, replicas of European churches, or Georgian residential areas. The tendency to make the past contemporary with the present is part of what Shakespeare means when he says, addressing Time:

> Our dates are brief, and therefore we admire
> What thou dost foist upon us that is old,
> And rather make them born to our desire,
> Than think that we before have heard them told. [Sonnet 123, ll. 5–8]

In a sense every physical artefact is a protest against time, an expression of a desire for permanence in a world of change. This is especially true of the huge monuments put up by kings, priests, and dictators, either to their own glory or to the glory of their gods or nations. We notice a persistent association between such monuments and death, and from the pyramids to our own war memorials there has run the constant realization that death is the nearest that life can get to permanence. One of the better chapters in *Parkinson's Law* remarks on the tendency of institutions to put up their largest and most impressive buildings at the moment when they are passing out of existence, so that the building instantly becomes a kind of cenotaph.[6] In a national capital like this, one could perhaps think of more examples than it would be tactful to mention. In general, the kind of artefact that posterity usually finds the most expendable culturally is also the hardest to remove physically.

In every age great artists attach themselves to the social establishment, and make their living from it, or, at least, live without questioning or quarrelling with it. Many of the artists we most deeply revere today, Bach, Shakespeare, Michelangelo, were busy professional men with commissions to fill and deadlines to meet. And yet, as time goes on, this view of culture, in which the artists are dependent on the patronage of their societies, begins to reverse its perspective. In nearly forty years of teaching literature in a university, I have found that William Morris is a writer and artist whose interest for me has never palled, and whose influence on my own social attitude has remained central. In Morris there is an apparent inconsistency between his fascination with medieval culture and his very left-of-centre political views. The inconsistency disappears when we realize that for Morris the creators of a culture, and those who give it its style, are not warriors or kings or priests, or the political or religious ideas they stand for, but architects and sculptors and poets. The ideal world that he presents in *News from Nowhere* is a world where everyone has become something of an artist, though it is the quality of design in the so-called minor or functional arts that he is primarily interested in, and regards as the essential clue to a culture's vitality. Morris' future world is not very interested in history or in preserving its past: it is too happy designing and making things in the present, though there is an indication at the end of the story that its historical perspective is going to expand. But even without this indication Morris makes an important point for those who do wish to preserve their past. Our sense of the need for preservation has in it a certain distrust in the integrity of our own cultural tradition: once things are gone, we have little confidence in our ability to replace them with new things equally good. The trouble is, once again, not the lack of creative people, but the lack of response to creativeness in our society. The rudder, so to speak, that guides our philosophy of preservation ultimately has to be the continuing vitality of our cultural tradition. Without that, the task of preserving our heritage will have in it a quality of desperation unhealthy both for it and for us.

Our museums preserve objects of the past, and by preserving them, if William Morris is right, they also express a potentially revolutionary view of history. I spoke earlier of the developing countries who are so proud of the achievements of their own regime and so impatient with the culture of their reactionary past. Even in China, deeply interested as it is in archaeology, a friend of mine, inspecting some of the great cultural monuments of Peking a few years ago, was accompanied by a guide who remarked that if she had her way she would cover them all up with posters explaining how badly exploited the workers were in those days. The point is, I think, that the social milieu of any culture will always be full of human folly and cruelty, but that whatever is beautifully designed always remains in the state of innocence, always a symbol of the kind of thing that human struggles for freedom and happiness are about.

In a sense it is a considerable advantage to Canada not to have so much history to live with as the European countries, to say nothing of the Middle Eastern ones. In so small and thickly settled a country as England, archaeology has to be largely a salvaging operation, a matter of keeping one jump ahead of the steam shovel. There is no way out of this, short of an atomic war that would cut the world's population in half, and in the meantime the preservation of visible monuments has its own kind of panic. However strongly we may condemn Henry VIII's dissolution of the monasteries, it might have been a crushing burden for the National Trust if all those abbeys had survived. Similarly, it is exceptional when the actual site of an important or interesting event, like the murder of Becket in Canterbury Cathedral, still remains: most of what historical markers remind us of has vanished forever into Newtonian space. Here again what is of primary importance is the quality of our historical imagination, the ability, if I may try to express something very difficult to express, to see things, not merely as objects confronting us, but as growing in time, as having come out of our own past and moving towards our own future.

The title of my talk speaks of Canada as a new world without revolution. As you have gathered, there is a certain irony in this: we have fully participated in all the social and cultural consequences of the American Revolution, and its advantages and disadvantages are equally ours.

Even Quebec, so long preoccupied with maintaining the traditions of its past, has gone through a remarkably complete cultural revolution, though alleged to be a quiet one.[7] Yet it is still perhaps the absence of a revolutionary tradition in Canada, the tendency to move continuously rather than discontinuously through time, that has given Canadian culture one very important and distinctive characteristic. This is its respect for the documentary. Canadian painting began with documentary painters like Krieghoff and Paul Kane, who may have kept an eye on the European market but were nevertheless keen observers of what was around them. Group of Seven painting, along with that of Thomson and Emily Carr, was documentary painting to an unusual degree, almost an imaginative mapping and survey of the remoter parts of the country; and we have also the extensive "war records" of painting from both wars. What Jackson and Thomson did for landscape, Riopelle and Pellan and their contemporaries are doing for the Cartesian culture that we live in now. Canadian film has always been remarkable for its sensitive documentary feeling, applied to everything from Eskimo and Indian life to the urban cultures of Toronto and Montreal. Canadian literature, in the nineteenth century as well as this one, and in both poetry and fiction, has had a distinctive attachment to a sober narrative technique, a clear sense of fact, and a curious tendency to itemize, to make a functional use of lists and catalogues and inventories. The implication is, perhaps, that the Canadian consciousness is one peculiarly adapted to preserving its own heritage, not like a miser guarding his hoard or a watchdog snarling at a burglar, not like a man living among his memories and reshaping them in a form more attractive to his ego, but like one who understands that all coherent action, as well as all moral integrity, depends on the continuity of the present with the past.

68

Conclusion to the Second Edition of *Literary History of Canada*

1976

From Literary History of Canada: Canadian Literature in English, *2nd ed., in 3 vols., ed. Carl Klinck et al. (Toronto: University of Toronto Press, 1976), 3:318–32. Reprinted in* University of Toronto Graduate, *4 (Winter 1976): 6–7, in DG, 71–80, in RCLI, 99–117, in ECLI, 97–115, and, partially, as "The American Way of Life Is Slowly Being Canadianized" in* Chelsea Journal, *3 (July–August 1977): 190–3. Typescripts are in NFF, 1988, box 5, files s–u.*

The essays Frye refers to are as follows: Michael Cross, Dalhousie University, "Canadian History"; George Woodcock, University of British Columbia, "Poetry"; William New, University of British Columbia, "Fiction"; Claude Bissell, University of Toronto, "Politics and Literature in the 1960s"; Desmond Pacey, University of New Brunswick, "The Course of Canadian Criticism"; Henry B. Mayo, Carleton University, "Writing in the Social Sciences"; John Chapman, Department of Communications, Ottawa, "The Physical Sciences and Engineering"; Sheila Egoff, University of British Columbia, "Children's Literature"; William Swinton, University of Toronto, "The Biological Sciences"; Malcolm Ross, Dalhousie University, "Critical Theory: Some Trends"; Thomas Goudge, University of Toronto, "Philosophical Literature"; John Webster Grant, Emmanuel College, Victoria University, "Religious and Theological Writings"; Clara Thomas, York University, "Biography"; John Ripley, McGill University, "Drama and Theatre"; Lauriat Lane, Jr., University of New Brunswick, "Literary Criticism and Scholarship."

It is difficult to know what to say, as a general conclusion, to this part of the *Literary History* that is not already said or implied in my previous conclusion. Ten or twelve years is not a generation, much less, even in these future shock days, a historical period. The logical starting point, I think, has to be the reason for producing a volume of this size so few years after the original one, and the reason is not difficult to grasp. Mr. Cross, writing on history, says that five hundred books in that field were produced during five of the years he covers; Mr. Woodcock counts over a thousand volumes of verse, excluding anthologies; nearly every contributor says or implies something about the colossal verbal explosion that has taken place in Canada since 1960. Such a quantitative increase eventually makes for a qualitative change: this change cannot, in so short a time, reveal much essentially new to the critical observer, but it does mean that the trends I studied in the previous conclusion have reached something of a crisis since then. All I can do here is to try to characterize that crisis: there can be no question of attempting any rounded general survey of the period.

Our reviewers are comprehensive to the verge of omniscience, and with all their selectivity they have little space to do more than mention a great number of books which are not simply entertaining, interesting, or instructive, but are richly rewarding to read. Such critical comments as they are able to make are often tantalizingly brief, like Mr. New's remark about the influence of structuralism and linguistics on the prose style of Canadian fiction. The fact that the book is something of a catalogue is nothing against it, but is on the contrary essential to its usefulness. Part of the total verbal explosion is the information explosion, and one of the more efficient ways of trying to cope with that is the "review of recent scholarship" article, a genre which this book closely approximates.

Critical methods, confronting such an avalanche of material, have to become rather more subtle than they were in the old days of collecting Canadians, putting the authentic specimens of Loyalist descent (or "stock," in the E.K. Broadus anthology)[1] in the centre of a penumbra of immigrant, expatriate, transient, and tourist writers, some of whom, like Grove and Grey Owl, turned out to be masks of quite different people. The mask in Canadian literature would make a good thesis for somebody, and doubtless has done. Twenty years ago, the Canadian critical scene was full of schools and orthodoxies and heresies and divergences and conflicting theories, the prevalence of which, in literary criticism no less than in religion or psychology, indicates a general failure to understand what is being talked about. It would be an affectation for me to pretend not to notice that I am extensively featured in this book myself, and among the many things I am grateful for and deeply appreciate, one is the fact that the phrase "the Frye school of mythopoeic poetry" is so briefly dismissed by Mr. Woodcock. There is no Frye school of mythopoeic poetry; criticism and poetry cannot possibly be related in that way; the myth of a poem is the structural principle of that poem, and consequently all poems that make any sense at all are equally mythopoeic, and so on and so on: the phrase, as Borges remarks about something in Fichte, is almost inexhaustibly fallacious.[2] The concreteness of this book, the absence of anxiety and special pleading, the constant awareness of the genuine authority of the literature the reviewer is dealing with, is reflected in the literature itself. Mr. Bissell notes that a good deal of recent political writing, even when strongly partisan, shows a real concern for objectivity and respect for facts; and similarly, the thesis novel, the assertive poem, the rib-nudging allegory, the assumption that literature can be "effective" only when it turns into subliterary rhetoric, seem to be receding from the literary scene.

For well over a century, and years before the satire in *Grip* that Mr. Pacey quotes,[3] discussions about Canadian literature usually took the form of the shopper's dialogue: "Have you any Canadian literature today?" "Well, we're expecting something in very shortly." But that age is over, and writing this conclusion gives me rather the feeling of driving a last spike, of waking up from the National Neurosis. There is much more to come, just as there were all those CPR trains still to come, but Canadian literature is here, perhaps still a minor but certainly no longer a gleam in a paternal critic's eye. It is a typically Canadian irony that such a cataract started pouring out of the presses just before Marshall McLuhan became the most famous of Canadian critics for saying that the book was finished. I doubt if one can find this in McLuhan, except by quoting him irresponsibly out of context, but it is what he was widely believed to have said, and the assertion became very popular, as anything that sounds anti-intellectual always does. Abandoning irony, one may say that a population the size of English-writing Canada, subject to all the handicaps which have been chronicled so often in Canadian criticism, does not produce such a bulk of good writing without an extraordinary vitality and morale behind it. At the same time, to achieve, to bring a future into the present, is also to become finite, and the sense of that is always a little disconcerting, even though becoming finite means becoming genuinely human.

Canadians, as I have implied, have a highly developed sense of irony, but even so, de Gaulle's monumental gaffe of 1967, "vive le Québec libre," is one of the great ironic remarks in Canadian history, because it

Conclusion to the Second Edition of *Literary History of Canada* 451

was hailing the emergence of precisely the force that Quebec had really got free from.[4] For the Quiet Revolution was as impressive an achievement of imaginative freedom as the contemporary world can show: freedom not so much from clerical domination or corrupt politics as from the burden of tradition.[5] The whole *je me souviens* complex in French Canada, the anxiety of resisting change, the strong emotionalism which was, as emotion by itself always is, geared to the past: this was what Quebec had shaken off to such an astonishing degree. It was accompanied, naturally enough, by intense anti-English and separatist feelings, which among the more confused took the form that de Gaulle was interested in, a French neo-colonialism. This last is dead already: separatism is still a strong force, and will doubtless remain one for some time, but one gets the feeling that it is being inexorably bypassed by history, and that even if it achieves its aims it will do so in a historical vacuum. I begin with French Canada because it seems to me that the decisive cultural event in English Canada during the past fifteen years has been the impact of French Canada and its new sense of identity. After so long and so obsessive a preoccupation with the same subject, it took the Quiet Revolution to create a real feeling of identity in English Canada, and to make cultural nationalism, if that is the best phrase, a genuine force in the country, even a bigger and more significant one than economic nationalism, which is, as Mr. Mayo notes, mainly a Central Canada movement.

The immense power of American penetration into Canada is traditionally thought of as either economic or subcultural: Canadians buy American cars and watch American situation comedies on television. Without denying the importance of these phenomena, in the last decade there has been a considerable growth of emphasis on more genuinely cultural aspects. This emphasis has affected Canadian attitudes to the publishing business, to the Canadian editions of *Time* and the *Reader's Digest*, to American television programs brought in, with their advertising, by cable, and to many other things; but perhaps the most widely publicized issue has been that of American appointments to Canadian universities. The reactions to these proposals, for quota systems and the like, may be theoretically untenable and practically impotent, but the kind of problem they try to meet is not an unreal one. Academics of course are a conservative breed, and they still try to keep explaining to one another that scholarship knows no boundaries. Scholarship may not, but culture does; and the only reason for having scholarship is that it is necessary to culture.

I am not a continentalist myself, although I have been called one,[6] and I can see that in the later work of Underhill, for instance, a writer whom of course I deeply respect and have learned much from, a naive admiration for things American amounts almost to a betrayal of his own liberalism. An independent Canada would be much more useful to the United States itself than a dependent or annexed one would be, and it is of great importance to the United States to have a critical view of it centred in Canada, a view which is not hostile but is simply another view. The United States has its share of fools like other countries, and just as fifty years ago senators would propose that Britain hand over Canada in payment of her war debt, so there are senators and others now (see Mr. Chapman's article) who tell us how lovely it would be if we placed all our resources unquestioningly in American hands. Resistance to such things is in the United States' own best interests. The nationalism that has evolved in Canada is on the whole a positive development, in which self-awareness has been far more important than aggressiveness. Perhaps identity only is identity when it becomes, not militant, but a way of defining oneself against something else. In any case problems of culture and of verbal articulation are the primary concern of this book. I see the kind of creative vitality which this book records as an emerging form of Canadian self-definition, and that involves looking at the difference from the American parallel development. The word "parallel" is important: Canada may be an American colony, as is often said, by me among others, but Canadians have never thought of the United States as a parental figure, like Britain, and analogies of youthful revolt and the like would be absurd.

To begin with a different kind of analogy: in countries where Marxism has not come to power, but where there is a strong Marxist minority, we see what an advantage it is to have a unified conceptual structure that can be applied to practically anything. It may often distort what it is applied to, but that matters less than the tactical advantage of having it. Defenders of more empirical points of view find their battlefronts disintegrating into separate and isolated outposts. They may demonstrate that this or that point is wrong, but such rearguard actions lack glamour. The same principle can be applied to the pragmatic, compromising, ad hoc, ramshackle Canadian tradition vis-à-vis the far more integrated and revolutionary American one. The coherence of the "American way of life" is often underestimated by Americans themselves, because the more thoughtful citizens of any country are likely to be more preoccupied with

Conclusion to the Second Edition of *Literary History of Canada* 453

its anomalies. Hence outsiders, including Canadians, may find the consistency easier to see. De Tocqueville, who didn't like much of what he saw in the United States, wrote his book [*Democracy in America*] very largely about that consistency, almost in spite of himself.

As Canada and the United States went their separate ways on the same continent, eventually coming to speak for the most part the same language, their histories took on a strong pattern of contrast. The United States found its identity in the eighteenth century, the age of rationalism and enlightenment. It retains a strong intellectual fascination with the eighteenth century: its founding fathers are still its primary cultural heroes, and the bicentenary celebrations of 1976, from all accounts, will be mainly celebrations of the eighteenth century rather than of the present day. The eighteenth-century cultural pattern took on a revolutionary, and therefore a deductive, shape, provided with a manifesto of independence and a written constitution. This in turn developed a rational attitude to the continuity of life in time, and this attitude seems to me the central principle of the American way of life. The best image for it is perhaps that of the express train. It is a conception of progress, but of progress defined by mechanical rather than organic metaphors, and hence the affinity with the eighteenth century is not really historical: it tends in fact to be antihistorical. Washington, Franklin, Jefferson, with their imperturbable common sense, are thought of, in the popular consciousness, more as deceased contemporaries than as ancestors living among different cultural referents. The past is thus assimilated to the present, a series of stations that our express train has stopped at and gone beyond.

In law and politics, new situations are met by reinterpreting, or in the last resort amending, an eighteenth-century document: proceeding, in other words, in a deductive direction, giving priority to the kind of logic which most clearly represents the mechanics of thought. In economics, there has been, and with qualifications there still is, a strong belief in laissez-faire, as a continuous and semi-autonomous process that will work by itself if left alone. The most characteristic American philosophical attitude is the pragmatism, so different from Canadian pragmatism, which sees truth as emerging from a course of consistent action. Its most characteristic attitude to education is the anticontemplative Dewey conception of learning through doing, or, again, through continuous activity. In religion, the real established church in the United States is that of eighteenth-century deism, where God is the umpire behind the competing churches, leaving man to justify himself by the continuity of his good works, which include the separating of church from state and the secularizing of education.

In attempting to characterize such a central driving force, one is bound to oversimplify and ignore powerful counter-forces. The United States is full of people deeply opposed to the attitudes I call characteristic. I see these attitudes, however, as symbols of something which has so far proved flexible enough to contain and absorb those counter-forces, greatly modifying itself as it has done so, but becoming stronger in consequence, and hence still in the driver's seat. What I am trying to describe cannot be reduced to a cliché, like the "Consciousness One" of *The Greening of America*,[7] or the naive optimism that perished with the 1929 crash, or a simple-minded trust in technology, much less "materialism," or a "worship of the almighty dollar." The traumas of Vietnam and Watergate have another side. The original impulse to go into Vietnam was part of a quite genuine political belief which, as a belief, is still there; and what carried public morale through the sickening revelations of Watergate was a loyalty to the constitutional tradition, which still functions much as the Torah does for Judaism. In the beginning the Americans created America, and America is the beginning of the world. That is, it is the oldest country in the world: no other nation's history goes back so far with less social metamorphosis. Through all the anxieties and doubts of recent years one can still hear the confident tones of its Book of Genesis: "We hold these truths to be self-evident." At least a Canadian can hear them, because nothing has ever been self-evident in Canada.

Canada had no enlightenment, and very little eighteenth century. The British and French spent the eighteenth century in Canada battering down each other's forts, and Canada went directly from the Baroque expansion of the seventeenth century to the Romantic expansion of the nineteenth. The result was the cultural situation that I tried to characterize in my earlier conclusion. Identity in Canada has always had something about it of a centrifugal movement into far distance, of clothes on a growing giant coming apart at the seams, of an elastic about to snap. Stephen Leacock's famous hero who rode off rapidly in all directions was unmistakably a Canadian.[8] This expanding movement has to be counterbalanced by a sense of having constantly to stay together by making tremendous voluntary efforts at intercommunication, whether of building the CPR or of holding federal-provincial conferences.

There is a novel called *Canadian Born*, by Mrs. Humphry Ward, written about 1908. In the opening pages we meet the heroine, Lady Merton, an Englishwoman whose father is important enough for her to be travelling across Canada in a private railway car. They are held up by a "sinkhole," described as "a place where you can't find no bottom,"[9] and which ten trainloads of dumping has failed to fill. Still, Lady Merton is deeply impressed with what she sees of "the march of a new people to its home" [48], especially after she meets an attractive Canadian male, and says to a less enthusiastic Britisher, "Don't you feel that we must get the natives to guide us—to put us in the way? It is only they who can really feel the poetry of it all" [45]. She later says: "We see the drama—we feel it—much more than they can who are in it," and quotes Matthew Arnold: "On to the bound of the waste—on to the City of God!" [49].

The author is a keen and intelligent observer, and her view of Canada in 1908 is consistent with many other contemporary views of it. She is also trying hard not to be patronizing. Nevertheless the great march of a new people can be seen better by visitors from higher civilizations, and the natives, poor sods, can only feel (not write) the poetry of it all. They may be headed for the City of God, but it is a very long way to the bound of the waste, and in the meantime there is that sink-hole. She has caught one of the essential Canadian moods, the feeling of apology for being so huge and tedious an obstacle on the way to somewhere more interesting, whether the City of God, the glittering treasures of the Orient, or the opulent United States. It seems to me very characteristic of Canada that its highest Order should have for its motto: "looking for a better country." The quotation is from the New Testament, where the better country really is the City of God, but the feeling it expresses has more mundane contexts.[10]

Such feelings of insecurity and inferiority are still with us: the brain drain has eased considerably, but there is the more serious issue raised in J.J. Brown's *Ideas in Exile*, referred to by Mr. Chapman;[11] and we still force pastoral myths on our children designed to reassure their elders, according to Miss Egoff. But transitions to something different are marked in this book. Some of the articles deal with nonliterary subjects, and there, what is important, for the present context, is not that many Canadians are distinguished chemists or engineers or whatever, but that all the nonliterary subjects have their role to play in creating the imaginative climate that this book is trying to put into isobars. If we look at Mr. Swinton's chapter, for instance, we see that there is no such thing as "Canadian biology": the phrase makes no sense. But the fact that Canada was, a couple of generations ago, regarded as possessed of "unlimited natural resources," and the later pricking of that gaseous balloon, gives biology a distinctive resonance in Canadian cultural life, and helps, for instance, to make Farley Mowat one of our best-known and best-selling authors. Much the same is true of the intense Canadian interest in geology and geophysics, reflected in Mr. Chapman's account of Tuzo Wilson.[12] I have often thought that Robert Frost's line, "The land was ours before we were the land's" [*The Gift Outright*, l. 1], however appropriate to the United States, does not apply to Canada, where the opposite seems to me to have been true, even in the free land grant days. Canadians were held by the land before they emerged as a people on it, a land with its sinister aspects, or what Warren Tallman, referred to by Mr. Ross, calls the "gray wolf,"[13] but with its fostering aspects too, of the kind that come into the phrase of Alice Wilson which one is grateful to Mr. Swinton for quoting: "the earth touches every life."[14]

Many of these themes illustrate the importance in Canada of the theme of survival, the title of Margaret Atwood's very influential book which is, as Mr. Pacey says, a most perceptive essay on an aspect of the Canadian sensibility. Mr. Ross points out some of its limitations: it does not have, and was clearly not intended to have, the kind of comprehensiveness that a conceptual thesis, like the frontier theory in American history, would need. But it is not simply saying that Canadians are a nation of losers. What the author means by survival comes out more clearly, I think, in her extraordinary novel *Surfacing*, where the heroine is isolated from her small group and finds something very archaic, both inside and outside her, taking over her identity. The word survival implies living through a series of crises, each one unexpected and different from the others, each one to be met on its own terms. Failure to meet the crisis means that some death principle moves in. From Mr. Goudge we learn that the theme of survival has had some odd extensions in Canadian philosophy: death itself may be simply one more discontinuity in existence.

This discontinuous sense of life is obviously a contrast to the American sense of continuity, and it affords more scope for the tragic, as distinct from the ironic, mood in Canadian literature. American fiction is prevailingly ironic for many reasons, but one reason is that irony (as a mode of fiction, not as an attitude) fits the American continuous perspective: it presents life as a horizontal continuum which stops rather than ends, like a car which may or may not go into the ditch but has run out of gas anyway. In tragedy, however dingy the hero may be, there is a fall through time, a polarizing of two levels of existence. They are equally valid forms, but there is a great deal more facile irony than facile tragedy, and the standard ironic formulas, the Slow Strangle, the Ouroboros, or Biting Oneself in the Tail, the Hateful Self-Discovery, are often used rather perfunctorily, as symbols of a serious literary intention. Tragic narratives are more structured, formalized, even contrived, reflecting as they so often do the sense of contrivance in outward circumstances. The affinity with the tragic is part of the affinity with formalism in Canadian writing, and both may be connected with the sense of discontinuity, the feeling for sudden descent or catastrophe, that seems to me to have an unusual emphasis in Canada.

The theme of descent may be as astringent as it is in *Surfacing* or as genial as in Robertson Davies's *Manticore*, where it takes the form of a Jungian analysis followed by images of caves and bears. But in the Zurich clinic, no less than in the Quebec forest, there is still something of the "gray wolf," even of the sink-hole. In the fall of the hero of David Knight's tightly constructed Nigerian story, *Farquharson's Physique*, in the Donnelly massacre at the end of Reaney's trilogy,[15] in the writhings of Margaret Laurence's Hagar and Rachel[16] (Mr. New points out the importance of the perspective on time in *The Stone Angel*), we realize that we are still in the country of Grove and Pratt. Some contributors have commented on the tragic tone of George Grant's *Lament for a Nation* and Creighton's *Canada's First Century*: the interest of such books does not end with the issues they deal with, because the tragic is always a major aspect of the human situation. Still, one may hope for a writer of equal power who will see a structure of comedy also in the Canadian story.

If we look at the three eighteenth-century events that defined the future of Canada (as of so much else in the modern world), the Quebec Act, the American Revolution, and the French Revolution, we see the whole range of a political spectrum that still confronts us.[17] The Quebec Act came close to an Edmund Burke model: it was an inductive, pragmatic recognition of a de facto situation, and the situation was one of those profoundly illogical ones that Burke considered typical of human life generally.[18] The two factors to be taken into account were: (a) the British have conquered the French (b) the British have done nothing of the kind. The only way out of this was a settlement that guaranteed some rights to both parties. The French Revolution, proceeding deductively from general principles, was what Burke condemned so bitterly as "metaphysical," and was also the forerunner of the dialectical Marxist revolutions. The American Revolution came in the middle, a strong contrast to the Canadian settlement, as we have seen, but keeping far more of the broadening-through-precedent British tradition than the French one did.

Hence although the United States itself got started on a revolutionary basis, it was a basis of a kind that made it difficult for that country to come to terms with the later Marxist revolutions. This produced a growing isolation from other revolutionary ideologies and societies, the climax of which was the maintaining, for so many years, of the grotesque fantasy that the refugee army in Formosa was the government of China. At the same time, the "melting pot" assumptions of the nineteenth-century United States, the ambition described in the inscription on the Statue of Liberty of making a united democracy out of the most varied social and racial elements, became profoundly modified. The conception of the "hundred per cent American" has been succeeded by a growing feeling that the various elements in American society can perhaps contribute more to it by retaining something of their original cultural characteristics. Here there is a growing similarity to the Canadian pattern, where the necessity of recognizing two major social elements at the beginning meant that nobody could ever possibly know what a "hundred per cent Canadian" was, and hence led to a much more relaxed ideal of a national "melting pot."

When the last edition of this book was published, the centenary of Canadian Confederation was coming up: the bicentenary of the American Revolution is the corresponding event on this horizon, if an anniversary is an event. It seems to me that a very conscious and significant exchange of identities between Canada and the United States has taken place since then. The latter, traditionally so buoyant, extroverted, and forward-looking, appears to be entering a prolonged period of self-examination. I am setting down very subjective impressions here, derived mainly from what little I know of American literature and literary criticism, but I feel that a search for a more genuinely historical dimension of consciousness has been emerging at least since Vietnam turned into a nightmare, and is still continuing. Part of it is a different attitude to the past, a re-examining of it to see what things went wrong when. This is not simply a reversing of the current of continuity, like a psychiatric patient exploring his childhood: there seems to be a growing tendency to think more in terms of inevitable discontinuities. Erik Erikson's book on identity, an attempt to clarify the psychology of the disturbances of a few years ago, is an example.[19]

Another part of the re-examination, and imaginatively perhaps the more significant part, revolves around the question: has the American empire, like the British empire before it, simply passed its climacteric and is it now declining, or at least becoming aware of limits? If so, the past takes on a rise-and-fall parabola shape, not a horizontal line in which the past is on the same plane as the present. This may not sound like much on paper, but changes in central metaphors and conceptual diagrams are symbolic of the most profound disturbances that the human consciousness has to face. After the strident noise and confusion of the later sixties, there was, for all the discussion, an eerie quietness about the response to Watergate, and to the irony of a President's turning into a cleaned-out gambler a few months after getting an overwhelming mandate. Even the violence of the now almost unmanageable cities seems to have caused less panic than one might reasonably have expected. Perhaps it is not too presumptuous to say, although few non-Canadian readers would understand what was meant, that the American way of life is slowly becoming Canadianized.

Meanwhile, Canada, traditionally so diffident, introverted, past-and-future fixated, incoherent, inarticulate, proceeding by hunch and feeling, seems to be taking on, at least culturally, an inner composure and integration of outlook, even some buoyancy and confidence. The most obvious reasons for this are technological. The airplane and the television set, in particular, have brought a physical simultaneity into the country that has greatly modified the older, and perhaps still underlying, blazed-trail and canoe mentality. As Mr. Cross says, we are now in a post-Laurentian phase of development. In the railway days, being a federal MP from British Columbia or a literary scholar in Alberta required an intense, almost romantic, commitment, because of the investment of time and energy involved in getting from such places to the distant centres that complemented them. Today such things are jobs like other jobs, and the relation to the primary community has assumed a correspondingly greater importance. This is the positive and creative side of the relaxing of centralizing tensions in modern society, of which separatism represents a less creative one.

The influence of television is often blamed for violence, and certainly there are television programs that are profoundly distasteful from this point of view. But there is another side to television: bringing the remote into our living room can be a very sobering form of communication, and a genuinely humanizing one. I remember the thirties, when so many "intellectuals" were trying to rationalize or ignore the Stalin massacres or whatever such horrors did not fit their categories, and thinking even then that part of their infantilism was in being men of print: they saw only lines of type on a page, not lines of prisoners shuffling off to death camps. But something of the real evil of the Vietnam war did get on television, and the effect seems to have been on the whole a healthy one. At least the American public came to hate the war, instead of becoming complacent or inured to its atrocities.

Similarly in Canada: Eskimos, blacks, Indians, perhaps even Wasps, cannot go on being comic-strip stereotypes after they have been fully exposed on television. Of course better knowledge can also create dislike and more tension; and when I speak of an exchange of identities I certainly do not mean that Canada will acquire anything of the simplistic optimism of an earlier age in the United States. Television is one of many factors which will make that impossible. Another is the curtailing of resources, already mentioned. Still another is the emergence of chilling technical possibilities in genetics, which raise questions about identity that make our traditional ones look like learning to spell cat. Another is the geography of the global village. In the nineteenth century the Canadian imagination responded to the Biblical phrase "from the river unto the ends of the earth" [Psalm 72:8], and one of the historians referred to by Mr. Cross, W.L. Morton, has written with great sensitivity about the impact, psychological and otherwise, of the northern frontier on the Canadian consciousness.[20] But now Canada has become a kind of global Switzerland, surrounded by the United States on the south, the European common market on the east, the Soviet Union on the north, China and Japan on the west.

In some essays in this book a distinctive Canadian bias shows through that may be culturally significant. The fact that Descartes is a French philosopher is not simply a biographical fact: Descartes is French in the sense that he is a permanent and central part of a tradition that makes France different in its cultural pattern from other countries. Similarly with Locke as a British philosopher, or Kant as a German one, or William James as an American one. Canada seems to have no philosopher of this defining kind: what Canadian philosophy does have is a strong emphasis on religion, so remarkable as to be worth pausing on for a moment.

Mr. Goudge, writing of philosophy, is compelled to deal with religion even though there is a separate chapter on religion; the only cult-philosopher in the country, Bernard Lonergan, referred to by Mr. Grant, is a religious philosopher; much is said in this book and elsewhere about the religious drive in George Grant, in McLuhan, in myself. In Creighton the drive may not be technically religious, but it is certainly prophetic. Here again French Canada established a pattern which English Canada to some degree imitated, of keeping church and state closer together, particularly in education, than was done in the United States. Mr. Grant's urbane treatment of ecumenical movements in Canada makes it clear that while religion is ideally a uniting force in society, it is more likely in practice to be a divisive one. Religion in Canada has closely followed the centrifugal and expanding rhythm of Canadian life, spearheaded by missionaries, from the seventeenth-century Jesuits to our own time—even Norman Bethune was a missionary in a sense. As it did so an intensely competitive spirit developed, as we can see if we walk through any Canadian town. The centrifugal movement came to a halt when the population started rolling back into the growing cities, and the urbanizing of Canadian mores greatly weakened the social influence of the churches, which long remained fixated on the earlier social values. The temperance movement, for example, as we find it in, say, Nellie McClung, was often associated with a very genuine political liberalism, even radicalism, in nineteenth-century Canada, but the growth of cities turned it into a horse-and-buggy phenomenon that could rouse no response except ridicule.

There is nothing here sociologically different from what happened in the United States, but the comparative absence of what I have called American deism may have made the impact of religion on the Canadian consciousness more direct. I remember a Spring Thaw skit of some years ago, where a Roman Catholic, an Anglican, and a United Church leader sang a song about charity and brotherly love, then each in turn, after glancing darkly at his confrères, stepped forward and informed the audience that of course *he* was God's accredited spokesman. The audience found the skit very funny, but I recall someone remarking that possibly only a Canadian audience would have done so.

I had long realized that the religious context of so many Canadian intellectuals had something to do with the peripheral situation of Canada, in the way that, for instance, Denmark was an appropriate place for a Kierkegaard in nineteenth-century Europe. Kierkegaard's hostility to what he called "Christendom" had a lot to do with the impact of the mores of bigger countries on his own. When I read Mr. Woodcock on the role of the Canadian poet as a counterculture hero, something else rang a bell, and enabled me to make a connection with literature.

Canada has always been a cool climate for heroes: Mr. Bissell speaks of the grudging support given to our last three prime ministers, all of whom, whatever one thinks of their policies, have compared very favourably, in intelligence and personal integrity, with some of those who adorned the White House in the same period; and Mrs. Thomas's survey of Canadian biography reveals very little response in Canada to any Carlylean great man conception of history. It would be interesting, and very typical of Canada, if Canadian literature had found its soul, so to speak, by defining the poet as a counter-hero or anti-hero. Of course this countercultural aspect of poetry is true of the United States also; but it seems to me that Canada has been steadily building up something like a North American counter-culture against the United States which is now big and complex enough to be examined on its own terms. Once more, "against" simply means differentiation.

It may be the end of the century before any real coherence will emerge from our cultural pattern: so far we are confined to what Eliot would call hints followed by guesses. But some things in the Canadian tradition are beginning to look very international. It seems to me that in the democracies generally today, the dialectical habit of mind is giving way to a tendency to think in containing terms, where the antithesis is included and absorbed instead of being defined by exclusion. This is really a conservative tendency in thought, although not directly connected with political conservatism: Mr Bissell quotes an example of it from Abraham Rotstein, who is very far from being a right-winger. At the same time, as we can see if we look carefully at what Mr Cross has to say about W.L. Morton, W.J. Eccles, and Carl Berger in particular, the tendency is conservative, in the sense of revolving around the question of what it is necessary or important to conserve. As such, it is a tendency that fulfils the tradition of Burke in Canada, in which opposition forms a larger synthesis instead of an apocalyptic separation of sheep and goats. The anti-Marxist attitude of mind suggested here, if I am right about it, is one of crucial importance for literature, in Canada and elsewhere. Marxism is a very remarkable intellectual achievement as well as the dominant moral force in the contemporary world, but, at least wherever it has come to power, it cannot really cope with the humanities or with the place of the arts in modern society.

Conclusion to the Second Edition of *Literary History of Canada*

When I read through the more purely literary chapters of this book, and check them against my own meagre first-hand knowledge, I am struck by a feature of Canadian writing that seems to me a literary parallel to the conservative tendency just spoken of. It might be called formalism or even classicism: I should prefer, however, to call it simply professionalism. Modern society has decreed that very few writers shall live by paper alone, and the great majority of our writers are part-time writers, but that is not what I mean. I mean writing from within literature and within its genres, as opposed to the "I've got something important to say" approach of the amateur, who then looks around for a fictional or poetic vehicle to put his important say into. The professional attitude has affinities, if we like, with the principle that the medium is the message. I should say rather that in fully realized writing there is no difference between structure and content, what is called content being the structure of the individual work, as distinct from the structure of the convention or genre to which it belongs.

Professionalism means technique and craftsmanship, which amateur writers often think of as a weakening of the moral fibre. Canadian criticism has been plagued a good deal by the foolish notion that imagination is a by-product of extremes, specifically emotional extremes. We can't have a great literature in Canada because we're too safe, sane, dull, humdrum—not enough lynchings, one critic suggested. The professional writer discovers from his experience that the imagination is the constructive element in the mind, and that intensity cannot be conveyed except through the structure, which includes design, balance, and proportion. Of all genres, this is perhaps most obvious in the drama, where the show has to go over or else, and Mr. Ripley has some trenchant observations about the importance of a professional attitude in the theatre.

Once technique reaches a certain degree of skill, it turns into something that we may darkly suspect to be fun: fun for the writer to display it, fun for the reader to watch it. In the old days we were conditioned to believe that only lowbrows read for fun, and that highbrows read serious literature to improve their minds. The coming of radio did a good deal to help this morbid situation, and television has done something (not enough) more. We now live in a time when Leonard Cohen can start out with an erudite book of poems called *Let Us Compare Mythologies*, the chief mythologies being the Biblical and the Classical, and evolve from there, quite naturally, into a well-known folk singer. Mr. Woodcock points out the immense importance of the revival of the oral tradition, the public speaking of poetry to audiences, often with a background of music, in making the serious poet a genuinely popular figure.

To be popular means having the power to amuse, in a genuine sense, and the power to amuse is, again, dependent on skill and craftsmanship. Mr. Woodcock speaks of an element in Earle Birney's poetry that might almost be called stunting, an interest in every variety of technical experiment, as though experiment were an end in itself. This is not a matter of panting to keep up with all the avant-garde movements: Birney is a genuinely contemporary poet, and his versatility expresses a central contemporary interest. Mr. Lane refers to the zany quality in Marshall McLuhan's style that has infuriated some people into calling him a humbug and a charlatan. James Reaney writes plays, sometimes tragic ones, full of the let's pretend devices of children's games, devices which, if they were described out of their context, might sound like Peter Quince and his wall in *A Midsummer Night's Dream*. The verbal wit that comes through in, say, Leonard Cohen's *Beautiful Losers*, in some of Needham's essays (see Mr. Conron's article), in the concrete poets, is a sign of the presence of seriousness and not the absence of it, the serious being the opposite of the solemn. We are a long way from the days when a bewildered Joyce, confronted with responses to *Finnegans Wake* which invariably treated it with either awe or ridicule, said: "But why couldn't they see that the book was funny?"

About twenty years ago I started trying to explain that the poet qua poet had no notion of life or reality or experience until he had read enough poetry to understand from it how poetry dealt with such things. I was told, in all quarters from Canadian journals (see Mr. Ross's article) to university classrooms, that I was reducing literature to a verbal game. I would not accept the word "reducing," but otherwise the statement was correct enough. Now that the work ethic has settled into a better perspective, the play ethic is also coming into focus, and we can perhaps understand a bit more clearly than we could a century ago why *Othello* and *Macbeth* are called plays. Play is that for the sake of which work is done, the climactic Sabbath vision of mankind.

A book concerned entirely with play in this sense passes over most of what occupies the emotional foreground of our lives at present: inflation, unemployment, violence and crime, and much else. The historian of Elizabethan literature, praising the exuberance and power of that literature, would not necessarily be unaware of the misery, injustice, and savagery that pervaded English life at the same time. What seems to come to matter more, eventually, is what man can create in the face of the chaos he also creates. This book is about what has been created, in words and in Canada, during the present age, and the whole body of that creation will be the main reason for whatever interest posterity may take in us.

69

View of Canada

6 April 1976

"View of Canada: Never a Believer in a Happy Ending." Extract from the soundtrack of the CBC television program Journey without Arrival: A Personal Point of View from Northrop Frye, *from the* Globe and Mail, *6 April 1976, 7. Subheads introduced by the newspaper have been omitted, and paragraphs have been made longer. The ellipses in the text are the* Globe and Mail's. *The program, in the Images of Canada series, was devised by Barbara Moon, Vincent Tovell, and Frye, and first broadcast on 6 April 1976. It was filmed in different parts of Canada.*

There have been many fables about people who made long journeys to find some precious object. The moral is often that the pot of gold at the end of the rainbow is in their own backyard. But this is not the Canadian moral. The Canadian identity is bound up with the feeling that the end of the rainbow never falls on Canada.

I spent the first five years of my life in Sherbrooke, close to the Vermont border, and all my childish constructs of the world grew up there. Some people say that they don't know where heaven is . . . or what it looks like. Well, I do know. It's the other side of the St. Francis River. Wherever I have gone since, my . . . roots will always be there.

After the First World War, my father, who travelled in hardware, went to Moncton, N.B., and that was where I had all my primary and secondary schooling. Moncton was, and still is, part English and part French: a language difference and to some extent a religious difference. But the English and the Acadian French have very similar attitudes to their environment . . .

When I was a boy at school, learning geography . . . my earliest image

View of Canada

of Canada was a flat map, which is handy for printing, but flat maps of Canada produce at least two distortions of reality. One is the blowing up of the whole North into an immense ghost that looms over the tiny inhabited strip along the border. The other is that Canada simply stops at the top of the page. There is nothing beyond that but the void. Now we may know that these impressions are false. But they still may condition our sense of where we fit into the scheme of things. It seems to me that the Canadian sensibility has been profoundly disturbed not so much by our famous problem of identity—"Who are we?"—as by some such riddle as "Where is here?"...

Let's go back to maps for a moment. The technique of transferring information from a sphere to a flat surface is called Mercator's projection. Mercator was the German map maker who hit on it in 1569. This (the flat map) was hailed as a most important new navigational aid by the explorers of the time. It sums up the frame of mind, the whole outlook of the country's founders. Galileo had already expressed the outlook.

"The language of mathematics." It makes an immense difference when a country enters on its history. It's interesting to speculate on what we'd have been like if the first Norse settlements had taken hold and we'd grown up with medieval roots. But that didn't happen. Instead we were launched into history by men confident of the power of the mathematical mind to master space and nature. We are marked by that confidence to this day.

Let's look at the country's founders for a moment. A monument that hails them officially as founders was erected here in Orillia in 1915. Champlain, the explorer. And along with him the other two founders: the trader, the missionary.[1] When we don't think of Canadian history as dull we think of it as theatrical. We think of it as a pageant of canoes and furs and tortures. And, when we think of it as a pageant, of course, we put it at a distance from us, and make it unreal. We forget that what Champlain brought—and what the explorer, trader, and missionary all brought—was our own consciousness and our own attitudes.

We're closer to them than we may think. The missionaries: forget, for a moment all the zeal and heroism and look at their organization. What we might call multinational corporate managements grew up in the seventeenth century, and they were what made possible Europe's extension into the New World. With the missionaries came a hierarchy and a chain of command leading from Rome through Paris and Quebec out to the advance posts of Ste. Marie among the Hurons. The idea of a chain of command was built into this country from the beginning: the respect for authority. The feeling that head office is somewhere else, in London, Paris, Rome, or Washington, and that the individual gets his dignity from his place in the organization.

The missionaries had other assumptions that had profound effects on our attitudes. The missionaries brought with them the ordered universe they inherited, and when they came up against the people they called the Indians, Les Sauvages, they felt that they were faced with something like a blank in the cosmos. They weren't racist, but they believed that they were bringing revelation, that is, they were bringing the light of the sun to the darkness . . .

The traders were concerned merely to plunder the continent and take its goods back home. Timber, copper, and fish. Later, furs led to the Hudson's Bay Company, and then came the "rushes" on minerals. Canada is full of ghost towns: visible ruins unparalleled in Europe. But in seventeenth-century Europe the ransacking of colonies to fatten the mother country was an absolute obligation. Hewers of wood and drawers of water for others: right from the beginning Canada understood her station in life. All this reinforced the sense that the head office was elsewhere and the attachment to a bureaucratic structure stretched deep into the wilderness . . .

Perhaps we have used honesty and balance sheets as a substitute for brilliance and riches. Americans like to make money; Canadians like to audit it. I don't know of any other country where the accountant enjoys a higher social and moral status.

Champlain is the leading figure in the seventeenth-century pageant and so he should be. He was to some extent a missionary and an entrepreneur, but he was also an explorer. There are two reasons for his central place in our history. His astrolabe stands for one of them. It is a symbol of the language of mathematics of which Galileo spoke, the belief that you could catch and control a universe in a net of abstractions and predictabilities. The explorer, with his astrolabe, and his compass, and his globe—printed for convenience as Mercator's flat map—trusted his life and his hope of glory to geometry. In no other age would the belief in the power of mathematics have launched us on so unquestioned a path. And hence, the human landscape of the New World shows a conquest of nature by an intelligence that does not love it. In Winnipeg, or in any other North American city, if you watch people stopping at red lights and crossing at green ones, you can see how much unconscious organization there still is in our life, and how much geometry we still act out.

As an explorer, Champlain also stands for the voyageur, the journeyer, the eternal seeker in Canadians. Those who first came here were looking for Cathay. What they found simply got in the way. Farther south it was easier to adjust. The Spaniards found gold in Mexico and Peru; the Americans found the American Dream and settled for it, instead. But here? ... We have never lost the feeling that Cathay is always over the horizon, a journey away. We have never been a culture that believed in happy endings. The real ending is ironic because it's here.

The Americans over there, and the Canadians here, are both stuck with the emotional results of discovering and settling this continent at a certain point in history. But at a later point their paths diverged. And this seems as good a place as any to talk about it.

Queenston Heights. So far as that incredible bungle of the War of 1812 had any meaning at all for Canada, it was Canada's War of Independence and this was where it began. The war didn't settle anything as a war, but it made clear what was already true, that the two halves of the continent were embarked on separate destinies ... In Canada nothing has ever been self-evident. The English and the French in Canada spent the eighteenth century battering down each other's forts, so we missed out on the enlightenment.

It may look on the map as though Canada was the most absurd idea ever conceived, but when you think of that tremendous east-west thrust, our obsessive one-dimensional drive across the continent makes sense. Confederation itself makes sense. We're not, as some people insist, seven fishing rods tied together by their ends but an organic unit with a spine articulated by that great probing waterway and its extension, the transcontinental railway ... In the mind of Sir John A. Macdonald what really made Confederation and the railway viable was their importance to the global communications link that began and ended at home in Britain: the link of empire. He was as representative of Canada's nineteenth century as Champlain was of its seventeenth: Macdonald forged the dominion. Yet, life long, his own sense of its identity remained colonial, bound up in the relation to a head office somewhere else ...

There are two aspects to the nineteenth-century Canadian imagination, one public and official, the other private and romantic. Victorian aggressiveness, its energy, confidence, and faith in science and progress, continued the westward expansion and produced Confederation. But there was another side to the nineteenth century: the Romantic sense of nature as a symbol or counterpart of man's inner life. This Romantic expectation opened up chasms in the Canadian imagination. It's all very well in the abstract to be thrilled by moonlit dark forests, and nature's grand design. But the reality in Canada was all too often . . . terrifying. No-man's land. Terra incognita . . .

And so we developed that curious streak of anxiety that distinguishes us from other North Americans. Which we kept trying to sweep under the carpet. Our Romantic painters translated the raw reality into picturesque European-style landscapes. Notice how Paul Kane first paints what he sees and then reshapes it for European sensibilities. The writers too. In the popular Jalna books, Mazo de la Roche manages to make life in Canada seem a pastoral idyll. The Whiteoaks are a British county family transplanted to the colonies . . .

It took Canadians a long time to get imaginative possession of their own space. The early settlers simply felt overwhelmed and beleaguered. The physical forts of the seventeenth century had changed by the nineteenth into the cultural attitudes that I call the "garrison mentality." The garrison mentality is defensive and separatist. Each group walls itself off and huddles inside, taking warmth and reassurance from numbers, but keeping its eyes fixed apprehensively on what's outside. The social attitudes are pretty simple and discourage any break in the ranks. Each member draws his sense of worth not from within himself, but from his allegiance. Pressure raises temperature, and the immanent pressure of nature in Canada raises the intensity of the community: tensions develop and garrisons are multiplied within garrisons . . . Each suspicious of the others. Intolerant of outsiders. Quick to blame "them" for misfortunes: the Americans, the Eastern Money Barons, the French, the hairy radicals. Them! . . .

I think (poet) Ned Pratt was a landmark figure in the development of the Canadian imagination. Somehow he had acquired an infallible instinct for what was central in the Canadian consciousness—the confidence of the seventeenth-century, and the anxiety of the nineteenth-century experience. It's very difficult for somebody inside Canada to explain how important Pratt is to a person who has never shared the Canadian heritage. It was Pratt who explained the central tragic theme of the Canadian imagination in his monumental poem, *Brébeuf and His Brethren.* . . . He shows that the Canadian attraction to the documentary

View of Canada

form is still with us: apparently we're still in the process of taking inventories and rendering accounts . . .

We came into this century without any agreement on what kind of people we were—or even, whether a Canadian could be identified. Nine-tenths of our land mass existed as a kind of vague miasma. The working sense of the country was one-dimensional: pinpoints strung along the railway line, St. John's here, and Tadoussac there, and Estevan there. And perhaps we're still in that phase, of a country without landmarks and without a silhouette. But somehow I don't think so. All that is beginning to change. And Pratt is the symbol of the change . . . The people who have followed Pratt—the Earle Birneys, the Margaret Atwoods, and James Reaneys—they're the map makers of the Canadian imagination. They're putting us in possession of our past and our shared responses . . .

He wasn't interested in planes though. That's curious, because it's the airplane, I think, that has made one crucial difference to the Canadian consciousness. The airplane supplied a perspective that began to pull the country together . . . The airplane gave us an outline—two dimensions instead of one; every part of the country imaginatively available at once instead of just centres connected by east-west ground links. Elsewhere the plane may mean a loosening of bonds, a way of escape; in Canada it is a means of tightening the country into a recognizable shape.

Here we are: not an obstacle on the route to Cathay, not on the edge of the earth, not on the sidelines, but ringed by the world's great powers: Japan and China here; the USSR here; the European Common Market here, and the United States here. And here is Canada, in the middle. The situation may not quite have sunk in yet, but it will. And it means that the entire country is now a garrison, and there are signs that it is being organized to behave like one . . .

Who is a Canadian? Well, the political answer is that he is an American who avoided revolution. Whatever national sense of unity we have is still very largely that cohesion along the east-west axis. But increasingly, I suspect, that's being replaced by the sense of occupying our particular garrison on our part of the globe.

70

Haunted by Lack of Ghosts

26 April 1976

"Haunted by Lack of Ghosts: Some Patterns in the Imagery of Canadian Poetry," in The Canadian Imagination: Dimensions of a Literary Culture, *ed. David Staines (Cambridge, Mass.: Harvard University Press, 1977), 22–45. Reprinted in RCLI, 117–39, and ECLI, 117–35. Typescripts are in NFF, 1988, box 5, file w, and box 6, file g. This was originally given as a lecture at Harvard University.*

Very few historical and cultural statements can be made about Canada that do not have obvious counterparts in the United States. At the same time, social developments in a country which has amassed a huge population and has become a great imperial power may have a quite different imaginative resonance in a country with a sparse population and a minor world influence. For example, railways were built across the United States to the Pacific, and the romance of railway building, along with the accompanying scandals and exploitations, have been factors of unquestionable importance in American culture. But in Canada the building of a single railway line was a matter of life and death to the infant nation, and the completion of it, against almost insuperable obstacles, was not one of many incidents of expansion but a central devouring obsession. Similarly, in the nineteenth century, an American boasting of the great size of America was helping to increase his own feeling of identity with it, whereas in Canada the background of immense rivers, lakes, and islands that very few Canadians had ever seen tended rather to weaken the sense of an identity that was already precarious.

In the United States, expansion into the West brought with it almost everywhere a sense of new opportunities for life in a new land. But while the Canadian expansion into the North looks vast enough on a map, the inference that there is unlimited room for people in Canada is an illusion. As the Canadian historian, W.L. Morton, says in *The Canadian Identity*, "The great staple trades have been extensive, in-gathering trades ... most of Canada is simply a hinterland extensively exploited from the soil base of the St. Lawrence and Saskatchewan valleys, and from the delta of the Fraser."[1] Increased immigration, in Canada no less than in Australia, means primarily an increase in the population of two or three cities which are already too big. The fact that the country grew up from two peoples speaking different languages meant that nobody could ever know what a "hundred percent Canadian" was, and hence the population became less homogeneous. An ethnic minority in any case is more conspicuous in a smaller population. And while we hear a good deal about separatism in Quebec, every part of Canada has strong separatist feelings: the Atlantic Provinces and Western Canada also tend to feel that they are, vis-à-vis central Canada, in the same mercantile bind that the United States was in before 1776, and that they are forced to export at a lower price, and import at a higher price, than they would do if they had more autonomy.

Canada was first settled, like the United Sates, in the seventeenth century, but, in striking contrast to the United Sates, there was nothing culturally distinctive about Canada's eighteenth century, and the country went directly from seventeenth-century Baroque expansiveness to nineteenth-century Romantic expansiveness. There are some curious reversals of American historical movements in Canadian history. The Americans had first a revolutionary war against a European power, followed by a civil war within the country itself. Canada had a civil war first, which was a struggle of European powers on its soil, followed by a war of independence against the United States—at least, so far as the War of 1812 had any meaning at all for Canada, that was its meaning. A generation or two ago, girls in Quebec convent schools were taught that the British conquest was the will of God, saving them from the atheistic horrors of the French Revolution. It might have been added, with some justification, that the British conquest also preserved the French language and culture itself in Canada. The French lost the country primarily because they had very little interest in keeping it, and if they had held it they would doubtless have sold it, as they did Louisiana.

In any case Canada was founded on the Quebec Act of 1774,[2] which recognized the *de facto* situation that while the British were technically the conquerors, the country could not survive as a British possession unless a settlement was made which guaranteed rights to the French.

The Quebec Act was a conservative measure, conforming to Edmund Burke's principle of a synthesis containing opposed principles, in contrast to the revolutionary, and therefore more dialectical, attitude established by the victorious Whigs in the United States. Its revolutionary basis, along with the written constitution which was an integral part of that basis, makes for a deductive and continuous pattern in American life, as the constitution is reinterpreted or, in the last resort, amended. In Canada a discontinuous, *ad hoc*, illogical series of bargains and compromises succeeded the Quebec Act. Margaret Atwood's book on the spirit of Canadian literature, *Survival*, has become very influential partly through its inspired choice of a title: the word "survival" in itself implies a discontinuous series of crises, each to be met on its own terms, each having to face the imminent threat of not surviving.

For all its centrifugal expansion, the American consciousness revolves around one or two centripetal symbols of the nation as a whole, notably the President and the flag. In Canada the parliamentary system of election places much less emphasis on the party leader as a personality, and it is even more significant that Canada had no official flag of its own until the middle of the twentieth century. Francis Sparshott, in a poem called *Episode in Frederick, Md.*, muses obliquely about this:

> "Spare, if you must, this old grey head,
> But shoot your country's flag!" she said.
> "You've got it wrong, you stupid bag.
> You mean, '*Don't* shoot your country's flag.'"
> "Yes, yes, young man, that's what I said:
> Shoot if you must this old grey head."
> "Pardon me, lady, that is not
> What you first said you wanted shot."
> Then down the street the General came,
> His sword unsheathed, his eyes aflame.
> "Sergeant! Don't contradict the lady.
> Holes in the head she's got already;
> Six more won't make no never mind.
> Present! . . . Aim! . . . FIRE:"
>   Still down the wind
> Streams the bright symbol of her honor
> But Mrs. Fritchie is a goner.
> So now the Yanks have both a flag
> And a distinctive national hag.

The author tells me that he was not aware, in writing the last line, that Canada also has had, in a sense, a distinctive national hag. No genuine portrait of English Canada's best known heroine, Laura Secord, exists, and the deficiency is made up for by a grisly reproduction of a male elder statesman, with the beard removed and a shawl put over the head, purporting to represent her in old age. I mention this because it illustrates so clearly the perennial Canadian problems of publicizing the heroes of a country which has manifested a great deal of remarkable courage but has never responded with much warmth to charismatic leadership. Canadian heroes include such ambiguous figures as William Lyon Mackenzie, leader of the 1837 rebellion against the "Family Compact" (the Tory establishment in nineteenth-century Ontario), whose role became very unheroic when the shooting started, but who nonetheless still stands for the nonconformist conscience of Canada, an unwillingness to knuckle under to any kind of foreign or domestic domination. Thus Dennis Lee, in a poem called *1838*:

> The British want the country
> For the Empire and the view.
> The Yankees want the country for
> A yankee barbecue.
> The Compact want the country
> For their merrie green domain.
> They'll all play finder's-keepers till
> Mackenzie comes again.
>
> Mackenzie was a crazy man.
> He wore his wig askew.
> He donned three bulky overcoats
> In case the bullets flew.
> Mackenzie talked of fighting
> While the fight went down the drain.
> But who will speak for Canada?
> Mackenzie, come again! [ll. 17–32]

Seventeenth-century Europe brought three cultural imports into the New World of North America. One was the revolutionary monotheism of Christianity, with its horror of "idolatry," that is, the sense of the numinous in nature. For Christianity, the gods that had been discovered in nature were all devils: man could raise his consciousness toward the divine only through human institutions. It followed that a natural religion like that of the Indians simply had to be extirpated if the Indians were to realize their human potential. The second was the Baroque sense of the power of mathematics, the results of which can still be seen in the grid patterns of our cities, in the concession lines in rural areas, and in the great burden of geometry that North American life in particular carries. The third was the Cartesian egocentric consciousness, the feeling that man's essential humanity was in his power of reasoning, and that the nature outside human consciousness was pure extension: a turning away from nature so complete that it became a kind of idolatry in reverse.

A friend of mine, watching two Western farmers driving fence stakes and hearing one say to the other, "Put 'er in a coupla inches west," remarked that a consciousness as closely geared to the points of the compass as that was obviously in intimate touch with the land. I was inclined to disagree, feeling that it was a consciousness of nature as a territory but not as a home. It goes with the feeling that improved human communications means a straighter and therefore less interesting path through nature, until with the airplane the sense of travelling through nature itself disappears. I said in an earlier article on Canadian literature that the Canadian problem of identity seemed to me primarily connected with locale, less a matter of "Who am I?" than of "Where is here?"[3] Another friend, commenting on this, told me a story about a doctor from the South (that is, from one of the Canadian cities) travelling on the Arctic tundra with an Eskimo guide. A blizzard blew up, and they had to bivouac for the night. What with the cold, the storm, and the loneliness, the doctor panicked and began shouting, "We are lost!" The Eskimo looked at him thoughtfully and said, "We are not lost. We are here." A vast gulf between an indigenous and an immigrant mentality opened at that point; the possibility of eventually closing this gulf is the main theme of what follows.

Yeats speaks in one of his prose works of the Port Royal logicians, followers of Descartes, who cut up animals alive because everything outside man was a machine to them and they simply could not believe that anything without human consciousness could feel pain.[4] The attitude of the Canadian fur trade, spreading traps over the North to catch animals, was not very different: for it, the mink, the beaver, and the silver fox were not living creatures but only potential fur coats. A growing sense of guilt about this attitude gives a peculiarly haunting resonance to the theme of the death of an animal in Canadian literature. (See, for example, Al Purdy's *The Death of Animals* in *Poems for All the Annettes* [1962], a poem too long to quote and too intricate to quote from.) Similarly, the destruction of the native culture, more particularly of its religion, leaves us with the feeling well described by the philosopher George Grant in *Technology and Empire* (1969): "That conquering relation to place has left its mark within us. When we go into the Rockies we may have the sense that gods are there. But if so, they cannot manifest themselves to us as ours. They are the gods of another race, and we cannot know them because of what we are, and what we did. There can be nothing immemorial for us except the environment as object."[5] Much the same thing is said in poetry by Douglas LePan, in a poem significantly called *A Country without a Mythology*:

> No monuments or landmarks guide the stranger
> Going among this savage people . . .
>
> And not a sign, no emblem in the sky
> Or boughs to friend him as he goes; for who
> Will stop where, clumsily constructed, daubed
> With war-paint, teeters some lust-red manitou?   [ll. 1–2, 33–6]

A parenthetical remark in Leonard Cohen's novel *Beautiful Losers* links a similar feeling of guilt to the colonial mentality of Canadians: "Some part of the Canadian Catholic mind is not certain of the Church's victory over the Medicine Man. No wonder the forests of Quebec are mutilated and sold to America."[6]

From my study of Canadian literature, in particular, I have found much evidence for the critical principle of the fallacy of imaginative projection, that is, the notion that a poet can confront some impressive object like Niagara Falls or Lake Louise and become "inspired" by it. An egocentric consciousness, Pascal's thinking reed,[7] in the centre of a country as huge and unresponsive as Canada finds the environment less impressive than oppressive. It is not only that nature is so big and the winters so cold, but also that there is a lurking feeling that if anything did speak to the poet from nature it would speak only to condemn. That is why I have adopted for my title the last line of Earle Birney's poem

Can. Lit.: "It's only by our lack of ghosts we're haunted." There are gods here, and we have offended them. They are not ghosts: we are the ghosts, Cartesian ghosts caught in the machine that we have assumed nature to be. Hence the characteristic Canadian feeling noted by the scholar and critic Robert McDougall: "In our literature, heroic action remains possible but becomes so deeply tinged with futility that withdrawal becomes a more characteristic response than commitment. The representative images are those of denial and defeat rather than fulfilment and victory."[8]

One obvious corollary of this feeling is the sense that "civilized" man, with his economy of waste, his relentless plundering of a nature which he thinks is there only to be exploited by him, his infinite capacity to litter his surroundings with every conceivable variety of excrement, is the essential principle of pollution in nature, a monstrous deformation or cancer that nature itself has produced by mistake. Thus Margaret Atwood, in a poem called *Backdrop Addresses Cowboy*, where the cowboy is perhaps less a cowboy than a symbol of the more fatuous forms of mass culture:

> I am also what surrounds you:
> my brain
> scattered with your
> tincans, bones, empty shells,
> the litter of your invasions.

James Reaney, studying *Winnipeg Seen as a Body of Time and Space*, makes an explicit contrast with the native relation to nature:

> Winnipeg, what once were you. You were,
> Your hair was grass by the river ten feet tall,
> Your arms were burr oaks and ash leaf maples,
> Your backbone was a crooked silver muddy river,
> Your thoughts were ravens in flocks, your bones were snow,
> Your legs were trails and your blood was a people
>   Who did what the stars did and the sun . . .
>
> Then on top of you fell
> A boneyard wrecked auto gent, his hair

> Made of rusted car door handles, his fingernails
> Of red Snowflake Pastry signs, his belly
> Of buildings downtown; his arms of sewers,
> His nerves electric wires, his mouth a telephone,
> His backbone—a cracked cement street. His heart
> An orange pendulum bus crawling with the human fleas
> Of a so-so civilization—half-gadget, half flesh—
>   I don't know what I would have instead—
> And they did what they did more or less.   [ll. 1–7, 13–23]

The phenomenon described is hardly peculiar to Canada, but again it has a distinctive resonance in a country where there is so much nature that ought to be unspoiled. The theme celebrated in science fiction, of nature's eventual revenge, seems to be less frequent in Canadian poetry, although E.J. Pratt, in a late poem called *The Good Earth*, notices in passing that the death-wish in man himself is partly a form of that revenge:

> Hold that synthetic seed, for underneath
> Deep down she'll answer to your horticulture:
> She has a way of germinating teeth
> And yielding crops of carrion for the vulture.   [ll. 21–4]

A curious schizophrenia can be seen in a good deal of nineteenth-century Canadian poetry, the sense of loneliness and alienation urgently demanding expression along with a good deal of prefabricated rhetoric about the challenge of a new land and the energetic optimism demanded to meet it. The latter mood often attempts to suppress or, failing that, to outshout the former one, but with little consistent success. Again, Margaret Atwood, who has inherited Pratt's instinct for what is imaginatively central in Canadian sensibility, studies this split consciousness in her *Journals of Susanna Moodie*. This book of poems follows the life of the redoubtable Susanna Strickland, who after her marriage came out to Ontario in the 1830s and wrote *Roughing It in the Bush*. Toward the end of the sequence, in a poem called *Thoughts from Underground*, the poet describes the conflict in her heroine's mind between her very real hatred for the country that had caused her so much suffering and the rhetoric that she thought she ought to be producing about its material progress and cultural enlightenment:

> Then we were made successful
> and I felt I ought to love
> this country.
>   I said I loved it
> and my mind saw double.
>
> I began to forget myself
> in the middle
> of sentences. Events
> were split apart.   [ll. 15–23]

A similar rhetorical epilepsy may be observed in some of the semi-official poets of the Confederation period and later, notably Charles G.D. Roberts and Bliss Carman. Roberts begins a poem called *Canada* thus:

> O Child of Nations, giant-limbed,
>   Who stand'st among the nations now
> Unheeded, unadorned, unhymned,
>   With unanointed brow,—

This apostrophe is also an invocation, not a genuine invocation, such as Homer would make to a Muse or some shaping spirit of poetry asking it to take over the poem, but one addressed to Roberts himself and intended to help him work himself into the proper emotional state for a sublime ode. The rest of the poem illustrates the principle that invocations addressed to oneself are seldom answered. Here is Bliss Carman, at the close of a poem [*Spring Song*] which has become perhaps less celebrated than notorious in Canadian literature:

> Only make me over, April,
> When the sap begins to stir!
> Make me man or make me woman,
> Make me oaf or ape or human,
> Cup of flower or cone of fir;
> Make me anything but neuter
> When the sap begins to stir!

Haunted by Lack of Ghosts

The critic E.K. Brown remarks on this passage that the tone is "jaunty" and that the jaunty cannot also be poetic. I think myself that Carman has fallen foul of another well known literary principle, the positive force of the negative statement. One who says "the day was not hot and stifling" has said something much hotter than he means; and when Carman prays to be made "anything but neuter" he is sowing a doubt in his reader's mind whether, when the sap rises in the spring, the poet will be able to rise with it. Both poets, especially Carman, wrote a good deal of verse dedicated to the power of positive thinking, but the tone is almost invariably forced, and invites Emily Dickinson's dry comment on Joaquin Miller, "Transport is not urged."[9] Yet both Roberts and Carman could be haunting and eloquent poets as long as their tone was nostalgic, elegiac, or plangent: Carman's *Low Tide on Grand Pré* is a fine example. So the question naturally comes to mind: why were these poets so much better at whimpering than at banging?

The answer has already been implied: the nostalgic and elegiac are the inevitable emotional responses of an egocentric consciousness locked into a demythologized environment. Wherever reason is regarded as the distinctively human element in consciousness, the impulse to write poetry remains rhetorical (in the sense of oratorical), preoccupied with versifying prose statements and talking about emotional attitudes instead of presenting them. Eventually it becomes clear that the focus of such a response, in such conditions, is the moment of death. Death is the one point at which man and nature really become identified; it is also, in a sense, the only event in which the genuinely heroic aspect of human life emerges. A life in which energy is expended in subduing a tiny fraction of space has little room for the heroic, until death rounds off the total effort and gives it another dimension. Without death, the struggle would seem only unending and hopeless. John McCrae, the author of *In Flanders Fields*, was a poet much possessed by death, and he has a poem called *The Unconquered Dead* in which one chilling phrase identifies the heroic with the ability to die:

> We might have yielded, even we, but death
>   Came for our helper. [ll. 13–14]

In such a setting the Indian appears as a noble savage in the sense that his life is so largely one of stoically enduring both the sufferings imposed by nature and those he inflicts on himself and others. In Duncan Campbell

Scott's *The Forsaken*, an Indian woman, trying to get food for her baby in winter, baits a fishhook with her own flesh. Later, as an old woman whom the tribe can no longer afford to feed, she is abandoned and left to lie down in the snow to die. Similarly, in Pratt's *Brébeuf and His Brethren*, the martyrdom of the Jesuit missionaries is nothing that they are seeking for itself, but it is the one real triumph of their service of Christ.

While some nineteenth- and early twentieth-century Canadian poets were rhetoricians, others understood better that the central poetic impulse is imaginative and not rhetorical, and that its most direct product is mythology, which is essentially the humanizing of nature. Charles Mair, author of *Tecumseh*, produced in 1901 a rather maundering poem called *Summer*, of this general texture:

> Or, if Fancy still would trace
> Forms ideal, forms of grace,
> Still would haunt, in dreamy trance,
> Kindred regions of Romance,
> Let her now recall the sweet
> Image of lorn Marguerite.   [ll. 73–8]

What is interesting about this poem is that it is a completely rewritten version of a poem written in 1868, which was both explicitly mythological and very much livelier:

> And let nymph-attended Pan
> Come in habit of a man,
> Singing songs of reeds and rushes,
> Elder brakes and hazel bushes.
> See him swing and jig about,
> Whilst the merry, rabble rout
> Chases round with joinèd hands,
> Twitching slily, when he stands,
> At his back, his garments tearing,
> All his swart, brute-buttocks baring.   [ll. 78–87]

Mair eventually came to realize that his 1868 muse was the authentic one, and her genteel 1901 sister a phoney. In Isabella Crawford's extraordinary narrative poem *Malcolm's Katie* (1884), there is an explicitly mythical section beginning "The South Wind laid his moccasins aside," which contains the following passage:

> In this shrill Moon the scouts of Winter ran
> From the ice-belted north, and whistling shafts
> Struck maple and struck sumach—and a blaze
> Ran swift from leaf to leaf, from bough to bough;
> Till round the forest flash'd a belt of flame
> And inward lick'd its tongues of red and gold
> To the deep, tranced inmost heart of all.
> Rous'd the still heart—but all too late, too late.
> Too late, the branches welded fast with leaves,
> Toss'd, loosen'd to the winds—too late the Sun
> Pour'd his last vigor to the deep, dark cells
> Of the dim wood. The keen, two-bladed Moon
> Of Falling Leaves roll'd up on crested mists
> And where the lush, rank boughs had foil'd the Sun
> In his red prime, her pale, sharp fingers crept
> After the wind and felt about the moss,
> And seem'd to pluck from shrinking twig and stem
> The burning leaves—while groan'd the shudd'ring wood.   [pt. 2, ll. 50–67]

There are several things to notice here. In the first place, the progression of seasons, with its great cycle of colour that emerges in spring, bursts into flame in the fall, and dies out in the winter, is seen as a kind of battle of Titans. Nature here is not a Cartesian extension in space, but a field of conflicting energies which are seemingly just about to take on the forms of mythological beings. Second, for all the riot of colour, the "inmost heart of all" does not quite come to life: something makes that "too late," and we are pulled around to death and winter again. The process is almost an allegory of the Canadian poetic imagination, making a tremendous effort to rouse itself and create a reborn mythology out of the abandoned Indian one, an effort still premature and collapsing before its fulfilment, but indicating that something new is on the way. The direct vision of nature in this passage is equally remarkable. Isabella Crawford has done in words much what the painter Tom Thomson was later to do in his art: evoking a dissonance of colour that seems like an autonomous force of life itself bursting through the tree trunks, the sumach, and the sky.

Speaking of painting, the British painter and writer Wyndham Lewis, who spent some years in Canada during the Second World War, makes this comment about A.Y. Jackson, one of the twentieth-century Group of Seven landscape painters, perhaps with an underlying allusion to the Carman poem already cited: "Jackson is no man to go gathering nuts in May. He has no wish to be seduced every Spring when the sap rises—neither he nor nature are often shown in these compromising moods. There is something of Ahab in him: the long white contours of the Laurentian Mountains in mid-winter are his elusive leviathan."[10] The Leviathan also recurs in Wilfred Watson's fine poem on another Canadian painter, the British Columbian Emily Carr:

> Like Jonah in the green belly of the whale
> Overwhelmed by Leviathan's lights and liver
> Imprisoned and appalled by the belly's wall
> Yet inscribing and scoring the uprush
> Sink vault and arch of that monstrous cathedral,
> Its living bone and its green pulsing flesh—
> Old woman, of your three days' anatomy
> Leviathan sickened and spewed you forth
> In a great vomit on coasts of eternity. [*Emily Carr*]

The image of being swallowed by the Leviathan is an almost inevitable one for Canada: the whole process of coming to the country by ship from Europe, through the Strait of Belle Isle and the Gulf of St. Lawrence and then up the great river, suggests it, again a marked contrast to the United States, with its relatively straight north-south coastline. In Pratt's narrative poem on the building of the Canadian Pacific Railway, *Towards the Last Spike*, the dragon image appears, the symbol of a nature so totally indifferent to man and his concerns that it is irrelevant to wonder whether it is dead or alive:

> On the North Shore a reptile lay asleep—
> A hybrid that the myths might have conceived,
> But not delivered, as progenitor
> Of crawling, gliding things upon the earth . . .
> This folded reptile was asleep or dead:
> So motionless, she seemed stone dead—just seemed:
> She was too old for death, too old for life . . .
> Ice-ages had passed by and over her,

Haunted by Lack of Ghosts

> But these, for all their motion, had but sheared
> Her spotty carboniferous hair or made
> Her ridges stand out like the spikes of molochs . . .
>
> Was this the thing Van Horne set out
> To conquer?   [ll. 870–3, 882–4, 890–3, 899–900]

Van Horne was the builder of the Canadian Pacific Railway, and the stretch of Precambrian shield in northern Ontario was one of his most formidable obstacles.

In the Bible, of course, the Leviathan swallows Jonah, a prototype not only of Emily Carr but of the Jesus who descended to the world of death and hell for three days. In the closely related myth of St. George and the dragon, St. George dies along with the dragon he kills, and has to be separately brought to life. What such myths appear to be telling us is that the Leviathan is the monster of indefinite time and space surrounding us on all sides: we are all born inside his belly, and we never escape from it; he is the body of death from which we cannot be delivered. The Christian, Baroque, Cartesian attitude that the white invaders brought from Europe helped to ensure that in Canada the sense of being imprisoned in the belly of a mindless emptiness would be at its bleakest and most uncompromising. As we have seen, the ego's one moment of genuine dignity in such a situation is the moment either of death or of some equally final alienation. Among the poets of the generation of Roberts, Carman, and D.C. Scott, Archibald Lampman achieved the highest consistent level of poetry, partly because he was prudent enough to stick to elegiac moods. His poems are almost invariably those of a solitary watcher of the nature around him: the idiom is strongly Wordsworthian, but the greater sense of indifference in the landscape makes him more conscious of his solitude than Wordsworth:

> I sat in the midst of a plain on my snowshoes with bended knee
> Where the thin wind stung my cheeks,
> And the hard snow ran in little ripples and peaks,
> Like the fretted floor of a white and petrified sea.
>
> And a strange peace gathered about my soul and shone,
> As I sat reflecting there,
> In a world so mystically fair,
> So deathly silent—I so utterly alone.   [ll. 5–12]

The poem, called *Winter-Solitude*, expresses a kind of serenity that Lampman constantly sought. Margaret Avison presents us with a similar landscape but a different response to it:

> But on this sheet of beryl, this high sea,
> Scalded by the white unremembering glaze,
> No wisps disperse. This is the icy pole.
> The presence here is single, worse than soul,
> Pried loose forever out of nights and days
> And birth and death
> And all the covering wings.   [ll. 9–15]

I have quoted this passage elsewhere, but keep returning to it because, apart from its great eloquence, the poem from which it comes is called *Identity*, and what it shows us is an identity driven into a last stand of such total isolation that it can define itself only by extinction, unless it can make some effort of rebirth.

I earlier quoted George Grant as saying that the gods of the Rockies are the gods of another race, and that we can make no contact with them because of what we are, and what we did. The statement sounds irrefutable, at least in prose, but it is not what the present generation of poets is saying. John Newlove, for example, in a poem called *The Pride*, says,

> not this handful
> of fragments, as the indians
> are not composed of
> the romantic stories
> about them, or of the stories
> they tell only, but
> still ride the soil
> in us, dry bones a part
> of the dust in our eyes,
> needed and troubling
> in the glare, in
> our breath, in our
> ears, in our mouths,
> in our bodies entire, in our minds, until at
> last we become them

> in our desires, our desires,
> mirages, mirrors, that are theirs, hard-
> riding desires, and they
> become our true forebears, moulded
> by the same wind or rain,
> and in this land we
> are their people, come
> back to life.   [ll. 194–216]

In this poem the Indians symbolize a primitive mythological imagination which is being reborn in us: in other words, the white Canadians, in their imaginations, are no longer immigrants but are becoming indigenous, recreating the kind of attitudes appropriate to people who really belong here. We may remember that "primitive" poetry, which is created in a society where the poets are the custodians of culture and learning, is very direct in its impact, sometimes needing footnotes for those outside its orbit of allusions, but not at all inclined to talk around or avoid its subject. Thus a Haida song as translated, or adapted, by Hermia Fraser:

> I cannot stay, I cannot stay!
> The Raven has stolen the Child of the Chief,
> Of the Highest Chief in the Kingdom of Light.
>
> The Slave Wife born from the first clam shell
> Is in love with the boy who was stolen away,
> The lovers have taken the Raven's fire.
>
> The Slave who was born from the first clam shell
> Has made love to the wife who was born from the shell,
> This Slave man has stolen her treasures away.
> [*Song to the Wanderer*, stanzas 3–5]

The Haida lived on the Queen Charlotte Islands off the coast of British Columbia. Living there now is the extraordinary poet Susan Musgrave, who has produced four volumes of verse in the first twenty-five years of her life, and who shows throughout them strong imaginative links with a people whom she clearly thinks of as poetically her ancestors. In a poem called *Witchery Way* the sense of an indigenous creative power reforming in the present and immediate future seems indicated in the phrase about "the dark seed of their coming":

> Sometimes an old man
> crouches at the river—
> sometimes he is someone
> whose bones are not formed.
>
> Sometimes an old woman
> with fisher-skin quiver,
> sometimes on the low bank
> is hungry after blood . . .
>
> Sometimes an old man
> whispers down the smoke hole,
> sometimes an old woman
> furrows in the wind.
> My skin is thick
> with the dark seed
> of their coming—
> the blade of a fine axe
> wedged between my eyes.   [ll. 1–8, 33–41]

It should go without saying that I am not speaking of the content or subject matter of such poems, but of the imaginative attitude that produces their structures.

A poetic consciousness formed within the Leviathan of Canadian nature, feeling that it belongs there and can no longer think of itself as a swallowed outsider, would naturally be preoccupied with two themes in particular: the theme of descent into the self and the theme of forming, within that self, an imaginative counterpart of what is outside it. The sense of a responding imagination which is part of its surroundings, and not a detached consciousness rolling over it like so much tumbleweed, already appears in Lampman and is in fact the reason why so much of his work is focused on the theme of serenity. Thus in a poem called *Storm*:

> O Wind, wild-voicèd brother, in your northern cave,
>   My spirit also being so beset

With pride and pain, I heard you beat and rave,
    Grinding your chains with furious howl and fret,
Knowing full well that all earth's moving things inherit
The same chained might and madness of the spirit,
    That none may quite forget.   [ll. 43–9]

The same kind of microcosmic imagery continues in Irving Layton's *The Cold Green Element* and in A.M. Klein's very central poem, *Portrait of the Poet as Landscape*, which concludes:

Therefore he seeds illusions. Look, he is
the nth Adam taking a green inventory
in the world but scarcely uttered, naming, praising . . .
For to praise

the world—he, solitary man—is breath
to him . . .

These are not mean ambitions. It is already something
merely to entertain them. Meanwhile, he
makes of his status as zero a rich garland,
a halo of his anonymity,
and lives alone, and in his secret shines
like phosphorus. At the bottom of the sea.

The closing lines echo Eliot on the poet as catalyst and Keats on the poet's lack of identity, but the final phrase comes out of the belly of the Canadian Leviathan, for the Leviathan, as no one knew better than Klein, is a sea monster.

Earlier Canadian poetry was full of solitude and loneliness, of the hostility or indifference of nature, of the fragility of human life and values in such an environment. Contemporary Canadian poetry seems to think rather of this outer Leviathan as a kind of objective correlative of some Minotaur that we find in our own mental labyrinths. The mind has become a dark chamber, or *camera obscura*, and its pictures are reflections of what is at once physical and human nature. A poem of Gwendolyn MacEwan, *Dark Pines under Water*, explicitly links the poetic consciousness with reflection and descent:

> This land like a mirror turns you inward
> And you become a forest in a furtive lake;
> The dark pines of your mind reach downward . . .
>
> There is something down there and you want it told.

Similar themes of descent are in Margaret Atwood's work, especially *Procedures for Underground*, in Eli Mandel's *Fuseli Poems*, and, very remarkably, in Jay Macpherson's *Welcoming Disaster*, a sequence in which the sections have such titles as *The Way Down* and *The Dark Side*. The imagery of this book, of a perilous descent into a world which is at once a world of fear and of love, of horror and of creation, recurs in Alden Nowlan's *Genealogy of Morals*:

> Take any child dreaming of pickled bones
> shelved in a coal-dark cellar understairs
> (we are all children when we dream) the stones
> red-black with blood from severed jugulars.
>
> Child Francis, Child Gilles went down those stairs,
> returned sides, hands and ankles dripping blood,
> Bluebeard and gentlest saint. The same nightmares
> instruct the evil, as inform the good.

The conception of nature as a mechanism, which began to take its modern form in the seventeenth century, meant, of course, that Western man was developing an increasingly mechanistic civilization. Canada was opened up by the technology of navigation and surveying and held together by the technology of transportation, which has left its mark in the great bridges and railways and seaports and in the network of canals in Southern Ontario. Up to, say, the Second World War, the inarticulate aspect of communication was the one that had top priority. Pratt's fascination with the rumbling and creaking of machinery, his constant awareness of the throbbing engines at the heart of the ship, indicated that poetry had with him become sufficiently aware of its surroundings to make poetic imagery out of technology. The development of technology makes for a growing introversion in life, with the high-rise apartments and office buildings, the superhighways, where falling asleep is one of the hazards, the tunnel-like streets, with pedestrians hustled out of the way of motor traffic as peasants used to be on the approach of nobility. Even in Pratt, society is held together only by the emergencies of "survival."

Culturally, this introversion reached its height with the blind man's medium of the radio and the deaf man's medium of the silent movie, the latter being a close relative of the puppet show. The television set is technically even more introverted, setting up a round-the-clock fantasy world that we can stay in without even making the effort of joining an audience. And yet the centring on both sound and vision sets limits to the introversion. Turn off the sound, and we are in the world of the puppet show again, totally uninvolved; turn off the screen and listen to the sound track, and a similar detachment occurs. But in the fully centred medium, for all the avoiding of reality, we are occasionally compelled to see glimpses of an actual and very human world. Whether cabinet ministers or Eskimos, people are ultimately compelled to look like people on television, instead of like abstractions of charisma or legend. The television set seems to me to provide an analogue, in the mass media, to the imagery of descent that I have been trying to trace in poetry, which ends not in introversion but in an intensely centred vision.

Besides television, the airplane is a technological development which has begun to make more human sense of the colossal space of Canada. Nature as seen from a plane forms patterns reminding us of the more abstract painters, Borduas and Pellan and Harold Town, who have succeeded the Group of Seven, but it figures less in the imagery of poetry, poets being, for the most part, children of the earth mother rather than the sky father. An analogy to the aerial perspective, which I think may be something more than an analogy, is the attitude to tradition in contemporary Canadian poetry. Tradition is usually thought of as linear, and as forming a series of conventions which continually go out of date, so that a poet has to be careful not to become associated with an obsolete fashion. In Canada tradition has become, in the last generation or so at least, a much more simultaneous and kaleidoscopic affair, reminding us perhaps of the welter of historical allusions in the costumes of young people. The echoes of Spenser in James Reaney's *A Suit of Nettles*, of descent themes from Ishtar to Boris Karloff movies in Macpherson's *Welcoming Disaster*, of prosodic devices from Old English to concrete poetry in Earle Birney, while they certainly assume a cultivated reader, are both unforced and unpedantic, and illustrate very clearly the advantage, for a Canadian poet, of being able to look down on tradition all at once, instead of being pushed ahead of it like the terminal moraine of a glacier. In the words of the critic Milton Wilson: "But one of the advantages of a poetry less than a hundred years old is that all the things that couldn't happen when they should have happened keep happening all the time... Having begun a millennium too late, there is not much point being correctly fashionable."[11]

Canadian literature has always been thought of as having its centre of gravity in the future. Now that it has come into the present also, it may, by being where it is as well as what it is, help to make its own contribution to the future that we all hope for—not the apocalyptic future of fantasy and nightmare, but a future in which Western man has come home from his exile in the land of unlikeness and has become something better than the ghost of an ego haunting himself.

71

National Consciousness in Canadian Culture

6 June 1976

An address delivered to the Royal Society of Canada's symposium on "The Revolutionary Tradition in Canadian and American Society." From Transactions of the Royal Society of Canada, *4th series, 14 (1976): 57–69. Reprinted in* RCLI, *63–79, in* ECLI, *147–60, and in part in* DG, *41–55. Italian translation by Silvia Albertazzi printed in* Argomenti canadesi, *ed. Amleto Lorenzini (Rome: np, 1978), 26–42, and in abridged form in* Vita, *18 June 1979, 3. Typescripts are in NFF, box 5, files y–z.*

One disadvantage of living in Canada is that one is continually called upon to make statements about the Canadian identity, and Canadian identity is an eminently exhaustible subject. I have written a dozen or so articles about it, which I warmly commend to your attention if you feel that what follows is too full of dry and sucking noises indicating that the straw has reached the bottom of the glass. Several aspects of the question are constants in any case. A year or two ago I was present at a public hearing of the Canadian Radio-Television Commission [CRTC], when leaders of the Cree Indian and Eskimo peoples in the far North were protesting against the destroying of their cultures by the mass media. One of them said that the overwhelming impression made on them by the media was that life in the south was "soft, violent, and sick." Some months later I was present at another CRTC hearing, on violence in television. There it was said that violence was an American phenomenon, being a cheap way of producing programs for a huge mass market, and not a problem in Canada, except as a result of importing American programs into Canada by cable. The conclusion of the second hearing was oddly similar to that of the first. There is no question of one group of people being inherently less violent than another: the principle involved is simply the elementary arithmetic of original sin. More people are always worse than fewer people.

At the same time more people are more aggressive and highly organized, and can force that organization on less populous communities. It seems doubtful at present that much of what is distinctive about the indigenous cultures of the North will long survive. One of their spokesmen asked us on the CRTC if we realized what an in-joke such a program as "All in the Family" seemed in Frobisher or Aklavik. But probably, before long, that unpleasant family will become part of their family too. Similarly, our undefended border is very effectively defended on one side, the United States being a highly protectionist country in culture as in other aspects of life, and the Canadian instinct for compromise has to make the best of it. If a Canadian novelist writes about people in Manitoba and wishes to find an American publisher, it is relatively easy for him (or her: I am thinking particularly of the ill-starred career of Martha Ostenso)[1] to push them over the border into North Dakota, in deference to the publisher's conviction that his readers will have a nervous breakdown if they pick up a novel with a Canadian setting. Some of Stephen Leacock's most unmistakably Canadian vignettes, in *Arcadian Adventures with the Idle Rich* and elsewhere, have American settings for the same reason. Again, if Canadian university graduates are excluded from the American job market and Canadian universities are full of Americans who make no concessions to their Canadian environment, it is easy for Canadians to rationalize the situation by saying that scholarship, like Canada, has no defended boundaries. Perhaps only intellectuals worry about cultural distinctiveness, and perhaps only because they have invented most of it themselves. The CRTC has constantly been reminded, first by broadcasters and later by cable operators, that the majority of Canadians prefer American programs, including the brutal ones.

And yet this represents a temptation to be fought against. I detected a certain desperation in the statements of the Cree and Eskimo leaders, a feeling which was more than simply a fear that their cultures were being exterminated by the high-powered death-wish of southern civilization. It was rather a feeling that their own people might not care very much if they did lose their distinctive identity and simply merged into the Canadian mass. There would be strong economic arguments for their doing so, if not cultural ones. One hears the same tone among French-speaking Canadians, opposing the way that Canadian French so often breaks down into an English dialect, or the way that so many ambitious young Francophones accept English as their career language. One hears it among spokesmen for ethnic minorities, including Jewish leaders who seem almost to regret the decline of anti-Semitism, and of course among English-speaking Canadians, where the threat to distinctiveness is regularly associated with America. But when we look at the United States itself, we can see that there is nothing American in the debasing of standards: that is simply human inertia, and such inertia destroys everything distinctive in American life equally with Canada. The fight for cultural distinctiveness, from this point of view, is a fight for human dignity itself, for the variety in life that nothing but genuine culture can ever produce, for the unity that is at the opposite pole from uniformity. Many years ago Toynbee defined one of the central problems of society as the need to foster what he called creative minorities without allowing the emergence of what he called a dominant minority.[2] Our current struggles for "affirmative action," our repudiation of "elitism," and the like, get this issue very confused at times, but it remains a genuine issue, especially when it is not recognized to be one, as is so often true of the United States vis-à-vis Canada. And to distinguish what is creative in a minority from what attempts to dominate, we have to distinguish between cultural issues, which are inherently decentralizing ones, and political and economic issues, which tend to centralization and hierarchy.

It is easy for those outside Canada to exaggerate the influence and persistence of the British connection on Canadian cultural development. It often comes as a surprise to my American friends that Canadians need passports to enter Great Britain, even though when they get there they go through a special door marked "Commonwealth." The British connection in Canada was culturally most important in the period between Confederation and the First World War. At that time Canada was trying to think of itself as a single nation extending "from sea to sea." As there was so much empty space in between, the Canadian consciousness could hardly match the American sense of a vast society slowly pushing a frontier westward until it reached the Pacific. Canada had to think of itself rather as part of a world-circling empire, its railways filling the gap in communication between Europe and the East, its natural resources contributing to a global technology, its young men taking part in the only social activity they were really wanted for outside Canada, imperial wars. As Charles G.D. Roberts says:

> And some Canadian lips are dumb
> Beneath Egyptian sands. [*Canada*, ll. 47–8]

The American influence on Canadian literature in English has always been at least as direct and immediate as the British influence, and often more so. Cultural connections with Britain were of course close all through the nineteenth century, but they were no closer than those in the New England of Emerson and Henry James. In fact Canadians felt that there was far less attention paid to them in Great Britain than they would have got if they had come from a sovereign state. There is a story, recorded in Smollett's *Humphry Clinker*, of the delight of George II on being told that a rumour that the French had marched on Louisburg from Acadia must have been false, because Cape Breton is an island.[3] This story symbolizes much in the British connection that still rankles in the Canadian consciousness. I have elsewhere made the obvious but often overlooked observation that the French lost Canada mainly because they had very little interest in holding it, and that if they had held it they might well have sold it as they did Louisiana. The British took a less parochial view of their empire, but still their flaccid attitude to Canadian interests, from the Treaty of Ghent in 1814 through all the nineteenth-century boundary disputes, gave Canada a strong sense of not getting the support it needed for its unusually difficult problem of identity. Nobody has much use for a colony, apparently, or at least for the human part of it.

It is a standard practice of universities in settled areas, like Harvard or Yale or Toronto, to send its graduates out to civilize the boondocks and then recall them when they have become "established" scholars with nothing much more to say. This is the situation that looms large in the writings of Haliburton, early in the nineteenth century. For all his commitment to the colonial position, Haliburton felt that it developed laziness and over-dependence on the mother country, and he thought that his Yankee peddler Sam Slick was a model of what greater energy could do for Nova Scotia, however detached a view he took of Sam Slick's opinions and language. But the greater energy would be useless unless it coincided with a more actively concerned response from Britain, and Haliburton felt that Britain should be much more active and discriminating in rewarding outstanding service in the colonies, beginning with him. Of the Church of England, for example, he makes Sam Slick say: "Remove the restrictions on colonial clergy, so that if they deserve promotion in the church to Britain, they needn't be shut out among big bogs, black logs, and thick fogs, for ever and ever."[4] In other words, the colonies are essentially penal settlements, and should be regarded as, at least for the well-meaning and deserving, a purgatory rather than a hell.

Another passage in this same paper, from *The Attaché*, is even more striking. At the end of his life Haliburton went to Britain and entered politics there, joining the Conservative party because he thought it was conservative, though by his Bluenose standards of conservatism it was practically a Communist front. We may remember the book called *White Niggers of America*, a recent manifesto of radical French Canadian protest.[5] It is interesting that identically the same metaphor had been used over a century earlier by the deeply conservative Haliburton to describe the English-speaking colonists in British North America: "The slave is a slave, and that's his condition. Now the English have two sorts of niggers—American colonists, who are free white niggers; and manufacturers' labourers at home, and they are white slave niggers.... A colonist and a free nigger don't differ in anythin' but color: both have naked rights, but they have no power given 'em to clothe those rights, and that's the naked truth."[6]

It seems to me better to think of Canada, not simply as British America, but as culturally descended from the Tory opposition to the Whig triumph at the time of the Revolutionary War. This is a view of it that would, *mutatis mutandis*, include French Canada, which still flies the prerevolutionary flag of the lilies. The American assumption that freedom and national independence were inseparable never took as deep root in Canada, and the uninhibited American development of entrepreneur capitalism was hardly possible in a country equally large but so sparsely populated. Hence it was natural for Canada to combine Tory attitudes with radical ones, just as it was possible, in fact necessary, for it to achieve a fairly high degree of socialization. Most Canadian politicians, whatever their parties or personal beliefs, are compelled to be middle-of-the-road trimmers, for obvious reasons we do not need to go into. But many leading Canadian intellectuals, English or French, could be described as one form or other of Tory radical.

The distinctive is not the unique: what is distinctive is an emphasis, a special proportioning of elements that other societies may have in different proportions. I see something distinctive, in this sense, in the remark of R.H. Bonnycastle, writing in 1841, when he speaks of "the United States, where from the great mixture of races, British feelings and British connection have given way before a flood of undefinable notions about liberty and equality, mixed with aristocratic wealth, slavery, and bigotry in religion."[7] I am quoting this not for its insight but for its commonplaceness. What the writer dislikes is not only American democracy but American oligarchy, the inequalities of wealth and opportunity. The criticism attacks from both sides of the Whig establishment. In the literature of social protest in Canada we find, over and over, a kind of radicalism that seems closer to Tom Paine than to Jefferson, often because, like Paine, it has immediate British roots.

Similarly in Susanna Moodie's *Roughing It in the Bush* (1852), the positive virtues of what I have elsewhere called a garrison society show up with great clarity: the constant fight to be clean, fully clothed, disciplined in speech and manner, to maintain any number of standards that we may think unnecessary even though now they would be easy to maintain, emerges with a singular intensity of dedication. Susanna Moodie's effort to remain a gentlewoman in the backwoods makes her the exact opposite of what Carlyle means by an unworking aristocracy. She felt that she belonged to the gentry, and devoted all her waking moments to dramatizing her social status. But to do so she was often forced to accept conditions of life that were primitive to the point of squalor. It is no good saying that she had servants to help her put on her show: servants were the most disheartening of all her problems.

A culture founded on a revolutionary tradition, like that of the United States, is bound to show very different assumptions and imaginative patterns from those of a culture that rejects or distrusts revolution. First, an underlying assumption of a successful revolution is "violence pays," and the violence in American life, through the opening of the West to the gangsterism in the immense cities, is part of its revolutionary heritage. In Canada, developing as it did through a series of military occupations, where the red-coated "Mountie," half policeman and half soldier, has become a national symbol, the violence has been mainly repressive violence. This means that nine-tenths of it never gets beyond the individual himself, or at most his immediate family. For details of how this self-destructive violence operates, see Canadian fiction, more or less passim: Margaret Atwood's lively book, *Survival*, is written largely about these indecisive "victor-victim" conflicts in Canadian novels. Such a mood, so largely disseminated through society, does not always make for colourful history. Dennis Lee, in his *Civil Elegies*, studies the curious paralysis of the 1837 rebellion, which took the form of

> the first
> spontaneous mutual retreat in the history of warfare [*Civil Elegies 1*, ll. 42–3]

because the rebels did not believe in the logic of rebellion, and their opponents did not believe in the logic of repression. And today, when not only Quebec but Western and Eastern Canada have strong separatist sentiments, separatism is neutralized by a feeling, affecting separatists and federalists alike, that the issue is not really important enough to go beyond the stage of symbolism. Even symbolism has had a curiously muted life in Canada. Older cultural nationalists, for example, warned us against the dangers of "flag-waving," disregarding the fact that Canada at the time had no flag to wave. A Newfoundlander told me once that he thought his people had most in common with the Poles, and like them tended to celebrate defeats rather than victories. This was some years before the publication of Ray Smith's story, "Cape Breton Is the Thought Control Centre of Canada," which makes the same point for Canada generally.[8] Certainly Canada has been quite as persistently partitioned throughout most of its history: the penalty it pays for having natural resources.

Then again, a revolutionary tradition is a deductive one: it implies a written constitution, which has to be reinterpreted or amended as time goes on, with major premises about human rights, the sense of a break with the past and of continuity with the future. The United States was fortunate in achieving this articulating process in the eighteenth century, perhaps the only time in Western history when reason looked reasonable. The contemporary Quebec Act was the opposite of all this:[9] it consolidated the past, recognized the *de facto* equality of two groups of people divided by language, legal tradition, and very largely by religion, and made an *ad hoc* settlement on the basis later developed theoretically by Burke, of resolving a conflict by recognizing some of the interests on both sides. It provided no blueprint for an indefinite future: it merely solved one crisis with some hope that it would last until the next one. The two countries, with their national birthdays only two days apart, were born under much the same stars, but have reacted to them very differently. In the United States there has been, until recently, a sense of progressive and linear advance, a progress like that of an express train into a future logically related to the past. Everyone quotes the penultimate sentence in *Huckleberry Finn* about lighting out for the Territory, but less attention is paid to the even more significant last sentence: "I been there before." There can be no creative return to the past: the past is absorbed into the future, or, as Whitman says:

> As a projectile form'd, impell'd, passing a certain line,
>   still keeps on,
> So the present, utterly form'd, impell'd by the past.
>
> [*Passage to India*, pt. 1, ll. 14–5]

    This sense of progress derives from a society which has defined its aims and is aware of its assumptions, and the individual defines himself against that society, usually as some kind of explorer or pioneer, whether the frontier implied is physical or cultural. Canada never defined itself as a unified society in this way: there is no Canadian way of life, no hundred per cent Canadian, no ancestral figures corresponding to Washington or Franklin or Jefferson, no eighteenth-century self-evident certainties about human rights, no symmetrically laid out country. Washington became a capital because it was in the logical place for one, between the North and the South: Ottawa became a capital because it was not Montreal or Kingston. A sardonic commentator, writing in 1868, remarks that its name was obviously derived from "Hoot awa," or out of the way. The Canadian sense of the future tends to be apocalyptic: Laurier's dictum that the twentieth century would belong to Canada[10] was, even then, implying a most improbable and discontinuous future. The past in Canada, on the other hand, is, like the past of a psychiatric patient, something of a problem to be resolved: it is rather like what the past would be in the United States if it had started with the Civil War instead of the Revolutionary War.

    American culture has followed the Western pattern, which grew out of the Biblical rejection of what it called "idolatry," that is, the belief that there was something numinous or potentially divine in the natural world. For the Western tradition, man must seek his God or his ideals through his social institutions. Nature is not to be worshipped or even loved: it is to be dominated. Canada tried hard to follow the same pattern, but its society has been less cohesive, and the individual poet or painter finds that it keeps disintegrating: it is hard for him to visualize either the audience in front of him that he is trying to reach or the audience behind him out of which his imagination has grown. In this situation the natural world keeps pushing insistently through the gaps in the mental society. I see constantly in Canadian culture, more particularly in its poetry, a sense of meditative shock produced by the intrusion of the natural world into the imagination. I say intrusion, because it so often looms up with a greater urgency than the poet's social, political, or religious outlook is prepared to allow for.

I imagine that W.L. Morton is right in connecting this sense in Canada with the role of the northern frontier in the Canadian imagination. An American who had never seen the Mississippi would not be regarded as a widely travelled man, at least in his own country; but few Canadians have ever seen the largest river in Canada, the Mackenzie, and the existence of a vast hinterland which is both a part of us and yet not a part of us creates something curiously self-alienating. Morton says: "And because of this separate origin in the northern frontier, economy, and approach, Canadian life to this day is marked by a northern quality, the strong seasonal rhythm which still governs even academic sessions.... The line which marks off the frontier from the farmstead, the wilderness from the baseland, the hinterland from the metropolis, runs through every Canadian psyche."[11] The last sentence might be equally true of the psyches in Colorado or Arkansas or Oregon: what is different is that in the United States wilderness and baseland can be assimilated by a uniting consciousness. In Canada the wilderness, symbolized by the North, creates a kind of *doppelgänger* figure who is oneself and yet the opposite of oneself. I remember being at a "church supper" in a rural area of Saskatchewan, and hearing one woman say to another: "You know, this last rain wasn't necessary, in the least." It nearly split my own Canadian psyche to hear, in so middle-class a gathering, the murmur of a timeless peasantry scolding its household gods. But such sudden atavisms are almost a commonplace in Canadian literature, whether the setting is rural or urban.

I have often spoken of the presbyopic sense in Canadian culture, the vast distances of river and sky that confer nobility on faraway looks. Donald Creighton, a great master of Canadian rhetoric, ends the first volume of his biography of John A. Macdonald with this sentence: "They [the parliament buildings] stood out boldly against the sky; and far behind them, hidden in darkness, were the ridges of the Laurentians, stretching away, mile after mile, towards the north-west." The last sentence of the second volume reads: "Beyond the dock lay the harbour and the islands which marked the end of the lowest of the Great Lakes; and beyond the islands the St. Lawrence River began its long journey to the sea."[12] I have previously noted the same perspective in Canadian painters, notably in Tom Thomson's canoeist's eye that is continually scanning the horizon for some break into still greater distance. The tree in the centre of Thomson's *West Wind* seems deliberately out of visual focus: the eye is led to something behind it. Yet it seems also to be saying: "Look, I belong here: I'm not just an obstacle on the way to the horizon." It is an emblem of Canada itself, so long apologetic for being so big an obstacle on the way to somewhere more interesting, yet slowly becoming a visible object in its own right.

At the very beginning of Canadian literature in English, we have Frances Brooke's *The History of Emily Montague* (1769), in which the narrator remarks: "Nothing is, in my opinion, so favorable to the display of beauty as a ball. A state of rest is ungraceful . . . never any human being had such an aversion to still life as I have."[13] A very innocent and light-hearted remark; but a great deal of Canadian cultural history is summed up in it: the obsession with movement and transportation, the eye that passes over the foreground object, the restlessness that solves all social difficulties by moving somewhere else, the commitment to a society that involves constant movement up and down an immensely long and narrow corridor. I remember glancing through Herbert Marcuse's book, *One Dimensional Man*, and wondering what he would have made of the modern world if he had had to live in a one-dimensional country. Two centuries later than Emily's proclamation of her aversion to still life, E.J. Pratt wrote a poem called *Still Life* which uses that phrase as a term of contempt for poets who do not deal with the great moving issues of society. It is the only poem of his I know with a real tone of hostility in it. Still later we have Gwendolyn MacEwen, in a poem called *The Portage*, commenting on the same feature in the Canadian sensibility:

> But now we fear movement
> and now we dread stillness;
> we suspect it was the land
> that always moved, not our ships . . .

I spoke of Susanna Moodie and her struggle to maintain the social perspective to which she had become accustomed in the unrelenting surroundings of the Canadian bush. Her sister Catharine Parr Traill is, at least superficially, a more attractive personality, making the best of her hardships and cultivating an interest in the nature around her that makes her a kind of miniature Thoreau, especially in her studies of flowers. She says: "To the person who is capable of looking abroad into the beauties of nature, and adoring the Creator through his glorious works, are opened stores of unmixed pleasure, which will not permit her to be dull or unhappy in the loneliest part of our Western Wilderness."[14] The word "her" is worth pausing on for a moment: it seems to be assumed that a woman's life, however arduous the conditions, will show a relatively civilized balance between work and leisure, whereas the male, whether hunter or fisherman or farmer, will merely oscillate between work and idleness. As an early (1818) writer in Newfoundland remarks: "all ranks of society appear to consider debauchery as the only antidote to the *taedium vitae* which prevails between the month of December and the recommencement of the fishery in the May following."[15] Perhaps we have a clue here to the large proportion of women among the best Canadian writers. Mrs. Traill's capacity for detailed attention to "still life" is exceptional, if not unique, in early Canadian writing: at the same time she sometimes gives the impression of having too fixed a smile, too determined a cheerfulness, too resolute to exclude many things she doesn't want yet knows to be there. One suspects that the two qualities are psychologically close together.

What I mean by a meditative shock produced by the natural world in Canadian poetry is not easy to explain, but some examples may clarify it. Let us first take a passage in Isabella Valancy Crawford's *Malcolm's Katie* (1884) that rather upset E.K. Brown, in his pioneering study of Canadian poetry:

> And Max car'd little for the blotted sun,
> And nothing for the startl'd, outshone stars;
> For Love, once set within a lover's breast,
> Has its own Sun—its own peculiar sky,
> All one great daffodil—on which do lie
> The sun, the moon, the stars—all seen at once . . .   [pt. 2, ll. 182–7]

The metamorphosis of distant nature into a single "great daffodil" inside the mind is a kind of imaginative explosion, in which the overlooked and peripheral suddenly turns into something overmastering and central. Or take Frederick Philip Grove's description of a July storm on the prairies in *The Turn of the Year*. There is a flash of lightning followed by thunder, as there so often is in thunderstorms: nothing really happens, and a minute later a "little girl comes out, barefooted, to splash in the pools." What is left in the narrator's mind is very curious: "Like a desert of barren snow is my mind, a white blank, stunned into unconsciousness of all things about me. But like a scarlet patch of blood shed on a real snowfield there lies on the white impassive background of my vision the memory of that frightful clap of wrath."[16] The image has nothing clearly to do with summer storms: it is the central image of Canadian fear and guilt: the blank world of white snow stained with the blood of murdered animals. In Irving Layton's *A Tall Man Executes a Jig*, a man watches a wounded grass snake "that lugged / Its intestine like a small red valise." It finally dies, and there follows an extraordinary conclusion:

> Meanwhile the green snake crept upon the sky,
> Huge, his mailed coat glittering with stars that made
> The night bright, and blowing thin wreaths of cloud
> Athwart the moon; and as the weary man
> Stood up, coiled above his head, transforming all.

A poem of James Reaney, *The Heart and the Sun*, describes a love affair in which the heart swallows the sun but then dies, the sun escaping with the final remark:

> "Alas, my Love, it is your fate and mine
> That I someday smother whom I kindle
> And give birth to those I'll someday kill."

In these passages something casual and expected in nature goes through a vortex or gyre into the mind, and creates there a riddle of experience which cannot be assimilated to any set of human or social values. Like the gods of polytheism, it is neither good nor evil, but may be either or both. It is usually an object of involuntary contemplation, something that the mind has not consciously attended to but has forced its way in anyhow. It looks almost as though the fear of still life in the Canadian imagination were a fear of, so to speak, catching Nature's eye, as seen not merely in the eye of a dying animal but in the autumnal blaze of a dying leaf, or even, in Pratt's *Towards the Last Spike*, in the glitter of metals blasted by dynamite out of the Precambrian shield.

National Consciousness in Canadian Culture

The unbroken violation of nature in Canada, the economy founded on the trapping and mutilating of animals, the destroying of trees, the drying up of rivers and the polluting of lakes, began inspiring guilt and uneasiness long before the contemporary ecology movement. In Canadian poetry there is a special pathos in dying animals and falling trees, and in many tragic narratives, such as Duncan Campbell Scott's *At the Cedars* and Birney's *David*, where people are killed in log jams or on glaciers, there is a lurking sense not only of the indifference of nature to man, but almost of its exasperation with this parasite of humanity that has settled on it. In one of Ernest Thompson Seton's stories, a hunter is obsessed with the desire to kill a great mountain ram, simply because it is the most beautiful thing he has ever seen. He finally shoots it; reaction sets in; he cuts the head off and puts it on the wall of his cabin with a curtain over it and sits down to wait for the ram, as he says, to get even. Eventually a landslide buries him and his cabin.[17] Modern ecology-conscious writing like that of Farley Mowat merely puts this conception of the nemesis of nature on a less fanciful basis.

We may also notice how often contemporary poets take the traditional Canadian theme of the identity of the hunter and the hunted, and turn it into the theme of metamorphosis, where the victorious human actually becomes the defeated animal, as in the story of Actaeon. We find this in Margaret Atwood's latest book of verse *You Are Happy*, especially in the sequence called "Songs of the Transformed," and the series of "Circe/Mud" poems which follows it. It is also prominent in Gwendolyn MacEwen's *Magic Animals*, in Susan Musgrave's Haida poems, and in the many poems about the descent to the darker levels of one's own consciousness, as in Jay Macpherson's *Welcoming Disaster* and Eli Mandel's Minotaur poems. Every so often this theme manifests the split within the psyche that Morton mentions. The poet becomes both a daylight consciousness and a dark shadow of that consciousness which identifies, very often, with a continuously martyred nature. In Francis Sparshott's remarkable long poem, *Rhetoric for a Divided Voice*, we have a dialogue between two halves of the same person, one questioning, the other more elusive and yet more certain of its knowledge. The part called "Half" says:

> I challenge your world to atone
> For my unmerited pain   [ll. 1-2]

and the "Other Half" answers:

> Breath is the wraith of frost,
> And breath drawn in to hold
> In the temple of the ghost
> The marriage of dark and cold.
> Deep over hands and head
> Welcoming snow is thrown;
> Deep over head and hands
> To the levelling of broken lands,
> To the burial of the dead.   [ll. 30–8]

It is perhaps worth noticing that the best piece of science fiction in Canadian literature, James De Mille's *A Strange Manuscript Found in a Copper Cylinder*, not published until 1888 but written much earlier, describes a society dedicated to the opposite of all normal human ideals, to darkness, death, poverty, and pain.

One could go on with many other examples, but these should make the point. The Tory opposition to the American way of life, which spoke as often from the left of it as from the right, was a strangled and muted voice as long as the United States was progressing, like Whitman's projectile, in more or less a straight line. Now the United States seems to be entering a period of self-examination, of taking a more retrospective look at its past and its traditional assumptions. It is even possible that American development has reached a climax and will see its past and future as more of a parabola. There are, of course, many movements of imaginative opposition within American literature itself paralleling the Canadian one. But simultaneously with the growth of a new feeling in the United States, there has been in English-speaking Canada, since about 1960, a great upsurge of creative power, both within the conventional forms of poetry and fiction and outside them. In French Canada the parallel upsurge, though equally remarkable, has taken more explicitly political forms. The Canadian recurring themes of self-conflict, of the violating of nature, of individuals uncertain of their social context, of dark, repressed, oracular doubles concealed within each of us, are now more communicable outside Canada in the new mood of the world. The assumption that exploiting nature is the only way to human advancement has lost much of its authority, and so has the geometry, reflected in the grid patterns of our cities and the like, that has ordered so much of our lives since the eighteenth century. Around 1900 the word "square" was a general term of approval; today it means something we are trying to get away from. I imagine that in another ten years there will be very little difference in tone between Canadian and American literature; but what there is now in Canada is a literature of extraordinary vigour and historical significance.

72

Canadian Culture Today

2 February 1977

From the typescript in NFF, 1988, box 6, file d. Files c and e have some preliminary drafts. Printed in somewhat compressed form in Voices of Canada: An Introduction to Canadian Culture, *ed. Judith Webster (Burlington, Vt.: Association for Canadian Studies in the United States, 1977), 1–7, and, with fewer but different omissions, as "Canada's Emerging Identity,"* Toronto Star, *28 June 1980, b1, b4. Typescript printed without the first paragraph as "Sharing the Continent" in DG, 57–70. This was given originally as the keynote address to the Symposium on Twentieth-Century Canadian Culture at the Hirshhorn Museum and Sculpture Garden, Washington, D.C., organized by the Association for Canadian Studies in the United States.*

I have been called upon to make a fair number of speeches about Canadian culture, mainly to Canadian audiences. The subject itself no doubt is inexhaustible, but my comprehension of it is not; and I find that each time I speak many of the same points insist on being repeated. I assume that this is mainly a different audience, but those of you who have heard or read me on these themes may feel that you have been here before. On the other hand, whatever I repeat I believe to be substantially true.

Practically all Canadians have friends or relatives in the United States, and have spent a good deal of time there. Hence it is generally assumed, in both countries, that English-speaking Canadians, at least, cannot be told apart from Americans. This was a view that I held myself until I spent a couple of years in England as a student. Then I realized that there was a difference, but I found it hard to put the difference into words, and because our civilization is tied up in words, we are apt to think that whatever we can't verbalize is unreal. After that, I began an academic career, and have taught briefly at several American universities. My American students often ask me if I notice much difference between teaching them and teaching Canadians in Toronto. They usually expect the answer to be no, but my answer is yes. Here is, perhaps, something that it is possible to put into words. American students have been conditioned from infancy to think of themselves as citizens of one of the world's great powers. Canadians are conditioned from infancy to think of themselves as citizens of a country of uncertain identity, a confusing past, and a hazardous future. Nine-tenths of the time the responses of my American students are identical with those of Canadian students, but the tenth time I know that I'm in a foreign country and have no idea what the next move is. The sensation must be rather similar to that of a Dane in Germany or a Finn in Russia; or, on a smaller scale, of a Welshman in England. What I should like to try to do here is to define the areas of likeness and of difference a little more precisely. The history and the geography of the two countries have been so different that the cultural response to them has to be different too.

I begin with the geographical differences. Some years ago I first saw Herbert Marcuse's *One Dimensional Man* in a bookshop, and what came into my mind was a quite irrelevant reflection: "I wonder what he'd say if he had to live in a one-dimensional country?" For Canada, through most of its history, has been a strip of territory as narrow as Chile, besides being longer and more broken up. In the United States, the general historical pattern has been based on a north-south axis with a western frontier that moved gradually across mountains and rivers and prairies to the Pacific. In Canada there is a single gigantic east-west thrust down the St. Lawrence, up the Great Lakes, and across the prairies, then through whatever holes a surveyor could find in the Rockies to the west coast. Consider the emotional difference between coming to the United States by ship from England and coming to Canada. The United States presents a fairly symmetrical coastline, with relatively few islands, apart from a minor group in the mouth of the Hudson, and one is reminded of the old remark about Columbus's discovering America; "How could he have missed it?" One enters Canada through the Strait of Belle Isle into the Gulf of St. Lawrence, where five Canadian provinces surround us, with enormous islands and glimpses of a mysterious mainland in the distance, but in the foreground only sea and sky. Then we go down the waterway of the St. Lawrence, which in itself is only the end of a chain of rivers and lakes that starts in the Rockies. The United States confronts the European visitor; Canada surrounds and engulfs him, or did until the coming of the airplane.

In the United States, the frontier has been, imaginatively, an open-ended horizon in the West; in Canada, wherever one is, the frontier is a circumference. Every part of Canada is shut off by its geography, British Columbia from the prairies by the Rockies, the prairies from the Canadas by the immense hinterland of Northern Ontario, Quebec from the Maritimes by the upthrust of Maine, the Maritimes from Newfoundland by the sea. A generation ago, Hugh MacLennan took a phrase from Rilke, "two solitudes," as the title for a novel about the mutual isolation of English and French in Montreal. But everywhere in Canada we find solitudes touching other solitudes: every part of Canada has strong separatist feelings, because every part of it is in fact a separation. And behind all these separations lies the silent North, full of vast rivers, lakes, and islands that, even yet, very few Canadians have ever seen. The Mississippi, running north to south through the middle of the country, is a symbol of the American frontier and its steady advance into the sunset. The largest river in Canada, the Mackenzie, pouring silently into the Arctic Ocean at what seems the end of the earth, is a symbol of the *terra incognita* in Canadian consciousness, or what Rupert Brooke called the "unseizable virginity" of the Canadian landscape.[1] Or, as another British visitor, Wyndham Lewis, remarked: "this monstrous, empty habitat must continue to dominate [this nation] psychologically and so culturally."[2]

In looking at two countries as closely related as Canada and the United States, no difference is unique or exclusive: we can point to nothing in Canada that does not have a counterpart, or many counterparts, south of its border. What is different is a matter of emphasis and of degree. In the United States, exploration and the building of railways have naturally been of central importance in the imagination of the country. In Canada they have been obsessive. The Confederation of 1867 depended on the building of a railway from one ocean to the other: the political necessity to keep the CPR entirely within Canada meant that the railway had to be built in the face of almost unimaginable natural obstacles. The CPR remained a private corporation, but the great difficulty of establishing communication in Canada meant that Canada became accustomed very soon to nationalized railways, broadcasting corporations, film boards, air lines, and similar efforts of deficit financing. Canadian culture has reflected the same preoccupations. The first wave of exploration was mainly religious and economic, carried on by missionaries and *voyageurs* and fur-traders, along with the explorers who worked in their interests. The second wave was technological and scientific, an age of railway building and geological surveys. The third wave was cultural, and was spearheaded by painters, from the earliest travelling and military artists of the nineteenth century, Krieghoff, Paul Kane, Thomas Davies, to the Group of Seven and their contemporaries a generation ago.

A strong documentary interest in painting, in films, even in literature, is an obvious and distinctive feature of Canadian culture, and it follows the tradition of the early explorers and missionaries, of the Jesuit Relations and the reports of the Hudson's Bay Company. But it is painting in particular that expresses this interest: painting, the art that began in the deep caves of palaeolithic times, has always had something of an unborn world about it, the projecting on nature of colours in the dark, this last phrase being the title of a Canadian play by James Reaney. Painting is in the front line of imaginative efforts to humanize a nonhuman world, to fight back, in a sparsely settled country, against a silent otherness that refuses to assimilate to anything human.

A fascination with landscape is the dominant feature of Canadian painting down to about 1930. Even in later and more abstract painters, Riopelle, for example, it seems to me that there is a strong basis of landscape in the underlying vision. The exploring and pioneering aspect of this is clearest in Tom Thomson, Emily Carr, and the Group of Seven, where we are still very largely in the Canada of the blazed trail and the canoe. The painter keeps shifting our eye from the foreground into the opening in the woods, the bend of the river, the break through the distant hills. The use of expressionist and fauve techniques, with powerful colour contrasts exploding against one another, suggests a natural world that is unconscious of man and is absorbed in an internecine battle of titans. In historical perspective another element emerges which is much more sinister than simply the unblinking stare of a stark "solemn land," as J.E.H. MacDonald called one of his best-known paintings. Just as, in a crowded country like Great Britain, the practice of archaeology is a matter of keeping one jump ahead of the bulldozer, so these precious records of nature in her "unspoiled" loveliness of snow and rock and red sumach and maple seem to be hastily jotted notes of a hunted refugee, set down before civilization arrives and turns the scene into one more garbage dump.

Literature during this period did not fare so well as painting, because this long-range perspective in literature is very apt to turn rhetorical, in a rather bad sense. Thus Charles G.D. Roberts:

> Awake, my country, the hour is great with change!
>   Under this gloom which yet obscures the land,
> From ice-blue strait and stern Laurentian range
>   To where giant peaks our western bounds command,
> A deep voice stirs . . .   (*An Ode for the Canadian Confederacy*)

I quote this because it is typical of what made so much Canadian poetry of a century ago immature and colonial. The poet is not expressing his feelings but talking about the feelings he thinks he ought to have, and the clue to his poetic insincerity is the remote surveying vision that is really focused on nothing but a map. In other contexts this kind of rhetoric turns didactic, as in Bliss Carman's rather forced praises of the strenuous life. No poets of this period gave us the sense of an inward struggling nature that Thomson and Emily Carr do, except for some brilliant flashes in one writer, Isabella Crawford, who died unknown at thirty-seven. English Canadian poetry had to wait for E.J. Pratt to convey the real sense of this centrifugal and linear rhythm in Canadian life. His themes are those that are most closely connected with this rhythm: the martyrdom of the Jesuit missionaries, the building of the CPR, the stories of whale hunts and shipwrecks that bring out the sense of a beleaguered and surrounded garrison.

    I have been speaking of one direction in the Canadian imagination: the direction that followed the east-west Laurentian movement and responded emotionally to the national motto *a mari usque ad mare*. This was both a romantic and a conservative movement: romantic because it sought the new and the unknown, conservative because its original impetus was in Europe. The Confederation that took shape around a transcontinental railway was part of a global chain of communication that started in London and linked together all the pieces of an empire on which the sun never set. But as settlement in the country advanced, a more longitudinal and north-south consciousness developed. This perspective focused on the American connection rather than the British Empire, and tended to see the country as a series of northern spurs of the United States. When I was growing up in the Maritime Provinces during the nineteen-twenties, there was a strong political loyalty to Confederation, but an even stronger sense that Boston was our real capital, and that the Maritimes formed the periphery of New England, or what was often called "the Boston states." In the nineteenth century, at least, the Liberal party reflected the north-south North American outlook, as the Conservative party reflected the Laurentian one.

Once again it is painting that gives us the clearest sense of the contrast. If we turn from the Group of Seven to the Quebec landscape painters, to Maurice Cullen, Suzor-Côté, Clarence Gagnon, and the very little of Morrice that was done in Canada, we are in a world of softer and gentler outlines where the sense of being lived in shows through. The painter's eye is more restricted and at the same time more precise. The landscape is receding from a human eye, not absorbed in itself. Quebec is the only part of Canada which has been settled long enough for a sense of imaginative digestion, so to speak, to emerge. When E.J. Pratt spoke of a kind of poetry he disapproved of, a poetry that avoided social issues and cultivated an easy self-indulgence, he described it in the pictorial metaphor of "still life." In his use of this phrase there is, perhaps, something of that odd fear of catching nature's eye that is very characteristic of that stage in Canadian development. It is significant, first, that the best still-life painter in the earlier period, Ozias Leduc, lived and died in Quebec, and, second, that the still-life perspective, where the imagination has completely surrounded the subject, begins to emerge rather later than the Group of Seven, with David Milne, and further west, Lemoine Fitzgerald.

What has been gradually revealed in this development is the fact that cultural movements are different in direction and rhythm from political and economic ones. Politically and economically, the current of history is toward greater unity, and unity in this context includes uniformity. Technology is the most dramatic aspect of this development: one cannot take off in a jet plane and expect a radically different way of life in the place where the plane lands. But culture has something vegetable about it, something that increasingly needs to grow from roots, something that demands a small region and a restricted locale. The fifty states of the Union are not, in themselves, a cultural entity: they are a political and economic entity that provides a social background for a great variety of cultural developments. We speak for convenience of American literature, but its real cultural context usually turns out to be something more like Mississippi or New England or Chicago or an expatriate group in Paris. Even in the much smaller Great Britain we have Thomas Hardy largely confined to "Wessex," Dylan Thomas to South Wales, D.H. Lawrence to the Midlands. Similarly in Canada: as the country has matured, more and more of its local areas have come to life imaginatively.

This fact has given French Canadian writers, in particular, one considerable advantage. The French Canadian poet or novelist knows that he is contributing to the articulateness of a beleaguered language, hence he need have no doubt about his social function or the importance of being a writer in such a situation. He has no competitors closer than European France, and they live in a very different social context. The English Canadian writer has not had this advantage, and the tedium of a permanent identity crisis has afflicted English Canada for a century. Soon after the Second World War, French Canada entered what has been called the Quiet Revolution, an awareness of belonging both to itself and to the modern world, which shook off most of the isolating features that had been previously restricting its cultural life. I think it was partly a response to the French act of self-definition that made for a sudden and dramatic emergence of English Canadian culture after about 1960. Since then there has been a tremendous cultural explosion, in literature and painting particularly, which has produced a mood that is often called cultural nationalism.

This is a most misleading phrase, and for two reasons. First, nationalism suggests something aggressive, like a nineteenth-century jingoist waiting for the next war to start, or a twentieth-century third-world revolutionary. But culture in itself seeks only its own identity, not an enemy: hostility only confuses it. Second, contemporary Canadian culture, being a culture, is not a national development but a series of regional ones, what is happening in British Columbia being very different from what is happening in New Brunswick or Ontario. Even there we find an increasing decentralization: one reason why Montreal has been so lively a cultural centre is that there are a good many Montreals, each one with its own complexities and inner conflicts. Then again, while a certain amount of protection may be needed for Canadian writers and artists, cultural products are export products. If we look at, say, the literature that has come out of Ireland during the last century, we can see that culture, like a grain or wine crop, is produced in a local area but is not necessarily consumed there.

Politically, economically, and technologically, the world is uniting; Canada is in the American orbit and will remain so for the foreseeable future. Canadians could not resist that even if they wanted to, and not many of them do want to. Culturally, both nations should run their own show, and the way to run a cultural show is to let a thousand flowers bloom, in Mao's phrase.[3] Things go wrong when cultural developments are hitched on to economic or technological ones. That gives us, on this continent, a subculture dominated by advertising and distributed through the mass media. The influence of this in our lives is often spoken of, both inside and outside the United States, as an Americanizing influence. Ten years ago, during the centenary of Confederation, a sour little joke was circulating in Canada to the effect that what had been aimed at in Canada was a combination of British political institutions, American economic buoyancy, and French culture, and that what we had, after a century, was French politics, British economic buoyancy, and American culture. However, the growth of an anonymous, mass-produced, mindless subculture is American only to the extent that the United States is the world's most highly industrialized society. Its effect on genuine American culture is quite as lethal as its effect everywhere else, and its main features are as Japanese or German or Russian as they are American.

Things go wrong in the opposite direction when economic or political developments are hitched on to cultural ones, as has happened in the Quebec separatist movement. It is a part of M. Lévesque's sales pitch to speak of separation as inevitable, and to compare it with the American Revolution. It seems to me a retrograde and counterhistorical movement, both in its neocolonial attitude to France and in its arrogant attitude to French Canadians outside Quebec. As for the American analogy, what was of permanent importance there was not the separation from Britain but the principle of *e pluribus unum*: politically and economically, the colonies had to unite, though culturally there was no reason why Massachusetts and Virginia should not be quite different. Separatism in Quebec is an intellectuals' movement, a *trahison des clercs*: it has dominated the communications media for some years, and bypasses economic issues with a simple emotional construct in which Confederation equals bondage and separation freedom. As an intellectuals' movement, even a revolutionary one, it may settle for a purely symbolic separation: if it goes beyond that, whatever is distinctive in the culture of Quebec will be its first casualty.

My reasons for thinking so take me into the second group of conditioning differences from the United States, the historical ones. The pattern of Canadian history has been almost the opposite of the pattern of American history. The United States had a War of Independence against a European power in the eighteenth century, and a civil war on its own soil a century later. Canada had a civil war of European powers on its own soil in the eighteenth century, and a movement of independence against its American partner in the nineteenth. This started with the invasion of 1775 and continued in the War of 1812, which had very little point as a war with Britain, but was in many respects a war of independence for Canada. I discover that Americans, while they know about the bombardment of Washington and the battle of New Orleans, are often hardly aware that this war involved Canada at all, much less that the bombardment of Washington was a reprisal for the burning of what is now Toronto. All through the nineteenth century, up to and beyond Confederation, there continued to be a certain edginess about the aggressive expansion of America, as it came through in Fenian raids and boundary disputes, and Confederation itself completed what the American invasions had begun, the sense that there was an identity on the north side of the border that could be brought into being only by some kind of political unity.

Another historical contrast is even more important. The United States reached its peak of articulateness in the latter part of the eighteenth century, the age when it became a nation, the age of Washington, Adams, Jefferson, and Franklin. The United States is today the oldest country in the world: that is, no other nation has lasted so long with so relatively little social change. The party now in power is the world's oldest political party,[4] and the American flag is one of the world's oldest flags. Canada, by contrast, had no eighteenth century. It started with the expansion of French Canada in the seventeenth century, and started again with the influx of defeated Tories into Ontario and the Maritimes after the Revolution, going directly from Baroque to Romantic expansion, but never achieving the moment of self-definition that the United States achieved.

It would be a great mistake to exaggerate the strength of the British connection in Canada, even in the nineteenth century. There was a great deal of superficial loyalty, or at least a good many expressions of it, but there was also much resentment, and a feeling that colonials would have been treated with more respect in London if, like Americans, they had represented an independent nation. Some years ago a book appeared in Quebec called *White Niggers of America*, meaning the French Canadians, an expression of strong separatist feelings in Quebec; but the same metaphor had been used over a century earlier by the deeply conservative Haliburton of Nova Scotia, who makes his Sam Slick remark that a colonial and a freed black slave differed in nothing but colour: they had theoretical rights but no power to enforce them.[5]

It would, I think, make for a clearer sense of Canada if we thought of it, not as British North America, but as a country that grew out of a Tory opposition to the Whig victory in the American Revolution, thus forming, in a sense, something complementary to the United States itself. This may sound like a very English-based view of Canadian history, but I am not sure that it is. Not long after the British conquest came the French Revolution with its strongly anticlerical bias. The clergy remained the ideologically dominant group in Quebec down to a generation ago, and the clergy wanted no part of the French Revolution or anything it stood for. Quebec still flies the prerevolutionary flag of lilies. Nor, from that clergy's point of view, was the American Revolution really so different from the French one. But apart from the clerical influence, French Canada had excellent and foresighted reasons for accepting a conservative *modus vivendi* which, from the Quebec Act[6] in the eighteenth century to Confederation in the nineteenth, had as its central idea the uniting of a French and an English community on a basis that guaranteed some cultural integrity for both.

Historically, the Tories stood for the supremacy of the crown and the established church, and for a society closely connected with the land. Conservatives in both Britain and Canada are called Tories, but the real Tories were pre-Conservative: they revolved around a domestic economy and a personal relationship to the working class that was destroyed by the Industrial Revolution. Expressions of Canadian opposition to American ideology, all through the nineteenth century, attack from the left quite as often as from the right. One writer, in 1841, spoke of "the United States; where from the great mixture of races, British feelings and British connection have given way before a flood of undefinable notions about liberty and equality, mixed with aristocratic wealth, slavery, and bigotry in religion."[7] I quote this not because it is profound but because it is commonplace; and we notice that what the writer dislikes is not only American democracy but American oligarchy, the inequalities of wealth and opportunity. It is not surprising, then, that so many of Canada's intellectuals, both English and French, should be one form or another of Tory radical. One of these, and also one of the ablest commentators on the Canadian scene, George Grant, writes near the end of his *Lament for a Nation*: "The impossibility of conservatism in our era is the impossibility of Canada. As Canadians we attempted a ridiculous task in trying to build a conservative nation in the age of progress, on a continent we share with the most dynamic nation on earth. The current of modern history was against us."[8]

Yet before we write off Canada as an abortive and quixotic culture that has failed to break through the heavy snow-crust of a technological world, it might be worth asking what there is, in this Tory devotion to crown and church and land, that can be translated into terms of the 1970s. Human ideas have an extraordinary power of metamorphosis, and many things that are outdated or absurd in their original context may reappear later in a very different aspect. For instance, no church has ever been established in Canada, but there has been a much closer connection between church and state, especially in education, which has given Canadian culture a distinctive colouring. Again, there may be advantages in having the personal symbol of the Queen instead of the impersonal one of the flag, which Canada did not have until recently, and would hardly miss if it still did not. But I think something rather different is involved here, which I shall illustrate by an example. When I first came to Toronto, in 1929, it was a homogeneous Scotch-Irish town, dominated by the Orange Order, and greatly derided by the rest of Canada for its smugness, its snobbery, and its sterility. The public food in restaurants and hotels was of very indifferent quality, as it is in all right-thinking Anglo-Saxon communities. After the war, Toronto took in immigrants to the extent of nearly a quarter of its population, and large Greek, Italian, Portuguese, Central European, West Indian communities grew up within it. The public food improved dramatically. More important, these communities all seemed to find their own place in the larger community with a minimum of violence and tension, preserving much of their own cultures and yet taking part in the total one. It has always seemed to me that this very relaxed absorption of minorities, where there is no concerted effort at a "melting pot," has something to do with what the Queen symbolizes, the separation of the head of state from the head of government. Because Canada was founded by two peoples, nobody could ever know what a hundred per cent Canadian was, and hence the decentralizing rhythm that is so essential to culture had room to expand.

Still more important is the Canadian sense of the close relation of the people to the land. Everywhere we turn in Canadian literature and painting, we are haunted by the natural world, and even the most sophisticated Canadian artists can hardly keep something very primitive and archaic out of their imaginations. This sense is not that of the possession of the land, but precisely the absence of possession, a feeling that here is a nature that man has polluted and imprisoned and violated but has never really lived with.

Canada does not have quite so heavy a burden of guilt toward red and black peoples as the United States, and the French record with the Indians was rather better than the British or Spanish record. Even so there is little to be proud of: in Newfoundland, for instance, a gentle and inoffensive people, the Beothuks, were exterminated as casually as though they were mosquitoes. But still the main focus of guilt in Canada seems to fall on the rape of nature. The deaths of animals seem to have an extraordinary resonance in Canadian literature, as though the screams of all the trapped and tortured creatures who built up the Canadian fur trade were still echoing in our minds. One of the silliest of Tory fetishes, the preserving of game, seems to be taking a very different role in the Canadian imagination.

The seventeenth-century invaders of both countries brought with them the Cartesian ego, the sense of man as a perceiving subject, totally different from everything else in nature by virtue of his consciousness. It was a long time before the philosophers got around to realizing that egocentric consciousness is primarily a consciousness of death, but the poets had always known that: even the nineteenth-century rhetorical poets I spoke of wrote their best poetry in elegiac or nostalgic or other moods that were close to the sense of death. The narrative poets gave us stories of death in log jams, on glaciers, in hunting expeditions where the hunter seems to identify with his victim. This was not of course confined to Canada: one thinks of Whitman, who also wrote his best poetry about death and his worst rhetoric about democracy. But it was so strong in Canada as to give most of its serious literature, especially its poetry, a very sombre cast.

In 1948 a group of Quebec artists, headed by Paul-Émile Borduas, produced a surrealist manifesto called *Refus Global*, which seems to me a most important breakthrough in Canadian culture, not because of what it said, which was naive and confused enough, but because it was a sign that the old antithesis between a conscious mind and an unconscious nature was breaking down. For Borduas, the human mind contained an It as well as an I or ego, and this It was what he felt needed expression. In more recent painting, in the quasi-realism of Alex Colville and Christopher Pratt, in the ghostly figures of Jean-Paul Lemieux, there is often a feeling of loneliness and emptiness, as though the conscious mind were deliberately draining itself of its contents, and waiting for something else to move in. Meanwhile an interest in Indian and Eskimo art, with all their nature-spirits, has grown into a fascination, and many of our younger poets—Susan Musgrave, John Newlove, Gwendolyn MacEwen—write as though Indians and Eskimos were our direct cultural ancestors whose traditions continue in them and in us. In fiction, there are some curious stories, such as Margaret Atwood's *Surfacing* and Marian Engel's *Bear*, of heroines turning away from their civilized heritage toward an identity with nature. It seems clear that for Canadian culture the old imperialist phrase "going native" has come home to roost. We are no longer an army of occupation, and the natives are ourselves.

The first half of the twentieth century saw a bitter dispute between democratic and Marxist conceptions of the best way to minimize the exploitation of man by man. Nobody seemed to notice that both sides were exploiting nature with equal recklessness. It seems to me that the capitalist-socialist controversy is out of date, and that a détente with an outraged nature is what is important now. Canada is still a place of considerable natural resources, but it is no longer simply a place to be looted, either by Canadians or by non-Canadians. It is of immense importance to the United States itself that there should be other views of the human occupation of this continent, rooted in different ideologies and different historical traditions. And it is of immense importance to the world that a country which used to be at the edge of the earth and is now a kind of global Switzerland, surrounded by all the world's great powers, should have achieved the repatriating of its culture. For this is essentially what has happened in the last twenty years, in all parts of Canada; and what was an inarticulate space on a map is now responding to the world with the tongues and eyes of a matured and disciplined imagination.

73

Culture as Interpenetration

16 September 1977

An address to the UNESCO International Council of Philosophy and Humanistic Studies, Montreal. From DG, 15–25. Reprinted in RCLI, 139–51, and in ECLI, 137–46. Typescript is in NFF, 1988, box 6, file f.

As long as I have been a literary critic, I have been interested in the relations between a culture and the social conditions under which it is produced. It has always puzzled me why so little seems to be known about this, when so much work, even so much first-rate work, has been done in what seem to be all the relevant areas. I have also been watching the Canadian cultural scene for about forty years, and I feel that Canada is perhaps as interesting and valuable a place as any to study such a question. What follows is a series of observations that might conceivably lead to some more general principles on the subject. I am confining the term culture, because of limited space, to the creative arts, and to painting and literature within those arts.

There is an aged and now somewhat infirm joke to the effect that the United States has passed from barbarism to decadence without an intervening period of civilization. A parallel and possibly more accurate statement might be made of Canada: that it has passed from a prenational to a postnational phase without ever having become a nation. It very nearly became one in the two decades following the Second World War, when it took an active part in international politics, acquired a national flag, and was for a time a perceptible military and naval power. But it never shook off its role as an American satellite sufficiently to be taken very seriously as a distinctive political presence even then. As third-world nations began to emerge in Africa and Asia, Canada's much more low-keyed nationalism became increasingly inaudible, like a lute in a brass band. Two books with highly significant titles appeared at the beginning and end respectively of this period: A.R.M. Lower's *Colony to Nation* in 1946 and George Grant's *Lament for a Nation* in 1965. When Trudeau became prime minister and adopted Marshall McLuhan as one of his advisors, Canada reverted to tribalism.

The settlement of America was a centrifugal movement out from Britain and France, and to centralize is to create a hierarchy. The top of the hierarchy is the central city, London or Paris, which is where all the cultural action is. In Elizabethan England, for example, literary culture was a London culture. If a writer were upper class, he would write Petrarchan love lyrics and send them around to his friends in manuscript, prior to arranging for a publisher to steal them. If he were middle class, he would turn to the theatre or to pamphleteering. But qua writer he could hardly live or work for long outside London: one thinks of Herrick, for instance, a parson stuck in Devonshire, writing nostalgically of jewellery, perfume, women's clothes, and his happy times with the "tribe of Ben." This situation lasted until late in the eighteenth century. Wordsworth was the first major English writer to set up his headquarters outside London, and of course by Victorian times, with the rise of the great Midland cities, the cultural picture was quite different. In France, with its more limited industrial development, culture remained fixated on Paris for a much longer time. As late as my own student days, I remember seeing in Paris an exhibition of a sculptor who lived in (I think) Dijon, advertised under the slogan "France is not Paris."

Discussions about Canadian literature began, in English Canada, about a hundred years ago, when it was still uncertain whether the condition was one of genuine pregnancy or merely wind. At that time the commonest argument advanced was that in a young and newly settled country the priorities were material ones, and that literature and the other arts would come along when economic conditions were more advanced. This argument makes very little sense: in a genuinely primitive community, like that of the Eskimos, where food and shelter are requirements that have constantly to be met, poetry (and other arts, such as carving) leaps into the foreground as one of the really essential elements of life. Something similar may be true of new societies that are not primitive: seventeenth-century Puritans in Massachusetts wrote poetry and carried on with their pamphlet war against the Anglican establishment. It is also possible, in modern times, for the centrifugal movement

Culture as Interpenetration

from the main centres to reverse itself, for works of culture to be export goods coming out of a small community. One thinks of the amount of Anglo-Irish literature produced in the last century, which was certainly never intended for the Dublin market.

No: Canadian assumptions about the low and late priority of creative activity were mercantilist assumptions, and signified the acquiescence by Canadians in their role as producers of raw materials for manufacturing centres outside Canada. What got the priority were the engineering modes of communication, the fantastically long and expensive railways, bridges, and canals that sprouted out of the nineteenth-century Canadian landscape. It was no more natural for Canada to produce such things than to produce major developments in literature or painting, but they were produced because they fitted the premises of Canadian mythology at that time. But while the prevailing mood was one of expansion into a bountiful future, other directions were indicated by the turn of the century, when the Boer War was fought. In the First World War there was a patriotic picture called *Canada's Answer*, depicting battleships on the ocean. The point of the picture was, of course, Canada's willingness to defend the mother country by sending soldiers over the sea. But the subject of the picture was again an engineering mode of communication, except that this time it was associated with a feeling that the noblest destiny for a human Canadian life was to become a sacrificial object in a European war. The assumptions here are getting a little more sinister than the purely mercantilist ones, and need more looking into.

One of the most remarkable works of fiction in our time, Thomas Pynchon's *Gravity's Rainbow*, suggests that the human instinct to see humanly intelligible pattern and design in nature is a form of paranoia. That is, man cannot endure the thought of an environment that was not made primarily for his benefit, or, at any rate, made without reference to his own need to see order in it. Man describes his total environment as a "universe," something that all turns around one centre, though often mentally suppressing the fact that that centre is himself. He clings to the argument of design as long as he can, projecting the notion of a man-related universe on God: when he is forced to give that up, he plunges into a mathematical order, the animated algebra of technology. As he goes on, it becomes increasingly clear that his "rage for order," in Stevens's phrase,[1] is linked to a death-wish—Pynchon's symbol for it is the V-2 rocket bomb of the Second World War.

However, to live without the sense of a need for order, Pynchon suggests, requires an inhuman detachment that is not possible nor perhaps desirable. What fights effectively against the destructive impulse can only be a "counter-force" or creative paranoia, a unifying power that works towards life and the fulfilment of desire instead of towards death. Such a creative force would naturally be closely allied to the work of the dream. Freud, in the *Traumdeutung*, remarks more than once on the curious compulsion in the dream work to unify a great variety of disparate experiences and themes. For Pynchon the opposite of this creative drama, the anti-dream, so to speak, is Kekulé's famous dream of the ouroboros that turned into the benzene ring,[2] and thereby inaugurated a new and deadly era of technology. There are other vivid episodes in the book making the same point. We are told of a madman who exterminated the dodoes in Mauritius because, being awkward and unadaptable, they seemed to him an offence against the argument for design. This modulates to a hideous picture of the formerly German colony of Southwest Africa, where the native population was slaughtered to the verge of extinction out of the bloodthirsty superstition known as social Darwinism, the belief that some people are better fitted to survive than others because they possess greater powers of destruction. It seems to me that this argument in *Gravity's Rainbow* affords an instructive parallel to some of the social conditions underlying Canadian literature.

New France and New England were colonized in the Baroque phase of European development. Certain religious and philosophical assumptions that they brought with them explain a good many features of that colonization. Let us take the religious ones first. Christianity is a revolutionary and urban religion, and, like Marxism in our day, it started with all the revolutionary characteristics: the belief in a specific historical revelation, a canon of sacred texts, an obsession with the dangers of heresy, and, above all, a dialectical habit of mind, a tendency to polarize everything into the for and the against. Such an attitude is by no means essential to a religion. When Buddhism came to Japan it collided with the indigenous Shinto cult, and after a good deal of tension, a Buddhist theologian suggested that the *kami*, the gods and nature-spirits of Shinto, could be thought of as emanations of the Buddha: in short, that Shintoism could be regarded as a positive analogy of Buddhism. As a result the two religions have coexisted in Japan ever since. But for Christianity, as for Islam and Marxism later, nothing will go right until the entire world is united in the right creed, and whatever place there may be in Christian thought for natural religion, no non-Christian faith can ever be anything but a negative analogy, a demonic parody, of Christianity. And when even saints and martyrs firmly believe that the only good heathenism is a dead heathenism, it becomes very easy for others to infer that the only good heathen is a dead heathen. What is particularly horrifying about the extinction of, say, the Beothuks in Newfoundland is the casualness with which it was done, the ability to murder people of a different ethnical group without losing five minutes' sleep over it. It is rather curious that the Eichmann trial of a few years ago should have come to so many people as a shocking discovery.

The differences between the Puritan Protestantism of New England and the Jansenist Catholicism of New France are of very little importance here. Both felt equally that there could be no truck with any nature-spirits or with any sense of identity between human and animal life, such as we have in some aspects of totemism. The horror of idolatry, the feeling that there could be nothing numinous in nature and that all the spiritual beings man had discovered in nature were really devils, was deeply rooted in Christianity, as was the feeling that man had to depend solely on human and social institutions for any improvement in his status. Nature became therefore an unrestricted area for human exploitation. God had said to Noah after the flood, at the very beginning of history: "The fear of you and the dread of you shall be upon every beast of the earth . . . into your hand are they delivered" [Genesis 9:2]. Hence the savage and superstitious custom of apologizing to the spirits of the fish or the deer and explaining that their human hunters were taking only enough for their own food was replaced by the enlightened and civilized custom of slaughtering everything in sight until one species after another disappeared from the earth forever.

Such traditional tendencies had been increased by the Baroque sense, most articulate in Descartes, that the consciousness of man created an immense gap between him and all other living creatures, who belonged primarily in a world of mechanism. The newly discovered power of mathematics, too, was at its clearest at the exploring and pioneering periphery of Baroque culture, in the astrolabes and compasses that guided the explorer, in the grid-patterns that eventually were imposed on city and country alike. Every "improvement" in communication since then, in railway, highway, or airway, has meant a shorter and straighter path through nature until, with the plane, the sense of moving through nature practically disappears. What does not disappear is the attitude of arrogant ascendancy over nature. For the white conquerors of this continent, creation does not begin with an earth-mother who is the womb and tomb of all created things, but with a sky-father who planned and ordered and made the world, in a tour de force of technology. The despoiling of nature has now reached the point at which the white settlement of America begins to look like a very clear example of what Pynchon means by his death-wish paranoia, a destructiveness increasing in efficiency and ferocity until it finally began to turn on itself.

Baroque Christianity still maintained the rigidly authoritarian world-picture inherited from medieval times, in which there is a downward movement from God to man and an upward movement from man towards God. For a natural religion like that of most of the native peoples, evil, suffering, and above all death do not cause a problem: death belongs in the cycle of nature from the beginning. But for a religion thinking in terms of an omniscient God planning and making the world, the world as originally made could not have had any evil or death in it, and hence a myth of fall was necessary to account for the contrast between the model world that God must have made and the actual world that surrounds us. The gap caused by the fall was closed by the Incarnation, when a principle of authority descended from the divine world to the human one. This principle of authority continues in the secular power focused in the monarchy. Man's response to divine authority is to raise his status from the lower nature into which he fell to the higher nature symbolized by the garden of Eden. But he can do this only through unswerving obedience to the sacraments of the church, the principles of morality, and the canons of secular law. Once again, there is no significant difference on this point between the Quebec Catholic and the Massachusetts Puritan. The Puritans were revolutionaries, but not for liberal or democratic reasons: they looked forward to a rule of the elect in which, to paraphrase Paul, the powers that be would not be ordained of God for man's sins, but ordained *by* God for his redemption.[3]

The first white man to write poetry in what is now Canada, Marc Lescarbot, wrote a poem in 1606 addressed to some Frenchmen returning to France from Port Royal. He says (in F.R. Scott's translation):

> 'Tis you who go to see congenial friends
> In language, habits, customs and religion
> And all the lovely scenes of your own nation,
> While we among the savages are lost
> And dwell bewildered on this clammy coast.[4]

Then he pulls himself together and speaks of what may yet be made of the country, after, perhaps, missionaries will have come

> And bring conversion to this savage nation
> That has no God, no laws and no religion.

Lescarbot thus defines a kind of cultural primal scene for Canada. In front of him, as he gazes wistfully at it, is the ship going back to rejoin the centre of culture and good life in France. Behind him is the great gap in existence, like one of the black holes of modern astronomy, created by the indigenous people—that is, of course, created by his view of them. We notice how the cultural situation exactly fits the religious and political one. In culture, as in religion and politics, the homeland is the source of authority, and the first duty of a colonial culture is to respond to it.

Lescarbot's verses inaugurate the first period of Canadian culture, the uncomplicated provincial or colonial period. One may distinguish three main phases in its development. In the first phase the provincial culture tends to imitate externally rather than by absorption, accepting certain standards and trying to meet them. It confines its attention to what is established in the homeland and has become a principle of cultural authority there. It is obvious that cultural lag is built in to such a process. In poetry of the Confederation period and earlier, while the ostensible echoes may be from Tennyson or Victor Hugo, the actual texture of the verse is usually closer to James Thomson or Béranger. Such external imitation is a self-defeating enterprise because a writer cannot meet external standards, but can only establish his own. Gradually, however, the first phase evolves into the second phase. The more mature colonial writing gets, the more contemporary the influences become: the writer has got out of the schoolroom and has joined a community. It is still a mercantilist situation, but some initiative has gone into the provincial manufactures.

These two phases represent different and contrasting ways of dealing with a sense of urgency connected with content, with a need to grapple directly with the new stimuli and situations encountered in a new land. Content is often regarded, even by artists themselves, as dictating its own forms, but this is an elementary fallacy: the forms of every art are generated from within the art. In the first phase it is obscurely felt that the more traditional the form, the better adapted it is to containing the new experience. The second phase swings to the opposite extreme and assumes that only the latest models are equipped to do the same job.

Poetry in Canada did not fare very well under these imitative phases, although naturally we can see a steady maturing process going on as, in English, pre-Raphaelite formulas are replaced by the influence of Eliot and the later Yeats, and, in French, a good deal of yawny verse about the *terroir* gives way to livelier echoes of Paul Fort and Claudel. Fiction was even more retarded. Painting is by far the most interesting art in Canada up to about 1960. Here the urgency of new content could find its place in a remarkable documentary development, which begins with the military and exploring painting of the age of Paul Kane and Thomas Davies, and continues through Thomson and the Group of Seven in Ontario, along with Emily Carr in British Columbia and a number of painters in Quebec. It is often said that these later groups broke with stale pictorial conventions and began to look directly at the country in front of them. There clearly must be some truth in this, as I have said it myself: however, the fallacy of content shaping form lurks within it. The lapse of time brings with it a decreasing attention to subject matter and an increasing awareness of convention. It is this lapse of time that makes us more conscious of the Barbizon and Dutch pastoral influences on the older landscape painters, and the continuing of the lapse that turns our interest from the "solemn land" of northern Ontario as painted by Thomson and MacDonald towards the fauve and art nouveau conventions that controlled their vision of it.

The final phase, in which provincial culture becomes fully mature, occurs when the artist enters into the cultural heritage that his predecessors have drawn from, and paints or writes without any sense of a criterion external to himself and his public. Here the anxieties about meeting proper standards or being up to date or expressing a distinctive subject matter with enough emphasis (or what was once called, in connection with Hemingway, false hair on the chest) have all disappeared. While I was reviewing English Canadian poetry during the fifties, I noticed how many of the best people were turning erudite, allusive, even academic. I felt that this indicated the growth of an unforced and relaxed sense of a cultural tradition, one which could now be absorbed instead of merely imitated or echoed. Of course all the anxieties listed above were still in the air, and I was widely regarded as encouraging a new form of inhibited provincialism. But what I saw in, for example, Leonard Cohen's *Let Us Compare Mythologies*, Jay Macpherson's *The Boatman*, Margaret Avison's *Winter Sun*,[5] James Reaney's *Suit of Nettles* seemed to me an attitude to cultural tradition that looked forward rather than back.

In 1952 some people in a small town in Ontario, simply because it was called Stratford, decided to put on some Shakespeare, and a Shakespeare festival began there the next year. The director was Tyrone Guthrie and the leading actors were Alec Guinness and Irene Worth—not precisely what the CRTC would call Canadian content. Those who think in pigeonholes could hardly point to anything more obviously parochial and colonial. Yet there are three factors to be considered. First, the beginning of the Shakespeare festival at Stratford turned out to be a very important event in the history of *Canadian* drama: it helped to foster a school of Canadian actors, and the lift in morale it represented fostered Canadian play-writing as well. Second, it represented an extraordinary recreation of the power and freshness of Shakespeare himself: one almost felt sorry for the British, who, having no Stratford except the one that had actually produced Shakespeare, would find it harder to make this kind of rediscovery of him. And third, Shakespeare at Stratford does not stand alone, because Molière played a very similar role in the development of French Canadian drama, at roughly the same time.

In proportion as Canada shook off its external and subordinating assumptions about its English and French cultural heritages, the genuine form of cultural development became more obvious. This genuine form is what I mean by interpenetration. As Shelley demonstrated in his *Defence of Poetry*, the language of the creative imagination is a language that cannot argue: it is not based on propositions that do battle with their implied opposites. What it does is to create a vision that becomes a focus for a community. This means that it has, at least at the beginning, a limited range. Shelley himself, writing in a culture that had been London-dominated for a thousand years,[6] suggests (in his preface to *Prometheus Unbound*) that for the best future developments in culture England should break down into about forty republics, each with a central city about the size of Periclean Athens or Medicean Florence.

Shelley was writing at a time when there was a strong liberal sympathy with self-determinism of nations as opposed to empires, with Italy against the Austrian empire, with Greece against the Turkish one. Since then it has become increasingly obvious that political and economic organization tends to centralize and unify. But Shelley seems to be right about cultural matters. Literature and painting do appear to depend on decentralization in a very subtle way. The artist seems to draw strength from a very limited community: American writers, for instance, generally turn out, under closer analysis, to be southern writers, New England writers, expatriate writers, New York writers, and so on. They need a certain cultural coherence within their community, but the community itself is not their market. This is where the principle of interpenetration operates: the more intensely Faulkner concentrates on his unpronounceable county in Mississippi, the more intelligible he becomes to readers all over the world.

We are back to the question of the challenge of content. Contemporary painting and writing, whatever the language, speak an international idiom, and the capitals where that idiom is established are still, as they have always been, the big centres, London, Paris, New York. Trying to ignore this international idiom is, experience suggests, futile, and leads only to a kind of archaism. The general principle appears to be that a painter or writer who is self-conscious about his immediate context will be likely to sound provincial, whereas a painter or writer who accepts a provincial milieu, in, say, Newfoundland or southern British Columbia, will be much less likely to do so. A Canadian artist may leave Canada to live and work in one of the big centres, like the painter Riopelle, but this does not affect the matter. Within the last twenty years we have been seeing more and more areas of this huge and sparsely settled country become culturally visible through painters and writers who belong, as creative people, less to Canada than to the prairies, the Pacific coast, the Atlantic coast, southern Ontario or Quebec. The process has been aided by Canada's more relaxed attitude to ethnical groups: there is no such thing as a hundred per cent Canadian, and the homogenizing of immigrants has been less intense than in the United States. But if we look at the pictures of Kurelek on the prairies or Jack Chambers in Ontario, or read Buckler on the Maritimes or Rudy Wiebe on Alberta Mennonites, we can see the "provincial" aspect of Canadian culture going into reverse, from inarticulate form to articulate content.

74

A Summary of the "Options" Conference

15 October 1977

From University of Toronto Bulletin, *31, no. 8 (24 October 1977): 6–7. Reprinted in* Options: Proceedings of the Conference on the Future of the Canadian Federation *(University of Toronto, 1977), 436–48, and in the French version of the same, 401–9. Partially reprinted as "Lively Culture the Answer to Canadian Unity?"* Globe and Mail, *18 October 1977, 7. Also recorded on videocassette as* Options *(Media Centre, University of Toronto, 1977). Typescripts are in NFF, box 6, files h–i.*

Frye's remarks were given as an overview at the Conference on the Future of Canadian Confederation—a conference at the University of Toronto born of a sense of crisis in Confederation, especially after the triumph of the separatist Parti Québécois (PQ), under René Lévesque, in the Quebec election of November 1976. The scholars referred to by Frye, with their essays, are as follows: Marcel Rioux, University of Montreal, "Communities and Identities in Canada"; Claude Castonguay, Imperial Life Assurance Co., "Back to the Principles!" (the summary following Frye's); John Meisel, Queen's University, "Who Are We? Who Are They? Perceptions in English Canada"; Denis Stairs, Dalhousie University, "Devolution and Foreign Policy: Prospects and Possibilities"; Ramsay Cook, York University, "Nationalist Ideologies in Canada"; Anthony Scott, University of British Columbia, "An Economic Approach to the Federal Structure"; Manon Vennat, Business Linguistic Centre, "The Francization of the Private Sector in Quebec"; Yves Martin, University of Sherbrooke, "Quebec Society and Political Power"; Richard Lipsey, Queen's University, "The Relation between Economic and Political Separatism: A Pessimistic View"; Peter Ernerk, Northwest Territories, "Native Political Participation"; Roma Dauphin, University of Sherbrooke, "The Economic Base for the Idea of Independence and Economic Association"; Robert Lacroix, University of Montreal, "The Regions and Unemployment: The Canadian Problem"; Michael Oliver, Carleton

University, "A New Regional Basis for Confederation"; Leslie Harris, Memorial University, "The Atlantic Region: An Expedient Fiction"; Harry Meredith, P.S. Ross and Partners, and Donald Fowke, Hickling-Johnston, "Delivering Public Services: Territorial Issues"; Thomas Courchene, University of Western Ontario, "The New Fiscal Arrangements and the Economics of Federalism"; Stanley Roberts, Canada West Foundation, "A Realistic Perspective of Canadian Confederation: A Revised Report"; Gilles Paquet, Carleton University, "Federalism as Social Technology"; Clarence Barber, University of Manitoba, "The Customs Union Issue"; and provincial perspectives on Canadian federation from politicians Alexander Campbell of Prince Edward Island, Darcy McKeough of Ontario, and Rafe Mair of British Columbia.

I could hardly have realized, when I accepted this assignment, how far outside the area of my scholarly competence many of the papers at this conference are. I am not even cheered by Marcel Rioux's remark that in a social crisis academics serve as the translators of esoteric texts. However, a certain impartiality in quoting other people's opinions may be one possible virtue of ignorance, and in any case the buck now stops with M. Castonguay and not with me.

The foreground of our discussion has been what may be called an exercise in hypothetical futurology, speculations beginning with the question, what would happen if? The science fiction writer John Wyndham said that that question was where all his writing began,[1] and this conference has a certain affinity with science fiction. But in the background is a much wider and more suggestive question, connected with the fact that Canada seems to have moved from a prenational to a postnational phase of existence without ever having been a nation. It almost became one in the two decades following the Second World War, when it acquired a national flag and was even briefly a perceptible military power. But it never shook off its role as an American satellite sufficiently to be taken very seriously by the rest of the world as a distinctive political presence. Arthur Lower's book, *Colony to Nation*, marks the optimistic beginning of this period; George Grant's *Lament for a Nation* the pessimistic end of it. What this conference of "options" is primarily about, I think, is the different ways there are of conceiving a postnational way of living.

For, of course, this postnational trend is a worldwide one, and if Canada works out its present crisis successfully it could serve as a pilot project for an emerging new mode of human life. In the United Kingdom

Irish separatism has been followed by Scottish and Welsh separatist movements; Quebec separatism is endorsed by French politicians who regard similar movements in Brittany or Corsica as an unmitigated nuisance; we read of planes being highjacked by people who wish to demonstrate the intensity of their desire to separate somewhere from somewhere else. And, of course, every part of Canada has strong separatist feelings. The tendency seems politically to be closest to a kind of anarchism, with all the ambivalence between violent and peaceful tendencies that anarchism has always shown. Even the United States, now one of the world's relatively few viable national federations, is likely to face similar developments as it decentralizes from its unmanageably violent cities, and the unrest of the late sixties was probably a portent of them.

My own feeling, summarized by John Meisel, is that in our world political and economic developments tend to centralize, whereas cultural movements tend to decentralize. To attach a cultural development to political or economic expansion produces an empty and pompous imperialistic culture; to attach political or economic revolution to a cultural revolution becomes, in such a context as Canada, a form of what Denis Stairs calls symbolic politics. I mention my own view, partly so that you can be aware of it and allow for it, and partly because it seems to have a large support from speakers at this conference. Marcel Rioux reminds us of a traditional distinction between a *Gemeinschaft* and a *Gesellschaft*, a community and a political federation; Ramsay Cook adds a European distinction between aggregate nations and nations that have tried to think of themselves as culturally or even racially uniform. Anthony Scott speaks of people who value their historic struggles for freedom more than they value the benefits obtained from them, and Denis Stairs says, "The independence movement is above all an ethnic and cultural revolt, in which the stakes have much more to do with psychic rewards than with economic organizational change." Manon Vennat and Marcel Rioux also agree that a cultural revolution is the dominant feature in contemporary Quebec. Even Yves Martin, though he says that the question is fundamentally one of power, and that the PQ wants a lot more of it, also says, in what may be, if I have understood it correctly, one of the most significant remarks made at this conference, that the November election was "the result of a collective quest for a new pattern of coherence within a collectivity which still admits its distinctiveness, but also now its pluralism."

I am aware that the separating of cultural issues from political and economic ones is, if one takes it no farther, facile and simplistic. And yet the political and economic adjustments that have to be made, even to provide for a cultural revolution, may often be separable, and are nearly always distinguishable, from the cultural issues themselves. And I do wish that there had been a section on the cultural situation at this conference, if only to emphasize the emotional contrast. The political, and still more the economic, picture is one of deep gloom, lightened by an occasional gleam of neurosis. Like the map of Canada that you have been contemplating in Convocation Hall, it is a recognizable but oversimplified picture of a country coming apart at the seams. It reminds me of a *New Yorker* cartoon of two explorers caught in quicksand, one, who is already up to his neck, saying to the other: "Say what you will, I've half a mind to struggle." The cultural situation, on the other hand, is a very exhilarating one. By a culture I mean the whole lifestyle of a people, starting with the language they speak, and not merely the creative arts. But the arts are the representative part of a culture and the best index of its quality. The growth of literature and painting, especially, in all parts and ethnic groups of Canada, particularly during the last two decades, indicates that the area we still call Canada is a very exciting place to live in.

I recently said this to an American audience in Washington, when introducing an exhibition of Canadian pictures.[2] The audience was puzzled, partly because the exhibition showed very little of the real vitality and variety of Canadian painting, and partly because the blue-ruin news stories they had read about Canada seemed to contradict my euphoria. I have long suspected, from my literary studies, that the social conditions underlying a culture are seldom good conditions. But they are usually lively conditions if the culture is lively, and Canada, for all the despair and apprehension and identity crises in the country, is no exception. Painters and writers are not acts of God: they come out of specific communities, and are the individual points where those communities have become articulate. Richard Lipsey said, in his personal statement this morning, that Canadian identity is an obsolete problem, being already here. The reason why it is still so much discussed, I think, is that it is being confused with another identity crisis, one which relates to regions emerging into articulate lifestyles. There is something vegetable about a culture: it needs roots and a limited environment. It needs a Newfoundland for a Christopher Pratt, Ukrainian prairie settlements for a Kurelek, a Cape Dorset for a Kenojouak. Everywhere I look in Canada, I get an impression of immense energies trying to find their proper regional outlets, continually thwarted by unreal political abstractions.

John Meisel says, "That a majority of citizens of any country feels that they have more in common with foreign nations than with their compatriots suggests that the strains on national unity are likely to go very deep." This is true, but such feelings of alienation may sometimes be the other side of a genuine creative vitality. Much is said about the alienation of French life in Quebec under English dominance, but Quebec's very impressive record in literature has a great deal to do with the fact that a writer who writes in a beleaguered and threatened language knows that he has an essential social function. Genuine culture is always and instinctively separatist: this fact affords a tentative answer to the question glanced at by Ramsay Cook, a question which also so bedevilled the Southern States in the American Civil War: where does a separatist movement stop separating? There is no limit as long as the separation is on a cultural basis, but of course a political sub-separation is a deadly threat to any separatism. We have been brought up to think of culture as a frill or nonessential, something to be added as a luxury after the essential things have been met, and this, I think, leaves us without the real clue to the present situation. For example, southern Ontario, formerly one of the most brutally inarticulate communities in human history, now finds itself in possession of James Reaney, Alice Munro, Robertson Davies, Margaret Laurence, Margaret Atwood, Al Purdy, and a dozen other people. The community as a whole has not grasped the importance of this fact, and no wonder; but scholars ought to have more insight.

A culture which is the expression of a specific community is in contrast to a mass culture, which tends towards uniformity rather than unity, and towards the obliterating of the specific and distinctive. A mass culture, so regarded, is an alienating culture, and when we think of mass culture we usually think of it as coming from or belonging to somewhere else. In Canada we speak of it as Americanization, although its effect on genuine American culture is quite as lethal as it is here; an English Canadian culture imposed on French Canada would be thought of there as mass culture. When Peter Erneck was speaking yesterday my mind went back to a CRTC hearing on the CBC renewal of licences, when spokesmen of Inuit and Cree groups asked us if we in the South realized that what we thought of as Canadian content was to them the invading of their culture by something not only alien to it but unconsciously bent on destroying it.

In the present debate the PQ's political aims assume what may be a disproportionate emphasis, partly because of certain tactical advantages of the moment. The PQ is still, for all practical purposes, an opposition party, not yet charged with the full responsibilities that bring so much obloquy with them. It can exert immense ideological pressure through the rhetorical device of identifying separatism with freedom and confederation with a subordinate status: as Marcel Rioux says, "Quebec cannot be culturally sovereign as long as it is dominated politically by Canada." Hence many of its most able political opponents within Quebec are still demoralized, as though advocating national unity had suddenly become disloyal within Quebec. And the PQ cause is greatly helped by the built-in flunkeyism of the news media, which, whatever their point of view, are forced by their own rigid conventions to build up a picture of René Lévesque as the only Canadian leader with genuine vision.

What is really at issue here, I think, is the fact that cultural identity results from an act of social will, whereas economic conditions are much less affected by will, at least in Canada. Political conditions come somewhere in between. Whatever political or economic deals could conceivably be arranged between Canada and Quebec, the overriding economic conditions are those of an American-dominated continent, and there is no greater will to resist this domination in French than in English Canada. Roma Dauphin and Robert Lacroix speak of the lower average income in Quebec as compared with Ontario, and the former adds that the Québécois, being normal human beings, want the same standard of living for themselves that other people have, and will not follow any leadership that deviates from this wish. There is a strong feeling among many speakers here, expressed with great sincerity by Alexander Campbell, that the Confederation of Canada not only can provide a viable political context for French culture in Quebec, but is in fact the only possible context for it. Deprived of this context, it is felt, Quebec will be exposed to the full force of American economic penetration, and without any ill will on the part of the United States, the first casualty of separation would be the integrity of French culture in Quebec itself.

It is remarkable, and a touching tribute to the Canadian temperament, that the PQ proposals of customs unions and economic association with the rest of Canada, even in the event of separation, seem to assume so much good will, even good humour, on the part of Canada. Of course, as in any other divorce, it is easiest for those who are getting what they want to behave like rational beings. But it is also true, to paraphrase Denis Stairs, that, while the threat to secede is undeniably a trump card, it will take only one trick in a highly vulnerable grand-slam bid. At the same time, to centralize is to create a hierarchy, and we have clearly reached the phase of democracy where the balance of federal and provincial interests has got badly dislocated. Many, if not most, of our contributors speak of certain positive aspects of decentralization, and regard it as a tendency that goes far beyond Quebec.

Michael Oliver remarks that while in the early sixties a deal might have been made with Quebec alone, the only option now open to us is devolution towards all the provinces. Leslie Harris reminds us that there is no monolithic English Canada, though there may have been a monolithic English Ontario a century ago. This point was well emphasized last night by the two Western speakers. John Meisel notes that anglophone Canadians think of their country as multicultural, and certainly a resident of Montreal, Toronto, Winnipeg, or Vancouver would have to be remarkably introverted to be unaware of the multicultural character of those cities. It is also Leslie Harris who speaks of the way in which Quebec has gained control of resources that belong to Newfoundland, which raises an important issue: concessions to a separating Quebec may involve selling out the interests of other provinces that are staying with Confederation. The implication is that, however the Quebec situation is resolved, we have to think in terms of applying all the PQ slogans of legitimate aspirations, self-fulfilment, mastery in one's own house, and the like, with equal seriousness to the rest of Canada.

John Meisel quotes Herschel Hardin as saying that Canadians differ from Americans in that the United States is a private enterprise country and Canada is a public enterprise one. Certainly Canadians have always shown an unusual aptitude for deficit financing. Canada has always been preoccupied with communication, because of its almost unique difficulties with it, and the most remarkable Canadian achievements, in the previous century, were with its inarticulate forms: the vast railways, bridges, and canals that sprouted out of the Canadian landscape on all sides. It was no more natural for Canada to produce such things than to produce major literature or painting, but they were produced because they fitted the mercantile mythology which Canada then accepted: the belief that its primary role was to get its natural resources moved to other centres. Confederation itself, on its economic side, was still within the mercantilist orbit. This phase was followed, in our century, by a nationally subsidized airline and the CBC. The result has been to leave us with a kind of communications overkill, so to speak, leading to a highly centralized machinery of government which in many areas is now cumbersome and inefficient.

Darcy McKeough, speaking as a minister, says: "Don't tell us how to do things. We're experts at that. Tell us what to do." The "what" of this conference seemed to centre on the question of the roles that should be assigned to federal and provincial authority. Ramsay Cook remarks that "our liberal heritage assures us that national self-government is preferable even to good government," but obviously many Canadians are prepared to re-examine that axiom. Meredith and Fowke speak of Ottawa as a company town removed from the mainstream of Canadian life, and Anthony Scott, referring to the Holy Roman Empire, says that centralized authority can sometimes become so unwieldy as to lose all real power. Voltaire said that the Holy Roman Empire was not holy, not Roman, and not an empire;[3] and some of our speakers seem to think that the time is fast approaching when the federal government at Ottawa will not be federal, not a government, and, considering the number of departments being exiled to Hull, not in Ottawa. There are many other suggestions about the greater efficiency of provincial autonomy in some areas. Thomas Courchene gives a list of them, emphasizing health care; Meredith and Fowke insist on the dangers of habit-thinking, of assuming that we *must* have a federal broadcasting system and federal control of that elephants' graveyard the post office. Anthony Scott also comments on the fact that citizens make more reasonable demands on local governments because they can see who pays for them, "whereas their demands on central governments are more irresponsible and carefree."

Even the federal Parliament, technically the supreme ruler of Canada, comes under the critique of overcentralizing, and there are suggestions for bypassing it to some degree. Stanley Roberts suggests a senior legislative body with relatively short-term appointments; Anthony Scott recommends an *ad hoc* assembly, and Thomas Courchene, referring to David Smiley, speaks of an "executive federalism," "the cornerstone of which is the federal-provincial conference." Gilles Paquet is cooler about these devices, but equally emphatic about the need to fight against what Darcy McKeough calls "mindless centralism."

It seems clear, then, that a considerable degree of political change is possible, and our speakers tell us that the Constitution is not an obstacle.

Meredith and Fowke speak of the Constitution as a non-issue in this respect, and of course economists tend to be tax-determinists. Authority lies where the taxes are paid, and Thomas Courchene says, "A major change in the funding arrangements is tantamount to a change in the constitution itself." If I am right, however (and here I am not speaking specifically of this conference), the principle on which political regionalism has to proceed is that it should conform to the underlying cultural realities of Canadian regionalism, and nobody seems to know what those cultural realities are. The only one even frequently alluded to is the language issue in Quebec, and that has in my view been treated so simplistically as to throw everything else out of proportion.

In any case political regionalism is bound to include a good deal of economic change as well. But, while I am not competent to follow their analyses in detail, it seems clear that most of the economists take a dim view of economic regionalism as such. It appears, from their accounts, to be like one of those rivers in Central Asia that can't find the sea, and have to dissipate in desert sands. Clarence Barber says that Quebec's interest in economic association with Canada would be much stronger than Canada's; that the centres of American manufacturing are moving away from the Canadian border towards the south and west, and that, as Canadians cannot compete with low-labour-cost countries like South Korea, they will have to shift over to skill-intensive goods requiring a highly trained labour force. He concludes that separation is economically a retrograde step. Robert Lacroix and Richard Lipsey are both highly sceptical about the possibility of combining economic co-operation with political separation. The view from outside Canada is still more negative. If even a united Canada failed to become a distinctive nation, a fragmented one would have about the rating of a banana republic, even if Canada's exports seem more basic than bananas. Denis Stairs, whose subject this is, mentions, among other things, the importance of the Great International Handicap, the feeling that it is parasitic not to impose a crushingly heavy defence budget even on nations too small to be effective in modern warfare.

I think the conference got rather stampeded in the direction of provincial rights, because clearly nobody believes that devolution towards the provinces is a panacea. The social elements that need strong federal control have to be studied with equal care, an obvious if seldom referred to example being ecology. I am not the only one who regrets the absence of a federal spokesman at the meeting last evening. Besides, various people, from Leslie Harris at one end of the country to Rafe Mair at the other, tell us that the provinces want a more equitable share in federal control even more than they want autonomy. This may well be true of the majority of Québécois also. One can understand the dream of young people in Quebec that Alexander Campbell speaks of, of taking part in the building of a new nation. But in a postnational world there are no new nations. All that is possible is what Ramsay Cook calls decolonization, or becoming a community in one's own right, no longer derivative of some other community. Without questioning that this is a worthy ambition, it makes sense only in cultural terms. Politically and economically, the general answer of the conference to Robert Bonner's question, "Is there regional life after national death?" is clearly no.

It would be easy to say that the conference was only a lot of talk, but, as Winston Churchill said, it is better to jaw than to war,[4] and more consistent with human dignity to exchange information than feed prejudice. The cultural life of Canada indicates that there is a buoyant and unquenchable vitality in the country, and a widespread tolerance for, or rather a delight in, ethnical variety. Culturally, there is no reason why Canada should not become a patchwork "geographical expression," like Germany or Italy before 1870. Vitality of this kind is not afraid of change. Gilles Paquet speaks of the need to adopt a functional rather than a structural approach to economic questions, and it is significant that this conference has revolved around the metaphor of destroying a structure. Much of that structure, it is also clear, should be, if not destroyed, at least redistributed and reassembled, if the real energies of Canada are to be set free.

It is, of course, possible that through bungling, rigid thinking, short-run expediency, and the like, Canada will re-enact the story of the tower of Babel, obliterating itself and its role in history because of a confusion of tongues. I think something rather more exciting than that is going on. I was once on a bus tour in Iceland, visiting the site of the national assembly that met there in the ninth century. If you care about democracy, the guide said, you will remember that you have seen the place where it all began. I think the next century may see a general slaughter of state leviathans, a breaking down of petrified bureaucracies, and the emergence of a more decentralized ideal of a full and creative human life. And perhaps our descendants, if they still care about history, may come back to the low-keyed and unflapped discussions like this one that are taking place all over Canada, and say, "Something started here."

75

Introduction to *Arthur Lismer*

1979?

From the clean typescript in NFF, 1988, box 47, file 1, marked 1979. The same file contains an earlier typescript with a few corrections marked April 23/49. Frye's piece was an introduction to Norah McCullough's Arthur Lismer: Watercolours, *but did not appear in the published work (Guelph, Ont.: Macdonald Stewart Art Centre, 1987). McCullough, an art teacher and associate of Lismer, helped establish art centres in South Africa.*

In my first term as an undergraduate in Victoria College in the fall of 1929, I took a course in English literature from John D. Robins. In those days any references to contemporary culture had to be bootlegged into lectures by digressions, and in one such digression Robins told us that there was an Art Gallery in Toronto, that a very lively movement in Canadian painting was being displayed there, and that it was an important part of our education, coming as most of us did from small towns outside Toronto, to get in touch with it. The response, as I recall, was very straggly, at least at first. True, the painters had names like Harris, Thomson, Jackson, and Macdonald—very reassuring names for timid and immature Wasps. But still they were "modern," and one never knew where that might lead.

Where it led me, in course of time, was to my first sight of an extraordinary man with long flying hair and loose limbs conveying a group of children across the gallery floors. Lismer was always a hit with children, mainly because he never thought of them as a separate human species, but talked to them in the same relaxed and simple way that he talked to adults. As I came to realize that Robins and Lismer were close friends, through their association with the Arts and Letters Club, and as, later, my wife became involved in the adult side of Lismer's program at the Art Gallery of Toronto (as it was then), I did a good deal of revolving in Lismer's orbit. I soon realized that he was not simply a very generous man and a selfless worker, but was one of those rare people who can persuade others to release whatever is creative within them—the quality that made Socrates call himself a midwife. This is a quality of the best kind of teacher, and Lismer was a very great teacher. But he had the same powers as a friend and a personal influence. An early article of mine on Tom Thomson took off directly from a lecture of Lismer's—it may not have been an important article in itself, but it was important to me to write it at that time.[1] Lismer's lecture has not to my knowledge been published, but I should be surprised if there were much verbal connection between it and my article. That was not the way Lismer influenced people.

When talking to students in the gallery about painting, he would keep drawing rapid sketches, for which he had an extraordinary facility, recalling some painters of an older generation—Charles W. Jeffreys, for example—who used to illustrate newspapers in the days when photography was still cumbersome. He was prodigal with such sketches, and would entertain parties with them: Robins had a large collection of drawings done at Arts and Letters Club luncheons, and I remember a brilliant caricature of A.Y. Jackson done with a diamond on a windowpane in Jackson's house in Manotick. He did not integrate this skill with his landscape painting, and doubtless the conventions of twentieth-century painting did not allow him to do so. But the remark often made about Group of Seven painters, that their sketches tend to be livelier than their finished paintings, was especially true of him. He was the opposite of monumental: he caught things in process and as it were in midair: things sprang into life wherever he was. He talked pictorially as well, though he was not a writer, and the verbal content of what he said was not always worth preserving. It was being under his personal spell that was the essential experience, and it was an unforgettable one. And because his talk was pictorial, as well as consistently dry and witty, there was nothing in it, or in his painting either, of the cosmic fuzziness that often sentimentalized Lawren Harris and Varley.

Group of Seven paintings command immense prices now, but even so I feel that Lismer's contribution to Canadian painting is still underestimated. In his later years such movements as abstract expressionism came into fashion, and he made no concessions to them: he was never a man to cover a large canvas with white paint and put a red spot in one corner. To bring my own prejudice into the open, abstract expressionism is a genre I have always distrusted, mainly because so much of it seems to me to express a violent reactionary anarchism, a repudiating not so much of the traditions as of the community of painting. Such pictures as those of Clyfford Still, for example, however magnificent in themselves, can hardly be hung in a gallery with any other pictures except his. But Canadian landscape of Lismer's generation readily combines with anything in the whole documentary tradition of Canadian painting from Paul Kane to Kurelek and Kenojuak. Many of Lismer's pictures are quite frankly cluttered, but they are cluttered for a good pictorial reason, which is the painter's enthusiasm for all objects with shape and colour. A study of boats in a dock will show ropes, anchors, and stanchions twisting in all directions like the ganglia of an elephant; a Vancouver Island landscape will have lichen climbing over rocks and ivy growing out of stumps with no regard for formal symmetry. Those who want decorative pictures conforming to preconceived patterns will have to leave Lismer alone. His pictures can be tangled or even incoherent, but when they are it is through excess of vitality and not through lack of it. In his painting, as in everything else, he was attentive and respectful to anything that had the spark of pictorial life in it. He disliked manipulating and arranging his subjects, and considered it facile to do so: he looked for the *objet trouvé*, the pictorial subject that said something just by being where and what it was.

Miss McCullough records his mixed feelings on seeing a retrospective show of his own work. He was the least retrospective of men, and threw all his energy into the present moment. But we need such shows, and we need Miss McCullough's book, to show us how solid and permanent an achievement he built up over the years. He was not a brilliant comet streaking across the Canadian sky, but, apart altogether from his achievement as a painter, a teacher who guided so many young hands and eyes into the pictorial world as to make a major and lasting impact on the growth of civilization in Canada.

76

Roy Daniells

24 May 1979

From English Studies in Canada, *5 (Winter 1979): vii–ix. Two typescripts are in NFF, 1988, box 47, file 1. Frye's remarks, read at the annual general meeting of the Association of Canadian University Teachers of English (ACUTE), are a tribute on the death of Daniells, a colleague who taught at Victoria University 1935–37 before becoming department head at the University of Manitoba and then at the University of British Columbia. The books by Daniells that Frye alludes to are* Alexander Mackenzie and the North West *(1969) and two books of poetry,* Deeper into the Forest *(1948) and* The Chequered Shade *(1963).*

I first met Roy when I was a graduate student and he, also a graduate student though a much more advanced one, sat at the circulating desk in the University of Toronto Library. We fell into conversation about Spengler, as I remember, and about theories of cultural history. In the university at that time, the words "medieval" and "Renaissance" were accepted, but using the words "Baroque" and "Rococo," to describe the next two centuries, was new and regarded with some suspicion as chi-chi, if not downright mystical. Roy's main interests in English literature revolved around Milton then, as they did all his life, and he was already interested in seeing Milton within a "Baroque" context. The Milton establishment in Toronto, presided over first by Malcolm Wallace and later by Woodhouse,[1] was committed to the history of ideas, to the historical and theological context of Milton, so Roy's choice of topic showed a good deal of independence in him and of tolerance in his supervisors.

This interest of Roy's puzzled me at first: it seemed a bit out of character for him, however legitimate in itself. I have since come to understand it better, I think. Milton is a poet of overwhelming power, and the power loses nothing even in a context of the crudest literalism. Roy's background had been a very intense and rather narrow evangelical one: this had given him a positive sense of the reality of what Milton was talking about, but he was anxious to break away from the narrowness, not merely in his own life but as a scholar, and so looked for a secular and more aesthetic context in which to place his formidable subject. As Milton himself worked with very different categories from the secular and aesthetic, to say nothing of the Baroque, Roy's approach to Milton brought out very unexpected aspects of his poet's design, colouring, sensitivity, and humour. The delightful essay on "A Happy Rural Seat," contributed to the *Paradise Lost* volume edited by Balachandra Rajan, illustrates this very well.[2]

While we were colleagues at Victoria, I felt very close to Roy, not merely because I loved and admired him, but because he seemed to me to dramatize, in his whole way of life, the attitude of a scholar dedicated to the humanities. A small point, but a significant one, was that he invariably spoke in elegantly formed prose sentences, something one does not often hear even among professors of literature. And whatever the subject he was speaking of, we were never far away from a pervasive but totally unmalicious humour. The word that comes closest to describing this side of him is, perhaps, the word urbanity. He was naturally in great demand as a master of ceremonies on both social and academic occasions, and could give a lightness and sense of exuberance to anything from a dinner in honour of a colleague to a meeting of Section 2 of the Royal Society. A hobby that he cultivated with great skill was the writing of occasional light verse for such occasions, and the word "light" conceals an unobtrusive craftsmanship that many heavy poets have failed to match.

His later scholarly interest in Canadian literature, recorded in his Mackenzie study and in four essays in the *Literary History of Canada*, defined him as a leading critical spokesman for his own country. To study Canadian literature one has to stand on its own level: to stand above it and sneer at it, or to stand below it and exaggerate it, are equally unscholarly procedures. Roy understood the limitations of the Canadian cultural scene, especially in the nineteenth century, and because he understood them he also understood the genuineness of the Canadian achievement. Two volumes of his own poetry belong to that literature, and their imagery revolves around the Canadian sense of creative isolation. In the earlier volume we begin with the figure of Anthony, plucking the golden bough that begins the initiate's journey, and move on to the locale of the title poem, *Deeper into the Forest*, clearly the typical place of his own imagination.

The depth of the forest is lonely and frightening, and those who have faced it, like Isabella Crawford, face also the disappearance of everything that gives their lives meaning, as a poem on Crawford in the second volume, *The Chequered Shade*, reminds us:

> Light once extinguished dies in deprived air,
> The past is self-effacing and soon gone.   [*Isabella Valancy Crawford*, ll. 11-2]

But it is also a place of discovery, when the sense of a lost cultural heritage is succeeded by the sense of a new world all around, as with Adam and Eve taking their "solitary way" into the forest of fallen nature, with a place of rest still to choose. It was the immediacy of this feeling in Duncan Campbell Scott that made Roy call him, in the *Literary History of Canada*, one of the "ancestral voices" of the Canadian imagination. The piercing accuracy of this phrase does not eliminate its humour: Scott lived so recently that many people still living knew him, but Canada needs a considerably speeded-up ancestry to get any sense of its cultural identity. Now Roy has become one of our ancestral voices himself. Once again, our first feeling is one of loss, loneliness, and regret. But, once again, this must give place to a grateful acceptance of what he has left us.

77

Across the River and out of the Trees

Fall 1980

From University of Toronto Quarterly, *50, no. 1 (Fall 1980): 1–14. Reprinted in* The Arts in Canada: The Last Fifty Years, *ed. W.J. Keith and B.Z. Shek (Toronto: University of Toronto Press, 1980), 1–14, in RCLI, 151–63, in ECLI, 161–74, and in part in DG, 26–40. Typescript is in NFF, 1988, box 47, file 4.*

I

The first issue of the *University of Toronto Quarterly* appeared in 1931. Its appearance was not exactly a breathtaking novelty: *Queen's Quarterly* and the *Dalhousie Review* were already in existence, and there had even been an earlier version of the *Quarterly* itself. But it was an important historical event none the less. The opening editorial statement attached the journal's traditions firmly to those of the "gentleman's magazine" of the eighteenth and nineteenth centuries. It was *not* to be a specialized learned journal: there were already enough of those, the editor implied, perhaps meaning that there were too many. Nor was it to be an outlet for creative talent in poetry or fiction: it published a poem or two at the beginning, but apologized editorially for the digression. It tried to cover a broad spectrum of academic interest for a while, but soon restricted itself in effect to the humanities, though it did not acknowledge this by calling itself "A Canadian Journal of the Humanities" until some years later. Within a very short time it had inaugurated "Letters in Canada" as an encyclopedic critique of everything published in Canada, so for all its exclusion of poetry and fiction it clearly had no intention of slighting the Canadian cultural scene, much less ignoring it.

There were some remarkable people first associated with the journal.

There was G.S. Brett, the first editor, a philosopher of vast erudition whose *History of Psychology* is still a standard work on the subject. There was E.K. Broadus, one of an extraordinary group of scholars in Alberta, and an early Canadian anthologist. There was Pelham Edgar, interested mainly in what was then contemporary fiction, author of a pioneering work on Henry James, and deeply concerned with Canadian writing as well. There was E.K. Brown, whose book on Canadian poetry was crucial in consolidating the sense of the context and tone of Canadian poetry up to that time. There was Watson Kirkconnell, whose prolific output and fantastic linguistic abilities enabled "Letters in Canada" to include a survey of Canadian writing in languages other than English and French, all of which he could read. A malicious but admiring legend said that when he became president of Acadia he took to shaking hands with his left hand so as not to interrupt his writing. An early issue contained an article by Kirkconnell on "Canada's Leading Poet," who according to Kirkconnell was Stephen Stephansson, a poet living in Manitoba and writing in Icelandic up to his death in 1927.[1]

I was preoccupied with getting through my sophomore year when the *Quarterly* first appeared, and I should perhaps not have been aware of its existence for some time if Brett and Edgar had not been teachers of mine. If I adopt a personal, even to some extent an autobiographical, tone in what follows, the reason is not simple egotism or garrulity: one needs a point of view for a survey, and a personal point of view is the obvious one for a surveyor who has lived entirely within the territory he surveys. In retrospect, the *Quarterly*'s early editorial policy decisions seem to me to have been prophetic of my own interests in criticism, and objectified much of what I have tried to do since. They also seem to me to mark a most significant cultural change, which was among other things a change in the university's relation to society, and which was already taking place, in Canada as elsewhere.

The learned journals the *Quarterly* was separating itself from belonged mainly to the philological tradition, with its headquarters in nineteenth-century Germany, that had dominated American scholarship for half a century. The scholars who wrote in them generally knew the standard Classical and modern languages, and for the most part did not include contemporary literature in their purview—at least not as scholars, whatever their general level of cultivation. Their scholarship thus gave the impression of being an activity independent of the creative life of their time. This was particularly true of Canadian scholars in 1930, many of whom had not only moved to Canada from elsewhere but had done much of their seminal work before they arrived. But the number of university people who gathered around the *Canadian Forum*, established in 1920, indicated that other things were happening.

My own college of Victoria had produced a monument of philological scholarship, Andrew Bell's *The Latin Dual and Poetic Diction* (1923), a work so obsessively specialized that the Classicists themselves hardly knew what to do with it. Yet the genial and urbane scholarship of Douglas Bush, another graduate of Victoria, who in his early years was a lively contributor to the *Canadian Forum*, grew directly out of this environment. Edgar's contemporary interests I have noted: he also influenced Brown's interest in twentieth-century American and Canadian writing, besides getting E.J. Pratt into his own English department at Victoria. Pratt was not a "writer in residence," but a full-time teacher until his retirement, and all the more influential as a link between creative and scholarly interests for both students and colleagues. He was a portent of the modern university's acceptance of some responsibility for encouraging writers and fostering a discriminating public for them.

In 1930 Canadian literature was still in a provincial state. Pratt and Morley Callaghan had established themselves as twentieth-century writers, and in 1936 a little anthology of six poets, including Pratt, called *New Provinces*, indicated that newer and more contemporary poetic idioms were taking shape. Morley Callaghan's books, I think I am right in saying, were sometimes banned by the public library in Toronto—I forget what the rationalization was, but the real reason could only have been that if a Canadian were to do anything so ethically dubious as write, he should at least write like a proper colonial and not like someone who had lived in the Paris of Joyce and Gertrude Stein. More recent scholarship has revealed that there was a good deal of remarkable, even astonishing, writing produced in Canada before 1930, but a mass of writing with good flashes in it is still not a literature. Articles proclaiming the imminent advent of literary greatness had been appearing for a long time, giving to Canadian literature, or its history, the quality that Milton Wilson has described, in a practically definitive phrase, as "one half-baked phoenix after another."[2] But the writing that got most direct public response tended to be subliterary rhetoric, like the Confederation poetry which was really inspired by a map and not by a country or a people, or the yawny French verse about the *terroir* which seemed to be written out of duty rather than discovery.

The excuse normally given for this state of affairs was that Canada was a "young" country, that its priorities had to be material ones, and that literature and the other arts would come along when economic conditions were more advanced. First the primary forms of communication—railways, bridges, canals—then the secondary ones. This argument makes very little sense: seventeenth-century Puritans in Massachusetts wrote poetry and carried on with their pamphlet war against the Anglican establishment. And in a genuinely primitive community, like those of the indigenous peoples, poetry leaps into the foreground as one of the really essential elements of life, along with food and shelter. It was no more "natural," and no more in accord with the historical process, for Canada to build the Victoria Bridge or the Welland Canal than to have produced major poets and novelists. But the argument was accepted because it was a mercantilist argument, and was part of Canada's acceptance of its role as a provider of raw materials for manufacture in larger centres. The reverse movement of imported goods brought the standards of culture set up in London and Paris back to the boondocks, and efforts were made there to imitate them. Trying to meet an externally imposed standard in the arts is a futile procedure in itself, and it is obvious that cultural lag is built into it. In nineteenth-century Canadian poetry, for instance, the ostensible echoes may be from Tennyson or Victor Hugo, but the texture of the verse is much closer to James Thomson or Béranger.

In 1930, again, the Depression settled into Canadian life, and the Depression was also a hampering and delaying influence on culture. There was not only the difficulty of getting books and pictures marketed (A.Y. Jackson remarked to me some time before his death that he still had guilt feelings when a picture of his sold for more than thirty-five dollars), but a theory of culture developed which was a modified form of mercantilism. According to it the creative person was to produce the raw material of his experience as part of an attempt to affect the ownership of production. There has always been a strong realistic and documentary slant to Canadian writing and painting, for obvious reasons, and this stereotype, after confusing a number of writers and spoiling one or two quite decent painters, hung around for several decades, though it shifted to a more psychological basis in the 1950s. Clearly this was still another way of reducing literature to rhetoric, and focusing attention on content, or what a writer thinks he is saying, rather than on what he constructs, or says in spite of himself.

When I was reviewing Canadian poetry in the fifties, I noted the emergence of a curiously interconsistent language of symbolism and imagery among the poets who most obviously knew what they were doing. The language had close affiliations with that of contemporary British and American poets, but was a quite distinctive language, a direct response, as I felt, to an environment that was taking on a new significance for them. I have spoken of what I call a garrison mentality and of the alternating moods of pastoral populism and imaginative terror (which has nothing to do with a poet's feeling terrified) in earlier Canadian writing. These were set up mainly as historical markers, like roadside plaques telling a motorist that something happened here two centuries ago, but they also attempted to define elements in a cultural tradition that was taking clearer shape as the contemporary writing matured. For those who felt that a poet ought primarily to express either sexual passion or social indignation, and was doing so if he said he was loudly enough, my comments on the emergence of a new variety of symbolic language sounded like a preference for poetry that was academic and inhibited. I myself felt that a quality was forming in Canadian poetry that I could only call professional. In an immature society culture is an import; for a mature one it is a native manufacture which eventually becomes an export. One thinks of the amount of major literature produced in the last century by Anglo-Irish writers who were certainly not writing for the Dublin or Belfast market. I finished my survey in 1960 convinced that Canadian literature was about to become a phoenix again, and a properly cooked one this time.

Well, I think I was right: Canadian literature since 1960 has become a real literature, and is recognized as one all over the world. We are told that there are Canadian authors who sell better in Holland or Germany than they do in their own country—and it has never been fair to say that the Canadian public has ignored its own literature, as far as buying and reading books goes. I doubt if there are any real causes for such a development, but there are some obvious conditioning factors. The Massey Report, published in 1951,[3] was a landmark in the history of Canadian culture, not merely because it recommended a Canada Council, but because it signified the end of cultural laissez-faire and assumed that the country itself had a responsibility for fostering its own culture. Back in 1930, Edgar was trying to organize voluntary societies for the relief of indigent authors, and there was an all too frequent assumption that society should concern itself with literature only when it felt like denouncing or censoring it. But the principle of social responsibility was established with the Massey Report, and without that principle Canadian literature would perhaps still be in its nonage. Federal support has been supplemented in the wealthier provinces, to the advantage of all concerned.

In his book *Odysseus Ever Returning* George Woodcock quotes a review by Oscar Wilde in which Wilde praises an American writer for being concerned with the literature he loves rather than the country in which he lives, adding "the Muses care so little for geography."[4] As usual, Wilde's critical instinct is sound: a writer cannot try to be anything except a writer, and a poet must adhere to literature, which is where his technical equipment comes from, not to the false rhetoric of the factitious and the *voulu*. But the last comment seems to me dead wrong. No Muse can function outside human space and time, that is, outside geography and history. Wilde himself owed his whole being as a writer to the tiny area of Anglo-Irish ascendancy which provided his own space and time. So while a Canadian writer may go anywhere and make any sort of statement about the place of Canada in his life, positive or negative, his formative environment and his ability as a writer will be interdependent, however different.

What affects the writer's imagination, however, is an environment rather than a nation, and an environment is limited in range. I have often noted the fact that regionalism and literary maturity seem to grow together. In the days of expanding nations and empires culture followed the centralizing movements of politics and economics, and to centralize is to create a hierarchy. In Elizabethan England, for example, literary culture was a London culture, and a writer qua writer found it hard to write long outside London. One thinks of Herrick, a parson stuck in Devonshire, writing nostalgically of jewellery, perfume, women's clothes, and his happy times with the "tribe of Ben." This situation lasted until late in the eighteenth century. Wordsworth was the first major English writer to set up his headquarters outside London, and of course by Victorian times, with the rise of the great Midland cities, the cultural picture was quite different. The twentieth century showed a Hardy largely confined to "Wessex," a Dylan Thomas to south Wales, a Hugh MacDiarmid to Scotland, and so on. Similarly with American literature, which has always been strongly regionalist.

Hence the increase in authority and precision in Canadian writing goes along with the sense of a clearly defined environment, in which one local area after another becomes culturally articulate through its authors. Just as we learn about American life inferentially, through what, say, Faulkner tells us about Mississippi or Frost about northern New England, so our knowledge of "Canada" is inferred from what, for example, Jack Hodgins tells us about Vancouver Island or Robertson Davies about southwestern Ontario or Roger Lemelin about the *pente douce* in Quebec City. A writer working outside Canada, like Mavis Gallant, is evidence that Canadian literature is diversified enough to have its expatriates as well, as American literature had its Eliot and Gertrude Stein.

So in a way it was an advantage for Canadian literature that Canada seems to have gone from a prenational into a postnational phase without ever having been a nation. It very nearly became one in the Pearson period, when it took an active part in international politics, acquired a national flag, and was for a time a perceptible military and naval power. But it never shook off its role as an American satellite sufficiently to be taken very seriously as a distinctive political presence even then. As third-world nations began to emerge in Africa and Asia, Canada's much more low-keyed nationalism became increasingly faint, like a lute in a brass band. Two books with highly significant titles appeared at the beginning and end respectively of this period: A.R.M. Lower's *Colony to Nation* in 1946 and George Grant's *Lament for a Nation* in 1965. When Trudeau became prime minister in 1968 and adopted Marshall McLuhan as one of his advisers, Canada reverted to tribalism.

French Canadian literature is also of necessity regional, and achieved its maturity rather earlier, I think, than its English counterpart. The reasons for this are not hard to see. A poet or novelist writing in a beleaguered and culturally threatened language has no doubts about his social function, and a French Canadian writer does not have his sense of identity so confused by the intrusive presence of an English-speaking American mass culture. The debates over the use of *joual* are, it seems to me, of immense benefit, whatever the attitude taken towards it, in sharpening the sense of what is going on in language and in the relation of oral to written French. I am also convinced, and have said elsewhere, that the discovery of a new French Canadian identity through the Quiet Revolution was the crucial factor in consolidating a similar sense in English Canada.[5] To document this statement fully, however, one would need to have a much more thorough knowledge of both literatures than most Canadians do, even though I am not speaking of direct literary influence. English and French Canada are still far too ignorant of each other's culture, and I think this fact indicates in itself that mutual translation is a more realistic handling of the problem than leaving it to "biculturalism."

If culture is regional and environmental rather than national, the writer comes somewhere in between the maple tree, which pays no attention to the national boundary line, and the customs official, who is created by it. Cultural movements, I have suggested, tend to decentralize and regionalize, while political and economic ones tend to centralize and build up expanding empires. Hence one is not inconsistent if one sympathizes warmly with French Canadian cultural aspirations and still opposes separatism, which is, in my view, a quite mistaken yoking of a progressive cultural movement to a regressive political one. But no sooner have we stated this principle than we realize how complex an issue is involved.

The publishing and selling of books, for instance, is an economic operation as well as a cultural one, and many Canadian writers have felt from the beginning that their final accolade of success was a New York publisher. The United States being a highly protectionist country, in literature as elsewhere, this often meant that a fiction writer would have to alter his settings. The publishing careers of Ernest Thompson Seton, Martha Ostenso, and Stephen Leacock afford three instructively different ways of meeting this issue. But apart from that, the border often introduces an unreal casuistry about the real ambience of Canadian writers into the picture. More recently it has become the basis of a strident nationalist rhetoric which has very little content and no cultural significance. The word "Canada" has a political meaning, but its cultural counterpart, which we also call "Canada" for convenience, is the federation of Canadian communities, in all their rich variety from sea to sea.

In an "instant world" of communication there is no reason for cultural lag or for a difference between sophisticated writers in large centres and naive writers in smaller ones. A world like ours produces a single international style of which all existing literatures are regional developments. This international style is not a bag of rhetorical tricks, but a way of seeing and thinking in a world controlled by uniform patterns of technology, and the regional development is a way of escaping from that uniformity. If we read, say, Wilson Harris's *Palace of the Peacock* and then Robert Kroetsch's *Badlands* one after the other, we find that there is no similarity between them, and that one story is steeped in Guyana and the other in Alberta. But certain structural affinities, such as the fold-over in time, indicate that they are both products of much the same phase of cultural development.

II

In 1930 native Canadian scholarship in the humanities was, as suggested above, spotty, and in a state of uneasy transition from nineteenth- to twentieth-century conceptions of humanism. Within the next twenty years a remarkable change had taken place. In 1950 I had a year off on a Guggenheim Fellowship and went to Harvard, and on my first visit to the bookstores I was startled at the prominence in them of books by my colleagues at home. I knew about the books, naturally, but seeing them in that context was a different experience. There were Cochrane's great book on Christianity and classical culture, Barker Fairley's second book on Goethe, Kathleen Coburn's edition of Coleridge's *Philosophical Lectures*, F.E.L. Priestley's edition of Godwin's *Political Justice*, my own book on Blake, Woodhouse's edition of the Clarke papers with its epoch-making introduction, Arthur Barker's book on Milton and Puritanism, still standard after nearly forty years—there were several others, but I remember seeing those.[6] Not a bad showing, I thought, for Canadian scholarship with its very inadequate libraries and travel grants (I am speaking of 1950). There were other signs too, like the establishment of the Pontifical Institute of Medieval Studies under Gilson, which indicated that Canadian scholarship in the humanities had become a genuine presence in the world. The scholarship had come to maturity rather earlier than the literature, and the fact nagged my subconscious for the next decade.

The expansion of scholarly activity represented by the setting up of "Letters in Canada" in the *Quarterly* meant that some scholarship, at least, was becoming assimilated to reviewing, even to journalism. And this kind of criticism has been traditionally regarded as a subordinate, even a parasitic activity. It was recognized that writers needed honest and informed criticism, but such criticism was the blest office of the epicene, of the bee who carries the pollen for the flower but does not fertilize it himself. I felt that when criticism and scholarship were the same activity (and an academic critic surely ought to apply the same principles to whatever he writes about) this parasitic relation to the writer disappeared. The academic critic is primarily concerned with the expansion of knowledge and sensitivity rather than with evaluation and "maintaining standards," which the writer must meet or else. He and the writer represent rather, I thought, the theory and practice respectively of the same activity. That did not mean, and could never possibly mean, that the critic's function was to influence the poet or tell him how he should write or what he should write about. But I felt that poetry and criticism, *Dichtung* and *Wahrheit*, imaginative expression and conceptual expression, were linked on equal terms in a dialectical relationship none the less, whenever they appeared in the same culture.

It was clear that to follow up this conviction one would need to expand and redefine the conception of criticism. If I was right, what I said would be confirmed by the cultural developments taking place around me. Matthew Arnold, in his essay on "The Function of Criticism at the Present Time" and elsewhere, had spoken of the essential role of criticism in the maturing of a culture, from which the poet would directly benefit. But he also assumed that the critical faculty was "lower" than the creative one, and I felt that this Romantic baggage of high and low metaphors was getting to be a nuisance. Some of my colleagues, notably A.S.P. Woodhouse, were absorbed by a scholarly interest to which they gave the name "history of ideas." It seemed to me that these "ideas" were really elements or units in what Tillyard calls a world picture,[7] the conceptual aspect of a kind of cosmology of imagery and metaphor that every poet who works on a large scale seems to work with, and that seems to preserve its main outlines for centuries, however much it may alter in detail from one age to another. Earlier poets could take such a world picture for granted, as something already formed by religious and political thought. In such passages as Ulysses' speech on degree in *Troilus and Cressida* [1.3.75–137] we glimpse something of the framework of theoretical assumptions that Shakespeare depended on his audience's possessing. But these traditional frameworks had largely collapsed by the end of the eighteenth century, and new poetic structures would need new conceptual ones. Hence when Arnold spoke of "criticism," he meant partly what was traditionally meant by that word, but he was also speaking of something new, something just coming into being that had barely taken form in his day.

Reviewing, of which I did a good deal in the fifties, is a *hermeneutic* activity, which means that it is a form of writing in which understanding and the articulating of that understanding become the same thing. It is also a species of translation: the poet writes in a specific language of symbolism, myth, imagery, and metaphor, and the reviewer renders that language in a different conceptual framework. Literature is one of the practical imaginative arts: criticism is one of the scholarly areas loosely called the humanities. It was clear that a great deal of shifting and regrouping of forces in the humanities was taking place. Toronto has always emphasized the importance of undergraduate teaching, and the undergraduate teaching of English literature is a very large activity, as it will be for the foreseeable future. But literary scholarship was beginning to resemble the well-known caterpillar, staring at a butterfly and saying, "You'll never catch me going up in one of those things." As a student in the early 1930s I had had to answer vague examination questions about a writer's "style"; as a teacher in the early forties I had to learn something quite specific about stylistics and rhetorical devices. No colleague or student of Woodhouse could avoid the challenge of the fact that history and philosophy were not just "background" for literature but were an essential part of literary criticism itself. Writers beyond the Toronto horizon at that time told me that anthropology and psychology were no less relevant.

The question then arose, what was this larger body of criticism of which literary criticism, as traditionally practised, seemed to be forming a smaller and smaller part? It was evidently something like "human science" of the kind adumbrated by Dilthey and others, but its total shape was still vague. The social scientists would have nothing to do with the suggestion that they were the applied humanities, nor did psychologists and anthropologists take much interest in the kind of use literary critics made of their material. I was aware of the rapid rise and influence of linguistics, especially synchronic linguistics, but, in striking contrast to the humane flexibility of nineteenth-century philology, linguistics was still a somewhat sectarian activity, not greatly interested even in literature, which it sometimes seemed almost to regard as a disease of language. But other movements were overriding this attitude, if I am right in thinking it existed. Gadamer, who is naturally thinking in a German context, says that the modern hermeneutic attitude, based on identifying *intelligere* and *explicare*, was established by the Romantic philosophers following Kant, and he adds that the effect of this was to move language from the periphery into the centre of the human sciences.[8]

It was not until the mid-sixties, with the rise of European structuralism and the conception of the "linguistic model," that I began to see something of the shape of what was emerging, and to see also where such figures as Wittgenstein and Heidegger belonged in the pattern. I am not sure how deeply Canadian criticism even yet has been affected by these developments: Dennis Lee's *Savage Fields* is an example of a critical approach that one hopes will soon be less exceptional. But I did learn three things of relevance to this question while writing about Canadian culture. One came from the editorial committee that had gathered under Carl Klinck to plan the *Literary History of Canada*. It was obvious to all of us from the start that a history of what would conventionally be called Canadian literature would be an utterly pointless cream-skimming operation. The book had to be an exhaustive survey of *writing* in Canada, whatever the subject written about, if the real "literary" element in Canadian culture was to be captured. The second came from the fact that I was drawing support and suggestions and insights from such writers as George Grant, Abraham Rotstein, Carl Berger, Frank Underhill, who represented a great variety of academic "disciplines," but whose writing I could not think of as anything but Canadian "criticism." The third came from my personal knowledge of Canadian scholars, such as the authors of the books I saw at Harvard. I could not feel that their scholarship would have been exactly the same wherever they lived. I knew that my own interest in Blake had been sparked by the way he made imaginative sense out of the Nonconformist attitude that I had been brought up in myself. And whenever a Canadian scholar makes a personal statement, as, say, Kathleen Coburn does in her autobiography, *In Pursuit of Coleridge*, it becomes clear that scholarship, no less than poetry, grows out of a specific environment and is in part a response to it.

It is no great credit to me that I entirely missed the significance, at the time, of the later work of Harold Innis, which appeared around 1950–52. I found the prose style impenetrable and the subject-matter uncongenial. But, of course, as is widely recognized now, Innis was defining a central issue in the Canadian imagination which ultimately affected the interests of practically everyone concerned with words. Innis had first, as an economist, studied the fur trade and the fishing industry, and had gained from that study a vision of the "Laurentian" centrifugal economic development of the country, with the traders and trappers fanning out from the Great Lakes into the far North. This in turn provided him with the underlying pattern of the primary modes of communication in Canada, the network of railways and canals mentioned above. After that, he asked himself the fateful question, "OK, what happens next?" This took him into a panoramic vision of secondary communication through words, as conveyed by papyrus, paper, parchment, clay bricks, manuscripts, books, and newspapers. He saw that verbal communication was an essential instrument of power, and that an ascendant class will naturally try to control and monopolize it. In *Empire and Communications*, and in the more accessible essays in *The Bias of Communication*, he sketched the outlines of a philosophy of history, based on the theme of the production and the control of the means of communication, on a scale as comprehensive, at least potentially, as anything since Marx. Like Marx, too, he left a large mass of *Grundrisse* to be published after his death.

Innis's influence, in Canada as elsewhere, will grow steadily, because with practice in reading him he becomes constantly more suggestive and rewarding. He was a curiously tentative writer, which may account for something of his rather spastic prose rhythm. He saw that every new form or technique generates both a positive impulse to exploit it and a negative impulse, especially strong in universities, to resist it, and that the former of course always outmanoeuvres the latter. But he had something of what I call the garrison mentality in him, the university being still his garrison for all the obscurantism in it that he comments on so dryly. Perhaps it is not possible to hold a vision of that scope and range steadily in one's mind without a more passionate commitment to society as well as to scholarship.

Marshall McLuhan, a literary critic interested originally in Elizabethan rhetoric and its expression in both oral and written forms, followed up other issues connected with the technology of communication, some of them leads from Innis. His relation to the public was the opposite of Innis's: he was caught up in the manic-depressive roller-coaster of the news media, so that he was hysterically celebrated in the 1960s and unreasonably neglected thereafter. It is likely that the theory of communications will be the aspect of the great critical pot-pourri of our time which will particularly interest Canadians, and to which they will make their most distinctive contribution. So it is perhaps time for a sympathetic rereading of *The Gutenberg Galaxy* and *Understanding Media* and a reabsorption of McLuhan's influence, though no adequate treatment of this topic can be attempted here.

I have often noted that many nineteenth-century writers in Canada, especially poets, spoke in what could be called, paraphrasing the title of Francis Sparshott's remarkable poem, the rhetoric of a divided voice.[9] Up above was vigour and optimism and buoyancy and all the other qualities of life in a new land with lots of natural resources to exploit; underneath were lonely, bitter, brooding visions of cruelty without and despair within. This division in tone is still in Pratt, in a different way, and can even be traced in later writers, such as Layton, though the context naturally changes. It is by no means confined to Canada, as a reading of Whitman would soon show, but it is traditional here. McLuhan put a similar split rhetoric into an international context. On top was a breezy and self-assured butterslide theory of Western history, derived probably from a Chestertonian religious orientation, according to which medieval culture had preserved a balanced way of life that employed all the senses, depended on personal contact, and lived with "tribal," or small community units. Since then we have skittered down a slope into increasing specialization (McLuhan defines the specialist as the man who never makes a minor mistake on his way to a major fallacy), a self-hypnotism from concentrating on the visual stimuli of print and mathematics, a dividing and subdividing of life into separate "problems," and an obsession with linear advance also fostered by print and numbers. The electronic media, properly understood and manipulated, could reverse the direction of all this. Below was a horrifying vision of a global village, at once completely centralized and completely decentralized, with all its senses assailed at once, in a state of terror and anxiety at once stagnant and chaotic, equally a tyranny and an anarchy. His phrase "defence against media fallout" indicated this direction in his thought.[10]

In the 1960s both the anti-intellectuals, who wanted to hear that they had only to disregard books and watch television to get with it, and the "activists," pursuing terror for its own sake, found much to misunderstand in McLuhan. Many of his theses involved research in linguistics, anthropology, sensory psychology, and economics which has still to be done or established even in those fields, and his recurring tendency to determinism involved him in prophecies not borne out by events. Media may be hot or cool, but societies do not turn hot or cool in consequence of adopting them. Canada is a cool country with cool people in it, hence all its media are cool. But McLuhan raised questions that are deeply involved in any survey of contemporary culture, and in any attempt to define the boundaries of the emerging theory of society that I call "criticism" in its larger context.

Meanwhile Canada's own involvement with new media, more particularly film and radio, had been a decisive influence in maturing the culture of the country and giving it a place in the international scene. I have no space or expertise to tell the story of the golden age of the N[ational] F[ilm] B[oard] and CBC radio in the forties and early fifties. That has been done before, and it is generally recognized that film and radio are the media of much of the best work produced in Canadian culture. The benefits extended into literature, through radio plays and such programs as "Anthology," and Andrew Allan and Robert Weaver are names of the same kind of significance in Canadian writing that publishers like Briggs had in the nineteenth century.[11] Radio also influenced, I think, the development of a more orally based poetry, more closely related to recitation and a listening audience, and popular in a way that poetry had not been for many centuries. As I write this, an anthology of "sound texts" comes in, poems based on sound and removed from ordinary syntax, and I notice that Canadian poets are deeply involved in this movement.

But there were difficulties that the coming of television made painfully obvious. These three new media, film, radio, and television, are mass media, and consequently follow the centrifugal and imperial rhythms of politics and economics more readily than the regionalizing rhythms of culture. This was not too crucial a problem for CBC radio, though it was certainly there, but the NFB had to struggle with problems of distribution created by the fact that movie houses had been monopolized by American syndicates. I remember a *Spring Thaw* skit which was a takeoff of an NFB film, ending with the line "on view in your local Sunday-School basement." So when television came, the government passed a Broadcasting Act and set up the CRTC as a regulating agency for both radio and television, and both private and subsidized networks. I became an advisory member of the CRTC in 1968, when the Broadcasting Act still made a good deal of sense. The feeling was that the distribution of books, newspapers, movies, and magazines had been very largely sold out to American interests, and that if television went the same way there would be no Canadian identity left.

For the next decade what seemed like a completely autonomous technological development started to explode: microwave, cable, satellite, and now a metamorphosis of pay-TV. It was not autonomous, of course, but Canadian identity, in that area, began to look as desperate as a Spartan at Thermopylae. Nor could a regulating agency even count on the support of public opinion: when Canada was, in the stock phrase, "flooded with American programs," it was clear that the majority of Canadians preferred the flood to any Canadian ark that would float above it. Further, television is expensive to produce, and there have been many complaints that not only the CBC but the educational stations set up by the wealthier provinces have become mired in real estate, bureaucracy, and vested interests. Many viewers living in or near Toronto say that they cling to the PBS station in Buffalo, looking for a standard of programming from it that they no longer expect from Canadian sources, and some of them, noting the frequent PBS appeals for money, draw the inference that limited funds may be a stimulus of livelier thinking. The provinces are demanding a larger share of control of communications, but their motives for doing so are not cultural ones.

So a "mass culture" which follows expanding economic rather than regionalizing rhythms complicates the situation I have been outlining very considerably. Certainly there is much in it at present which is not Canadian in any sense and expresses very little creative energy. On the other hand all the mass media seem to have an entire cultural history to recapitulate, from the most archaic crudity to the greatest technical, and eventually creative, sophistication. There are still bad movies and dull radio programs, just as there are still bad books, but a listener to FM radio today or a movie-goer is a long way from the world of Amos and Andy or the Keystone Cops. Television is more frustrating and is still largely formulaic, but it too seems to be maturing in obedience to an inner process of development. I think the inherent tendency of television, as of film and radio, is to decrease the distinction between highbrow and lowbrow listeners, and within its widening central area of appeal to find more room for a greater variety of tastes.

In the 1960s a resistance movement against the mass culture of (mainly) television grew up in the United States, and the magic word that explained everything that was then going on in this area was the word "subculture." But a subculture, whether its interest was in rock or drugs or meditation, showed a strong tendency to become mass news, featured on television networks or being reflected in fashion advertising. In other words these subcultures seemed to be really specialized forms of mass culture. Perhaps genuine culture is also the genuine form of subculture. No matter how complex the technical means of communication, the elements communicated are still words, tones, and images, the same elements that have been around since the earliest stone age. And I feel there is hope that the genuine article will continue, quietly but persistently and increasingly, to filter through the new technology.

In this overview there are many subjects, such as painting, that cannot be touched on here, even though painting was perhaps the liveliest of all Canadian arts up to about 1960 at least, and is still very much in a foreground position. Other articles to follow will deal with the situation in detail, and will show the reader, I think, that Canada today is a far more exciting place to live in, culturally speaking, than its demoralized economy and demented political leadership would suggest. I do not know what the social causes of a culture are, or if there are any causes apart from conditioning factors, but half a century of contemplating its development, in Canada as elsewhere, has convinced me that it is the force that underlies both real social change and real social stability.

78

Beginnings

3 January 1981

From Today Magazine, *3 January 1981, 3, based on a tape-recorded interview by Susan Gabori.*

I was always a devourer of books. I'd gone through the Victorian writers Thackeray and George Eliot and the Scott novels by the time I was fifteen. I can't remember a time when I couldn't read. My mother taught me to play the piano very early, and to some degree that was my refuge. I was never well coordinated and always myopic, so I wasn't very good at games and sports. I was given the nickname "professor" because of my glasses.

Under Mother's influence I acquired a knowledge of the Bible quite early. My mother had an intensely strong and religious personality—her whole emotional life was bound up with religion. Like so many women of her generation, she didn't have any other outlets for her energy. She had a tremendous contralto voice that could have been quite spectacular, but as one of eight children in a Methodist minister's family you don't get far with musical training.

There was a good deal of chaos and confusion in my early years. I was born in 1912 and spent the first five years of my life in Sherbrooke, Quebec. Then we moved to Lennoxville. I was brought up essentially as an only child. My sister was twelve years older than I and my brother was thirteen years older; he was killed in World War I at the Battle of Avignon when I was six. My mother started going deaf very soon after my brother was killed, and I was conscious of a barrier between us from then on. Deaf people tend to withdraw into themselves.

My father had a hardware store in Sherbrooke, but with the slump in the economy, in 1918, his business failed and he moved to New Brunswick as an agent for various central Canadian hardware companies. He took relatively little part in influencing me; he tended to leave that to my mother. As I grew up and got more and more bookish he must have wondered occasionally what the hell he had spawned. Because we were shuffling between Quebec and New Brunswick, trying to find accommodation, I didn't start school till I was eight years old, then I started in the fourth grade. Of course my mother's teaching at home had given me the basics of reading and counting.

I was bored to death in public school. I liked literature and history but I couldn't stand mathematics. My public school career was very undistinguished—I always regarded it as one of the milder forms of penal servitude. High school was a little better. I greatly admired my music teacher and, when I was thirteen, started taking piano lessons from him after school. He was very competent and he had a complete devotion to music. It was his impersonal approach that appealed to me; the important thing was the music itself and not his relation to me or to my performance.

My sister got a job in Chicago and she invited me to visit her in the summer of 1927. That was quite an experience. It was the first big city I had seen and I was overwhelmed by city life. I stayed in a house where the people had a piano so I had that as well—I never wanted to be away from a piano.

I did some writing when I was young. I wrote sketches modelled on what I happened to be reading, and that perhaps gave me one of the bases for my critical theory that literature is born out of other literature. Gradually the notion dawned on me that you have to write hundreds of thousands of words just to get technique.

I always thought of adolescence as something to grow away from. I think I suffered from an impatience to get on with my own job. I knew I had books in me, but in Moncton I felt I had no specific function in the community. An adolescent whose physical coordination is all right can play sports, which can fill up his life and give him a function; with me, everything was geared toward a "not yet" feeling. I don't mean I had an unhappy childhood—it was just a waiting period.

I had moments of mental enlightenment when I glimpsed my own potential abilities. While walking to school one day, that claustrophobic, evangelical, Christian environment that I was brought up in just lifted from my shoulders. It just vanished and has never come back. Ever since then I have been interested in religion solely as a means of expanding the mind, not of contracting it.

Nevertheless, when I was fourteen or fifteen I decided to become a candidate for the ministry. To me, religion symbolized a cultivated life. I felt it would allow me to lead my own rather introverted lifestyle. So I enrolled at Victoria College in Toronto with the ministry in mind. But as soon as I got to university I knew that was where I wanted to stay. I found myself in a community where I felt I had something to contribute. I plunged into everything: the dramatic society, the debating society. It was a sudden, extroverted reaction from my rather withdrawn adolescence.

I met my wife about the second year of my undergraduate career. She was the pianist of the music club. When the club put on its Gilbert and Sullivan opera at Hart House, I was operating an arc light and she was on the other side of the stage, in the wings, with the prompt book. It wasn't love at first sight, but it was certainly a very effortless operation.

Before I was ordained I went to Saskatchewan for one summer as a student preacher. This was in the southwestern part of Saskatchewan, where there were three communities called Stone Pile. I got around on the back of Katie, the mare, who was slightly older than I. The services were held in the schoolhouses. By then I had realized that, although I felt honour-bound to complete the theological course, I didn't want to stay in active parish work. Going into the ministry required social qualities I knew I didn't possess. I never found it easy to meet people and make small talk. The only thing I could do was to preach service, and that is a very small part of the job. I did become an ordained minister, but I'm on a sort of permanent leave of absence from the United Church.

I remember thinking in my later twenties, when I'd been appointed to the English department at Victoria, "Now I've got the wife I want and I've got the job I want. Why the hell couldn't my life have begun at this point instead of stomping all the way up here?"

79

Criticism and Environment

3 September 1981

From Adjoining Cultures as Reflected in Literature and Language *(Proceedings of the Fifteenth Triennial Congress of the Fédération Internationale des Langues et Littératures Modernes), ed. John X. Evans and Peter Horwath (Tempe: Arizona State University, 1983), 9–21. Reprinted in* EAC, *139–53. A preliminary typescript with corrections is in NFF, 1991, box 38, file 2, and a retyped version in 1988, box 47, file 4. Frye's remarks were originally an address at the FILLM Conference, Phoenix.*

I

It seemed to me that I could contribute most usefully to this conference by speaking out of my experience as a resident of Canada. An American hardly needs to concern himself much with problems of adjoining cultures in the ordinary sense, unless he has a special interest in them: if he does have such an interest, Mexico will provide him with far more dramatic examples than Canada will. But in Canada the cultural situation represented by the word "adjoining" is present and continuous, and there are many elements in the Canadian situation that are of great interest and relevance to the general questions of critical theory that arise from it. They are, in my view, of all the greater interest for being so muted and camouflaged.

In 1950 I was asked to make an annual critical review of all the English poetry published in Canada during the previous year. I did this for ten years, when by a combination of good luck and instinctive cunning I retired just before it became humanly impossible to continue it, because of the phenomenal increase in quantity. During this period I acquired my own sense of the context, in time and space, that Canadian culture inhabits. More important for me, these reviews formed a body of "field work" which entered into my more general critical attitudes, modifying some and strengthening others. In other words the Canadian scene became a kind of cultural laboratory in which to study the relation of criticism to its environment. What I have to say, especially in the next few moments, I have often said before, if not to this audience, and I apologize to anyone who may be familiar with my other writings on Canada for the repetition.

We may begin with the geographical or spatial environment. In Canada there is nothing corresponding to the north-south frontier that has been so conspicuous in American culture. Entering Canada from Europe by ship—through the Straits of Belle Isle into the Gulf of St. Lawrence, and down the river to the Great Lakes—has no counterpart in the American Atlantic coastline. This movement is the centre of the east-to-west thrust that Canadian economists and historians call (or used to call, there being fashions in such matters) the "Laurentian axis." The Laurentian axis suggests a mercantile economy, with sparse settlements along the waterway and long canoe and forest trails probing the hinterland for furs and other raw materials to be shipped to more populous markets.

Several features inherited from this economy may be traced in Canadian life down to our time. In the treatment of the indigenous peoples, the French record is considerably better than the British or Spanish record. The main reason for this was that the early Canadian economy depended on the co-operation of Indians for the long canoe and forest trails, and the close economic relation led to a good deal of intermarriage. In the opening up of the Canadian West, an embattled situation arose with the "Métis," or French-Indian half-breeds, which was not an Indian war but a collision with another part of French Canada. The trauma left by the crushing of the Métis rebellion and the hanging of their leader Louis Riel still forms part of the tension between English- and French-speaking parts of the country.

Two aspects of the inheritance of mercantilism may be noted. First, there was a long period, a century at least, when there were extensive analyses of Canadian cultural production, and critical articles with such titles as "Is There a Canadian Literature?," to which the answer, as a rule, was a highly qualified yes. That is, the answer was usually accompanied by a prophecy that a much greater literature was just about to begin. The rationalization given for the late arrival of major poetry and fiction was that Canada was a "young" country, and had to establish a material basis for its culture first. The real reason, that Canada had accepted the mercantilist conditions against which the United States revolted, of providing raw materials and resources to be consumed by wealthier centres, seldom emerged into the foreground. But the sense of cultural inferiority left from the conviction that the head office is always somewhere else is obvious enough to the least reflective of Canadians.

Second, we notice in early Canadian literature something that continues to our own time: the predominance of women among the more serious writers. The centrifugal rhythms of hunting, fishing, trapping, farming, and ranching were the "men's work": it was the centripetal rhythms presided over by the women directed toward hearth and home, which in more elaborate societies expanded to parties and other social gatherings, that belonged to the embryonic culture. One of the first novels written in the New World, and certainly the first in Canada, is *The History of Emily Montague*, published in London in 1769, and written by Frances Brooke, the wife of a clergyman attached to the British military garrison in Quebec after its capture from the French. This is an epistolary novel of sensibility in the Richardson tradition, and is earlier than either Henry Mackenzie's *Man of Feeling* or Fanny Burney's *Evelina*. The world it describes is, in the words of one of her letter-writers, "like a third or fourth rate country town in England; much hospitality, little society; cards, scandal, dancing, and good chear."[1] It is not greatly different from many aspects of the world of Jane Austen, where there are also handsome officers to be flirted with, but certain tones betray a greater sense of desperation. The same correspondent, whose name, Arabella Fermor, evokes an echo from *The Rape of the Lock*, remarks: "Those who expect to see `A new Athens rising near the pole' will find themselves extremely disappointed. Genius will never mount high, where the faculties of the mind are benumbed half the year.... I suppose Pygmalion's statue was some frozen Canadian gentlewoman, and a sudden warm day thawed her."[2]

It is significant that Canada's first work of fiction is about life in a garrison, for the garrison encapsulates a great deal of imaginative feeling in Canada, even down to the twentieth century. What corresponded to the frontier in American life was never a border in Canada. It was a circumference: a frontier surrounded and enclosed all the tiny communities wherever they were. The sense of alienation from nature was nowhere distanced in space from the cultural centres. Canada is still divided by natural or political obstacles which even a world of instant communication does not wholly overcome psychologically. As the population increased with immigration, specific ethnical cultures appeared, like Icelandic in Manitoba, which were enclave cultures, totally surrounded by alien linguistic influences. It is clear that the culture of French Canada is, in the North American context, simply the largest of these enclave cultures. Still, an enclave culture with its own language has at least no problem of identity, and French writers in Canada, however limited their markets or audiences, have always had the advantage of knowing that they had a social function in carrying on the fight to preserve a threatened and beleaguered language. English Canada has lacked the advantage of an easily defined identity without much to compensate for it.

The particular problems of space in Canada, along with those of a terrifying climate, are naturally dissolving under modern technology. Problems of time and of cultural tradition are much more elusive. In its history, Canada has reversed the American sequence of a revolutionary war against Europe followed by a civil war to preserve its own federation. Canada had a civil war of European immigrants, English and French, on its own soil first, followed by the War of 1812 against its North American neighbour. This war, for all its grotesque muddle, was still from the point of view of the Canadas something of a war of independence, at any rate an indication that the two halves of upper North America were to have different directions and destinies.

One consequence of this inverted history was that Canada missed the eighteenth century, with all its confidence in reason and progress. English and French in Canada spent the eighteenth century battering down each other's forts, and Canada went directly from the Baroque expansion of the seventeenth century to the Romantic expansion of the nineteenth. There are no culture-heroes corresponding to Washington, Jefferson, or Franklin, and no sense of a detachment from history and a fresh start such as the American Revolution provided. Much of English Canada was settled by disaffected Tories from America, and there was a strong reaction against the Whig spirit that won the American Revolution, with its liberal mercantile values, its confidence in laissez-faire, its equating of freedom with national independence. A good many English Canadian intellectuals, even yet, are some form of Tory radical, and when anti-American sentiments are expressed in nineteenth-century Canada, they tend to attack from the left and right at the same time. That is, they decry both the absence of distinctions in American democracy and the inequalities of wealth and privilege, especially in the slave-owning states, in American oligarchy. The Nova Scotian writer Thomas Haliburton has his Yankee peddler Sam Slick describe a Fourth of July celebration as "a splendid spectacle; fifteen millions of freemen and three millions of slaves a-celebratin' the birthday of liberty."[3] But the positive side of this critical attitude is harder to find.

A cultural tradition founded, as the American one is, on a successful revolution tends to be deductive, drawing up a constitution based on "self-evident" principles, and continually revising and amending that constitution without discarding it. This deductive pattern has no counterpart in Canada, where nothing has ever been self-evident. Canadians usually try to resolve social tensions and conflicts by some form of compromise that keeps the interests of both parties in view, in the conservative spirit of Edmund Burke.[4] The result is that the country seems to an outsider, and often to insiders as well, to be perpetually coming apart at the seams, with nothing to sustain it but a hope that some *ad hoc* settlement will keep it together until the next crisis. As a result there is a greater preoccupation with history in Canada, especially French Canada (the motto of Quebec, recently revived, is *je me souviens*), and much less of the sense of emerging from history that was so characteristic of American popular feeling down to about 1950, and was one of the central themes of Walt Whitman.

The fact that a revolution is based on the success of violence is doubtless connected with much of the lawlessness in American history; the lynchings, the labour violence, the anarchy at the frontier as it proceeded through an increasingly wild West. Canada was controlled first by the British military occupation, after which a military police force moved into the North-West to keep order there. As a result violence in Canada has tended to be mainly a repressive, or "law-and-order" violence. The effect on Canadian fiction has been very marked, because the obvious place for outbreaks of violence in such a society is the family.

II

We may distinguish three main phases in the development of Canadian literature, each phase having its distinctive interest for a student of the relation of criticism to environment. The first is the colonial or provincial stage, where culture is one of the things to be imported from more populous centres, and where the standards of culture are assumed to be established in those centres. It is characteristic of a provincial culture to think in terms of meeting an external standard. But as no mature standards can ever be met externally like an examination, but have to be established by the writer for himself, it is obvious that frustration and cultural lag are built in to this kind of imitation.

In August, 1606, a poet named Marc Lescarbot, one of the settlers in the tiny French outpost of Port Royal, or what is now Annapolis, Nova Scotia, wrote a nostalgic poem on seeing a shipload of his fellow-countrymen returning to France. It was published in France the following year. There is some perfunctory rhetoric about expanding the glory of France in a new world and the like, but the pervading tone is one of almost unbearable desolation as he sees the ship go, taking so much of everything that makes life worth living along with it. There is nothing, he says, for those who remain stranded in Acadia except a rabble of savages who have no God, no laws, and no religion. We should be inclined to say only that the Micmac Indians did not have *his* God or laws or religion, but for a spokesman of Baroque Europe there is little difference between the two statements. Indians frequently appear for picturesque effect in Canadian literature down to our own time, but the notion of learning anything from their culture hardly appears before the middle of this century.

One does not obliterate a native culture with impunity, however, no matter how alien it may seem. In the United States this process was rationalized as a kind of crusade; in Canada it formed part of an excluding view of culture that I have often spoken of as a garrison mentality. The basis of this is a sense of the need for constant vigilance against attack that leaves one with no time to cultivate the kind of imaginative flexibility that is needed for culture. As a society, the garrison is under rigid discipline and class distinction; as a culture it forms a kind of mob rule that is alert to stamp out any expression of consciousness or opinion that might weaken the sense of social cohesion.

In a provincial situation one of the most illuminating forms of literature is the book written by a relatively sympathetic outsider who feels that the onlooker may see more of the game being played than the participants. Thus Mrs. Humphry Ward, a British novelist of the turn of this century, has a story called *Canadian Born* (1908), in which the British heroine, impressed by the energy of the country and by an attractive young Canadian male she has met, remarks: "I am only a spectator. *We* see the drama—we feel it—much more than they can who are in it."[5] Similarly, perhaps the best-known work of French Canadian fiction, *Maria Chapdelaine* (1914), was written by a European Frenchman, Louis Hémon, whose first novel, incidentally, was written in English and had an English setting.

This story is centred on a group of *habitant* farmers in Quebec, whose instinct it is to retreat from the more urbanized forms of life as they encroach. The heroine, brought up in a *habitant* household, has to choose between a suitor who will take her to Boston and a suitor who can offer her only more of the gruelling pioneer life she has known. Judging from the statistics of emigration from both English and French parts of Canada to New England in this period, we can say with some confidence that practically any Canadian girl would have bought a one-way ticket to Boston before her deliverer had had time to reconsider. But Maria Chapdelaine is the exception: she stays with the tiller of the soil.

What Louis Hémon discovers in Quebec *habitant* life is in large part a literary convention. He is fascinated by a way of life that reminds him of certain aspects of French literature: he has a sharp ear for any *vieux parler* phrase he hears, and encloses his action within a framework of assumptions about the mystique of the *terroir* and of the peasant's feeling for the soil. Nobody in Quebec could reasonably be called a peasant, even then, but the emotions of the Chapdelaine family are assimilated to literary conventions about peasantry. It is also significant that the book was attacked by French Canadians in its day for presenting *habitant* life in so primitive a form. There were many counterparts to such attacks in English Canada: they are part of a typical response of a provincial culture to an external view of it. Its insecurity takes the form of resentment at being thrust on a larger stage before it has had time to put on its best clothes. One is reminded of the Irish reaction to Synge's *Playboy*. It is not the genuineness of the heroine's decision to remain on Quebec soil that is in question: the same type of resolution recently appeared in the film *My Brilliant Career*, which was based on an Australian story. It is rather the ambiguity of a vision of a certain limited area of life that looks like the exposures of realism to those within it and like the concealments of literary convention to those outside it.

The second stage of cultural development in Canada revolves around the Confederation of 1867, the union of the two Canadas, now Ontario and Quebec, with two Maritime Provinces, and eventually British Columbia. This stage is characterized by a search for a distinctively "Canadian" identity, more particularly in English Canada, and attached to this search are a number of critical fallacies that are important to diagnose. The first and most elementary of these is the fallacy of the exclusive characteristic, or nonexistent essence, the attempt to distinguish something that is, in this case, "truly Canadian," and is not to be found in other literatures. There are no exclusive or even defining characteristics anywhere in literature: there are only degrees of emphasis, and anyone looking for such characteristics soon gets as confused as a racist looking for pure Aryans. It is not hard to ridicule the fallacy of the distinctive essence, and to show that it is really a matter of looking for some trade mark in the content. A satirical revue in Toronto some years ago known as *Spring Thaw* depicted a hero going in quest of a Canadian identity and emerging with a mounted policeman and a bottle of rye. If he had been Australian, one realizes, he would have emerged with a kangaroo and a boomerang. One needs to go deeper than ridicule, however, if one is to understand the subtlety of the self-deceptions involved.

The search for a distinctive Canadian identity was, naturally, a remote and minor development of Romanticism. Like other forms of Romanticism, it often fell into another critical fallacy that might be called the "harnessing of Niagara Falls" fallacy, the notion that literature derives its energy from nature or experience, and that a new literature is bound to arise in a new country simply because there are new things to look at, and types of experience with no direct counterparts elsewhere. Getting really clear of this fallacy is a more difficult enterprise than it sounds. Man never lives directly in nature: he lives inside the construct of culture or civilization, of which the verbal aspect is a mythology. Literature is a constant recreation of this mythology, and derives its forms from it. The writer is not "inspired" by nature or even by experience: these things may supply incidental content, but the forms of literature develop out of literature itself, and are only projected on experience and nature. The shaping spirit of literature is literature, and a writer's quality is determined primarily by what he makes of what he has read, not by the differentiating factors in his environment. Writers often tend to resist this conclusion, because their imaginative attitudes seem to them to be directly shaping forces, and they are often unaware of the extent to which literary conventions are controlling those attitudes. Often too it is better for them as writers to be unaware of it, but it is part of the critic's business to see more clearly what is happening.

In English Canada, in the wake of Confederation, there was a certain amount of patriotic and rather phoney poetry about a great emerging nation stretching from sea to sea, but the social reality corresponding to this was less a country than a means of transportation, a waterway and a railway, which formed part of the network of communications within the British Empire. In proportion as Canadian writers began to realize their own environment on the North American continent, the effective contemporary influences became American rather than British. Haliburton, the author of *Sam Slick* referred to earlier, writing in pre-Confederation times, was fanatically loyal to the British connection, but he uses his Yankee mouthpiece to express a good deal of ambivalence about that loyalty. It seems clear, both from him and from other writers, that many Canadians felt that they would be treated with more respect elsewhere if they represented an independent country, and that cultivated people in Great Britain had a strong tendency, only partly unconscious, to think of the colonies as essentially penal settlements. There is also the irony of the fact that no Canadian in this period could dream of living by his writing without a London or New York publisher, implying a mainly non-Canadian audience.

One very shrewd novel that reflects this change in perspective is Sara Jeannette Duncan's *The Imperialist* (1904). The author was born and brought up in the community she portrays in her book, but she had lived outside Canada a good deal and was a devotee of William Dean Howells and the earlier Henry James. Here one of the two central male characters develops a strong enthusiasm for Canada's role in the British Empire, which he sees as fulfilling both the destiny and the identity of Canada, but his somewhat incoherent expressions of this fail to impress the young woman he wishes to marry, and it is obvious that the cause to which he devotes himself will be short-lived. This story is all the more striking in that Sara Duncan herself was something of an "imperialist," but she was also a good enough writer to detect the false ring of a rhetoric that had no social reality behind it.

French Canada had at first an exceptional disadvantage in the severing of the political link with France. After the departure of the aristocracy, a very conservative form of Roman Catholicism came to be the dominant cultural influence, one that repudiated the ideology of the French Revolution and clung to the romantic blood-and-soil values reflected more obliquely in *Maria Chapdelaine*. (One may compare the later career of Haliburton, who retired to England in later life and entered the Conservative party there, only to find it far too radical for *his* conservativism.) There have also been cultural tensions connected with the spoken language, which for many French Canadians is a patois now called *joual* (the word is derived from its alleged pronunciation of *cheval*). Anyone at all familiar with English writing in Nigeria or Guyana or Pakistan will realize that English, like Latin a thousand years ago, is developing different dialect forms that are trying hard to become separate languages, and would do so practically over night if it were not for the conservative grip of the written language and the news media. *Joual* represents an analogous development in French, and, like its English counterparts, has been both condemned as sub-standard illiteracy and defended as a genuine popular idiom. The defence has also taken the form of some lively literary productions, mainly in drama. I mention *joual* here because it is a particularly clear example of the change in environmental conditions in this century, and has gone through the normal stages of resistance followed by gradual acceptance. There are many other aspects of this change which have turned what seemed at first insuperable odds against French Canada's ever producing a literature of any significance into a major advantage. In my opinion, the maturing and intensifying of French Canadian imaginative life in mid-century, with the so-called "Quiet Revolution" and the turn to a more secularized culture, was the event that touched off a similar development in English Canada around 1960.

III

One of the difficulties in developing a "Canadian" literature is that Canada is too big and heterogeneous a country to be unified imaginatively. In other words, the assumption that cultural developments always follow political and economic ones does not work, at least in its more simplistic forms. Political and economic developments tend to centralize and to build up increasingly large entities, as national units combine into great continental powers. But there seems to be something vegetable about the creative imagination, something that needs roots and a limited environment. This contradictory movement of centralizing economy and decentralizing culture makes the twentieth century a difficult but fascinating time for a critic. The emptiness of the "Canadian" rhetoric of the previous century, we can now see, was the result of trying to annex a cultural development to a political one, just as the separatist and neo-Fascist movements of today represent the opposite fallacy of attaching a political movement to a cultural one.

In the first half of the century Canada was preoccupied with becoming a nation, but it had only just become one when the postnational developments of the modern world caught up with it. These developments have been, significantly, much more favourable to culture than to other aspects of Canadian life. Another possible critical principle appears dimly in the background: we do not know what social conditions produce good literature, except that we have no reason to suppose that they are good conditions. Canadian economic and political development today is that of a fully matured Western democracy, but its culture is that of an emergent nation. To put it another way, as the Canadian economy becomes increasingly chaotic and its political leadership increasingly schizoid, its cultural life becomes proportionately more varied and lively.

Within the last twenty years a verbal explosion has taken place in English Canadian literature, a quantitative increase so dramatic as to amount to, or include, a qualitative change. The Canadian critic George Woodcock, reviewing English Canadian poetry for the decade 1960–70, found himself confronted with a thousand volumes, exclusive of anthologies. This does not of course mean that they were all printed by solvent publishers: most of them were produced by what amounts to a resistance press. The implications of the word "resistance" will meet us again in a moment. Much of this increase is a by-product of a socially decentralizing movement, especially in fiction. As one previously inarticulate region after another has formed an orbit for the imagination, we discover that "Canada," culturally speaking, is really an aggregate of smaller areas stretching from Vancouver Island to the Avalon peninsula in Newfoundland. Here Canada has followed the rhythm of American literature, which has always been strongly regional. It seems to be a law of literature that the more strictly limited its environment is, the more universal its appeal. Faulkner writes of his unpronounceable county in Mississippi and gets the Nobel Prize in Sweden, while novelists writing of the dilemma of modern man would get nowhere.

However, American literature is no less American for being an aggregate of New England literature, Mississippi literature, and dozens of other areas. Similarly, English Canada now has a literature with an imaginative coherence that is recognized outside the country, so that some Canadian writers sell as well in Germany and Italy as they do at home. Within the country, Canadian literature, ignored in Canadian universities in my student days, is now an academic heavy industry. The main positive result of this has been to make contemporary Canadian writers aware of the tradition behind the work they are producing, and thereby to give that work the rounded dimension of continuity without which no literature can be mature, whatever the merits of its earlier products.

So far we have been speaking of criticism in its traditional form as a servomechanism of literature. Poets and novelists, according to this view, produce literature, and then the critic comments on their work, explains it, and retails it to at least the academic part of its audience. This conception of criticism has always reminded me of an early Chaplin film, in which Charlie Chaplin was portrayed as a street cleaner, in the days before automobiles, wearily trudging up one street after another in pursuit of the horses. It has been out of date for a century, but it lingers like other obsolete notions. I have known several academics who could have been fine scholars, but forced themselves to become indifferent poets or novelists because their egos demanded that they concern themselves only with the primary or "creative" process of literature. Nobody denies that commenting on pre-existing literature is still a central function of criticism, but what with all the linguistic and semiotic developments of the last quarter-century a new perspective on it is overdue.

It was a Canadian economic historian, Harold Innis, who, in his studies of the fur trade and fishing industry in Canada, along with an earlier study (his thesis) of the Canadian Pacific Railway,[6] laid the groundwork for the "Laurentian" view of Canadian development mentioned at the beginning of this paper, a view carried on and elaborated by the historian Donald Creighton, who also wrote a biography, or rather a personal sketch of Innis.[7] Innis then became interested in other contexts of communication, a word which enters the titles of two of his later books, *Empire and Communications* and *The Bias of Communication*. Here he is concerned mainly with verbal or written communication, the role of the printing press, the book, the codex, the pamphlet, the newspaper, the periodical, and of paper itself and the other materials used for writing, throughout history. In these books a vision of history emerges in which an ascendant class tries to monopolize the means of communication, and in which every power struggle includes an effort to get control of it, to promote an ideology and censor or repress rival ones.

In our world the control of communications is connected with what is called advertising in some contexts and propaganda in others, depending on the economic context involved. A somewhat unlikely disciple of Innis, Marshall McLuhan, published his first and I think his best book, *The Mechanical Bride*, in 1951. This is a study of the psychological appeals and responses in advertising. As its title indicates, it seizes on that curious identification of the erotic and the mechanical that seems so central to the sensibility of our age: Eros and Thanatos locked together in a peculiarly twentieth-century embrace. My copy of this book classifies it as "sociology," but McLuhan was a literary critic who remarks in his introduction that it is high time for the techniques of criticism, in literature and the other arts, to be applied to the analysis of society.

The Mechanical Bride has no specific reference to Canada, but it was, I think, written in Canada, and reflects the perspective of a country committed to observing rather than participating actively in the international scene. The career of Innis indicates even more clearly that Canada affords some unusual perspectives for relating criticism to its social environment. As criticism expands in range and variety of subject, it will merge with communications theory, and the sprawling and disunited Canada, from its very beginning, has been preoccupied—obsessed would be a better word—with means of communication, whether animate or inanimate. As its literature has developed, it has formed an adjoining culture in time to the whole British tradition from *Beowulf* to Eliot and Joyce. From the point of view of a new culture using an old language, that tradition is not a moving belt in time but a kaleidoscope, all of it available for simultaneous study and imitation. One suggestion arising from this situation is that a major task facing criticism today is that of attaining a synoptic view of language.

I do not mean primarily the different languages spoken, with all their untranslatable idioms pointing to many different habits of thought. I mean rather the different modes of language which have entered into our speech, many of which have become obsolete although they still contain great potential powers of utterance. There is a metaphorical language of immanence, of a kind we find in the poetry of so-called "primitive" societies, where subject and object are not clearly separated and where words are words of power that can affect the environment directly. There is a metonymic language of transcendence of a kind that we find in theology or metaphysics, where language points in the direction of something beyond itself. There is a language of objectivity and description and clear definition, such as we find in expository prose. There is a meditative language for which all physical objects become foci of converging forces, as in some of the later essays of Heidegger. There is the language of what is called ordinary speech, where meaning bursts through the words and is eked out by gesture and body language, of the kind studied in the later works of Wittgenstein. There is the disguised and hieratic language of the kind typical of the dream, which makes its way into the waking world in all sorts of disconcerting ways. And there are dozens of other kinds. The investigating of these different aspects of language forms what is probably the liveliest area of criticism today, but the subject is still in its scholastic period, undermining the postulates of other critics without arriving at an interconnected view. When that interconnected view begins to show some of its outlines, criticism will be a much more central subject than it is now.

The name of McLuhan also reminds us of the growth of electronic media. *The Mechanical Bride* appeared before the main impact of television, and in trying to grapple with that McLuhan lost the distinction between the positive and negative aspects of his global village. What is positive about the world opened up by the electronic media is the sense of all the time and space known to us as simultaneously present to us. What is negative about it is the control of it, along with so much of the press, by advertising, in our culture, with its ready access to our reflexes and its power of manipulating them.

Advertising is closely allied with what is called mass culture, which demands passivity of response and acceptance of unexamined clichés. Mass culture is a most misleading phrase for what it describes because it is something imposed on the so-called "masses" and is not produced by them. To call it "popular culture" is clearly still more misleading. During the unrest of the 1960s there was some confused understanding of this, and at that time the magic word that explained everything then going on was the word "subculture," meaning something in revolt against the dominant or imposed culture. But there turned out to be no such thing as a subculture: what was called that was invariably a sucker of mass culture, and was quickly absorbed into it. The situation was rather that what is called mass culture, supported as it is by advertising and working through advertising's control of television and the press, is really anticultural. Not because it wishes or intends to be, but because its social context is anticreative. Hence all genuine products of the creative imagination, in literature, in the other arts, in film or television, are forced by the dialectic of their social function into an adversary relationship to mass culture. In other words, in our day genuine culture has to take the form of a counter-culture. It is one of the tasks of criticism now to help mobilize it in the direction of its ultimate goal, which is the creating of a counter-environment, the opposite of the one being built by the architects of desolation.

Canada is sufficiently close to the United States to feel these mass-cultural influences as a threat to its identity, while being also sufficiently distinct from it to feel them as foreign influences. In any case the phenomena are much the same everywhere. Culturally, we are glutted with possible influences: all the resources of human space and time are available to us. But we lack the hard core of knowing what we want to use them for. Every culture is an adjoining culture, in space or time: isolated or "buried" cultures may be common enough in romance, but history and archaeology, so far as I am aware, know nothing of them. Everything of value to us has grown out of conflicts and mutual influences among individual cultures. Some cultures have arisen as spatial frontier revolts, as the cultures of Periclean Athens and Elizabethan England were frontier revolts against worlds dominated by Persia and by the Papacy and Empire respectively. Some have tried to recreate a culture in time, as the Renaissance tried to recreate late Classical culture. In our world, as we saw, most cultures grow up as decentralized enclaves in a technologically unified world, struggling for a voice of their own. All of them have had to fight against some threat to their existence, though in our day actual war only perverts the real issues. On the horizon appears the larger task of criticism for the future: to realize that our culture adjoins every other culture in time and space, to become aware of our particular cultural conditioning, and then to help in the fight against the passivity and paralysis of will that block up creative power.

80

Introduction to *A History of Communications*

1982

From the typescript in NFF, 1991, box 40, file 3, which breaks off at "social vision of a" on p. 595; the rest of the concluding paragraph is taken from the printed text in EAC, *set from an unknown typescript. A typescript of an early draft with extensive corrections is in the same file in NFF. This is the general introduction to the incomplete typescript of Harold Innis's projected* A History of Communications, *a 1200-page typescript that was left in a state somewhat between organized reader's notes and a first draft at Innis's death in 1952. (The typescript is in the University of Toronto Archives. It covers chaps. 4–11 of the projected book.) The CRTC, which was in charge of the work, planned to publish it in two or perhaps three volumes, with Frye's general introduction at the beginning of the first volume; however, in the event the book never appeared. Another introduction by Frye to the second volume, in the same file of NFF, appears in vol. 10 of CW.*

It seems only a short while ago that André Martin and Rodrigue Chiasson of the CRTC's Research Branch went, along with myself, to call on the late Mary Quayle Innis to obtain permission to edit the great block of unfinished manuscripts of Harold Innis's projected history of communications, which had been left in that state by his death. Our aim was eventual publication, so our next stop was the University of Toronto Press, which of course at that stage could do nothing but express general interest. On the way André remarked that he felt like a Renaissance humanist salvaging Classical manuscripts out of monastic libraries.

We were aware that shortly after Innis's death a group of scholars chosen by Mrs. Innis had examined the manuscript and had recommended against trying to publish it in any form beyond microfilm. But, first, the CRTC was willing to make very considerable editorial efforts to put the manuscript in publishable condition, and it is doubtful whether anywhere else in Canada one could find people who either could or would make such efforts. Those who could were mostly academics who would have found the task an impossible addition to their working schedule. Although I am listed as editor of the book, there has been a great deal of detailed and painstaking editorial work done on the manuscript which I have not and could not have done. Second, after so many years Innis was no longer a contemporary thinker but a landmark in the cultural history of Canada, and for such a figure the conception of what was publishable was radically different. So the CRTC Research Branch went ahead, although a crushing administrative load made it impossible for years to direct enough organizational time and energy into completing the task. Mr. Chiasson has paid tribute to those who encouraged the project and to those who made it possible, and I can only endorse him on the point.

I can say with some confidence, however, from having seen various stages of the manuscript in progress, that the editorial work, extensive as it is, has gone in Innis's own direction, and its effort has consistently been to bring out his own theses from the materials he used. The original manuscript contained a great deal that was not Innis but his sources, as is inevitable with an unfinished work, and naturally this feature had to be essentially retained. One would not take advantage of his death to rewrite his book, and what is here offered, I think, comes as close as is humanly possible to indicating what Innis would have wanted to do himself.

There is at least one disadvantage inherent in the whole operation, however, and it is better to be frank about it. Even if Innis had lived to complete his own work, it would not now be a contemporary work of scholarship. The work of a scholar who died thirty years ago has to be based on sources even older than that, and the information explosion since then has made many of those sources questionable or obsolete. It is, perhaps, no more than amusing to find him quoting G.G. Coulton as saying that bilingualism "implies a lack of clearness of speech and therefore of thought."[1] But there are certain areas, such as critical and cultural theory, where what was available to him can only be described as primitive. The manuscript must be read with a good deal of historical imagination in the 1980s, with the realization that whatever issues do not seem central now must have been central once, and if they were once they are still potentially so. The function of the historical imagination in reading is to change "potentially" into "actually" whenever possible.

In the preface to *The Bias of Communication* Innis remarks that he is starting with the methodological question: why do we attend to the things to which we do attend? He then says that changes in communication follow changes in the things to which we attend. I do not understand the word "follow," as it clearly seems to be Innis's view that changes in communication are involved in, or accompany, or in many cases are even the causes of, historical changes of attention. The first question relevant to Innis's own work, in any case, is rather: why was it communication to which he was brought to attend? This is primarily a historical (and more incidentally a biographical) question relating to the period around 1950. He has answered the question himself, and all we need do here is summarize him. But next there is the problem of how to incorporate him into the background and tradition of our contemporary preoccupations. That will take a good deal of critical effort still, to which the present essay can be only a minor contribution. Yet I think it is essential for an introducer of the present volume, if he is to be genuinely useful, to exploit the hindsight of thirty years, so far as his knowledge permits. Everybody interested in the subject knows that Innis was a pioneer in his own day: we need not discuss that, only the relevance of his pioneering to "the things to which we attend" a generation later.

Innis was concerned primarily with verbal communication through the written word. For such communication to flow freely in society certain things are essential. One is a cheap, accessible, and practical material medium, which turned out to be paper. Another is an alphabetical system of writing. Third is a mechanical power of reduplication, such as we have in the printing press and its later technological developments. The Chinese invented paper but not the alphabet. The Hebrews had a consonantal syllabary that was practically an alphabet, and the Greeks had a true alphabet of both consonants and vowels. But they were still dependent on scribal transmission, and paper took a long time to establish itself in the West. We have paper, an alphabet, and a printing press, but that very fact has created a new set of difficulties.

Innis began as a Canadian economic historian, studying such areas as the fur trade and the fishing industry. He learned from this study that Canadian history, Canadian imagination, and the way of Canadian life had all been profoundly affected, in many respects determined, by the fact that the Canadian economy was based on the exporting of staples to foreign markets. The last major staple was that of pulp and paper, and at the opening of *Empire and Communications* (really the beginning of the total history of which the present volume is the continuation)[2] he gives us a brief sardonic vision of the interminable churning out of written documents in British and American life through the last century, with Canadians obediently supplying the paper to write them on. But the ramifications of verbal communication were so vast that Innis found himself examining not merely the economy of exported staples but the larger question of the cultural use of the staple. Here he moved from economic history into a field where he was, in effect, taking all knowledge for his province.

Economic history demands immense assembling and patient sorting through of facts. Marshall McLuhan, in his preface to the reprinted edition of *The Bias of Communication* (1964), assimilates this technique to the "mosaic" type of discontinuous writing in which each detail is to be related to a total context as well as to the narrative sequence in which it is embedded. That is, each detail is separately symbolic of the whole argument, just as each story on a newspaper's front page is separately symbolic of the editor's notion of what should be front-page news for that day. Such a technique can be found in twentieth-century poetry, for example in the Ezra Pound *Cantos*, especially the more purely historical ones like the early Malatesta group.

Where one finds this "mosaic" writing in Innis, however, is not so much in his continuous books as in the collection of notes recently edited by William Christian as *The Idea File of Harold Adams Innis* (1980), which will be a constant and invaluable resource for the reader of this book as well. The omnivorous intellectual curiosity revealed in this work is something unique in Canadian culture, so far as I know. There cannot be many academics in any age who are so highly integrated that they can hardly have an idea on any subject whatever that is not, or may not be, or may not produce something, relevant to their scholarly work. This is scholarship as not merely a total commitment but a total way of life, and few there be that find that way. Of course such flexibility of reference is a quality of the subject as well as of the temperament of the scholar—anything may be relevant to communication. This is particularly true of the more plastic time when Innis became interested in it. In a very few years communications theory had become an academic discipline like other academic disciplines, congealing into a specialized jargon that prescribes the way one thinks about it. But for Innis communication was something more like the challenge to an author of science fiction: if there is too little left to discover in one world, explore another. Or, as e.e. cummings would say, there's a hell of a good universe next door: let's go![3] Not many scholars are attracted to such endlessly ramifying themes, however, or can sustain the Leacockian energy needed for riding madly off in all directions.[4]

The disadvantages of exploration of this sort are of course equally obvious. It is not possible for any scholar to acquire scholarly expertise in unlimited areas. Hence while much of the present work is an amassing of factual details, as in the passages dealing with the spread of paper manufacturing in Renaissance Europe, there is much of it also in which generalizations, sometimes very simplistic generalizations, are being used as though they were facts. What this primarily means is that Innis is negatively as well as positively seminal. He will always be rewarding to study, but he will also be in constant need of modification, revision, and updating.

There is a general "bias" (a word Innis uses in several senses and contexts) predisposing the societies of the past either towards time or towards space. To emphasize time is also to emphasize tradition and continuity, and time-bound societies tend to use cumbersome or expensive materials for writing—clay and stone in the Near East, parchment in the Middle Ages—and to associate writing with secrecy and elitism, the ascendancy of a priesthood or other "oligopoly" that wants to keep knowledge in its own hands. Sometimes a special hieratic language, like Latin in the Middle Ages, is employed for the same purpose. When communications acquire one or more of the three attributes of free movement mentioned above (paper, an alphabet, a mechanical reproducer of copy), they become more accessible to a wider group. More people write and more people read, and the media of communication spread more widely in space. This spatial expansion has become worldwide since the Industrial Revolution. In the background of this "bias" thesis there seems to be a lurking analogy with military history, where the stonewalling defences of a declining empire are usually destroyed by the rapid outflanking movements of the more mobile societies outside.

The general principle involved is that every ascendant class, in fact every pressure group within society, tries to establish a dominant or if possible a monopolized control over communications. Such monopolies are never permanently successful, because new techniques of communication, as well as new forms of knowledge and thought that require a different content for it, keep springing up even in the most stagnant societies. In ancient Egypt, at the very dawn of history, there was still a tension between the royal and the priestly power, of a kind that recurred in late medieval Europe between the papacy, with its claims for both spiritual and temporal control of Christendom, and the secular princes. This latter struggle eventually became absorbed into the Reformation, with the Protestants demanding wide distribution of the Bible and its translation into the vernacular languages, and such resistance as that of Pope Gregory VII in the eleventh century, pronouncing that the Bible must on no account be put into the hands of ordinary people, as they would be certain to get its meaning wrong. Whatever the theological rights and wrongs of the issue, the central feature of it, from Innis's point of view, was a struggle within communications, between the classifying of information and the dissemination of it. The latter tendency grew spectacularly with the printing press, and now "freedom of the press" is so established that it has developed a monopoly in its turn.

One factor in Innis's time and space thesis is that time-bound societies, with their emphasis on continuity and tradition and elitism, are bound to the monumental as well, to erecting vast buildings and public works that express their devotion to the spiritual and temporal authority of their times. The trouble is that, as Shelley's Ozymandias failed to discover, the monumental turns out to be surprisingly fragile. It is the verbal that has the real power of survival in time, and this power is inseparable from the spatial power of cheap and expendable material and devices for multiplication. In other words, it is only the temporary that attains a real control of time.

A famous passage in Victor Hugo's *Hunchback of Notre Dame* contrasts the David of print with the Goliath of the cathedral.[5] *Ceci tuera cela*, Hugo says, "ceci" being the printing press and "cela" monuments like Notre Dame. Innis suggests in the *Idea File* that Hugo has exaggerated the power of print, but I think the facts support Hugo. Not only are medieval cathedrals very expensive to keep in repair, but the creative architectural impulse behind them is gone. Even if fifty new cathedrals were built this year, the cathedral would still be as dead as the step pyramid, at least as an imaginative power in our culture. Every city today exhibits churches dwarfed with high-rise buildings, but the latter are so prominent because it is relatively easy to knock them down again. An even more dramatic example of the *ceci tuera cela* situation is in the Book of Jeremiah [36:20–3], where the prophet's secretary reads the prophecy from a papyrus scroll to the infuriated king of Judah, who every so often cuts off a piece of the scroll with a knife and throws it into the fire. The Book of Jeremiah still exists, but the king's palace does not. One wonders what could be left to present a real challenge to the monopoly of the written word.

It is clear that the general attitude of Innis is rooted in what is called, in a somewhat foolish phrase, old-fashioned liberalism. He thinks of the Middle Ages as a rather sleepy period (despite the fact that he was working in the same university as Etienne Gilson), and of history since the Renaissance as revolving primarily around the relation of the individual to his society. The individual's opportunity comes when the power struggles over communication reach a deadlock.

In the sixteenth century the Reformed Church regarded itself as the fulfilment of the Catholic Church, as itself the Catholic Church purified of corruptions, so that the natural tendency of the Catholic Church, if unobstructed by selfish interests, would be to expand into the Reformed framework. That did not happen: Catholic societies seldom turned Protestant except when forced to do so by their princes, and Catholicism and Protestantism remained in a simply antithetical and adversary relationship. Renaissance humanism, Cinquecento painting, and Elizabethan drama came somewhere out of the middle. Later, Communism was conceived by Marx as the logical outcome of capitalism, after capitalism had reached a certain crucial point of contradiction in which a guided revolutionary act would permit of its transformation. Nothing like that happened: Communism got established only in preindustrial societies with a weak middle class, and the two systems have remained in a simply antithetical and adversary relationship. Twentieth-century science and literature have got what benefits they could from the absence of a final victory for either side. We may call this process of imaginative wriggling out of a power struggle by Innis's own phrase, "the strategy of culture."

One looks in every period of history for a *tertium quid*, for some cultural element in the middle that escapes from the competing pressure groups by having something of its own to communicate that neutralizes the conflicts of interest. For Innis there seem to be three aspects of this *tertium quid* of particular importance. One, as indicated above, is the creative and imaginative culture a society produces in the middle of all its power struggles: we shall return to this aspect in a moment. Another is law.

Law has always been an instrument of power for ascendant classes, and a great deal of law consists of various ways of rationalizing the existing power structure. It is interesting that one of the most incisive quotations in this book is from the sixteenth-century French jurist Jean Bodin. "It rarely happens, that any parties, even the best and purest, will, in the strife to retain or recover their ascendancy, weaken themselves by a scrupulous examination of the reasoning or the testimony which is to serve their purpose." Bodin should know, for he is said to have had one of the finest legal minds in history, and was also both a strong advocate of absolutism and a gullible and vicious witch-hunter.

At the same time law, often against the will of the lawmakers, has evolved a technique of guaranteeing rights to both sides of a dispute. This quality in law was expanded into a theory of social contract, in fact an entire social philosophy, by Edmund Burke. Nobody could have cared less about British freedom broadening slowly down from precedent to precedent than the barons who forced King John to sign the Magna Carta, but they started something that carried on with its own momentum. This tendency is much older than King John: Sir Henry Maine's *Ancient Law* is one of Innis's favourite and most frequently quoted books, and he makes a good deal of the interplay of "bookright" and "folkright": law as a written code and law as partly a matter of oral tradition. Keeping a balance between them has been a feature of the more empirical Anglo-Saxon tradition of law, in contrast to the revolutionary American and French procedures of starting with a written constitution and proceeding deductively from it.

It would be nonsense to think of any aspect of law as being in any way sacrosanct, autonomous, or detached from social influences or historical conditions. But to think of it as nothing but an instrument of social power would be equally wrong: it still contains an objective quality that lifts it clear of that. An island is certainly conditioned by the fact that it is surrounded by water, but still it is an island and not water, even when flooded by the storms of tyranny. There can hardly be a society that does not at least pretend to provide some legal rights for its citizens, and when a totalitarian state resorts to arbitrary violence it is still breaking its own laws.

The maintaining of the inner objectivity of law, therefore, is one of the ways by which the strategy of culture attempts to keep something going in society that is not simply a conflict of pressure groups, which are always and by nature anticultural. The language is stronger than the language Innis uses, but I think it reflects his view, that the alternative to the strategy of culture is simply systematized mob rule. What Innis says about law in the present book is supplemented by the third essay in *Changing Concepts of Time* (1952), on Roman law and the British Empire.

Another aspect of the cultural *tertium quid* is the objectivity of scholarly and scientific knowledge, which today is mainly institutionalized in the university. Once again, keeping the objectives of the university alive in society is part of the strategy of culture, part of the fight for human freedom. Again, it would be nonsense to regard the university simply as a secure bastion of such freedom in a hysterical world. But it does have some right to be called that, and it would be equally wrong to join the simple-minded chorus of those, many of them within the university, who maintain that objectivity in knowledge is a mere illusion.

Of course the very structure of the university, with its hierarchies and protocols, revives the "time-bound" tendency to emphasize tradition and continuity and the confining of knowledge to an elite. Innis is deeply attached to the university in modern society, and he is not merely aware but sharply critical of its tendency to become a small-scale monopoly of communication in its turn, blocking new openings of knowledge by declaring that they are a distraction to the existing scholarly structure. But he has little use for political activism within the university, of the kind at least where liberalism and concerned citizenship cross the line into bourgeois masochism. Many intellectuals have a constant itch to try to help turn the wheel of history, to support social movements that are going in what they feel are the right directions, to show that in the power struggles of history ideas do after all count for something. They do, but for Innis not in that context: this kind of activism is what Julien Benda called, in a book Innis often refers to, the *trahison des clercs*, the betrayal, by the intellectuals, of their own standards in the interest of some form of mass movement. The university helps society by communicating with it on a solid two-way street in which, if the university is accountable to society, society is also accountable to the university. At least, that seems to be the implication of such essays as the one on adult education which forms an appendix to *The Bias of Communication*.

The history of science gives us perhaps the clearest examples of how an element of culture, springing from the concerns of society and conditioned by them, nonetheless may acquire an authority of its own that rises above its conditioning. Thus the new astronomy of Galileo's time struggled through to a heliocentric view of the solar system although the religious and political concerns of society demanded a geocentric one, and the new biology of Darwin's time eventually established an evolutionary view of the order of nature in spite of the agonized protests of those who felt that without a divine creation there could be no real source of authority. Similarly in scholarship, where the accepted picture of a subject may be challenged by another that explains more facts, or facts previously inexplicable. The conflict of authority resulting is entirely within the area of that scholarship, or at least the effective part of it is.

It is more difficult to see that the painter, the writer, the creative artist in whatever field, also makes technical discoveries in that field, and that the serious writer or painter owes a loyalty to the authority of his art as well as to the concerns of his social patrons. When we look at the great works of art of the past, we know that they are products of a society as full of tyranny and folly as any other, and in fact may even reflect many of their contemporary social evils. But they have established their authority within their own area, while the tyranny and folly have vanished into nothingness. There are several reasons why it is more difficult to recognize such authority in the arts. The arts are weaker and less organized than the universities, hence more vulnerable to social bullying, and more directly dependent on patronage: "they that live to please must please to live," as Samuel Johnson said.[6] Then again, critics of the arts, whose function it is in part to establish the authority of the arts they study, have tended to assume that the real authority belongs to them and the judgments they make about it.

Even allowing for Innis's vacuum-cleaner techniques of quotation, it is still startling to find in *The Bias of Communication* a remark of such stupefying imbecility as one ascribed to Sir James Mackintosh: "After art had been toiling in India, in Persia, and in Egypt to produce monsters, beauty and grace were discovered in Greece."[7] One point here is that the statement is roughly contemporary with the introduction of the Elgin marbles into England (Mackintosh died in 1832), and hence in its day would have been considered a cultivated and perceptive thing to say. I find the remark very significant, however, because it points up the failure of the critical function so dramatically. The context is that of the nineteenth-century assumption, to which Innis recurs more than once, that great periods of art come very rarely and last only a very short time. There is some truth in this, from some points of view, but nine-tenths of the assumption is based not on the qualities of art but on the attention span of critics. Such provincialism in art criticism comes from the exaggeration of the importance of value judgments, which are always expressions of the dominant ideology of the time, and so tell us much more about the concerns and anxieties of that time than they do about the art. It is only when we begin to adopt more flexible standards of judgment, and realize that art is there to be studied and understood, not pronounced on, that its authority is recognized and it becomes another aspect of the *tertium quid* of culture.

As remarked above, Innis's earlier books were on specifically Canadian topics, and if he had moved to Chicago, as he could have done, his social vision would have had a different perspective, however similar in general outline. He realized the importance of the east-west Laurentian axis, the thrust up the river to the Great Lakes, fanning out from there into the far West and the North, that makes sense of the map of Canada, and accounts for its having a political development distinct from that of the United States. The Laurentian axis has vanished into the past, but its cultural consequences have not. An economy founded on the export of staples leaves behind it a profoundly colonial mentality, proud of its natural resources but very diffident about its human ones, conditioned to accept somewhere else as the place where the main action is.

Several of Innis's essays about the growing cultural monopoly of print in Britain and the United States during the last two centuries allude to Canadian difficulties in taking part in this. (I am speaking now of English Canada: the French problem, though in some ways more difficult, is more clear-cut.) Without major publishers, except those controlled from outside the country, a Canadian, if he is to live as a writer, must write for a mainly non-Canadian audience, like Stephen Leacock or Mazo de la Roche. He must also conform to the conventions of these larger markets. Innis has a footnote on a Canadian writer who was told by a prospective British publisher to expand his manuscript and by a prospective American one to shorten it. Canadians, mutters Innis, ought to make good accordion-players. The essay of Innis that is specifically called "The Strategy of Culture" is largely a response to the Massey Report, which recommended setting up an agency to subsidize and encourage Canadian culture without trying to direct or control it.[8] Such a procedure aligns itself very well with the strategy of culture by recognizing that the arts have an essential authority in society, that society has some responsibility for recognizing that authority, and that Canada faces exceptional difficulties in trying to find a place for its own culture.

Introduction to *A History of Communications* 593

We are now back to the question raised earlier. The technical achievements of the printed word today have made it an unchallenged medium of communications. This means a mass monopoly, the "propaganda" that we decry so much in totalitarian countries, without much noticing the effectiveness of a slightly different kind of propaganda in our own. Where are we to turn to find a liberating agency from this monopoly? At the beginning of *Empire and Communications* Innis refers, with a vagueness and imprecision unusual in him, to the "oral tradition" as something to set over against the monopoly of the printed word. His regard for the oral tradition is partly an appreciation of the metaphorical vividness of folk poetry and of Homer. He took an interest in the work of Milman Parry on the close relation of Homer to the half-improvised formulaic oral poetry still extant in Slavic countries,[9] and he also refers to the parallel work of Eric Havelock, though Havelock's *Preface to Plato* (1963) is later than Innis.[10] It is partly also, I think, an unconscious use of something in his religious background. The world's great religious teachers tend to avoid writing and keep to direct discourse, leaving the writing down of their teachings to secretaries. The claim of oral authority made by Jesus ("but I say unto you") seems especially to have impressed Innis. But how can oral communication be revived in a world like ours, except with the aid of mechanical reproduction? Innis knew very well how the devil had inspired Hitler to use the radio as a means of mass control, a fact Hitler recorded in *Mein Kampf* with all his usual contempt for the people he was bamboozling. So, not unnaturally, Innis adds a footnote on Hitler explaining that that is not at all the kind of thing he is talking about. But what is he talking about? Oral communication in its original form belongs to an ancient world that can never come back.

We are reminded here of Marshall McLuhan and of Innis's interest in McLuhan's *The Mechanical Bride* (1951). McLuhan in turn has described his own major books as a "footnote" to Innis's investigations: these books developed a large-scale revolutionary thesis about the displacing of linear and time-bound print by the simultaneous many-sided impact of the electronic media. For McLuhan this was primarily a psychological difference: still later he tried to suggest that it was a physiological one as well. What is disappointing about McLuhan's work, however, is the absence of any clear sense of the kind of social context in which electronic media function. Television in particular is geared to the rhythms of the social economy: however striking the psychological difference between its impact and that of print, the absence of any real social difference neutralizes nearly all of it. The usual television program, as the CRTC keeps rather irritably reminding Canadian broadcasters, is simply a talking journal, as the phrase "magazine format" indicates, a way of conveying the same words and images for the same social purposes. McLuhan felt, at least at first, that the electronic media would bring in a social revolution so pervasive that one could describe its social context only in terms of the future. But, as with other prophetic revolutionary theories, the existing power structures have refused to wither away on schedule.

I think "oral tradition" is being used by Innis as a symbol for something that he failed to identify, and if I venture a suggestion about it, it is because some aspects of the question have clarified a good deal since Innis's death, in Canada as elsewhere. Within the last twenty years a quantitative explosion has taken place in Canadian literature (and in other fields as well) which amounts to a qualitative change. In short, there is such a thing as Canadian literature now. But, on further examination, it seems to have developed a strongly regional quality, as though the creative imagination needed a smaller and more coherent unit than the vast sprawl of "Canada" affords. In this, Canada has followed the rhythm of American literature, which has always been strongly regional, so that we learn about American literature by adding together Mississippi writers, New England writers, Middle Western writers, and so on. It looks as though the "counter-culture" we used to hear so much about is really the "strategy of culture" itself, decentralizing where politics centralizes, differentiating where technology makes everything uniform, giving articulateness and human meaning to the small community where economy turns it into a mere distributing centre, constantly moving in a direction opposite to that of the political and economic tendencies of history.

If this counter-movement of culture to political and economic developments is true of space, it is likely to be true of time as well. Innis's "time-bound" societies are obsessed with continuity, with handing down the authority of institutions to new generations with as little change as possible. The arts too often follow an established convention closely, even slavishly; but as time goes on, a greater variety of traditions appears. Nothing is more striking today than the expanded variety of influences available to the artist. In this situation culture tends to move backward in time, away from the merely continuous, and towards the constant recapturing and rediscovery of the imaginative life in neglected tradition. It continues to do so even when "time-bound" institutions are replaced or supplemented by "spatial" or marketplace monopolies. We have Mackintosh in one era asserting that everyone produced monsters in the ancient world except the Greeks, and fifty years later we have Gauguin speaking of the Greek tradition as "the great error."[11] The second statement is quite as silly as the first one, but indicates the variety of responses involved.

In the present book there is a good deal of data about the way in which the printing press established a market, with Renaissance humanists using it to provide scholarly editions of the Classics, despite what one would think would be the economic impossibility of doing so. They were fighting according to the directives of the strategy of culture, in the opposite direction from the tendencies of the market. Today, apart from our writers and painters and other artists, there are many profoundly creative people in film, radio, and television who are continuing the same fight. The evocation of the phrase "oral tradition" thus begins to make sense as indicating the headwaters of tradition, the end of the recreating backward movement in time that, in all forms of creation, brings the past to life as a new and enlarged form of present experience.

I hope this introduction has done something at least to show that the present book, for all its often bewildering masses of detail and its many outmoded sources, is still an integral part of a social vision of a scope and comprehensiveness unparalleled in Canadian culture. Such a *Nachlass* [legacy] would be, I think, well worth publishing if for no other reason than to indicate the proportions of the whole conception. Innis was always a difficult and sometimes a dull writer, and he was not interested in exploring the resources of rhetoric. He often seems to feel that where the facts do not speak for themselves, one should be silent. But, of course, facts do not speak: it is only the ordering and arranging of them that speaks, and the editorial effort that has gone into this book has been directed towards giving it its author's real voice. There are limits, as explained, to what can be done in this way. But in looking through the present volume, along with its successors and the books completed in the author's lifetime, one is often impelled to echo Goethe, when examining the interpolated and corrupt text that is all we have left to us of Marlowe's *Faustus*: "How greatly it was all planned."[12]

81

The Chancellor's Message

Spring 1982

From Acta Victoriana, *106 (Spring 1982): 9. Frye's message was the first article in a special number of* Acta *celebrating the centenary of the birth of Pratt with archival material and recollections of present and former staff. Typescripts are in NFF, 1988, box 47, file 5, and box 48, file 4.*

It is a bit of a shock to find oneself observing the centenary of someone who has been a teacher, friend, and colleague over so large a part of one's own lifetime. But then Ned was never in a hurry: his life had the leisurely rhythm of the scholar who takes a long time to mature, rather than the hectic rhythm more typical of the poet, who so often produces his best work early in life. Pratt was forty when *Newfoundland Verse* appeared, and had already soaked up several academic disciplines: psychology, theology, English literature. Very little of this was obvious in *Newfoundland Verse*: what was obvious was the sudden clearing of vision, the sense that a Canadian poet was actually looking at Canada instead of idealizing it or dreaming about fairyland. With the hindsight of another half-century, we can see that what he was really doing was restoring the native Canadian tradition of bleak narrative and austere lyric that, even yet, are the primary modes of the imaginative reaction to Canada.

Knowing Ned as a colleague, with his hospitality and his absentminded kindliness, his unobtrusive work in the college as a teacher, and his unfailing sense of proportion, one found it hard to realize what was going on in his mind: visions of "pliocene Armageddons," of ships torn to pieces by storms and rocks, of Brébeuf at the stake bellowing his Master's unconquerable death-song, of steel-clad dragons huffing and puffing through mountains and over prairies. He was a pure Romantic, not an idealizing Romantic, but a Romantic who accepted heroism as a poet's theme. A Newfoundlander recently asked me if Ned ever told Newfie jokes. I said no: their vogue was later than his time, and in any case he would not have liked them because they are mainly ironic, and Ned was not an ironist. Like his colleague John Robins, he liked the tall tale, the expression of the undying Paul Bunyan titanism in the human spirit. Even when writing of the wreck of the *Titanic*, his eye is not on the incredible bungles that made it such a disaster: it is on the extra dimension of dignity that facing death gives to human life. Centenary or no centenary, Ned is as much alive now as he ever was, and his presence is as much a part of the community he served as it was when he was visible.

82

E.J. Pratt

25 November 1982

From a tape in E.J. Pratt Library (also available in the CBC radio archives), transcribed by Monika Lee and slightly edited to remove oral characteristics. Frye's lecture was arranged by "The Intellectual Life Committee of Victoria College" and given at the college. It was introduced by his colleague, professor emeritus Christopher Love.

I might begin, perhaps, with a picture which hangs in our dining room and which is a portrait of Ned Pratt by Barker Fairley. It is a very early portrait of Barker's, done around the 1940s. It presents Ned in middle life, and it is a rather sombre and even a grim face, and you would never recognize it as the same person that you have a photograph of in the *Collected Poems* with that genial, welcoming, and perhaps rather wistful face. Somebody said to Barker once, "that picture doesn't look very much like Ned." Barker said, "No. It doesn't look like Ned, but it looks like the man who wrote Ned's poems." Well that, perhaps, starts you off with one of the difficulties in talking about Ned, the personal legends, which are so very vital to us here at Victoria, and the author of *The Collected Poems of E.J. Pratt*. He emerged from Newfoundland and his original training was training for the ministry. He didn't go on with that. It is possible, as some of his critics insist, that there was a crisis of faith. It could very well have been, because crises of faith were extremely fashionable at that time. But perhaps the crisis was less in his personal beliefs than of what he could say to a congregation, and it seems clear that, while he was a teacher, he was not naturally a preacher, nor was he interested in the kind of administrative work that would involve. At the same time, there was a growing shift in religious thinking at Victoria at the time. Both the Higher Criticism and the doctrine of evolution had made their way very deeply into Victoria, and Ned was also interested and much influenced by Thomas Hardy, among others, and had learned from him that the popular god of Providence, the god projected into the sky as the president and general manager of the corporation of the universe, was not a very convincing-looking deity. There are many poems of Hardy's which indicate how extremely inefficient God is, if you think of him as the manager of the universe, and of how much you have to use implicit faith rather than reason. So he went from theology, after writing a work on St. Paul, to psychology or what the University of Toronto, at the time, was convinced was psychology, and that provided him largely with the mechanical metaphors of Wundt, which he disliked,[1] and later on with the hydraulic metaphors of Freud. He learned from his training in philosophy a good deal about stimulus and response, which was useful to him later in his communication poems. Otherwise, he seems to have had relatively little use for his career in that field. He was then appointed to the Department of English by Pelham Edgar on a basis which would now be regarded as heretical, that is the basis of personal knowledge. If you can imagine what would be thought now of a chairman of an English department who would appoint a demonstrator in psychology in his late thirties, who had published virtually nothing, on the ground that he would not only make an excellent teacher of English, but a distinguished poet, you would naturally assume that he was insane. But Pelham Edgar was not insane, and exercised the same curious ESP with regard to Pratt that he did later with a number of his students.

At Victoria there was, of course, the legend which grew up very quickly of the absent-minded duffer. It was readily accepted, because poets and professors are supposed to be that, and Ned, I think, cultivated it deliberately, because it enabled him to carry on his own schedule in his own way. The people who accepted the legend of his incompetence usually did not know that he was carrying on a very complex schedule, social and teaching and writing, without any secretarial assistance at all, and that he built up this legend as a means of getting out of the enormous resources for wasting one's time that the modern university can provide. And everyone loved to tell the story of how he drove his car down the middle of the street, stopped at a red light in front of a streetcar, got out of the car to talk to a friend on the sidewalk, walked down to the college with him, and remembered that he had left his car in the middle of traffic later. That, if my information is correct, was something which actually did happen to Professor Norman DeWitt in the Department of Classics, but it was, of course, instantly transferred to Ned because he attracted that kind of story as honey attracts flies. His hospitality again was a legendary feature of Victoria life. It was rather touching, I think, that that long table in the senior common room at Burwash had, at that time, a place on the end, and that that place was left vacant for Ned to sit at long after it was clear that he would never return to that table, because of the general feeling that Ned could not sit anywhere except at the head of a table. His hospitality, I think, had something to do with a feeling that the community, which is so precious an asset of the university, was beginning to weaken as the city grew larger and social relations became more impersonal.

He was also a legendary soft touch for panhandlers of various kinds and, there again, Ned's liking for people was so genuine that I should not be surprised if he felt a trifle guilty when he was approached by people to whom he actually was indifferent. In any case, there used to be a progression of people up the staircase of Victoria College where they had the choice of turning left at Ned's office or turning right at Professor De Beaumont of the Department of French, who would fix them with a cold stare and say, "Of course you have received your authorization from the college office to canvas me?" If Ned had adopted that excellent strategy, he would have been considerably less out of pocket.

Ned was, of course, a popular poet, who wanted to be liked. I would not say he was the best reader of his own poetry, but he was a poet who wanted and needed the direct response of an audience. He was a pioneer in something which actually grew up after his time, the revival of poetry which is read aloud to a listening audience. At the time when he began to write poetry, poetry had got very badly bogged down in the book, and the features of oral poetry are still quite discernible in Ned's work. That meant, of course, confining himself to Canada and isolating himself, at least for a long time, from the more fashionable poets in the rest of the world. His poems entered Canadian high schools and he helped to introduce a love of poetry to a great many young Canadians, but I can remember the mixture of amusement and contempt with which a professor at an American university asked me if I really thought that Pratt was an important poet or was this simply a patriotic gesture. But he took his own time, and his reputation has, in the course of time, taken care of itself. So we are not surprised that there is something almost hostile about the private poet who retreats from the world around him, as in the opening of *Still Life*:

> To the poets who have fled
> To pools where little breezes dusk and shiver,
> Who need still life to deliver
> Their souls of their songs,
> We offer roses blanched of red
> In the Orient gardens,
> With April lilies to limn
> On the Japanese urns—
> And time, be it said,
> For a casual hymn
> To be sung for the hundred thousand dead
> In the mud of the Yellow River.   [ll. 1–12]

It was characteristic of Pratt that he could never forget the hundred thousand dead in the river or any other of the massacres and disasters of contemporary history.

There is also a certain edginess in an early poem called *The Epigrapher* where he is speaking of someone who devotes his life to the deciphering of dead languages, certainly an honourable enough career, but the tone, which is not typical of Pratt, nevertheless does indicate the energy with which it might have been sent in a different direction. He says of this epigrapher

> And thus he trod life's narrow way—
> His soul as peaceful as a river—
> His understanding heart all day
> Kept faithful to a stagnant liver.   [ll. 36–9]

Somehow or another the resonance of that phrase, "his understanding heart," really makes that quatrain for me.

He wrote relatively little in free verse, the most notable free verse poem being the one called *Silences*. He stuck to what most contemporary poets in the thirties had decided was no longer poetic material, the octosyllabic couplet and the iambic pentameter, blank verse, and other standard metrical forms which are the only forms that it is possible to use for narrative. The use of narrative form itself, of course, was very much out of fashion in his own generation. I suppose the poem on the *Roosevelt* and the *Antinoe* is the finest straight piece of story-telling in all his work, but the narrative is a form where you get your best effects from understatement; that is, if you have a real story to tell, the poet who knows how to make the flat statements that belong to the story and then get out of the way of his story is the one who succeeds in the narrative genre. And hence you get the extraordinary starkness of *Behind the Log*, which simply follows a convoy to Murmansk during the war with about half of the ships sunk on the way and that is really the story. There is no metaphysical comment, no introduction of either fatality or expressions of patriotism; it is simply the story of this convoy.

W.H. Auden has remarked, in connection with Homer's catalogue of ships, that if we really like catalogues and lists of names in poetry, it is probably a sign that our interest in poetry is a serious one,[2] and one can think of poets like Whitman, who are otherwise so different from Pratt, who have recognized the importance of the catalogue as an element in verse. That is the way in which Pratt conveys the sense of the universality of the gathering together of the demoralized British at the time of the escape from Dunkirk:

> A Collingwood came from Newcastle-on-Tyne,
> Trewlawney and Grenville of the Cornish Line,
> And Raleigh and Gilbert from the Devon Seas
> With a Somerset Blake. They met at the quays—
> McCluskey, Gallagher, Joe Millard,
> Three riveters red from Dumbarton Yard,
> And Peebles of Paisley, a notary clerk,
> Two joiners from Belfast, Mahaffy and Burke,
> Blackstone and Coke of Lincoln's Inn,
> A butcher from Smithfield, Toby Quinn,
> Jonathan Wells, a Sheffield bricklayer,
> Tim Thomas of Swansea, a borough surveyor,
> Jack Wesley, a stoker, by way of South Shields,
> And Snodgrass and Tuttle from Giles-in-the-Fields.   [*Dunkirk*, ll. 114–27]

It goes on and on, and the building up this slow accumulation of all of these various heterogeneous names gives you the impact of the kind of thing Dunkirk was in a way that I doubt anything else would do as effectively.

It is a familiar fact about Canada that it has always been obsessed by communications. The building of a railway to the Pacific was not just a building of a railway to the Pacific; it was also a national neurosis, an obsession. The sense of communication as really the key to the history of Canada can be found in the works of Harold Innis and Donald Creighton, which start out with things like the fur trade and the deep exploration of the waterways through canoes and progress through the building of canals and railways and so on to radar and underseas communication. This is one of the things that Pratt is fascinated by, and he is one of the most successful poets of the twentieth century, I think, in rendering the language of technology, in which so much of our emotional life is bound up, whether we realize it or not. His poem on the railway, *The 6000*, for example, ends:

> A lantern flashed out a command,
> A bell was ringing as a hand
> Clutched at a throttle, and the bull,
> At once obedient to the pull,
> Began with bellowing throat to lead
> By slow accelerating speed
> Six thousand tons of caravan
> Out to the spaces—there to toss
> The blizzard from his path across
> The prairies of Saskatchewan.   [ll. 84–93]

It's one of the finest railway poems that I know, and he is also fascinated by the way in which technology seems to repeat the rhythms of past evolution in nature, the ways that dinosaurs and pterodactyls and the like seem to be recreated in the submarines and airplanes of our own day. In a poem called *The Dying Eagle*, for example, there is a vision at the end of the passing of the empire of the peaks from the eagle to the airplane:

> So evening found him on the crags again,
> This time with sloven shoulders
> And nerveless claws.
> Dusk had outridden the sunset by an hour
> To haunt his unhorizoned eyes.
> And soon his flock flushed with the chase

> Would be returning, threading their glorious curves
> Up through the crimson archipelagoes
> Only to find him there—
> Deaf to the mighty symphony of wings,
> And brooding
> Over the lost empire of the peaks. [ll. 70–81]

And it is hardly necessary to remind you that one of his most celebrated poems is *The Cachalot*, a poem about a whale. Canada is deeply preoccupied with whales. There was an anthology produced a few years ago called *Whale Sound*, and practically every Canadian poet you've ever heard of is in it.

At the same time, Pratt realized that communication moves from the silent and mechanical forms, like waterways, to the articulate communication of the human consciousness, and that that has its climax in words as an instrument of communication. You would expect a poet to have a horror of the kind of disease of debased language which is so often employed in political and other circles. In *The New Organon*, he is speaking of a conference held in 1937 about disarmament, and he says,

> But flaws were hidden in the predicates,
> And in the pips of the adverbials,
> And the rhetorical adjectives
> Assumed the protective colouring
> Of the great cats against the jungle grass . . . [ll. 7–11]

That is, the use of words for something that words should never be used to do is what emerges there. Similarly, at the beginning of *Dunkirk*:

> Appeasement is in its grave: it sleeps well.
> The mace had spiked the parchment seals
> And pulverized the hedging *ifs and wherefores*,
> The wheezy adverbs, the gutted modifiers.
> Churchill and Bevin have the floor,
> Whipping snarling nouns and action-verbs
> Out of their lairs in the lexicon,
> Bull-necked *adversatives* that bit and clawed,
> An age before gentility was cubbed. [ll. 7–15]

But behind the social and political use of words, there is, of course, the whole process of human work and human energy. The anonymous worker is the hero of *Towards the Last Spike*. It is the gangs who build the railway who represent the heroism of that particular kind, but behind the workers are the commanders who pronounce the word of command. This poem gives a great deal of its attention to the Parliamentary debates, which result in the countermanding of these orders, and, in the course of this, the political leaders, chiefly Macdonald and Blake, and then later the leaders of the building of the railway itself, like Van Horne, begin to swell to something like titanic size. Here is his description of that rather nervous little man, Blake, who was the Liberal leader of the House of Commons at the time:

> The odour of the bills had blown his gorge.
> His appetite, edged by a moral hone,
> Could surfeit only on the Verities. [ll. 275-7]

It's a most extraordinary description, I think, of the kind of debate that you might read any day still in the morning paper. In two of his fantasies, *The Witches' Brew* and *The Great Feud*, there is the same general scheme, a tremendous brawl, in which one immensely destructive force emerges called "the cat from Zanzibar" in the one and "Tyrannosaurus Rex" in the other, and the scheme of *The Fable of the Goats* is not very dissimilar. He refused to reprint *The Fable of the Goats* in the second edition of his poetry, but I don't think that the texture of it is really inferior to the other poems, although the general scheme of the poem is perhaps a bit forced, as he himself came to think. But what impresses one about such a poem as *The Great Feud* is the almost childlike delight in collecting words and shooting the whole resources of his vocabulary....[3]

The thing is that the story of *The Great Feud*, which is pure fantasy, is not a turning away from life or the facts of evolution or anything of that kind. What it does is to set up a rich texture of words and that texture of words manages to convey the inner energy, which is what I suppose any poet would feel in contemplating the whole process of evolution. It's that sense of inner energy, which is not clouded up by reflections about the grimness of the struggle to survive and so forth, which lets the humour get through in Pratt. There's a nineteenth-century Canadian narrative poet, Charles Heavysege, whose name was, unfortunately, most appropriate. What he wrote showed a great deal of poetic ability, but again he was obsessed by the grimness of nature, the terror and fear that it inspired— "Nature, red in tooth and claw"[4]—and his concentration on that means that his poetry is much more monotonous in texture. It suffers from what Eliot calls "a dissociation of sensibility."[5] Not only are Canadians interested in all matters having to do with communication, but obviously for a poet whose imaginative world was formed in Newfoundland, themes of navigation and also of shipwreck would be central. When the *Titanic* sank, there were responses both from Hardy and from Joseph Conrad. Hardy wrote a poem about Fate and Conrad wrote some furiously angry essays, in which he drew on his own experience in the seas, to say what utter damn fools the people in charge of the *Titanic* were, how they seemed to have aimed deliberately at the iceberg in order to prove to themselves that the ship was unsinkable, which, of course, no ship can ever be.[6] In Pratt's treatment of the story of the *Titanic*, he is obviously impressed by the fatality which it involved, and he says so in his prose introduction to it, but the fatality again he sees as a projection of the human hubris, the human self-complacency, which made the tragedy both fatal and, at the same time, utterly unnecessary. Sandra Djwa, in her book on Pratt, has pointed out that, in the story of the lifeboats coming to take off the women and children, there is a curious ambiguity in the way Pratt describes the various people there.[7] It is not simply the melodramatic emergence of heroism and sacrifice. He speaks, for example, of Isidor and Ida Straus:

> At the sixteenth—a woman wrapped her coat
> Around her maid and placed her in the boat;
> Was ordered in but seen to hesitate
> At the gunwale, and more conscious of her pride
> Than of her danger swiftly took her fate
> With open hands, and without show of tears
> Returned unmurmuring to her husband's side;
> *"We've been together now for forty years,*
> *Whither you go, I go."*
>   A boy of ten,
> Ranking himself within the class of men,
> Though given a seat, made up his mind to waive
> The privilege of his youth and size, and piled
> The inches on his stature as he gave
> Place to a Magyar woman and her child.   [ll. 859–72]

That just teeters on the verge of being sentimental, but it isn't, because there are phrases like "more conscious of her pride/Than of her danger," and the reflection of the boy that, in a situation where the boys and the men are separated, he has joined the men. In other words, it is not a melodramatic situation. These are human beings and their motivations are as mixed and obscure to themselves as human motivations always are.

I have spoken of the conception of evolution as something which was naturally very much in the air at the time that Pratt was a student. Pratt renders this in his poetry as something which has gone through various levels, rising finally to human consciousness, and is now a spiritual process, which can carry on only through the suffering and the endurance of human beings. That is the theme of a poem, *The Highway*:

> What aeons passed without a count or name,
> Before the cosmic seneschal,
> Succeeding with a plan
> Of weaving stellar patterns from a flame,
> Announced at his high carnival
> An orbit—with Aldebaran!
>
> And when the drifting years had sighted land,
> And hills and plains declared their birth
> Amid volcanic throes,
> What was the lapse before the marshal's hand
> Had found a garden on the earth,
> And led forth June with her first rose?
>
> And what the gulf between that and the hour,
> Late in the simian-human day,
> When Nature kept her tryst
> With the unfoldment of the star and flower—
> When in her sacrificial way
> Judaea blossomed with her Christ!
>
> But what made *our* feet miss the road that brought
> The world to such a golden trove,
> In our so brief a span?
> How may we grasp again the hand that wrought
> Such light, such fragrance, and such love,
> O star! O rose! O Son of Man?

That is, the process of evolution has produced what, in the Middle Ages, was called the primate at various levels of existence: the rose among flowers, the Christ among humanity. From here on, the upward course of evolution is the course which is taken by Brébeuf the martyr, dying under torture from the Iroquois.

In the poem called *The Truant*, the representative of mankind stands in front of the great Panjandrum, that is, the power of nature, who is really the devil disguised as God, and hurls defiance in his teeth. He finally swears by the rood that he will not join the unconscious and mechanical dance of atoms, which is all that the Panjandrum stands for. What is not evolving in that sense, what is not going through the suffering and endurance of conscious beings, is simply a mechanical repetition, which is the basis of the evolutionary movement, but is not taking on any form as it goes. One gets the contrast between the two in the very first poem in his *Collected Poems, Newfoundland*:

> Here the tides flow,
> And here they ebb;
> Not with that dull, unsinewed tread of waters
> Held under bonds to move
> Around unpeopled shores—
> Moon-driven through a timeless circuit
> Of invasion and retreat;
> But with a lusty stroke of life
> Pounding at stubborn gates,
> That they might run
> Within the sluices of men's hearts,
> Leap under throb of pulse and nerve,
> And teach the sea's strong voice
> To learn the harmonies of new floods,
> The peal of cataract,
> And the soft wash of currents
> Against resilient banks,
> Or the broken rhythms from old chords
> Along dark passages
> That once were pathways of authentic fires.   [ll. 1–20]

There is the meaningless, mechanical repetition of the water pounding on the shore. There is also the unceasing energy that reappears in the human bloodstream and in the forms of organic life that succeed it. In human life, this mechanical repetition carries on in the mechanical ferocity of the Iroquois in seventeenth-century Canada, in the Mongols sweeping across the Steppes of Asia, and in the Nazis in modern Europe, and Pratt is quick to point out how little evolution there has been in certain aspects of human existence:

> The snarl Neanderthal is worn
> Close to the smiling Aryan lips,
> The civil polish of the horn
> Gleams from our praying fingertips. [From *Stone to Steel*, ll. 5–8]

This is a theme that recurs frequently in Pratt. It comes again in the poem about the prize cat which suddenly pounces on a bird, and in the poem *Silences*, where the silent struggles under the sea of big fish eating little fish are the pattern for a great deal of human existence afterwards.

I hardly need to read the famous passage from *Brébeuf* about the driving force of Brébeuf's courage and endurance as coming from the two right-angled boards hung on a Jewish hill, and the conclusion of *The Truant* is something that I cannot read in public, but there is a less well known poem, the poem called *The Mystic*, which I think conveys the sense of the life that goes on building itself up. This process becomes increasingly painful as life becomes more conscious, because the suffering of a conscious being is presumably more acute than that of an unconscious being. In *The Mystic* Pratt says,

> Where do you bank such fires as can transmute
> This granite-fact intransigence of life,
> Such proud irenic faith as can refute
> The upstart logic of this world of strife—
> Its come-and-go of racial dust, its strum
> Of windy discords from the seven seas,
> Its scream of fifes and din of kettle-drum
> That lead the march towards our futurities?
> The *proof*, that slays the reason, has no power
> To stem your will, corrode your soul—though lime
> Conspire with earth and water to devour
> The finest cultures from the lust of slime;
> Though crumbled Tartar hordes break through their sod
> To blow their grit into the eyes of God.

The mystic becomes the person with the certainty which is transfigured faith, because he no longer believes, he merely knows. He no longer wishes to strive, he merely does so. The fact that the evidence is all against him, that death seems everywhere to be so infinitely stronger than life, does not alter the fact that life is still with us for all its precariousness and its fragility, and that it will outlast death, just as, in a different category of existence altogether, death outlasts life.

83

Margaret Eleanor Atwood

14 June 1983

Speech for the conferring of the honorary degree of Doctor of Letters by the University of Toronto. From the typescript in NFF, 1988, box 48, file 1.

It is now some years since a reporter referred to Margaret Atwood as the reigning queen of Canadian letters, and there is no question yet of abdication. Born in Ottawa and growing up in Toronto, in an academic family, she took her first degree here, at Victoria College. Principal Johnston, on my right, was a classmate.[1] She then went to Harvard for graduate work, and began a thesis on nineteenth-century Romantic fiction, under the supervision of Professor Jerome Buckley, an earlier graduate of Victoria. I imagine that by now doctoral theses are more likely to be written on her than by her, but she showed an original and independent interest in writers of off-beat and "Gothic" romances, such as Rider Haggard, that is reflected in some of her own fictional techniques, notably perhaps in *Lady Oracle*.

She had begun to write in her undergraduate days at Victoria, and it was not long before she emerged as one of the most brilliant, distinctive, and photogenic figures in the cultural landscape. Early reviews of her work grudgingly admitted that she really wrote very well for a Canadian, and when her novel *Surfacing* appeared in paperback it carried a blurb on its back cover asserting that it was one of the most shattering novels ever written by a woman. Margaret Atwood, like the CN Tower, is a free-standing structure, and needs no patronizing props of reference to her sex or her nationality. But that, of course, does not prevent her from writing with great cogency about the ambiguous status of women and Canadians, both explicitly in essays and implicitly in poetry and fiction.

Her production to date, by my own unreliable reckoning, includes nine volumes of verse, five novels, a book of short stories, and a critical study of Canadian literature, *Survival*. This last year saw a volume of essays[2] and a new edition of the *Oxford Book of Canadian Verse*, selected and edited by her. Clearly a fallow year. She has been translated into at least fourteen languages, and is as well known and as eagerly studied in Germany, Italy, and Scandinavia as she is on this continent. She works tirelessly for professional organizations related to literary interests, such as the Writers' Union, and is invariably prominent in Harbourfront readings and similar efforts to connect Canadian literature with its audience. An intrepid explorer of her own society, she has penetrated the jungles of Empire and Canadian Club luncheons, and a sharp inquiring mind, combined with a mordant wit, has made her in great demand as a public speaker for a wide variety of occasions. You will understand this more clearly in a moment. Like Goldsmith, she has touched nothing that she has not adorned,[3] and she shows no signs of peaking or of starting to repeat herself. She keeps constantly maturing, discovering, articulating deeper strata of her vision.

Her critical essay on Canadian literature, *Survival*, provoked a good deal of hostile comment because it appeared to be saying that Canadians are a nation of losers. I don't think it did say that, but there was another dimension to its argument that many people seemed to miss. In a world like the 1980s, the *writer* is a survivor. Galileo and Bruno owed a loyalty to their science even when it conflicted with the demands of their society, and similarly the serious writers have a loyalty to their vision no matter how many of their books get banned or denounced. Most people admit by now the authority of science, because it makes bombs and things, but are very unwilling to concede the independent authority of literature. Marxist countries refuse to admit any such authority as a matter of dogma. If Canada is a land of survival, it may, for the moment, be a good place for writers also.

Margaret Atwood's essays are full of her concern for the professional writers around her equally with herself: concern for the pitfalls in their economic situation, for the immense difficulties in being popular without writing junk, in maintaining standards without losing contact with one's readers. She is constantly aware that a few hours away on a plane there are police states where all the serious writers have been jailed or killed as a matter of perverted principle. She often recurs to such figures as Ishmael in *Moby-Dick* or the messengers in Job who say, "I alone am escaped to tell thee." It is that sense of being set apart, not to withdraw from society but to communicate a unique message to it, that gives vocation to a writer.

But if the message expresses urgency or fear it fails of its purpose, because then it betrays its authority to something else. Her first novel, *The Edible Woman*, written in her early twenties, is a lethal satire on a consumer society, without a word of moralizing in it. It looks at first like a trivial story: at the second glance we see that it is the world reflected in it that is trivial. In her earlier books of verse, such as *Power Politics*, we can see, without her telling us, how all the brutalities that get loose in a totalitarian state are just under the surface of commonplace life in our own society. Her later works, if more expert, are still built on the same insights. It may sound like an anticlimax to say that a writer's authority comes from the truth told in the writing, but the truth about ourselves is the source equally of wit in comedy and of pity and terror in tragedy.

In her impressionable years Margaret Atwood read Robert Graves's *The White Goddess*, which told her that it was the function of men to write poetry and of women first to inspire and then cannibalize them for doing so. Women are most truly women, Mr. Graves asserts, when their treatment of males assimilates to that of the black widow spider or the female praying mantis. In Margaret Atwood's book of poems *You Are Happy*, the theme is metamorphosis and the central figure Circe, the enchantress, who traditionally embodies Graves's thesis. What Margaret Atwood does with her you must read the book to discover, if you have not already done so, but in the amazing sequence called *Circe/Mud Poems* we hear at the end of the first poem the voice of the enchantress summoning us to her island, and behind it the voice of a personality which is neither male nor cannibal:

> You move within range of my words
> you land on the dry shore
>
> You find what there is.

84

Culture and Society in Ontario, 1784–1984

7 September 1984

From the typescript in NFF, 1988, box 48, file 5; a preliminary typescript is in 1991, box 39, file 1. First printed in OE, 168–82, and reprinted in ECLI, 175–89. Originally given as an address to the Ontario Historical Society.

Most of the cultural factors that exist in Canada as a whole also exist in Ontario in a reduced but identical form. Geographical displacement is the most obvious. The entire province is half as large again as Texas, but most of its people are huddled near the American border, in a territory no larger than Michigan. The hinterland in the North has been explored by painters, but in this paper I have time and space only for the literary aspect of Ontario culture, and northern Ontario does not seem as yet to have found a Rudy Wiebe to interpret it. The chief exception, so far as I know, is Wayland Drew's remarkable but rather neglected story *The Wabeno Feast*, and Drew has also written essays on what this vast territory ought to be contributing to our imaginations. It is a type of irony familiar in the modern world that in most respects it is easier to get from Toronto to Moscow or Tokyo than to get to Moosonee, at the other end of the province. It may be an irony more typical of Ontario that it seems to be easier to get into genuine social contact with Asians or Africans than with the indigenous peoples. The impact of native Indian consciousness on white settlers has been remarkably narcissistic: Pauline Johnson was very much a whitecomer's Indian, and when Grey Owl turned out to be an Englishman obsessed with noble savage ideology he repeated a pattern set up in Ontario's earliest historical novel, *Wacousta*, where the allegedly Indian hero is actually a rejected suitor of the heroine's mother, back in Great Britain.

In the nineteenth century the central activity was the clearing of the land for farming. "Clearing" meant for the most part cutting down trees, the trees being regarded not as a potential resource but simply as obstacles. Catharine Parr Traill remarks in her book *Backwoods of Canada*: "Man appears to contend with the trees of the forest as though they were his most obnoxious enemies; for he spares neither the young sapling in its greenness nor the ancient trunk in its lofty pride; he wages war against the forest with fire and steel."[1] Anna Jameson makes the same observation, but carries it a step further: "A Canadian settler *hates* a tree, regards it as his natural enemy, as something to be destroyed, eradicated, annihilated, by all and any means. . . . [She goes on to say that there are two ways of killing a tree, by burning it and by draining the sap out of it.] Is not this like the two ways in which a woman's heart may be killed in this world of ours—by passion and by sorrow?"[2] Leaving this terrifying remark to speak for itself for the moment, we note that clearing the forest means, among other things, a slaughter of the animals who are thereby made homeless. Here is Samuel Strickland, the male literary representative of that celebrated family:

> The deer are not now (1853) nearly so numerous as they formerly were. . . . To give my readers some idea how plentiful these wild denizens of the forest were, some years since, I need only mention that a Trapper with whom I was acquainted, and four of his companions, passed my house on a small raft, on which lay the carcasses of thirty-two deer—the trophies of a fortnight's chase near Stoney Lake. The greater number of these were fine bucks.
>
> I once had seventeen deer hanging up in my barn at one time—the produce of three days' sport, out of which I had the good fortune to kill seven. . . . I do not know anything more pleasant than these excursions. . . . This is one of the great charms of a Canadian life, particularly to young sportsmen from the Mother Country, who require here neither license nor qualification to enable them to follow their game; but may rove about in chase of deer, or other game, at will.[3]

There are any number of ways in which such activities can be defended or rationalized; but to begin one's culture by severing so many links with nature and the earlier inhabitants poses the most formidable problems for its development. As Anna Jameson suggests, can one really destroy so many trees without stunting and truncating human lives as well? I have often had occasion to notice the curiously powerful resonance that the killing of animals has for Canadian writers: Irving Layton invests the death even of a mosquito with dignity. Among Ontario writers, we notice how the action in Margaret Atwood's *Surfacing* is directed toward reversing the current of the destroying and polluting of nature: the heroine, searching for what is both her father and the as yet unspoiled source of Canadian life, wants "the borders abolished . . . the forest to flow back into the place his mind cleared."[4] Al Purdy's *The Death of Animals*, a very intricate and subtle poem among many of his that deal with similar themes, shows us how the real horror in man's attitude to nature is not so much deliberate cruelty as total indifference, a feeling that man and nature have no life in common whatever:

> When mouse died, a man coughed, stirred,
> went to the bathroom. No connection, of course.
> When the lady slit her lover's throat with a nail file,
> owl was already dead. Again, no connection.
> Fox screamed, but the lady with lacquered nails
> already owned a fur coat. No real connection.
> Deer died later of a bullet wound, having trailed
> a broken leg through miles of red snow . . .
> What's the point of all this? None at all, really.

It is also Purdy who, in *Watching Trains*, depicting some Indian boys staring at a railway train, shows us, without wasting a syllable on moralizing, an abyss between two ways of life too wide even for conflict: the boys might as well be on a different planet, as in some respects they are. And I doubt if any other book on the First World War calls our attention more distinctly to the sufferings of animals than Timothy Findley's *The Wars*, when describing a situation in which men have started to treat each other the way they have always treated wild animals. The slaughter of animals, so often ignored as a feature of war, is one of the major elements in the demoralizing of the hero, and toward the end of the book we have a description of a mare and a dog, mute and helpless victims in a nightmare, and remember that this episode is repeated verbatim from the opening page, as a central emblem of the story.

It is often said that if it hadn't been for Niagara Falls, Ontario would have been a most idyllic and pastoral community. Of course the sense of something idyllic and peaceful represents only a pause, a sort of plateau, in the "clearing" of nature. Technology, however, is a second twist in the destruction of so many of its features, and the cultural opposition to it is vocal and versatile. Lampman's poem *The City of the End of Things* is a familiar example, as is Grove's late Ontario novel, *The Master of the Mill*, where the theme is mechanophobia hitched to a sorcerer's apprentice myth, the mill compulsively continuing to grind flour after the world has been smothered with it. George Grant's *Technology and Empire* approaches a similar theme philosophically. Canada, as I have often had occasion to remark, missed out on eighteenth-century enlightenment, and has no counterparts to such cultural heroes as Jefferson and Franklin. But, as Grant insists, it did participate, very fully, in the Hegelian antithesis that the enlightenment turned into, the oligarchic exploiting of the country. It is probably Grant's influence that lies behind the sombre brooding opening poem of Dennis Lee's *Civil Elegies*:

>Buildings oppress me, and the sky-concealing wires
>bunch zig-zag through the air. I know
>the dead persist in
>buildings, by-laws, porticos—the city I live in
>is clogged with their presence, they
>dawdle about in our lives and form a destiny, still
>incomplete, still dead weight, still
>demanding whether Canada will be.   [*Civil Elegies I*, ll. 46–53]

Marshall McLuhan is often regarded as a prophet on the opposite side, but actually he thought of the coming of electronic media as bringing about a political reversal of development from technological imperialism back to a new form of tribalism, and was sustained by that belief as long as it was possible for him to hold it. No one has spoken more strongly of the dehumanizing effects of technology than he has: "When the perverse ingenuity of man has outered some part of his being in material technology, his entire sense ratio is altered. He is then compelled to behold this fragment of himself 'closing itself as in steel' [the quotation is from Blake]. In beholding this new thing, man is compelled to become it."[5]

The question that this paper faces me with is one that I have never seen dealt with in depth, and trying to cut through the jungle of jargon in contemporary critical theory will give one no help whatever. The question is this: when a new society begins to develop some cultural interests, that culture is bound to be, for some time, a provincial culture—I am not using this as a putdown term but as a characterizing one. After a culture has matured, it begins to show a decentralizing movement, as more and more communities become articulate through the writers that grow up in them. For about 150 of the 200 years I am considering, Ontario had mainly a provincial culture, and a rather sparse one at that. For the last 25 years, at least, with the writers I have mentioned and others I have still to mention, it has had a regional culture, and a remarkably rich and varied one. Obviously there are affinities as well as contrasts between the provincial and the regional: what are they, and how does one get from one to the other? The central social process at work is the shift from a rural-based to an urban-based lifestyle, but the cultural changes accompanying this must involve more complex factors than that. I should say at once that I am not going to solve this question, merely to raise it, along with a few suggestions that I hope will be useful.

I arrived in Toronto to take up what turned out to be permanent residence there, in September of 1929. Toronto was then mainly a quiet Scotch-Irish town, its Yonge Street a curious mixture of an English midland and a middle-west American appearance, both of them deceptive. It was English midland in its array of second-hand bookshops and small grocery or butcher shops, with what appeared to be practically live rabbits hanging from the ceiling. The mean architecture, the grid plan, and the uniformity of the drug stores and branch movie houses were middle-western American features. It was a homogeneous city, with very little of the ethnical mix that Montreal and Winnipeg had: perhaps this is connected with the fact that the Jewish community in Toronto did not make the impressive contributions to Canadian literature that its counterparts in the other two cities did.

Toronto's spiritual life began on Saturday evening, where many downtown corners had a preaching evangelist, and continued through Sunday, a day of rest of a type I have never seen paralleled except in Israeli Sabbaths. One could then learn from a celebrated preacher that God was in his heaven and that the only events that bothered him were produced by the machinations of the Roman Catholic hierarchy. The Orange Order kept a firm grip on municipal government, demonstrating Communists, who began to appear in the Depression, went to jail with broken heads, and, in imitation of the United States, the work ethic had expanded to the point of making any form of alcoholic drink illegal, drinking being bad for working-class morale. Outside Toronto there was a good deal of ridicule of "Hogtown's" somnolence and sexual prudery. It is still true that Ontario gives too much authority to censors, originally out of panic, though the real reason now is probably that censoring is a genuinely popular sport, with many votes to be got out of it. Even so, prudery in Ontario at its worst is mild enough compared to what one would find in Islamic or most Communist countries today.

What one noticed at once was the curious double-think about the loyalty to the British connection. There had been a good deal of resentment in the nineteenth century about some of the more spectacular ineptnesses of British colonial rule, and its obviously greater respect for American than for Canadian interests. One might have expected the aftermath of the First World War to have weaned Canada from much of its colonial fixation, the casualties being so hideously large in proportion to the population of the country. A holocaust is not less a holocaust for being a voluntary one. George Grant, speaking of Canada after 1918, says, "Those who returned did not have the vitality for public care, but retreated into the private world of moneymaking."[6] Yet this was mainly imitative of American life in the 1920s, where the Republicans, who thought of a president as an idol carried in the processions of big business, had a permanent majority. The imperialism which thought of Canada as one more exit from the globe-girdling highway of the British Empire was already in decline: its epitaph had been written, though few realized it at the time, in Sara Jeannette Duncan's *The Imperialist* (1904), where one of the main characters, an earnest but fairly articulate bore, keeps flogging what is clearly the very dead horse of "imperial federation."

So by 1929 the loyalty to the British connection in Ontario began to have a suspiciously vociferous quality to it: obviously it masked the fact that Canada was rapidly ceasing to be a British colony and was becoming an American one. A few years later, Frank Underhill said this openly, and the furore that resulted showed, first, that he had hit a social neurosis squarely in the bull's-eye, and, second, that tenure is a genuine necessity for academic freedom, even though he left the university early to disappear into the civil-service vortex in Ottawa.[7] I remember that the fiercest condemnation of Underhill I heard came from Charles G.D. Roberts, who had spent much of his productive career in the United States, but had received a new lease of imperial loyalty along with his knighthood.

And yet the ignoring of Canada by Americans effectively prevented much loyalty from going in that direction. American arrogance was all the more galling in that it was so largely unconscious. Apart from a few Fenians, who, like the murderers of the Donnellys, had brought their feuds from Ireland with them, there was little awareness in the United States that a different country bounded them on the north. In the year 1826 the citizens of Ancaster were insulted by a travelling American exhibition showing a diorama of the glorious American victory over the British at New Orleans ten years earlier. Doubtless, like their descendants today, the showmen had forgotten or never realized that the war that ended at New Orleans had begun with an invasion of Upper Canada.

It was much more important, of course, that in proportion as the United States began to exert its strength as a world power, the continentalism of the Liberals, as expressed in the later Underhill and elsewhere, began to look increasingly reactionary. Nineteenth-century Canadian critics of the American way of life had tended to attack from both the right and the left, criticizing the absence of social standards in American democracy but also reflecting on the gross inequalities, including the retention of slavery in the South, in American oligarchy. In the Depression the new CCF party, which hoped to become the Labour party of Canada and force the Conservatives and Liberals to unite against them, represented a new kind of British-centred ideology. The British model faded along with the party, but an uneasy kind of Tory and radical mixture, expressed in very different ways by Donald Creighton, George Grant, and Dave Godfrey, continues the fight to try to define just what kind of social contract Canada in general, and Ontario in particular, does have to hold it together. The fight has not been made any easier by the more childish aspects of French separatism, which tends to divide the continent into Quebec and the United States.

With so much agreement that Ontario probably does not exist, it is hardly surprising that earlier studies of its culture, such as E.K. Brown's *On Canadian Poetry* (1943), should have expressed some wonder, not that it had a provincial culture, but that it had any at all. Tracing the criticism of Canadian literature back into the nineteenth century, it is extraordinary to find so unflaggingly persistent a desire to produce a literature, so constant a hope that a few contemporary seeds will burgeon into a bumper crop. The desire and the hope were genuinely heroic, and right in that our provincial heritage has become an essential cultural asset, not something to repudiate or get away from. The continuity between provincial and regional literature is primary: if we understand something of that, most of the differences will fall into line. An English friend once remarked to me that a Canadian's conversational opening gambit seemed to be invariably, "Where you from?" Two of our most memorable novels, Margaret Atwood's *Surfacing* and Margaret Laurence's *The Diviners*, trace the development of their heroines backward to its source, in an effort to answer the same question to the satisfaction of the heroine herself. Both novels are Ontario-based, even though one heads east to Quebec and the other west to Manitoba. Often such a journey to the source includes the cultural sources. Margaret Atwood's *Journals of Susanna Moodie* indicates how creative an act it can be to absorb and exploit one's own cultural tradition, and Susanna's sister Catharine Parr Traill plays a significant role at the end of *The Diviners*.

These two novels employ, in reverse, the commonest formula of Canadian fiction, the *Bildungsroman*. The theme of "How I Grew Up in Zilch Corners" is inevitable for the young writer who as yet knows nothing except his own impressions, and of course the great bulk of all writing, in every age, consists of filling up prescribed and fashionable conventions. You will note that I fell into the idiom myself a moment ago. Even so, the theme seems to have an unusual intensity for Ontario writers: the best and most skilful of them, including Robertson Davies and Alice Munro, continue to employ a great deal of what is essentially the Stephen Leacock Mariposa theme, however different in tone. Most such books take us from the first to the second birth of the central character. Childhood and adolescence are passed in a small town or village, then a final initiation, often a sexual one, marks the entry into a more complex social contract.

In Ontario literature the large proportion of women writers comes out of a tradition established at the very beginning of settlement. It was not that nineteenth-century women had any more leisure than their husbands, or that the physical effort involved in the work they did was less intense. But they did have a more creative notion of what to do with the leisure they had: we may compare Samuel Strickland's three-day orgy of deer-killing with his sister Catharine's delighted discoveries of new plants and birds in her environment. The Strickland sisters worked mainly in a genre which had an actual market, of sorts: diaries, journals, reminiscences aimed, not at readers in Ontario, but at prospective immigrants "back home." We owe many of our clearest insights into the social and cultural development of the country to such work. Very occasionally we see some awareness of its function: thus Anne Langton, writing in 1840:

... The bride looked much better than on ... her first appearance. Her dress was of another shade, richer than the former. I think it would have stood erect by itself. ... If the follies and extravagances of the world are to be introduced upon Sturgeon Lake, we might as well, I think, move on to Galt Lake. I am afraid women deteriorate in this country more than the other sex. As long as the lady is necessarily the most active member of her household she keeps her ground from her utility; but when the state of semi-civilization arrives, and the delicacies of her table, and the elegancies of her person become her chief concern and pride, then she must fall, and must be contented to be looked upon as belonging merely to the decorative department of the establishment and valued accordingly.[8]

The woman who loses her commanding position in a household to become part of the furniture is familiar enough today: in the literature we are considering, the dead end of the process is reached by the heroine of Margaret Atwood's *The Edible Woman*, the victim of a cellophane-wrapped consumerism. It is more common, however, for Canadian fiction writers to feature the woman who is determined to hold on to that commanding position even after her real function is past. Male-dominated societies are constantly turning into matriarchies and vice versa, and some reflection of this is perhaps what has produced the literary convention described, again, by Margaret Atwood in *Survival*: "If you trusted Canadian fiction you would have to believe that most of the women in the country with any real presence at all are over fifty, and a tough, sterile, suppressed and granite-jawed lot they are. They live their lives with intensity, but through gritted teeth."[9]

One of the earliest of such women, though not one she mentions, is the mother of the heroine of Raymond Knister's novel, *White Narcissus* (1929), a book I shall come to again in a moment. This is a story of how a young man's love for a young woman is frustrated by the latter's parents, who are emotional vampires sucking all the life out of her. They are feuding with each other for some reason, communicate only through her, and the mother retreats into an epic sulk and raises white narcissi. The funereal colour, the sickly-sweet smell, and the mythical overtones of "Narcissus" provide the central image of the novel. A rather forced ending breaks up this pattern of frustration, but the type itself marches across Canada from sea to sea. I have occasionally wondered if some psychological transfer from a political dependence on a "mother country" has affected Canadian feeling about female establishments. Scott Symons's *Place d'Armes*, for example, has castrating mother symbols all over it, and ends in an apocalyptic prophecy of the fall of the "mommy bank," the Bank of Montreal. The setting is Montreal, but the psychological focus is clearly Ontario.

In writing a *Bildungsroman* about one's early surroundings, especially if one is not thinking of the people one writes about as forming any large part of one's readership, it is often difficult to avoid a patronizing tone that isolates the characters from the rest of the world. That is, the author knows that his milieu is provincial, and his knowledge is apt to work against him into identifying with it. Hence a certain self-conscious archness in earlier Canadian fiction, in Ralph Connor, even in Leacock's *Sunshine Sketches*. Leacock, however, is aware of this tone and feels defensive about it, and so adds a sentimental epilogue to the book, describing a returning railway journey to Mariposa after a life misspent in the big city: "Don't bother to look at the reflection of your face in the window-pane shadowed by the night outside. Nobody could tell you now after all these years. Your face has changed in these long years of money-getting in the city. Perhaps if you had come back now and again, just at odd times, it wouldn't have been so."[10]

It is easier to locate, and still easier to caricature, the limitations of a provincial culture. There is, for example, its resentment of realism, its feeling that it should not be studied before it has had time to put on its best clothes. There are the querulous complaints against academic critics, who know how it should be done but can't do it, through which one can always hear the voice of the provincial appeal, "Please go away until we get better." And there are all the fallacies engendered by the wrong kind of literary study, such as the notion that poetry is an elegant varying of meaning instead of a higher concentration of it. Thus Wilson MacDonald in *The Song of the Ski*:

> I land erect and the tired winds drawl
> A lazy rune on a broken harp

where the skier may have landed erect but his metaphors are a basket case. I am more interested, however, in the genuine difficulties encountered by dedicated and isolated writers. May I turn again to *White Narcissus*:

> He smiled bitterly. "It is always of her you speak," he added, with a surprising acrimony, for his thwarted feeling was being transferred to annoyance in behalf of the representative of his own sex in this generation-

long quarrel. "Doesn't your father feel? Do you think he doesn't know the bitter of loneliness and misprision as well as your mother?"

"Father, of course. I know that, and it is why things are as they are. Possibly if I could take sides, there could be some outcome, even to strife. But I see, I understand too well, so that there is no hope. I see the sadness of both, and how oblivion awaits it all . . . across a mist of pathos like dreaming."[11]

This is provincial style: the heightening of tone, so that the conversational idiom is smothered in rhetorical rhythms, and the conscientious tracing of motive, indicate a writer who thinks of the highest standards of his craft as being already established outside his community (Henry James is the chief ghost haunting this passage, I should think), and as having to be met by very deliberate efforts.

It was a similar concern about meeting external standards that produced the dream of "The Great Canadian Novel," by which was apparently meant a Victorian type of character-crowded panorama, on the model of *Bleak House* or *Middlemarch*, or, if one ventured to hope so high, *War and Peace*. But such forms now exist, so far as they do, chiefly in historical romance, which is an international commercial product for the most part, though Antonine Maillet's *Pélagie-la-Charrette* indicates that something much more could be made of it. In any case, as we saw, prose in Ontario began with the documentary realism of journals and memoirs, and when fiction developed, that was the tradition it recaptured. Documents, when not government reports, tend to have short units, and the fact may account for the curious ascendancy in Canadian fiction of the novel which consists of a sequence of interrelated short stories. This form is the favourite of Alice Munro, and reaches a dazzling technical virtuosity in *Lives of Girls and Women*.

As a way of approaching cultural through social phenomena, let me give one example of how a provincial situation is affected, first, by the rural-urban population shift, and then expands into a more complex social issue. I remarked earlier that it was impossible to get legally any kind of alcoholic drink in Toronto in 1929. I forget whether the first tentative post-Prohibition beers were available then or not, but I should not consider them an exception if they were. Many Protestant churches, at least, seemed to attach more importance to abstaining from liquor than they did to all the clauses in the Apostles' Creed together. Whenever we have a token anxiety symbol of this kind, we should look for an unacknowledged change in the social process. The process here, as mentioned, was the rapid shift to an urban-based ethos. The churches adhered almost obsessively to the rural one, and in rural communities there was some justification for assuming that one either did not drink or took to drink. Where the industry was strongly seasonal, as with Newfoundland fishing, this was proportionately more true. However, according to Catharine Parr Traill: "Intemperance is too prevailing a vice among all ranks of people in this country; but I blush to say it belongs most decidedly to those that consider themselves among the better class of emigrants."[12] The word "emigrants" goes a long way to annotate the remark: the "better class" in Ontario at that time had not come to Canada so much as left Britain or the United States, and like other refugees they felt a lack of social context, especially in moments of leisure. Ontario is a place to stand, we are told: the cultural complications begin with sitting down.

So "temperance," meaning total abstinence, may have been so vigorously supported by the more evangelical churches partly as a native protest against manners imported by the self-styled gentry. If so, this would explain why the political affinities of temperance movements were liberal to the verge of radical. A very easy generalization from denouncing "the liquor interests" and their control of politicians and the press would soon bring one to radicalism, or at any rate a kind of radical populism. The alliance between the evangelical and the populist was noted as early as Tiger Dunlop: "It is long since the French reproached the English with having twenty religions, and only one sauce. In Canada, we have two hundred religions, and no sauce at all. . . . The mode by which religion and politics are joined is, I believe, peculiar to the American continent, *viz.* by newspapers inculcating the tenets of a sect, and at the same time the politics of the leaders of it; and this unholy alliance have the Methodists set up to blend treason with the Gospel."[13]

I became aware of the blending of "treason" and the Gospel from some of my contemporaries who came from missionary families, and had spent much of their childhood in China or Japan. The Student Christian Movement, a very influential organization among students at that time, drifted rapidly leftward, partly under their influence. The tragic career of my classmate Herbert Norman is perhaps too well known to need more than a reference.[14] So it should not be surprising that if, on a Sunday afternoon in 1931, there were 18,000 people at Denton Massey's York Bible Class in Maple Leaf Gardens, the children or grandchildren of those people should be listening to left-wing speakers imported from third-world countries in the same place in the late sixties.

If we add to this issue a dozen others, we can begin to understand how it was that Toronto was able, in half-a-dozen years after 1945, to transform itself from the "Hogtown" of the thirties into a cosmopolitan city with a minimum of ethnical tension. The immigration of those years was not of course confined to Toronto, though it was most dramatic there, and it was not the cause of the contemporary transformation of Ontario literature from the provincial to the regional, though it accompanied it and has many connections with it. The process itself by which a provincial writer isolated in a part of the world becomes a regional writer who from a sense of being in the world strikes his roots in his social environment remains a mysterious one. James Reaney has a poignant poem called *The Upper Canadian*:

> I shall always sit here in this hovel
> Weeping perhaps over an old Victorian novel
> And hear the dingy interwinding tunes
> Of country rain and wind
> And lame fires of damp wood.
> Especially shall I hear that starved cricket
> My mind, that thinks a railway ticket
> Could save it from its enclosed, cramped quality.
> That mind where thoughts float round
> As geese do round a pond
> And never get out.

Alvin Lee, in his book on Reaney, identifying the narrator of this poem with Reaney himself, remarks that his way of handling the problem "was not to export himself elsewhere but rather to learn an order of words or literary language comprehensive enough to swallow up the place and society which had brought him into being."[15]

Lee is certainly right in pointing to language as the key to the process: it is a new sense of language that makes a writer realize that he must establish his own standards and not try to meet those of someone or somewhere else. There are many other factors: sometimes a railway ticket does help, as a ticket to Toronto helped E.J. Pratt to become a Newfoundland poet. Sometimes one can see a definite influence. One of the first Ontario writers to whom this metamorphosis occurred was

Morley Callaghan, and the impact of Maritain on Ontario Catholic culture was operative there. But critics, when they identify such an influence, are apt to exaggerate it, because the actual process eludes them as much as it does the writer himself.

The point is that the transformation did occur, however it occurred. If the Nobel Prize Committee were to ask for Canadian nominees, anyone reasonably conversant with the field could name eight or ten people in English Canada alone, without feeling in the least apologetic about any of them, and a good proportion of them would be Ontario writers. At the beginning Ontario struggled along in what Douglas LePan calls a country without a mythology, having both obliterated the Indian mythology and discarded its own. A mythology is a framework of thematic imagery within which a literature operates, hence a country without one is a country with a provincial literature and a largely undeveloped imaginative potential. A mythology emerges when the mental landscapes of a group of writers begin to fuse with their physical environment.

In another article I have tried to show this process at work among some contemporary Canadian poets.[16] If I had another hour of your time and another month of my own (which I do not), I might attempt a similar study of Ontario fiction, showing how the *Bildungsroman* form, and others closely related to it, so often works through to some intuition or private epiphany that is an aspect of an emerging coherent mythology. LePan's own novel *The Deserter* affords an impressive example, as does each of the three Deptford novels of Robertson Davies, especially *Fifth Business*. Fable and fantasy forms, such as Marian Engel's *Bear*, Timothy Findley's new novel *Not Wanted on the Voyage*, or in a still different way Graeme Gibson's *Perpetual Motion*, have an important role to play here. Predictably, perhaps, the unifying theme of the fantasies is nearly always a renewed relation between humanity and nature. And there is also, of course, the ironic version of the *Bildungsroman*. To win through to a genuine mythical vision means casting off any number of false ones, and the failure of some characters to do this is quite as significant as the success of others. An example would be the heroine of Margaret Atwood's *Lady Oracle*, who exchanges a physical obesity for equally overstuffed myths, because, as she says, "the truth was not convincing."

When an imaginative coherence of this kind emerges within a literature, it becomes genuinely communicable, and provokes an immediate response in other parts of the world. It is not geographical curiosity about Canada, and certainly not its political importance, that has caused universities in Germany and Italy, in China and Japan, in Holland and Scandinavia, to set up centres of Canadian studies. Perhaps, as has been suggested, Canada has passed up or abandoned a genuinely political identity. But as long as it retains its imaginative one, it will do infinitely more for the benefit of the world.

85

Tribute to Robert Zend

16 July 1985

From the typescript in NFF, 1988, box 49, file 2. Frye used the first paragraph and the last three (with a few minor changes) for his Afterword to Zend's Daymares: Selected Fictions on Dreams and Time, *ed. Brian Wyatt (Vancouver, B.C.: Cacanadada Press, 1991), 184. His tribute was originally given in a ceremony at Harbourfront after Zend's death. Zend, who had come to Canada after the Hungarian Revolution of 1956, had worked as a writer and producer for the CBC; his chief books of poetry are* From Zero to One *(1973),* Beyond Labels *(1982), both translated with John Robert Colombo, OĀB.1 (1983), and OĀB.2 (1985).*

I first got to know Robert Zend through a CBC program I was in and he was producing. As Samuel Johnson said of Edmund Burke, if you were caught in a shower under a doorway with him you'd still know you'd been with a remarkable man,[1] but I don't recall much that got said except such things as his impassioned defence of Velikovski, where he was ready to take on all comers.

I don't know when I've been more bowled over than when I began seeing the OĀB material. One can call it anything: concrete poetry, shape poetry, or just straight doodling, but nothing you call it even starts to describe what it is. Zend tells us that he's created someone or something called OĀB, then another entity, IRDU, gets into the act, and the two of them tumble around a hundred pages of verbal designs and puzzles, playing games like endlessly resourceful children. In the second volume, which has just appeared, a third character, ARDO, appears, evidently a split-off of IRDU.

I've forgotten the details, but I remember vaguely that a publisher once offered to produce extracts from it, and I said that extracts wouldn't do: the cumulative effect of the whole thing was what one had to have. Zend himself is partly a creating God and partly a bothered father who can't answer all the importunate questions of his small children, but both roles land him in an encyclopedic context, and without that context the book loses its point.

I remember reading once about a woman travelling in Tibet and studying magic there. She created a human phantom, a monk, who took on an independent life and started giving her the eye, in this case a rather unpleasant eye. So she had to get rid of him, but it was harder to dissolve him than to create him in the first place. Yeats said something similar about his Crazy Jane. I had something of the same feeling when following the lives of OĀB and IRDU, except that they were so utterly good-natured and innocent. Apparently they'd been made out of nothing and had only a purely subjective existence. But that never really happens. Whatever is created takes on an autonomous life of its own, and becomes objective as well as subjective. That's why it can be communicated to others. The fancies of a brain assimilate with what in the past have been called gods or ghosts or muses or spirits of nature. You're never sure when you're creating them and when you've invoked or summoned something that's started to recreate you.

This happens to every writer, I think, but it seems to have happened to Zend with a unique vividness and power. I was interested that so many of the people who wrote to him to express interest in what he was doing—Borges, Marcel Marceau, Norman McLaren—kept coming back to the same point: what you're doing is somehow like what I'm trying to do.[2] That means, I think, that he'd hit a central nerve of the whole creative process.

Like all fine humorists, he had a deeply serious side to him: one can find plenty of that in the book *Beyond Labels*. There's one epigram in particular in that book that I like:

> The pseudo-poet uses the medium
> of poetry to speak;
> the true poet is used as a medium
> through whom poetry speaks.

But I like that at least partly because I agree with it. The relation of creator to creature is the main subject of the OĀB books, and if Zend had cast himself in the role of creature, instead of creator, he'd have become a most disturbing religious poet. There are many hints of this in his work: I think of a poem called *Psalm*, which he did me the honour to dedicate to me, and where he says to God: "You are the hatred in my heart—against those who cut through my circles—and that which was before this hatred—and that which remains untouched by its flames [para. 4]."

If I go on in this vein I'll get solemn and sententious, and that's what Zend never did. He never forgot that every creative act was first and foremost an act of free play. And playing with words, which you can do on any level from crossword puzzles to *Finnegans Wake*, is something he did with a variety and scope I've seldom seen equalled.

It's his humour that stays with us, and the paradox of humour behind it. The humorous vision sees things in proportion because it sees them out of proportion. That means that the customary proportions of things are somehow all wrong. Probably that's why we have dreams: to remind us every night that we've spent the previous day in a world of petrified nonsense. There are not many people beyond the age of five who carry this sense into the waking world: most of those who do are graphic artists: Klee, Chagall, Escher, and, temperamentally closer to Zend, Saul Steinberg, to whom Zend has addressed an impressive tribute.[3] The verbal people are more apt to get tangled up in the conventional meanings of words: perhaps Zend's detachment from English was a help.

He was a notably free and unfettered spirit who was among us for a while, and who, now that he is gone, is irreplaceable. All we can do is read and admire what he has left us.

86

Opening of Lawren Harris and Arthur Lismer Exhibitions

26 September 1985

From the typescript in NFF, 1988, box 49, file 1. A sound cassette of Frye's talk is in NFF, 1991, box 64. He was introducing two exhibitions to be shown at the Art Gallery of Ontario in Toronto, 27 September to 24 November 1985: "Atma Buddhi Manas," consisting of 88 works of Lawren Harris, and "Canadian Jungle," 98 paintings and drawings of Arthur Lismer.

When creative artists form groups and issue manifestos and rely on the support of each other for encouragement, it is usually a sign that they have not achieved full recognition or maturity. In proportion as their authority increases, they tend to pull away from one another and make their public impressions as individuals. It is very remarkable how firmly the name "Group of Seven" has stuck, although the painters it refers to diverged in very different directions, and had increasingly less in common as they went on.

Lawren Harris, for example, began by searching for the simplifying aspects of the landscapes he studied, bringing out their geometrical underlying forms, and finally going on into pure abstraction. In his abstract period there is at first a preponderance of tightly controlled outlines, where the mountains and lakes of the earlier paintings have become triangles and circles, but are clearly still related to landscape. Then there is a final period of remarkable exhilaration and spontaneity, where, like Kandinsky or Turner in their final periods, he seems absorbed by form and colour for their own sakes. In all this he was strongly influenced by his theosophical studies, and the title given this exhibition, *Atma Buddhi Manas,* as I understand, refers to three stages of theosophical enlightenment, ranging, apparently, from the highest possible to the highest conceivable. We are reminded of the days when the Theosophical Society on Isabella Street was a power centre in the city's culture; and I understand too that the title "Group of Seven" grew out of his feeling for the sacredness of the number seven, at a time when the painters involved were effectively a group of five.

With Arthur Lismer we have precisely the opposite: a delight in all the complexity and clutter of the objective world, whether on Nova Scotia fishing docks or British Columbia forests. His landscapes show us Canadian vegetation doing all kinds of un-Canadian things, pushing, scrambling, getting in each other's way, living off one another, yet directing all this energy to the great Canadian aim of survival. So the title *Canadian Jungle* is less of a paradox than it seems. The contrast in technique reflects a contrast in personality: Harris retired and scholarly, Lismer a teacher striding through galleries first here and later in Montreal, and followed by swarms of fascinated children.

It is somewhat disconcerting to find two such lively and vibrant personalities turning, within one's own lifetime, into legends and national monuments. Disconcerting, at least, until we look at the pictures themselves. Then we realize that all the liveliness and vibrancy are still there, still being presented to us and still mirrors of their creators. From that I shall not keep you any longer, but simply declare both of these exhibitions officially open.

87

Barker Fairley

21 May 1986

From the typescript in NFF, 1991, box 39, file 7. Frye's speech was delivered at a dinner for Fairley on his ninety-ninth birthday; he died later that year. Fairley had been head of the German department at the University of Toronto from 1936 to 1957. The portrait of Ned Pratt mentioned below, along with Fairley's portrait of Frye, is now hung in the Senior Common Room of Victoria University.

It seems to me very typical of Barker Fairley that his first appearance on this campus should have been in the role of a professor of German during the First World War. Not many of us are old enough to remember the hysterical anti-German frenzies of that time, but it has always taken some courage and a good deal of faith in one's subject to remain a Germanist in this century through so much prejudice and so many periods of dropping enrolments.

Barker was, in any case, an unusual Germanist for those times, one who had clearly read a book or two in English, and who produced a study of Charles Doughty, who has been largely ignored even by English scholars and has never, so far as I know, been featured on an English course here.[1] But Barker has never been one to back away from any subject because it was unpopular or widely misunderstood. He showed this also in his own field in the book he produced, many years later, on the neglected nineteenth-century German novelist Raabe.[2] It was the same sympathy for minority causes that impelled him, within a very short time after his arrival, to take so active a role in the new student magazine the *Rebel*. The *Rebel* folded before long, as perhaps was fitting for a periodical with so un-Canadian a title, but was immediately succeeded by the *Canadian Forum*, which still exists, through a great variety of changes, and of which Barker was a founding member. The amount and quality of work he devoted to it was a major factor in its survival.

At the same time he was active in the golden age of the Arts and Letters Club, and was a friend of and helped publicize the Group of Seven painters, at that time struggling for recognition. He was never much attracted to the theosophical interests of Lawren Harris or Jackson, and perhaps for that reason he was able to explain to the Canadian public what these painters were up to more articulately than they did. But, of course, his central interest as a Germanist scholar and teacher steadily developed. When he came to Toronto he had already had a distinguished scholarly career that embraced Leeds, Jena, and Alberta, and through his books on Goethe particularly he established himself as one of the most admired and respected Germanists on the continent. The second of these books, *A Study of Goethe* (1947), consolidated his reputation: it is a book I have read many times, always with increased insight and profit.

Even before his retirement in 1957, his interests were shifting from literature to painting, and again he threw himself into the minority movement of portrait painting, in reaction to the overwhelming emphasis on landscape favoured by Canadian painters. His portraits of well-known characters on the university scene showed uncanny insight, so much so that sitters occasionally refused to have anything to do with the result. I particularly cherish his portrait of Ned Pratt, which I own. It is a portrait of the poet who told the tragic stories of Brébeuf and the wrecked *Titanic*, and makes no effort to reproduce the jovial mask that the poet turned on the outer world. Portraiture was followed by a renewed interest in landscape, an incredibly prolific and already legendary period in which an exhibition could be sold out almost before it was hung, and might even be taken off the walls and replaced by another exhibition before the end of the showing period.

In his book on Goethe that I mentioned there is a comment on Goethe which is so startlingly true of Barker himself that I cannot resist applying it to him. He is speaking of how Goethe continued to work on the second part of *Faust* in his eighties (it was in *his* eighties that Barker completed his racy and idiomatic prose translation of *Faust*). Goethe, says Barker, "was no friend of last words."[3] That is our view too, as we gather to celebrate, with equal affection and admiration, the renewal of his ninety-nine-year lease, and honour the man who has contributed as much, in variety and value, as any other single member of the university he has served and distinguished for seventy years. Let us drink a toast to his continued health and activity.

88

Don Harron

October 1987

From the typescript in NFF, 1991, box 39, file 7, which is headed "A Unique Achievement." Frye's tribute to Canadian entertainer Don Harron was composed for a banquet intended to celebrate Harron's fiftieth anniversary in show business; in the event the banquet failed to take place.

My memories of Don Harron as a student are so vivid partly because he stood out so prominently in a quite extraordinary year—Vic '48, full of stellar characters with a great variety of talents and interests. Don's interests were obviously connected with drama and entertainment generally, and he naturally took a leading part in such things as an undergraduate. He was an excellent student, but I felt that success in his studies came rather too easily to him: that is, his studies weren't giving him the right kind of stimulus. I told him he had unusual gifts as a popularizer, which for me was by no means a condescending word: I am a popularizer myself, in a different way, and take that side of my work very seriously.

I was not surprised when he took to drama professionally, and not surprised either, my view of education being what it is, by the way in which his academic background was absorbed in it, and reflected from it. We had a brief collaboration in trying to adapt Webster's *Duchess of Malfi* as a radio drama: the project came to nothing, perhaps fortunately, except that I learned a good deal from it about both Webster and radio drama. I remember also, soon after his graduation, his appearances in the early *Spring Thaw* revues, both as performer and as author. As author, making puns in three languages, he asked a good deal of his audience. I recall what was alleged to be a French version of *Macbeth*, with Macbeth shouting "je t'aime! je t'adore!," and a door being slammed offstage. I recall also how a local metropolitan schemozzle became the subject of an operatic spoof ending with "the blood-chilling duet, Todmorden." But what I recall most is his sensitivity toward his variety of audiences and his unvarying respect for them, along with his awareness of the dangers of being taken over by too facile a response. In a profession where so many feel that they have to develop the ego of a piranha to keep going, he retained a receptive quality that was the outward sign not merely of a high level of culture but of a very real gentleness. It was a quality that later made him in great demand as a host for radio and television talk shows, but was there from the beginning.

I was not surprised either by the fact that while he could do the stand-up comic routine with its series of wisecracks as well as anyone else, he was not content with that stage. He went on to develop his famous personae, of whom Charlie Farquharson is doubtless the best known.[1] Like Gélinas in French Canada, he realized that such projected types are not simple caricatures, but dramatize genuine elements in the society they are assumed to have come from. So they can help the rest of us, whatever we talk or sound like, to become more conscious of the attitudes and assumptions that surround us, and so more conscious too of the Charlie Farquharson inside us who reads the morning paper.

Don's career has been a quite extraordinary achievement, and what this occasion calls for is not mere congratulation but tribute and gratitude. When the poet Cocteau told the scientist Poincaré that poets often felt inferior to scientists because scientific work seemed to be more important, Poincaré said that they should not feel that way, because "the chance of a rhyme may cause a system to emerge from darkness." I am not sure what that means, but it reminds me of something I have felt when listening to Don: that at any time the chance of a joke may bring something else along with it, a shift of vision, perhaps, that will suddenly turn one into a different person, before the old one has stopped laughing.

89

Speech at the New Canadian Embassy, Washington

14 September 1989

From the typescript in NFF, 1991, box 38, file 10. Three other typescripts in the same file show stages of revision. Printed as "Levels of Cultural Identity" in Northrop Frye Newsletter, 2, no.1 (Winter 1989–90): 2–12, and reprinted in EAC, 168–82, RCLI, 179–94, and ECLI, 191–205. Frye's speech was given to open the Embassy of Canada's lecture series in the theatre of the new Embassy building designed by Arthur Erickson, 501 Pennsylvania Avenue, Washington, D.C.

I

I suppose that nowhere in the world is there a relationship between two countries even remotely like that of Canada and the United States. The full awareness of this relationship is largely confined to Canada, where it has churned up a good deal of speculation about "the Canadian identity," the extent to which Canadians may be said to be different from non-Canadians, meaning, ninety per cent of the time, Americans. I am not concerned with this approach to the question, which seems to me futile and unreal. A nation's identity is (not "is in") its culture, and culture is a structure with several distinct levels. On an elementary level there is culture in the sense of custom or lifestyle: the distinctive way that people eat, dress, talk, marry, play games, produce goods, and the like. On this level culture in Canada, including both English and French Canada, has been practically identical with the northern part of American culture for a long time. This fact is not, in my view, one of any great significance. The time is past when we could speak of the "Americanizing" of this aspect of Canadian life: what faces us now is the homogenizing of the entire world, including the United States, through twentieth-century technology. Today Canadians, like other people, are hardly more Americanized in their lifestyle than they are Japanned or common-marketed.

Then there is a middle level of cultural identity, which is the product of tradition and history, and consists of the distinctive political, economic, religious, and other institutions that shape a nation's life and give direction to the main currents of its ideology. This *is* an area where Canadians have always felt beleaguered and threatened by American influences, and where, by an inevitable irony, that influence keeps increasing through divisions among Canadians themselves. In every part of Canada there are strong separatist feelings, and separatism can lead only to increased American penetration, especially economic and ideological. This is not to say that such penetration must be sinister, merely that it is the opposite of what separatism aims at.

Finally, there is an upper level of culture as the product of a nation's specialized creative powers. In Canada it seems to be particularly literature, painting, film, and radio drama that have attracted most attention, both within the country and outside it, and we should now add architecture, as this building is one of three at least to achieve such recognition in the present year. In theory, culture in this more specific sense is the product of the people as a whole and the shared heritage of all the people. In practice, it is the product of an often neglected minority, and in its appreciation there is a strongly elitist element. To bridge this gap between theory and practice is largely what the process known as education is all about.

The middle level, the specific nation formed by a historical process, is the place where the conception "Canada" is to be found, but it is not the place to look for cultural symbols. Those come from either the lifestyle level or the creative level. On the lifestyle level, Canada has shown an extraordinary ability to absorb ethnical groups without essentially violating their folkways. The treatment of the indigenous peoples is an exception to this that I shall return to later. But the Icelandic and Ukrainian immigrants of the nineteenth century, the Italians and Portuguese and Jamaicans of the twentieth, have been able to preserve much of their lifestyle cultures: the extent to which they have been eroded, as just said, is due to worldwide rather than national pressures. The same thing was true of the original British and French groups: in fact John Kenneth Galbraith, with no sense of incongruity, wrote a book called *The Scotch* which was concerned entirely with a community of Scottish origin in southern Ontario.

In lifestyle culture there is little that is typical of Canada as a whole: a satiric revue of forty years back called *Spring Thaw* pretended to make a search for authentic Canadian symbols, and emerged with a mounted policeman and a bottle of rye. Canada is the Switzerland of the twentieth century, surrounded by the great powers of the world and preserving its identity by having many identities. Its distinctive identity is represented by its creative culture, in its literature and painting and the other arts just mentioned.

As for the American awareness of Canada, one may say that Americans are conscious of Canada first of all as insulation. And, perhaps, one should not ignore the importance of Canada as a geographical object, apart from its inhabitants, in sealing in the United States on one point of the compass, much as the oceans seal it in on two others. The physical existence of Canada helped to confirm the American sense of separateness from the world up to the earlier decades of this century, and perhaps later had something to do with the fact that the Cold War remained relatively cold. But of course there are people in Canada, and it has been of immense benefit to the United States, whether it knows it or not, to have across its northern border not merely a friendly ally but another nation with a different history and traditions, closely related to and yet contrasting with its own.

The contrasts relate to what I have called the middle level of culture, the distinctive paths formed by history. The American Revolution was a Whig revolution, and one of the things it revolted against was the mercantilist theory that the function of colonies was merely to produce raw materials. English Canada was settled, in upper Canada and much of the Maritimes, largely by disaffected Tories. These made common cause, to some degree, with their former enemies in French Canada, who felt doubly betrayed, first by the lack of interest in Canada shown by the government of prerevolutionary France, and secondly by an atheistic French Revolution. It is perhaps fair to say that France has never shown any real concern for Canada since, except when promoting its own interests. And English-speaking Canadians, even those who remained uncritically loyal to Britain, had to put up with massive ineptitude, indifference, and an attitude that showed much more respect for the independent United States than the dependent colonies. The feeling of not being wanted, except as a place of exploitation, forms a ground bass under Canadian themes, and among other things has forced Canada to retain the dependence on commodity exports which makes its economy so different from the American one.

One always has to oversimplify situations like this, unless one is writing scholarly history, but in the forming of Canada there *was* something like this Tory-Whig division of ideology, and one that went much deeper than the Republican-Democrat or Conservative-Liberal divisions arising later in the separate countries. The revolution produced a written constitution and a deductive attitude to social problems, whereas the Canadians, in rejecting the revolution, adopted something more like an Edmund Burke theory of a continuous contract including the dead, the living, and the unborn, an unwritten constitution based on precedent, and a tendency to look for solutions to crises by safeguarding the rights of both sides. Canadian history is a series of ad hoc compromises, in contrast to the American practice of reinterpreting and amending an eighteenth-century document. Each crisis brings with it a settled belief, in the minds of many Canadians, that this is really the end, that the country is at last irremediably torn apart by its own inner contradictions. So far such feelings have proved to be mistaken, but if a sculptor were making a statue symbolizing Canadian loyalty to Canada, he might well portray someone holding his breath and crossing his fingers.

The entrenched Tory oligarchy in nineteenth-century Ontario, known as the Family Compact, provoked a rebellion of sorts in 1837, though the history of that rebellion, at least in Ontario, makes very curious reading. Canadians have always refused to believe in any kind of political logic, whether the logic of revolution or the logic of repression. The liberal opposition that began to take shape was continentalist in tendency, and some of the more myopic liberals, such as the English Goldwin Smith, who resided for some time in Toronto before going to Cornell, assumed that the union of the British colonies was a chimerical fantasy, and that annexation to the United States was only a matter of time. But even Toryism in Canada has always had a radical element in it, that opposed American tendencies from the left as well as the right. This element emphasized the gross inequalities of wealth and privilege building up in the United States, and it was more aware than the liberals of the aggressive and imperialistic side of American development. The Monroe doctrine, through much of the nineteenth century, seemed to imply that Americans were claiming the right to exploit the New World for themselves.[1] The effects in Canada included the War of 1812, the Fenian raids, the "Fifty-four forty or fight" crisis,[2] and various other incidents. But as regards Canada the United States seems to have realized very early that, to paraphrase Clausewitz, economic penetration is the continuing of war by other means,[3] and with a far greater chance of success.

There was also the Canadian opposition to slavery. During the Civil War, the liberal John Stuart Mill in England attacked the Tories of his time for supporting the South and rejoicing over the apparent disintegrating of the great republican experiment. One might have expected Canadians to take a similar [Tory] view, and some did, but Canadian volunteers produced a sizeable contingent for the Union army. Much earlier, the Nova Scotian writer Haliburton, who was about as Tory as one could get, made his stage American Sam Slick refer to the Fourth of July as "fifteen millions of free men and five millions of slaves a-celebratin' the birthday of liberty."[4]

The point all this is leading up to is that the continuity of certain British elements in Canadian life is not simply a vestigial relic of Canada's colonial past or reactionary nostalgia. One very obvious example is the retaining of the monarchy, along with a Governor-General as, so to speak, the resident Canadian crown. When there is no question of British rule any more, keeping this memento of the fact that we were once a British colony is one way of qualifying the extent to which we are now an American colony. In any case the monarchy in both Britain and Canada seems to be genuinely popular, its connection with an aristocratic class having largely disappeared.

The monarchy is a symbol of a national unity transcending the conflicts of all political and religious pressure groups. The corresponding symbol of such a unity in the United States is the flag, something Canada did not even have until it acquired one along with the new third-world nations a quarter-century ago. The real point about a monarchy is that it puts the cult of personality where it belongs, in the area of ceremonial symbolism. A flag, however useful for covering the mental nakedness of political speeches, lacks the accessibility of a personal symbol like a royal family: it is pointless to complain about it, and impossible to gossip about it. A parliamentary system, where a leader stands or falls with his party, reduces the personality cult in other ways, although there is a growing emphasis on leadership conventions and the like in Canada which reflects American influence.

Then again, Canada has had, for the last fifty years, a Socialist (or more accurately Social Democrat) party which is normally supported by twenty-five to thirty per cent of the electorate, and has been widely respected, through most of its history, for its devotion to principle. Nothing of proportional size or influence has emerged among socialists in the United States. When the CCF, the first form of this party, was founded in the 1930s, its most obvious feature went largely unnoticed. That feature was that it was following a British rather than an American tendency, trying to assimilate the Canadian political structure to the British Conservative-Labour pattern. The present New Democratic Party, however, never seems to get beyond a certain percentage of support, not enough to come to federal power. Principles make voters nervous, and yet any departure from them towards expediency makes them suspicious.

The American ideology of assimilation, expressed in such phrases as "hundred per cent American," "un-American activities," and the like, can hardly operate in Canada, with its roots in a coalition of two founding groups. Recently Canadians have become aware that a large proportion of the population, including of course the indigenous peoples, come from an ethnical and linguistic background which is neither English nor French. Hence the policy of bilingualism, so sharply intensified in the Trudeau era, has been qualified by the newer buzzword of "multiculturalism." In Toronto, for example, where the teaching of French in elementary schools is heavily stressed, the Italian-speaking population is much greater than the French-speaking one. The result, or so an irritated educator once remarked to me, is to send an Italian child to school to destroy his native language and make him illiterate in two others. Not that it is all that easy to destroy a native language.

I am entering an area here which is thickly sown with emotional minefields, and any advance into it has to be cautious. I have first to return to my three levels of culture, a level of lifestyle, a level of ideology and historical process, and a level of creativity and of education in the arts and sciences. On the level of lifestyle there are immense pressures towards uniformity, including uniformity of language. Economic forces in particular make for increasing centralization. One frequently sees the statement that such trends are changing and becoming more decentralized, but applied to Canada the statement is nonsense.

The creative arts, on the other hand, have to be planted in a very limited environment. Literature, in particular, is intensely regional in Canada, as it is in the United States, and even in the much smaller Great Britain. Canadian critics have realized for a century that the more Canadian a writer tries to be, the less chance he has of becoming a really distinguished writer. The reason is that the conception "Canadian" belongs to a different aspect of culture, and can have little direct or positive influence on the creative one. At the same time, the *aggregate* of writers in Canada will produce a Canadian body of literature, which is felt by both Canadian and non-Canadian readers to be distinctive of the country.

Regional literature grows out of provincial literature. The provincial writer assumes that literary standards have been established for him outside his environment. English and French writers in nineteenth-century Canada both tended to follow models in their ancestral countries. But the notion of meeting established external standards is a fallacy: literature changes too rapidly, and standards are no longer mainstream influences by the time the provinces get around to imitating them. As a provincial culture matures, it becomes more aware of the variety of new ideas and ideologies, new techniques of narrative, new forms of imagery, that are sweeping across the world, and it begins to respond to them and become part of an international idiom. Such an idiom does not, like lifestyle fashions in food or clothing, make for uniformity or mass production: it works in quite the opposite direction, though in ways too complex to go into here. What it does not do either, or does very seldom, is uproot the writer from his localized place in his own community. There is a curious law in culture, at least literary culture, which says that the most specific settings have the best chance of becoming universal in their appeal.

It is clear that a multiplicity of ethnical backgrounds is highly favourable to a culture, and any writer or artist will exploit everything he has that is distinctive in his regional, ethnical, or religious background. But as he matures as a writer and his horizon expands, he wants to be read on his own merits and not as an ethnic specimen, however unusual. Similarly with the consumer. A reader interested in Canadian literature may feel in the position of one who has bought a box of candy and discovered from the fine print on the box that he has acquired a melange of twenty-three food, chemical, and additive substances. But he still expects some unity of taste in the final product, not a mere recognition of the subtle contributions made by invertase or lecithin. As for minority languages, they seem to be one area where privatization actually does seem to work. I think that among the Celtic languages in the British Isles, Welsh has fared better than Irish, because Welsh has been spoken and studied by the people who wanted to speak and study it, whereas Irish was made compulsory in schools and given the rank of an official language, to the great detriment of its popularity.

There remains, however, the unique historical development which has made Canada a bilingual country with two recognized Canadian languages. I suppose no reasonable Canadian denies the extraordinary advantages of a bilingual culture, despite all the complaints one may hear in English Canada about "shoving all that French down our throats," though those who use such phrases are unlikely to have much French in their throats. Corresponding complaints can be heard in French Canada. But one should keep in mind the different aspects of cultural life already referred to, and the fact that a creative benefit may be a political burden. The conception "Québécois," for example, belongs culturally to the area of political leverage, not to anything genuinely creative.

II

Many languages, including earlier English, have no word for space but only for place, or space-*there*. For the imagination of, say, Shakespeare's original audience, the entire cosmos was filled up by objects or beings with assigned places. Nature abhors a vacuum, the philosophers said, at a time when vacuum and empty space meant much the same thing. But as the influence of Copernicus and Galileo began to make itself felt, the imaginative responses changed. The French who settled Quebec and Acadia belonged to the seventeenth-century world of Descartes and Pascal. Descartes was, I think, the first to make the conception of space as pure extension, apart from whatever it contained, functional in philosophy. Pascal, certainly no Cartesian, expressed his terror of "these empty spaces" and their silence, in one of the most famous epigrams ever uttered.[5] By "these empty spaces" he meant much more than what is now called "outer space" beyond the sky, but the phrase reflects a time when, to adapt a remark of Blake, the human imagination was beginning to be more impressed by the amount of space between the stars than by the stars themselves.[6]

It was the sense of space without place, descended to earth to become the natural environment, that confronted the Canadian imagination in its formative years. A universe of places means a hierarchical universe: earlier human imagination was dominated by the sense of a natural hierarchy, with everything occupying the place that God had assigned it. As the sense of natural hierarchy waned, distinction of ranks in human life seemed increasingly to be imposed simply by human will expressed in violence. Some time ago I used the phrase "garrison mentality" to describe the psychological effects in Canada of the Anglo-French wars, fear of Indian attacks, and protection against an implacably indifferent nature, with its cycle of intense heat, intense cold, and the coming of spring along with the black flies. I grew up in a town in the Maritimes about thirty miles from where, in the eighteenth century, a French and a British fort scowled at each other across the isthmus that separates New Brunswick from Nova Scotia. It was an eloquent if primitive symbol of the "two solitudes" that Hugh MacLennan later described in his novel of that name about Anglo-French relations in Montreal. Similar survivals of this "two solitudes" construct were still all around me in my early years. My phrase however has been rather over-exposed since, and like other over-exposed images has got blurred and fuzzy, its specific historical context being usually ignored.

As I understood it, a garrison brings social activity into an intense if constricted focus, but its military and other priorities tend to obliterate the creative impulse. In one brief interval of relaxation, after the peace of 1763, a novel called *Emily Montague* was written by a woman named Frances Brooke in the garrison town of Quebec. It is not only the first novel written in Canada; it is one of the earliest novels to be written anywhere. But a more typical garrison attitude survived psychologically in the rural and small-town phase of Canadian life, with its heavy pressures of moral and conventional anxieties. Canadians are now, however, one of the most highly urbanized people in the world, and the garrison mentality, which was social but not creative, has been replaced by the condominium mentality, which is neither social nor creative, and which forces the cultural energies of the country into forming a kind of counter-environment.

The same paradox of space without place confronted American life too, but the Americans lived in a two-dimensional country, and were able to fill up their empty space more systematically, with the aid of a frontier. Canadians were compelled by geography to live in much more scattered communities, the main divisions of the country being widely separated from one another. The writers or speakers who eventually emerged from this environment were confronted first of all by the physical problems of being able to communicate at all. De Tocqueville, in his magisterial survey of democracy in America, says only one thing about Canada, but what he says bears on our present point. "In Canada," he says, "the most enlightened, patriotic and humane inhabitants make extraordinary efforts to render the people dissatisfied . . . more exertions are made to excite the passions of the citizens there than to calm them elsewhere."[7] He is speaking mainly of French Canada, but the remark applies to the whole country. One reads between the lines the desperate frustrations of the earlier communicators, and the massive indifference of those they attempted to address. The silence of the eternal spaces remained at the bottom of the Canadian psyche for a long time, and in many respects is still there. Communication is of course a major preoccupation, almost an obsession, with Canadians, but in the nineteenth century the impressive part of it was a matter of building railways and bridges and canals. Articulate communication has now taken its normal place in Canadian life, but with rare exceptions Canada has avoided the movements of mass hysteria that have swept over the United States so frequently during the last century.

Some time ago, in looking through an anthology of American poetry, I came across Theodore Roethke's poem *Journey to the Interior*. The "interior" in this poem is both a landscape and a psyche, but the journey is out of the self and not into it. We begin with the image of driving a car or jeep over rough and dangerous roads. Then the car goes faster, and soon we are travelling at a breakneck speed past a place where "some idiot plunger" had previously met his death. The car disappears and the poet's spirit expands to become merged with the nature around him, as all the dormant powers within him break into renewed life. I had read the poem before, but had not realized how superbly it caught a dominant mood in American imaginative experience: the conquering of nature through the sheer force of technology, the exhilaration of danger and high speed that comes as technology develops, and the arrival through the speed at an ecstasy of an expanding consciousness.

I remembered too that there was a Canadian poem also called *Journey to the Interior*, in Margaret Atwood's first volume, *The Circle Game*, so I turned to it. Here the "interior" is again both psychic and physical, but the journeying narrator is apparently walking through woods, moving very cautiously, as much aware of the rough going and the tangles of branches as her counterpart, but with a total uncertainty about her direction. The Atwood narrator wonders if she is going in circles: Roethke speaks only of "detours" in a straightforward quest. But if the Atwood traveller has no trust in direction she is intensely aware of presences, which may be menacing presences. It is important, she says, to keep one's head but useless, perhaps dangerous, to call out or utter words in such a wilderness. Roethke, in contrast, is aware of no presence except his expanding self.

I am not of course comparing the poems in merit, merely looking at them as documents illustrating two kinds of sensibility. Both poems come from the 1960s, Roethke's being a late poem, composed near his death, and Atwood's being early and experimental. I know how easy it is to deceive oneself in such matters, but I feel sure that one sensibility represents something centrally American as it was twenty years ago, and the other something centrally Canadian. One is preoccupied with speed, machinery, progress, and intensity of consciousness, the other with loneliness, diffidence, uncertainty of direction, and a divided consciousness. In the twenty years since then great changes have come over the imaginations of both countries, to the point almost of a merging of attitudes.

According to the Canadian economist Harold Innis, the development of techniques of communication tends to create a "bias" in culture. There are two main biases according to Innis, a bias toward time and a bias toward space. Innis felt that the Canadian sensibility had a time bias and the American a spatial one. This is not as a rule the type of observation that I find very cogent, but let us follow it up for a moment. It may seem to contradict what I said earlier about the impact of space on the Canadian imagination, but the contexts are very different.

Countries that have a long record of oppressive foreign rule are intensely aware of their history: Ireland and Poland are obvious examples. Nations expanding into empires think in terms of acquiring space, and English Canada felt something of this by proxy when it was a part of a British Empire on which the sun was alleged never to set. French Canada, on the other hand, has been very conscious of its history and traditions: Quebec automobile license plates still bear the motto *je me souviens*, I remember. But in fact all Canada, with its sense of precedent and continuous contract, seems oriented to history in a way that the United States, until quite recently, never has been. The sense of irreversible progress that has been so central in American imagination seems to carry with it the sense of an escape from history itself.

The bias toward time may become neurotic, preoccupied with Don Quixote's vision of some imaginary historical ideal that ought to exist now. Ideological terrorism in particular is usually inspired by an obsession with reshaping the past. But the same bias may go in a genuinely creative direction, recognizing that it is tradition more than anything else that creates identity. From about 1960 on, English Canada began to achieve something of the sense of self-definition that French Canada had had for much longer, and a renewed historical sense began to realize how much Canadian cultural traditions had been mutilated by the coming of two European peoples who refused to continue, in fact did their best to extinguish, the culture of the Indian and Inuit peoples already there.

Of course appreciation for the arts and culture of native peoples has not been lacking. The Haida mask from the early documentary *The Loon's Necklace* has been practically a Canadian logo for some time,[8] and the outpouring of Inuit (Eskimo) sculpture and painting has been one of the most remarkable cultural developments in modern history. A great deal of scholarship has been devoted to collecting the oral literary culture of the indigenous peoples, who of course still produce it. What is more recent is the sense of the absurdity of regarding native peoples as foreigners, and their culture as an exotic curiosity. Clearly it forms a tradition which should be at the headwaters of our own, and should be absorbed into our traditions in the same way that English and French traditions are. In Canadian literature, one could point to many examples of such absorption in the work of Susan Musgrave, John Newlove, Robert Kroetsch, M.T. Kelly, Yves Thériault, and others. Even careless popularizers are more hesitant about writing such sentences as "Jacques Cartier was the first man to set foot on Canadian soil," which were fairly frequent usage not so long ago. Even when the word "white" was inserted, the implication "first genuine human being" was often there.

But the new sense of cultural kinship with the indigenous people was not really an expanded historical or temporal awareness: it was part of a new attitude to space, specifically the space within Canada. The closer relationship of the indigenous peoples to their natural environment was what gave them a new significance in Canadian imagination. The nineteenth-century sense of a hostile and amoral nature, the early twentieth-century sense of a land of mystery with its huge and so seldom visited lakes, rivers, and islands, has been almost reversed in a world where anything that is natural may be precious. Rupert Brooke spoke seventy years ago of the "unseizable virginity" of the Canadian landscape,[9] but this will hardly apply to a situation in which even uninhabited land may still be polluted.

Of course a concern for the environment is a worldwide movement, politically as well as culturally, but the Canadian economy has been marked by a peculiarly reckless exploiting of natural resources, in which trees, fish, and fur-bearing animals were sacrificed on a scale that has left a cultural residue of intense guilt feelings in the Canadian consciousness. There has hardly ever been a time when Canadian writing has not expressed some resentment or apprehension at the treatment of the environment. But it is fairly recently that large numbers of people have come to feel that the exploiting of nature is just as wrong and immoral as the exploiting of other human beings. There is an essay by Heidegger, "The Origin of a Work of Art," which has been a strong influence on two very distinguished works of Canadian criticism, Dennis Lee's *Savage Fields* and Bruce Elder's *Image and Identity*, the latter concerned mainly with film. Heidegger's argument turns largely on a distinction between "World" and "Earth." "World" means the universe of human consciousness, "Earth" the universe of animals, plants, and inanimate nature. "World" tries to dominate and enslave "Earth," but "Earth" has its own modes of survival, and it is dangerous to violate it beyond a certain point.

In a poet of an older generation, E.J. Pratt, the main themes are still "World" themes. He wrote narrative poems about whaling expeditions, shipwrecks, the building of the Canadian Pacific Railway, the martyrdoms of Jesuit missionaries in which the Iroquois are assimilated to a mindless and ferocious nature. But even he has a late poem called *The Good Earth* in which he warns:

> Hold that synthetic seed, for underneath
> Deep down she'll answer to your horticulture:
> She has a way of germinating teeth
> And yielding crops of carrion for the vulture. [ll. 21–4]

In the last two or three decades there has been a remarkable growth of the feeling that "nobody owns th earth," as bill bisset says (a poet who chooses lower case and unconventional spellings). There have been startling works of fiction, such as Marion Engel's *Bear*, where an erotic relation between a woman and a pet bear has clearly an allegorical implication that Canadians have to learn to love their environment instead of exploiting or ignoring it. Some poets, again, have internalized the nineteenth-century landscape, with all its fears and loneliness, realizing that the real fears are there and not outdoors. The development in painting has run closely parallel. When I spoke in Washington some years ago, there were two exhibitions of Canadian painting on view, representing two phases of "World" culture in Canada. One was concerned with the early twentieth-century painters, the "Group of Seven" and their contemporaries, who were the pictorial successors of the explorers and missionaries of earlier centuries. The other and more highly publicized exhibit gave us the Clement Greenberg version of painting in Canada, the trend to abstraction which was at once the climax of the "World" view and the beginning of something else, although the something else was even then much more present in Canada than the exhibit suggested.[10] Techniques in painting and film of directly confronting natural imagery, such as the one often called "magical realism," are part of the evidence that a new kind of spatial consciousness has come into Canadian imagination, in all its arts, and has given it a new confidence and stability.

I spoke earlier of the Tory ideology in early English Canada: it was never associated with an aristocracy, though some of the Family Compact may have regarded themselves in that light. But of course their Tory counterparts in England did include a good many of the aristocracy, who devoted a large part of their energy to preserving their game, working up anxieties about poachers and the like. Consciously, there was nothing to this but the selfishness and arrogance of privilege, a subculture of what Matthew Arnold accurately called "Barbarians." But in unconscious symbolism there was some preservation of "Earth" from the encroachments of "World." Canadian consciousness may be slowly moving toward a conception of Canada as something like a gigantic national park, with a string of cities along or near its southern border. Some years ago Buckminster Fuller used the metaphor of "spaceship earth," but this suggested an overcrowded ship with all its space outside.[11] The writers, painters, and film-makers whose function it ought to be, in part, to tell us what the rest of the public will be thinking fifty years later, are providing us with a different metaphor, an internal reservoir of space, an "Earth" that can live with "World."

Great changes have come over the American consciousness too in the last few decades, and I suspect that the more strident and readily politicized issues, such as feminism or racial prejudice, are not the really underlying ones. I spoke earlier of a certain sense, in American imagination up to about 1950, of outrunning history, of a linear progress that would still move in a straight line even if it were headed for disaster. It seems to me that the Vietnam War has brought about the beginning of a profound shift of perspective. In the days when I taught for brief periods in American universities, my students would ask me if I noticed any difference between American and Canadian students. I said that students conditioned from infancy to be part of a world empire must necessarily be very different from students conditioned to be part of a secondary power, observing history from the sidelines rather than playing a major role in it. But I think American consciousness since then has acquired a new sensitivity to history, including its own history, and seeing its recent ascendancy as part of a parabola that goes up and comes down. History has no record of any empire that did not, qua empire, decline and fall, and the process is still inevitable, even though the decline and fall of the Russian and Chinese empires has still to come. There is nothing to regret in this, because the phrase decline and fall, in this context, means only the straightening out of priorities, throwing away phoney ones and, with luck, acquiring more genuine ones.

Of course it takes some effort to become more self-observant, to acquire historical sense and perspective, to understand the limitations that have been placed on human power by God, nature, fate, or whatever. It was part of President Reagan's appeal that he was entirely unaware of any change in consciousness, and talked in the old reassuring terms of unlimited progress. But the new response to the patterns of history seems to have made itself felt, along with a growing sense that we can no longer afford leaders who think that acid rain is something one gets by eating grapefruit. I wish I could document this change from recent developments in American culture, but I am running out of both time and knowledge. It seems clear to me, however, that American and Canadian imaginations are much closer together than they have been in the past.

I make no apology for having talked mainly in terms of the creative aspect of culture. In the first place, you can get better informed political commentary by turning on a television set. In the second place, imaginative developments give one the real clues to political and economic ones. Third, and most important to me, fifty years of teaching have only confirmed my conviction that only the arts and sciences are stable social realities: everything else simply dissolves and re-forms. The world of 1989 is no more like the world I was born into in 1912 than it is like the Stone Age, but nothing has improved since then except scientific and scholarly knowledge, and nothing has remained steady except human creative power. The students crushed under tanks in Tienanmen Square may have been, in a way, as much in the grip of illusion as the thugs who crushed them. But they showed very clearly that all human beings want the same things, freedom and dignity and decent living conditions, that those are very simple and reasonable things to want, and that nothing but the release of the power to apply our knowledge and creative energies can get them. If the process I have tried to trace in the cultural history of Canada and the United States has any validity, that is what it has for its moral.

90

Afterword to *Hetty Dorval*

1990

From the New Canadian Library edition of Ethel Wilson's Hetty Dorval *(Toronto: McClelland & Stewart, 1990), 105–8. The typescript is in NFF, 1991, box 40, file 2.*

Ethel Wilson's work is mainly in the form of what Henry James called "the beautiful and blest novella," the short novel with a streamlined narrative aimed from the beginning at a specific resolution.[1] *The Innocent Traveller* is longer and less shapely, doubtless because its scatterbrained gabbling heroine lasts for a hundred years. This book, however, began as Ethel Wilson's first sustained effort, and gave her an unusual amount of trouble. But *Hetty Dorval*, the two stories in *The Equations of Love*, *Swamp Angel*, and *Love and Salt Water* are exquisite examples of the novella form. The dénouement of *Hetty Dorval*, with its old-style recognition scene, may seem over-designed for contemporary readers accustomed to finding such things only in detective stories and the like, but perhaps contemporary tastes could do with some expanding.

Besides, it is easy to miss the real irony of Hetty Dorval's servant turning out to be her mother. Part of the irony is that Hetty is no freak in this respect: Mrs. Broom is typical of the millions of mothers of adolescent and arrested-adolescent sons or daughters who have never been recognized as anything but servants. Then again, most of us, up to a point, take Longfellow's advice and act in the living present,[2] but for normal people the present is at the end of the past: it is seen in a continuous temporal dimension. Hetty lives in an abstract present and her past keeps disappearing from her awareness: she can remember having seen people before but she cannot remember friendships, much less obligations. She has the charm of the self-absorbed narcissist who inspires admiration but is never touched by it, a fascination endearing in a baby or a housecat but frightening in an adult human. She is constantly spoken of as though her worst quality was her instinct to walk out of situations as soon as they involve her in responsibilities; but what makes her sinister is rather the way she walks into them. Wherever she is, some male in her orbit will move toward her, and the praying mantis will soon have another meal. But when nemesis is finally outraged beyond endurance, and confronts her with her entire past in accusation and righteous wrath, there is no melodrama: she merely stares at it innocently and waits for it to go away. It does: that is not how the Hettys of this world are caught. If they are caught, it is by totally unrelated accidents, like the one indicated unobtrusively in the last two sentences.

If the book were, as its title threatens, the story of Hetty Dorval, it might become tedious. But it is really the story of how the narrator Frankie grows from a child of thirteen into a mature woman. She has a decent father, a shrewd careful mother, and some good friends ready to help her over the rough spots. But they are dead or absent when the crisis comes, and it is Hetty, who never did anything in her life except help herself, Hetty who is not a friend but keeps turning up like an apparition in a Victorian ghost story, who actually becomes the midwife in Frankie's second birth. Of course her help is purely negative, but it is help none the less.

We first see Frankie and Hetty in the tightly constricted society of a small town in the British Columbia hinterland, where the impetuous Thompson River plunges into the devious and dangerous Fraser. Why Hetty went there and how her reputation preceded her we are not clearly told, but the fact that she is cut off from her community is mainly her own doing. No man is an island, says John Donne in the great meditation that forms the motto of the book [*Devotions*, 17], but Hetty is determined to be and remain an island. Frankie is naturally enchanted by a much older stranger from the outside world, and one who gives her some sense, however shallow, of what it would be like to be a complete individual in her own right. Even the pact to keep their friendship secret, though silly and creating a rift with her family, helps in a way to develop this sense. Gradually the relation changes, until at the end Hetty, temporarily in trouble, comes to Frankie and asks to share her bed, lying down in it in a (what else?) S-curve that takes up all the room. Frankie gives her a hard smack on the posterior and tells her to move over: this does not get her a fair share of the bed, naturally, but it marks the final reversal of the adult-child relation between the two.

In the background is the close proximity of nature, the genius loci as the author calls it, and the loving descriptions of it give the story a most distinctive beauty. But for all the beauty there is a predatory side to nature, a total indifference of every living thing to the welfare or comfort of others, with which Hetty's self-absorption blends. It is the seasonal flight of wild geese that makes the most lasting impression on both: doubtless it suggests directed flight to Frankie and simple escape to Hetty.

Hetty Dorval establishes Ethel Wilson's world, a world bounded on the west by Vancouver Island and on the east by the Okanagan valley, which links up readily with the rest of Canada and with England, but seldom crosses the United States boundary. In *Hetty Dorval* many themes are embryonic that are more deeply explored in later works. It is interesting to contrast Hetty with the heroine of "Lilly's Story" in *The Equations of Love*, who starts out as a kicked-around alleycat but forms an iron resolution to live "like folks," to achieve bourgeois respectability for herself and her daughter, and finally succeeds. She too obliterates her past, but with a vision of a future society to counterbalance it. The evocations of the British Columbia landscape, with its hills and alfalfa fields and fishing streams, have a symbolic relevance to the action, but no real "objective correlative" emerges, like the series of images which (as a somewhat defensive prefatory note tells us) are correlated with Topaz in *The Innocent Traveller*, much less anything like the revolver that gives its name to *Swamp Angel*. Carefully limited, quiet and unpretentious, *Hetty Dorval* is a typical first novel of a writer of great ability and a sure sense of direction.

91

Foreword to Viola Whitney Pratt Papers

1990

From Viola Whitney Pratt: A Testament of Love, *ed. Mildred Claire Pratt (Toronto: Lugus Productions, 1990), ix. The same foreword appears, with the substitution of "collecting and editing these essays" for the phrase "editing this diary for publication," in the companion volume,* Viola Whitney Pratt: Papers and Speeches, *issued simultaneously by the same publisher and editor. Viola Pratt, who died in 1984, was the wife of E.J. Pratt and in her own right a teacher, accomplished speaker chiefly on Biblical and literary topics, and editor of a children's magazine.*

Everyone who knew Vi Pratt, as well as a great many who did not, will be most grateful to Claire Pratt for editing this diary for publication. For a woman of her generation even the most able and articulate had to work without adequate recognition, and I hope that this book will bring her extraordinary range of interests and her eloquent style into focus and public attention.

92

Italy in Canada

1990

Text taken from Frye's disk, printed with some errors as the Preface to Italy in Canada *(Toronto: Istituto Italiano di Cultura, 1990). This was the catalogue of a festival of Italian art in Toronto held from November 1990 to January 1991.*

"Italy in Canada" is an overwhelming display of Italian culture in all its variety, an enlarged and expanded version of the highly successful "Italy on Stage" of 1987, and the further result of an agreement on cultural co-operation between Canada and Italy that goes back to 1984. Its variety and quality speak wholly for themselves in the following pages: all an introduction can do is to suggest what its significance is to the country.

The most positive event in Canadian history was the Confederation of 1867, which formed a nation of the immense and sparsely populated mass of land in northern North America. Confederation envisaged an essentially British Canada, with French and indigenous groups forming picturesque variations. It was a romantic and imperialistic conception, by no means an ignoble one, but its cultural basis was so impoverished that it collapsed very quickly, leaving English Canada to wonder about its real identity for several decades.

Canada is no longer at the end of the earth: it is at the centre of the present world, the U.S. on its south, the U.S.S.R. on its north, Japan and China on the west, the European common market on the east. Like Switzerland in nineteenth-century Europe, it can maintain its identity only by having many identities. Its population has become urbanized and its larger cities transformed from homogeneous English and French communities into great cosmopolitan centres. It is clearly time to start creating a second positive event in our history: Reconfederation. The only basis for such a Reconfederation that will count for anything—and this is the one reason for writing this introduction—is a cultural basis that is in accord with the present cultural situation in Canada. This includes a greatly increased number of ethnic groups, the refusal of French and indigenous Canadians to retire into a picturesque background, and the fairly recent emergence of an English Canadian literature whose integrity and power is recognized over the world.

Every ethnical group in Canada—British, French, Inuit, Caribbean, Vietnamese, Sikh, whatever—requires a tension of cultural loyalties: one to its origin, the other to its Canadian context. By tension I do not mean straining in opposite directions, and by loyalty I mean nothing uncritical. I mean simply a context in both time and space. Every one should be proud of being what he is and of where he is, otherwise something has gone seriously wrong. Such a festival as this should, as the text of the program says, make Canadians proud if they are of Italian origin, and fascinated if they are not.

Of all the major ethnical groups in Canada, I think the Italians are the most aware (though the Japanese run them a close second) of the interlocking relevance of everything that we normally call culture. This includes culture as a lifestyle, its food and drink and clothes; culture as entertainment, its games and films and puppet shows and concerts; and culture as the creative arts, both contemporary and historical. Whatever your personal cultural interests, you can hardly fail to find some of them here.

It increasingly seems obvious to me that nothing can improve in the modern world except science, to the extent that science has no boundaries (to the extent that it does have boundaries, in other words is politically controlled, it is evil and dangerous). The arts of culture do have boundaries: they are intensely localized and specific, but their boundaries (unless also politically controlled) are infinitely porous and open to influences from all over the world. So just as science is our only source of improvement because it operates in one world, so the cultural arts are our only source of stability because their boundaries welcome invasion, which of course is not invasion but transfusion. It is such a transfusion, on an extraordinarily rich and lavish scale, that is here being presented to the Canadian public.

93

Tribute to Don and Pauline McGibbon

12 June 1990

From the typescript in NFF, 1991, box 34, file 4. Frye made his remarks at a dinner honouring the McGibbons. Pauline McGibbon had been Lieutenant-Governor of Ontario, 1974–80.

My friendship with Don and Pauline goes back for sixty years, when we were classmates in the same year at Victoria College—1932 for Don, 1933 for Pauline. To explain how that got to be the same year would take another half-hour. I have just been sitting at a table with seven members from that year at it, and others are scattered through the room. It is a year that has stayed together more closely than perhaps any other graduating year at Victoria, and you will perhaps not be surprised to learn that the hospitality of the McGibbons, in holding a reception at every reunion year, is the central reason for that fact. It was a very incestuous year, with thirty-two people marrying within it, but naturally most of those met their husbands and wives at college. Not Don and Pauline: they came apparently straight from high school with a marriage made in heaven but rooted in Sarnia.

They may not have been model students by the standards of that time and place: they occasionally got away to dance halls with names like The Silver Slipper, which sounds harmless enough now, but was way out for the somewhat overprotected young women in Victoria residences in 1930. Then came graduation, Don's study at the School of Business Administration in Harvard, and a rapidly expanding social program of volunteer work, at first mainly in the IODE for Pauline,[1] in the university alumni for both of them. Their interests, however widely spread, have always revolved around university life and the awarding of scholarships: Don served long and faithfully on the Board of Regents at Victoria University; Pauline has been chancellor of two universities and, as you have heard already, has a dozen or so honorary degrees. They have always been most loyal to Victoria, but when Pauline became chancellor of the University of Toronto she made special efforts to show that she was interested in every aspect of the larger institution.

Their work for Canadian drama has always been a central part of their activities: the Drama League expanded into the Dominion Drama Festival under them. If my memory serves me, Pauline was the first president of the festival, with Don treasurer; then Don was the second president. Sounds like an interlocking directorate. It is easy enough to be what is called stage struck, but one doesn't always realize what a vast amount of self-sacrificing and anonymous work has to be done behind the scenes before the novice can get on the stage and utter his immortal first line: "The dean, my lord, is cwed."[2] The immense amount of dramatic activity in Ontario, apart altogether from the Stratford and Niagara festivals, owes as much to the McGibbons as to any other single persons.

Even those who have barely heard of the McGibbons have been fascinated by them, very largely, I think, because of their uniquely civilized lifestyle. Many people have been interested in drama, in music, in painting, in university work and scholarships. But to see a Canadian businessman with a socially active wife take such an interest in these things, and to cultivate that interest with such energy for such a long time, is like finding two green and living trees in a developer's desert.

Pauline in particular seems to be useful as a precedent-breaker: her career is peppered with the phrase "first woman," as though she were Ontario's Eve. Being honorary colonel of a regiment is perhaps not unique for someone who has been Lieutenant-Governor, but to be on the board of governors for Upper Canada [College] and, even more, to be on the selection committee for Rhodes scholarships, is enough to send Rhodes spinning in his grave like a dynamo. There is no word in the English language to describe what Pauline is: the word "socialite" would be ridiculous, because it suggests someone who doesn't work very hard, and Pauline has worked like a galley slave at every job she's tackled. I once met her at a house in Edmonton, where she'd just come back from Aklavik, or some equally unlikely place, to find alumni of the University of Toronto, but finding them and talking to them was what she was doing at the time, and she was doing it with her invariable thoroughness. Years later, when as Lieutenant-Governor she was covering the smaller centres in Ontario, I saw a news item on her that aroused the kind of affectionate admiration that only Pauline can inspire. The question had come up of a second term as Lieutenant-Governor, and Pauline had remarked that it would be nice to have a bit more time, as then she would be able to get to Wawa.

There are many people who for one reason or another, political or otherwise, do not approve of having a representative of the Queen in a Canadian province, but I imagine that most of them, at least in Ontario, came to feel that when such a person as that held the office, there was a lot to be said for the office. Not that everyone knows what the office is: an American friend of mine, formerly a lootenant in the American Navy, said to me with a most puzzled expression: "But what *is* a left-handed Governor?"

Anyone looking over the list of things Don and Pauline have done, and thinking of the innumerable things they have also done that have never been recorded, may well wonder how they could have done it without being quintuplets at least. What keeps them going is not simply the genuineness of their interest in people, but a genius for friendship. Like anyone else, their radius of friends stretches from the close to the casual, but at no point does it cut out or exclude: nothing in their relationship to anyone builds up cliques or factions or divisions. I think of that particularly in contrast to so much in Canadian public life. For the last few weeks we've been watching that curious one-sided football game that Canadians seem to be preoccupied with—eleven men kicking around a compromise.[3] (I should think Pauline's work in connection with art and drama centres in Montreal was itself a powerful argument against separatism.) And I think of the futility and fantasy of so much of such activity: people promoting visions of society as much out of touch with reality as Don Quixote's age of chivalry; hard-working public servants writing reports and drafting resolutions to be ignored and thrown in the waste basket.

Don and Pauline have undoubtedly sat through many tedious discussions and have been bored as often as anyone else. But they have concentrated on the things that last: drama, the arts, the universities: what will still be here when all the fantasy and futility has gone. So what we pay tribute to tonight is not only these two extraordinary people; it is not only even the work they have done. It is also in part a tribute to the genuine and permanent value of what they have worked for with so much energy and efficiency: to the activities and institutions that will continue to be important, and will be carried on by people who will always remember who it was that helped them so much when they most needed help.

94

The Cultural Development of Canada

17 October 1990

Text from the booklet The Cultural Development of Canada *(Toronto: Massey College and the Vice-President, Research, 1991). Reprinted in the 2nd edition of Frye's* The Modern Century *(Toronto: Oxford University Press, 1991); as "Northrop Frye's Canada,"* Globe and Mail, *15 April 1991; and in* Australian-Canadian Studies, *10, no. 1 (1991): 9–16. A typescript with corrections is in NFF, 1991, box 38, file 8. Frye's piece was originally given as an address to a luncheon meeting of the Social Sciences and Humanities Research Council of Canada (SSHRCC) at Hart House, University of Toronto.*

Canada has had a far less bloody and violent history than most countries, but Canadians have lived through as much history as any other nation, and the pattern of that history is closely related to events everywhere else in the world. The pivot around which our history turns is, of course, the Confederation of 1867, which was a romantic and imperialistic idea, consolidating into a nation a group of British-controlled colonies and territories. In many respects it was by no means an ignoble idea, and the documents leading up to it, such as the Quebec Act and the Durham Report,[1] were, by the standards of their time, based on sane and balanced conceptions.

The main thing wrong with Confederation was its impoverished cultural basis. It was thought of, however unconsciously, as a British colony and a Tory counterpart of the United States, with French and indigenous groups forming picturesque variations in the background. Treaties were made with the indigenous people, but as it was widely assumed that they would soon become extinct or assimilated it made little difference what the treaties said. Students of my generation were taught in school to sing *The Maple Leaf Forever*, which almost attained the status of a national anthem in English Canada, though its attitude to British imperialism sounds pathetic enough in 1990.

There are, as I see it, three aspects of the word culture. First, there is culture as a lifestyle, shown by the way a society eats, drinks, clothes itself, and carries on its normal social rituals. The British pub and the French bistro represent a cultural difference in lifestyle of this sort. Second, there is culture as a shared heritage of historical memories and customs, carried out mainly through a common language. Third, there is culture in the shape of what is genuinely created in a society: its literature, music, architecture, science, scholarship, and applied arts. In the years following Confederation, Canada could hardly be said to have had a culture in any of these areas. There was no distinctively Canadian lifestyle; there was some sense of a common tradition in French Canada, but not much elsewhere; the arts and sciences were minor and provincial. On the Mercator maps usually studied in school, Canada was a huge land mass extending to the ends of the earth, full of rivers, lakes, and islands that few Canadians had ever seen; the inhabited part of the country looked only like what the United States had left, a country longer and more divided than Chile. To make a nation out of the stops on the Intercolonial and Canadian Pacific lines seemed as chimerical a notion as building an African civilization on a Cape-to-Cairo railway.

In the eighteenth century the French lost Canada largely because they had no interest in holding it: they sold Louisiana to the United States a few years later, and that probably indicates what the fate of a French Canada would have been. With no social structure left of its own, French Canada fell under the control of the Catholic Church, which was profoundly alienated by the atheistic and anticlerical French Revolution. As for the British, once they succeeded in occupying Canada their interest in it remained lukewarm, and Canadians in England constantly felt that they would have been regarded with more respect if they had belonged to an independent nation like the United States. The pioneering literature of the nineteenth century continually conveys the feeling that Canada was a kind of noncriminal penal colony, designed for remittance men and Irish housemaids. The Americans made two attempts to occupy the country by military force, both of them beaten off, but violence and the threat of violence continued in the Fenian raids and such things as the "fifty-four-forty-or-fight" crisis. They then tried economic penetration, in which they were brilliantly successful. Why go to the trouble of annexing a country that is so easy to exploit without taking any responsibility for it? A society valued mainly for its beaver pelts, its softwood forests, and the soldiers it can supply for other countries' wars, is unlikely to develop any cultural phenomena beyond a problem of identity, a general state of wondering why it exists.

Part two of this history begins with the close of the Second World War. Up to 1945 immigration from countries other than the United Kingdom had been largely rural-based. But now an urbanized immigration started pouring into the larger cities: half a dozen large ethnic groups appeared in Toronto, which up till then was mainly a Wasp reservation. French Canada went through a secularizing "Quiet Revolution" that deprived the Catholic Church of most of its political influence, and gave Quebec a new sense of status. The indigenous people showed a strong prejudice against extinction or assimilation, and began to develop a new professional class, including lawyers, to examine such questions as whether building a golf course across land previously guaranteed to them was really in the spirit of that agreement. Meanwhile Canada had ceased to be a British colony and had become effectively an American one, which made at least more geographical sense in a postnaval world. In the sixties many American students opposed to the Vietnam draft discovered that Canada was not merely an insulation of ice against the Soviet Union but was an actual country that could be lived in.

All these developments created a cultural imbalance that exploded in the crisis of the Meech Lake controversy in 1990 and continued in the Oka confrontation a few weeks later.[2] I am not competent to discuss the incidental problems involved here. But I feel that directly in front of us lies a primary need for what I shall call Reconfederation, and which I think of essentially as providing a cultural skeleton for the country that fits its present conditions. Without a cultural Reconfederation there can be only continued political tinkering of the most futile kind. True, I think the best political context by far for Reconfederation is a renewed political Confederation, which means abandoning all the jockeying for power that proposes trade barriers or separate currencies. I hope that the greatest of all political forces, inertia, will manifest its majestic power here.

A political entity, in any case, is not a cultural one. French-speaking Canada is a cultural reality of the highest importance: "Quebec" is a province like other provinces, and always will be: the more separatist its policies, the more inevitably provincial their characteristics. Such pedantic fatuities as outlawing English signs on the outsides of buildings are typical of the way that the political mind works when dealing with a cultural problem. A distinct society can be only a cultural unit where a language is spoken and a culture fostered by those genuinely interested in it for its own sake, and such societies are the only possible architects of a reconfederated Canada. Quebec had been an architect of Confederation in 1867, and it has no higher destiny now than to become an architect of Reconfederation on a renewed cultural basis.

It is a curious law, or seems to be one, that a neglected or oppressed culture will sooner or later fulfil itself. No culture could have been more submerged than that of black America in the nineteenth century, yet it was that culture whose jazz transformed the music first of America and then of the world. Similarly, the Inuit peoples of the North turned out to have astonishing resources of highly prized creative abilities in sculpture and painting; something very similar has happened with the Indian people, and after the Quiet Revolution French-speaking Canada began to develop a poetry and fiction of extraordinary intensity and power. Finally, English Canada, the land nobody wanted, the land that seemed unable to communicate except by railways and bridges, began, from about 1960 on, to produce a literature of a scope and integrity admired the world over. Not that such things take place simply as mysteries or miracles. Canada cannot afford private universities, and must have subsidies in all areas related to scholarship and creativity, and without the present organization [SSHRCC] and the Canada Council earlier none of this would have happened.

The Meech Lake conference was so administratively clumsy in its set-up that it was certain to fail, and the main issue involved was, as just explained, partly an illusory one. What was amazing about the conference was that it very nearly succeeded, and of the two final roadblocks one had nothing to do with the "distinct society" issue at all. The Québécois were told by their leaders to interpret the Meech Lake débâcle as a rejection of their special status by English Canada, but I think it represented the exact opposite: a sense of urgency about the cultural renovation of the country, of which the distinct society clause was at least a symbol. It was a curious irony that Quebec found a sovereignty-association issue of its own on its doorstep a few weeks later. I am aware how many qualifications are involved here, but both crises were nearly hysterical by Canadian standards, which they would not have been, I think, if they had been concerned with cultural realities instead of political fictions.

The Cultural Development of Canada

The bilingual program emphasized in the Trudeau era seems to me on the whole a sensible and pragmatic policy, and its general shape will doubtless remain in place for some time. The unwillingness of speakers of a majority language to learn a minority one certainly exists, but is by no means confined to Canada, and, apart from an occasional foolish demonstration, English Canada's tolerance has been remarkable. Flemish is not, to put it mildly, popular in French-speaking Belgium; Irish, whatever the sentiments behind it, is not really popular in Ireland; and the immense social pressure on French Canadians to speak English is part of a North American situation, in fact of a world situation, that affects Norway and Pakistan as much as it affects Quebec. The spearhead of invasion of English into Quebec does not come from English Canada but from American television. Meanwhile the language and culture of French Canada is in flourishing shape, in no danger except when politicians refuse to leave it alone. Culture and language are an area—perhaps the only area—where privatization really does work.

The variety of ethnical mix in the bigger Canadian cities brought the buzzword "multiculturalism" into the foreground, and a variety of problems with it. An Anglo-French bilingualism seems more problematic in a city where, as in Toronto, the Italian-speaking population is eight to ten times greater than the French one. Behind this lies the contemporary geographical situation of Canada, which is no longer at the ends of the earth but in the centre of all the great powers, the United States on the south, the Soviet Union on the north, Japan and eventually China on the west, and the European common market on the east. Two of these, the Soviet Union and Europe, are in the process of becoming primarily cultural federations. Like Switzerland in nineteenth-century Europe, Canada must now preserve its identity by having many identities.

May I revert for a moment to my conception of three aspects of culture, as a lifestyle, as a shared heritage, and as the pursuit of scholarship, the sciences, and the creative arts. There is hardly a distinctive Canadian cultural lifestyle, which has been largely identical with that of northern United States for a long time. This in turn has been part of the general homogenizing of lifestyles everywhere. In Canada we say, or have said, that we are being Americanized; but America itself has become Americanized in the same way, and the original contrasts in, say, Philadelphia, St. Louis, and Atlanta have long since been largely obliterated.

The process here is that of the growing uniformity of technology, in which Americans have naturally had a leading role. We cannot take off in a jet plane and expect a radically different way of life in the place where the plane lands. Uniformity of standards and measurements is of course essential in all technological or mechanical areas: in other aspects of human life we seek a unity or coalescence of various things. Unity, which always possesses a quality of uniqueness, is the opposite of uniformity, where there is only likeness or similarity.

As for culture in the sense of a shared heritage, this is an outgrowth of a provincial stage where there is a sense of only one community. As the provincial grows into the genuinely cultural, the conflicts of the past become the positive elements of a common experience. *Je me souviens* is an ambiguous motto: everything depends on what one is expected to remember. If it means preserving the continuity of a cultural tradition within a larger context, it is a basic principle of human dignity; if it means brooding on suppressed resentments in the past, it is quixotic nonsense. In contrast to the United States and France, which began with revolution and the deductive approach to unity that a revolution inculcates, Canada has had a history of compromise and *ad hoc* agreements, with a fairly constant attempt, whatever the lapses, to preserve the rights of both sides. At any rate, Canada seems to impress non-Canadians as a moderate and reasonable country, potentially as happy a country to live in as the world affords. It is a peculiarly poignant irony that Canada should reach such a point when its political leadership seems to have been attacked by an epidemic of Alzheimer's disease.

The twentieth century has been mainly a period of war and tyranny: these are evil things, and there is always something unreal about evil, not for the victims, unfortunately, but in the sense of disappearing from history with no structure left behind. Nothing has improved in this century except science and scholarship, which have improved because they have no boundaries. If they do have boundaries, in other words if they are politically controlled, they soon become sinister and dangerous. And just as only science and scholarship have improved, so nothing has remained stable except the arts, including the arts of language. These do have boundaries: poetry and fiction particularly are usually limited to a very specific locale. But they are infinitely porous boundaries, open to influences from anywhere in the world. The prominence of Zola, Erasmus, Disraeli, and Mill in Canadian humanist scholarship may have started accidentally through the presence of qualified scholars here, but they represent a Canadian presence in world culture, and are part of the only contribution we can make to the world that the world is likely to have much permanent respect for.[3]

The Cultural Development of Canada

Sometimes the influence is from the same country. There are many poets and novelists in Canada of white ethnical origin who think of themselves as cultural descendants of indigenous people and helping to carry on their traditions. It is sometimes said that, for example, whites should not write about blacks or Gentiles about Jews, but that is only froth on the surface of controversy. The more vigorous the literature, the more it thrives on cross-pollination. One thinks of Yeats and his dependence on a Celtic and Irish mythological tradition of which he knew next to nothing at first hand. A different type of cross-pollination occurs when a Canadian writer has a Japanese or Caribbean or Czech or Sri Lankan background.

A few weeks ago I was in Yugoslavia, travelling by train from Zagreb in Croatia to Ljubljana in Slovenia. The journey was about as far as from Toronto to Kingston, but when I got off the train I was in a different country which spoke a quite different language. For seventy years this tiny landlocked community had been a rather down-graded part of Yugoslavia, and for centuries before that an even more down-graded part of the Austrian empire. And why was I in Ljubljana? Because the university there had decided to open a school of Canadian studies. I thought to myself that this is typical of what a culture is: it is the indestructible core of a human society, so far as it is a human society and not a mere aggregate of atoms in a human mass. Such a culture can resist century after century of invasion, conquest, infiltration, and neglect; yet it remains open to influences and experiences from anywhere in the world, even Canada.

The institutions of culture, museums, art galleries, and above all universities, reflect this boundary-without-walls aspect of culture in their combination of local and worldwide interests. Cultural institutions are educational as well, because what I have been calling culture is the social manifestation of the educational system. It is not only the present audience, but a rapidly increasing number of concerned Canadians, who realize that Canadian educational standards are far below what they ought to be. This question has been discussed endlessly: I have only one point to make here about it.

A very central and important aspect of education, and probably the part that stays with us longest, is what comes, not from what we are taught or read, but from what we learn from one another. The more homogeneous and provincial the community, the more of what we learn in this way is simply the repeated prejudices of our friends, backed up by similar repetitions in the news media. Canada has now become cosmopolitan to a degree that would have been incomprehensible fifty years ago. If Toronto is a world-class city, it is not because it bids for the Olympics or builds follies like the Skydome, but because of the tolerated variety of the people in its streets.

Society must have loyalty, but in a democracy there are no uncritical loyalties. There must always be a tension of loyalties, not in the sense of opposed forces pulling apart, but in the sense of one feeling of belonging attached to and complemented by another, which is very often the relating of a smaller ethnical community to a larger one. It is through some such process as this that the cultural development of Canada must make its way.

Appendix
Canadian Criticism

From the typescript in NFF, 1991, box 58, file 8. This undated statement is in a file labelled "The Canadian Forum—Reviews by Frye." The two other pieces in the file appeared in the Forum *in the late 1940s. This piece has not been found in the printed journal; its themes suggest it originated at about the same date.*

Criticism may be anything from scholarship to journalism. Both of these are international, and very few branches of either in Canada give any unusual amount of attention to Canadian subjects. So I suppose Canadian criticism means criticism of Canadian culture: otherwise it just means the critical work that has accidentally got written here. You notice that I begin by quibbling about the meaning of "Canadian," which is what most Canadian critics do. And it's harder than one would think to say just what that word does mean, because there is no Canadian language or dialect, and Canada is not a geographical unit. A good many of our critics say that to worry about this question is the sign of a provincial mind, and they have my sympathy; but usually they write just as much about it as anyone else.

Our critics have done most of their best work on painting and poetry, and there the word "Canadian" could be, perhaps not defined, but at least described, as a fairly distinctive kind of experience. That is the sense of an unusually exposed contact with nature. Most of our best painting is pure landscape, and our poetry is full of the tragedy and irony that grow out of a pioneer's struggle with nature. I don't say that this is the primary fact of Canadian life: I say that Canadian painters and poets seem to be fond of dealing with it, and so it becomes the subject-matter of our criticism. It doesn't follow that our critics all like what they have to write about: they often complain that the Canadian artist is unwilling to come to grips with the real social problems of Canada, and takes refuge in a romantic escape. They say that the Canadian painter is too fascinated by icebergs and rocks and trees, and the Canadian poet too absorbed in the lyrical possibilities of the climate. This doesn't apply so much to our fiction, and criticism of the best Canadian fiction seems to me to be, except in details, just like the criticism of any other fiction. That is what a lot of our critics wish were true of the criticism of everything else produced in Canada.

Notes

Introduction

1 *NFC*, 135.
2 George Johnston, "Northrop Frye: Some Recollections and Observations," *CEA Critic*, 42, no. 2 (January 1980): 25.
3 Notebook 3, par. 174 (NFF, 1991, box 22).
4 Quoted in David Staines, introduction to E.K. Brown, *Responses and Evaluations: Essays on Canada* (Toronto: McClelland & Stewart, 1977), xiii–xiv.
5 *NFC*, 135.
6 Malcolm Ross, "Northrop Frye," *University of Toronto Quarterly*, 41 (Winter 1972): 173.
7 Margaret Atwood, "Fifties Vic," *CEA Critic*, 42, no. 1 (November 1979): 21.
8 This was a one-hour-a-week course offered to senior students in certain honour courses, though not to those in English. See Jay Macpherson, *The Spirit of Solitude* (New Haven: Yale University Press, 1982), 321, n.3.
9 NF, "The Search for Acceptable Words," *Daedalus*, 102 (Spring 1973): 19.
10 For a discussion of the meaning of the term in Frye, see Jean O'Grady, "The Poetic Frye," *Journal of Canadian Studies*, 34, no. 4 (Hiver 1999/2000 Winter): 15–26.
11 *Voices of Canada: An Introduction to Canadian Culture*, ed. Judith Webster (Burlington, Vt.: Association for Canadian Studies in the United States, 1977), 19, 21. This interchange was brought to my attention by Thomas Willard's essay "Gone Primitive: The Critic in Canada," forthcoming in *Northrop Frye: Eastern and Western Perspectives*, ed. Jean O'Grady and Wang Ning (Toronto: University of Toronto Press, 2003), 110–20.
12 Wayne Grady, *Chasing the Chinook: On the Trail of Canadian Words and Culture* (Toronto: Viking, 1998), 113. Malcolm Ross describes the puzzlement of his foreign students when confronted with Frye's characterization of the dominant note of Canadian literature. See "The Impossible Sum of Our Tradi-

tions" (1982), in *The Impossible Sum of Our Traditions: Reflections on Canadian Literature* (Toronto: McClelland & Stewart, 1986), 186.

13 Susan Glickman, *The Picturesque and the Sublime: A Poetics of the Canadian Landscape* (Montreal & Kingston: McGill-Queen's University Press, 1998), 45.

14 Sandra Djwa, "Forays in the Bush Garden: Frye and Canadian Poetry," in *The Legacy of Northrop Frye*, ed. Alvin A. Lee and Robert D. Denham (Toronto: University of Toronto Press, 1994), 130–45. NF himself recognizes this literary connection, e.g. at 103.

15 For two recent discussions of NF's changing response to nature, including his handling of the gendered terminology that sees nature as female, see Caterina Nella Cotrupi, "Against a Separate Nature," in *Northrop Frye and the Poetics of Process* (Toronto: University of Toronto Press, 2000); and Margaret Burgess, "From Archetype to Antitype: A Look at Frygian Archetypology," in *Northrop Frye and the Afterlife of the Word, Semeia*, 89 (2002): 103–24.

16 Desmond Pacey, "The Course of Canadian Criticism," in *Literary History of Canada*, ed. Carl F. Klinck et al., 2nd ed. (Toronto: University of Toronto Press, 1976), 3:22.

17 David Staines, "Northrop Frye in a Canadian Context," in *Visionary Poetics: Essays on Northrop Frye's Criticism*, ed. Robert D. Denham and Thomas Willard (New York: Peter Lang, 1991), 53.

18 Malcolm Ross, "Critical Theory: Some Trends," in *Literary History of Canada*, 2nd ed., 3:162.

19 Frank Davey, "Surviving the Paraphrase," in *Surviving the Paraphrase: Eleven Essays on Canadian Literature* (Winnipeg: Turnstone Press, 1983), 3.

20 Barry Cameron and Michael Dixon, "Mandatory Subversive Manifesto: Canadian Criticism vs. Literary Criticism," introduction to special issue of *Studies in Canadian Literature*, 2 (Summer 1977): 138, 139.

21 Paul Stuewe, *Clearing the Ground: English-Canadian Literature after "Survival"* (Toronto: Proper Tales Press, 1984), esp. 12–14. See also W.J. Keith, "The Thematic Approach to Canadian Fiction," in *Taking Stock: The Calgary Conference on the Canadian Novel*, ed. Charles R. Steele (Toronto: ECW Press, 1982), 71–90.

22 Russell Brown, "Critic, Culture, Text: Beyond Thematics," *Essays on Canadian Writing*, 11 (1978): 181.

23 Heather Murray, "Reading for Contradiction in the Literature of Colonial Space," in *Future Indicative: Literary Theory and Canadian Literature*, ed. John Moss (Ottawa: University of Ottawa Press, 1986), 75.

24 This is the term used by Branko Gorjup in his introduction to *ECLI*, 10, and in his introduction to an as yet unpublished collection of critical reactions to Frye's Canadian writings. Many of the works mentioned here will be found

in this useful volume. I am grateful to Professor Gorjup for letting me read its introduction and table of contents.
25 Leon Surette, "Here Is Us: The Topocentrism of Canadian Literary Criticism," *Canadian Poetry*, 10 (Spring/Summer 1982), 44–57.
26 Eli Mandel, introduction to *Contexts of Canadian Criticism* (Chicago: University of Chicago Press, 1971), 7.
27 David Jackel, "Northrop Frye and the Continentalist Tradition," *Dalhousie Review*, 56, no. 2 (1976): 221–39. Cf. also Robin Mathews's *Canadian Literature: Surrender or Revolution* (Toronto: Steel Rail Educational Publishing, 1978), which accuses Frye of being part of an insidious Americanization of Canadian culture, though not specifically because of geographical determinism.
28 George Bowering, "Why James Reaney Is a Better Poet (1) Than Any Northrop Frye Poet (2) Than He Used to Be," *Canadian Literature*, 36 (Spring 1968): 40–9.
29 Jackel, "Northrop Frye and the Continentalist Tradition," 238, n.20.
30 Eli Mandel, "Northrop Frye and the Canadian Literary Tradition," in *Centre and Labyrinth: Essays in Honour of Northrop Frye*, ed. Eleanor Cook et al. (Toronto: University of Toronto Press, 1983), 286. Louis Dudek, "Frye Again (But Don't Miss Souster)," *Delta*, 5 (October 1958): 26–7.
31 Milton Wilson, "Frye as Reviewer of Canadian Poetry," in *The Legacy of Northrop Frye*, 146–54.
32 George Woodcock, "Poetry," in *Literary History of Canada*, 2nd ed., 3: 311, 294.
33 George Woodcock, "Diana's Priest in the Bush Garden: Frye and His Master" (1974), in *The World of Canadian Writing: Critiques and Recollections* (Vancouver: Douglas & McIntyre, 1980), 234. In "Away from Lost Worlds" (1964), the first essay in *Odysseus Ever Returning* (Toronto: McClelland & Stewart, 1970), Woodcock suggested that Frye's criticism was "largely responsible" for the emergence of the mythopoeic school (2).
34 James Reaney, editorial introducing *Alphabet*, no. 1 (September 1960).
35 For the anthologies, entitled *Literature: Uses of the Imagination*, see Jean O'Grady, introduction to *WE*, xli–xlii.
36 Woodcock, "Diana's Priest in the Bush Garden," 234.
37 E.g., Eleanor Cook, "Against Monism: The Canadian Anatomy of Northrop Frye," in *Ritratto di Northrop Frye*, ed. Agostino Lombardo (Rome: Bulzoni Editore, 1989), 288–9; Linda Hutcheon's introduction, "The Field Notes of a Public Critic," to a new edition of *BG* (Toronto: Anansi, 1995), ix–xi.
38 NF, interview with Peter Gzowski on the CBC's "Morningside," 30 March 1987, transcribed from the CBC tape by Monika Lee.
39 Sandra Djwa, "'Canadian Angles of Vision': Northrop Frye and the *Literary History of Canada*," *English Studies in Canada*, 19, no. 2 (June 1993): 133–49. A revised version of this essay is forthcoming in *Northrop Frye: Eastern and Western Perspectives*, 95–109.

40 Murray, "Reading for Contradiction in the Literature of Colonial Space," 72–3. A similar point is made by Mathews, *Canadian Literature*, 136–7.
41 A.J.M. Smith, "Eclectic Detachment," *Canadian Literature*, 9 (Summer 1961): 7, quoting from his introduction to the *Oxford Book of Canadian Verse in English and French* (1960).
42 Milton Wilson, "*Other Canadians* and After," in *Masks of Poetry*, ed. A.J.M. Smith (Toronto: McClelland & Stewart, 1962), 137–8.
43 Eli Mandel, introduction to *Contexts of Canadian Criticism*, 13.
44 Surette, "Here Is Us," 48.
45 Ross, "Critical Theory," in *Literary History of Canada*, 2nd ed., 3:165. See NF's remarks at 361–2 below.
46 For a recent discussion of this shift, see Philip Kokotailo, "From Father to Sun: Northrop Frye and the History of English-Canadian Poetry," *American Review of Canadian Studies*, Spring 1999, 43–66.
47 *StS*, 61.
48 See two essays by Malcolm Ross, "The Imaginative Sense and the Canadian Question" (1977), and "Canadian Culture and the Colonial Question" (1982), in *The Impossible Sum of Our Traditions*.
49 Murray, "Reading for Contradiction in the Literature of Colonial Space"; Wang Ning, "Northrop Frye and Cultural Studies," forthcoming in *Northrop Frye: Eastern and Western Perspectives*, 82–91. Wang points out both the postmodernism inherent in Frye's jettisoning of the conventional standards of judgment, and the postcolonialism of Frye's championing of a marginal literature. On the latter point, see also Jan Gorak, *The Making of the Modern Canon* (London: Athlone, 1991), 142.
50 Linda Hutcheon, "Frye Recoded: Postmodernity and the Conclusions," in *The Legacy of Northrop Frye*, 105–21.
51 Eleanor Cook, "Against Monism: The Canadian Anatomy of Northrop Frye," 293–4. Her other examples, such as the novels of Margaret Atwood and the dramas of James Reaney, would be considered "similar" to *AC* only by someone with a Frygian taxonomy of literary form.
52 Margaret Atwood, "Eleven Years of *Alphabet*," *Canadian Literature*, 49 (1971): 62–3.
53 A.C. Hamilton, "Northrop Frye as a Canadian Critic," *University of Toronto Quarterly*, 62, no. 3 (Spring 1993): 309–22.
54 NF, interview with Carl Mollins, *Northrop Frye Newsletter*, 4, no. 2 (Summer 1992): 5.

1. Lord Dufferin

1 Both Tennyson's and Browning's poems are titled *Helen's Tower*.
2 Noel Coward's *Cavalcade*, chronicling English history, consists of twenty-one short scenes spanning a period of thirty years.

3. Canadian Art in London

1 "Canadian Art in London," *The Times*, 15 October 1938, 9–10.
2 Louis Jobin (1845–1928) was a Quebec sculptor known mainly for large religious statues in metal-covered wood.
3 *New Statesman*, 22 October 1938, 610. Jan Gordon, "Canadian Art: Exhibition at Tate Gallery," *Observer*, 16 October 1938, 15.

4. Canadian Water-Colours

1 With funding from the Federal Arts Project, the WPA (Works Progress Administration) printed about two million posters from 1935 to 1943.
2 Hagan's *Susanna at the Bath* is a parody of Rembrandt's *Susanna and the Elders*.

5. Gordon Webber and Canadian Abstract Art

1 See the anecdote of the artist Tschuplitski in chap. 12 of Aldous Huxley's *Crome Yellow* (1921).

8. Canadian Chapbooks

1 Dr. Lorne Pierce was editor of the Ryerson Press from 1920 to 1960.

9. Canadian Writing: *First Statement*

1 *PM; An Intimate Journal for Production Managers, Art Directors and Their Associates* (New York: 1934–40).
2 John Sutherland, Betty Sutherland, Robert Simpson, Keith MacLellan, and Audrey Aikman.
3 "Editorial," no. 1, p. 1.
4 John Sutherland, "On a Story Published in Preview Magazine," no. 1, p. 5.
5 See Alan Creighton's review of Bliss Carman's *Pipes of Pan*: "There is also, in these poems, a continual quest for phrases of startling quality . . . and this—the mere beauty of a phrase—seems to dominate the intention of his work." *Canadian Forum*, 22 (October 1942): 221.
6 John Sutherland, "On Certain Obscure Poets," no. 2, p. 3.
7 Neufville Shaw, *Edwardian and the War*, no. 3, p. 3.

10. Canadian Poets: Earle Birney

1 *Anthology of Canadian Poetry (English)*, ed. Ralph Barker Gustafson (Harmondsworth: Penguin Books, 1942).

11. Canada and Its Poetry

1 Gabriel Harvey, *Gabriel Harvey's Marginalia*, ed. G.C. Moore Smith (Stratford-upon-Avon: Shakespeare Head Press, 1913), 161.
2 Richard Hovey was an American poet who collaborated with Carman on *Songs from Vagabondia* (1894) and subsequent volumes.
3 The passage "the wandering Pedlar" from *The Rising Village*, ll. 199–216.
4 Spoken by Lefroy, act 4, sc. 6, l. 94.

12. Review of *A Little Anthology*

1 In a letter to the editor, Gustafson responded to this review by claiming that poetry did not require "an apologia, a platform, and an atlas," and that Canadian poetry was not readily available in the U.S. (March 1944: 287).
2 See no. 10, n. 1.
3 The two A.M. Klein poems are *Heirloom* and *The Still Small Voice* (from *Haggadah*, ll. 72–87).

14. Water-Colour Annual

1 Yvonne McKague Housser, "Canadian Group of Painters—1944," *Canadian Art*, 1 (1944): 142–7. The exhibition was on display from 21 April to 21 May 1944.

16. Undemocratic Censorship

1 There was a surge of book-banning in Boston in 1927, involving such books as Sinclair Lewis's *Elmer Gantry*. NF alluded to this as the Boston Book Massacre in an article in *Acta*, 56, no. 5.
2 The editors of the *Little Review* began to publish *Ulysses* serially in the United States, but stopped midway, in February 1921, under threat of legal action. Although American publication became possible again in December 1933, the book was not admitted into Canada until 1950.

17. Canadian Authors Meet

1 James T. Farrell's novel *Bernard Clare* (1946) was banned in Canada in June 1946.

20. The Narrative Tradition in English Canadian Poetry

1 See the opening of pt. 2 of *Malcolm's Katie*.

2 The holding of the Long Sault against the Iroquois occurred during May 1660. Tecumseh died on 5 October 1813 and Riel on 16 November 1885. The 1837 rebellion was led by William Lyon Mackenzie in Upper Canada and Joseph Papineau in Lower Canada. The fight at St. Julien occurred on 24 April 1915, the Battle of Amiens on 8 August 1918, and the fight at Dieppe on 19 August 1942.
3 See *The Battle of Maldon* (ll. 312–13) and *The Song of Roland* (ll. 1320 ff.).
4 This is an interpretation of Johnson, who said that the spectators at a public execution were "gratified by a procession" and "the criminal was supported by it." See *Boswell's Life of Johnson*, ed. George Birkbeck Hill, rev. L.F. Powell (Oxford: Clarendon Press, 1934), 4:188–9.
5 Pt. 1, act 4, sc. 4, ll. 209–72.
6 The hero's song is in pt. 4, ll. 39–56, and the villain's reply in ll. 57–136.

25. Duncan Campbell Scott

1 John Masefield, "Foreword," *The Poems of Duncan Campbell Scott* (London: J.M. Dent & Sons, 1927).
2 The reference is to the flat-footed amateur poet, the "Sweet Songstress of Saskatchewan," invented by Paul Hiebert in *Sarah Binks* (1947).

26. David Milne: An Appreciation

1 In *David B. Milne: Catalogue Raisonné of the Paintings*, ed. David Milne Jr. and David P. Silcox (Toronto: University of Toronto Press, 1998), this painting is titled *Red Church VI*.
2 In the same catalogue, this painting is titled *Waterlilies and the Sunday Paper*.
3 David Milne, "The Colour Dry-Point," *Canadian Art*, 4, no. 4 (1947): 144–7.

27. Canadian Dreiser

1 Desmond Pacey, *Frederick Philip Grove* (Toronto: Ryerson Press, 1945).
2 "Apologia pro Vita et Opere suo" in the *Canadian Forum* for August 1931. [NF]

29. Dean of Critics

1 A.J.M. Smith, preface to *The Book of Canadian Poetry*, iii.
2 The book was *Henry James, Man and Author* (Toronto: Macmillan, 1927). In the "present uproar over James," NF is perhaps alluding to the perception of James as a great artist in such critical studies as F.O. Matthiessen's *Henry James: The Major Phase* (1944). James was placed among the major novelists in F.R. Leavis's *The Great Tradition* (1948).

30. *The Book of Canadian Poetry*, Second Edition

1 See no. 10, n. 1.

32. The Pursuit of Form

1 S.T. Coleridge, *Religious Musings*, ll. 243–8.

33. Culture and the Cabinet

1 The National Film Board or NFB, which still exists, was founded in 1939 by John Grierson. NF was perhaps looking back nostalgically to the days of the war when the NFB turned out more than five hundred films. By 1949 the board had come under attack by some private Canadian film producers and Conservative members of Parliament.
2 George Alexander Drew, *Globe and Mail*, 29 January 1949, 1–2. Drew was the leader of the Conservative opposition.

34. Letters in Canada: Poetry

1 Canadian Authors' Association, Edmonton Branch, *Alberta Poetry Year Book, 1949–50*; *Alberta Poetry Year Book, 1950* (Edmonton, n.p.); Saskatchewan Poetry Society, *The Saskatchewan Poetry Book, 1950–51* (Regina, n.p.).
2 *Contemporary Verse*, no. 36 (Fall 1951); *Poetry Commonwealth*, no. 8, ed. Earle Birney.
3 See no. 25, n. 2.
4 E.K. Brown, "Duncan Campbell Scott," *On Canadian Poetry*, rev. ed. (Toronto: Ryerson Press, 1944), 118–43.
5 Archibald MacMechan. See his "'The Best Sea Story Ever Written,'" *Queen's Quarterly*, 7, no. 2 (October 1899): 120–30.
6 V.B. Rhodenizer, review of *The House of Orseoli* by Laurence Dakin, *Dalhousie Review*, 33, no. 1 (Spring 1953): xiii.
7 William Edwin Collin, "Difficult, Lonely Music," *The White Savannahs* (Toronto: Macmillan, 1936), 235–66. The phrase is from Smith's poem *Like an Old Proud King in a Parable*, l. 16.
8 An allusion to no. 347 in Blaise Pascal's *Pensées* (1670): "Man is but a reed, the weakest in nature, but he is a thinking reed."
9 From the preface to the 1st ed. of *Leaves of Grass* (1855).
10 *The Boatman* won the Governor-General's award for poetry in 1957.
11 See 110 above (1953).
12 See *The Waste Land*, especially ll. 423–5.
13 In the poem *A Country without a Mythology*, quoted at 477 below.

14 Robert Graves, *The Greek Myths*, 2 vols. (Penguin, 1955).
15 Milton Wilson, review of *The Carnal and the Crane* by Daryl Hine, *Canadian Forum*, 37 (February 1958): 257.
16 See the closing lines of *Li Revived* in Jones's *Frost on the Sun*.
17 Hans Christian Andersen, "The Red Shoes," *Fairy Tales* (London: Dent, 1906), 66–8.
18 The Stratford Festival Theatre (Tyrone Guthrie) production of Marlowe's *Tamburlaine the Great*, with Anthony Quayle in the title role, played at the Winter Garden Theater in New York in January 1956. It played for twenty performances and made no profit.
19 Raymond Gushue was president and vice-chancellor of Memorial University.
20 Ned O'Gorman, review of *The Boatman* by Jay Macpherson, *Poetry*, 91, no. 4 (January 1958): 272.
21 Walt Whitman's sentiment is from the opening of his *Song of Myself*; for Ralph Waldo Emerson's remark, see *The Apology*, l. 12.
22 T.S. Eliot, "Matthew Arnold," *The Use of Poetry and the Use of Criticism* (London: Faber & Faber, 1933), 106. Eliot says that it is the poet's advantage "to see the boredom, and the horror, and the glory."
23 John Milton, *Samson Agonistes*, l. 1642.

35. Pelham Edgar

1 E.K. Brown, *Matthew Arnold: A Study in Conflict* (Chicago: University of Chicago Press, 1948) and *Studies in the Text of Matthew Arnold's Prose Works* (Paris: P. André, 1935).
2 Pelham Edgar, "Matthew Arnold As a Writer of Prose," *Dalhousie Review*, 1 (1921–22): 248–62; and "Matthew Arnold As Poet," *Transactions of the Royal Society of Canada*, ser. 3, sec. 2 (1914): 309–20.
3 In the acknowledgments of *Across My Path*, Frye thanks Margaret Ray, who was a librarian of Victoria University, for her assistance and the bibliography she provided of Edgar's writings.
4 See no. 29, n. 2.
5 See for example W.B. Yeats, *A Vision*, 2nd ed. (London: Macmillan, 1937), 73 ff.; and "The Death of Synge," *Autobiographies* (London: Macmillan, 1955), 503–4.
6 Matthew Arnold, "Equality," in *Essays Religious and Mixed*, ed. R.H. Super (Ann Arbor: University of Michigan Press, 1972), 297.
7 Pelham Edgar, "The Changing Aspects of Poetry," *Queen's Quarterly*, 44 (1937): 339.
8 Pelham Edgar, "Virginia Woolf's New Book," *Acta*, 56, no. 6 (April 1932): 25–6.

37. John D. Robins

11 *A Book of Canadian Humour*, ed. John D. Robins and Margaret Ray (Toronto: Ryerson Press, 1951).

38. Turning New Leaves: *Folk Songs of Canada*

1 The music of *Huron Carol* (or *Jesous Ahatonhia*) is that of a sixteenth-century French carol, *Un jeune pucelle*, and the words were probably written by Father Jean de Brébeuf.
2 *The Squid-Jiggin' Ground* is by Arthur R. Scammell.
3 *Songs and Ballads from Nova Scotia*, ed. Helen Creighton (1932); *Ballads and Sea Songs of Newfoundland*, ed. Elisabeth Bristol Greenleaf (1933); and *Folk-Songs of Old Quebec* (1935) and *Alouette!*, ed. Marius Barbeau (1946).

39. English Canadian Literature, 1929–1954

1 See no. 34, n. 7.
2 No trace has been found of the radio dramatist Graham Ferguson. The name is probably a mistake for Max "Rawhide" Ferguson.

40. Introduction to *I Brought the Ages Home*

1 Homer A. Thompson, who taught Classical archaeology at the University of Toronto (1933–47) and at Princeton (1947–77), was assistant director of the Royal Ontario Museum (1933–47). He wrote a foreword to Currelly's book.

41. Preface to an Uncollected Anthology

1 Earle Birney, *Images in Place of Logging*, l. 3; A.M. Klein, *Grain Elevator*, ll. 4–5.
2 "Canaday-I-O," *Folk Songs of Canada*, ed. Edith Fulton Fowke and Richard Johnston.
3 Norman Levine, *Letter from England*, ll. 19 and 53.
4 Norman Corwin is a writer and producer of radio dramas: among them is "On a Note of Triumph," the V-E Day broadcast. In speaking of "lugubrious inspirationalism," perhaps NF is referring to the self-confessed optimism of Corwin's work. In the forward to *"Untitled" and Other Radio Dramas* (1947), Corwin writes: "I have no apology to make for the affirmative tone of these scripts. I am convinced that ultimately we will get where we want to go. It will be grim en route, but I think there is nothing to be said for cynicism and despair, and everything to be said for getting out and working towards a better world."

5 Honoré de Balzac, *Père Goriot*, trans. A.J. Krailsheimer (Oxford: Oxford University Press, 1991), 124.
6 *A Great Big Sea Hove in Long Beach, Folk Songs of Canada*, ed. Fowke and Johnston, 177.
7 In the battle of Crysler's Farm, 11 November 1813, the invading Americans were defeated. See no. 20, n. 2 for the other battles.
8 See no. 20, n. 4.
9 See no. 11, n. 4.
10 Frye's reference is to the Jindyworobak club, founded in 1938 by poet Rex Ingamells and active until 1953.
11 Quintilian, *Institutio Oratoria*, 12.1.1, and 12.2.1.
12 See no. 20, n. 1.

42. Culture and the National Will

1 Claude T. Bissell was president at Carleton, 1956–58. Carleton College was established in 1942, gained university status in 1952, and changed its name to Carleton University in 1957.
2 The phrase "the solemn duty of interfering" is used by Miss Clack in chap. 7. See Wilkie Collins, *The Moonstone: A Romance* (London: Dent, 1944), 224.
3 William Blake, *Jerusalem*, pl. 55, ll. 60–1.
4 David Low was a political cartoonist whose recurring character, Colonel Blimp, first made an appearance in the *Evening Standard* in 1934.
5 William Wordsworth, *It is not to be thought of that the Flood*, ll. 11–13.

43. Poetry

1 John Keats, letter to George Keats, 19 February 1819, in *The Letters of John Keats*, ed. Hyder Edward Rollins (Cambridge: Harvard University Press, 1958), 2:67.
2 See no. 34, n. 7.
3 See the opening of pt. 2 of Crawford's *Malcolm's Katie*, and ll. 389–90 of Heavysege's *Jephthah's Daughter*.

44. Preface and Introduction to Pratt's Poetry

1 William Blake, *Milton*, pl. 30; the inscription is in mirror writing above the title of book 2.
2 Henry James, "The Art of Fiction," *The Art of Criticism*, ed. William Veeder and Susan M. Griffin (Chicago: University of Chicago Press, 1986), 173.
3 Thomas Hardy, *The Convergence of the Twain*; and Joseph Conrad, "Some Reflections on the Loss of the *Titanic*" and "Certain Aspects of the Admira-

ble Inquiry into the Loss of the *Titanic*," *Notes on Life and Letters* (New York: Doubleday, Page, 1921), 213–48.
4 Edward Blake (1833–1912) was the leader of the Liberal party; the quoted line is an elaboration of his opinion, in response to Sir John A. Macdonald's vision for a transcontinental railway, that "It can't be done." See NF's comment at 104–5.
5 Hart Crane, "Modern Poetry," *The Complete Poems and Selected Letters and Prose of Hart Crane*, ed. Brom Weber (New York: Liveright, 1966), 261–2.
6 Stephen Leacock, "Gertrude the Governess," *Nonsense Novels* (1911). The hero is Lord Ronald.

45. Introduction to *The Stepsure Letters*

1 Benjamin Franklin, *Autobiography*, ed. J.A. Leo Lemay and P.M. Zall (New York: Norton, 1986), 49 (pt. 1).
2 Henry David Thoreau, *Walden* (London: Dent, 1908), 180 (chap. "Baker Farm").
3 The Eighteenth amendment to the American Constitution in 1919 authorized the legislation which, in the following year, introduced Prohibition.
4 The chapter "English Niggers" in *The Attaché*, 2nd ser. (1844). For further comments on this, see 497.
5 Haliburton's Sam Slick papers were published from 1836 to 1855 under the titles *The Clockmaker; or, The Sayings and Doings of Samuel Slick, of Slickville* (3 series, 1836–40), *The Attaché; or, Sam Slick in England* (2 series, 1843–44), *Sam Slick's Wise Saws and Modern Instances* (1853), and *Nature and Human Nature* (1855).
6 Victor Chittick, *Thomas Chandler Haliburton ("Sam Slick"): A Study in Provincial Toryism* (New York: Columbia University Press, 1924), 378–9.
7 Thomas Chandler Haliburton, *Sam Slick the Clockmaker: His Sayings and Doings* (Toronto: Musson, n.d.), 312 (3rd ser., chap. 5, "The Great Unknown"). This book was in NF's library.
8 Haliburton, *Sam Slick the Clockmaker*, 247 (2nd ser., chap. 18, "Taking Off the Factory Ladies").

46. John George Diefenbaker

1 The Canada Council granted Victoria $375,000, or half the cost of the building up to that amount, for its new library.

47. Haliburton: Mask and Ego

1 NF is including Haliburton's last book, *The Season-Ticket* (1860), not actually a Sam Slick book. For the titles of the other seven, see no. 45, n. 5.
2 Lord Durham's *Report on the Affairs of British North America* (1839), an inves-

tigation into the causes of the 1837 rebellions. It led to the union of Upper and Lower Canada under a form of responsible government, and recommended also union with the Maritime provinces.
3 See no. 35, n. 5
4 See no. 45, n. 7.
5 See for example Haliburton, *Sam Slick the Clockmaker*, 53 (1st ser., chap. 16, "Mr. Slick's Opinion of the British").
6 Ibid., 260 (2nd ser., chap. 20, "The Wrong Room").
7 Ibid., 130 (2nd ser., chap. 1, "The Meeting").
8 Victor Chittick, *Thomas Chandler Haliburton ("Sam Slick")*, 334, 337–8.
9 Haliburton, *Sam Slick the Clockmaker*, 34 (1st ser., chap. 12, "The American Eagle").
10 See no. 45, n. 8.
11 Haliburton, *Sam Slick the Clockmaker*, 200 (2nd ser., chap. 11, "Italian Paintings").
12 Ibid., 149 (2nd ser., chap. 4, "Nick Bradshaw"). NF has changed the pronoun references to the cow to "her."
13 Ibid., 273 (2nd ser., chap. 22, "Keeping Up the Steam").
14 Haliburton, *Nature and Human Nature* in *The Sam Slick Anthology*, ed. Reginald Eyre Watters (Toronto: Clarke, Irwin, 1969), 257 (chap. "Holding Up the Mirror").

48. Governor-General's Awards (I)

1 William Blake, annotations to Wordsworth's *Poems* (1815), *The Complete Poetry and Prose of William Blake*, ed. David V. Erdman (Berkeley, University of California Press, 1982), 665.
2 In the campaign leading up to the election of 8 April 1963, the main issue was whether Canada should accept American nuclear warheads for its Bomarc missiles, which were part of the NORAD air defence plan. Dissension within the government over defence policy and relations with the U.S. had already led to the resignation of three cabinet ministers.

50. Ned Pratt: The Personal Legend

1 W.B. Yeats, *Among School Children*, l. 8.

51. Silence Upon the Earth

1 See no. 50, n.1.

53. Conclusion to First Edition of *Literary History of Canada*

1 The Jalna books are a series of sixteen novels by Mazo de la Roche, published from 1927 to 1960, about the Whiteoak family, who lived in a house

called Jalna. Finch Whiteoak is the misunderstood second-youngest brother, who becomes a concert pianist and composer of international reputation.
2 John Milton, *Paradise Lost*, bk. 9, ll. 44–5.
3 Goldwin Smith, *Reminiscences*, ed. Arnold Haultain (New York: Macmillan, 1910), 421. Smith attributes the remark to a Mr. Dunkin, not otherwise identified.
4 See, e.g., no. 58–9, 69–70.
5 Non-Canadian readers may not be aware of the traditional application to Canada of Psalm 72:8: "And he shall have dominion from sea to sea, and from the river unto the ends of the earth." Canada was called the "Dominion" of Canada for many years; the motto on the Canadian coat of arms is *a mare usque ad mare*, and the vertical red stripes on the Canadian flag were originally blue to represent the two oceans. Canadian politicians seem to be endeavouring to obliterate this symbolism for reasons which elude me. [NF]
6 Rupert Brooke, *Letters from America* (London: Sidgwick & Jackson, 1916), 119.
7 Jay Macpherson is quoting from Frederick Philip Grove's *In Search of Myself*.
8 Prime Minister Sir Wilfrid Laurier's celebrated remark—that whereas the nineteenth century had been the century of the United States, "the twentieth century belongs to Canada"—was made with variations in wording in several speeches in 1904 and 1905.
9 The allusion is to *Next Year Country*, by Jean Burnet (1951), a sociological study of Alberta. [NF]
10 Ralph Waldo Emerson, journal entry for October 1841, *Selected Prose and Poetry*, ed. Reginald L. Cook (New York: Rinehart, 1950), 477. The passage is marked in the copy in NF's library.
11 *Deeper into the Forest*, by Roy Daniells (1948), who, like Emily Carr, is from British Columbia. [NF]
12 See Charles G.D. Roberts, *Tantramar Revisited*.
13 One may also compare the last sentences of the two volumes of Professor Donald Creighton's biography of John A. Macdonald [*John A. Macdonald: The Young Politician* and *John A. Macdonald: The Old Chieftain*] (1952, 1955). [NF] For the endings, see 501–2.
14 Thomas McCulloch, author of the *Stepsure Letters* (see no. 45), was a teacher and first president of Dalhousie University, who wrote widely on educational and theological subjects. George Sidney Brett taught NF as professor of philosophy at the University of Toronto.
15 Edward Braddock (1695–1755) was a Scottish-born soldier who served in America as commander-in-chief of British forces during the last year of his life. He attacked Fort Duquesne (in what is now Pittsburgh) but was outflanked by French troops and Indians. Refusing to order his men to seek

Notes to pages 351–7

16 Sir John Franklin (1786–1847) was a British naval officer who led several Arctic expeditions, the last of which never returned.

cover in the trees, he allowed them to remain an open target for three hours while half were killed and he was mortally wounded.

17 The title (a phrase from Rilke) of Hugh MacLennan's novel (1945) about the English and French communities in Montreal. [NF]

18 W.B. Yeats, *Per Amica Silentia Lunae*, in *Later Essays*, ed. William H. O'Donnell (New York: Charles Scribner's Sons, 1994), 8 (sec. 5).

19 Stephen Leacock, "The Rival Churches of St. Asaph and St. Osoph," *Arcadian Adventures with the Idle Rich* (Toronto: Bell & Cockburn, 1914), 208.

20 When reprinting this text in *BG*, NF amended "George" to "the Canadian philosopher George," presumably to distinguish James George, professor of philosophy at Queen's University, from the better-known American theorist Henry George. John Watson was also a philosophy professor at Queen's; the quotation is from the preface to his *Outline of Philosophy* (1898).

21 This is the subtitle of a book significantly called *Hegel not Haeckel*: the allusion is to Ernst Haeckel's *The Riddle of the Universe*, trans. McCabe, 1900, a book much refuted in clerical circles. [NF] Frye's phrase "cited by Mr. Thomson" was rather confusingly retained when the conclusion was reprinted in the second ed. (2:344), although both James S. Thomson and the book had disappeared from this ed. when Thomson's chapter had been replaced by John Webster Grant's "Religious and Theological Writings (to 1960)." In *BG* and *StS* Frye omits Thomson but still does not mention the theologian's name. The index to the *Literary History* gives it as W.J. Penton (1890).

22 Sara Jeannette Duncan, *The Imperialist: A Critical Edition*, ed. Thomas E. Tausky (Ottawa: Tecumseh Press, 1996), 79 (chap. 11).

23 W.B. Yeats, letter to Lady Elizabeth Pelham, 4 January 1939, *The Letters of W.B. Yeats*, ed. Allan Wade (London, 1954), 922.

24 Samuel Johnson, "Cowley," *Lives of the English Poets* (Oxford: Clarendon Press, 1905), 1:45.

25 American lawyer and politician Ignatius Donnelly (1831–1901) is best known for his supposed discovery, by means of a cipher in Shakespeare's work, that much of it had been written by Francis Bacon. His *Caesar's Column* (1890), a combination of Utopia and anti-Utopia, benefited from the vogue for Utopian fiction that had been started by Edward Bellamy's *Looking Backward* (1888). William Morris's *News from Nowhere* (1891) was a favourite of NF's.

26 Douglas Bush, *Mythology and the Renaissance Tradition in English Poetry* (Minneapolis: University of Minnesota Press, 1932), 19.

27 The exact phrase has not been found, but cf. Franz Kafka, *Letters to Felice*, ed.

Erich Heller and Jürgen Born, trans. James Stern and Elisabeth Duckworth (New York: Schocken, 1973), 389.
28 As Kenneth Windsor points out in *Literary History*, the word was used in *The Archaeology and Prehistoric Annals of Scotland* (1851) by Sir Daniel Wilson, who emigrated to Canada in 1853.
29 NF probably has in mind Eliot's remark, in "The Music of Poetry," "that a poem, or a passage of a poem, may tend to realize itself first as a particular rhythm before it reaches expression in words, and that this rhythm may bring to birth the idea and the image" (*On Poetry and Poets* [London: Faber & Faber, 1957], 38). NF quotes this assertion in *TSE*, 38.
30 Duncan, *The Imperialist*, 50 (chap. 7).
31 The Massey Report was the *Report of the Royal Commission on National Development in the Arts, Letters and Sciences, 1949–1951* (1951), which attempted to evaluate the current state and present recommendations for the future state of culture in Canada. For the commission's formation, see no. 33.
32 The novels are by William Kirby and Gilbert Parker respectively. The remark on the few arpents or acres of snow is generally attributed to Voltaire.
33 The opposing commanders in the battle for Quebec in 1759: the Marquis de Montcalm, and James Wolfe, who is said to have read Gray's *Elegy, Written in a Country Churchyard* on the eve of the battle and to have declared that "I would rather have written those lines than take Quebec tomorrow."
34 See no. 20 (55–63).
35 See 350 above.
36 John Robins, *The Incomplete Anglers* (Toronto: Collins, 1943), 187–8.
37 *The Plough and the Pen: Writings from Hungary 1930–1956*, ed. Ilona Duczynska and Karl Polyani (Toronto: McClelland & Stewart, 1963). This book is in NF's library in NFF.
38 See no. 47, n. 6.
39 Marshall McLuhan, *The Gutenberg Galaxy* (Toronto: University of Toronto Press, 1962), 32.
40 W.B. Yeats, *Sailing to Byzantium*, l. 14.

54. Foreword to *The Prospect of Change*

1 Conservative Republican senator Barry Goldwater had been defeated in the 1964 presidential election by Lyndon B. Johnson; former Democratic vice-president Henry A. Wallace, an extreme liberal, ran for the Progressive party in the 1948 presidential election when Truman was elected.
2 John XXIII, pope from 1958 to 1963, called the twenty-first ecumenical council, commonly known as Vatican 2 (1962–65), which began a process of Catholic renewal.
3 Gerard Manley Hopkins, *God's Grandeur*, "It gathers to a greatness, like the ooze of oil / Crushed."

55. A Poet and Legend

1 E.J. Pratt, *Studies in Pauline Eschatology and Its Background* (1917).
2 Wilhelm Wundt was a psychologist who carried on the theory of association; for Pratt's interest in him, including reference to a letter from Frye, see Sandra Djwa, *E.J. Pratt: The Evolutionary Vision* (Vancouver: Copp Clark, 1974), 88–90.
3 John Allan Irving, chair of the Department of Ethics and Social Philosophy at Victoria since 1945, had died earlier that year.
4 See no. 35, n. 5.

56. Edwin John Pratt

1 See no. 55, n. 1.

57. Silence in the Sea

1 W.H. Auden, "Making, Knowing and Judging," *The Dyer's Hand and Other Essays* (London: Faber & Faber, 1963), 47.
2 T.S. Eliot, "The Metaphysical Poets," *Selected Essays* (London: Faber & Faber, 1986), 289.
3 *A Defence of Poetry* [by] Percy Bysshe Shelley. *The Four Ages of Poetry* [by] Thomas Love Peacock, ed. John E. Jordan (Indianapolis: Bobbs-Merrill, 1965), 80, 4.
4 T.S. Eliot, conclusion to *The Use of Poetry and the Use of Criticism* (London: Faber & Faber, 1933), 152. Eliot says, speaking as a poet, "I myself should like an audience which could neither read nor write."
5 See 305 above.
6 Charles Haddon Spurgeon (1834–92) was a fiery English Baptist who preached to large crowds at the Metropolitan Tabernacle in London.
7 Samuel Johnson, "Yalden," *Lives of the English Poets* (Oxford: Clarendon Press, 1905), 2:303.
8 John Sutherland, *The Poetry of E.J. Pratt* (Toronto: Ryerson Press, 1956), 104–5.

58. Lawren Harris

1 The allusion is to J.E.H. MacDonald's painting *The Solemn Land* in the National Gallery of Canada.

60. Dialogue on Translation

1 Gerard Manley Hopkins, letter to Alexander William Mowbray Baillie, 14 January 1883, *Further Letters of Gerard Manley Hopkins*, ed. Claude Colleer Abbott, 2nd ed. (London: Oxford University Press, 1956), 252.

61. Rear-view Crystal Ball

1 Marshall McLuhan usually applies the phrase "rear-view mirror" to himself and his readers: see *Counterblast* (Toronto: McClelland & Stewart, 1969), 22; and *The Medium Is the Massage* (New York: Bantam, 1967), 75. He also applies it specifically to Marx and Marxism: see *Counterblast*, 96 and 140.
2 William Carlos Williams, *The Autobiography of William Carlos Williams* (New York: New Directions, 1967), 390.

62. Preface to *The Bush Garden*

1 There was no federal election campaign in 1956; NF perhaps had in mind the campaign which led to Diefenbaker's becoming leader of the Conservatives in December 1956. Here and in the federal election of spring 1957 he emphasized his "Northern vision"—to develop the Canadian North into a full partner in Confederation as John A. Macdonald had done for the West. In a report for the CRTC, Frye remarks that when Diefenbaker faced north he soon found himself "a mere agent of expanding American capital" (*LS*, 267). The books referred to are George Grant's *Lament for a Nation* (1965), for which see 517–18 below, and Peter Newman's *Renegade in Power: The Diefenbaker Years* (1963).
2 The Front de Libération du Québec was an ultranationalist organization in that province. In October 1970, cells in that movement kidnapped James Cross, a British diplomat, and Pierre Laporte, minister of labour in Quebec; Laporte was eventually murdered.
3 Louis Dudek, "Frye Again (But Don't Miss Souster)," *Delta*, 5 (October 1958): 26–7.

63. Canadian Scene: Explorers and Observers

1 See no. 53, n. 3.

64. Lester Bowles Pearson, 1897–1972

1 Pearson married Maryon Moody on 22 August 1925.
2 See no. 46.

65. *Cold Green Element*

1 W.B. Yeats, *Vacillation*, l. 88.
2 William Blake, *The Book of Urizen*, pl. 13, l. 53.

66. Douglas Duncan

1 NF is slightly conflating two texts. *The Loved One* (itself first published in *Horizon* in 1948) does allude to an imaginary *Horizon* article on current cultural figures including "Scottie" Wilson, but does not mention Duncan. The quotation comes from the article by E.L.T. Mesens, "'Scottie' Wilson," *Horizon*, 13 (June 1946): 400–2. Wilson was a British self-taught painter whom Duncan found running a second-hand furniture store during a temporary sojourn in Toronto; Duncan encouraged him to become a full-time artist.

67. Canada: New World without Revolution

1 René Descartes, *A Discourse on Method*, trans. John Veitch (London: Dent, 1912), 27.
2 Margaret Atwood, *Surfacing* (Toronto: McClelland & Stewart, 1972), 176 (chap. 23).
3 Earle Birney, *Can. Lit*, final line.
4 Thomas Chandler Haliburton, *Sam Slick the Clockmaker*, 242–3 (2nd ser., chap. 18, "Taking Off the Factory Ladies").
5 J.S. Mill, "Coleridge," *Essays on Ethics, Religion and Society*, ed. John M. Robson (Toronto: University of Toronto Press, 1969), 119–20.
6 C. Northcote Parkinson, *Parkinson's Law* (Boston: Houghton Mifflin, 1957), chap. 6.
7 The Quiet Revolution is the period during which Quebec modernized, lessening church influence in politics and developing economically. It is associated with the Liberal government of Jean Lesage, premier 1960–66.

68. Conclusion to the Second Edition of *Literary History of Canada*

1 E.K. Broadus and Eleanor Hammond Broadus, *A Book of Canadian Prose and Verse* (Toronto: Macmillan, 1923; rev. ed. 1934).
2 Jorge Luis Borges refutes J.G. Fichte's assertion, in *Speeches to the German Nation* (1809), that Germans' superiority is due to "their uninterrupted possession of a pure language." See "Two Books" (1941), *Selected Non-Fictions* (New York: Viking, 1999), 209.
3 *Grip*, 32 (6 April 1889): 213. The Toronto-based satirical magazine offers "rules for aspiring Canadian critics," including being born abroad, using a formal, stilted style, and writing articles entitled "Have We a Canadian Literature?"
4 Gen. Charles de Gaulle's words, spoken from the balcony of the Montreal

City Hall during an official visit in July 1967, seemed a deliberate encouragement of Quebec separatists, and resulted in a stern rebuke from Prime Minister Pearson.

5 See no. 67, n.7.
6 E.g. by Eli Mandel in his introduction to *Contexts of Canadian Criticism* (Chicago: University of Chicago Press, 1971). This was to be the theme of David Jackel's "Northrop Frye and the Continentalist Tradition," *Dalhousie Review*, 56, no. 2 (1976), 221–39.
7 This is how Charles Reich characterized the shallow, traditional outlook of the American farmer and small businessman in his *Greening of America* (1970), a book hailing a revolution in consciousness supposedly initiated by the protest generation of the 1960s.
8 See no. 44, n. 6.
9 Mrs. Humphry Ward, *Canadian Born* (London: George Newnes, 1908), 21 (chap. 2). Page references in the text are to this edition.
10 The motto of the Order of Canada is *Desiderantes meliorem patriam* (They desire a better country) from Hebrews 11:16.
11 In his *Ideas in Exile: A History of Canadian Invention* (1967), J.J. Brown's theme is the fact that ideas resulting from scientific research in Canada cannot be developed for lack of a native technical industry.
12 John Tuzo Wilson is a Canadian geophysicist, best known for the theory of continental drift, one of the bases of plate techtonics. He was a professor at the University of Toronto, 1946–74, and director of the Ontario Science Centre.
13 Warren Tallman, "Wolf in the Snow," *Canadian Literature*, 6 (Autumn 1960): 43.
14 Alice Wilson, Canada's first woman geologist and paleontologist, worked for the Geological Survey of Canada beginning in 1909.
15 James Reaney's three plays about the Donnelly family who were massacred in 1880 are *Sticks and Stones* (1974), *The St. Nicholas Hotel, Wm. Donnelly, Prop.* (1976), and *Handcuffs* (1977).
16 Heroines respectively of *The Stone Angel* (1964) and *A Jest of God* (1966).
17 The Quebec Act of 1774 followed upon the British conquest of Canada in 1763. In response to the demands of the new British settlers, the act instituted British criminal law, but maintained French civil law and safeguarded Catholic rights.
18 Burke did not comment on the Quebec Act itself, but his opposition to settling political questions by appeals to abstract rights and *a priori* metaphysical reasoning is found throughout his works. See, e.g., *Reflections on the Revolution in France*, ed. L.G. Mitchell (Oxford: Clarendon Press, 1989), 111.
19 Erik H. Erikson, *Dimensions of a New Identity* (New York: Norton, 1974).
20 William L. Morton, *The Canadian Identity* (Madison: University of Wisconsin Press; Toronto: University of Toronto Press, 1961).

69. View of Canada

1 The monument by sculptor Vernon March, meant to be finished by 1915 but actually unveiled in 1925, features Champlain alone on top of the monument, with a robed priest below on one side, a fur trader on the other, and natives at the base.

70. Haunted by Lack of Ghosts

1 William L. Morton, *The Canadian Identity*, 91.
2 See no. 68, n. 17.
3 See 346 above.
4 W.B. Yeats, *A Vision*, 2nd ed., 255.
5 George Grant, *Technology and Empire* (Toronto: Anansi, 1969), 17.
6 Leonard Cohen, *Beautiful Losers* (Toronto: McClelland & Stewart, 1966), 58.
7 See no. 34, n. 8.
8 Robert McDougall, "The Dodo and the Cruising Auk," *Canadian Literature*, 18 (Autumn 1963): 11.
9 Emily Dickinson, *The Letters of Emily Dickinson*, ed. Thomas H. Johnson (Cambridge, Mass.: Belknap Press, 1958), 2:491 (letter 368).
10 Wyndham Lewis, "Nature's Place in Canadian Culture," *Wyndham Lewis in Canada*, ed. George Woodcock (Vancouver: University of British Columbia Publications Centre, 1971), 52.
11 Milton Wilson, "*Other Canadians* and After," *Tamarack Review*, no. 9 (Autumn 1958), 91.

71. National Consciousness in Canadian Culture

1 Martha Ostenso was a Winnipeg writer who gained some fame for *Wild Geese* (1925); she had moved to New York in about 1921 and thereafter lived in the United States.
2 Arnold Joseph Toynbee, *A Study of History* (1934–61).
3 Tobias Smollett, *The Expedition of Humphry Clinker* (Oxford: Oxford University Press, 1984), 111.
4 Thomas Chandler Haliburton, *The Attaché* in *The Sam Slick Anthology*, ed. Reginald Eyre Watters (Toronto: Clarke, Irwin, 1969), 191 (2nd ser., chap. "English Niggers").
5 Pierre Vallières, *White Niggers of America: The Precocious Autobiography of a Quebec "Terrorist"* (1968; English trans. 1971).
6 T.C. Haliburton, *The Attaché*, 190.
7 Richard Henry Bonnycastle, *The Canadas in 1841* (London: Henry Colburn, 1841), 2:103.

8 The leading short story in the collection of the same name (Toronto: Anansi, 1969). For the Polish comparison, see 25–8.
9 See no. 68, n. 17.
10 See no. 53, n. 8.
11 William L. Morton, *The Canadian Identity*, 93.
12 See no. 53, n. 13 for the titles of Creighton's two volumes.
13 Frances Brooke, *The History of Emily Montague* (Toronto: McClelland & Stewart, 1995), 26 (letter 6).
14 Catharine Parr Traill, *The Backwoods of Canada; Being Letters from the Wife of an Emigrant Officer, Illustrative of the Domestic Economy of British America* (Toronto: McClelland & Stewart, 1989), 12 (Introduction).
15 Edward Chappell, *Voyage of His Majesty's ship Rosamond to Newfoundland and the Southern Coast of Labrador* (London, 1818), 52.
16 Frederick Philip Grove, *The Turn of the Year* (Toronto: McClelland & Stewart, 1923), 109 (chap. 50).
17 Ernest Thompson Seton, "Krag, the Kootenay Ram," *Lives of the Hunted* (1901).

72. Canadian Culture Today

1 See no. 53, n. 6.
2 Wyndham Lewis, "Nature's Place in Canadian Culture," *Wyndham Lewis in Canada*, 53.
3 Mao Tse-Tung, Chairman of the People's Republic of China, ushered in an abortive campaign of intellectual debate, 1956–57, with the slogan "Let a hundred flowers bloom, let a hundred schools contend." He had used the first half of the slogan earlier in a lesser-known campaign to reform literature and drama in 1951.
4 The Democratic party was in power, with James Earl [Jimmy] Carter as president.
5 See 497 above.
6 See no. 68, n. 17.
7 See no. 71, n. 7.
8 George Grant, *Lament for a Nation: The Defeat of Canadian Nationalism* (Toronto: McClelland & Stewart, 1965), 68 (chap. 6).

73. Culture as Interpenetration

1 Wallace Stevens, *The Idea of Order at Key West*, last stanza.
2 The allusion is to German chemist Friedrich Kekulé von Stradonitz (1829–96). He attributed his discovery of the circular structure of the benzene molecule to a dream of the ouroboros, or serpent with its tail in its mouth.

3 Romans 13:1: "The powers that be are ordained of God."
4 Marc Lescarbot, *Farewell to the Frenchmen Returning from New France to Gallic France*, ll. 18–22, in *Poems of French Canada*, trans. F.R. Scott (Burnaby, B.C.: Blackfish Press, 1977).
5 Avison's *Winter Sun* was actually published in 1960, after NF had given up his *UTQ* reviewing. He was nevertheless familiar with her poetry, and regrets in his last review, for 1959, that she was one of those poets who had not received her due because she had not published a volume (227 above).
6 NF's remark should be taken with a grain of salt, as the Anglo-Saxon period was not London-centred. For the period after 1066, one could begin to make such a case.

74. A Summary of the Options Conference

1 John Wyndham, foreword to *The Seeds of Time* (London: Penguin, 1959), 8.
2 See no. 72, particularly the closing pages. The exhibition Frye refers to at the Hirshhorn is "14 Canadians: A Critic's Choice," showing recent work by artists such as Jack Bush, Charles Gagnon, Dorothy Knowles, and Daniel Solomon.
3 Voltaire, *Essai sur les moeurs*, ed. René Pomeau (Paris: Garnier, 1963), 1:683 (chap. 70).
4 "To jaw-jaw is always better than to war-war." Winston Churchill, impromptu luncheon speech at the White House, 26 June 1954, reported in the *New York Times*, 27 June 1954, 1.

75. Introduction to *Arthur Lismer*

1 Presumably this is no. 6 above.

76. Roy Daniells

1 Malcolm Wallace was head of the University College English department, 1926–44; he was succeeded by A.S.P. Woodhouse, 1944–64.
2 Roy Daniells, "A Happy Rural Seat of Various View," in *"Paradise Lost": A Tercentenary Tribute*, ed. Balachandra Rajan (Toronto: University of Toronto Press, 1969), 3–17.

77. Across the River and out of the Trees

1 Watson Kirkconnell, "Canada's Leading Poet: Stephen G. Stephansson (1853–1927)," *University of Toronto Quarterly*, 5 (1935–36): 263–77.
2 Milton Wilson, *Recent Canadian Verse*, A Queen's Quarterly Publication (Kingston, Ont.: Jackson Press, [1959]), 6.

3 See no. 53, n. 31.
4 Woodcock's allusion to Oscar Wilde has not been found in *Odysseus Ever Returning: Essays on Canadian Writers and Writing* (1970), or in his *The World of Canadian Writing* (1980). Wilde makes basically the same remark about the Muse of Poetry in his lecture "The English Renaissance of Art." See *The Uncollected Oscar Wilde*, ed. John Wyse Jackson (London: Fourth Estate, 1991), 14–15.
5 See 451, 514 above.
6 Charles Norris Cochrane, *Christianity and Classical Culture* (1940); Barker Fairley, *A Study of Goethe* (1947); S.T. Coleridge, *Philosophical Lectures*, ed. Kathleen Coburn (1949); William Godwin, *Political Justice*, ed. F.E.L. Priestley (1946); NF, *Fearful Symmetry* (1947); A.S.P. Woodhouse, *Puritanism and Liberty: Being the Army Debates (1647–9) from the Clarke Manuscripts with Supplementary Documents* (1938); Arthur E. Barker, *Milton and the Puritan Dilemma* (1942).
7 E.M.W. Tillyard, *The Elizabethan World Picture* (1943).
8 Hans-Georg Gadamer, *Truth and Method*, 2nd ed. (New York: Crossroad, 1990), 388 (pt. 3, sec. 1).
9 Francis Sparshott, *Rhetoric for a Divided Voice*, in the collection *A Divided Voice*.
10 Marshall McLuhan, *Understanding Media* (New York: McGraw-Hill, 1964), 195.
11 Allan and Weaver were CBC producers; Allan's "Sunday Night Stage" (begun in 1944) broadcast many Canadian radio dramas, and Weaver's "Anthology" (begun in 1953) broadcast readings of Canadian literature. For Briggs, see 352 above.

79. Criticism and Environment

1 Frances Brooke, *The History of Emily Montague*, 99 (letter 45).
2 Ibid., 103, 105 (letter 49).
3 See no. 47, n. 6.
4 See no. 68, n.18.
5 Ward, *Canadian Born*, 49 (chap. 3).
6 Innis, *The Fur Trade in Canada* (1930), *The Cod Fisheries: The History of an International Economy* (1940), and *A History of the Canadian Pacific Railway* (1923).
7 Donald Creighton, *Harold Adams Innis: Portrait of a Scholar* (Toronto: University of Toronto Press, 1957).

80. Introduction to *A History of Communications*

1 British cultural historian G.G. Coulton (1858–1947) made the remark in his

Europe's Apprenticeship: A Survey of Mediaeval Latin with Examples (London: Nelson, 1940), 14, while discussing the difficulties of the coexistence of medieval Latin and the vernacular. (Nevertheless, he himself was an advocate of foreign-language training.)

2 In fact *Empire and Communications* uses some of the material in the 1200-p. TS NF is dealing with. In the University of Toronto Archives, filed with the *Empire and Communications* material, is an 800-p. TS which constitutes the missing chaps. 1–3 of *A History of Communications*; it too had been "mined" in the writing of *Empire and Communications*.
3 As he did in the poem *1x1 [One Times One]*, ll. 14–15.
4 See no. 44, n. 6.
5 Victor Hugo, *The Hunchback of Notre Dame*, bk. 5, chap. 2.
6 Samuel Johnson, *Prologue Spoken at the Opening of the Theatre in Drury-Lane, 1747*, l. 53.
7 James Mackintosh (1765–1832) was a British lawyer, writer, and Whig politician who had served as a judge in Bombay.
8 See no. 53, n. 31.
9 Milman Parry, "Whole Formulaic Verses in Greek and South Slavic Heroic Song" (1933), in *The Making of Homeric Verse: The Collected Papers of Milman Parry*, ed. Adam Parry (Oxford: Clarendon Press, 1971).
10 Eric Alfred Havelock's work on orality issued later in a number of books: *Origins of Western Literacy* (1976), *The Literate Revolution in Greece and Its Cultural Consequences* (1982), and *The Muse Learns to Write: Reflections on Orality and Literacy from Antiquity to the Present* (1986).
11 Paul Gauguin, *Oviri: écrits d'un sauvage*, ed. Daniel Guérin (Paris: Gallimard, 1974), 156.
12 Johann Wolfgang von Goethe quoted in *Henry Crabb Robinson on Books and Their Writers*, ed. Edith J. Morley (London: Dent, 1938), 1:369.

82. E.J. Pratt

1 See no. 55, n. 2.
2 See no. 57, n. 1.
3 At this point most of another sentence is lost while the tape is turned over.
4 Alfred Lord Tennyson, *In Memoriam*, st. 56, l. 15.
5 T.S. Eliot, "The Metaphysical Poets," *Selected Essays*, 3rd ed. (London: Faber & Faber, 1957), 288.
6 See no. 44, n. 3.
7 Sandra Djwa, *E.J. Pratt: The Evolutionary Vision*, 90.

83. Margaret Eleanor Atwood

1 Alexandra Johnston, principal of Victoria College, 1981–91.

2 Margaret Atwood, *Second Words: Selected Critical Prose* (Toronto: Anansi, 1982).
3 This was Samuel Johnson's tribute to the English Oliver Goldsmith. See *Boswell's Life of Johnson*, 3:82 (22 June 1776).

84. Culture and Society in Ontario, 1784–1984

1 Catharine Parr Traill, *The Backwoods of Canada*, 162 (letter 12).
2 Anna Brownell Jameson, *Winter Studies and Summer Rambles in Canada* (Toronto: McClelland & Stewart, 1990), 64–5 ("Trees in Canada").
3 Samuel Strickland, *Twenty-Seven Years in Canada West; or The Experience of an Early Settler* (Edmonton: Hurtig, 1970), 178–9.
4 Margaret Atwood, *Surfacing*, 186 (chap. 25).
5 Marshall McLuhan, *The Gutenberg Galaxy*, 265–6. The parenthesis is NF's.
6 George Grant, *Technology and Empire*, 70.
7 The allusion is to Professor Frank Underhill's urging Canadian isolationism and non-participation in British wars (in a CCF convention and *Forum* writings). In 1939 members of the Ontario legislature and the Board of Governors of the University of Toronto tried to have him dismissed on the grounds that he had insulted the imperial connection.
8 Anne Langton, *A Gentlewoman in Upper Canada: The Journals of Anne Langton*, ed. H.H. Langton (Toronto: Clarke, Irwin, 1950), 154 (14 June 1840).
9 Margaret Atwood, *Survival: A Thematic Guide to Canadian Literature* (Toronto: Anansi, 1972), 199 (chap. 10).
10 Stephen Leacock, *Sunshine Sketches of a Little Town* (Toronto: McClelland & Stewart, 1982), 152 ("L'envoi").
11 Raymond Knister, *White Narcissus* (Toronto: McClelland & Stewart, 1962), 36–7 (chap. 3).
12 Catharine Parr Traill, *The Backwoods of Canada*, 220 (letter 15).
13 William ("Tiger") Dunlop, *Statistical Sketches of Upper Canada for the Use of Emigrants* (1832), in *Tiger Dunlop's Upper Canada* (Toronto: McClelland & Stewart, 1967), 123, 127 (chap. 9).
14 Herbert Norman, Canadian ambassador to Egypt, committed suicide in Cairo on 4 April 1957 after having been accused of being a security risk as an alleged Communist sympathizer.
15 Alvin Lee, *James Reaney* (New York: Twayne, 1968), 121.
16 See especially the closing pages of no. 70.

85. Tribute to Robert Zend

1 See James Boswell, *Boswell's Life of Johnson*, 4:275.
2 Jorge Luis Borges was a postmodernist writer, Marcel Marceau a mime

artist, and Norman McLaren a Canadian animator who made experimental films.
3 Steinberg is a Romanian-born American cartoonist and illustrator who was often featured in the *New Yorker*. The poem *The Line Runs On* in *Beyond Labels* is dedicated to him.

87. Barker Fairley

1 Barker Fairley, *Charles M. Doughty: A Critical Study* (London: J. Cape, 1927). Charles Doughty (1843–1926) is remembered for his *Travels in Arabia Deserta* (1888), and forgotten for his volumes of eccentric verse.
2 Barker Fairley, *Wilhelm Raabe: An Introduction to His Novels* (Oxford: Clarendon Press, 1961).
3 Barker Fairley, *A Study of Goethe* (Oxford: Clarendon Press, 1947), 272.

88. Don Harron

1 Harron introduced Charlie Farquharson, a down-to-earth Parry Sound farmer, in the 1952 *Spring Thaw*, and later he appeared on television and in *Charlie Farquharson's Histry [sic] of Canada* (1972).

89. Speech at the New Canadian Embassy, Washington

1 The Monroe Doctrine was the doctrine, proclaimed by the fifth U.S. president, James Monroe, in 1823, that the American continents were not to be considered as subjects for future colonization by any European power.
2 "Fifty-four forty or fight" was the slogan adopted by supporters of Democratic presidential candidate James J. Polk in 1844, signifying their determination to claim the land in the disputed Oregon territory up to this parallel. By the Oregon Treaty in 1846, the 49th parallel was established as the western boundary between Canada and the U.S.
3 Military strategist Karl Marie von Clausewitz had said in his *Vom Kriege* (1833) that war was a carrying out of political relations by other means.
4 See no. 47, n. 6.
5 No. 206 of his *Pensées* (1670), normally translated as "The eternal silence of these infinite spaces terrifies me."
6 In *Jerusalem*, pl. 91, ll. 36–7, Blake comments that Los reads the stars of Albion and the Spectre reads the voids between the stars.
7 Alexis de Tocqueville, *Democracy in America*, ed. Phillips Bradley (New York: Knopf, 1960), 1:296–7, (chap. 17). There are several other brief references to Canada in chap. 8.
8 *The Loon's Necklace* was a 1948 film made by director Radford Crawley for

the Canadian Educational Association. The film, which retells the Indian legend of how the loon received his distinctive neckband, makes use of the collection of Indian masks in what is now the Museum of Civilization.
9 See no. 53, n. 6.
10 "The Group of Seven" was showing at the Phillips Collection, 29 January to 19 February 1977; the abstractionist exhibition already referred to [see no. 74, n. 2], "14 Canadians," opened at the Hirshhorn Museum 3 February and was the occasion for the address in no. 72. Clement Greenberg was an American critic who favoured abstract expressionism.
11 See especially Buckminster Fuller, *Operating Manual for Spaceship Earth* (1969), chap. 4.

90. Afterword to *Hetty Dorval*

1 Henry James, preface to the New York edition of "The Lesson of the Master" and other stories, *Literary Criticism* (New York: Literary Classics of the United States, 1984), 2:1227. James uses the term *novelle*.
2 Henry Wadsworth Longfellow, *A Psalm of Life*, l. 23.

93. Tribute to Don and Pauline McGibbon

1 The Imperial Order Daughters of the Empire, an organization of British loyalists involved largely in philanthropic work.
2 A nervous Spoonerism for "the queen, my lord, is dead."
3 A reference to the attempt to alter Canada's constitution, usually called the Meech Lake accord, between Canada's prime minister and the ten provincial premiers. It proposed to recognize Quebec as a "distinct society." The accord was not ratified by the provinces.

94. The Cultural Development of Canada

1 For the Quebec Act, see no. 68, n. 17; for the Durham Report, see no 47, n. 2.
2 The Oka confrontation, in Oka, Quebec, in 1990, involved a stand-off lasting for several months between Canadian troops and heavily armed Mohawks, who were resisting the attempt to use their land for the golf course alluded to above. For Meech Lake, see no. 93, n.3.
3 *Correspondance d'Emile Zola* (Presses de l'Université de Montréal, 1978-95); *Collected Works of Erasmus* (University of Toronto Press, 1974-); *Benjamin Disraeli Letters* (University of Toronto Press, 1982-); *Collected Works of John Stuart Mill* (University of Toronto Press, 1967-91).

Emendations

page/line
4/17   fashionable *for* fashioned
7/17   Beaucourt *for* de Beaucourt
14/27   Fraser *for* Frazer
16/5   wilderness. *for* wilderness as she had those of La Verendrye. (as in *BG*; in letter to Joan Murray, NFF, 1988, box 63, file 8, NF points out that statement was in error)
23/14   allusions *for* illusions
36/1   *A Death* for *The Death*
63/10   poets seems *for* poets seem
81/27   Malcolm Lowry and *for* Malcolm Lowry,
164/39 Cohen's *for* Cohen
241/39 Newfoundland *for* Newfound
244/20 1943 *for* 1944
246/18 *Strait* for *Straights*
261/33 *The 6000* for *No. 600*
274/25 help *for* held
281/34 (1841) *for* (1842)
281/35 (1865) *for* (1869)
305/8–9 as though *for* as through
311/30 brother *for* fiancé
333/3–4 Under the liquidating tally / Of the cat-and-truncheon bastinades *for* Under the cat-and-truncheon bastinades
333/20 struggle *for* struggles
347/15 even ultimately as *for* even as
348/30 miles on miles *for* miles and miles
354/33 are a permanent *for* is a permanent
362/22 *La petite poule* for *La poule*
405/31 genuine America *for* genuine American

429/12	make *for* makes
436/25	of aggressiveness or imperialistic domination *for* of aggressiveness of imperialistic domination (as in *Heritage Canada*; DG corrects to of aggressiveness, of imperialistic domination)
437/15	inhabited *for* inhibited (as in TS, *DG*)
439/27	who *for* whom
466/27	was *for* is
477/21	constructed *for* contrived
493/17	Radio-Television *for* Radio and Television
519/11	deaths of animals seem *for* deaths of animals seems (as in *Voices of Canada*)
530/8	speak *for* speaks
535/38	spokesmen *for* spokesman
536/18	conditions *for* condition
536/37	customs *for* custom
558/38	*Communications* for *Communication*
569/2	the real reason, that *for* the real reason that
583/38	1980s *for* 1908s
573/3	1914 *for* 1913
574/20	derives *for* drives (as in TS)
577/10	the Canadian *for* Canadian
578/27	*Communications* for *Communication*
592/13	up *for* down
604/11	*Whale* for *Whale's*
615/30	a Canadian *for* Canadian
615/32	rove about *for* rove
621/9	indicates *for* indicate
635/38	friend of *for* friend to
643/16	is not simply a *for* are not simply
650/10	*Loon's* for *Moon's*
662/34	like a galley *for* like galley
662/34	she's tackled *for* she'd tackled
662/35	she'd just *for* she's just
663/1	covering *for* covering up
663/21	cut out *for* cut our
670/4	unity or *for* unity of (as on NF's disk)
671/7	pollination *for* pollenization
689/5	1945 *for* 1946

Index

Birth and/or death dates are given for individuals when available. Books are indexed under their author's name. Dates of works are for the first edition; for foreign works translated into English, the date is that of the English translation.

Abstract Expressionism, 542–3
Actaeon, 505
Acta Victoriana, xxiv
Adam, 172; and Eve, 546
Adams, John (1735–1826), 516
Adams, Myrtle Reynolds (1889–1977), 149, 201
Advertising, 578–9, 580; and propaganda, 404, 410
Aeschylus (ca. 525–ca. 456 B.C.): *Agamemnon*, 64
Aesthetics, judgment in, 253
Africa, 521, 553
Afrikaans, 268
Airplanes, 471, 476, 491, 533
Alberta, 347, 459, 530
Alcohol, 618, 624–5
Aldwinckle, Eric (b.1909), 84
Alger, Horatio (1832–99), 307
Algonquins, 437
"All in the Family," 494
Allan, Andrew Edward Fairbairn (1907–74), 560
Allen, Ralph (1913–66), 249
American Constitution, 405
American literature, 462, 506, 507; influence on Canadian literature, 88, 182, 244, 258–9, 276, 496, 575; irony in, 456; nature in, 37; poetry in, 114–15; popular, 277; primitivism and traditionalism in, 32–3; regionalism in, 412, 513, 529–30, 552–3, 577, 594, 644; tradition in, 345
American Revolution, 106, 258, 345, 370, 415, 446, 457–8, 471, 497, 515, 516, 517, 570; bicentenary of, 453, 458
Amos, Book of, 278
Amoss, Harold Edwin (b. 1880), 182
Andersen, Hans Christian (1805–75), 177
Anderson, Patrick (1915–79), 68, 120; poetry of, 34, 36, 39, 51, 82, 218, 246, 262, 289–90; *The Colour as Naked* (1953), 115–17, 226, 246, 290
Anderson, Violet Louise (b. 1906), 204
Anglo-Saxon (language), 107, 130, 288

Anglo-Saxons; cultural situation of similar to Canada's, 101, 236–7, 266, 345, 385; poetry of, 24–5, 56–8, 170, 285, 386
Animals, 363; death of, 477, 505, 519, 615–16
Anthropology, and criticism, 557
Antiques, 443
Apprentice, idle vs. industrious, 306–8, 312
Apuleius, Lucius (b. ca. A.D. 125): *The Golden Ass*, 220
Archaeology, 435–6, 444, 446; development of, 252–3
Archetypes, xli, xliii; in Glassco, 191; in Pratt, 302
Architecture, 268, 414
Aristophanes (ca. 448–388 B.C.): *The Frogs*, 64
Aristotle (384–22 B.C.), 71, 345
Arnold, Matthew (1822–88), 230, 231, 455, 652; on criticism, 556; on Goldwin Smith, 233
Art(s): authority in, 591–2; cross-cultural influences in, 660, 670–1; and environment, 14; importance of, 653–4; magic as, 401; manifestos in, 632; primitive, 443; and reality, 399; and social imagination, 402; and tradition, 594–5. *See also* Painting
Art Gallery of Toronto, 10, 14, 41, 541–2
Arthur, Eric (1898–1982): *Toronto: No Mean City* (1964), 441
Arts and Letters Club, 409, 541, 542, 635
Asia, 521, 553
Asselin, Olivar (1874–1937), 27
Athens, 581
Atlantic Provinces. *See* Maritimes
Atwood, Margaret Eleanor (b. 1939), 95, 471, 535; achievement of, 611–13; on NF, xxx, xlviii; poetry of, xl, 478, 490, 505, 648–9; *The Edible Woman* (1969), 613, 622; *The Journals of Susanna Moodie* (1970), 420, 479–80, 621; *Lady Oracle* (1976), 611, 627; *Power Politics* (1971), 613; *Surfacing* (1972), 439, 456, 457, 520, 611, 616, 621; *Survival* (1972), xxxviii–xxxix, 456, 474, 498, 612, 622; *You Are Happy* (1974), 613
Auden, W(ystan) H(ugh) (1907–73), 108, 158, 165, 176, 233; influence of, 115, 120, 173, 213, 268; on catalogues, 386, 602
Austen, Jane (1775–1817), 569
Australia, 473; aboriginal language in, 268
Authority, in scholarship and art, 590–2, 612
Automobiles, 436
Avison, Margaret (b. 1918): poetry of, xl, 37, 39, 227, 246, 271, 285, 367, 486; *Winter Sun* (1960), 528

Babylon, 436
Bach, Johann Sebastian (1685–1750), 445
Bailey, Alfred Goldsworthy (1905–97): in *Literary History of Canada*, 340, 341, 346, 362; poetry of, 108–10, 267, 286, 287
Bailey, Philip James (1816–1902): *Festus* (1845), 59
Ballads, 58–9, 239, 357, 442
Balzac, Honoré de (1799–1850), 260
Barbeau, Marius (1883–1969): *Alouette!* (1946), 242; *Folk-Songs of Old Quebec* (1935), 242
Barber, Clarence (b. 1917), 539
Barbizon school, 528
Barker, Arthur E. (1911–90), 555

Baroque age: assumptions of, 436–7, 476, 485, 524–6; Daniells and, 544
Bates, Ronald Gordon Nudell (1924–95), 213–15
Battle of Maldon, The, 58
Baudelaire, Charles Pierre (1821–67), 55, 121; *Correspondances* (1857), 56
Bayer, Mary Elizabeth, 179, 222
Beattie, Alexander Munro (b. 1911), 353, 355, 366, 369, 371
Beaucourt, François (1740–94), 7
Beaupré, Jean, 157–8
Beauty, in art, 197–8
Becket, Thomas à (1118–70), 446
Beckett, Samuel (1906–89), 413
Beddoes, Thomas Lovell (1803–49), 27
Beerbohm, Max, Sir (1872–1956): 'Savonarola' Brown (1919), 59
Bell, Andrew James (1856–1932), 549
Bellamy, Edward (1850–98), 354
Benda, Julien (1867–1956): *La trahison des clercs* (1927), 590
Beothuks, 519, 525
Beowulf, 24, 57, 64, 579
Béranger, Pierre Jean (1780–1857), 527, 550
Berger, Carl (b. 1939), 462, 558
Bethune, Norman (1899–1937), 461
Bible, 424, 485, 564; as foundation of literature, 277; interpretation of, 252–3, 294; in *Stepsure Letters*, 310; translation of, 587. *See also* individual books
Bickersteth, (John) Burgon (1888–1979), 83
Bildungsroman, in Canadian literature, 621, 623, 627
Bilingualism, 644, 646, 669
Binks, Sarah. *See* Hiebert
Biology, in Canada, 455–6
Birney, Earle (1904–95), 100, 183, 330, 332, 337, 369, 409, 471; as academic poet, 267, 288, 491; on lack of ghosts, 440, 477–8; poetry of, xli, 17, 30, 33, 35, 108, 246, 256–7, 464; *David and Other Poems* (1942), 23–5, 34, 63, 246, 264, 266, 288, 505; *Trial of a City* (1952), 106–8, 226, 246, 247, 267, 288, 370; *Turvey* (1949), 246; ed. *Twentieth-Century Canadian Poetry* (1953), 123
Bishop, Mary Davidson (1905–57), 201
Bissell, Claude T. (1916–2000), 272; in *Literary History of Canada*, 340, 341, 450, 462
bisset, bill (b. 1939), 651
Black culture, 668
Blake, Edward (1833–1912), 104, 299, 417, 605
Blake, William (1757–1827), 172, 302, 418, 617, 646; influence of, 157, 168, 191; on minute particulars, 274; NF and, xxxi, 555, 558; on pity, 432; on poets, 322; on simplicity, 294
Bland, Salem Goldworth (1859–1950), 86, 399
Blasted Pine, The. See Scott, F.R.
Blavatsky, née Hahn, Helena Petrovna (1831–91), 87
Blostein, David Avrom (b. 1935), 153
Bodin, Jean (1530–96), 589
Boer War, 523
Bonner, Robert (b. 1920), 540
Bonnycastle, Sir Richard Henry (1791–1847), 497, 517
Borduas, Paul–Émile (1905–60), 81, 491, 519
Borges, Jorge Luis (1899–1986), 450, 630
Boston, 47, 344
Bourinot, Arthur Stanley (1893–1969): poetry of, 94, 123–4, 136, 150, 222; *Five Canadian Poets* (1954), 136

Bowering, George (b. 1935), xl
Bowles, Richard Pinch (1864–1960), 426
Bowman, Louise Morey (1882–1944): *Characters in Cadence* (1938), 5–6
Boxer, Avi (b. 1932), 153
Braddock, General Edward (1695–1755), 349–50
Braden, Bernard (1916–93), 247
Bradshaw, Thecla, 148–9
Bradstreet, Anne Dudley (ca. 1612–72), 33
Brandtner, Fritz (1896–1969), 43
Braque, Georges (1882–1963), 12
Brett, George Sidney (1879–1944), 349; *History of Psychology* (1912–21), 548
Brewster, Elizabeth (b. 1922), 100, 136, 181
Briggs, William (1836–1922), 352, 561
British Columbia, 31, 138, 413, 439, 459, 510
Broadus, Edmund Kemper (1876–1936), 548; and Broadus, Eleanor Hammond: *A Book of Canadian Prose and Verse* (1923), 449
Brooke, Frances (1724–89): *The History of Emily Montague* (1769), 351, 502, 569, 647
Brooke, Rupert Chawner (1887–1915): on Canada, 346, 510, 650
Brooker, Bertram (1888–1955), 328
Brown, Audrey Alexandra (b. 1904), 336
Brown, E(dward) K(illoran) (1905–51), 418, 481; on Arnold, 230; NF's tribute to, xxvii, 101; *On Canadian Poetry* (1943), 101, 244, 283, 503, 548, 620; ed. *Selected Poems of Duncan Campbell Scott* (1951), 101
Brown, J.J. (b. 1916): *Ideas in Exile* (1967), 455

Brown, John (1800–59), 350
Brown, Russell Morton (b. 1942), xxxix
Browning, Robert (1812–89), 4, 185; *Sordello* (1840), 353
Bruce, Charles Tory (1906–71), 33, 97–8; *The Flowing Summer* (1947), 67
Brueghel, Pieter (ca. 1525–69), 7
Bruno, Giordano (1548–1600), 612
Bucke, Richard Maurice (1837–1902): *Comic Consciousness: A Study of the Evolution of the Human Mind* (1901), 353
Buckler, Ernest (1908–84), 530; *The Mountain and the Valley* (1952), 249, 361
Buckley, Jerome (b. 1917), 611
Buddha, 431
Buddhism, 524
Bunner, Freda Newton (b. 1904), 155
Bunyan, Paul, 57, 105, 271, 597
Burke, Edmund (1729–97), 3, 349, 457, 462, 499, 571, 589, 629, 642
Burnet, Jean (b. 1920): *Next Year Country* (1951), 688n9
Burney, Fanny (1752–1840): *Evelina* (1778), 569
Burns, Robert (1759–96), 94, 304, 389, 390
Bush, Douglas (1896–1983), 230; on great thoughts, 356
Butler, Samuel (1612–80): *Hudibras* (1663), 295
Butler, Samuel (1835–1902), 183
Butterslide theory of history, 560
Byron, Lord (George Gordon) (1788–1824), 109, 276, 302, 423; *Don Juan* (1819–24), 295

Callaghan, Morley (1903–90), 49, 549, 627; fiction of, 249, 359; on Toronto, 384; *The Loved and the Lost* (1959),

363; *Such Is My Beloved* (1934), 348, 363; *They Shall Inherit the Earth* (1935), 354; *The Varsity Story* (1948), 83–4
Cameron, Allen Barry (b. 1940), xxxix
Cameron, George Frederick (1854–85), 136
Campbell, Alexander Bradshaw (b. 1933), 536, 540
Campbell, Thomas (1777–1844), 423
Campbell, Wilfred (1858–1918), 26–7, 34, 164, 264
Campion, Thomas (1567–1620), 147
Canada Council, 314, 323, 324, 381, 551, 668; rationale for aid to culture from, 273, 274, 276, 323
Canada: characteristics of, 253; contrast with and relation to U.S., *see* United States and Canada; as country without mythology, 172; ecological problems of, 435–6; and fallacy of "new country," 31, 55–6, 276, 356, 522, 527, 550, 569; folk songs of, 238–42; French, *see* French Canada; ghost towns in, 440; as Grove's ideal America, 258, 364; growth of, 305; heroes in, 462, 475; identity of, 344–7, 403–5, 412–17, 419–20, 452, 454, 466–71, 472, 476, 493, 534, 574, 639–41, 659; importance of communications in, 243, 261, 348, 349, 579, 603, 648; landscape of, 14–15, 256; language problem in, *see under* French Canada; nature in, *see* Nature; necessity for change in, 363–6; NF and, xlviii, 412; N–S and E–W axes in, 512 (*see also* Laurentian axis); Pearson's vision of, 428; political situation of, 322–3, 424–5, 419–20, 663, 667–8, 670; as possible model, 532, 540; in postmodern world, 371–2; postnational future of, 532–40; prenational to postnational, xlvi, 521–2, 532, 553; small population of, 78, 183, 314, 461. *See also* North America

– culture of, 308, 508; and assimilation of native tradition, 650; CBC's role in, 247–8, 560–1; church and state in, 518; colonial phase in, 526–8, 666–7; Currelly's contribution to, 253–4; documentary and realistic interest in, 511, 550; effect of media on, 560–2; English stimulated by growth of French, 451, 514, 553, 576; future of, 672; government role in, 88–90, 273–4, 668; history of, 243–4; importance of, 244, 312, 325–6, 663–4; Innis on, 592; intrusion of natural world in, 500–7; NF on, xxxi–xxxvi; as pioneer culture, 347–8; Pratt's role in, 305; provincialism to regionalism in, 530; question of distinctiveness of, 102–3, 106; regionalism in, 514, 540, 576–7; repatriating of, 520; Robins and, 236–7; romantic vs. pastoral tradition in, 417, 434; three levels of, 639–41; vitality of contemporary, 534

– economy of, 536, 539, 666–7; Innis on, 584–5, 592; mercantilism in, 347–8, 523, 550, 568–9

– history of, 104, 665; Baroque beginnings of, 436–7; compromise in, 642; as discipline, 244, 449; foreshortening of, 345–6; as pageant, 467; and Quebec, 450–1; reflected in ballads, 240; in romances, 356, 362–3; shortness of, 446; summary of, 243–4; Toryism in, 517–18; typical incidents in, 58, 61, 262, 349

- literature of, 40, 66, 522, 524, 650; American influence on, *see under* American literature; animals in, 363, 477, 519, 616; British influence on, 88, 423 (*see also* form and content in); Brown on, xxvii; colonial or provincial phase of, 29-31, 549, 571-3; Confederation period of, 573-6; contribution of Pratt, Edgar, and Robins to, 336; cross-cultural pollination in, 671; critical stance required in, 255-6, 284-5, 449-50; Daniells and, 545-6; developing themes in, 462; Edgar's contribution to, 79-80, 231-2, 234, 336; egocentric consciousness in, 477-9; enlarged conception of, 341; form and content in, 275-6, 356-7; in *First Statement*, 21; garrison mentality in, 350-5, 360; and the government, 88-9; and Governor-General's Awards, 322-3, 326; Grove on, 76; growth of, 448-50, 551, 577-8, 668; and Jewish writers, 618; language question in, 345; late development of, 568-9; myth and, 356, 361-2, 520; nature in, *see* Nature; NF on, xxxi-xxxiii, xxxvi-xl, xlii-xlviii; pastoral myth in, 362-9, 371; position of writer in, 89, 343; primacy of scholarship in, 244, 352, 555; professionalism in, 49-50, 463-4; from provincial to regional, 620-1, 644-5; Pratt's status in, 379, 381-2; question of its distinctiveness, xlvii, 28-9, 250, 645; question of its merit, 249-50; realism and irony in, 358-9, 360, 361; regionalism in, 514, 552-4, 594; respect for fact in, 447; and the tradition, 276, 345-6, 357-8, 372, 579; tragic themes in, 456-7; value judgments in, 255, 340-1, 342; value of, 341-2, 372, 465, 492, 507, 628, 660; women in, 503, 569. *See also* Canada, culture of; and individual genres

Canadian Authors' Association, 49-50, 80, 231, 323

Canadian Club, 612

Canadian Forum, 22, 23, 68, 235, 285, 549; aims of, 77-8; Fairley and, 635; NF and, xxiv, 417, 418; reflections on after fifty years, 408-11; Robins and, 236

Canadian Group of Painters, 41

Canadian Poetry Magazine, 99, 328

Canadian Society of Painters in Water Colour, 41

Canadian Writers' Foundation, 231

Cape Breton, 496, 499

Cape Dorset, 535

Capitalism, 408, 440, 588; American, 404-5

Cappon, James (1854-1939), 353

Careless, James Maurice Stockford (b. 1919) 325, 326

Carleton University, 272-3, 278-9

Carlyle, Thomas (1795-1881), 462, 498; *Sartor Resartus* (1833-4), 291

Carman, William Bliss (1861-1929), 22, 79, 126, 136, 231, 353, 485; influence of, 129, 149, 155, 164, 286; poetry of, 27, 31, 33, 37, 129, 132; rhetorical and elegiac impulses in, 233, 366, 480-1, 484, 512; as Romantic lyric poet, 126-8, 135, 264, 280, 304

Carpenter, Edmund Snow (b. 1922): ed. *Anerca* (1959), 220-2

Carr, Emily (1871-1945), 8, 12, 57, 73, 85, 102, 138, 140, 281, 348, 417, 423, 434, 447, 484, 485, 511, 528; *Klee Wyck* (1941), 249

Carroll, Lewis (Charles Lutwidge Dodgson) (1832–98), 187
Carsley, Sara Elizabeth (b. 1887): *The Artisan* (1941), 19–20
Cartesianism, xlv, 399, 447, 476, 478, 483, 519, 646
Cartier, Jacques (1491–1557), 271, 650
Castonguay, Claude (b. 1929), 532
Catullus, Gaius Valerius (ca. 84–ca. 54 B.C.), 57, 267
CBC, 305, 409, 538, 629; and Canadian unity, 413; contribution to Canadian culture, 247–8, 283, 285, 343, 560–1
CCF, 420, 620, 644; and *Canadian Forum*, 409
Celts, culture of, 258
Censorship, 47–8, 50; in Canada, 278, 619
Cézanne, Paul (1839–1906), 72, 401
Chadwick, Charles McKenzie, 153
Chagall, Marc (1889–1985), 74, 144, 631
Chambers, Jack (1931–78), 530
Champlain, Samuel de (1567–1635), 467, 468–9
Chaplin, Charles Spencer (1889–1977), 578
Chapman, George (ca. 1559–1634) et al.: *Eastward Ho!* (1605), 306
Chapman, John H. (b. 1940), 452, 455, 456
Chappell, Edward (1792–1861): *Voyage of His Majesty's ship Rosamond to Newfoundland* (1818), 503
Chateaubriand, François René (1768–1848), 281
Chaucer, Geoffrey (ca. 1345–1400), 56, 59, 180, 296
Chiasson, Rodrigue, 582, 583
Chicago, 565

Child, Philip (1898–1978): *The Victorian House* (1951), xxix, 95–6, 226
Chile, 243, 422, 509, 666
Chilton, Vina Bruce, 111
China, 458, 584, 625, 653; antiquities in, 446; Canadian studies in, 628
Chirico, Giorgio de (1888–1978), 86
Chittick, Victor Lovett Oakes (b. 1882): *Thomas Chandler Haliburton ("Sam Slick")* (1924), 310, 318
Christian, William (b. 1945): *The Idea File of Harold Adams Innis* (1980), 585, 587
Christianity; attitude to nature, 437, 475–6, 485, 525–6; attitude to other religions, 524–5; Pratt and, 159–60, 294, 302, 392–3; principle of authority in, 526
Church of England, 496
Church: role of, 273; and state, 461
Churchill, Sir Winston Leonard Spencer (1874–1965), 105, 540; oratory of, 299, 392
Civil War, American, 535, 643
Clarke, George Herbert (1873–1953), 128
Classics, 277
Claudel, Paul (1868–1955), 528
Clausewitz, Karl Marie von (1780–1831), 643
Cobbett, William (1763–1835), 311, 370
Coburn, Kathleen (1905–91), 555; *In Pursuit of Coleridge* (1977), 558
Cochrane, Charles Norris (1889–1945), 555
Cocteau, Jean (1889–1963), 638
Cogswell, Fred (b. 1917): in *Literary History of Canada*, 348, 350, 351; poetry of, 136, 156, 180, 217–18
Cohen, Leonard (b. 1934): *Beautiful Losers* (1966), 464, 477; *Let Us*

Compare Mythologies (1956), 164–6, 463, 528
Coleman, Herbert Thomas John (1872–1964), 201
Coleridge, Samuel Taylor (1772–1834): on poetry, 86
Colgrove, Rogers G., 416
Collie, Michael (b. 1929), 224–5
Collin, William Edwin (1893–1984): *The White Savannahs* (1936), 129, 244, 245, 286
Collins, William (Wilkie) (1824–89): *The Moonstone* (1868), 273
Colombo, John Robert (b. 1936), 206, 207, 225
Colonialism, 408; in Canada, xliii–xlvii, 30–1, 68, 346–7, 403, 414, 416, 468, 469, 496–8, 526–7, 592; European attitude to, 468; reflected in de la Roche, 248. *See also* Provincialism
Columbus, Christopher (1451–1506), 509
Colville, Alex (b. 1920), 519
Comfort, Charles Fraser (1900–94), 10
Communication, 410–11; Innis on, 584–8, 593, 603; Innis and McLuhan on, 558–9, 578–9. *See also under* Canada
Communism, 105, 122, 355, 402, 408, 588, 619; persecution of, 618
Condominium mentality, 647
Confederation, 3, 89, 90, 101, 240, 417, 495, 516; and Canadian identity, 346; centennial of, 349, 375, 425, 458, 515; cultural basis of, 517, 659, 665; economic aspect of, 537–8; Haliburton on, 316; and Laurentian axis, 469; literature of, 527, 549, 573–6; Quebec and, 515, 536, 537; and railroad, 510, 512; and Reconfederation, xlvii, 659–60, 667–8

Connor, Ralph (Charles William Gordon) (1860–1937), 352, 623
Conrad, Joseph (1857–1924), 14, 103; on the *Titanic*, 298, 606
Conron, Brandon (b. 1919), 361, 362, 464
Consciousness, Cartesian, 437, 476, 519, 525
Conservatism, 462; Conservative party, 89, 513
Contact Press, 285
Contemporary Verse, 17–18, 100, 285
Contract, social, 589
Convention, 29, 98, 155, 171, 443
Cook, Eleanor (b. 1933), xlviii
Cook, Ramsay (b. 1931), 375, 533, 535, 538, 540
Cooke, Jack Kent (1912–97), 235
Copernicus, Nicolas (1473–1543), 646
Corwin, Norman (b. 1910), 259
Coulter, John (1888–1980), 247, 361–2
Coulton, George Gordon (1858–1947), 583
Courchene, Thomas (b. 1940), 538, 539
Coward, Noel (1899–1973): *Cavalcade* (1931), 4
CPR (Canadian Pacific Railway), 454, 510; Pratt on, 381, 386, 484–5, 512
Crane, (Harold) Hart (1899–1932), 173, 301
Crawford, Isabella Valancy (1850–87), 187, 546; poetry of, 27, 30, 365, 369, 512; mythopoeia in, 57, 127, 288, 304; *Malcolm's Katie* (1884), 57, 60–1, 259–60, 270, 281, 287, 482–3, 503
Crawley, Alan (1887–1975), 285
Crawley, Alec, 224
Creation, process of, 630–1
Cree, and mass media, 493–4, 535–6
Creighton, Alan (b. 1903), 22, 410

Creighton, Donald Grant (1902–79), 344, 350, 419, 461, 603, 620; *Canada's First Century, 1867–1967* (1970), 457; *John A. Macdonald* (1952, 1955), 501–2, 688n.13; *Harold Adams Innis* (1957), 578

Creighton, Helen (1899–1989): ed. *Songs and Ballads from Nova Scotia* (1932), 242

Crémazie, Octave (Claude-Joseph-Olivier) (1827–79), 32

Criticism, 281; and amateur poetry, 150–1; Canadian, 463, 557–60, 673–4; Edgar's approach to, 232–4; and environment, 568; NF and, 548; NF's place in Canadian, 419; relation to literature, 555–7, 578; schools of, 449; and task of critic as reviewer, 114, 209, 227–8, 229, 449–50; and test of genuine poetry, 132–3; value judgments in, 253, 340, 591–2; wider concept of, 557, 579–81

Crockett, David (Davy) (1786–1836), 57, 318

Cromwell, Oliver (1599–1658), 444

Cross, Michael S., 449, 459, 460, 462

CRTC, 493–4, 529, 535–6, 561, 594; and Innis's *History of Communications*, 582–3

Cuba, 415

Cullen, Maurice Galbraith (1866–1934), 513

Culture: as adjoining, 581; and counterculture, 580; Edgar on, 234; importance of genuine, 495; Innis on strategy of, 588–95; mass, 535, 562; persistence of, 668, 671; and politics and/or economics, 268, 273–4, 280, 325–6, 513–15, 527, 529–30, 536, 540, 533–4, 554, 576, 594; provincial into mature, 670; rootedness of, 513, 529–30, 534; and social conditions, 341, 342, 345, 445–6, 521, 534, 563, 577; and subculture, 562, 580; and technology, 258; three levels of, 639–40, 644, 660, 666, 669. *See also* Canada, culture of; Oral culture

cummings, e. e. (Edward Estlin) (1894–1962), 108, 153, 209, 586

Currelly, Charles Trick (1876–1957), 439, 443; *I Brought the Ages Home* (1956), 251–4

Daglish, Peter, 200

Dakin, Laurence, 123

Dalton, Annie Charlotte (1865–1938), 36

Daniells, Roy (1902–79): in *Literary History of Canada*, 340, 341, 353, 364, 366, 368, 545, 546; poetry of, 267, 286, 287, 545–6, 688n.11; tribute to, 544–6

Dante Alighieri (1265–1321), 174

Darwin, Charles Robert (1809–82), 591

Darwinism, social, 353–4, 524

Dauphin, Roma (b. 1942), 536

Davey, Franklin Wilmot (b. 1940), xxxix

Davies, Robertson (1913–97), 535, 553, 621; Deptford trilogy, 627; drama of, 247; *The Manticore* (1972), 457; *Tempest-Tost* (1951), 360

Davies, Thomas (ca. 1737–1812), 511, 528

Davis, Herbert J. (1893–1967), 409

De la Roche, Mazo (1879–1961), 358, 359, 592; Jalna novels, 248, 342, 470; *Delight* (1926), 363

De Beaumont, Victor (1881–1954), 600

De Gaulle, Charles (1890–1970), 450–1

De Mille, James (1833–80): *A Strange Manuscript Found in a Copper Cylinder* (1888), 506
Death, 481–2, 660
Debussy, Claude Achille (1862–1918), 59, 70, 101, 266, 345
Defoe, Daniel (1660–1731), 306; *Moll Flanders* (1722), 307
Deism, in U.S., 453–4
Deloney, Thomas (ca. 1550–1600), 306
Democracy, 405, 520, 672; achievement of, 375–6; aid to art in, 274; need for theory of, 314
Denmark, 461–2, 509
Depression, 183, 354, 409, 550, 618, 620
Descartes, René (1596–1650), 437, 460, 476, 525, 646. *See also* Cartesianism
Descent themes, 489–90, 491
Detective stories, 151
Dewdney, Selwyn H. (1909–79), 249
Dewey, John (1859–1952), 453
DeWitt, Norman Wentworth (1876–1958), 600
Dialectic, 462
Dickens, Charles (1812–70): *Bleak House* (1852–53), 624
Dickinson, Emily Elizabeth (1830–86), 94, 371, 481
Diefenbaker, John George (1895–1979), 313–15; and the North, 416; and Pearson, 427
Diespecker, Richard Alan (b. 1907), 158–9
Dilthey, Wilhelm (1833–1911), 557
Dilworth, Ira (1894–1962), 222
Dinn, M.F., Monsignor, 201
Direction, 40
Disraeli, Benjamin (1804–81), 670
Dixon, Michael F.N. (b. 1937), xxxix
Djwa, Sandra (b. 1939); on NF, xxxvii, xlii–xliii; on Pratt, 606

Dobbs, Kildare (b. 1923): *Running to Paradise* (1962), 321–2, 323
Dominion Drama Festival, 662
Donne, John (?1572–1631), 231, 656; influence of, 44, 92, 121, 129, 191
Donnelly, Ignatius (1831–1901), 353; *Caesar's Column* (1890), 55
Doughty, Charles Montagu (1843–1926), 634
Douglas, Gilean (1900–93), 124
Downes, Gwladys (sic) (b. 1915), 148
Drama, Canadian, 347, 409, 463, 529; McGibbons and, 662; between 1929 and 1954, 246–7
Drayton, Geoffrey (b. 1924), 93–4
Dreams, 524, 580
Dreiser, Theodore (1871–1945), 248
Drew, George Alexander (1894–1974), 89–90
Drew, Wayland (1932–98): *The Wabeno Feast* (1973), 614
Drummond, Ian M. (1933–94), 375
Drummond, William Henry (1854–1907): *The Wreck of the 'Julie Plante'* (1897), 35, 58, 239
Dryden, John (1631–1700), 343
Dudek, Louis (1918–2001), 68, 165, 183, 200, 202; on NF, xli, 419; poetry of, xli, 44–5, 111–13, 145–6, 196–8, 246, 260, 290; ed. *Canadian Poems* (1953), 123; ed. *Delta*, 182; *East of the City* (1946), 246, 285, 290; ed. Raymond Souster's *Selected Poems*, 160–1; *The Transparent Sea* (1956), 161–2, 226, 290
Dufferin, Lady (Helen Selina Sheridan) (1807–67), 4
Dufferin, Lord (Frederick Temple Hamilton Temple Blackwood) (1826–1902), 3–4; *Letters from High Latitudes* (1857), 3

Duhamel, Roger (b. 1916), 326
Duncan, Douglas Moerdyke (1902–68), 433–4
Duncan, Sara Jeanette (1861–1922): *The Imperialist* (1904), 353, 360–1, 575, 619
Dunlop, Dr. William ("Tiger") (1792–1848), 625
Durham Report (1839), 108, 316, 665
Duvar. *See* Hunter-Duvar

Earth mother, 526
Eastern Townships, 416
Eastward Ho! (1605). *See* Chapman, George
Eccles, William John (b. 1917), 462
Ecology, 505, 539; in Canada, 435–6; natural and human, 441. *See also* Nature
Edelstein, Hyman (1889–1957), 95
Edgar, Pelham (1871–1948), 126–7, 389, 551; achievement of, 79–80, 231–4, 548–9; hires Pratt, 379, 380, 599; influence on NF, xxii–xxiv, 335–6, 384–5; *Across My Path* (1952), 230–4; *The Art of the Novel* (1933), 230; *Henry James, Man and Author* (1927), 79, 230, 232, 232–3, 548
Education: aim of, 640; in Canada, 90, 151–2, 275, 375, 442, 518, 671–2; and the cultural tradition, 277–8; Currelly's approach to, 252; separation of church and state in, 461; in U.S., 258, 453–4
Egoff, Sheila A. (b. 1918), 455
Egypt, 436, 441; royal vs. priestly power in, 587
Eichmann, Karl Adolf (1906–62), 525
Eighteenth century: in Canada, 457–8, 469, 666; in the U.S. and Canada, 453–4, 473, 499, 516, 570, 617

Eisener, Charles R. (b. ca. 1943), 152
Eisenhower, Dwight David (1890–1969), 374
Elder, Bruce (b. 1947): *Image and Identity* (1989), 651
Elijah, 411
Eliot, George (Mary Ann Evans) (1819–80), 564; *Middlemarch* (1871), 624
Eliot, Thomas Stearnes (1888–1965), 56, 97, 115, 167, 176, 229, 233, 278, 335, 356, 383, 391, 430, 462, 553, 579; on difficulty, 388; on dissociation of sensibility, 606; influence of, 108, 121, 128–9, 139, 158, 197, 245, 286, 366, 528; on literacy, 390; on the poet, 489; as royalist, 68; *After Strange Gods* (1936), 330; *Gerontion* (1920), 140; *The Waste Land* (1922), 140, 168, 169
Elizabeth I (1533–1603), 342
Elizabeth II (b. 1926): as head of state, 518
Elizabethan age, 581
Elizabethan literature, 306, 522; London centred, 552; social conditions of, 464
Ellenbogen, George (b. 1934), 200–1
Emerson, Nan Macpherson (1892–1968), 201
Emerson, Ralph Waldo (1803–82), 33, 127, 219, 307, 496; on provincialism, 348
Empire Club, 612
Endymion, 172
Engel, Marian (1933–85): *Bear* (1976), 520, 627, 651
England: archaeology in, 446; attitude to Canada, 8; Haliburton on, 319–20; NF in, 508; poetry in, 114; typical Englishman, 275. *See also* Great Britain

English language, 429, 576; dominance of, 669
English literature: mythopoeic periods in, 418; teaching of, 557
Enooesweetok (1890–1950), 220–1
Environment, obliteration of, 414. *See also* Ecology; Nature
Epiphany, NF's, 565–6
Erasmus, Desiderius (1466–1536), 670
Erikson, Erik H. (1902–94): *Dimensions of a New Identity* (1974), 458–9
Ernerk, Peter (b. 1947), 535
Escher, Maurits Cornelius (1898–1971), 631
Eskimos. *See* Inuit
Europe, 669; contribution to New World, 475–6, 485
Evangeline. See Longfellow
Everson, Ronald Gilmour (1903–92), 178–9, 192–3
Evolution, 252–3, 591; Pratt and, 294, 300–1, 393, 599, 603, 605, 607–9
Existentialism, 355
Expressionism, 511
Ezra, Isaac Ben (b. 1896), 101, 150

Fairley, Barker (1887–1986), 409, 555; achievement of, 634–6; his portrait of Pratt, 598, 635
Fall of man, 526
Family Compact, 316, 352, 475, 642, 652
Farley, Tom (b. 1917), 111
Farrell, James Thomas (1904–79): *Bernard Clare* (1946), 50
Fascism, 375, 408
Fashion, cycle of, 443
Faulkner, William (1897–1962), 278, 530, 553, 577
Fauvism, 424, 511
Feminism, 652
Fenians, 620, 642

Ferguson, Graham (Max?), 247
Ferne, Doris Maud (née Napper) (b. 1896): *Ebb Tide* (1941), 20
Ferron, Jacques (1921–85): *Contes du pays incertain* (1962), 322–3
Fiamengo, Marya (b. 1926), 153, 199
Fichte, Johann Gottlieb (1762–1814), 450
Fiction, Canadian, 528, 674; and "great Canadian novel," 358, 624; between 1929 and 1954, 247–9
Fiddlehead, 182, 285
Field, Erastus Salisbury (1805–1900), 369
Films. *See* Movies
Finch, Robert (1900–95), 33, 39, 245, 371; as academic poet, 246, 267, 286, 287
Findley, Timothy (1930–2002): *Not Wanted on the Voyage* (1984), 627; *The Wars* (1977), 616
Finland, 509
Finnigan, Joan (b. 1925), 179
First Flowering. See Frisch
First Statement (1942–45), 21–2, 40, 68, 285
Fitzgerald, Lemoine (1890–1956), 424, 434, 513
Flaherty, Robert J. (1884–1951), 221
Flaubert, Gustave (1821–80), 224
Fleming, May Agnes (1840–80), 358
Flemish, 669
FLQ, 415
Folk songs, 239–42, 277, 357, 442, 463
Ford, Henry (1863–1947), 307
Ford, R(obert) A(rthur) D(ouglas) (1915–98), 163–4
Form, and content, 137, 265, 268–9, 275–6, 356–7, 463, 527, 530
Fort, Paul (1872–1960), 528
Fortner, Dora P. (b. 1894), 207
Foster, Stephen Collins (1826–64), 277

Fournier, Jules (1884–1918): *Anthologie des Poètes Canadiens* (1920), 27
Fournier, William Robert, 153
Fowke, Donald (b. 1937), 538, 539
Fowke, Edith Fulton (1913–96), 357; and Richard Johnston (b. 1917) ed. *Folk Songs of Canada* (1954), 238–42, 418
Fox, Dr. Sherwood William (1878–1967), 123
France, 460; art in, 9; as colonial power, 436, 473, 496, 519, 522, 527, 568, 641, 666; separatism in, 533
Franklin, Benjamin (1706–90), 453, 500, 516, 570, 617; *Autobiography* (ca. 1760), 307; *Poor Richard's Almanac* (1732–57), 311
Franklin, Sir John (1786–1847), 351, 386
Fraser, Hermia Harris (b. 1902), 180, 270, 487
Fraser, Simon (1776–1862), 14, 372
Frazer, Sir James George (1854–1941), 286; *The Golden Bough* (1890–1915), 187
Freedom: academic, 273, 274, 279, 314; individual and corporate, 235
French (language), 406, 407, 576; teaching of in Canada, 644, 646
French Canada, 461, 497; Cartesiansim in, 646; conquest of, 422; conservatism in, 517, 575, 641, 666; creative upsurge in, 506; introversion in, 375; language question in, 268, 345, 473, 494–5, 539, 576, 669; and *Maria Chapdelaine*, 30, 573; preoccupation with history in, 571, 649
– literature of, 27, 343, 576; ballads, 239, 241, 242; English translations of, 157–8; maturity of, 553–4; parochialism in, 31; "quaintness" in, 30; social function of writers in, 514, 570. *See also* Quebec
French Revolution, 457–8; French Canadian attitude to, 473, 517, 575, 641, 666
Freneau, Philip Morin (1752–1832), 33
Freud, Sigmund (1856–1939), 113, 286, 599; on dreams, 524
Freudianism, social, 355
Frisch, Anthony (b. 1921): poetry of, 101, 136; ed. *First Flowering* (1956), 152, 163
Frith, William Powell (1819–1909): *Derby Day* (1858), 13
Frost, Robert Lee (1874–1963), 98, 189, 202, 308, 391, 456, 553; on translation, 406
Frye, Catherine Mary Maud Howard (Cassie) (NF's mother; 1870–1940), 564
Frye, Eratus Howard (NF's brother; 1899–1918), 564
Frye, Helen Kemp (1910–86), 433, 438, 566
Frye, Herman Edward (NF's father; 1870–1959), 440, 564–5
Frye, Herman Northrop (1912–91), 461; childhood reading, 358; early life, 564–6; Edgar on, 231; Layton on, 113; supposed school of poetry, 449–50; *AC* (1957), xxvi–xxvii, xxxi, xli, xlii, xliii, xlv, xlviii, 418; *BG* (1971), xxi, xxxiii–xxxiv, xxxvi, xli, 412–19 passim; "Canada and Its Poetry" (1943), xxxvi, xxxvii, xxxviii, 417; "Canadian and Colonial Painting" (1941), xxv, xxxvii, 417, 542; "Canadian Culture Today" (1977), xxxvi; ed. *Collected Poems of E.J. Pratt*, 2nd ed. (1958), 208; "Conclusion" to *Literary*

History of Canada (1965), xxxii–xxxiii, xxxvi, xxxvii–xxxviii, xliii, 340, 419, 448–9; "Conclusion" to *Literary History of Canada* (1976), xxxiv, xxxv–vi, 448–9; "David Milne: An Appreciation" (1948), 417; *FS* (1946), xxvi–xxvii, xxxi, xxxvii, 418, 555; "Haunted by Lack of Ghosts" (1977), xxxv, xxvii, xlvi; ed. *I Brought the Ages Home* (1956), 251; Lawren Harris: An Introduction" (1969), 417; "Letters in Canada: Poetry" (1951–60), xxvii–xxx, xl–xlii, 150–1, 226–9, 418–19, 551, 567–8; "The Narrative Tradition in English Canadian Poetry" (1946), xxv, 418; "Preface to an Uncollected Anthology" (1956), xlii–xliii, 418; "Silence in the Sea" (1969), 417; ed. unpublished *History of Communications*, 583

Frye, Vera Victoria (NF's sister; 1900–66), 564, 565

Fuller, Buckminster (1895–1983), 652

Future, 442; and past, 408; shock, 442

Gadamer, Hans-Georg (1900–2002), 557

Gagnon, Clarence A. (1881–1942), 27, 513

Galbraith, John Kenneth (b. 1908): *The Scotch* (1964), 640–1

Galileo (Galileo Galilei) (1564–1642), 467, 468, 590, 612, 646

Gallant, Mavis (b. 1922), 553

Galloway, David (b. 1919), 343

Galois, Évariste (1811–32), 232

Garneau, Hector de Saint-Denys (1912–43), 157

Garner, Hugh (1913–79), 249, 325, 326

"Garrison mentality," xxxii–xxxiii, xxxvi, xxxviii, xlv, 351–2, 355, 360, 470, 471, 551, 559, 569–70, 572, 647

Gaugin, Paul (1848–1903), 595

Gauthier, David P. (b. 1932), 374

Gélinas, Gratien (1909–98), 638

Genius, 342

Geography, and map-making, 466–7

Geology, in Canada, 456

George, St., 485

George II (1683–1760), 496

George, James (1818–70), 352

German (discipline), 634

Germany, 460, 515, 540; art in, 9; Canadian literature in, 551, 577, 612; Canadian studies in, 628; scholarship of, 548

Ghana, 413

Gibson, Graeme (b. 1934): *Perpetual Motion* (1982), 627

Gilson, Étienne (1884–1978), 555, 588

Glassco, John (1909–81), 189–92, 202

Glendinning, Alexander (fl.1871), 183

Glickman, Susan (b. 1953), xxxvii

Glooscap, 57

Gnarowski, Michael (b. 1934), 225

Godfrey, Dave (b. 1938), 620

Godfrey, Eleanor (d. 1977), 409

Goethe, Johann Wolfgang von (1749–1832), 595, 635; *Faust* (1808), 635

Goldsmith, Oliver (of Canada) (1794–1861): *The Rising Village* (1825), 33, 59

Goldsmith, Oliver (of England) (1730–74), 612

Goldwater, Barry Morris (1909–98), 374

Good Housekeeping, 279

Gothicism, 611

Goudge, Thomas A. (1910–99), 456, 460

Governor-General's Awards, 321–6, 381

Index

Grady, Wayne (b. 1948), xxxvi–xxxvii
Graham, Gwethalyn (1913–65), 249
Grant, Douglas (1921–69), 328
Grant, George Parkin (1918–88), 419, 461, 558, 619, 620; *Lament for a Nation* (1965), 415, 457, 517–18, 522, 532, 553; *Technology and Empire* (1969), 477, 486, 617
Grant, John Webster (b. 1919), 461
Graves, Robert Ranke (1895–1985): *The Greek Myths* (1955), 172; *The White Goddess* (1948), 613
Gray, James Martin (b. 1930), 207–8
Gray, Thomas (1716–71): *Elegy, Written in a Country Churchyard* (1751), 363
Great Britain, 78, 259, 283, 346, 460; archaeology in, 511; Canada's relation to, 495–7, 575, 619, 620, 643–4, 649; as colonial power, 452, 519, 522, 568, 641, 666; cultural influence of, 243, 276, 344–5, 516–17, 592; Haliburton on, 318, 319; politics in, 374; regional literature in, 283, 413, 513–14, 644; separatism in, 532–3. *See also* England
Great man, 427–8
Greece, ancient: art in, 14, 591, 595; and alphabet, 584
Greenburg, Clement (1909–94), 652
Greenleaf, Elisabeth Bristol (1895–1980): ed. *Ballads and Sea Songs of Newfoundland* (1933), 242
Gregory VII (Hildebrand), St., Pope (ca. 1020–85), 587
Grey Owl (Archibald Stansfield Belaney) (1881–1938), 362, 449, 614
Grip, 450
Groom, Ida Sutherland, 149
Group of Seven, 10, 126, 280, 353, 409, 417, 422–3, 424, 484, 491, 513, 541, 542, 635; aims of, 398–9; colour in,

8–9; documentary interest in, 447, 511, 528, 652; landscape in, 73; as name, 632, 633; perspective in, 102; reaction to, 401–2
Grove, Frederick Philip (1879–1948),102, 357, 449, 457, 688n.7; achievement of, 75–6, 248; *The Master of the Mill* (1944), 248, 354, 617; *Over Prairie Trails* (1922), 364; *A Search for America* (1927), 258, 363–4, 371; *The Turn of the Year* (1923), 364, 504
Grube, George Maximilian Anthony (1899–1982), 409
Guinness, Sir Alec (1914–2000), 529
Gushue, Raymond (1900–80), 201
Gustafson, Ralph Barker (1909–95), xxxvi; ed. *A Little Anthology of Canadian Poets* (1943), 39; ed. *Anthology of Canadian Poetry (English)* (1942), 24, 39, 81; ed. *Canadian Accent* (1944), 66
Guthrie, (Sir William) Tyrone (1900–71), 529

Haeckel, Ernst Heinrich Philipp August (1834–1919): *The Riddle of the Universe* (1900), 689n. 21
Hagan, Robert Frederick (b. 1918), 11
Haggard, (Sir Henry) Rider (1856–1925), 611
Haida, 487, 505, 650
Haig-Brown, Roderick (1908–76), 249
Hale, Katherine (Amelia Beers Warmock Garvin) (1878–1956), 94
Haliburton, Thomas Chandler (1796–1865), 344, 346; on British connection, 496–7; life of, 316–17; *The Clockmaker* (1836–40) and other Sam Slick papers, 33, 105, 308, 310–11, 316–20, 370, 440, 516–17, 571, 575, 643; *The Old Judge* (1849), 316

Hambleton, Ronald (b. 1917): poetry of, 33, 44–5, 68, 120–2; ed. *Unit of Five*, 44–6, 91
Hamilton, A(lbert) C(harles) (b. 1921), xlviii
Harbourfront, 612
Harden, Verna Loveday (b. 1904), 222
Hardin, Hershel (b. 1936), 537
Hardy, Thomas (1840–1928), 103, 230, 302, 413, 513, 552, 599; on the *Titanic*, 298, 606
Harris, Bess, and R.G.P. Colgrove, ed.: *Lawren Harris* (1969), 398–402 passim
Harris, Lawren (1885–1970), xxxv, 8, 10, 12, 73, 417, 541, 542, 635; achievement of, 85–7, 398–402, 632–3
Harris, Leslie (b. 1929), 537, 540
Harris, Wilson (b. 1921): *Palace of the Peacock* (1960), 554
Harron, Don (b. 1924), achievement of, 637–8
Hart House, 361, 409
Harvard, NF at, xxxiv–xxxv, 555
Harvey, Gabriel (1550?–1631): on scholars, 32
Havelock, Eric Alfred (1903–88), 409, 593
Haworth, Colin Reid (1916–98), 178, 193
Haworth, Peter (1889–1986), 43
Hazelton, Ruth Cleaves, 111
Heath, John (1917–51), 203–4
Heavysege, Charles (1816–76): poetry of, 27, 35, 36, 304, 365, 605–6; *Count Filippo* (1860), 59, 263; *Jephthah's Daughter* (1865), 59–60, 62, 263, 264, 266, 281, 287; *Saul* (1857), 59, 60, 263
Hébert, Anne (1916–2000), 407
Hebrew (language), 268, 584

Hebrews, culture of, 258. *See also* Jews
Hegel, Georg Wilhelm Friedrich (1770–1831), 352, 353
Heidegger, Martin (1889–1976), 108, 557, 579, 651
Heine, Heinrich (1797–1856), 95, 193
Hemingway, Ernest Millar (1899–1961), 384, 528
Hémon, Louis (1880–1913): *Maria Chapdelaine* (1914 and 1916), 30, 275, 356, 362, 573, 575
Hénault, Gilles (b. 1921), 157
Henry, Marion Kathleen (neé Waddell) (1893–1973), 155
Henry VIII (1491–1547), 446
Henryson, Robert (1430–1506), 180
Hermeneutics, 557
Heroes, in Canada, 462, 475
Herrick, Robert (1591–1674), 522, 552
Hicks, Edward (1780–1849), 371
Hiebert, Paul Gerhardt (1892–1987), 183; *Sarah Binks* (1947), 70, 101
Higher Criticism, 599
Hine, Daryl (b. 1936),153; poetry of, 146–7, 154, 173–6, 225, 271, 291
History, 325; American attitude to, 652–3; American vs. Canadian attitude to, 649; and criticism, 557; of ideas, 544, 556; Innis on, 559, 578; Pearson on, 427. *See also* Canada, history of
Hitler, Adolf (1889–1945), 299, 431; and radio, 593
Hodgetts, Bernie (1911–87): *What Culture? What Heritage?* (1968), 442
Hodgins, Jack (b. 1938), 553
Hoey, Elizabeth Wilkes, 238
Hogarth, William (1697–1764), 307
Holland, Canadian studies in, 551, 628
Holy Roman Empire, 538

Homer (8th century B.C.), 32, 333, 386, 480, 593; *Iliad*, 276, 386; *Odyssey*, 104, 129
Homo ludens, 352
Hopkins, Gerard Manley (1844–89), 129, 356, 374; influence of, 24, 92, 139, 204, 268; on overthought and underthought, 407
Hopwood, Victor George (b. 1918), 351, 356
Horizon, 433
Hornyansky, Michael (b. 1927), 99–100
Housman, Alfred Edward (1859–1936), 92, 220, 240
Housser, Yvonne McKague (b. 1898), 41
Hovey, Richard (1864–1900), 33
Howe, Joseph (1804–73), 36, 316, 317, 365; *Acadia* (1874), 59, 281
Howells, William Dean (1837–1920), 575
Hudson's Bay Company, 468, 511
Hugo, Victor Marie (1802–85), 55, 527, 550; *The Hunchback of Notre Dame* (1833), 587
Humour, 631
Humphrey, Jack Weldon (1901–67), 43
Hunter–Duvar, John (1821–99), 304, 365; *De Roberval* (1888), 59, 281; *The Enamorado* (1879), 59
Huron Carol, 239
Hutcheon, Linda (b. 1947), xlvii
Huxley, Aldous Leonard (1894–1963): on abstract art, 13
Hyde, Laurence (1914–87), 146

Ibsen, Henrik (1828–1906), 231
Iceland: immigration from, 640; NF in, 540
Identity, personal, 460

Ideology, 375, 592, 649
Images, in poetry, 109, 114, 115
Imagination: function of, 420; rooted in a locality, 412–13, 576
Imagism, 109, 184–5
Immigration, 443, 473, 518, 660, 667
Imperialism, 29–30, 533; American, 345, 404, 405, 424, 472; British, 30, 31, 364, 575, 619, 666
Impressionism, 13, 424
Incarnation, 526
India, 415
Indians, North American, 350, 422, 447, 527; assimilation of traditions of, 520; in Canadian literature, 362; colonizers' attitude to, 437, 439, 468, 476, 477, 519, 568, 572, 665; culture of, 668; imaginative assimilation of, 487–8, 650; in literature, 481–2, 572; myths of, xlvi, 57, 138, 270, 357, 483; poetry of, 180; professionalism in, 667; religion of, 526; relation of with settlers, 614, 616; songs of, 239. *See also* individual tribes
Individual, and society, 361, 588
Industrial Revolution, 517, 586
Infeld, Leopold (1898–1968), 232
Innis, Harold Adams (1894–1952), 103, 603; chief ideas of, 584–95; significance of, 558–9, 578–9; *The Bias of Communication* (1951), 349, 558, 578, 584, 585, 590, 591, 649; *Empire and Communications* (1950), 558, 578, 585, 593; projected history of communications, 582–4, 585–95 passim
Innis, Mary Quayle (1899–1972), 582
Intellectuals, modern, 329–30, 337, 373–4
International idiom, 530, 554, 645
Interpenetration, 529, 530

Introversion, modern, 410–11, 438–9, 490–1
Inuit, 447, 476; art of, 520; culture of, 650, 668; and mass media, 493–4, 535–6; poetry of, 220–2, 522; sculpture of, 443; songs of, 239
IODE, 661
Iphigeneia, 263
Ireland, 649; literature of, 232, 514, 523, 551
Irish (language), 268, 645–6, 669
Irving, John A. (1903–65), 377, 349, 352
Irving, Washington (1783–1859): "Rip Van Winkle" (1819–20), 277, 309
Isaiah, Book of, 371
Ishtar, 491
Islam, 439
Israel, 618
Italian (language): Layton in, 429
Italy, 529, 540; Canadian studies in, 577, 612, 628; Italians in Canada, 640, 644, 659–60, 669

Jackel, David (b. 1941): on NF, xl–xli
Jackson, A(lexander) Y(oung) (1882–1974), 12, 73, 272, 278, 398, 484, 542, 550, 635; painting of, 275, 417, 447, 541
Jacombe, Grace M., 95
Jake and the Kid. See Mitchell
Jamaica, immigration from, 640
James, Helen. *See* Weaver
James, Henry (1843–1916), 295, 496, 575, 624, 655; Edgar's study of, 79, 230, 232–3, 548; *The Jolly Corner* (1908), 224
James, William (1842–1910), 377, 460
Jameson, Anna Brownell (1794–1860): *Winter Studies and Summer Rambles in Canada* (1838), 615

Jameson, Edward A., 101
Japan, 515, 625, 660; Buddhism and Shinto in, 524; Canadian studies in, 628
Jaques, Edna (1891–1978), 124–6
Jeffers, (John) Robinson (1887–1962), 24, 33, 259, 391
Jefferson, Thomas (1743–1826), 405, 453, 498, 500, 516, 570, 617
Jeffreys, Charles W. (1869–1952), 542
Jeremiah, Book of, 442, 587–8
Jesuits, 439, 461, 512; *Jesuit Relations*, 511
Jesus, 431, 439, 485; as oral teacher, 593
Jews, Canadian, 289, 495, 618
Job, Book of, 36, 612–13
Jobin, Louis (1845–1928), 7
John XXIII (Angelo Giuseppe Roncalli), Pope (1881–1963), 374
John, King (1167–1216), 589
Johnson, E. Pauline (1861–1913), 362, 614
Johnson, Samuel (1709–84), 60, 263, 395, 591, 629; on generality, 353
Johnston, Alexandra Ferguson (b. 1939), 611
Johnston, George Benson (b. 1913), 285; on NF, xxvi; *The Cruising Auk* (1959), 209–13, 226
Johnston, Richard. *See* Fowler
Jonah, 343, 485; Book of, 102, 440
Jones, D(ouglas) G(ordon) (b. 1929): poetry of, 153–4, 175, 176–8, 225; *Butterfly on Rock* (1970), xxxviii–xxxix
Joual, 345, 576
Joyce, James Augustine Aloysius (1882–1941), 233, 267, 289, 335, 356, 385, 549, 579; censorship of, 47; *Finnegans Wake* (1939), 107, 153,

Index

172, 187, 464, 631; *Ulysses* (1922), 153, 246
Judaism, 454
Jung, Carl Gustav (1875–1961), 286

Kafka, Franz (1883–1924), 167, 357
Kandinsky, Vasily (1866–1944), 401, 424, 632
Kane, Paul (1810–71), 7, 422, 447, 470, 511, 528, 543
Kant, Immanuel (1724–1804), 460
Karloff, Boris (1887–1969), 491
Kaye, Leslie Lonker (b. 1936), 225
Keats, John (1795–1821), 19, 55, 57, 105, 274; on genius, 284; on the poet, 489; *Endymion* (1818), 208; *La Belle Dame Sans Merci* (1820), 56
Kekulé von Stradonitz, Friedrich August (1829–96), 524
Kelly, M(ilton) T(erence) (b. 1946), 650
Kennedy, Leo (b. 1907): poetry of, 17, 36, 59, 129, 142, 245, 246, 271, 286, 366; *The Shrouding* (1932), 245, 285
Kenojouak (b. 1927), 535, 543
Kent, George Edward Alexander Edmund, Duke of (1902–42), 7
Kent, Rockwell (1882–1971), 12
Khrushchev, Nikita Sergeyevich (1894–1971), 374
Kierkegaard, Søren Aabye (1813–55), 108, 461–2
Kilbourn, William M. (1926–95), 344, 350
Killins, Ada Gladys (ca. 1901–63), 11
Kipling, Rudyard (1865–1936), 29, 94, 304, 389; *If*, 277, 390
Kirby, William (1817–1906): *The Golden Dog* (1877), 363
Kirkconnell, Watson (1895–1977), 548
Klee, Paul (1879–1940), 13, 631
Klein, Abraham Moses (1909–72), 183; poetry of, 32, 39, 245, 257, 262, 267, 288–9, 489; *Hath Not a Jew* (1940), 245, 289; *Hitleriad* (1944), 245; *The Rocking Chair* (1948), 245, 289; *The Second Scroll* (1951), 246, 288–9, 349
Klinck, Carl Frederick (1908–90): ed. *Literary History of Canada* (1965), xxxii, xlii–xliii, 340–72 passim, 419, 458, 545, 546, 558; 2nd ed. (1976), 448–65 passim. *See also* Frye, "Conclusion" to *Literary History of Canada*, 1965 and 1976; Wells, Henry W.
Kline, Marcia B., xxxviii–xxxix
Knight, David (1926–2000): *Farquharson's Physique* (1971), 457
Knight, George Wilson (1897–1985), 328
Knister, Raymond (1899–1932), 79, 187, 231, 336; *White Narcissus* (1929), 369, 622, 623–4
Korea, 539
Kreisel, Henry (1922–91), 203; *The Rich Man* (1948), 248–9
Krieghoff, Cornelius (1815–72), 7, 423, 447, 511
Kroetsch, Robert (b. 1927), 650; *Badlands* (1975), 554
Kubrick, Stanley (1928–99): *2001: A Space Odyssey* (1968), 439
Kurelek, William (1927–77), 530, 535, 543

La Vérendrye, Pierre Gaultier de Varennes, sieur de (1685–1749), 400
Lacey, Edward A. (b. 1938), 207, 225, 226
Lacroix, Robert (b. 1940), 536, 539
Laissez-faire, 453
Lake Louise, 477
Lamb, Charles (1775–1834), 219

Lampman, Archibald (1861–99), 32, 69, 134, 136, 173, 183; his attitude to landscape, 262–3, 368, 485–6, 488–9; poetry of, 27, 35, 57, 61, 62, 91, 269–70, 283, 284, 363, 365; as Romantic lyric poet, 126, 266, 280, 287; *The City of the End of Things* (1894), 36, 57, 260, 286, 368, 617

Lanctôt, Gustave (1883–1975), 325, 326

Landor, Walter Savage (1775–1864), 179

Lane, Lauriat, Jr. (b. 1925), 464

Langland, William (ca. 1330–ca. 1400), 107

Langton, Anne (1804–93), 621–2

Language: different modes of, 579–80; importance of, 557; minority, 645–6; and regionalism, 626; subject and object in, 399

Languirand, Jacques (b. 1931), 323

Lapointe, Gatien (b. 1931): *Ode au Saint-Laurent* (1963), 325, 326

Lapointe, Jeanne (b. 1925), 406

Latin, 576, 586

Laurence, Margaret (1926–87), 535; *The Diviners* (1974), 621; *A Jest of God* (1966), 457; *The Stone Angel* (1964), 457

Laurentian axis, xl, 414, 422, 459, 469, 471, 512, 513, 558, 568, 578, 592

Laurier, Sir Wilfrid (1841–1919), on Canada, 347, 500

Law, Innis on, 589–90

Lawrence, D(avid) H(erbert) (1885–1930), 166–7, 335, 385, 432, 513–14

Laycock, Joseph E. (b. 1910), 375

Layton, Irving (b. 1912), 68, 183, 202, 355, 616; *personae* of, 217, 229; poetry of, 112, 113, 122, 145, 166–7, 173, 256, 260, 287–8, 290–1, 368, 369, 504; poetry vs. rhetoric in, 99, 559; *The Black Huntsmen* (1951), 99; *The Blue Propeller* (1955), 166, 290; *The Bull-Calf and Other Poems* (1956), 166; ed. *Canadian Poems* (1953), 123; *The Cold Green Element* (1955), 139, 144–5, 166, 271, 429–32, 489; *Here and Now* (1945), 51; *The Improved Binoculars* (1956), 166, 290; *In the Midst of My Fever* (1954), 133–4, 166, 173, 226, 290; *A Laughter in the Mind* (1958, 1959), 193–5; *The Long Pea-Shooter* (1954), 132–3, 166, 290; *Music on a Kazoo* (1956), 166; *A Red Carpet for the Sun* (1959), 216

Lazechko-Haas, Myra, 110–11

Le Claire, Gordon (b. 1905), 182

Leacock, Stephen (1869–1944), 183, 554, 592; on the hero, 304, 454, 586; *Acadian Adventures with the Idle Rich* (1959), 352, 494; *Sunshine Sketches of a Little Town* (1912), 136, 309, 316, 360, 362, 621, 623

Leadership, changing conceptions of, 374

League for Social Reconstruction, 409

Leduc, Ozias (1864–1955), 513

Lee, Alvin A. (b. 1930): *James Reaney* (1968), 626

Lee, Dennis (1939): poetry of, xl, 475; and BG, xxi; *Savage Fields* (1977), xxxviii–xxxix, 557, 651; *Civil Elegies* (1968), 498–9, 617

Lee, Hope (1929–98), xlii

Leggatt, Alexander (b. 1940), 207

Lemelin, Roger (1919–92), 553

Lemieux, Jean-Paul (1904–90), 519

Lennoxville, 564

LePan, Douglas Valentine (1914–98), xxxvi, 81; on country without a mythology, 172, 256, 361, 477, 627; poetry of, 173, 246, 271; *The De-*

serter (1964), 627; *The Net and the Sword* (1953), 117–20, 226, 246, 262, 291, 369
Lescarbot, Marc (1570?–1630?), 526–7, 572
Leslie, Kenneth (1892–1974), 37
Lévesque, Réné (1911–87), 515, 536
Leviathan, 484–5, 489
Levine, Norman (b. 1923), 93, 257
Lewis, Wyndham (1882–1957): on Canada, 510; on A.Y. Jackson, 484; on vocabulary, 384
Liberalism, 409, 588; Liberal party, 89, 513, 620
Lincoln, Abraham (1809–65), 258, 364
Lindsay, (Nicholas) Vachel (1879–1931), 33
Linguistics, 449, 557
Lipsey, Richard G. (b. 1928), 534, 539
Lismer, Arthur (1885–1969), 11, 73, 85, 398, 417; achievement of, 541–3, 633
Literary History of Canada. See under Klinck
Literature: authority in, 612; disturbing impact of, 278–9; economic position of writer, 274; form and content in, xliii, 265; importance of, 231; and life, 356, 574; longevity of, 442, 443; and myth, 357, 359, 361–2, 574, 627; popular, 276–8, 359–60; relation to criticism, 555–7, 578; and social conditions, *see under* Culture; and truth, 613; as verbal game, 464; writer's life, 324. *See also* Canada, literature of
Livesay, Dorothy Kathleen May (1909–96): poetry of, xli, 18, 35, 37, 148, 183–5, 246, 260, 285; *Call My People Home* (1950), 93, 247
Lochhead, Douglas (b. 1922), 223
Locke, John (1632–1704), 460

London, England, 374; as cultural centre, 522, 529, 530, 550, 552
Lonergan, Bernard, J.F. (1904–84), 461
Longfellow, Henry Wadsworth (1807–82), 33, 277, 389, 390, 655; *Evangeline* (1847), 191, 281; *The Song of Hiawatha* (1855), 136, 281
Loon's Necklace, The (1948), 650
Lorne Pierce Medal, 381
Los Angeles, 436, 438
Lovell, R.G., 94
Low, David (1891–1963), 275
Lowell, Amy Lawrence (1874–1925), 5, 184
Lowell, Mass., 440
Lower, Arthur Reginald Marsden (1889–1988): *Colony to Nation* (1946), 522, 532, 553
Lowry, Malcolm (1909–57), 81–2
Loyalists, 362, 449
Lucas, Alec (b. 1913), 363, 364, 367

McCarthyism, 106
McClelland & Stewart, 285
McClung, Nellie Letitia (1873–1951), 461
McCourt, Edward Alexander (1907–72), 248
McCrae, John (1872–1918), 481; *In Flanders Fields* (1915), 58, 262
McCulloch, Thomas (1776–1843), 349; *The Letters of Mephibosheth Stepsure* (1821–23), 308–12
McCullough, Norah (1902/3–93), on Arthur Lismer, 543
MacDiarmid, Hugh (Christopher Murray Grieve) (1892–1978), 552
MacDonald, Goodridge (1897–1967), 93, 94, 149, 181
MacDonald, J(ames) E(dward) H(arvey) (1873–1932), 8, 10, 398, 400, 511, 528, 541

Macdonald, Sir John Alexander (1815–91),103, 104, 105, 299, 417, 469, 604
MacDonald, Wilson Pugsley (1880–1967), 183, 264, 284, 623
McDougall, Robert (1918–2000), 478
McDowell, Marjorie, 363
MacEwan, Gwendolyn (1941–87), 489–90, 502, 505, 520
McGibbon, Donald (1910–96) and Pauline (1910–2001), 661–4
MacGillivray, James Robertson (1902–92), xxvii, 418
MacInnes, Thomas Robert Edward (1867–1951), 35, 36
Macintosh, Sir James (1765–1832), 591, 595
MacKay, Louis Alexander (b. 1901), 100, 110, 183; poetry of, 33, 246, 267, 286, 288
Mackenzie, Henry (1745–1831): *The Man of Feeling* (1771), 569
Mackenzie, Sir Alexander (1755?–1820), 14, 372, 400
Mackenzie, William Lyon (1795–1861), 475
Mackenzie River, 501, 510
McKeough, (William) Darcy (b. 1933), 538
McLachlan, Alexander (1818–96), 183, 259, 370
McLaren, Floris Clark (1904–78), 17, 100
McLaren, Norman (1914–87), 630
MacLeish, Archibald (1892–1982), 33
MacLennan, Hugh (1907–90): *Barometer Rising* (1941), 249; *Two Solitudes* (1945), 249, 510, 647, 689n. 17; *The Watch That Ends the Night* (1959), 367–8
McLuhan, Herbert Marshall (1911–80), 323, 328, 349, 461, 522, 553, 585; on death of book, 450; on global village, 371, 580; influence of, 559-60; on print vs. media, 593–4, 617; on rear-view mirror, 408; style of, 464; *The Gutenberg Galaxy* (1962), 559; *The Mechanical Bride* (1951), 578–9, 580, 593; *Understanding Media* (1964), 559
MacLure, Millar (1917–90), 352, 353
MacMechan, Archibald (1862–1933), 362, 682n. 5
McNaught, Carlton (1888–1963), 409
McPherson, Hugo (1921–99), 358, 359, 375
Macpherson, (Jean) Jay (b. 1931), xlii, 153, 209, 347; and Emblem Books, 146, 204; poetry of, xl, xli, 110, 147, 154–5, 176, 225, 271, 369, 420; *The Boatman* (1957), 168–72, 209, 210, 226, 291, 528; *The Spirit of Solitude* (1982), xxxviii–xxxix; *Welcoming Disaster* (1974), 490, 491, 505
McRobbie, Kenneth (b. 1929), 207
Magna Carta, 589
Maillet, Antonine (b. 1929): *Pélagie-la-charrette* (1982), 624
Maine, 510
Maine, Sir Henry James Sumner (1822–88): *Ancient Law* (1861), 589
Mair, (Kenneth) Rafe (b. 1931), 540
Mair, Charles (1838–1927), 365, 482; *Tecumseh* (1886), 34, 61, 264, 281
Mallarmé, Stéphane (1842–98), 267, 286
Mandel, Eli (Elias Wolf) (1922–92), xliv; on NF, xl, xli; poetry of, 134–6, 227, 269–70, 490, 505
Manitoba, 570; French in, 416
Mao Tse-tung or Zedong (1893–1976), 515
Maple Leaf Forever, The, 666
Marceau, Marcel (b. 1923), 630

Marcotte, Gilles (b. 1925), 323
Marcuse, Herbert (1898–1979): *One Dimensional Man* (1964), 422, 502, 509
Maritain, Jacques (1882–1973), 627
Maritime provinces, 312, 319, 346, 348, 413, 415, 510, 512–13, 530, 647; literature in, 351–2; separatism in, 416, 473, 499
Marlowe, Christopher (1564–93), 120; *Tamburlaine* (1590), 105, 188; *Dr. Faustus* (1604), 595
Marriott, Anne (1913–97), 30, 36, 63, 260
Marshall, Joyce (b. 1913): *Presently Tomorrow* (1946), 53–4
Marshall, William E. (1859–1923), 136
Martin, André (b. 1925), 582
Martin, Yves (b. 1929), 533
Marvell, Andrew (1621–78), 51, 52, 116
Marx, Karl (1818–83), 113, 559
Marxism, 98, 355, 431, 458, 520, 588; art in, 354, 462, 612; Christianity and, 437, 524; democracy and, 314; dogma in, 452; as revolutionary, 439. *See also* Communism
Masaccio (Tomasso de Giovanni di Simone Guidi) (1401–28?), 72
Masefield, John (1878–1967), 69
Mask: in Canadian literature, 449; Yeats on, 232
Massachusetts, 258
Massey, (Charles) Vincent (1887–1967): at Victoria College, 426
Massey, Denton (1900–84), 625
Massey, Raymond (1896–1983), 158
Massey, Walter Edward Hart (1864–1901), 252
Massey Report (1951), 362, 551–2, 592; genesis of, 88, 89

Mathematics, 87; in Baroque age, 436, 467, 468–9, 476, 485, 525
Matisse, Henri (1869–1954), 73
Mauritius, 524
Mayakovsky, Vladimir (1893–1930), 164
Mayo, Henry B. (b. 1911), 451
Meaning, derived from context, 406–7
Media, mass: influence on culture, 560–2; McLuhan on, 560, 617
Meech Lake crisis, 663, 667, 668
Meisel, John (b. 1923), 533, 535, 537
Melodrama, 360
Melting pot, 421, 458, 518
Melville, Herman (1819–91), 103; *Moby-Dick* (1851), 64, 149, 612
Memory, 125
Mercator, Gerhardus (1512–94), 467
Meredith, George (1828–1909), 233
Meredith, Harry (b. 1931), 538, 539
Metaphor, 269, 271
Methodism, 294, 296, 336, 352, 380, 625
Métis, 568
Mexico, 567
Michelangelo (Michelagniolo di Lodovico Buonarroti) (1475–1564), 445
Middle Ages, 586, 588; papacy and princes in, 587; painting in, 72
Middle class, social mythology of, 306–8
Mill, John Stuart (1806–73), 670; on liberal and conservative, 441; on liberty, 279; on U.S. Civil War, 643
Miller, Mary Margaret, 21
Miller, Peter (b. 1920), 200, 218–19, 226
Milliken, Lorene Frances (1907–90), 124
Milne, David (1882–1953), 8, 11, 15,

43, 417, 424, 434, 513; achievement of, 71–4
Milton, John (1608–74),172, 199, 278, 418; Daniells on, 544–5; *Paradise Lost* (1667), 389; *Samson Agonistes* (1671), 229
Minneapolis, 344
Miró, Joán (1893–1983), 13
Missionaries: their attitude to natives, 439, 468; hierarchy in, 467–8. *See also* Jesuits
Mississippi River, 501, 510
Mitchell, William Ormond (1914–98): *Jake and the Kid* (1961), 362; *Who Has Seen the Wind* (1947), 248, 348
Modern age, 670; art in, 10; debased language in, 208; introversion in, 410–11; obliteration of environment in, 414
Mohammed (570–632 A.D.), 439
Moholy-Nagy, Laszlo (1895–1946), 12
Molière (Jean-Baptiste Poquelin; 1622–73), 529
Monarchy, 526; in Canada, 643, 663
Moncton, 416; NF in, 466, 565
Monroe doctrine, 642
Montcalm, Louis Joseph, Marquis de (1712–59), 363
Montgomery, Lucy Maud (1874–1942): *Anne of Green Gables* (1908), 362
Montreal, 416, 438, 447, 510, 514, 537, 618, 663
Moodie, Susanna (1803–85), 240, 345, 347, 621; *Roughing It in the Bush* (1852), 360, 479, 498, 502
Moore, Henry Spencer (1898–1986), 13
Moore, Marianne Craig (1887–1972), influence of, 134, 158, 162, 219
Moore, Thomas (Tom) (1779–1852): influence of, 268, 276, 281, 423; *Canadian Boat Song*, 239

Moosonee, 614
Morant, Mollie (neé Wilde): *The Singing Gypsy* (1941), 19
Morrice, James Wilson (1865–1924), 7, 8, 27, 73, 424, 513
Morris, Louis A. and Kay, 410
Morris, William (1834–96), 24, 127, 354, 445–6; *News from Nowhere* (1891), 445
Morton, William L. (1908–80): *The Canadian Identity* (1961), 460, 462, 473, 501, 505
Moscovitch, Henry (b. 1941), 157
Moss, John George (b. 1940), xxxviii–xxxix
Movies, 347; Canadian documentary, 447; silent, 491
Mowat, Farley (b. 1921), 456, 505
Multiculturalism, 644, 669
Munro, Alice (b. 1931), 535, 621, 624
Munro, Kathryn (Mrs. Tupper), 93
Murray, Heather (b. 1951), xxxix, xliii, xlvii
Musgrave, Susan (b. 1951), 487–8, 505, 520, 650
Music, 13, 87, 413; form and content in, 265; NF and, 565; program, 72; twelve-tone, 268
My Brilliant Career, 575
Myth/mythology: and Canadian literature, 356, 351–2, 520; in Canadian poetry, xl–xlii, xlvi, 57, 128–9, 137, 165, 172, 173, 176, 199, 218, 270–1, 287–8, 291, 366, 394–5, 397, 418–19, 449–50, 482–3, 486–8; and literature/poetry, 269, 271, 357, 359, 361–2, 574, 627; social, 306–8, 359–60, 362. *See also* Pastoral myth

Nash, Paul (1899–1946), 13
National Film Board, 89, 560–1

Index

National Gallery of Canada, 10
Nationalism, cultural, xlvi, 414, 451, 514
Natives. *See* Indians
NATO, 427
Nature: and the artist, 400, 401; Canadian attitude to, 349–50, 436–8, 470, 476–9, 500–7, 518–19, 569–70, 615–16, 646–7, 650–2, 673–4; in Canadian literature, xxxvi–xxxix, 24, 33–8, 56–63 passim, 164, 256, 263, 365–9, 482–92 passim, 651; Christianity and, 475–6, 485; ecological attitude to, 441; Layton on, 432; need to preserve, 520; North American attitude to, xlv–xlvi, 24, 500, 525–6; Pratt on, *see under* Pratt; and progress, 353–4. *See also* Ecology; Environment
Naziism, 9, 36, 37, 302
NDP, 354
Nebuchadnezzar, 252
Needham, Richard (1912–96), 464
New, William H. (b. 1938), 449, 457
New Brunswick, French in, 416
New England, 416, 496, 513
Newfoundland, 413, 415, 444, 499, 503, 510, 534, 625; ballads in, 239, 240, 241–2; Beothuks in, 519, 525; folk song in, 260; Pratt and, 294, 367, 378, 383, 385, 391–7 passim, 396–7, 597, 606, 626; Quebec and, 537
New Frontier (1936–37), 354
Newlove, John (b. 1938), 486–7, 520, 650
Newman, Cardinal John Henry (1801–90), on university, 438
Newman, Peter C. (b. 1929): *Renegade in Power* (1963), 415
Newton, Sir Isaac (1642–1727), 279
New Orleans, Battle of, 620

New Provinces (1936), 129, 158, 173, 245, 246, 285, 286, 288, 289, 549
New Republic, 29
New Statesman, 8
New Testament, 455
New Voices (1956), 152–3, 155
New York, 530
New Yorker, 29, 534
Niagara Falls, 477, 616
Nichols, Ruby, 155
Nicholson, Sir Harold George (1886–1968): *Helen's Tower* (1937), 3–4
Nineveh, 440
Niven, Frederick (1878–1944), 248
Noah, 525
Nobel Prize, 427, 577, 627
Norman, Herbert (1909–57), 625
North America: assumptions of settlers of, 475–6, 485; social mythology of, 307–8; view of nature in, 500, 525–6
North, Canadian, 414–15, 501, 505, 510; in Ontario, 485, 528, 614
North, Peter, 94
Northern Review, The (1945–56), 68, 285
Norway, 415
Norwegian (language), 268
Nova Scotia: ballads in, 239, 240, 241; Haliburton on, 311, 316, 319–20, 344, 346, 496–7; McCulloch on, 308
Nowlan, Alden (1933–83), 205–6, 369, 490
Nursery rhymes, 277

O'Casey, Sean (1884–1964), 217
O'Gorman, Ned (b. 1929), 683n. 20
O'Grady, Standish (fl.1793–1846), 183, 240; *The Emigrant* (1841), 35, 59, 257, 281
Observer, The, 8
Occultism, 87

Oka confrontation, 667
Old English. *See* Anglo-Saxon
Old Testament, 32
Oliver, Michael (b. 1925), 537
Ontario, 239–40, 253, 413, 415, 416, 444, 490, 510, 530; culture of, from provincial to regional, 617–28; growth of, 614–17; McGibbons and, 662–3; once monolithic, 537; painting in, 422; southern, once inarticulate, 189, 535
Oral culture, role of poetry in, 385–6, 387, 391
Oral tradition, Innis on, 593–5
Orange Order, 518, 618
Order of Canada, 455
Orient, art in, 72, 73, 253
Orpheus, poet as, 401
Ostenso, Martha (1900–63), 494, 554
Ottawa, 89, 500, 538
Ouspensky, Peter Demianovich (1878–1947), 87
Ovid (Publius Ovidius Naso) (43 B.C.–17 A.D.), 57
Oxford, NF in, 105

Pacey, Desmond (1917–75): in *Literary History of Canada*, 340, 341, 348, 358, 363, 367, 450, 456; on Livesay, 183, 185; on NF, xxxviii; ed. *A Book of Canadian Short Stories* (1949), 247–8; *Creative Writing in Canada* (1952), 244; *Frederick Philip Grove* (1945), 75; ed. *Selected Poems of Sir Charles G.D. Roberts* (1955), 138
Page, P(atricia) K(athleen) (b. 1916): poetry of, 18, 34, 44, 45, 68, 173, 260, 289–90; *The Metal and the Flower* (1954), 131–2, 271, 290
Paine, Thomas (1737–1809), 259, 498
Painting, 94, 124, 413; abstract, 12–13, 87, 268, 401; Fairley and, 635; form and content in, xxix, 137; isolation vs. engagement in, 71; oil vs. water-colour in, 41–3; perspective in, 71–2. *See also* Art(s)
– Canadian, 89, 562; Anglo-Saxon features of, 101; colour in, 413; compared to U.S. art, 421; documentary interest in, 447, 528; European influence on, 423, 470; exhibitions of, 7, 10, 14, 41, 534, 651–2; landscape in, 8, 12, 41, 72–3, 85, 126, 173, 424, 511, 673–4; NF on, xxiv–xxv, xxxv; NF studies, 417; oil vs. water-colour in, 10–11; perspective in, 15, 102, 348, 422–3; two traditions in, 434; urbane tradition in, 424. *See also* Group of Seven; Quebec; and individual artists
Paisley, Ian Richard Kyle (b. 1926), 403
Pakistan, 415
Paquet, Gilles (b. 1936), 538, 540
Paris, as cultural centre, 522, 530, 550
Parker, Sir Gilbert (1862–1932), 358; *The Seats of the Mighty* (1896), 363
Parkinson, Cyril Northcote (1909–93): *Parkinson's Law* (1957), 445
Parry, Milman (1902–35), 593
Parsons, Richard Augustus (1893–1981), 201
Parti Québécois, 533, 536, 537
Pascal, Blaise (1623–62): on spaces, 646; on thinking reed, 139, 477
Past: attitudes to, 670; in American social mythology, 453, 458–9; Canadian vs.U.S. attitude to, 500; and future, 408; preservation of, 441–7
Pastoral myth, in Canada, 362–9, 371
Patchen, Kenneth (1911–72), 99
Pater, Walter Horatio (1839–94), 233

Paul, St., 352, 353, 526; Pratt on, 377, 380, 599
PBS, 561–2
Peacock, Thomas Love (1785–1866), 389
Pearson, Lester Bowles (1897–1972), 71, 426–9, 553
Pearson, Maryon Elspeth (née Moody) (1901–89), 426
Pellan, Alfred (1908–88), 81, 447, 491
Penn, William (1644–1718), 371
Penton, W.J.: *The Riddle of the Universe Solved* (1890), 353
Perry, Martha Eugenie (1880–1958), 150
Peterson, Leonard Byron (b. 1917), 247
Pharis, Gwen (Gwendolyn Pharis Ringwood) (1910–84), 247
Philology, 548, 557
Philosophy, 388; in Canada, 352–3, 456, 460–1; and criticism, 557
Picasso, Pablo (1881–1973), 11, 12, 85
Pickthall, Marjorie (1883–1922), 79, 231; poetry of, 185–6, 282, 304
Pierce, Dr. Lorne (1890–1961), 19, 352; on Pickthall, 185; ed. *Canadian Poetry in English* (1954), 136–7; ed. *Selected Poems of Bliss Carman* (1954), 126–8, 138
Pincock, Jenny O'Hara (1890–1948), 95
Plato (ca. 428–ca. 348 B.C.), 87, 279, 332
Play, work and, 464
Plough and the Pen, The (1963), 369
PM (1934–40), 21
Poe, Edgar Allan (1809–49), 35; on long poem, 105, 286
Poetry Commonwealth, 100
Poetry: concrete images in, 109; convention in, 29, 155, 171; and criticism, 227–8; Edgar on, 233; form and content in, 137, 463; free verse, 123; importance of, 105, 227, 228, 279; importance of minor, 19, 27, 150–1, 151–2; language of, 20; and life, 31–2, 288; lyric, 58, 63, 126, 208; and meaning, 23, 24, 26, 45, 65, 137, 114–15, 407, 623; modern, 23, 24, 26, 45, 65, 114–15, 137, 407; myth and, 172, 269, 271, 419; naive, 94, 124; narrative, 59, 63, 65, 602; popular, 389–90; primitive, 487; revival of oral, 389, 391, 463–4, 561; and role of poet, 232, 355, 385–6, 388–90, 394–5, 397, 420; simplicity in, 208–9; of social protest, 98–9, 122–3; translation of, 406–7, 429–30
– Canadian: absence of mythopoeic school in, 449–50; academic tradition in, 267–8, 286–8, 291; advance of, 114; Anglo-Saxon character of, 101; on CBC, 283, 285, 561; comic and satiric themes in, 258–62; of Confederation period, 527, 549; contrasting moods of in nineteenth century, 479–83, 519, 551, 559; development of, 226–7; form and content in, 265–71, 527–8; garrison mentality in, 423; magazines for, 182, 285; "modern" vs. Romantic, 137–8; myth in, 270–1, 291, 366, 418, 482–3, 486–8; narrative in, 59–63, 65, 82, 266, 281–2, 304, 365, 281–2, 286–8; nature in, xxxvi–xxxix, 24, 33–8, 55–7, 164, 350, 365–9, 503–5, 673–4; neo-Romantic movement in, 289–90; NF's approach to, xxv–xxxi, xl–xlii, 228, 418–19; between 1929 and 1954, 244–6; as poetic conversation of cultivated people, 151; position of poet in, 283–5, 291–2; Pratt's status in, 596; professionalism in, 172–3, 551; question of

distinctiveness of, 28, 102; reasons for studying, 255–6, 281; rhetoric in, 512; Romantic lyrical tradition in, 58–9, 126–7, 244, 245, 280–90 passim, 304; satire and light verse in, 183; Smith's importance in, 417–18; Sutherland on, 68; and the tradition, xliii–xlv, 32–3, 55, 244, 491–2, 528–9, 550; tragic themes in, 262–5. *See also* Canada, literature of
Poets 56 (1956), 153–5
Poland, 499, 649
Pompadour, Jeanne Antoinette Poisson, Marquise de (1721–64), 363
Pontifical Institute of Medieval Studies, 555
Pope, Alexander (1688–1744): *Moral Essays* (1731–35), 306–7; *The Rape of the Lock* (1714), 569
Popular culture, 418
Portugal, 436; immigration from, 640
Postmodernism, NF and, xlvii–xlviii
Pound, Ezra Loomis (1885–1972), 79, 145, 185, 390, 405, 431; *Cantos* (1917–59), 585
Pragmatism, 453
Prairies, 367, 413, 415, 416, 510, 530, 534
Pratt, (John) Christopher (b. 1935), 519, 534
Pratt, E(dwin) J(ohn) (1882–1964), 79, 100, 183, 185, 186, 231, 247, 284, 286, 288, 355, 417, 457, 559, 626, 635; achievement of, 244–5, 282–3, 304–5, 329–30, 381–2, 470–1; chief themes of, 297–304, 332–3, 337–8, 349, 351, 378, 391–7, 490–1, 512, 603–10; comic and tragic themes in, 261–2, 264–5; influence of, 150, 246, 287; influence on NF, xxiii–xxiv, xxxvii, 327–8, 330, 332, 335–6, 337, 384–5; life and character of, 294–5, 327–9, 331–2, 334–7, 377–9, 380, 383–5, 549, 596–600; as narrative poet, 59, 61–3, 266, 365; nature in, 24, 35, 36, 62–3, 103, 264, 265, 366, 367, 392–4, 395–6; as oral poet, 385–91, 600; poetry of, 27, 64–5, 127, 380–1, 479, 502, 513, 601–2, 651; style of, 295–7; Sutherland on, 159–60, 287; *Behind the Log* (1947), 103, 104, 261–2, 283, 293, 296–7, 298, 299, 329, 381, 387, 395, 602; *Brébeuf and His Brethren* (1940), 32, 36, 37, 62–3, 103, 185–6, 245, 265, 266, 282, 296, 298, 303, 304, 381, 386, 387, 470, 482, 609, 635; *The Cachalot* (1926), 36, 61, 298, 381, 386, 387, 604; *Collected Poems* (1944), 245, 283, 290, 380, 381, 598; 2nd ed., 208, 293, 381, 391, 605; *The Depression Ends* (1932), 302, 303, 338, 382, 387, 420; *Dunkirk* (1941), 62, 301, 302, 303, 381, 602, 604; *The Fable of the Goats* (1937), 36, 62, 266, 381, 605; *The Great Feud* (1926), 36, 61, 62, 271, 296, 300, 303, 381, 384, 605; *The Highway* (1932), 301, 302, 382, 393, 607–8; *The Iron Door* (1927), 381; *Newfoundland Verse* (1923), 295, 297, 304, 380, 381, 596; *The Roosevelt and the Antinoe* (1930), 266, 297, 337, 381, 386, 387, 602; *The 6000* (1932), 61, 261–2, 387, 603; *Studies in Pauline Eschatology* (1917), 377, 380; *The Titanic* (1935), 35, 62, 63, 64, 245, 261, 264, 265, 297, 298, 303, 366, 381, 387, 597, 606–7, 635; *Towards the Last Spike* (1952), 103–6, 226, 261, 265, 266, 271, 283, 293, 296, 299, 350, 381, 417, 484–5, 504, 605; *The Truant* (1942), 63, 103, 160, 265, 302–3, 330, 332–3, 337–8, 368,

372, 382, 392, 608, 609; *The Witches' Brew* (1925), 32, 36, 61, 64, 82, 265, 267, 296, 300, 379, 381, 386, 605
Pratt, Lenore (b. 1901), 155–6
Pratt, Mildred Claire (1921–95), 380, 658
Pratt, Viola Leone Whitney (1892–1984), 380, 658
Pre-Raphaelitism, 528
Present, 442, 447
Preview (1942–45), 40, 68, 285, 289, 354
Priestley, Christopher (Douglas Craig) (b. 1937), 207, 225
Priestley, F(rancis) E(thelbert) L(ouis) (1905–88), 555
Prodigal son, 277–8
Professor, changing role of, 232, 410
Prometheus, 395
Propaganda, 404, 410, 593
Prose, and poetry, 388
Protestantism, 183, 357; and the Bible, 587; and Catholicism, 588; and evolution, 252; and liquor, 624–5; NF and, 403. *See also* Religion
Proust, Marcel (1871–1922), 356
Provincialism, 250, 284, 527, 623–4; culture and, 234, 670; maturing of, 528, 530; and regionalism, 618, 645. *See also* Colonialism
Psalms, Book of, 460
Psychology: and criticism, 557; Pratt and, 294, 329, 377, 380, 384, 599
Publishing: Innis on, 592; U.S. influence on, 554
Purdy, Alfred Wellington (1918–2000), 149, 178, 224, 477, 535, 616
Puritans, 439, 522, 525, 526, 550
Pusey, Edward Bouverie (1800–82), 4
Pynchon, Thomas (b. 1937): *Gravity's Rainbow* (1973), 523–4, 526
Pythagoras (6th century B.C.), 87

Quebec, fortress of, 363, 416
Quebec (province), 349, 413, 510, 646; British Conquest of, 473–4; and distinct society question, 668; and French Canadian culture, 667–8; language and literature in, *see under* French Canada; nation-building aspirations of, 540; painting in, 422, 424, 513, 519–20; quiet revolution in, *see* Quiet Revolution; separatism in, 375, 403, 408, 415–16, 451, 473, 499, 515, 516, 533, 535, 536–7, 539, 554, 620, 663; writer's position in, 535. *See also* French Canada
Quebec Act, 457, 473–4, 499, 517, 665
Queen's Quarterly, 285
Quiet Revolution, 447, 451, 514, 553, 576, 667, 668
Quintilian, Marcus Fabius Quintilianus (ca. 35–ca. 100), 269

Raabe, Wilhelm Karl (1831–1910), 634
Rabelais, François (1483/94?–1553), 271
Raddall, Thomas Head (1903–94): *His Majesty's Yankees* (1942), 248
Radicals, and literature, 354–5
Radio, 274, 408, 463, 491; drama and literature on, 89, 247–8, 284, 288, 637; Hitler's use of, 593
Railways, 472, 510, 512
Rajan, Balachandra, 545
Rashley, Richard Ernest (b. 1909), 123, 223–4
Ray, Margaret Violet (1898–1982), 231. *See also* Robins
Reader's Digest, 279, 451
Reagan, Ronald Wilson (b. 1911), 653
Realism, 399; "magical," 652
Reaney, James (b. 1926), xlii, 202, 209, 323, 471, 535; as playwright, 464;

poetry of, xl, 173, 225, 258, 271, 291, 478–9, 504, 626; *Colours in the Dark* (1969), 511; Donnelly trilogy; 457; *Night Blooming Cereus* (1962), 369; *A Suit of Nettles* (1958), 186–9, 203, 205, 226, 291, 363, 491, 528
Rebel, The (1917–20), 236, 409, 634–5
Rebellion of 1837, 240, 498–9, 642
Reeves, John (b. 1926), 153
Reformation, 587
Refus Global, 519
Regionalism, xlvi–xlvii, 29–30, 31, 412–13, 417, 513–14, 529–30, 539–40, 552–4, 576–7, 587, 594, 618, 644–5
Reich, Charles A.: *The Greening of America* (1970), 454
Religion, 388, 408–9; in Canada, 352, 460–1, 625; Layton on, 430; NF and, 566; and oral teaching, 593; in Toronto, 618
Renaissance, 581; humanism in, 595
Republican party, 619
Reviewing, 555–7. *See also under* Criticism
Revolt of Islam. See Shelley
Reynard the Fox, 64
Reynolds, Ella Julia (1881–1970), 201
Rhetoric: in literature, 352–3, 355; in poetry, 268–9, 481
Rhodenizer, V(ernon) B(lair) (b. 1886), 207, 682n.6; ed. *Canadian Poetry in English* (1954), 136–7
Rhodes scholarships, 662
Richardson, John (1796–1852): *Wacousta* (1832), 362, 614
Richardson, Samuel (1689–1761): *Pamela* (1749), 307
Richler, Mordecai (1931–2001), 355
Riel, Louis (1844–85), 58, 350, 568
Riley, James Whitcomb (1849–1916), 390

Rilke, Rainer Maria (1875–1926), 116, 510, 689n. 17
Rimbaud, Jean Nicholas Arthur (1854–91): *Le Bateau Ivre* (1871), 56
Riopelle, Jean-Paul (1923–2002), 424, 447, 511, 530
Rioux, Marcel (1919–92), 532, 533, 536
Rip Van Winkle. *See* Irving
Ripley, John (b. 1940), 463
Rix, Karl, 122
Robb, Wallace Havelock (b. 1888), 201
Roberts, Dorothy (1906–93), 180–1, 226
Roberts, Sir Charles George Douglas (1860–1943), 79, 173, 231, 280, 304, 353, 485, 619; poetry of, 35, 138, 262, 348, 495; rhetorical and elegiac impulses, 233, 366, 480–1, 512; as Romantic lyric poet, 126, 264, 280, 304; *Orion* (1880), 365
Roberts, Stanley (1927–90), 538
Robins, John Daniel (1884–1952), 86, 231, 239, 409, 597; influence on NF, xxii, xxiii–xxiv, 335–6, 384–5, 541, 542; tribute to, 236–7; *Cottage Cheese* (1951), 236; *The Incomplete Anglers* (1943), 236, 367; ed. *A Pocketful of Canada*, 237; and Margaret Ray, ed. *A Book of Canadian Humour* (1951), 236
Roethke, Theodore (1908–63), 648–9
Rogers, Robert, 149–50
Roman Catholic Church, 357, 387, 618; in French Canada, 31, 183, 525, 526, 575, 666, 667; and Protestantism, 588. *See also* Religion
Romance: characteristics of, 360; and popular literature in Canada, 358–61
Romanticism, 3–4, 233, 418; in Canadian imagination, 469–70, 574; in

Canadian poetry, 58, 127, 129, 138, 244, 245, 266, 280–90 passim, 304; in Group of Seven, 399; idea of genius in, 342; myth in, 395; narrative poetry in, 281; NF studies, xxiv; and oral poetry, 389; in Pratt, 389, 596–7
Roper, Gordon (b. 1911), 358, 359
Ross, Eustace (W.W.E.) (1894–1966), 35–6, 158
Ross, James A. (1869–1945), 94
Ross, Malcolm (1911–2002), 77, 108, 456; on NF, xxx, xxxviii, xlv, xlvii, 464
Ross, Sinclair (1908–96): *As for Me and My House* (1941), 361
Rossetti, Dante Gabriel (1828–82), 127
Rotstein, Abraham (b. 1929), 462, 558; ed. *The Prospect of Change* (1965), 373–6
Rousseau, Henri (Le Douanier) (1844–1910), 42, 371
Rousseau, Jean-Jacques (1712–78), 116, 364
Roy, Gabrielle (1909–83), 49, 362
Royal Ontario Museum: Currelly and, 251–4 passim
Royal Society of Canada, 313, 381, 545
Russia, 415, 439, 515, 653. *See also* Soviet Union
Ryerson Press, 285

Sainte-Beuve, Charles Augustin (1804–69), 233, 234
Sandburg, Carl (1878–1967), 33, 202, 258
Sandwell, B(ernard) K(eble) (1876–1954), 361
Sangster, Charles (1822–93), 136, 281, 365
Sapir, Edward (1884–1939), 103
Saskatchewan, 501; NF in, 566
Satire, 275
Saturday Evening Post, 307
Saturday Night, sale of, 235
Saunders, Thomas (b. 1909), 98, 202–3
Scammell, Arthur R. (1913–95): *The Squid-Jiggin' Ground*, 239
Scandinavia: Canadian studies in, 612, 628
Scargill, Matthew Harry (1916–97), 345
Schiff, Mortimer, 154, 225
Scholarship: in Canada, 244, 352, 548–9, 555, 558, 670; Innis on, 590–1; as way of life, 585
Schull, Joseph (1910–80), 247
Sciences, 388, 612; improvement in, 660, 670, 653–4; and social pressures, 590–1
Scotland, immigration from, 640–1
Scott, Anthony (b. 1923), 533, 538
Scott, Duncan Campbell (1862–1947), 79, 136, 164, 173, 231, 336, 485; achievement of, 69–70, 101; poetry of, 58–9, 126, 281, 345, 365, 366, 368, 481–2, 546; as Romantic lyric poet, 280, 304; *At the Cedars* (1893), 61, 63, 70, 505; *The Piper of Arll*, 34–5, 69, 271
Scott, F(rancis) R(eginald) (1899–1985), 100, 197, 284; as neo-Romantic, 289; poetry of, 28, 49, 129, 130–1, 183, 245–6, 258, 260, 285, 370; on Pratt, 299; as translator, 406–7, 526–7; ed. *The Blasted Pine* (1957), 182–3, 202, 289
Scott, Frederick George (Archdeacon) (1861–1944), 35
Scott, Peter Dale (b. 1929), 153
Scott, Sir Walter (1771–1832), 3, 311, 564
Seafarer, The, 56

Secord, Laura (1775–1868), 475
Separatism, 410, 533, 576; in Canada, 351, 375, 403, 408, 414, 415–16, 422, 451, 473, 499, 510, 515, 516, 533, 536–7, 539, 554, 620, 640, 663; and sub-separation, 535
Service, Robert William (1874–1958), 113–14, 283, 390
Seton, Ernest Thompson (1860–1946), 505, 554
Shakespeare, William (1564–1616), 96, 129, 228, 277, 279, 294, 336, 385, 418, 445, 646; background of, 342; at Canadian Stratford, 529; expurgation of, 278; NF studies, xxii; values in, 388, 556; *Henry V* (1600), 64; *Macbeth* (1606), 29, 174, 464, 637–8; *A Midsummer Night's Dream*, 464; *Othello*, 464; *Sonnets* (1609), 444; *The Tempest* (1611), 309, 360, 401; *Troilus and Cressida* (1609), 556
Shaw Festival, 662
Shelley, Percy Bysshe (1792–1822), 302, 399; influence on Edgar, 232, 234; influence on Pratt, 389; *A Defence of Poetry* (1821), 389, 529; *Julian and Maddalo* (1824), 389; *Ozymandias* (1818), 587; *Prometheus Unbound* (1820), 234, 395, 529; *The Revolt of Islam* (1818), 105, 123
Sherbrooke, NF in, 416, 466, 564
Shintoism, 524
Short stories, 624
Sibelius, Jean (1865–1957): *Finlandia* (1899), 10
Siebrasse, Glen: ed. *Yes*, 182
Simcoe, John Graves (1752–1806), 69
Sinclair, Lister (b. 1921), 247
Sky father, 526
Slavery, 643
Slavic countries, 593
Slick, Sam. *See* Haliburton

Smiles, Samuel (1812–1904): *Self Help* (1859), 307
Smiley, David (b. 1916), 538
Smith, A(rthur) J(ames) M(arshall) (1902–80), 256; on Canadian poetry, xliii–xliv; on Edgar, 79; poetry of, 17, 27, 37–8, 59, 129–30, 245, 260, 286, 366; ed. *The Blasted Pine*, 182–3, 202, 289; ed. *The Book of Canadian Poetry* (1943), xxv, xxxvi, xxxvii, 26–38, 68, 81, 246, 284, 359, 417–18; 2nd ed., 81–2, 284
Smith, Goldwin (1823–1910), 233; on Canada, 344, 422, 642
Smith, Kay (b. 1911), 68, 97
Smith, Ray (b. 1941), 499
Smollett, Tobias (1721–71): *The Expedition of Humphry Clinker* (1984), 496
Social Credit, 354
Socialism, 440–1; in North America, 643–4
Socrates (ca. 469 B.C.–399 B.C.), 542
Song of Roland, The, 58, 64
Song of Songs, 172
Sonnet, 269
Souster, Raymond (b. 1921), 183, 202, 206, 285; poetry of, 40, 44, 45, 68, 100, 112, 113, 146, 160–1, 195–6, 198, 226, 260, 290, 355
South-west Africa, 524
Southwell, Robert (1561–95), 175
Soviet Union, 667, 669; culture in, 273–4. *See also* Russia
Space, 646. *See also* Time
Spain, 354, 355, 436; as colonial power, 469, 519, 568
Sparshott, Francis Edward (b. 1926), 225, 474–5; *Rhetoric for a Divided Voice* (1965), 505–6, 559
Spears, Heather (b. 1934), 153, 204–5
Spender, Sir Stephen (1909–95), 233

Spengler, Oswald (1880–1936), 286, 544
Spenser, Edmund (ca. 1552–99), 187, 418, 491; *The Faerie Queene* (1590–96), 406; *The Shepheard's Calendar* (1579), 186, 188
Spring Thaw, 561, 574, 637, 641
Spurgeon, Charles Haddon (1834–92), 392
SSHRCC, 668
Stairs, Denis (b. 1939), 533, 537, 539
Stalin, Joseph (1879–1953), 431, 460
Star Weekly, 217
Stein, Gertrude (1874–1946), 549, 553
Steinberg, Saul (Saul Jacobson) (1914–99), 631
Stephansson, Stephen (1853–1927), 548
Stevens, Wallace (1879–1955), 383, 391, 523; influence of, 162, 192
Still, Clyfford (1904–80), 543
Stoicism, 393, 437
Stratford Shakespearean Festival, 188, 529, 662
Strathcona, Lord (Donald Alexander Smith) (1820–1914), 104, 105
Street, Eloise (b. 1857): trans. *Sepass Poems* (1955), 138
Strickland, Samuel (1804–67), 615, 621
Structuralism, 449, 557
Student Christian Movement, 625
Stuewe, Paul (b. 1943), xxxix
Subject and object, 357, 361, 365, 368
Sunday observance, 618
Surette, Philip Leon (b. 1938), xl, xliv
Surrealism, 13, 144
Sutherland, John (1919–56): ed. *First Statement*, 21–2; ed. *Northern Review*, 285; ed. *Other Canadians* (1947), 68; *The Poetry of E. J. Pratt* (1956), 159–60, 287, 396

Suzor-Côté, Marc-Aurèle De Foy (1869–1937), 513
Swayze, Fred, 201–2
Sweden, 415
Swift, Jonathan (1667–1745), 216
Swinburne, Algernon Charles (1837–1909), 127, 185
Swinton, William Elgin (1900–93), 455, 456
Switzerland, and Canada, 403, 460, 520, 641, 659, 669
Sylvestre, Guy (b. 1918), 418
Symons, Scott (b. 1933): *Place d'Armes* (1967), 622–3
Synge, John Millington (1871–1909), 217, 573

Tait, Michael S. (b. 1931), 347, 361
Tallman, Warren (1921–94), 456
Tamarack Review, 155, 285, 369
Technology, 424–5, 440–1, 570; American attitude to, 648; culture and, 258, 561; effect of, 375, 442, 459; and introversion, 410, 438–9, 490–1; opposition to, 617; and uniformity, 513, 669–70
Tecumseh (ca. 1768–1813), 58
Television, 274, 284, 410, 463, 669; and culture, 561–2; effects of, 459–60, 491; and print, 593; violence on, 493–4
Temperance movement, 461, 625
Tennyson, Alfred, Baron (1809–92), 55, 103, 390, 527, 550; *Helen's Tower* (1884), 4; *In Memoriam* (1850), 123
Thackeray, William Makepeace (1811–63), 564
Themistocles (ca. 523–ca. 458 B.C.), 178
Theology, Pratt and, 329, 377, 380, 384, 599

Theosophy, 632–3
Thériault, Yves (1915–83), 650
Thomas, Clara McCandless (b. 1919), 462
Thomas, Dylan Marlais (1914–53), 278, 391, 413, 513, 552; influence of, 108, 115, 139, 141, 197, 246; *Under Milk Wood* (1954), 211
Thompson, Dr. Homer Armstrong (1906–2000), 254
Thomson, James (1700–48), 527, 550
Thomson, James (1834–82), 60; *The City of Dreadful Night* (1874), 36
Thomson, Theresa E., 100; and Don W., 149, 179, 222
Thomson, Tom (1877–1917), 8, 10, 12, 57, 73, 102, 126, 280–1, 400, 417, 434, 447, 541; colour in, 483; convention in, 528; distance in, 348, 422–3, 502, 511, 512; landscape in, 14–16
Thomson, Very Rev. James Sutherland (1892–1972), 527
Thoreau, Henry David (1817–62), 258, 398, 405, 503; *Walden* (1854), 307, 364, 371
Tienanmen Square, 653–4
Tillyard, E(ustace) M(andeville) W(etenhall) (1889–1962), 556
Time, 451
Time and space, as bias of society, 586–7, 594–5, 649
Times, The, 7, 8
Tocqueville, Alexis Charles Henri Clérel de (1805–59): *Democracy in America* (1835), 453, 647–8
Tolstoy, Count Leo Nikolayevich (1828–1910): *War and Peace* (1863–69), 624
Toronto, 438, 447, 537, 667, burning of, 516; culture in, 409; growth and change of, 438, 439–40, 441, 518, 626, 672; in 1929, 618; Italians in, 669; writer in, 384
Toryism: in Canadian history, 517–18; Canadian intellectuals as Tory radicals, 497, 570–1, 620, 642
Town, Harold Barling (1924–90), 491
Toynbee, Arnold Joseph (1889–1975), 286; on creative minority, 495
Tracy, Neil (b. 1905), 36
Traill, Catharine Parr (1802–99), 345, 367, 502–3, 621; *The Backwoods of Canada* (1989), 615, 625
Translation, of poetry, 406–7, 429–30
Treaty of Ghent, 496
Trees, 615
Trenka, Stephen (b. 1909), 7
Trotskyism, 409
Trudeau, Pierre Elliott (1919–2000), 644, 669
Turnbull, Gael (b. 1928), 134–5, 157, 158
Turner, Joseph Mallord William (1775–1851), 85, 632
Twain, Mark (Samuel Clemens) (1835–1910), 405; *Huckleberry Finn* (1884), 277, 318, 364, 371, 499–500
Tweed, Tommy, 247

Ukraine, immigration from, 640
Underhill, Frank H. (1889–1971), 344, 409, 558; on U.S., 452, 619, 620
UNESCO, 89
Unit of Five. See Hambleton
United Church: moderator in, 374; NF and, 566
United Nations, 427
United States, 244, 283, 415, 460, 469; and "American way of life," 452–4, 459; barbarism to decadence in, 521; black culture in, 668; changing consciousness in, 458–9, 652–3;

cultural tradition in, 258–9; deism in, 461; dominance of, 369–71, 514–15, 669–70; economy of, 404–5; frontier theory of history of, xl, 456; genuine, 405; Grove on, 363–4; Haliburton on, 317–20 passim; literature in, *see* American literature; painting in, 10; possible separatism in, 533; Prohibition in, 618; relations with natives, 519, 572; social mythology of, 458; wilderness in, 501
- and Canada, xlv, 28, 78, 408, 520; annexation question, 414–15; Canada as northern extension of U.S., 104, 243, 344, 416, 424, 512–13; contrasting histories of, 453–4, 515–16; cultural influence of U.S., 247, 344–5, 451–2, 493–5, 535, 561–2, 581, 592, 619, 639–40; difference in frontier and seaboard, 102, 243, 256, 343–4, 346, 422, 423, 484, 568, 569, 647–8; difference re law and order, 57, 350; different views of revolution, 106, 258, 345, 370, 421, 446–7, 471, 473–4, 497–500, 570–1, 670; economic domination of U.S., 536, 666–7; exchange of characteristics, 458–60, 653; financial differences, 468, 537; similarities and differences, 403–4, 472–3, 508–9, 510, 644, 648–9; tariff question, 375; U.S. consciousness of Canada, 619–20, 641; Whig vs. Tory, xxxiv, 517–18, 570–1, 641–3. *See also* North America

Unity, and uniformity, 416–17, 670

University of Toronto, 438; Callaghan's fictional portrait of, 83–4; English studies at, 544, 556–7; Graduate Department of English at, 379; McGibbons and, 661–2; NF at, 416, 544, 557. *See also* Victoria College/University

University of Toronto Press, 582

University of Toronto Quarterly, 244; founding of, 547–9; "Letters in Canada" section of, 547, 548, 555; NF's reviews in, xxvii, 418. *See also* Frye, "Letters in Canada: Poetry."

Universities: American influence on Canadian, 451, 494; changing status of, 410; government role in, 273, 314; hiring practices in, 496; Innis and, 559, 590; role of, 272–3; and society, 548, 590; and writers, 549. *See also* Professor

Upper Canada College, 662

Vallières, Pierre (b. 1938): *White Niggers of America* (1971), 497, 516

Value judgments, 253, 443–4, 591–2; in Canadian literature, xlii–xliii, 255, 340–1, 342

Van der Mark, Christine (1917–69), 249

Van Horne, William Cornelius (1843–1915), 103, 104, 105, 485, 605

Vancouver, 537

Vanzetti, Bartolomeo (1888–1927), 350

Varley, Frederick Horsman (1881–1969), 8, 542

Vaughan, Henry (1622–95), 116, 345

Veblen, Thorstein (1857–1929): *The Theory of the Leisure Class* (1899), 307

Velikovsky, Immanuel (1895–1979), 629

Vennat, Manon (b. 1941), 533

Victoria College/University: art at, 433–4; Atwood at, 611; class of 1933 at, 661; Edgar at, 231; NF as student at, xxii–xxiv, 566; NF at, 417, 541,

545; Pearson family at, 426–7; Pratt at, 294, 328–9, 331, 332, 334, 335, 380, 383–4, 598–600; Pratt, Robins, and Edgar at, 335–6; scholarship at, 549; Senior Common Room of, 251, 252, 328, 331, 600
Victorian age: fiction in, 307; restoration in, 444
Vietnam War, 454, 458, 460, 652, 667
Virgil (Publius Vergilius Maro) (70–19 B.C.), 29, 286, 288, 364; *Aeneid*, 174; *Georgics*, 268; *Second Eclogue*, 174
Vise, Gerald, 207, 226
Voltaire, François Marie Arouet de (1694–1778): on Holy Roman Empire, 538

Waddington, Miriam (b. 1917), 51–2, 139, 142–4, 198–9, 260
Wales, 509
Walker, Horatio (1858–1938), 7, 14, 16
Wallace, Henry Agard (1888–1965), 374
Wallace, J.S. (Joe) (1890–1975), 122, 156–7
Wallace, Malcolm William (1873–1960), 544
Walton, George, 219–20
Wanderer, The, 56, 57
Wang Ning (b. 1955), xlvii
War of 1812, 240, 421, 469, 473, 516, 570, 642
Ward, Mrs. Humphry (Mary Augusta) (1851–1920): *Canadian Born* (1908), 454–5, 572–3
Warr, Bertram (1917–43), 94
Washington, George (1732–99), 453, 500, 516, 570
Washington, DC, 436, 500, 516; NF in, 651–2
Wasp, NF as, 403

Watergate, 454, 459
Waterson, Elizabeth (b. 1922), 346, 347
Watkins, Melville H. (b. 1932), 375
Watson, John (1847–1939), 352–3
Watson, Wilfred (1911–98), 173, 484; *Friday's Child* (1955), 138–41, 226, 291
Watt, Frank W. (b. 1927), 208, 353–4
Waugh, Evelyn Arthur St. John (1903–66): *The Loved One* (1948), 433
Wawa, 663
Weaver, Robert (b. 1921), 560; and Helen James, ed. *Canadian Short Stories* (1952), 248
Webb, Phyllis (b. 1927), 134–5, 162–3, 225
Webber, Gordon McKinley (1909–66), 12, 13
Webster, John (ca. 1580–ca.1625): *The Duchess of Malfi* (1623), 637
Wells, Henry Willis (1895–1978) and Carl F. Klinck: *Edwin J. Pratt* (1947), 64–5
Welsh (language), 645
Western Canada, 240; separatism in, 499, 473
Whale Sound (1977), ed. Greg Gatenby, 604
Whalley, George (1915–83): ed. *Selected Poems of G. H. Clarke* (1954), 128
Wheeler, Frances, 225
"Where is here?" 346, 467, 476
Whipple, George, 153
White Niggers of America. See Vallières
Whitman, Walt (1819–91), 33, 113, 160, 219, 244, 258–9, 371, 386, 390, 398, 500, 506, 519, 559, 571, 602
Whittier, John Greenleaf (1807–92), 33
Wiebe, Rudy (b. 1934), 530, 614

Wilde, Oscar Fingall O'Flahertie Wills (1854–1900), 552
Wilder, Thornton (1897–1975): *The Cabala* (1926), 443–4
Wilkinson, Anne (1910–61), 96–7, 138, 141–2, 145, 173, 291
Williams, William Carlos (1883–1963), 383; on ideas, 410; on Layton, 166
Williamsburg, Va., 444
Wilson, Alice (1881–1964), 456
Wilson, Edmund (1895–1972): *Memoirs of Hecate County* (1946), 47
Wilson, Ethel (1888–1980): *The Equations of Love* (1952), 249, 655, 657; *The Innocent Traveller* (1949), 249, 659, 657; *Hetty Dorval* (1947), 249, 655–7; *Love and Salt Water* (1956), 655; *Swamp Angel* (1954), 655, 657
Wilson, John Tuzo (b. 1908), 456
Wilson, Milton Thomas (b. 1923): on Canadian poetry, xliii–xliv, xlvi, 492, 549; on Hine, 173; on NF, xli
Wilson, Scottie Robert (1899–1972), 433
Windsor, Kenneth Neville (1933–79), 344
Winnipeg, 468, 537, 618
Winter, Jack (b. 1936), 207
Wittgenstein, Ludwig Joseph Johann (1889–1951), 557, 580
Wolfe, James (1727–59), 363
Women: in Canadian literature, 503, 569, 621–3; and poetry, 613
Wood, Grant (1892–1942), 11
Woodcock, George (1912–94), 449, 462, 463–4, 552, 557; on NF, xlii, 449–50
Woodhouse, Arthur Sutherland Pigott (1895–1964), 544, 555, 556, 557
Woolf, Adeline Virginia (1882–1941), 385; *The Waves* (1931), 233

Wordsworth, William (1770–1850), 94, 127, 202, 281, 389, 522, 552; on freedom, 278; on nature, 56, 57, 256, 367, 368; tradition of, 115, 276, 399, 485
"World" and "Earth," 651–2
World War I, 243, 307, 426, 466, 495, 523, 564; effect of, 619; Findley on, 616; anti-German feeling in, 634
World War II, 243, 390, 409, 490, 521, 532, 667; art in, 42; defence of values during, 330, 332
Worth, Irene (1916–2002), 529
WPA, 10, 442–3
Wreford, James (J. Wreford Watson) (1915–90), 44, 45, 68, 91–2
Writers' Union, 612
Writing: effects of, 388; "mosaic" technique of, 585; threats to the writer, 612–13
Wundt, Wilhelm (1832–1920), 377, 599
Wyle, Florence (1881–1968), 222–3
Wyndham, John (1903–69), 532

Yeats, William Butler (1865–1939), 56, 185, 211, 215, 332, 391, 430, 476, 630, 671; drama of, 390; Edgar on, 230, 233; influence of, 139, 158, 199, 245, 286, 528; on mask, 232, 317, 378; on poetry, 352, 353
Yessenin, Sergei (1895–1925), 163–4
Young, Florrie Baxter, 222
Yugoslavia, 415; Canadian studies in, 671
Yule, Pamelia Vining (1825–97), 30–1, 183

Zend, Robert (1929–85), 629–31
Zionism, 349
Zola, Émile (1840–1902), 670